McGRAW-HILL SERIES IN MUSIC

Douglas Moore, CONSULTING EDITOR

America's music

McGRAW-HILL SERIES IN MUSIC

Douglas Moore, CONSULTING EDITOR

Chase: AMERICA'S MUSIC

(Other titles in preparation)

America's music

From the Pilgrims to the present

GILBERT CHASE

Author of *The Music of Spain* and *A Guide to Latin American Music*
Formerly Lecturer on American Music at Columbia University

McGRAW-HILL BOOK COMPANY, INC.

New York, Toronto, London

Seventh Printing

Library of Congress Catalog Card Number: 54-9707

Published by the McGraw-Hill Book Company, Inc.
Printed in the United States of America

This book is dedicated to my sons:

Paul, Peter, John

αἰχμὰς δ' αἰχμάσσουσι νεώτεροι, οἵ περ ἐμεῖο
ὁπλότεροι γεγάασι πεποίθασίν τε βίηφιν.

HOMER, ILIAD, IV, 324

tu ne cede malis, sed contra audentior ito
qua tua te fortuna sinet.

VIRGIL, AENEID, VI, 95

I' mi son un, che quando
Amor mi spira, noto, e a quel modo
ch'e' ditta dentro vo significando.

DANTE, PURGATORIO, XXIV, 52

Foreword

A serious study of American music is arrestingly important at this time. Music has become one of our leading industries; our performing standards are probably now higher than anywhere else in the world, and we are making rapid strides in music education. How large a part in all this activity is our own music to play? How good is it? How does it differ from European music?

There are many signs of an awakened interest in American composition. More of it is being performed, published, and recorded than ever before. This interest is not confined to the United States alone. During the past few years Europeans who have always liked our popular music have discovered that we have several composers in the serious field well worth their attention. As for the foundations, fortunes are being spent to discover, to train, and to encourage our native talent.

In *America's Music* Gilbert Chase, a musician and scholar who understands and enjoys all kinds of music, has collected all the strands that have gone into the fabric of our musical speech—and a fascinating web of incompatibles they turn out to be. Who could imagine a pattern which would include Billings, Foster, Gottschalk, Chadwick, and Gershwin? Each of them contributed substantially to our musical tradition, and when we can grasp their interrelationship we perceive that there is indeed an American music, a hardy one just beginning to feel its strength and destined to stand beside our other contributions to world culture.

There have been many problems, but apparently lack of public appreciation has not been one of them. From the time of the Pilgrims our people have liked music and made it a part of their lives. They have played and sung and fashioned their own songs for all occasions. There were, however, no European courts for the cultivation of art music and opportunities were rare for the training and development of individual talents. When sufficient numbers of professional musicians had arrived to establish centers of serious musical culture our role as a backward province of European music was firmly established. It was only natural that the imported arbiters of taste would regard any deviation from European musical thinking as deplorable savagery to be resolutely put down. Our emerging talent was packed off to Europe to learn civilized ways. Our wealthy patrons, as they invariably do in a frontier society, regarded the European label as the only sure means of achieving cultural prestige.

Small wonder, then, that a serious dichotomy developed in the field of American composition. Our educated young people, fresh from German or French influences, did their loyal best to write good German or French music. For subject matter they turned to "remote legends and misty myths" guaranteed to keep them from thinking about the crudities of the land which they found so excruciating upon their return from abroad. They did, however, bring back with them a professional competence which was to be their significant contribution to the American scene.

Meanwhile the uneducated creator, finding good stuff about him, carried on a rapidly developing music speech which was a blend of European folk music, African rhythm, and regional color, and discovered that the public liked his music and was ready to pay for it handsomely. As a result via the minstrel ballad, through ragtime into jazz, a genuine popular American music made its appearance and was given every encouragement by the entertainment industry. European musicians were quick to recognize the originality and value of this music and, beginning with Debussy, accepted it as a new resource.

The American serious group, however, anxious to preserve their new-found dignity, nervously dismissed this music as purely commercial (a lot of it was and is), and until it was made respectable by the attention paid to it by Ravel and Stravinsky there were only occasional attempts to borrow from its rhythms and melodies. The highly successful popular group, on the other hand, has developed the notion that the technique of composition is not only unnecessary but an affectation. Such needs as may arise for their concerted numbers, ballets, and orchestrations they can well afford to pay for from the hacks (the underprivileged literate musicians). Gershwin's contribution to the American scene is significant beyond his music itself in that he was able to reconcile the two points of view and achieve popular music in the large traditional forms.

America's Music for perhaps the first time attaches importance impartially to all the currents of musical thinking which have influenced our development. We are ex-Europeans, to be sure, and as such have responsibilities to the preservation and continuance of European culture, but we are also a race—and a vigorous one—and it is increasingly evident that we are capable of developing cultural traditions of our own.

Douglas Moore

Acknowledgments

In all places where I worked on this book I had occasion to appreciate the combination of friendliness and efficiency that characterizes the American librarian. So it is with pleasurable recollection of their helpful kindness that I extend my thanks to Dr. Carleton Sprague Smith and the staff of the Music Division of the New York Public Library; to Miss Gladys Chamberlain of the 58th Street Music Library in New York; to Mr. Arthur Cohn and the staff of the Music Division of the Free Library of Philadelphia; to Dr. Glen Haydon and the staff of the Music Department of the University of North Carolina; to the Director and the staff of the General Library of the same University; to Dr. Harold Spivacke and the staff of the Music Division of the Library of Congress, in particular Mr. Richard S. Hill, Mr. William Lichtenwanger, and Mr. Edward N. Waters.

I am especially grateful to those friends and colleagues who gave generously of their time to read the typescript of my book, in whole or in part, and to make valuable comments thereon. They are Dr. Glen Haydon, Dr. Douglas Moore, Dr. Hans Nathan, Dr. William S. Newman, Dr. Richard A. Waterman. Mr. John Kirkpatrick was kind enough to share with me his intimate knowledge of Gottschalk's music. Dr. Otto E. Deutsch helpfully tracked down for me a copy of Camidge's *Psalmody* that I had almost despaired of finding.

My thanks also go to Mr. Milo Sutliff of the American Recording Society and to Mr. Moses Asch of Folkways Records; the former placed at my disposal the comprehensive series of recordings of American compositions issued by ARS, and the latter made available to me the valuable Folkways Anthologies of Jazz and of American Folk Music.

My warmest gratitude is reserved for my editor, Mr. C. Gibson Scheaffer, whose constant encouragement, patience, helpfulness, and good judgment have put me greatly in his debt. He has proved, for me, to be the ideal editor. The fact that we have been separated by five thousand miles during the final stages of revision, editing, and proofreading has multiplied the difficulties of his task without in the least diminishing his friendly efficiency.

In the course of a historical work of such scope as the present one, an author inevitably accumulates many obligations to the scholarly writers who have preceded him. Specific acknowledgments of sources are made elsewhere in this book. But I wish here to pay tribute to the memory of such men as Oscar G. Sonneck, Waldo Selden Pratt, and George Pullen Jackson, who dedicated their industry, their talent, and their enthusiasm to exploring virtually unknown tracts of America's musical history. And it is impossible to handle such an impressive work of imaginative scholarship as Benson's *The English Hymn* without profound admiration and respect. Here, too, I should like to mention the admirable writings of Constance Rourke, especially *The Roots of American Culture* and *American Humor*, which, it seems to me, must always remain a source of inspiration to anyone trying to grasp what is really native and traditional in our culture. In a more specialized field, Percy Scholes, in his work on *The Puritans and Music in England and New England*, has made a valuable contribution, by which I have fully profited.

Finally, my thanks are due to those authors and publishers who have permitted me to quote from their books and compositions, as indicated by the appropriate credit lines in the text.

Contents

Foreword by Douglas Moore vii
Acknowledgments x
Introduction xv

one | **Preparation**

chapter 1. Puritan psalm singers 3
2. New England reformers 22
3. Singing dissenters 41
4. African exiles 65
5. Gentlemen amateurs 84
6. Professional emigrants 106
7. Native pioneers 123

two | **Expansion**

chapter 8. Progress and profit 149
9. The genteel tradition 164
10. The fasola folk 183
11. Revivals and camp meetings 207
12. The Negro spirituals 232
13. The Ethiopian business 259
14. America's minstrel 283
15. The exotic periphery 301
16. Europe versus America 324
17. A romantic bard 346
18. The Boston classicists 365

three | Fulfillment

chapter 19. Nationalism and folklore 385
20. Indian tribal music 403
21. The rise of ragtime 433
22. Singin' the blues 452
23. The growth of jazz 468
24. The Americanists 488
25. The eclectics 516
26. The traditionalists 548
27. The experimentalists 571
28. Twelve-tone composers 597
29. In the orbit of Broadway 617
30. Toward an American opera 634
31. Composer from Connecticut 653

Bibliography 679
A note on recordings 707
Index 711

Introduction

What a new world, with new processes and new ideals, will do with the tractable and still unformed art of music; what will arise from the contact of this art with our unprecedented democracy—these are the questions of deepest import in our musical life in the United States.

ARTHUR FARWELL, MUSIC IN AMERICA, INTRODUCTION (AUGUST, 1914).

Writing forty years ago, Arthur Farwell—himself one of the formative spirits that helped to shape America's music—could rightly speak of the "still unformed art of music" in the United States, and thus justify his dictum that "prophecy, not history, is the most important concern of music in America." Since those words were written, so much has happened in American music, there has been such an accumulation of accomplishments, that history and prophecy may now be said to hold a more equal balance in our concern. We have, to be sure, every reason to believe that our future will outweigh our past. By and large, our past has been a formative period: this is indicated by the subtitles given, respectively, to Parts I and II of this book: *Preparation* and *Expansion*. The confidence—certainly not complacence—displayed in the heading of Part III, *Fulfillment*, is based mainly on the achievements of the last two or three decades; but it also leans somewhat on prophecy, venturing to predict and anticipate what the second half of the twentieth century will bring. Beyond that, my crystal ball ceases to function, save that it clearly reveals there will be a great deal more musical history to concern ourselves with in America by that time. Meanwhile, my present concern in this book must be with that portion of America's music that has already become history at the moment when we find ourselves entering the second half of our confused but dynamic century.

Naturally, others before me have undertaken to write the history of American music or of music in America—we must suppose there is a difference of meaning or implication in those terms. Some seventy years ago, Frédéric Louis Ritter (1834–1891), an Alsatian musician who came to America in 1856, published the first comprehensive history of music in the United States, titled *Music in America* (New York, 1883). Divided into six "periods," it began with the "low state of musical culture" in New England, devoted much attention to the establishment of musical societies and orchestras, the rise of oratorio and opera, and "progress of vocal and instrumental music" in the large cities. In his last chapter, Ritter dealt with "The Cultivation of Popular Music." He stated roundly that "the people's song . . . is not to be found among the American people." And he asked rhetorically, "How are we to account for this utter absence of national people's music and poetry in America?" He accounted for it by the Puritanical "repression" of early New England. "From the hearts of such people, in whose eyes an innocent smile, a merry laugh, was considered a sin, no naïve, cheerful, sweet melody could spring. His [the American colonist's] emotional life was stifled and suppressed: therefore there are no folk-poetry and no folk-songs in America." The only concession that Ritter would make to "a people's song" in the United States was to acknowledge the existence and the merit of "the songs of the colored race."

The History of American Music by Louis C. Elson appeared in 1904 and gave relatively more attention to composers than to musical institutions. It bestowed a condescending chapter on "the folk-music of America," made a gallant bow to "American women in music," and concluded with an appraisal of the "qualities and defects of American music"—a procedure that might be described as a prenatal post-mortem. Out of the 423 pages of his book, Elson devoted sixteen to "The Folk Music of America," declaring, "It must be admitted that in this field America is rather barren." Six pages of this chapter dealt with Stephen Foster as "the folk song genius of America," and eight pages with Indian music. Elson concluded that "American folk song in its true sense can only be derived from Indian or plantation life."

Music in America, compiled by Arthur Farwell and W. Dermot Derby, was published in 1915 as volume four of a composite work called *The Art of Music.* A critical and interpretative study, it was the best treatment of the subject up to that time and the first work to show a grasp of the cultural foundations and creative trends of American music. In his introduction to this work, Farwell wrote:

> The chief danger which threatens the American composer is the tendency to accept and conform to the standards of the centers of conventional and fashionable musical culture . . . and to fail to study out the real nature and musical needs of the American people.

This danger still exists, perhaps will always exist; but it is less of a threat to the creative vitality of American music today than it was forty years ago, because the deep currents of American folk and popular music have been so powerfully set in motion that they can counteract the tendency toward conventional stagnation. Speaking of these vital currents in America's music, Farwell concluded:

> The new movement will call forth new and larger efforts on the part of American composers, who, with their present thorough assimilation of the various musical influences of the world, will lead the nation into a new and mature creative epoch.

In this passage Farwell proved that he was a true prophet as well as a perceptive critic.

In 1931 John Tasker Howard brought out his book *Our American Music,* in which, out of eighteen chapters, one was assigned to "Our Folk-Music," including the music of the North American Indian (which, strictly speaking, is not folk music) and a section on "Composers Who Have Used Our Folk-Songs." The character of this work was aptly summed up by Dr. Carleton Sprague Smith, who remarked of the author, "His approach is highly respectable, and implies that we have made aesthetic progress." As evidence of his highly respectable approach, we may take Mr. Howard's remarks on the "gospel hymn" as being a "cheap and tawdry" type of music "that appeals only to the emotions." On the other hand, he can solemnly declare that Ethelbert Nevin "represents one of the summits of American music" and that "The Rosary" is "an almost perfect work of art." Thus he exalts the genteel tradition, which prefers what is polite and pretty to what is vulgar but vital.

My own approach to America's music is not at all respectable—my bête noire is the genteel tradition, and I take my stand with that Connecticut Yankee, Charles Ives, whose most damning adjective is said to be "nice."

As for the doctrine of aesthetic progress, which, in the guise of a firm belief in "progressive improvement" has hitherto dominated the historical criticism of American music, I hold it to be fallacious. According to this doctrine, the music of one period—let us say the "fuguing tunes" of the eighteenth century—was surpassed and made obsolete by the "improved" products of the next age—let us say the hymns of Lowell Mason. And we can observe the implications of this doctrine at work in many other directions. For example, in the belief that the smoothly mechanized performances of the big "name bands" were an improvement over the small-band improvisations of early New Orleans jazz. The important thing, it seems to me, is to be aware, as T. S. Eliot says, "of the obvious fact that art never improves, but that the material of art is never quite the same." [1] Or, as stated by Wilhelm Worringer: "The stylistic peculiarities of past epochs are not to be explained by lack of ability, but by a differently directed volition." [2] To study objectively the peculiarities of style in a given phase of America's musical past—as Mr. Charles Seeger has done so perceptively in his study of "Contrapuntal Style in the Three-voice Shape-note Hymns" [3]—is to discover not merely a deficiency in knowledge (as might be supposed from the persistent use of "incorrect" progressions), or a product which should be either discarded as obsolete or improved by correction, but rather an authentic and traditional American musical style, with "a rigorous, spare, disciplined beauty" of its own. To discoveries, perceptions, and appreciations of this kind, reaching into the very core of America's music, the present work is chiefly dedicated.

Art changes, and it is the business of the historian to record those changes, to understand them if he can, to accept them whether or not he understands them, and not to presume to establish the pattern of his prejudices as objective truth. I have my definite likes and dislikes in music, as in everything else. I never try to admire what it is merely respectable to admire. I prefer "Beale Street Blues" to *Hora Novissima.* I do not think I am prejudiced in favor of our folk-popular music simply because I believe it has been the most important phase

[1] In "Tradition and the Individual Talent," *Selected Essays, 1917–1932.*

[2] In *Abstraction and Empathy* (1908). English translation by Michael Bullock (London, 1953), p. 9.

[3] In the *Musical Quarterly*, October, 1940.

of America's music. And if you ask what do I mean by "important," I will answer, in this case, "different from European music." And if we are now beginning to sense that difference in American art-music also, that is because of the subtle but pervasive influence of our folk-popular idioms; the American musical vernacular has been on the march through all these generations, and even our most academic composers are catching up with it, or being caught up by it.

In this book, some sixteen chapters deal, in whole or in part, with various phases of American folk, primitive, and popular music. This is in line with Charles Seeger's dictum that "when the history of music in the New World is written, it will be found that the main concern has been with folk and popular music." And this dictum, in turn, implies the recognition of historical and cultural factors that are discussed later in this Introduction. I make no apology for devoting much attention to types of music, such as the revival hymn and ragtime, that have hitherto not been regarded as "important" or worth the serious attention of the musical historian. What seemed "cheap and tawdry" to a writer yesterday may serve as material for some of the "best" music of today—as witness the skillfully creative use of gospel-hymn tunes by such composers as Ives, Cowell, and Thomson. A passage from the autobiography of the composer Nicolas Nabokov seems to me to express, better than anything else I have seen, the importance of exploring all kinds of music in a historical work that aspires to approximate the complexity and the movement of human life:

> . . . It seems to me that music came into my life in the way it came to the lives of most composers; through the illicit communication with that fertile subsoil, that vast underground of life where musical matter of all degrees of beauty and ugliness lives freely and is constantly being reinvented, rearranged, transformed and infused with new meaning by a universe of memories and imaginations.[4]

Perhaps I should attempt to explain how I came to write a book about America's music. As far as I can trace the circumstances that led me to the undertaking, the process was somewhat as follows. The first step was probably my appointment to the staff of the Music Division of the Library of Congress in 1940. My desk happened to face a portrait of Oscar G. Sonneck, the Division's former chief and pio-

[4] *Old Friends and New Music*, by Nicolas Nabokov. Copyright 1951 by Little, Brown & Company, Boston, Mass.

neer scholar in the field of early American musical history. It was he who painstakingly unearthed, from old newspaper files and other documents, the data that enabled him to reconstruct the musical life of the United States and of the thirteen colonies prior to 1800. The example of his industry, erudition, and enthusiasm could not fail to impress me profoundly, even though as yet I had no definite intention of following along the path that he had cleared.

Another influential factor that stemmed from my association with the Library of Congress was the stimulation of my interest in American folk music through contact with the library's Archive of American Folk Song. This archive housed a collection of tens of thousands of American folk tunes of all kinds. Many of these I had an opportunity to hear and to discuss with the folklorists and folk singers who visited the Library frequently. At that time the Library of Congress was also beginning to acquire recordings of folk music from Latin America, which was then my area of specialization, including notable examples of Afro-American music from Haiti and Brazil. It was thus that I acquired the hemispheric approach to Afro-American music and was led to recognize the underlying unity of Negro music in the New World. As a result of all this, I became definitely absorbed by the whole fascinating process of the development of musical culture in the Americas.

At this point I was invited to join the staff of the National Broadcasting Company's recently created "Inter-American University of the Air," of which Sterling Fisher was director. Consequently, in the summer of 1943, I went to New York to undertake the challenging task of putting America's music on the air. With the valuable assistance of Ernest La Prade, I planned the educational broadcast series known as "Music of the New World," for which I also wrote the scripts and accompanying handbooks. The resources that I had discovered in the Library of Congress, as well as my researches in the field of Latin American music, were tapped to provide a series of coordinated programs related to the backgrounds of American history and American folkways, with much music of the Americas that had hitherto been unheard or little known. The handbooks for "Music of the New World," though extremely concise and rapidly written, as everything for radio had to be, may be regarded as the seed that eventually produced the present work.

While I was on the staff of the NBC University of the Air, Dr.

Douglas Moore suggested that I give two courses at Columbia University, one on music of Latin America, the other on music of the United States. Now deeply committed to both of these subjects, I readily agreed to give the courses. My *Guide to Latin American Music*, published by the Library of Congress in 1945, served well enough as a textbook for the course on Latin American music. But when it came to a text on music in the United States, I found none that satisfied me completely, for reasons that have been largely explained earlier in this Introduction. I had reached the conviction that, for obvious historical and cultural reasons, the main emphasis in American music necessarily rested upon folk and popular idioms. There were specialized books on American folk and popular music; there was none that related these idioms to one another and to the whole cultural development of the United States from the earliest times to the present. This then, was the immediate incentive and *raison d'être* of the book that, after seven years of labor, I now offer to the reader.

It will be noticed that I do not call the book either a history of American music or of music in America, but simply *America's Music*. By *America's Music* I mean the music made or continuously used by the people of the United States, people who have come from many parts of the earth to build a new civilization and to create a new society in a new world, guided by ideals of human dignity, freedom, and justice. It takes all kinds of music to make America's music, just as it takes all kinds of people to make America's world. In these pages I have tried to depict the diversified world of America's music, rich in human and universal values. While trying to reveal this diversity by continually shifting from one phase to another of our musical culture, I have also attempted to demonstrate some basic relationships that give a large measure of organic unity to our music.

This work is not a conventional history, though it is based on historical principles. It is not a book about the performance of music or about musical institutions, though these matters may be touched upon incidentally. It is above all an attempt to understand, to describe, to illuminate, and to evaluate, the vital processes and factors that have gone into the making of America's music. When I say that it is based on historical principles, I mean that its form and content, the order and organization of its material, follow and are dependent upon the historical processes that determined the growth and direction of musical culture in the United States. This means, for example, that the first part of the book, and the earlier sections of Part II, are concerned largely with the various religious trends and impulses that dominated our musical expression for over two centuries and that continued to be powerfully felt even after the rise of secular music in the second half of the nineteenth century. Furthermore, until the closing decades of the nineteenth century, the overwhelming emphasis in America's music was upon song, upon vocal music in its simpler and more popular manifestations, rather than upon instrumental music; and this emphasis, too, is reflected in the book.

The twentieth century is characterized primarily by the rapid development of instrumental music, both in the popular and "serious" fields. It is, indeed, extremely interesting to observe the rise of ragtime, jazz, and the popular "name bands," paralleling that of our instrumental art music in both the smaller and larger forms, ranging from the piano sonata to the symphony. If jazz may be regarded as our most original and far-reaching contribution to the world's music, this should not blind us to the fact that our "serious" or fine-art music is at present capable of holding its own with most of the contemporary music that is being composed anywhere. And if the influence of jazz has succeeded in making some of our art music a little less "serious," that is all to the good. Certainly, we have not relinquished our search for the sublime in music; but we no longer consider it necessary to be completely solemn about the matter. And that, perhaps, is an encouraging sign of our musical maturity.

In the title of my book I have used the term "America" to designate the United States of America, while fully aware that the term is more properly applicable to the Western Hemisphere as a whole. Having worked for fifteen years in the field of inter-American relations, I could not fail to be aware of the larger sense that we of this hemisphere are bound to give to the term "America" as the symbolic name that binds us all to common ideals of peace, friendship, and cooperation. For my restricted use of the term in this case, I plead the needs of euphony and convenience, supported by a literary tradition that has ample precedent.

There are many aspects of America's music that I should like to explore further; and I hope that the reader, after finishing these pages, will also feel the urge to further exploration in this vast and fascinating field. I do not claim that this work is either perfect or complete (no book on American music will ever achieve completeness; the subject is too large and diversified), but in it I have sincerely endeavored to present my vision and my understanding of the growth of America's music. I trust that the reading of this book will prove to be an adventure less arduous, but no less stimulating and rewarding, than was the writing of it.

Gilbert Chase

one | Preparation

The stone which the builders refused is become the head stone of the corner. PSALM 118.

chapter one

Puritan psalm singers

Musick is an Art unsearchable, Divine, and Excellent . . . that rejoyceth and cheareth the Hearts of Men.

PLAYFORD, AN INTRODUCTION TO THE SKILL OF MUSICK, 11TH ED., 1687.

The Puritans who settled New England have been held up to history as haters of music, so that the story of America's music has always been darkened at the outset by the shadow of this sinister cloud. Ritter, in his *Music in America*, wrote: "The Puritans, who landed in 1620 at Plymouth Rock, brought with them their psalm-tunes and their hatred of secular music." The first part of this statement is true—the Puritans were psalm singers by tradition and predilection—but the second part is contrary to the facts: love of psalmody did not necessarily imply hatred of other kinds of music. The average Puritan was by no means as severe or ascetic as is generally supposed. Enjoyment of fine clothes, good food, wine, books, sociability, and music, was readily reconcilable with the Puritan conscience.

In order to clear away some prevalent misconceptions, it would be well to begin by making the acquaintance of a typical New England Puritan. We may meet one in the person of Judge Samuel Sewall (1652–1730), B.A. and M.A. at Harvard College; ordained minister; justice of the peace; member of the New England Council; member of the Court of Assistants (hence involved in the Salem witch trials); Chief Justice of Massachusetts from 1718; and father of fifteen children. It is easy for us to become intimately acquainted with Judge Sewall, to learn of his tastes and occupations and interests, because throughout nearly the whole of his long and busy life he kept a detailed diary that has come down to us just as he wrote it. From the pages of this diary emerges, not a Saint-Gaudens statue of gloom-ridden pride, but the lifelike portrait of a very human person.

First of all, the Judge—he weighs 193 pounds with his light coat on —will want good food, and plenty of it. Note with what relish he records a dinner in Cambridge, England: "Mr. Littel dined with us at our inn: had a Legg Mutton boiled and Colly-Flower, Carrets, Rosted Fowls, and a dish of Pease." Back home in New England there was no lack of good fare, including that famous apple pie, as the diary testifies on October 1, 1697: "Had first Butter, Honey, Curds and Cream. For Diner, very good Rost Lamb, Turkey, Fowls, Aplepy." Once, when the Judge stayed in the Council Chamber "for fear of the Rain," he "din'd alone upon Kilby's Pyes and good Beer." Besides beer, the Judge enjoys wine (both sack and claret), ale, and a dram or two of that "Black-Cherry Brandy" that Madam Winthrop gave him when he was courting her (after the death of his first wife, he courted four widows in succession, and married two of them). He prefers to dine and drink with a numerous and convivial company. Witness the diary for August 25, 1709: "In the even I invited the Govr. and Council to drink a glass of Wine with me; about 20 came. . . . Gave them variety of good Drink, and at going away a large piece of Cake Wrap'd in Paper."

Judge Sewall would be pleased to have some books at hand for leisurely browsing. He writes of a visit to a friend in Narragansett: "Din'd at Bright's: while Diner was getting ready I read Ben Jonson, a Folio." The play from which he read was Jonson's *The Poetaster*, and he quotes some lines from it in his diary:

> Wake, our Mirth begins to dye,
>   Quicken it with Tunes and Wine.
> Raise your Notes; you'r out, *fie, fie,*
>   This drowsiness is an ill sign.

This introduces the subject of music, which was very near to Sewall's heart. For him, no entertainment was complete without music. Once he was invited to a Council Dinner, and notes with disappointment: "Had no musick, though the Lieut. Govr. had promised it." On the occasion of the dinner in Cambridge, already mentioned, the music did not fail: "Three Musicians came in, two Harps and a Violin, and gave us Musick." During a visit to Coventry, on the same English trip, he notes: "Had three of the City Waits bid me good morrow with their Wind Musick." While in London he took the opportunity to attend a public concert: "Mr. Brattle and I went to Covent Garden and heard a Consort of Musick." But the Judge was not content merely to listen to music: he loved to raise a good tune himself. Referring to a former classmate at Harvard, he wrote: "We were Fellows together at College and have sung many a tune in Consort," which would be the early New England variety of barbershop harmony. In later life, Judge Sewall continued to enjoy part singing, as indicated by an entry in his diary for May 11, 1698: "In the new Room with the widow Galis and her daughter Sparhawk; sung the 114th Psalm. Simon catch'd us a base" (i.e., Simon sang the bass part). The Judge was fond of psalm singing, especially with widows.

Judge Sewall's fondness for psalm singing was shared by his fellow Puritans, both in old and new England. But here it is necessary to correct two prevailing misconceptions: one, that Puritans sang only psalms; two, that only Puritans sang psalms. The singing of metrical versions of the Psalms of David in the vernacular was a heritage shared by all Protestants outside of Germany, where the Lutheran chorale prevailed. Among the French Huguenots, in Switzerland, in the Low Countries, in Scotland and England, the use of psalmody was widespread. In England psalms were sung by both Puritans and "Cavaliers," that is, by nonconformists and by adherents of the established church. In 1559 Queen Elizabeth granted formal permission for psalms and spiritual songs to be sung in English churches "for the comforting of such as delight in music." In the following year appeared an enlarged edition of a famous English psalter destined to play an important role in the musical life of New England:

> Psalmes of David in Englishe Metre, by Thomas Sternhold and others: . . . Very mete to be used of all sorts of people privately for their godly solace & comfort, laying aparte all ungodly songes & ballades, which tende only to the nourishing of vice, and corrupting of youth.

Long before this psalter was brought to Massachusetts by the Puritans, English psalms were heard in America, and in a manner confirming that they were indeed "used of all sorts of people." In the year 1577, Sir Francis Drake sailed from England on his celebrated voyage around the world. In June, 1579, he landed on the coast of northern California, and lay there for five weeks, while his men camped ashore. The Indians proved friendly and frequently visited the encampment.

This is what we find in an account of the voyage written by Drake's chaplain, Francis Fletcher:

> In the time of which prayers, singing of Psalmes, and reading of certaine Chapters in the Bible, they sate very attentively: and observing the end of every pause, with one voice still cried, Oh, as greatly rejoycing in our exercises. Yea they took such pleasure in our singing of Psalmes, that whensoever they resorted to us, their first request was commonly this, *Gnaáh*, by which they intreated that we would sing.

It has been suggested that the word *Gnaáh* was intended to be an imitation of the English singing through their noses—a habit allegedly transmitted to New England somewhat later. Be this as it may, the passage quoted above will serve to dispel the notion that psalm singing was the exclusive preoccupation of Puritans.

As to whether the Puritans sang secular songs as well as psalms, that is a question bound up with the Puritan attitude toward music as a whole, into which we shall now inquire.

"Musick is a good gift of God"

The black legend of the Puritan hatred of music has been strangely persistent. Here is a sampling of American opinions on this subject ranging over the past fifty or sixty years: the Puritan looked upon music as fashioned by the evil designs of the Tempter; the Plymouth Pilgrims brought with them a hatred of music unparalleled in history; in the early days in New England, instrumental music was looked upon as a snare of the devil; secular music of all kinds was sternly interdicted as a menace to the salvation of souls; the Puritans were forbidden to invent new tunes; in the early days of the New England colonies psalm singing was the only note of music heard. And so on—one might fill several pages with similar excerpts. It would be nearer the truth to say that music as an art was cherished by the Puritans, but its abuse was not tolerated, and it was regarded as having its highest use as an aid to worship.

In other words, the Puritan attitude toward music was not antagonistic or intolerant, but it *was* moralistic. That is, they judged music according to the way it was used. They considered it wrong to sing bawdy or obscene songs—and a great many of these circulated in those times—and they objected to music as an incentive to wanton or lascivious dancing, of which there was also a great deal in those times. Their objection to instrumental music in churches was based on religious grounds: it smacked of the "ceremonial worship" and "popery" against which they stood. To the use of instrumental music on social occasions, or in the home, they did not object. To mention only a few prominent cases, John Milton was an amateur organist, Cromwell had a private organ and engaged a large band of musicians for his daughter's wedding, and John Bunyan had a "chest of viols" for his recreation.

Now, the judging of music according to its uses was by no means peculiar to the Puritans. This was the view held, for example, by the noted music publisher, composer, and theorist, John Playford, who brought out numerous widely used collections of secular music, both vocal and instrumental, including the often-reprinted *English Dancing Master* and Hilton's *Catch that Catch Can.* In his *Introduction to the Skill of Musick* (London, 1655), Playford writes:

> The first and chief Use of Musick is for the Service and Praise of God, whose gift it is. The second Use is for the Solace of Men, which as it is agreeable unto Nature, so it is allow'd by God, as a temporal Blessing to recreate and cheer men after long study and weary labor in their Vocations.

After lamenting that "our late and solemn Musick, both Vocal and Instrumental, is now justl'd out of Esteem by the new Corants and Jiggs of Foreigners" (a theme upon which every age makes its own variations), Playford concludes by saying, "I believe it [music] is an helper both to good and evil, and will therefore honour it when it *moves* to *Vertue*, and shall beware of it when it would *flatter* into *Vice*."

No better statement of the Puritan attitude toward music could be found; yet it was stated by a man who was not himself a Puritan, though his publications, including the one from which we have just quoted, were well known and highly esteemed by the Puritans, including those of New England. Philip Stubbs, a writer often cited as holding "puritanical" views, in his *Anatomie of Abuses* (1583), warns that music "allureth to vanitie," yet adds:

I grant that Musick is a good gift of God, and that it delighteth bothe man and beast, reviveth the spirits, conforteth the heart and maketh it redyer to serve God; and therefor did David bothe use Musick himselfe, and also commend the use of it to his posteritie, and being used to that end, for man's privat recreation, Musick is very laudable.

One of the most rabid ranters against worldly amusements, William Prynne, in his *Histrio-Mastix* (1633), affirms that "Musicke of itself is lawfull, and usefull and commendable."

In New England, we find the Rev. Increase Mather, in his *Remarkable Providences* (1684), praising "the sweetness and delightfulness of Musick" for its natural power to soothe "melancholy passions." In the poems of Anne Bradstreet (1612–1672), the most notable New England poet of the early colonial period, we find numerous references to music, mentioned in such a way as to make it obvious that this Puritan bluestocking had both an understanding and a love of musical art. Here is an example:

I heard the merry grasshopper then sing,
The black glad Cricket bear a second part,
They kept one tune, and plaid on the same string,
Seeming to glory in their little art.

Music was loved and skillfully practiced by that band of Separatists whom we call "Pilgrims." The founder of the Separatists was a certain Robert Browne, known to be very fond of music and reputed to be "a singular good lutenist." One of the Pilgrim Fathers, Edward Winslow, has left us an account of their departure from Holland, when they took leave of their exiled brethren:

They that stayed at Leyden feasted us that were to go, at our pastor's house, being large; where we refreshed ourselves, after tears, with singing of psalms, making joyful melody in our hearts, as well as with the voice, *there being many of our congregation very expert in music;* and indeed it was the sweetest melody that ever mine ears heard.[1]

We may conclude, then, that among the New England settlers there were as many music lovers as one finds in the average group of

[1] Winslow, *Hypocrasie Unmasked* (1646), quoted in Pratt, *The Music of the Pilgrims.* (Italics added.)

normal human beings; and that, while they had a predilection for psalm singing, they cultivated other types of music as far as circumstances permitted. Instrumental music and secular songs were by no means unknown to them.

Black legends and blue laws

Contrary to popular belief, instrumental music was not anathema to the Puritans, nor did they ever pass any laws, in Connecticut or elsewhere, forbidding the use of certain instruments. Instrumental music in religious worship was frowned upon because it smacked of "popery," but, as stated by the Rev. John Cotton in his *Singing of Psalms a Gospel Ordinance* (1647), "the private use of any Instrument of musick" was not forbidden. Specific references to musical instruments in New England before 1700 are rare, yet they *are* mentioned several times. The will of Mr. Nathaniell Rogers, of Rowley, Massachusetts, dated 1664, mentions "A treble viall" (viol), valued at ten shillings. The Rev. Edmund Browne, of Sudbury, at his death in 1678, left a "bass Vyol" and several music books. The Boston printer and engraver John Foster, a graduate of Harvard (1667), owned a guitar and a viol. On December 1, 1699, Judge Samuel Sewall noted in his diary, "Was at Mr. Hiller's to enquire for my wife's virginal." The virginal (or virginals) was a fashionable keyboard instrument of those times, and this Mr. Hiller must have been a tuner and repairer of musical instruments. It is unlikely that he would have long remained in business had Mrs. Sewall been his only client.

The alleged enactment of 1675 "that no one should play on any kind of music except the drum, the trumpet and the jewsharp," is, like many of the so-called "blue laws," a pure fabrication concocted by the Rev. Samuel Peters and originally published in his *General History of Connecticut* (1781), a work as fanciful as it is malicious.[2] The reason Peters exempted the drum, the trumpet, and the jew's-harp from the imaginary ban was that these instruments were so widely known and used in New England. Drums and trumpets were used for military and civil purposes, and the jew's-harp was a favorite item of barter with the Indians. The jew's-harp may also have served as "the poor man's viol," for it was inexpensive and easily carried about.

[2] See Scholes, *The Puritans and Music*, pp. 370–373.

Although antimusical laws never actually existed in New England, there are instances when music and dancing figure in court proceedings of that period. In such cases, however, the music is only incidental to what we would call "disorderly conduct," generally combined with drunkenness. Here are a few typical examples. In Salem, Massachusetts, in 1653, one Thomas Wheeler was "fined for profane and foolish dancing, singing and wanton speeches, probably being drunk." In July, 1678, Josiah Bridges deposed that he saw "an Indian drunk on brandy and cider" in Mr. Crod's house, and that "one night while he was there, there was music and dancing when it was pretty late." In 1679, also in Salem, Mary Indicott deposed that "she saw fiddling and dancing in John Wilkinson's house and Hue drinking liquor there." For one such case that came to the attention of the authorities, there were doubtless dozens or even hundreds that went unnoticed. Hence these court records testify that there *was* fiddling and dancing and profane singing among the common people of New England in early colonial times.

If we wish to know what kind of music they played and danced to, we have only to look into Playford's *The English Dancing Master* (1651; many later editions), a collection of the favorite popular tunes of that time, including such famous ones as "Sellinger's Round," "Trenchmore" and "Green-sleeves." These were tunes that circulated in oral tradition long before they got into print: we can be certain that the people of all the American colonies knew them well.

The Puritan attitude toward dancing was not sweepingly condemnatory. The Rev. John Cotton, very influential in New England, wrote in 1625: "Dancing (yea though mixt) I would not simply condemn. . . . Only lascivious dancing to wanton ditties and in amorous gestures and wanton dalliances, especially after great feasts, I would bear witness against, as great *flabella libidinis*." The Puritans' dislike of May Day celebrations was due not only to the fact that these were of pagan origin, being survivals of the Saturnalia of the ancients, but also to the fact that the Maypole dancings frequently led to sexual excesses of the most licentious character. (The Maypole itself is of phallic origin.) Romantic sentimentalism has made the Maypole a symbol of innocent merriment, but contemporary accounts give a more realistic picture. This point is mentioned here because of the widely diffused legend of "Merry Mount," the name given to Thomas Morton's settlement at Mount Wollaston (now Braintree, Massachusetts), which has been held up as a bright example of Cavalier freedom and gaiety contrasted with Puritan severity and gloom. In his tale *The Maypole of Merry Mount*, Hawthorne describes the May Day festivities at Merry Mount in the most glowing colors, and then goes on to say: "Unfortunately, there were men in the new world, of a sterner faith than these Maypole worshippers. Not far from Merry Mount was a settlement of Puritans, most dismal wretches, who said their prayers before daylight, and then wrought in the forest or the cornfield, till evening made it prayer time again." Unfortunate indeed that our country was settled by dismal wretches who believed in prayer and hard work!

William Bradford, in his *Of Plimmoth Plantation*, set forth some of the complaints of the Plymouth colonists against the settlement at Mount Wollaston:

> They also set up a May-pole, drinking and dancing aboute it many days together, inviting the Indean women, for their consorts, dancing and frisking togither (like so many fairies, or furies rather), and worse practises. . . . Morton likewise (to shew his poetrie) composed sundry rimes and verses, some tending to lasciviousness. . . .[3]

One of the songs used in the revels at Merry Mount has been preserved by Thomas Morton himself, in his *New English Canaan*, where he also tells us in what manner it was sung:

> There was likewise a merry song made, which, (to make their Revells more fashionable,) was sung with a Corus, every man bearing his part; which they performed in a daunce, hand in hand about the Maypole, whiles one of the Company sung and filled out the good liquor, like gammedes and Iupiter.

The Songe

Drinke and be merry, merry, merry boyes;
Let all your delight be in Hymens ioyes;
Jo to Hymen now the day is come,
About the merry Maypole take a Roome.

Make greene garlons, bring bottles out
And fill sweet nectar, freely about,

[3] Bradford, *Of Plimmoth Plantation*, ed. by W. C. Ford (Boston, 1912), vol. II, pp. 48–49.

Vncover thy head, and feare no harme,
For hers good liquor to keep it warme.
Then drink and be merry, etc.
Io to Hymen, etc.[4]

This conventional drinking ditty may well have come under the heading of "harmless mirth," as Morton claimed, but all was not harmless at Merry Mount, either morally or politically. The Puritans undoubtedly had ample reason for disapproving of the immoral conditions at Merry Mount; yet their main grievance against Morton was that he sold firearms to the Indians and instructed them in their use, thus creating a serious threat to the very existence of the newly established colonies. This was a grave crime that fully justified Morton's arrest and deportation.

Another phase of the anti-Puritan black legend is that these "dismal wretches" had no interest in artistic or intellectual matters, apart from theology. Yet the *Mayflower*, on its voyage to America, was well stocked with books, and not all of them were religious tracts. History, philosophy, travel, poetry, and music were all represented. Among the three hundred volumes in the personal library of William Brewster, one of the original Pilgrim Fathers, was a celebrated musical work by one of the most notable composers of the Elizabethan period, Richard Allison (or Alison). The title is worth quoting in full:

> *The Psalmes of David in Metre, the plaine song beeing the common tunne to be sung and plaide upon the Lute, Orpharyon, Citterne or Base Violl, severally or altogether, the singing part to be either Tenor or Treble of the instrument, according to the nature of the voyce, or for foure voyces. With tenne short Tunnes in the end, to which for the most part all the Psalmes may be usually sung, for the use of such as are of mean skill, and whose leisure least serveth to practize. . . . (London, 1599).*

This title is in itself an informative commentary on the musical practice of those days, and it indicates that Allison's book could be used for a wide variety of musical purposes, ranging from concerted vocal and instrumental performance to the simplest psalmody. Although the Plymouth settlers were certainly among those "whose leisure least

[4] Morton, *New English Canaan*, ed. by C. F. Adams (Boston, 1883), pp. 279–280.

serveth to practize," we know from Winslow's testimony that they were not among "such as are of mean skill." Whatever use Brewster and his companions may have made of Allison's volume, it unquestionably forms a direct link between them and the finest contrapuntal art of Elizabethan England.

The lute, orpharion, and cittern mentioned by Allison were elaborate, delicate, and costly stringed instruments scarcely practical for use in a frontier community. By the beginning of the eighteenth century, such wind instruments as the flute, flageolet, and oboe (then spelled haut-boy) came into general use, along with the violin, and were soon imported by the American colonies. In 1716, an advertisement in the *Boston News* announced the arrival of a shipment of instruments from London, consisting of "Flageolets, Flutes, Haut-boys, Bass-viols, Violins, bows, strings, reeds for haut-boys, books of instruction for all these instruments, books of Ruled Paper. To be sold at the Dancing School of Mr. Enstone in Sudbury Street near the Orange Tree, Boston." So by this time Boston had a fully equipped music store, and located in a Dancing School at that! The mention of ruled paper raises a question in my mind. Ruled paper is for writing music. If the paper was advertized it was probably sold, and if it was sold it was probably used. By whom and for what? Amateurs who studied instruction books for various instruments would perhaps carry their interest a step further and begin writing "Lessons" or other pieces for their favorite instrument. This supposition is strengthened by the fact that treatises on musical composition were available, *and were used in New England*, from the earliest times.

In 1720 the Rev. Thomas Symmes, of Bradford, Massachusetts, published an essay, *The Reasonableness of Regular Singing, or Singing by Note*, in which he writes, among other things, of music at Harvard (founded in 1636). Speaking of what he calls "Regular Singing," Symmes says:

> It was studied, known and approved of in our College, for many years after its first founding. This is evident from the Musical Theses which were formerly printed, and from some writings containing some tunes, with directions for singing by note, as they are now sung; and these are yet in being, though of more than sixty years standing; *besides no man that studied music, as it is treated of by Alstead, Playford and others, could be ignorant of it.*

The musical theses and writings to which Symmes refers were subsequently destroyed when the library of Harvard College burned. The passage I have italicized is what concerns us particularly, for Symmes clearly takes it for granted that educated men in New England would be familiar with the theoretical works on music that he mentions. The author whom he calls "Alstead" was Johann Heinrich Alsted (1588–1638), and the work in question is undoubtedly his *Templum Musicum: or, The Musical Synopsis, of the learned and famous J.H.A., being a compendium of the rudiments both of the mathematical and practical part of musick, of which subject not any book is extant in our English tongue. Faithfully translated out of Latin by J. Birchensha* . . . London, 1663.

In spite of this title blurb, Playford's book, *An Introduction to the Skill of Musick,* had been in print since 1654, and new editions appeared at frequent intervals until 1730. It included a section on composing music in parts, to which, after 1683, Henry Purcell contributed. The high standing enjoyed by Playford's book in New England is attested to by the fact that when, in 1698, music came to be included in the *Bay Psalm Book,* the tunes were taken from the eleventh edition of Playford's standard work, which was one of the best books of its kind ever written.

"Vayne and triflying ballades"

"Honest John" Playford was the leading English music publisher of his time, and we can safely assume that his numerous collections of vocal and instrumental music were well known in New England. There is ample evidence that secular songs circulated widely in New England, and the fact that most of the evidence is indirect does not make it any less valid. First of all, let us take an instance that rests upon direct evidence. The Rev. John Cotton had a son who was born at sea on the voyage to America. This son, aptly named Seaborn Cotton, in due course became a student at Harvard and, while there, found time to copy out in his "commonplace book" the words of several English ballads, which were currently sung to popular tunes of the day. Among these ballads are "The Lovesick Maid, or Cordelia's Lamentation for the Absence of Her Gerhard," "The Last Lamentation of the Languishing Squire, or Love Overcomes All Things," and "The Two Faithful Lovers." It is obvious that even in seventeenth-century New England, a young man's fancy turned to thoughts of love, and that even a divinity student at Harvard could find relaxation in sentimental "tear-jerkers." The ballad of "The Two Faithful Lovers," sung to the tune of "Franklin Is Fled Away," is a stilted tale of woe, in dialogue form, which tells of a lover who had to flee from England. Refusing to be parted from him, his sweetheart dresses as a man and goes on board; during the voyage to Venice the ship is wrecked and the girl is drowned. Whereupon the lover laments:

> You loyal lovers all
>   that hear this ditty,
> Sigh and lament my fall,
>   let's move you to pity:
> She lies now in the deep,
> In everlasting sleep,
> And left me here to weep
>   in great distress.

This is pretty poor poetry, evidently the work of some hack, and cannot compare with the magnificent old traditional ballads that undoubtedly circulated through oral tradition in New England. Benjamin Franklin, in a letter to his brother Peter, refers to "some country girl in the heart of Massachusetts, who has never heard any other than psalm tunes or 'Chevy Chase,' the 'Children in the Woods,' the 'Spanish Lady,' and such old, simple ditties"—mentioning in a breath three of the most famous English ballads. Franklin, it is true, was writing around the middle of the eighteenth century; but his remark indicates that ballad singing and psalm singing went hand-in-hand in New England. And if a country girl of his generation knew these ballads, we can be sure that her parents and grandparents sang them before her, because that is how they were handed down.

The Rev. Thomas Symmes, advocating the establishment of regular singing schools in 1720, argued that these would have "a tendency to divert young people . . . from learning idle, foolish, yea, pernicious songs and ballads, and banish all such trash from their minds." How often, in our own times, have the comics been denounced as trash and all kinds of alternatives been proposed for substituting more edifying reading matter for our youngsters. Yet the vogue of the comics continues unabated; and so, no doubt, it was in early New England with those "idle, foolish, yea, pernicious songs and ballads" which Reverend Symmes was so anxious to prevent young people from learning.

Geneva jigs and Puritan hornpipes

Although young people might naturally prefer a little more variety and spice in their vocal diet, the singing of psalms was by no means such a dull and solemn business as is generally supposed. In its heyday it was done with much verve and gusto. Shakespeare, in *The Winter's Tale*, has a character say, "But one Puritan amongst them, and he sings psalms to hornpipes." Now, the hornpipe was a lively dance, and the singing of a psalm to it would make it no less lively. Even if we are not to take Shakespeare's quip literally, the point remains that early Puritan psalm singing gave an impression of liveliness and vigor, which was turned to scorn and ridicule by the enemies of Puritanism. This is confirmed by a passage in John Cotton's treatise, *Singing of Psalms a Gospel Ordinance*, in which he answers objections to psalm singing raised by those who considered the melodies were made by "sinful men." Cotton writes:

> For neither the man of sinne . . . nor any Antichristian Church have had any hand in turning Davids Psalms into English Songs and Tunes, or are wont to make any Melody in Singing them; yea, they reject them as *Genevah Gigs;* and there be Cathedrall Priests of an Antichristian spirit, that have scoffed at Puritan-Ministers, as calling the people to sing one of *Hopkins Jigs*, and so hop into the pulpit.

Let us look more closely at some of the "Genevah Gigs," to see what truth may lie behind these gibing jests.

The Plymouth Pilgrims used a psalm book prepared especially for the Separatist congregation in Holland by Henry Ainsworth and first printed at Amsterdam in 1612 (five other editions followed, the last in 1690). This is the book that Longfellow describes in "The Courtship of Miles Standish," when he pictures Priscilla singing at home:

> Open wide in her lap lay the well-worn psalm-book of Ainsworth,
> Printed in Amsterdam, the words and the music together,
> Rough-hewn, angular notes, like stones in the wall of a churchyard,
> Darkened and overhung by the running vine of the verses.

The melodies are for one voice only, printed in the customary diamond-shaped notes of the period, and without bar lines. There are thirty-nine different tunes. Concerning the origin of the melodies, Ainsworth writes:

> Tunes for the Psalms I find none set of God; so that each people is to use the most grave, decent and comfortable manner of singing that they know. . . . The singing-notes, therefore, I have most taken from our former Englished Psalms, when they will fit the measure of the verse. And for the other long verses I have also taken (for the most part) the gravest and easiest tunes of the French and Dutch Psalmes.

By "our former Englished Psalms," Ainsworth meant the Sternhold and Hopkins version, which had been completed in 1562. Several years earlier an edition of "Sternhold and Hopkins" had been printed in Geneva for the use of English Protestants who had taken refuge in Switzerland; several of the tunes in this edition were taken from the French psalter, for which the music had been composed or arranged by Louis Bourgeois. Subsequent editions of "Sternhold and Hopkins" continued these borrowings from French sources, so that Ainsworth's psalter actually contained even more tunes of French origin than he suspected. To take one example, the tune for the 100th Psalm, as it appears in both "Sternhold and Hopkins" and "Ainsworth," is derived from the French setting of the 134th Psalm. And this, in turn, bears a striking resemblance to a French secular *chanson* of the sixteenth century, "Il n'a icy celuy qui n'ait sa belle" ("There Is None Here without His Fair One"). A number of other tunes in the French psalter, which eventually found their way, more or less altered, into English psalmbooks, appear to have had a similar origin.

Musically, the *Ainsworth Psalter* is of great interest. The tunes have considerable metrical variety and rhythmic freedom. Only a few of the psalms in Ainsworth's version use the four-line ballad stanza (so-called "common meter") that later became so tiresomely prevalent in English psalmody. Stanzas of five, six, eight, and twelve lines are frequently used by Ainsworth, and he has no less than eight different rhythms for the six-syllable line alone. In the words of Waldo Selden Pratt: "This music represents the folk-song style, with its symmetrical and echoing lines, each with a definite unity and all fused into a total enveloping unity. But it is folk song that has retained great freedom of inner structure. It may be that these thirty-nine melodies illustrate more than one strain of folk-song tradition." [5] Here, then, is a document fully worthy to be the cornerstone of America's music: stem-

[5] Pratt, *The Music of the Pilgrims.*

ming from folk traditions, international in background, marked by melodic freedom and rhythmic variety—qualities that will repay a careful study of the modest little psalter that the Pilgrims brought with them to Plymouth.

Below is a verse from the 100th Psalm, in Ainsworth's translation, together with the tune as he printed it:

Showt to Jehovah, al the earth;
  Serv ye Jehovah with gladness;
Before Him come with singing mirth;
  Know that Jehovah He God is.

This stirring tune, sung in a lively and jubilant spirit, became a favorite with the Pilgrims and Puritans in New England. "Jehovah," incidentally, was pronounced *Jehovay*. Nicknamed "Old Hundredth," the tune appears in modern hymnals as a setting for the Doxology, but in an altered form that causes the tempo to drag.

Another tune from the *Ainsworth Psalter*, known as "Old 124" or "Toulon," which is still used in truncated form in modern hymnals, demonstrates the type of melody used for the psalms with five lines and ten syllables to the line, as in this version of Psalm 124:

Our sowl is as a bird escaped free
  From out of the intangling fowler's snare.
The snare is broke and we escaped are.
Our succour in Jehovah's name shal bee,
That of the heav'ns and earth is the maker.

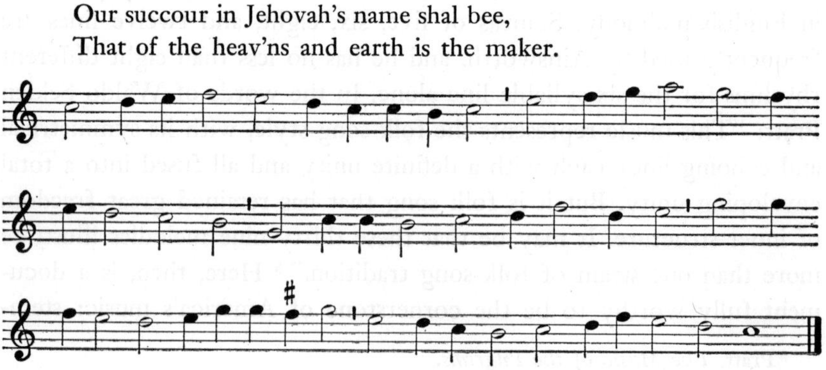

This tune was taken from the *Geneva Psalter* of 1560, and it appears as the "proper" tune for Psalm 124 in "Sternhold and Hopkins."

The early New England settlers really believed in coming before Him "with singing mirth." With St. James they said, "If any be merry, let him sing psalms." If jigs and hornpipes could be turned to the service of God, so much the better. They enjoyed psalm singing not only because it was edifying but also because it was fun.

The *Bay Psalm Book*

The Plymouth colonists continued to use the *Ainsworth Psalter* until 1692, a year after their merger with the larger and more powerful Massachusetts Bay Colony. They apparently found it increasingly difficult to cope with the long and varied melodies of Ainsworth. The prevailing trend was toward the jog-trot ballad stanza of common meter, with alternating lines of eight and six syllables, as illustrated in this translation of the 23d Psalm from the *Bay Psalm Book:*

> The Lord to mee a shepheard is,
> want therefore shall not I.
> He in the folds of tender grasse,
> doth cause me downe to lie.

The Massachusetts Bay colonists at first used the Sternhold and Hopkins Psalter, but they became dissatisfied with the translations, as not being sufficiently faithful to the original. For this reason a group of New England divines prepared a new version, which was printed at Cambridge, Massachusetts, in 1640, as *The Whole Booke of Psalmes Faithfully Translated into English Metre*. Commonly known as the *Bay Psalm Book*, it was the first book printed in the English colonies of North America and held sway in New England for several generations (the twenty-sixth edition appeared at Boston in 1744). Numerous editions were also printed in England and Scotland. A copy of the first edition was sold at auction in New York in 1947 for $151,000, said to be the highest price ever paid for any book, including the Gutenberg Bible.[6]

No music was included in early editions of the *Bay Psalm Book*, but an "Admonition to the Reader" contained detailed instructions regarding the tunes to which psalms in various meters might be sung.

[6] *The New York Times,* Jan. 29, 1947.

For example, "The verses of these psalmes may be reduced to six kindes, the first whereof may be sung in very neere fourty common tunes; as they are collected out of our chief musicians by Thomas Ravenscroft." The reference to Ravenscroft is significant, for it shows that the New England Puritans were acquainted with the best musical publications of that time. Ravenscroft's psalter had been printed at London in 1621, with the title: *The Whole Booke of Psalmes, with the Hymnes Evangelicall and Songs Spirituall. . . . Newly corrected and enlarged by Thomas Ravenscroft, Bachelar of Musicke.* This notable collection contains four-part settings by many of the most prominent English composers of the period, including Thomas Morley, Thomas Tallis, Giles Farnaby, John Dowland, John Farmer, Michael Cavendish, Richard Allison, and Ravenscroft himself—a total of 105 compositions. Note that the compilers of the *Bay Psalm Book* take pains to mention that Ravenscroft's collection enjoyed the collaboration of "our chief musicians," which would have been a matter of indifference to them had they lacked artistic appreciation.

By the time the ninth edition of the *Bay Psalm Book* was ready to appear, the editors had decided that it should be provided with a selection of the tunes most frequently used. Thus, music was included for the first time in the revised and enlarged edition printed at Boston in 1698, under the title:

> *The Psalms, Hymns, and Spiritual Songs, of the Old and New Testament. . . . For the use, Edification and Comfort of the Saints in publick and private, especially in New-England. The Ninth Edition.*

The music, in two parts (soprano and bass), with solmization syllables, is printed in five pages near the end of the book. The tunes are those known as "Oxford," "Litchfield," "Low-Dutch," "York," "Windsor," "Cambridge," "St. David's," "Martyrs," "Hackney," "119th Psalm Tune," "100th Psalm Tune," "115th Psalm Tune," and "148th Psalm Tune." For these tunes, the compilers of the *Bay Psalm Book* turned once more to an excellent English source, Playford's *Introduction to the Skill of Musick,* of which the eleventh edition had been published in London in 1687. The thirteen tunes included in the *Bay Psalm Book* are identical, save for two slight misprints, with those printed in this edition of Playford's famous work.[7] The instructions for singing the

[7] I am indebted to Dr. Carleton Sprague Smith for this identification.

psalms, with the classification in various meters, are also taken from Playford's book. No better guide than Playford could have been chosen.

In contrast to the metrical variety displayed in the melodies of the *Ainsworth Psalter*, nearly all the tunes printed in the *Bay Psalm Book* were in common meter. This was indicative of the trend toward regularity and standardization that made itself increasingly felt in New England psalmody and hymnody during the eighteenth century. But along with this trend toward standardization, as manifested in the movement for "Regular Singing," there was a countercurrent, stemming from the folk, that opposed the imposition of regular rules and standardized procedures in singing. Thus, near the very beginning of America's musical history, we encounter one of those clashes of conflicting cultural traditions that dramatize the creation of a people's music.

chapter two

New England reformers

They use many Quavers and Semiquavers, &c. And on this very account it is they are pleased with it, and so very loath to part with it.

REV. NATHANIEL CHAUNCEY, REGULAR SINGING DEFENDED, NEW LONDON, 1728.

It is important to understand the conditions under which psalmody and hymnody developed in New England during the eighteenth century and to comprehend, in particular, the nature of the divergent and conflicting cultural trends that made New England a virtual battleground between the zealous reformers who advocated and tried to impose "Regular Singing," and the common folk who preferred their own way of singing, handed down by oral tradition. The reformers, most of whom were clergymen educated at Harvard, held that "the usual way of singing" practiced by the people was an abomination and an offense against good taste. But many of the people clung tenaciously to their own way, for they thoroughly enjoyed it and were therefore "so very loath to part with it," as the Rev. Nathaniel Chauncey wrote. A typical argument of the opponents of the folk style of psalm singing is the following, which appeared in a pamphlet published by Chauncey: "It looks very unlikely to be the right way, because that young people fall in with it; they are not wont to be so forward for anything that is good."[1] This indicates, among other things, that the folk way of singing was not cherished only by die-hard oldsters, but that it also appealed to the younger generation.

The reformers referred to the style of singing to which they were opposed as "the usual way" or "the common way" of singing. The style of singing that they advocated they called "Regular Singing" or "Singing by Note." Each camp was evidently thoroughly convinced of the superior merits of its own kind of singing. There is no indica-

[1] Chauncey, *Regular Singing Defended.*

tion, however, that those who practiced "the common way" of singing endeavored to impose their convictions or their methods upon others. They simply wished to be left alone to sing as they pleased. It was the reformers, with their righteous zeal, who wanted to impose their standards on everyone else. The title of a pamphlet written by the Rev. Nathaniel Chauncey, of Durham, Connecticut, is revealing in this respect: *Regular Singing Defended and proved to be the only true way of singing the songs of the Lord.* . . . New London, 1728. "The ONLY TRUE WAY!"

In his pamphlet, Chauncey employs the method of "Objection" and "Answer." The arguments advanced in favor of "the common way" are listed as "Objections." Each objection is followed by an answer intended to refute the argument. For example:

> Objection. This way of singing we use in the country is more solemn, and therefore much more suitable and becoming.
>
> Answer. But suppose by solemn you mean grave and serious. Nothing makes more against the common way; for they will readily grant that they use many Quavers and Semiquavers, &c. And on this very account it is they are pleased with it, and so very loath to part with it; neither do we own or allow any of them [i.e., "quavers, semiquavers, &c."] in the songs of the Lord. Judge then which is most solemn.

Notice that in the Objection "the common way" of singing is referred to as the way of singing used in the country, which defines it as a rural folk tradition. As for the use of "many Quavers and Semiquavers, &c.," we shall deal with that presently when we undertake to describe the characteristics of the two opposed styles of singing, one upheld by the common folk, the other by the educated clergy.

The printed accounts of early New England psalm singing that have come down to us were all written by the advocates of Regular Singing. The common people sang but did not write. Hence the written accounts are definitely one-sided. It is upon these one-sided accounts, polemical and prejudiced as they are, that historians have based their descriptions of early New England psalmody. For example, in 1721 Cotton Mather wrote: "It has been found . . . in some of our congregations, that in length of time, their singing has degenerated into an *odd noise*, that has more of what we want a name for, than any Regular Singing in it." [2] In the same year, Thomas Walter wrote: "I have observed in many places, one man is upon this note while another is upon the note before him, which produces something so hideous and disorderly as is beyond expression bad." Seizing upon such expressions as "an odd noise" and "hideous and disorderly," modern writers have not hesitated to make sweeping generalizations regarding the manner of singing in New England, and have been content to dismiss it as deplorable. They have repeated as objective truth the words of men who were *attacking* something they did not like, something that was contrary to their own interests and inclinations. The procedure is about the same as that of a writer who would base a biography of a public man on material contained in the campaign speeches of his political opponents.

Once we accept the premise that the advocates of Regular Singing are polemical writers, that they are prejudiced and one-sided, we are in a position to use their writings more intelligently and more fruitfully. We may begin by discounting all that comes under the heading of sheer name-calling, which includes such expressions as "an odd noise," and such adjectives as "hideous," "disorderly," and "bad." The same expressions have always been applied to music by people who do not like it.[3] Their only objective value is to indicate that the music to which such terms are applied is *different* from the kind of music to which the name-callers are accustomed or which they regard as "the right thing." These abusive terms, then, serve to confirm the existence of a type of singing that was not "regular," that was not conventional or correct according to educated opinion in early New England.

The next question that we ask is: what were the characteristics of that "common way of singing" to which the reformers were so strongly opposed? Since the writings of the reformers are the only sources of *written documentation* that we possess, we must extract our information from them. But we must look for whatever objective information may be imbedded in the polemical verbiage. Chauncey's

[2] Mather, *The Accomplished Singer*, published in 1721 and "Intended for the assistance of all that sing psalms with grace in their hearts: but more particularly to accompany the laudable endeavours of those who are learning to sing by Rule, and seeking to preserve a REGULAR SINGING in the Assemblies of the Faithful."

[3] For a thorough (and entertaining) documentation of this statement, consult the *Lexicon of Musical Invective* by Nicolas Slonimsky (New York, 1953).

statement regarding the "use of many Quavers and Semiquavers, &c." (that *etcetera* is very important) is an example of objective information that may be extracted from a polemical context. This written documentation can be supplemented by the evidence of folklore, which, being a survival of archaic practices, is a valuable adjunct to cultural history. The evidence furnished by folklore will be discussed later in this chapter.

The reformers

The leaders of the reform movement in New England's singing methods were the Rev. Thomas Symmes (1677–1725), the Rev. John Tufts (1689–1750), and the Rev. Thomas Walter (1696–1725), supported by a number of other clergymen, such as the Rev. Cotton Mather and the Rev. Nathaniel Chauncey, who preached and wrote in favor of "Regular Singing" or "Singing by Note." The Rev. John Tufts, a graduate of Harvard, published a little work called *A Very Plain and Easy Introduction to the Singing of Psalm Tunes,* which may have been issued around 1714, though no edition earlier than the fifth (Boston, 1726) has been located. This went through eleven editions up to 1744. It was a modest pamphlet of only twelve pages, containing thirty-seven tunes set in three parts, with instructions for singing adapted from Ravenscroft and Playford. Instead of musical notation, Tufts used letters to indicate the notes of the scale, according to the system of solmization then prevalent: F (fa), S (sol), L (la), M (mi). The time value of the notes was indicated by a system of punctuation. A letter standing alone was equal to a quarter note; a letter followed by a period was equal to a half note; and one followed by a colon, to a whole note. Tufts thought he had introduced an "easy method of singing by letters instead of notes," but his system was not widely adopted.

The Rev. Thomas Walter of Roxbury was also a graduate of Harvard, though during his student days he thought more of social pleasure than of application to his studies. Fortunately he had a good memory and supplemented his education by listening to the remarkable conversation of his learned uncle, Cotton Mather. In 1721, Walter brought out *The Grounds and Rules of Musick Explained, or An Introduction to the Art of Singing by Note. . . .* Boston, Printed by J. Franklin (who, by the way, was James Franklin, older brother of

Benjamin, who was then an apprentice in the shop). Walter's book went through at least eight editions, the last in 1764. It was highly regarded and exerted wide influence for upwards of forty years. It was the first music book to be printed with bar lines in the North American colonies.

The alternate title of Thomas Walter's book, *An Introduction to the Art of Singing by Note*, claims closer attention at this point. As we observed above, "singing by note" was one of the terms used by the musical reformers to designate the "correct" or "regular" way of singing that they advocated, which in effect meant singing the notes as written or printed, without alterations, additions, or embellishments, and in strict time and pitch. In his preface, Walter asserts that he was thoroughly familiar with the common or country way of singing, and speaks of himself as one "who can sing all the various Twistings of the old Way, and that too according to the *genius* of most of the Congregations." By the latter statement he meant that each congregation had its own special manner of singing within the style of the old or common way. It was only natural that Walter should be familiar with this manner of singing, since it was the way practiced by most people. But as a college graduate, and an up-to-date, progressive young clergyman, he repudiated the old, common way of singing, and denounced it in the strongest terms. He writes of tunes which

> . . . are now miserably tortured, and twisted, and quavered, in some churches, into an horrid Medley of confused and disorderly Noises. . . . Our tunes are, for Want of a Standard to appeal to in all our Singing, left to the Mercy of every unskilful Throat to chop and alter, twist and change, according to their infinitely divers and no less odd Humours and Fancies. . . .

And he sadly concludes: "Our Tunes have passed through strange Metamorphoses . . . since their first introduction into the World." Metamorphosis, or change, is the fate of all folk music, and constitutes indeed one of its defining traits. So Walter is simply telling us, indirectly, that these tunes underwent what we would now call a process of folklorization. (The term "folklore," by the way, did not come into usage until after 1840.)

In defending the Regular Way of singing psalm tunes, Walter writes: "And this I am sure of, we sing them as they are prick'd down, and I am sure the Country People do not." Of course not; they never do.

The *New England Courant* for March 5, 1722, contains this significant item:

> On Thursday last in the afternoon, a Lecture was held at the New Brick Church [Boston], by the Society for Promoting Regular Singing in the worship of God. The Rev. Thomas Walter of Roxbury preach'd an excellent Sermon on that Occasion, *The Sweet Psalmist of Israel.* The Singing was perform'd in Three Parts (according to Rule) by about Ninety Persons skill'd in that Science, to the great Satisfaction of a Numerous Assembly there Present.

This sermon was afterwards printed, also by J. Franklin, under the following title: *The sweet Psalmist of Israel: A Sermon Preach'd at the Lecture held in Boston, by the Society for promoting Regular and Good Singing, and for reforming the Depravations and Debasement, our Psalmody labours under, In Order to introduce the proper and true Old Way of Singing. . . .* (Boston, 1722.)

Both of these citations are interesting for several reasons. The first reveals that there was a Society for Promoting Regular Singing at Boston in the early 1720s, and that there then existed large choral groups trained to sing in parts. The second defines the aims of the reform movement as the correction of the "depravations and debasements" of New England psalmody, and the introduction of "the proper and true Old Way of Singing." If the reformers stood for new methods and the correction of existing abuses, why did they speak of restoring the Old Way of Singing, and why was this the "proper and true" way? The Rev. Thomas Symmes will help us to answer these questions.

Symmes's anonymous pamphlet, *The Reasonableness of Regular Singing, or Singing by Note* (1720), is subtitled "An Essay to revive the true and ancient mode of Singing psalm-tunes according to the pattern of our New-England psalm-books." According to Symmes, singing by note was "the ancientest way" among the early New England settlers. Emphasizing this point, he writes:

> There are persons now living, children and grand-children of the *first* settlers of New-England, who can very well remember that their Ancestors sung by *note*, and they learned to sing of them, and

they have more than their bare words to prove that they speak the truth, for many of them can sing tunes exactly by note which they learnt of their fathers.

Symmes will also define for us Regular Singing or Singing by Note:

Now singing by note is giving every note its proper pitch, and turning the voice in its proper place, and giving to every note its true length and sound. Whereas, the usual way varies much from this. In it, some notes are sung too high, others too low, and most too long, and many turnings or flourishings with the voice (as they call them) are made where they should not be, and some are wanting where they should have been.

This is an extremely significant passage, for it sums up the two opposing styles of singing that were contending for supremacy in New England. Regular Singing was according to the pattern of the psalm-books: giving to every note its proper pitch and true length as "prick'd" in the book, and turning the voice only as required by the melody. This, according to the reformers, was the proper and true "Old Way of Singing." How and why, then, was it abandoned and allowed to undergo "depravations and debasements," to become incrusted with what Cotton Mather called "indecencies"? Again, the obliging Mr. Symmes has an explanation:

The declining from, and getting beside the rule, was *gradual and insensible.* Singing Schools and Singing books being laid aside, there was no way to learn; but only by hearing of tunes sung, or by taking the run of the tune, as it is phrased. The rules of singing not being taught or learnt, every one sang as best pleased himself, and every leading-singer, would take the liberty of raising any note of the tune, or lowering of it, as best pleased his ear; and add such turns and flourishes as were grateful to him; and this was done so gradually, as that but few if any took notice of it. One Clerk or Chorister would alter the tunes a little in his day, the next a little in his, and so on one after another, till in fifty or sixty years it caused a considerable alteration. If the alteration had been made designedly by any Master of Music, it is probable that the variation from our psalm-books would have been alike in all our congregations; whereas some vary much more than others, and it is hard to find two that sing exactly alike. . . . Your usual way of singing is handed down by tradition only, and whatsoever is only so conveyed down to us, it is a thousand to one if it be not miserably corrupted, in three or four-score years' time. . . .

The Rev. Thomas Symmes is truly invaluable; what he tells us is interesting, but what he reveals between the lines is priceless. He does not explain why the singing schools and singing books should have been laid aside by the early colonists, he just assumes that they were. However, he does trace very revealingly, though with no intention of doing so, the formation of a folk tradition. Let us note some of its characteristics: it is handed down by tradition only (that is, by oral tradition, since books had been set aside); the variation from the standard norm (that is, from the tunes as printed) is not uniform, but differs from congregation to congregation, so that hardly any two sing exactly alike; the singing was not learned by rule or lesson, but by ear, and everyone sang as best pleased himself; the leading-singer would raise or lower notes at will, and add such turns and flourishes as he pleased. In short, we have here the complete description of a folk tradition in singing. We may therefore call this the Early New England Folk Style.

Some musical historians account for the "decline" of New England psalmody by pointing to the difficult conditions of frontier life, aggravated by political dissension and military strife. This explanation falls through when we realize that a similar "decline" took place in England, which was not precisely a struggling colony. In the preface to his edition of *Psalms and Hymns in solemn musick* (1671), Playford vividly describes the sad state of psalm singing in England at that time, concluding with the assertion that "this part of God's service hath been so ridiculously performed in most places, that it is now brought into scorn and derision by many people." Apparently the "decline" continued for a long time, because in 1796 a letter in the *Gentleman's Magazine*, referring to psalm singing in England, states: "In some churches one may see the Parish Clerk, after giving out a couple of staves from Sternhold and Hopkins, with two or three other poor wights, drawling them out in the most lamentable strains, with such grimaces, and in such discordant notes, as must shock every serious person, and afford mirth to the undevout." [4] We gather from these quotations that, in every generation, there was a kind of singing going on, both in old and new England, that offended the taste and

[4] Quoted by Curwen, *Studies in Music Worship*, p. 30.

provoked the scorn and ridicule of educated persons because it failed to conform to the culturally dominant standards of "good" singing.

Summarizing the characteristics of the Early New England Folk Style as described by contemporary writers: the singing is very slow; many grace notes, passing notes, turns, flourishes and other ornaments are used; pitch and time values are arbitrarily altered; there is a lack of synchronization among the voices; everyone sings as best pleases himself. This is not to be taken as a complete description of the style, because the reformers were interested only in pointing out what they considered some of its most prominent faults: they cover up many details with an "&c." In order to spell out that *etcetera* we must find an analogous and more fully documented tradition. It will then be within the bounds of reasonable conjecture to assume that the New England Folk Style embodied the traits of the analogous tradition.

The logical place to look for this analogous tradition is in eighteenth-century England and Scotland, whence came the early New England settlers. We may begin by glancing at the old Gaelic psalmody of Scotland. Our earliest written documentation on this tradition dates from the 1840s, but its persistence from generation to generation enables us to reconstruct the eighteenth-century practice with reasonable fidelity. John Spencer Curwen, the English authority on congregational singing who wrote at a time when Gaelic psalmody could still be heard in Highland parishes in much the same manner as it was sung a hundred years earlier, summarized the main features of this tradition as follows: "There are five tunes—*French*, *Martyrs*, *Stilt* (or *York*), *Dundee*, and *Elgin*—which are the traditional melodies used for the Psalms. These have been handed down from generation to generation, amplified by endless grace notes, and altered according to the fancy of every precentor. When used, they are sung so slowly as to be beyond recognition." And he adds: "Each parish and each precentor had differences of detail, for the variations were never written or printed, but were handed down by tradition." Now, is this not, in all essential points, an exact counterpart of the description of the "usual" New England way of psalm singing as contained in the writings of Symmes and his colleagues?

Note that the traditional repertory consisted of five tunes. Writers on early New England psalmody have continually harped on the theme that only five or six tunes seem to have been commonly used in the Puritan congregations, and they have adduced this as further evidence of the musical impoverishment of Puritan New England. When we stop to consider that in England the number of psalm tunes in common usage in the second half of the seventeenth century had dwindled down to six or eight, we realize that New England enjoyed no position of privileged inferiority in this respect. Here, again, it is necessary to look at the matter from a different point of view, and to regard this limitation of repertory as characteristic of the folk tradition with which we are dealing; in England, in Scotland, in America, the same pattern prevails. This small inherited repertory of tunes provided a firm foundation for the improvisations and embellishments of the folk style. There was a core of unity with scope for endless variety. (Compare the core of "stock" tunes used in hot jazz improvisation, as another illustration of the same principle.)

Before going on to see what we can discover in eighteenth-century England, we may pause to discuss briefly the practice of "lining-out," a prominent feature of folk psalmody in England, Scotland, and New England. The nature of lining-out is explained by the ordinances of the Westminster Assembly of 1644 which recommend the adoption of the practice in English churches: ". . . for the present, where many of the congregation cannot read, it is convenient that the minister, or some other fit person appointed by him and the other officers, do read the psalm, line by line, before the singing thereof." The Rev. John Cotton, in his treatise *Singing of Psalms a Gospel Ordinance* (Boston, 1647), granted that "where all have books and can reade, or else can say the *Psalme* by heart, it were needless then to reade each line of the Psalme beforehand in order to singing." But where this is not the case, he adds, "it will be a necessary helpe, that the lines of the Psalme, be openly read beforehand, line after line, or two lines together, that so they who want either books or skill to reade, may know what is to be sung, and joyne with the rest in the dutie of singing." The practice of lining-out became fairly widespread in New England, to judge by a passage in Cotton Mather's *Church Discipline; or Methods and Customs in the Churches in New England* (Boston, 1726):

> In some [churches], the assembly being furnished with Psalm-books, they sing without the stop of reading between every line. But ordinarily the Psalm is read line after line, by him whom the Pastor desires to do that service; and the people generally sing in such grave tunes, as are the most usual in the churches of our nation.

The practice of lining-out has been deplored, condemned, and ridiculed by most writers on early American music. Once again, the important thing is to understand, not to sneer. Granted that the custom was introduced as a practical and temporary expedient, how shall we account for its persistence in circumstances where these practical considerations were not a factor? How shall we account for the tenaciousness with which the people clung to it, and their resentment of, and determined opposition to, all efforts to abolish the custom? How shall we account for the fact that it has endured, in one form or another, for more than three hundred years? John Cotton admitted—what is in any case quite obvious—that lining-out had no practical justification where the people knew the psalms by heart. Yet the custom prevailed even when the repertory of psalms was limited, orally transmitted, and learned by memory. We must, therefore, seek some other *raison d'être* for the practice of lining-out. This will be found if we can locate a tradition in which lining-out was not an expedient, but an organic element of style. For this we return momentarily to the Highlands of Scotland.

The Scottish church accepted the custom of lining-out reluctantly, under a directive from the Westminster Assembly in the middle of the seventeenth century. Yet, when attempts to abolish it were made a hundred years later, great resentment arose among the people of Scotland, and in some parishes the custom was not abandoned until well into the nineteenth century. As Curwen writes: "Lining-out, which had at first been resented as a concession to illiterate England, was clung to as a vital principle." Now, what had happened in the interval to transform lining-out from a foreign imposition to a "vital principle" of Scottish popular psalmody? The tradition of Gaelic psalmody will help us to answer this question. Dr. Joseph Mainzer published a monograph on *Gaelic Psalm-Tunes* in 1844, in which he collected vestiges of the traditional psalmody handed down through many generations. In these psalms the lining-out becomes an integral musical factor. The precentor gives out one line at a time, chanting it on the tonic or dominant, according to the key of the tune. According to Mainzer, the dominant is preferred, but if it is too high or too low for the voice, the tonic is taken. The recitative is not always on a monotone: it often touches the tone next above. The congregation then sings the line *with much elaboration of the melody*.

This shows the process by which an apparently extraneous element is incorporated into a folk tradition and becomes an organic stylistic factor. Because of this it is "clung to as a vital principle"—not because the people prefer what is "bad" in opposition to what the learned doctors from Oxford or Harvard tell them is "good." We have already seen that the Gaelic tradition of psalmody had several points of similarity with the Early New England Folk Style. We should not jump to the conclusion that the details of lining-out were identical in the two traditions. It is sufficient to have established, by analogy, that lining-out was an organic element in the folk tradition of New England psalmody. It should be pointed out, moreover, that lining-out constitutes a form of the "call-and-response" pattern that is basic in certain folk-song traditions, including the Afro-American. Lining-out still persists in the singing of some Negro congregations.

In 1724 the *New England Courant* published a curious satirical letter attacking the so-called defects of popular psalmody, written by an individual who signed himself "Jeoffrey Chanticleer" and who may have been James Franklin. Lining-out is the particular target of his attack, and in describing what he considers the evil results of this practice he sheds additional light on the Early New England Folk Style of psalmody. According to "Jeoffrey Chanticleer":

> . . . the same person who sets the Tune, and guides the Congregation in Singing, commonly reads the Psalm, which is a task so few are capable of performing well, that in Singing two or three staves the Congregation falls from a cheerful Pitch to downright *Grumbling;* and then some to relieve themselves mount an Eighth above the rest, others perhaps a Fourth or Fifth, by which means the Singing appears to be rather a confused Noise, made up of *Reading, Squeaking,* and *Grumbling,* than a decent and orderly part of God's Worship. . . .[5]

Translating this into unpolemical language, we get an aural image of a successive lowering of pitch among the main body of the congregation carrying the tune, while other voices sing above it at intervals of a fourth, a fifth, or an octave. Compare Curwen's account of "two old ladies in the North of England who were noted among their friends for their power of improvising a high part above the melody of the tune." This custom, he adds, had been common, "and it was

[5] Quoted by Foote, *Three Centuries of American Hymnody,* p. 376.

always considered a sign of musicianship to be able to sing this part." This last remark should be emphasized, for it underlines the point we are trying to establish throughout this chapter: that what is considered bad taste or "a confused Noise" by conventional standards may be regarded as a sign of musicianship and a source of pride in the folk tradition.

We must quote another brief passage from the letter of "Jeoffrey Chanticleer": "The Words are often murder'd or metamorphos'd by the *Tone* of the Reader. By this Means it happens in some churches, that those who neglect to carry Psalm Books with them, only join in Singing *like so many musical Instruments*, piping out the Tune to the rest. . . ." (The italics are mine.) Any reader acquainted with the history of opera will recognize the general trend of these remarks as being similar to criticisms leveled at the florid vocal style of Italian opera and oratorio: that the words could not be understood, and that the human voice was therefore used merely as an instrument. Compare, for example, Benjamin Franklin's remark on the vocal style of Handel and other contemporary composers, in which "the voice aims to be like an instrument" (see p. 96).

In England, where organs and other instruments were used in the established church, some observers commented adversely on what they regarded as the abuse of ornamentation in the organ accompaniments. A certain William Riley, who in 1762 published a book titled *Parochial Music Corrected*, complained that the parish organists introduced tedious variations in every line, indulged in ill-timed flourishes, and insisted on putting a "shake" (trill) at the end of every line. He quotes as an absurd example:

> The Lord's commands are righteous and (*shake*)
> Rejoice the heart likewise;
> His precepts are most pure and do (*shake*)
> Give light unto the eyes.

Instrumental music was, of course, forbidden in the Puritan churches of New England, though organs were used in such Episcopalian churches in America as King's Chapel in Boston (which acquired in 1713 an organ bequeathed by Mr. Thomas Brattle) and Bruton Parish Church in Williamsburg, Virginia. The reason I have made reference to organ playing in English parish churches is because of the obvious analogy with New England psalm singing suggested by "Jeoffrey Chanticleer's" previousy quoted remark that the people "join in Singing like so many musical Instruments, piping out the Tune to the rest." We may conclude that the people of New England, deprived of musical instruments in church, did their best to supply this lack by using their voices for the production of those shakes, flourishes, and variations that so annoyed the worthy Mr. Riley no less than the sarcastic "Chanticleer."

According to Curwen, congregational singing in English parish churches during the eighteenth century "was a string of grace-notes, turns, and other embellishments." This is exactly what Symmes, Walter, Chauncey, and other contemporary writers tell us about the popular psalmody of early New England, except that their statements are surrounded with polemical verbiage, which has to be cleared away before we can get at the truth. Though Curwen wrote in the 1870s, he interviewed informants whose memory and experience reached back to the early years of the century, and who spoke of traditional practices handed down from an earlier generation. One informant stated that in his early days, when the melody leaped a third, the women invariably added the intervening note; and if it leaped more than a third, they glided up or down, portamento, giving the next note in anticipation. Another informant confirmed the common use of appoggiaturas and gliding from one note to another. Another told of men in his congregation who "sing the air through the tune until they get to the end, and then, if the melody ends low, they will scale up in falsetto to the higher octave, and thus make harmony at the end." [6] I am not prepared to state categorically that these practices prevailed in eighteenth-century New England, but there is every reason to believe that they did, for they evidently belonged to the same tradition of folk psalmody and would doubtless have contributed to conveying an impression of what learned gentlemen like Cotton Mather called "an odd Noise."

[6] Curwen's informant also told him that "in the old times the people liked the tunes pitched high; the women especially enjoyed screaming out high G. It made the psalmody more brilliant and far-sounding." It should be observed that in those days it was the men, not the women, who carried the "tune" or principal air; therefore, the screaming on high notes may have been a compensatory means of feminine self-assertion.

Thus far we have relied upon analogy, conjecture, description, and tradition for our reconstruction of the Early New England Folk Style of psalmody. These methods are legitimate; yet it would be gratifying to be able to reinforce them with an actual musical document of the eighteenth century. Such a document exists, though from a slightly later period than the one we are discussing. Once again I am indebted to the admirable Curwen for putting me on its track. Let Curwen tell the story in his own words:

> Mr. John Dobson, of Richmond, has shown me an interesting publication by Matthew Camidge, organist of York Minster, bearing the date 1789. Camidge discovered in a library same psalm-tunes composed by Henry Lawes, a musician of the time of Charles I. He came to the conclusion that these tunes, if amended in accordance with modern feeling, might be revived for church uses. What did he mean by this amendment? Simply the addition of passing notes in the melody, trills, and such like devices. In order to show the reader how greatly he has improved Henry Lawes, Camidge prints the original and amended versions side by side throughout the book, and the result is ludicrous. The taste of today has returned to that of Lawes' time, but the old-fashioned tricks of vocalisation may still be heard from old people in remote country places.[7]

In other words, the once fashionable style of singing lived on as folklore, as an archaic survival, long after it ceased to be part of the dominant cultural pattern: a perfect example of the process of "folklorization." The result of Camidge's "improvement" of Lawes' music appeared "ludicrous" to Curwen, regarded solely from an aesthetic or artistic point of view. But from the historical point of view, Camidge's versions throw valuable light on the tradition of embellished psalmody in the eighteenth century.

Camidge's volume, entitled *Psalmody for a Single Voice*, is extremely rare. No copy exists in the United States, as far as is known, and until recently there was none in the British Museum in London. I was able to obtain a microfilm of the copy that is in the National Library of Scotland. The following musical example, a setting of Psalm 1 in the translation of George Sandys, illustrates both the original unadorned melody by Lawes and the "Variation" or embellished version of Camidge:

[7] Curwen, *op. cit.*, p. 66.

Original

Variation

That Man is tru - ly__ blest who_scorns to
stray By false ad-vice or walk the Sin - ners_ way, Or__
deigns to_min-gle_ with the_Sons of Pride Who God con -
temn_and_ Pi - e - ty de - ride.

Like most codified and printed versions of music that stems primarily from oral tradition, Camidge's version probably gives a schematic presentation of the actual traditional practice. Yet it is revealing as far as it goes.[8]

It remains to explain how New England psalmody, which among the original Plymouth Pilgrims and the first Puritan settlers was evidently "regular" (that is, according to the strict notes of the melody, and sung in a lively tempo), acquired the characteristics of embellished and slow-paced psalmody that we have been discussing. In the first place, the Pilgrims or Separatists, who had taken refuge in Holland, and the early Puritans, many of whom had lived in Geneva, were strongly influenced by the methods and customs of the French, Swiss, and Dutch Protestants, among whom the practice of lining-out was not used in psalm singing. My belief is that regular "singing by note" and the lively pace called for by the vigorous and varied tunes of the early psalters prevailed in New England, as in England and Scotland, until the spread of lining-out opened the door for the introduction of the florid style. The custom of lining-out in psalmody necessarily interrupted the free flow of the music and caused a slackening of the pace. To this may be added the natural tendency of some persons in an untrained and undirected group to sing more slowly than others —to take, as it were, their own time. This could have the effect of slowing up the whole group, but it could also have a more important effect in permitting the more skilled, or the more ambitious, or the bolder members of the group to indulge in the embellishments to which we have so often referred. The late G. P. Jackson aptly called this "a compensatory florid filling in." And why, it may be asked, did they indulge in these embellishments? Simply because they enjoyed it, because it was fun. The Rev. Nathaniel Chauncey is explicit on this point: "They use many Quavers and Semiquavers, &c. *And on this very account it is they are pleased with it, and so very loath to part with it.*"

When Henry W. Foote, in his history of American hymnody, writes that the old psalm tunes "which had once been sung with vigor and at reasonable speed, had become flattened with usage into weari-

[8] For other examples of the tradition of embellished psalmody and hymnody, the reader may wish to compare, in the present work, the ornamented versions of "Ah, Lovely Appearance of Death" (p. 49), "Amazing Grace" (p. 203), "I Stood Outside de Gate" (p. 250), and "Jordan's Stormy Banks" (p. 456).

some and dragging measures which had lost all their freshness and vitality," he expresses a modern opinion that actually distorts the whole situation by failing to take into account the values of the tradition which he is attempting to discuss. If the people who sang in that manner found it dull and wearisome, they would have sought some other manner of singing that pleased them better. But they did nothing of the sort. On the contrary, they clung tenaciously to their own style of singing. They liked it. And who is to say that they should have preferred something else?

It would be interesting to trace the transition from plain to embellished psalmody that took place in New England during the seventeenth century. But the available documentation scarcely permits us to trace the process in detail. We must not, in any case, assume that the process was complete and uniform; that is to say, that it occurred all at once and everywhere at the same time. Cultural processes are never as simple as that. As an illustration of this particular phase of cultural dynamics, let us take two representative dates and events. Symmes tells us that the Plymouth colonists took up the practice of lining-out at about the same time that they abandoned the *Ainsworth Psalter*, around the year 1692. And lining-out, as we have seen, prepared the way for the growth of responsorial, embellished, and improvisational psalmody. Now, only a few years later, in 1699, the practice of lining-out was abolished at the Brattle Square Church in Boston. In other words, the relatively backward and undeveloped colony at Plymouth was taking up a traditional practice which the relatively advanced and progressive city of Boston was on the point of abandoning. The sophisticated urban congregation was discarding a custom that already began to be associated with rural crudeness and backwardness. In the course of time, as urban culture tended to dominate the whole New England area, lining-out disappeared from that region and took refuge in the relatively undeveloped frontier sections.

The movement for Regular Singing led to the rise of singing schools. Reverend Symmes was one of the reformers who argued most persuasively in favor of regular musical instruction to improve the quality of singing:

> Would it not greatly tend to promote singing of psalms if singing schools were promoted? Would not this be a conforming to scripture pattern? Have we not as much need of them as God's

> people of old? Have we any reason to expect to be inspired with the gift of singing, any more than that of reading? . . . Where would be the difficulty, or what the disadvantage, if people who want skill in singing, would procure a skillful person to instruct them, and meet two or three evenings in the week, from five or six o'clock to eight, and spend the time in learning to sing? Would not this be an innocent and profitable recreation, and would it not have a tendency, if prudently managed, to prevent the unprofitable expense of time on other occasions? . . . Are they not very unwise who plead against learning to sing by rule, when they can't learn to sing at all, unless they learn by rule? [9]

As the eighteenth century advanced, more and more people decided that it was a pleasant recreation to come together at certain times to receive instruction in Regular Singing and to sing as a group the music that they learned. Thus the singing schools prospered and became an important institution during the second half of the century. The singing schools had to be provided with instruction books and collections of tunes. Hence the thriving trade in music books compiled and issued by the successors of Tufts and Walter. The singing schools did not exclusively promote the singing of psalms. Hymns, spiritual songs, and anthems were soon added to the repertory. Then came the exciting "fuguing tunes," which in turn proved to be the center of another controversy.

The singing school, as an institution, developed in two directions. In the cities it prepared the way for the formation of choirs and choral societies, such as the celebrated Handel and Haydn Society of Boston, devoted chiefly to the performance of music imported from Europe. In the rural areas, mainly in the South and Middle West, it formed the foundation for a homespun hymnody and for a communal type of singing that kept alive many of the old New England tunes along with the later "revival spirituals" and camp-meeting songs that were a distinct product of the American frontier.

The rise of evangelical hymnody, largely under the impulse of Methodism, and the transition from psalmody to hymnody, together with the musical activities of various dissenting sects and minority groups, will form the subject matter of the next chapter.

[9] Symmes, *The Reasonableness of Regular Singing.*

chapter three

Singing dissenters

Likewise in Amerikay
Shines the glorious Gospel-day.
JOSEPH HUMPHREYS, SACRED HYMNS.

The attitude of nonconformity represented by the Separatists and other Puritans who first settled in New England continued to manifest itself in many successive or simultaneous dissenting movements and groups that spread throughout the American colonies and had, in several instances, a lasting influence after the formation of the Republic. Through the inevitable irony of history, the nonconformists of one generation became the conformists of the next. Psalmody, which had been a symbol of Protestant and Puritan dissent, came to be regarded in the eighteenth century as a sign of adherence to restricted and arbitrary forms of worship. The nonconformist English divine, Dr. Isaac Watts (1674–1748), strongly objected to the old, strict, metrical psalmody, and even protested, in the preface to his *Hymns and Spiritual Songs* (1707), against the very contents of the psalms:

> Some of 'em are almost opposite to the Spirit of the Gospel: Many of them foreign to the State of the New-Testament, and widely different from the present Circumstances of Christians. . . .

On the other hand, those who clung to the old metrical psalmody, as opposed to the new hymns, were convinced that the word of God was being impiously replaced by "man-made" concoctions. Actually, a few hymns had been included in the appendixes of the metrical psalters as early as the sixteenth century. And the first supplement to Tate and Brady's *New Version of the Psalms*, issued in 1700, included three hymns for Holy Communion, two for Easter, and the familiar Christmas hymn beginning, "While shepherds watched their flocks by night," based on a passage from Luke (2:8–14). In the early years of the eighteenth century, the hymns of Dr. Watts swept like a flood over England and the North American colonies.

The influence of Dr. Watts in America was enormous. The first American edition of his *Hymns and Spiritual Songs* appeared in 1739, but his hymns and paraphrases of the psalms were known on this side of the ocean many years before that. As early as 1711 the Rev. Benjamin Colman of Boston wrote to Cotton Mather, saying: "Mr. Watts is a great Master in Poetry, and a burning Light and Ornament of the Age. . . . You will forgive me that I emulate, and have dared to imitate, his Muse in the Inclosed. . . ."[1]

Colman was not the only imitator of Watts in America. There were many others, among them that precocious literary ornament of New England, the famous Dr. Mather Byles, hailed by a contemporary as "Harvard's honour and New England's hope." In his early youth, Byles addressed the following admiring verses to Dr. Watts:

What Angel strikes the trembling Strings;
  And whence the golden Sound!
Or is it Watts–or Gabriel sings
  From yon celestial Ground?

Watts did not entirely discard the psalms. He selected those that he considered most appropriate for Christian worship and paraphrased them freely. In 1719 he brought out *The Psalms of David Imitated*, of which an American edition was printed at Philadelphia by Benjamin Franklin ten years later. The "System of Praise" of Dr. Watts continued to gain favor in America, though eventually the Revolution made it necessary to emend certain passages in which he alluded to British sovereignty and the glory of British arms. In 1784 the ingenious Mr. Joel Barlow of Connecticut was appointed to "accommodate" the psalms of Dr. Watts for American usage. Barlow, a poet of some reputation and one of the group of "Hartford Wits," aroused some opposition by making too free with Dr. Watts. For this he was censured by a fellow rhymster:

You've proved yourself a sinful cre'tur;
You've murdered Watts, and spoilt the metre;

[1] Cotton Mather, *Diary*, Dec. 2, 1711. Quoted by Foote, *Three Centuries of American Hymnody*, p. 65.

You've tried the Word of God to alter,
And for your pains deserve a halter.

But the alteration of "the word of God" had gone too far to be halted even by threats of a halter. Paraphrases of the psalms became so free that they could scarcely be distinguished from the new hymnody that soon prevailed almost everywhere in the English-speaking world. Timothy Dwight, president of Yale College, paraphrased a portion of the 137th Psalm ("If I forget thee, O Jerusalem, let my right hand forget her cunning") and produced what turned out to be a favorite hymn:

I love thy Kingdom, Lord,
The house of thine abode,
The Church our blest Redeemer saved
With his own precious blood.

The blood of the Redeemer was to be a recurrent theme of evangelical hymnody, and thence of the revival spirituals ("Are you washed in the blood of the Lamb?").

Later Dwight himself was commissioned to prepare another "accommodation" of Watts's version of the psalms, which he did with a characteristic combination of poetic and patriotic zeal. There is more of General Washington than of King David in Dwight's "accommodation" of Watts's paraphrase of the 18th Psalm:

When, fir'd to rage, against our nation rose
Chiefs of proud name, and bands of haughty foes,
He train'd our hosts to fight, with arms array'd,
With health invigor'd, and with bounty fed,
Gave us his chosen chief our sons to guide,
Heard every prayer, and every want supplied.
He gave their armies captive to our hands,
Or sent them frustrate to their native lands.

Such paraphrases of scripture, sometimes with local or topical allusions inserted, were frequently set to music by New England composers of the eighteenth century. But that is another chapter of our story; for the present we must return to the spread of evangelical hymnody, a movement which, receiving its initial impulse from Isaac Watts, was given an extraordinary impetus through the work and influence of the Wesleys, John and Charles.

The Wesleys in America

In the year 1735 Governor Oglethorpe of Georgia was in England seeking ways to strengthen his recently founded colony. Realizing the importance of religion as a stabilizing factor in a frontier settlement, he invited a serious-minded young minister named John Wesley to accompany him to Georgia and preach to the colonists there. John Wesley and his younger brother Charles were then active in Oxford as members of a group of religious zealots known variously as the "Holy Club," the "Bible Moths," and the "Methodists" (because they studied methodically–a strange innovation at the university). The elder Wesley accepted Oglethorpe's invitation, and Charles decided to go along with him. Together they embarked on the ship *Simmons*, bound for Savannah.

On board the ship was a group of twenty-six Moravian missionaries, members of a persecuted German Protestant sect, under the leadership of Bishop Nitschmann and Peter Boehler. These Moravian brethren were enthusiastic hymn singers, and their hymnody made a deep impression upon the Wesleys. The English brothers remembered one occasion particularly, when, during a severe storm that terrified most of the passengers, the Moravian missionaries calmly stood on the deck singing their hymns, entirely unperturbed by the raging storm and the towering waves. John Wesley began at once to study the hymnbooks of the Moravians, as attested by an entry in his journal for October 27, 1735: "Began Gesang Buch," referring to *Das Gesang-Buch der Gemeine in Herrnhut,* the principal hymnal of the Moravian brethren in their central community at Herrnhut, Germany.

When their ship sailed into the Savannah River, John Wesley was agreeably surprised by the sight of "the pines, palms, and cedars running in rows along the shore," making "an exceedingly beautiful prospect, especially to us who did not expect to see the bloom of spring in the depths of winter." The admiration was not all one-sided, for during his sojourn in Savannah, John Wesley apparently made a considerable impression upon a young lady by the name of Sophia Hopkey, a niece of the chief magistrate of that town. The young Methodist, however, balked at matrimony, and departed from the colony a free man.

Feminine allurements notwithstanding, Wesley's chief concern in the colonies was to spread the Gospel, and also to introduce the rather radical practice of hymn singing to which he had been converted by his contact with the Moravians. It will be recalled that during this period psalmody still held sway in the colonies, though the hymns of Dr. Watts were beginning to gain favor. In 1737 John Wesley published in "Charles-Town," South Carolina, *A Collection of Psalms and Hymns*, which is highly significant as containing the first of his translations of German hymns. Half of the seventy items in this book were by Dr. Watts, and the two Samuel Wesleys each contributed five hymns. Charles, who returned to England in 1736, was not represented in this collection. It is interesting to note that on the title page John Wesley is called "Missioner of Georgia." This octavo volume of seventy-four pages, printed by L. Timothy, forms a tangible link between Methodist hymnody and the American colonies, where the former was to have such far-reaching effects.

After his return to England in 1738, John Wesley frequented the meetings of the Moravian brethren in London, whose leader was his former shipmate Peter Boehler. This association led to a crucial experience in Wesley's religious development, namely, his so-called "conversion." This occurred during a reading of Luther's Preface to the Epistle of the Romans, as described by Wesley in his journal:

> About a quarter before nine, while he was describing the change which God works in the heart through faith in Christ, I felt my heart strangely warmed. I felt I did trust in Christ, Christ alone for salvation; and an assurance was given me that He had taken away my sins, even mine, and saved me from the law of sin and death.[2]

This might be called the basic text, the gospel, as it were, for the whole movement of evangelical and revivalist hymnody. Note the emphasis on direct salvation through faith in Christ, the conviction of salvation coming as an emotional and heartwarming personal experience, and the feeling of elation resulting from the taking away of sin. This type of emotional reaction, this attitude toward conversion and salvation, and this basic imagery of sin and death, are the seeds out of which grew American folk hymnody, including the Negro spirituals.

Soon after this experience, John Wesley made a visit to the headquarters of the Moravians at Herrnhut in Germany, where he met their patron and protector, Count Zinzendorf, himself a prolific writer

[2] John Wesley, *Journal*, ed. by Curnock, vol. 1, pp. 475ff.

of hymn texts (he is credited with over 2,000). The Moravians, officially known as "Unitas Fratrem," were a Pietist sect, stemming from the reforms of John Hus in the fifteenth century. After many vicissitudes and persecutions, the church of the "Unitas Fratrem" or the Moravian Brethren was revived by Count Zinzendorf, a Saxon nobleman who had been brought up under Pietist influence, and from the late 1720s its activity spread rapidly, including the establishing of missions and settlements in the American colonies. Like the Methodist movement initiated by the Wesleys, the Moravian church represented a blend of Puritan asceticism with emotional fervor, the latter strikingly expressed in their numerous hymns.

"The great awakening"

As a result of his visit to Herrnhut, John Wesley, upon his return to England, began with renewed fervor "to declare . . . the glad tidings of salvation" among his countrymen. His voice was also heard, indirectly, in America, where others were likewise engaged in spreading the glad tidings of salvation, soon to be embodied in a fast-growing hymnody, made largely by, and wholly for, the people. It was the time of "The Great Awakening," a popular mass movement in which the folk took religion into their own hands, though the initial impulse came from the emotional preaching of such powerful orators as John Wesley, George Whitefield, and Jonathan Edwards of New England, whose sermon on "The Reality of Spiritual Light" (1734) touched off the rather sensational Northampton revival of 1735. Shortly thereafter, George Whitefield, leader of the Calvinist Methodists, made the first of his several journeys to America and aroused tremendous enthusiasm by his preaching. Some idea of his eloquence and emotional appeal may be gained from the fact that when speaking in Philadelphia he cast such a spell upon the thrifty and prudent Franklin that the latter, intending at first to give only a few coppers to the collection, ended by pouring out all the money he had with him.

It will not be necessary to consider in detail the doctrinal difference and the multiple sectarianism that characterized the religious movements in England and America during the eighteenth century. Suffice it to say, in the words of Thomas C. Hall, that the gospel of the Wesleys and of Whitefield was in essence "the intensely individualistic proclamation of a way of escape for the soul from eternal damnation. The test of conversion was an emotional reaction rather than an intellectual acceptance of a creedal statement." If we bear in mind this double concept of individual salvation and emotional acceptance, it will provide us with the main thread for following the course of musical revivalism in America. We may further note that this individualism, through what might be called a process of collective individualism, proliferated into a great number of religious sects, offshoots of the main dissenting or reforming branches. Not all the evangelical reformers were dissenters. Wesley himself, for example, always remained nominally within the Church of England. John Wesley wished to reform the Church, not to break with it. But because his strongest appeal was to the masses, the working people, the downtrodden and economically distressed, the movement that he inspired drew further and further away from the established Church, nearer and nearer to the spirit and form of Dissent, with which eventually it became fully identified. It was characteristic of the religious ferment of that period that dissenting groups were continually breaking off from the main dissenting or reforming bodies and forming new sects.

Among the principal dissenting groups were the Quakers, the Moravians, the Baptists, the Presbyterians, and the Congregationalists. The Baptists split into "New Lights," "Free Willers," and "Separates." There were also the "Shakers," the "Shaking Quakers," and the "Dancing Baptists." The Presbyterians split into "Old Side" and "New Side," the latter going in strongly for enthusiastic revivalism. Dissenters were bitterly attacked, though here and there they had a sturdy champion, of whom the most notable was perhaps the Rev. Samuel Davies, a staunch upholder of religious toleration whom we shall later meet as a missionary among the Negroes in Virginia. Some idea of the prevailing acrimony may be gathered from the following passage in Davies's *Impartial Trial Impartially Tried:*

> Tho' the pulpits around me, I am told, ring with exclamatory harangues, accusations, arguments, railings, warnings, etc., etc., etc., against New-Lights, Methodists, Enthusiasts, Deceivers, Itinerants, Pretenders, etc., etc., etc., yet I never design to prostitute mine to such mean purpose.[3]

[3] Bost, *Samuel Davies,* p. 185.

And Reverend Davies adds: "Satires, etc., are published in the *Gazette*, to alarm the world of these dangerous animals." Strange as it may seem, among all these dissenting sects there was actually one who called themselves simply "Christians"—and it was founded by two men named Smith and Jones!

Before attempting to follow the singing dissenters along what one writer has called "the broad road of revivalism," it would be well to take a closer look at the development of Wesleyan hymnody in England, the indispensable background for musical revivalism in America.

Rise of the evangelical hymn

John Wesley found that the singing of hymns by his congregations was one of the most effective means for spreading the glad tidings of salvation. He and his brother Charles wrote the words of a great many hymns that were published in various collections. The first of these to include musical notation was *A Collection of Hymns . . . as they are commonly sung at the Foundry* (1742), generally known as "The Foundry Collection." Wesley and his followers had acquired for their meetings a building formerly used by the government for casting cannon, hence called "The Foundry." This collection was followed in 1746 by *Hymns on the Great Festivals and Other Occasions*, containing twenty-four tunes by a German bassoonist, resident in London, named John Frederick Lampe. In *Hymns on the Great Festivals* we have a fundamental document for the study of the antecedents of American popular hymnody, as regards both text and music. It contains hymns that have become part of America's folklore and that oral tradition has kept alive to the present day. The best-known of these hymns is probably the one that begins with the line "Ah, lovely Appearance of Death" (Hymn XXII) and is entitled "Over the Corpse of a Believer." Versions of this are widespread in American folk tradition.[4]

Musically, the tunes of John Frederick Lampe are remarkably interesting for their demonstration of the florid style in evangelical

[4] John A. and Alan Lomax, in *Our Singing Country*, p. 38, print a version of this hymn as sung for them by a deacon and a deaconess of the Hard-Shell Baptists in Clay County, Kentucky, in 1937. The Lomaxes refer to it as "George Whitefield's funeral hymn," and in their head-note they write: "Reverend George Whitefield . . . ten years before his death wrote this song to be sung at his own funeral." Whitefield died in 1770. He could not have written "this song" ten

hymnody. All the tunes are profusely ornamented, with grace notes, turns, trills, appoggiaturas, etc. Thus we can observe in this collection the extent to which embellished hymnody had gained ground in England through the spread of Wesleyan Methodism. Herewith is Lampe's setting of the hymn, "Ah, Lovely Appearance of Death." [5]

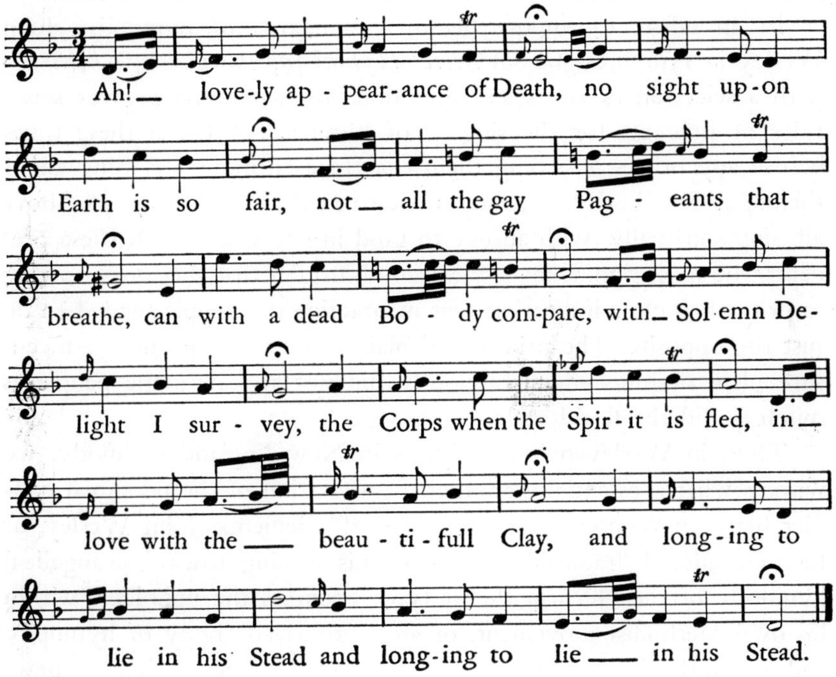

In 1753 Thomas Butts, a friend of the Wesleys, published his *Harmonia Sacra*, containing a large number of hymns with both words and tunes, many of the latter in florid style. This collection proved popular but did not entirely meet with the approval of John Wesley, who evidently felt that the trend toward embellished hymnody was getting out of hand. It was not long before Wesley expressly forbade the use of "vain repetitions" in congregational singing. He also condemned florid singing and fuguing tunes as being no better than

years before his death, because it was published in London in 1746. That this hymn may have been sung at Whitefield's funeral is possible, and there is evidently a tradition that links it with that event. Whitefield died at Newburyport, Mass., following an attack of asthma.

[5] From *Hymns on the Great Festivals and Other Occasions*, p. 56. Courtesy of the Library of Congress.

"Lancashire hornpipes"—a condemnation curiously reminiscent of the attacks made on Puritan psalm tunes as "Geneva Jigs"! [6] In opposing the popular trend toward florid singing of hymns, John Wesley, paradoxically, allied himself with the conservative and "respectable" elements who advocated a decorous and dignified type of congregational singing and would not tolerate any liberties taken with the tunes.

In an effort to impose his own standards of hymnody, John Wesley in 1761 brought out *Select Hymns for the Use of Christians*, with a selection of tunes and directions for singing. He gives seven rules or precepts for the singing of hymns: (1) Learn these tunes before any others, (2) Sing them exactly as printed, (3) Sing all of them, (4) Sing lustily, (5) Sing modestly, (6) Sing in tune, (7) Above all, sing spiritually, with an eye to God in every word. Of these precepts, the most significant is the second, urging that the tunes be sung as printed: a clear indication that in practice the people tended to do just the opposite. The printing of plain tunes was not enough to ensure plain singing, which obviously did not appeal to the people as much as did the florid style.

Thus, in Wesleyan hymnody, as in New England psalmody, we witness what is essentially another manifestation of the perennial conflict between "conservative" and "liberal" elements. John Wesley, at first considered "radical" because of his leaning toward evangelical hymnody of the German Pietist type, becomes the upholder, within his own Methodist movement, of an "authorized" body of hymnody and an "authorized" style of singing which he seeks to impose upon his followers but which is rejected or freely altered by the more radical or less conventional proponents of personal salvation and revivalism. We shall see, very shortly, the results of this conflict on the American frontier, but for the moment, we must turn our attention to two other significant figures in English evangelical hymnody: John Cennick (1718–1755) and John Newton (1725–1807).

John Cennick was a Quaker who became a follower of John Wesley and later (in 1745) joined the Moravian Brethren. His first collection of hymns was *Hymns for the Children of God* (second edition, London, 1741), and his second, *Sacred Hymns for the Use of Religious Societies, Generally Composed in Dialogues* (Bristol, 1743). The importance of Cennick is, in the words of G. P. Jackson, that he

[6] Benson, *The English Hymn*, p. 239.

"was destined to become the real founder of folksy religious song in the rebellious eighteenth century movement." Typical of his style is the hymn "Jesus My All to Heaven is Gone," which, again quoting the same authority, "was to become one of the most widely sung religious lyrics among the country folk of America during the entire 200 years which have elapsed since it appeared." [7] This is the highly characteristic final stanza:

> I'll tell to all poor sinners round
> What a dear Saviour I have found;
> I'll point to thy redeeming blood
> And say, behold the way to God.

The "dialogues" mentioned in the title of Cennick's second collection were pieces sung antiphonally by men and women who, at this time and for about a hundred years thereafter, sat on opposite sides of the meetinghouse (sometimes they used a "double-deck" meetinghouse, with the women below and the men above).

John Newton was a rather wild character who went to sea at the age of eleven, was flogged as a deserter from the Royal Navy, became servant to a slave dealer in Africa, and before long was in the slaving trade himself. While acting as captain of a slaving ship he was converted by reading Thomas a Kempis, and soon afterward he came under the influence of John Wesley and Whitefield, leading to his ordination as curate of Olney in 1764. Together with his friend, the unfortunate poet William Cowper, Newton undertook a remarkable collection of hymns, which was published in three books in 1779 as *Olney Hymns*. Cowper, stricken by insanity in 1773, wrote only 68 of the 280 hymns in the collection; the rest were by John Newton. This "old African blasphemer," as he called himself, drew largely upon his own experience in wrestling with sin and being snatched from damnation into eternal salvation. His hymns, like those of Cowper, are marked by what the critics call "excessive emotionalism" (as though emotion should be meted out by measure), by "morbidity" (that is, preoccupation with blood, sacrifice, and death), and by a perpetual swing from gloom to exultation, corresponding to the basic antithesis of sin and salvation. Cennick and Newton represent what might be called the "leftist" or radical tendency in evangelical hymn-

[7] Jackson, *White and Negro Spirituals*, p. 20.

ody, as compared with the relative conservatism of the Wesleys, and still more as compared with the "middle-of-the-road" hymnody of Watts.

This struggle between Wesleyan authority and the popular mass movement of religious dissent, including complete unrestraint in religious singing, continued in America, where it found, indeed, its most dramatic battleground. At a Methodist conference held in Virginia and in Baltimore in 1784, the fourteenth query on the agenda was: "How shall we reform our singing?" And the answer was: "Let all our preachers who have any knowledge in the notes, improve it by learning to sing true themselves, and keeping close to Mr. Wesley's tunes and hymns." This is essentially a repetition, or rather a continuation, of the same fundamental conflict that we found in New England psalm singing fifty or sixty years earlier: the conflict between Regular Singing and the free style of the folk. The situation has been aptly summarized by Benson:

> The entire course of Methodist Episcopal Hymnody may be viewed as a continuous effort to keep the Church on a level sufficiently described as Wesleyan, and a failure to cooperate therein on the part of a considerable section of the people who preferred the plane of the Revival Hymn and the popular Spiritual Song.[8]

That, of course, is written from a conservative and institutional point of view. The masses of people who preferred the lively revival hymns and the popular spiritual songs that sprang up in the American camp meetings after 1799 did not merely manifest a lack of cooperation with religious institutionalism: they were all out for freedom of song, freedom of expression to the utmost limits of the human spirit and body. And we shall see in a later chapter what were the results of this wild freedom of emotional expression that produced the "singing ecstasy" of the great revivals.

The Shakers

In some ways the most remarkable of all the dissenting sects were the Shakers, who established themselves in America about the time of the Revolution and grew from a mere handful to a large and flourishing organization with many communities scattered from Maine to

[8] Benson, *op. cit.*, p. 285.

Kentucky. The sect originated in England as an offshoot of the Quakers, and its adherents were at first popularly known as "Shaking Quakers." Their official designation was United Society of Believers in Christ's Second Coming. In England the society split into two groups, one of which came under the leadership of a young woman of humble origin and forceful character named Ann Lee, soon to be known to the faithful as "Mother Ann." Ann Lee was illiterate, had worked in a cotton factory in Lancashire, and had suffered from an unhappy marriage followed by the death of her four children. It is no wonder that she looked upon sexual relationships as the root of all evil, and imposed the rule of celibacy upon her followers. Mother Ann had the power of being spiritually "possessed" and of seeing visions. In one of these manifestations she had a vision of America. "I saw a large tree, every leaf of which shone with such brightness as made it appear like a burning torch. . . . I knew that God had a chosen people in America; I saw some of them in a vision and when I met with them in America I knew them. . . ."

To America, accordingly, Mother Ann went, accompanied by eight of her followers, in the year 1774. It was scarcely a propitious moment to arrive in America, especially from England. After some time, Mother Ann's band found their way to a small settlement near Albany, then called Niskeyuna (later Watervliet), where they suffered much persecution, including imprisonment on a charge of treason. After their release they settled in New Lebanon, New York, where they built their first meetinghouse. They recruited new members from the Baptists, who in 1780 were in the midst of a fervent revival. In 1784, Mother Ann died, but her work was continued by James Whitaker and Joseph Meacham, and, from 1796, by another remarkable woman, Lucy Wright. The Shakers believed in equality of the sexes and proved it in their leadership. By this time the society had some dozen communities, in New York, Connecticut, Massachusetts, New Hampshire, and Maine. Around 1805 communities were established in Kentucky and Ohio.

The spirit of Mother Ann continued to exert a strong influence on the Shakers. They followed her advice: "Put your hands to work and your hearts to God." They developed handicrafts; they were thrifty and practical and, as they grew stronger, resisted persecution and condemnation with vigor and determination. Music was important in their culture, not as sensuous delectation but as a means of expressing their faith. From Mother Ann they received a number of songs that had been revealed to her in visions.[9]

Mother Ann is also supposed to have revealed by inspiration the system of musical notation used by the Shakers. This consisted of designating the notes of the scale by the first seven letters of the alphabet, beginning with "a" for middle C. Differences in note values were indicated by different types of letters: roman letters for quarter notes, italics for eighth notes, and so forth. This was but one of many systems devised for using letters instead of notes, with some of which we have already become acquainted.

Singing, dancing, shaking, running, leaping—all these were means whereby the Shakers expressed the joy of their religious faith and their victory over the flesh and the devil. Mother Ann believed firmly in the reality of the devil. "The devil is a real being," she said, "as real as a bear. I know, for I have seen him and fought with him." This belief in the corporeal reality of the devil, this expression of faith and spiritual victory through song and the violence of bodily motion, found their full manifestation in the nineteenth-century revivals, where we shall again meet the Shakers and their songs and dances.

Music among minority sects

In addition to the predominantly Anglo-Saxon movements of dissent that made themselves felt in eighteenth-century America, there were a number of religious sects from continental Europe which established settlements in the New World and which gave varying degrees of importance to music in their worship and recreation. Though they remained relatively self-contained and isolated from the popular mass movement of religious dissent, their musical activities are part of the American experience and deserve, therefore, a place in our narrative.

According to chronological priority, we may mention first the Mennonites, followers of Menno Simon, who came from Switzerland and the German Palatinate and who emigrated to the American colonies from 1683 to 1748. The first small group of Mennonites came to Pennsylvania via Rotterdam and London in 1683 and settled in Germantown, near Philadelphia, where in 1708 they built a meeting-house. Their first pastor in America was Willem Rittinghuysen, great-grandfather of the celebrated astronomer and mathematician

[9] For examples of Shaker songs, see Chapter 11.

David Rittenhouse (the name having become thus anglicized). In 1770 they built a new stone church, which is still in use. The Mennonites used a hymnbook which had originally been printed at Schaffhausen in 1583 and which was reprinted at Germantown in 1742, under the title *Der Ausbund: Das ist Etliche Schöne Christliche Lieder* (later editions in 1751, 1767, and 1785). With regard to religious beliefs, the Mennonites were related to the Dunkers or German Baptists, but they practiced baptism by affusion rather than by immersion. They were opposed to instrumental music in church worship and their hymnody was not particularly important.

In 1694 a group of German Pietists under the leadership of Johannes Kelpius came to Pennsylvania and after a brief sojourn in Germantown settled on the banks of the Wissahickon, not far from Philadelphia. These Pietists became known as the Hermits or the Mystics of the Wissahickon. Their leader Kelpius, besides being a dabbler in Oriental lore and cabbalistic philosophy, was somewhat of a musician and hymn writer. He was only twenty-one when he sailed for America in 1694 with about forty other German Pietists, among whom there were evidently several musicians. This we gather from a sentence in Kelpius's own account of the voyage: "We had also prayer meetings and sang hymns of praise and joy, several of us accompanying on instruments that we brought from London." It is believed the instruments mentioned by Kelpius may have been those used at the ordination of Justus Falckner in Gloria Dei Church on November 23, 1703. For this occasion the Mystics of the Wissahickon provided music with viols, hautboys, trumpets, and kettledrums. The church already had an organ, which had been sent from Germany in response to a plea from Justus Falckner, written shortly after his arrival in Pennsylvania in 1700. The text of this letter is worth quoting, in part, for it shows the importance that Falckner attached to music and gives us an insight into the reactions of the Indians when exposed to European music. Speaking of the desired organ, he writes:

> It would not only attract and civilize the wild Indian, but it would do much good in spreading the Gospel truths among the sects and others by attracting them. . . . Thus a well sounding organ would prove of great profit, to say nothing of the fact that the Indians would come running from far and near to listen to such unknown melody, and upon that account might be willing to accept our language and teaching and remain with people who had such

agreeable things: for they are said to come ever so far to listen to one who plays even upon a reed pipe; such an extraordinary love have they for any melodious and ringing sound.

The Gloria Dei Church in Philadelphia, of which Falckner became pastor, was built by Swedish Lutherans, who had first settled on the Delaware River in 1638. Falckner himself was a German Lutheran, a native of Saxony, educated at the universities of Leipzig and Halle. He wrote several hymns, of which the best known is "Rise, Ye Children of Salvation," sung to the tune of "Meine Hoffnung."

Magister Johannes Kelpius, leader of the Wissahickon Hermits, has been put forward by some writers as the first Pennsylvanian composer, a claim based on his supposed authorship of some hymn tunes contained in a manuscript collection entitled *The Lamenting Voice of the Hidden Love, at the time when She lay in Misery & forsaken; and oprest by the multitude of Her Enemies. Composed by one in Kumber. . . . Pennsylvania in America 1705.*[10] "Kumber" or "cumber" is an obsolete English word for "distress." There is a possibility that Kelpius may have written the text in this manuscript (which is not in his handwriting), but there is no valid evidence that might substantiate a claim for him to be regarded as the composer of the music, most of which is taken from identifiable German sources. The words of the hymns are in German, with English translations that have been attributed to Dr. Christopher Witt, an Englishman who emigrated to America in 1704 and joined the Mystics of the Wissahickon. He seems to have been a musician, a portrait painter, and an amateur organ builder, for he is believed to have built the pipe organ that he owned —said to be the first private organ in the North American colonies. As for *The Lamenting Voice of the Hidden Love,* it has an antiquarian interest as containing, in the words of Albert Hess, "the earliest known practical example of a *continuo* realization in mensural notation." This realization of the figured bass or *basso continuo* is found in the hymn titled "Colloquium of the Soul with Itself." [11] The realization reveals lack of technical skill, and is characterized by the prevalence of three-part harmony.

[10] A facsimile reproduction of this manuscript will be found in *Church Music and Musical Life in Pennsylvania,* vol. 1, pp. 21–165.

[11] A transcription of this hymn, made by Hess, was printed in the *Journal of the American Musicological Society,* vol. 3, p. 221.

Francis Daniel Pastorius, who became the leader of a German Pietist colony in Germantown, Pennsylvania, was a friend of William Penn, whose liberal laws encouraged so many minority sects to settle in his colony. The Quakers themselves were generally opposed to church music, but it is curious to note that George Fox, after attending a Quaker meeting in 1655, wrote that those present "were much exercised by ye power of ye Lorde in Songes and Hymns & made melody and rejoiced." So apparently not all Quakers were antimusical. Pastorius wrote the words of a love song, "Come, Corinna, let me kiss thee," which has been given a modern musical setting for male quartet by Arthur L. Church. John Greenleaf Whittier's poem "The Pennsylvania Pilgrim" was written around the life and character of Pastorius.

We turn now to one of the most original of the Pennsylvania religious sects, the Ephrata Cloister or the Community of the Solitary, who under the leadership of Conrad Beissel and Peter Miller settled on the Cocalico River in 1720, in what is now Lancaster County. They were Seventh-day Baptists who believed strongly in music as an aid to worship. But instead of drawing upon established musical traditions, they used their own homespun music, based on principles set forth by Beissel in his curiously quaint *Dissertation on Harmony*. Beissel himself not only composed the hymns for the community, he also sang and played several instruments, including the violin, and organized the musical life of the Ephrata Cloister down to the most minute details. He established choirs and singing schools, and even prescribed special diets for different types of singers—one diet for altos, another for basses, and so forth. The singing of the Ephrata Cloister was usually in four parts, and their repertoire consisted of nearly a thousand selections. A visitor to the Ephrata Cloister in 1735 wrote "many of the younger sisters are just now constantly employed in copying musical note books for themselves and the brethren." These hand-copied songbooks were beautifully illuminated. In addition, the Ephrata Cloister used printed hymnbooks, of which several were printed by Benjamin Franklin in the 1730s. The main body of Ephrata hymnody was contained in a work entitled *Song of the Lonely and Forsaken Turtle Dove, the Christian Church*, more conveniently known as the *Turtel-Taube*, a manuscript volume with some 750 hymns, compiled in 1746. This unique book was at one time in the possession of Benjamin Franklin, who took it with him to England

and loaned it to the Lord Mayor of London in 1775. Eventually it was acquired by the Library of Congress. Beissel's last collection of hymns, the *Paradisiacal Wonder Music,* dating from 1754, was partly hand-written and partly printed.

Beissel's musical system was crude but doubtless effective for his purpose. There is no question that he made the Ephrata Cloister a community of musical enthusiasts, of whom many were amateur composers and nearly all singers. Beissel divided the notes of the scale into "masters" and "servants." The notes belonging to the common chord were the "masters," the others the "servants." In his metrical system he simply followed the rhythm of the words, the accented syllables having the longer notes and the unaccented ones the shorter notes. In setting the texts to music, he provided that the accent should always fall on a "master" note, while the "servants" took care of the unaccented syllables. With the help of chord tables for all the keys, compiled by Beissel, the art of musical composition became an easy exercise for the brethren of the Ephrata Cloister. The method thus evolved had no repercussions in the outside world and did not shake the foundations of established musical theory; but it did produce a remarkable example of "primitive" art that deserves a special niche among the curiosities of musical Americana.

From the point of view of musical production and continuous activity, the most important of the early religious colonies in Pennsylvania was undoubtedly that of the Moravians or Unitas Fratrem, about whom something has already been said in connection with their influence on John Wesley and Methodist hymnody. After the failure of their first colony in Georgia, the Moravian brethren in America moved northward to Pennsylvania and in 1741 established a settlement on the Lehigh River, which they called Bethlehem. There, under the personal leadership of Count Zinzendorf, Bishop of the Unitas Fratrem since 1734, they organized a communal society in which all worked for the common good and were provided for from a common store (private property, however, was not abolished, and the colonists were free to withdraw if they wished). Soon joined by other Moravians from Europe, the colony prospered, though it was never large.

Music at once assumed an important place in the life of the Moravians in Bethlehem. By 1743 they had a small orchestra consisting of violins, viola da gamba, viola da braccio, flutes, French horns, trombones, and a spinet. In December, 1744, they formed a musical society, or "Collegium Musicum," for the performance of chamber music and symphonies by such celebrated European composers as Haydn, Mozart, Johann Christian Bach, and Johann Stamitz. They also performed oratorios, among them Haydn's *Creation,* Handel's *Messiah,* and *The Israelites in the Desert* by C. P. E. Bach.

The Moravians were partial to trombones, which they organized in "choirs" (soprano, alto, tenor, and bass), and which they used both on festive occasions and for the sad duty of announcing the death of a member of the community. On such occasions it was customary for the trombone players to station themselves on the roof of one of the buildings, so that they could be heard far and wide. There is a tradition that during the French and Indian War a band of Indians was planning to attack the settlement and for this purpose lay in wait on Calypso Island until the coming of darkness. Just then the trombones sounded for the death of one of the brethren, and the Indians, thinking this strange noise from above must be the voice of the Great Spirit warning them away, decided to give up the attack. The story is also told that a certain Christian Ettwein, player on the bass trombone, on one Easter morn drank seventeen mugs of mulled wine. The effect this had on his performance has not been recorded.

Shortly after the founding of Bethlehem, a group of Moravians went to North Carolina, where they made several settlements, of which the most important was at Salem (now Winston-Salem). There they built churches with organs, formed trombone choirs, and continued their characteristic interest in both vocal and instrumental music. Typical of their experiences and customs is this passage from the diary of a Moravian settler in North Carolina, dated November 17, 1753:

> We drove three miles further on the new road, then turned to the left and cut a road for 2½ miles to the little house that the Brethren found yesterday. . . . We at once made preparations for a little Lovefeast, and rejoiced with one another. Brother Gottlob began singing, with the little verse:
>
> We hold arrival Lovefeast here
> In Carolina land,
> A company of Brethren true,
> A little Pilgrim band,

Called by the Lord to be of those
Who through the whole world go
To bear Him witness everywhere
And naught but Jesus know.[12]

To this day there remain notable examples of Moravian architecture in the state of North Carolina, as well as in Pennsylvania.

The Moravians were interested in carrying on missionary work among the Negroes and the Indians, and in 1763 they published a collection of hymns in the language of the Delaware Indians. In 1803 the Rev. David Zeisberger brought out *A Collection of Hymns for the Use of the Christian Indians of the Mission of the United Brethren in North America*. The Moravians were also a highly international group. On September 4, 1745, there took place in Bethlehem a remarkable example of polyglot singing, when the hymn "In Dulce Jubilo" was sung in thirteen languages simultaneously: Bohemian, Dutch, English, French, German, Greek, Irish, Latin, Mohawk, Mohican, Swedish, Welsh, and Wendish. A Dane, a Pole, and a Hungarian were also present but did not join in the singing. Here, surely, is a preview of the American melting pot.

The Bethlehem colony developed a rather notable group of composers, among whom were John Christopher Pyrlaeus, Christian Frederick Oerter, John Antes, David Moritz Michael (1751–1825), and John Frederick (Johann Friedrich) Peter (1746–1813), the chief member of the group. Peter, born in Holland of German parents, was educated in Holland and Germany, and came to America in 1770, where he joined the Moravian colony in Bethlehem. There he became organist of the church, director of music, and secretary of the Brethren's House. He brought to America manuscript copies that he had made in Germany of compositions by C. F. Abel, Johann Christoph Friedrich Bach, Johann Stamitz, and other European composers less known today. Later he copied a number of works by Haydn, who strongly influenced his own style of composition. In 1786 Peter left Bethlehem and was active for several years in Salem, North Carolina, where he married and where he composed the six String Quintets upon which chiefly rests his reputation as a composer (they are dated 1789). Returning to Bethlehem, he died there suddenly on July 19,

[12] *Records of the Moravians in North Carolina.* Publications of the North Carolina Historical Commission. Raleigh, N.C., 1922, p. 79.

1813. He was the teacher of John C. Till and of Peter Wolle, who in turn handed down the musical tradition of Bethlehem to future generations. The celebrated Bach Choir of Bethlehem continues to sustain the community's reputation as a music center.

All but one of Peter's quintets are in three movements. Following the classical tradition of Haydn and Stamitz, but with considerable harmonic freedom and boldness in modulation, the String Quintets of John Frederick Peter are well-written and attractive, and one might agree with Dr. Hans T. David, leading authority on American Moravian music, that they are at times "even brilliant." Certainly, when revived for performance today, they can be heard with pleasure and not solely for their historical significance. Peter also composed a number of interesting and effective anthems for chorus with accompaniment of organ and strings.

Music of the Catholic Church

The Catholic Church welcomed the aid of music, both vocal and instrumental, in its religious worship. The less wealthy Catholic churches in the English colonies could not match the musical ceremony in the churches of the Spanish colonies, especially those in the viceregal cities of Mexico and Lima. But the seduction of music in the Catholic Church, even in North America during the eighteenth century, is attested by several entries in the diary of John Adams. On October 9, 1774, Adams wrote: "Went in the afternoon, to the Romish Chapel [in Philadelphia]. The scenery and the music are so calculated to take in mankind that I wonder the Reformation ever succeeded . . . the chanting is exquisitely soft and sweet." On July 4, 1779, the French Ambassador Gerard arranged for a celebration of the anniversary of the signing of the Declaration of Independence with a ceremony in St. Mary's Church, Philadelphia, which was attended by members of the Congress and other important personages, and where "the great event was celebrated by a well-adapted discourse, pronounced by the Minister's chaplain, and a *Te Deum* solemnly sung by a number of very good voices, accompanied by the organ and other kinds of music."

The first hymnbook published for the use of Catholics in the United States was *A Compilation of the Litanies and Vesper Hymns and Anthems as They are Sung in the Catholic Church, Adapted to the Voice or Organ by John Aitken* (Philadelphia, 1787). The music was in two parts (treble and bass); in later editions a third part was added. Perhaps the most interesting selection in this book is "The Holy Mass of the Blessed Trinity," with the plainsong harmonized and with instrumental interludes (called "symphonies") in typical eighteenth-century style, including the standard Alberti bass.

Meanwhile the influence of the Catholic Church, with music always prominent in its missionary program, was spreading to other parts of North America then under Spanish domination but later destined to be incorporated in the territory of the United States. The Spanish missionary Cristóbal de Quiñones, for example, entered New Mexico between 1598 and 1604 and was therefore probably "the first music teacher who worked within the confines of the present United States" (L. M. Spell).[13] Fray Alonso de Benavides, whose *Memorial* was written in 1630, states that in New Mexico there existed "schools of reading and writing, singing, and playing of all instruments."[14] Fray Antonio Margil de Jesús went into Texas in 1716 and taught the Indians there to sing the *Alabados* and *Alabanzas,* simple songs of religious praise that remained in the musical folklore of the Southwest long after the end of Spanish control. The Spanish missionaries also introduced the *autos sacramentales* or religious plays with music, which likewise have survived in the folklore of the region, notably in the Christmas play *Los Pastores,* performed annually or at less frequent intervals in some communities of Texas and New Mexico.

The founding of the famous California missions, from 1769 to 1823, represented another phase of the cultural penetration of Spain and of Catholic church music within the borders of present-day United States. Music was a very important feature in the educational, recreational, and religious life of the missions. The Indians of the region, most of whom proved docile, were soon taught the rudiments of music, then formed into choirs and small orchestras, consisting usually of violins, violas, violoncellos, bass viols, flutes, trumpets, horns, *bandolas* (a kind of lute), guitars, drums, and triangles. The orchestra in the Mission of San Luis Rey consisted of forty players. Many of the instruments were made by the Indians themselves in the mission

[13] "Music Teaching in New Mexico in the 17th Century." In *New Mexico Historical Review,* II, 1 (Jan. 1927).

[14] *The Memorial of Fray Alonso de Benavides,* translated by Ayer, Chicago. 1916.

workshops. The most notable musician among the Franciscan missionaries in California was Padre Narciso Durán, choirmaster at the San José Mission, where in 1813 he compiled a choir book that constitutes our most valuable source of information for the study of Spanish mission music. Padre Durán is believed to be the composer of a Mass, *La Misa Catalana,* discovered at San Juan Capistrano a few years ago.

Among the valued possessions of the Franciscan friars of Mission San Juan Bautista was an "*órgano de tres cilindros*" that had been given to them by the British explorer Vancouver. This was nothing but an English barrel organ, with three barrels, each of which could grind out ten tunes. That these tunes were far from sacred in character may be judged by the following selections: "Spanish Waltz," "College Hornpipe," "Lady Campbell's Reel," and "Go to the Devil!"

This brief glimpse of early Catholic church music in North America has taken us far from the Eastern seaboard, where the principal forces that shaped the course of American music were developing not only in New England but also in the South. If the vocal-religious movement that dominated American music for two hundred years received its main impetus from New England, through the singing schools, the songbooks, and the revival fervor that spread thence to other sections of the country, the continuing impact of this movement, as the nation consolidated itself and expanded, was to be felt principally in the South, first along the seaboard, then in the piedmont, and later across the first barrier of mountains that marked the early frontier.

In this chapter we have traced the rise of evangelical hymnody up to the point where, largely taken over and remade by dissenting groups, it was ready to enter "the broad road of revivalism." And we have given some account of various minority sects which, more or less isolated from the predominant mass movements, managed to develop their own types of music within a limited sphere. Such were the Shakers, the Mennonites, the Ephrata Cloister, and the Moravians. These groups came to America of their own accord, though impelled to a certain extent by circumstances. In the next chapter we shall describe the backgrounds and the first American experiences of an important minority group that was brought to the New World against its will, and that was obliged to adapt itself to the new environment under the unfavorable conditions of slavery. The importation of Negro slaves into the North American colonies, and later the United States, has had profound and far-reaching consequences in America's music. Since the foundations of Afro-American music were laid in the eighteenth century, and since it has a direct connection with the spread of evangelical hymnody and the growth of revivalism, this is the appropriate place to take up the story of the Negroes in Africa and America.

chapter four

African exiles

Jove fix'd it certain, that whatever day
Makes man a slave, takes half his worth away.
HOMER, THE ODYSSEY XVII, 233 (QUOTED BY JEFFERSON, NOTES ON VIRGINIA).

Dutch ships landed a few African slaves in Virginia as early as 1619. A century later the American slave trade was in full swing. By 1727 there were 75,000 Negroes in the North American colonies, and by 1790 there were more than ten times that number. Ten years later, in 1800, there were over a million Negroes in the United States, of whom more than 100,000 were free—a significant fact to bear in mind. At that time the Negroes formed nearly 19 per cent of the population of this country. Such was the rapid growth of a socioeconomic system that resulted in the transplanting of a large measure of African culture on the continents of the New World.

What did enlightened Americans think of the institution of slavery? Patrick Henry, in a letter to a friend, expressed his views on the subject: "Every thinking honest man rejects it in Speculation, how few in practice. Would anyone believe that I am Master of slaves of my own purchase? I am drawn along by ye general Inconvenience of living without them; I will not, I cannot justify it. . . ." Henry's sister Elizabeth freed her slaves with the declaration that "it is both sinful and unjust, as they are by nature equally free as myself, to continue them in slavery." It was Thomas Jefferson who, in 1782, was instrumental in getting the Virginia legislature to pass an act making it lawful for any person "by last will and testament or other instrument in writing sealed and witnessed, to emancipate and set free his slaves." In his *Notes on Virginia*, Jefferson elaborated a scheme for gradually emancipating all slaves in Virginia and sending them to be "colonized to such places as the circumstances of the time should render most proper." Jefferson treated his own slaves kindly, but did not hesitate to sell them on the open market when the need arose.

Jefferson makes an unfavorable comparison between the Negro and the Indian, claiming that the latter was superior in imagination and artistic skill. Yet on one point he grants the superiority of the blacks, not only over the Indians, but over the white man also: "In music they are more generally gifted than the whites, with accurate ears for tune and time, and they have been found capable of imagining a small catch. Whether they will be equal to the composition of a more extensive run of melody, or of complicated harmony, is yet to be proved." This, and a footnote on the "banjar" (which will be quoted later), is all that Jefferson wrote about the Negroes and music in his *Notes on Virginia.* It is just enough to be tantalizing, not enough to be really enlightening. It corroborates what we already know: that even in slavery the Negroes cultivated their precious gift of music, and this with a skill that impressed even such a connoisseur as Jefferson.

Certain it is that the Negroes came from Africa singing, dancing, and drumming. This in spite of the horrible and cruel conditions under which they were transported in the slave ships. Harsh as were the methods of the slaver, it was not to his interest to let his human cargo pine and die. Music and dancing were used to keep up the morale of the miserable captives. In 1700 Thomas Starks of London directed the captain of the *Africa* to take on a cargo of 450 slaves, and included the typical admonition: "Make your Negroes cheerful and pleasant makeing them dance at the Beating of your Drum, etc." When weather permitted, it was customary to drive the slaves on deck for exercise. What better exercise than dancing, which of course had to be accompanied by drumming (tin pans would do if nothing else) and usually by singing also? It is said that "slave captains preferred happy tunes and frequently would resort to whips to exact their preference." Evidence from a later period, but surely typical of the whole slaving era, is found in a work titled *Captain Canot, or Twenty Years on an African Slaver (1827–1847)*: "During afternoons of serene weather, men, women, girls and boys are allowed while on deck to unite in African melodies, which they always enhance by an extemporaneous tom-tom on the bottom of a tub or tin kettle."

When no other instruments were at hand, a tub or tin kettle would do: this is characteristic of the Negro's knack for improvised percussion. He also had a knack for making musical instruments in a simple manner out of easily available materials. Writing of the Negroes and music in his *Notes on Virginia,* Jefferson says, "The instrument proper to them is the Banjar, which they brought hither from Africa, and which is the original of the guitar, its chords [i.e., strings] being precisely the four lower chords of the guitar." This is the instrument which came to be known as the banjo. Jefferson is not historically accurate when he says that it was "the original of the guitar," for there is evidence to indicate the contrary: namely, that the West African *bania* (as it was called) was a modification of the Arabian guitar (from which the European guitar is derived). The main point of interest, however, is that the African slaves brought to America a musical instrument that subsequently became so important in our folklore.

It is a pity that Jefferson did not describe the construction of the "banjar" as it existed in his time. Very likely it was made in the same primitive fashion followed by later generations of Negroes. The seeds were scooped out of a large gourd, and the bowl cut away so as to be level with the handle attached to it. Over the bowl of the gourd a tanned coonskin was tightly stretched, forming a drumhead. Four strings were passed over a bridge placed near the center of the drum and attached to the neck or handle of the instrument. The strings were made of any suitable material at hand.

The slaves at work and play

The Negroes were brought from Africa to America for the purpose of working. That truism is stated in order to remind the reader of an equally obvious fact; namely, that the desire to sing while working was the prime impulse for the growth of Afro-American folksong. The emphasis placed upon the "spirituals" has tended to overstress the religious factor in the origins of American Negro music. It is true, as we shall soon observe, that exposure to white psalmody and hymnody had a direct influence on the course of Afro-American folksong and determined one direction that it was to take. But this was a gradual and relatively late development, which did not attain significant proportions until the latter part of the eighteenth century. The Rev. Samuel Davies estimated that in 1750, out of about 120,000 Negroes in Virginia, only 1,000 had been converted and baptized. The

Virginia House of Burgesses, toward the end of the seventeenth century, declared that religious progress among the Negroes was impossible because of the "Gros Barbarity and Rudeness of their manners, the variety and strangeness of their languages, and the weakness and shallowness of their minds. . . ." No wonder that Du Bois speaks of "the spread of witchcraft and persistence of heathen rites among Negro slaves."

We know that the Negroes in Africa sang at their work; there was nothing to prevent them from doing the same in America. Neither the plantation owner nor the overseer cared whether the slaves sang, as long as they did their work. If anything, singing might be regarded with favor, since it tended to lighten the burden and tedium of labor, and thus might make the slaves more docile and contented; which is to say, from the owner's point of view, less troublesome. If slave-ship captains encouraged the Negroes to sing on shipboard, plantation overseers would have at least as much reason for doing likewise.

It was difficult enough to get the slaves to do a real day's work under any circumstances. No sooner was the overseer's back turned, than a slowdown would begin, and not even the most energetic overseer could be everywhere at once. An American slaveowner stated that "his Negroes never worked so hard as to tire themselves—always were lively, and ready to go off on a frolic at night. . . . They could not be made to work hard: they never would lay out their strength freely, and it was impossible to make them do it. . . ." [1]

In general, the slaveowner's attitude toward the singing and other pastimes of the Negroes was tolerant so long as these did not interfere with his own peace and comfort. The making of drums was discouraged, when not positively forbidden, because drums could be used as signals for uprisings, of which there was constant fear in the South. But makeshift drums could be improvised out of boxes, kegs, or kettles; and simple instruments of one kind or another, like the "banjar," could be readily made out of available materials. Then the clapping of hands, the stamping or tapping of feet, and every sort of rhythmic bodily movement, together with the voice used both melodically and rhythmically, could reinforce the primitive music-making of the first Africans who found themselves in a new world not of their choosing.

Although Jefferson recognized the superior musical gifts of the

[1] Quoted in Herskovits, *The Myth of the Negro Past,* p. 102.

Negroes, he remarked on their alleged inferiority to the Indians in arts and crafts. In this connection he wrote, "It would be unfair to follow them to Africa for this investigation." Today our approach is different. We believe it is both fair and necessary to follow the trail of the Negro's past into Africa, to learn what we can of his traditional values and ancestral folkways. We do not look upon the Negro as "a man without a past." His past is in Africa; it is an ancient past, and one not without deep influence upon European, and thence American, culture. Jefferson would have been surprised, for example, if he could have foreseen the effect of African sculpture upon modern art. Our next step, therefore, must be to glance at the African backgrounds of Negro culture in general and of music in particular.

African backgrounds

Although some slaves were taken from East Africa (Mozambique), from Angola, and from the region of the Congo, the majority of those shipped to the New World came from the coastal area of West Africa, along the Gulf of Guinea. The heart of the slave territory lay in Nigeria, Dahomey, western Congo, and the Gold Coast. This region is still inhabited, as it was in the time of the slave trade, by the Ashanti, the Congo, the Dahomeans, the Yoruba, and the Bini. Most of the African survivals found in the Americas can be traced to these main cultural-linguistic groups.

Music, dance, and religious beliefs and practices seem to be the phases of African culture that have left strongest traces in the New World. Music and dance, indeed, are often closely allied with African religion; hence an outline of the latter is pertinent to our subject. Persons not disposed to regard such matters objectively have dismissed African religions as gross superstition, a crude mixture of magic and idolatry. It is true that magic does play a very important part in West African beliefs, but it is only one aspect of a complex supernatural system that implies a definite world view, a profound conception of man's relation to Fate, and a highly organized relationship between human beings and the spiritual powers who are conceived as gods or deities. There is a hierarchy of gods, and the great gods, in the words of Herskovits, "are grouped in pantheons, which follow the organization of the social units among men, each member having specific names, titles, functions, and worshipers. The cult groups are organized in honor of these deities, and the outstanding religious festivals are held for them."

The spirits of ancestors are also worshiped, and those who were most powerful in life are believed to have retained that power—either for good or evil—after death. This leads to elaborate funeral rites, for it is necessary to appease the spirits of the departed and assure their good will by these observances. The cult of ancestor-spirit worship, in determining the attitude toward the dead and in setting the pattern for burial customs, has had a marked influence on Negro customs in the New World.

Something must be said about the fetish in connection with West African beliefs. Outwardly the fetish is represented by a charm worn around the neck, or elsewhere on the body, or hung up within a dwelling. Certain powers and taboos are associated with this charm. Fetishism is the belief that possession of the charm, and observance of the rituals and taboos associated with it, can procure the help and protection of the spirit that it represents. The charm itself, as a material object, is simply the symbol of a supernatural power. The fetish charm, in addition to doing good for its wearer or owner, can also work harm upon the latter's enemy. Hence it becomes an instrument of so-called black magic.

The cult of Fate or Destiny is extremely important in relation to the African world view. Fate rules the universe. Everything is predetermined, nothing happens by chance or accident. Nevertheless, the individual is believed to have a fighting chance to alter the course of destiny in his own case, provided he can be forewarned in time to invoke the supernatural intercession of some deity whom he has duly propitiated. If one is a faithful worshiper and observes all the rites of the cult, one may perhaps obtain a better deal from Fate. Because of this belief, the art of divining, or foretelling the future, is of the utmost importance. Knowing what lies in store, one can take steps to meet the situation.

Such, very briefly, are some of the beliefs that determined the world view, the attitude toward life and death, of those Africans who were forcibly brought to America as slaves, and which they used to cope with the new problems of fate and destiny that beset them in a strange environment. In the course of time we shall see some of these ancestral patterns reflected in their folklore and their music. For the moment, let us glance at the background of music in African life.

Music of West Africa

Song is the characteristic musical expression of Africa. There are songs for every occasion: for marriages and funerals, for ceremonies and festivals, for love and for war, for work and for worship. The African expresses all his feelings in song. He taunts his enemies or rivals with songs of derision. He propitiates or implores his deities with an infinite number of sacred melodies. The African sings while he works: at his labor in the fields, on the rivers, in his household, and in the communal tasks. The dances of Africa are usually accompanied by singing; the sounds of the ubiquitous African drums most often blend with human voices, providing a strong and complex rhythmical foundation for song.

The alternation between solo and chorus is a fundamental trait of West African singing. This is the "call-and-response" or antiphonal type of song that has been carried over into Afro-American folk music. Richard Waterman makes some highly interesting comments on the overlapping call-and-response patterns of African song:

> While antiphonal song-patterning, whereby a leader sings phrases which alternate with phrases sung by a chorus, is known all over the world, nowhere else is this form so important as in Africa, where almost all songs are constructed in this manner. A peculiarity of the African call-and-response pattern, found but infrequently elsewhere, is that the chorus phrase regularly commences while the soloist is still singing; the leader, on his part, begins his phrase before the chorus has finished. This phenomenon is quite simply explained in terms of the African musical tradition of the primacy of rhythm. The entrance of the solo or the chorus part on the proper beat of the measure is the important thing, not the effects attained through antiphony or polyphony. Examples of call-and-response music in which the solo part, for one reason or another, drops out for a time, indicate clearly that the chorus part, rhythmical and repetitive, is the mainstay of the songs and the one really inexorable component of their rhythmic structure. The leader, receiving solid rhythmic support from the metrically accurate, rolling repetition of phrases by the chorus, is free to embroider as he will.[2]

[2] Waterman, *African Influence on the Music of the Americas*, p. 214.

Contrary to a widespread notion, harmony is not unknown in African music, although there is no modulation from one key to another, and the feeling for harmony is less developed than in European music. Apart from the accidental harmony that may result from the overlapping song patterns described above, singing in parallel thirds, fourths, sixths, and octaves is common in West African music. The Babira of the Belgian Congo have been known to use *parallel seconds* in their choral singing! Of course, not all African music is uniform. Practices differ among the various tribes. In Dahomey, use of harmony is relatively rare, but two-, three-, and four-part harmony is frequent in the music of the Ashanti of the Gold Coast.

We are apt to think of African music as "weird." This is largely owing to peculiarities of intonation and to melodic practices to which we are unaccustomed. W. E. Ward writes illuminatingly on this point:

> The "weird" intervals are most noticeable at the beginning and end of the tune or of a phrase. Now it is at these places that the African, instead of endeavoring to end or begin with his phrase on a pure note as any European singer would, allows himself to slide on to the note or down from it. It seems to be left to the individual to decide the range of the slide, and whether to approach the note from above or below. A final note is always quitted in a downward glide.[3]

Notice the similarity between this procedure and the "dirty" notes of American jazz music.

Rejecting the hypothesis of an "African" scale of fractional or microtonal intervals,[4] Ward believes that "African melodies are essentially diatonic in structure, modified by a liberal, and unregulated, use of *portamento*" (i.e., sliding from one note to another). Waterman also asserts the diatonic character of the African scale, a fact which now seems beyond dispute; and he remarks that "the tendency toward variable intonation of the third and seventh of the scale has occasionally been noted in West African music." The diatonic scale with ambiguous intonation of the third and seventh degrees—usually somewhat flattened—is the so-called "blues" scale of American popular music.

[3] Ward, *Music of the Gold Coast.*

[4] Nicholas Ballanta-Taylor put forth the theory of an African scale based on a division of the octave into sixteen intervals.

The African conception of rhythm is more complex than the European. In European music different rhythms, as a rule, may be employed successively but not simultaneously; but in African music several rhythms go on simultaneously. Every piece of African music has at least two or three rhythms, sometimes four or five. A frequent combination is to have two percussion parts, one of which may be the clapping of hands, and one vocal part with its own metrical pattern. Often there are several metrical patterns in the percussion, played by drums of different sizes. Confusion is avoided by the presence of a fundamental underlying beat that never varies. If there are several drums, this regular beat is played by the largest drum. The diverse rhythms of all the other instruments must coincide on the first beat of the fundamental rhythm. Rhythm in African music, therefore, is conceived as a combination of time patterns that must coincide at a given moment.

In a recording of Gold Coast drums with gong, the following combination of rhythms appear, with the basic beat of the drum in 3/4 and that of the gong in 6/8 (in the background a second drum is heard in another rhythm, with what Waterman describes as "a fluttering beat in 12/8 time"—a rhythmic pattern frequently found in African music): [5]

The following example of an African song with accompaniment of hand clapping will serve to illustrate further some of the varied rhythmical patterns of this music: [6]

[5] In Alberts (ed.), *Tribal, Folk and Cafe Music of West Africa,* p. 7.

[6] From Ballanta-Taylor, *St. Helena Island Spirituals,* p. 19. Quoted by permission of Penn Community Services, Inc., Frogmore, S.C.

Commenting on this example, Nicholas Ballanta-Taylor remarks that the pattern 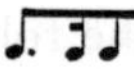 is a rhythmic figure popular among the Africans, its duple character being suited to their usual dance steps. It is one of numerous metrical patterns derived from the basic duple pulse (♩♩). Some of the more common patterns, together with their corresponding syncopated effects, are as follows: [7]

Fundamental duple vibrations: 

Variant Figures | Syncopated Effect

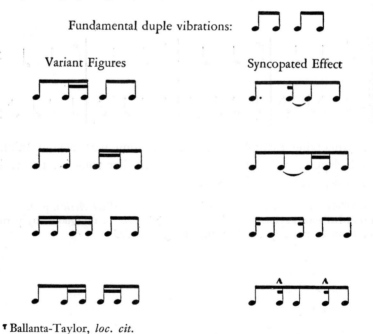

[7] Ballanta-Taylor, *loc. cit.*

These syncopated effects are frequently met with in Afro-American music.

The "metronome sense" is cited by Waterman as crucial for the understanding of African music; and, we may add, for the appreciation of Afro-American music also. In view of its importance, Waterman's explanation is given herewith:

> From the point of view of the listener, it entails habits of conceiving any music as structured along a theoretical framework of beats regularly spaced in time and of co-operating in terms of overt or inhibited motor behavior with the pulses of this metric pattern whether or not the beats are expressed in actual melodic or percussion tones. Essentially, this simply means that African music, with few exceptions, is to be regarded as music for the dance, although the "dance" involved may be entirely a mental one. Since this metronome sense is of such basic importance, it is obvious that the music is conceived and executed in terms of it; it is assumed without question or consideration to be part of the conceptual equipment of both musicians and listeners and is, in the most complete way, taken for granted. When the beat is actually sounded, it serves as a confirmation of this subjective beat.[8]

A grasp of this fundamental concept underlying the traditional values of African music enables us to understand readily how and why the Afro-American influence has had such a tremendous impact on the dance music of the Western world.

Notwithstanding the differences in the concept of rhythm that have been pointed out, there is a basis of unity between European and African music. The diatonic scale is common to both systems and forms, indeed, the strongest link between them, as well as the mark that distinguishes them from all other systems. Then there is the basic concept of harmony that they share. Though the harmonic sense may be less developed in African music, it exists as a concrete factor.

These considerations lead us to conclude, with Kolinski and Waterman, that African and European music have enough basic factors in common to facilitate the process of musical "syncretism" or blending when they are brought into contact with each other over a period of time, as occurred in America. This explains, as Kolinski observes, the homogeneous character of the American Negro spirituals and of

[8] Waterman, *African Influence on the Music of the Americas*, p. 211.

Afro-American music as a whole. We shall now observe some phases, secular and religious, of this process of musical syncretism.

Negro fiddlers and dances

With that remarkable musical aptitude that Jefferson observed, the Negroes in America soon learned to play various European musical instruments. It must be remembered that conditions in which Negroes lived in the American colonies and the early United States differed greatly according to circumstances, and accordingly provided different kinds and degrees of opportunity for the acquisition and display of musical skills. In some cases slaves employed as household servants were encouraged to develop musical skills that might contribute to the pleasure or social prestige of their masters. In 1753 the *Virginia Gazette* carried an advertisement for "an orderly Negro or mulatto who can play well the violin." The same paper also printed an advertisement offering for sale "A young healthy Negro fellow . . . who [plays] extremely well on the French horn." Another announcement requested the return of a runaway slave "who took his fiddle with him." Captain Richard Bailey, of Accomac County, Virginia, is reported to have had a Negro servant who fiddled for the whole neighborhood.

An aristocrat among Negro musicians was Sy Gilliat, body servant to Lord Botecourt, who was the official fiddler at state balls in Williamsburg. He wore an embroidered silk coat and vest of faded lilac, silk stockings, and shoes with large buckles. He also wore a powdered brown wig, and his manners were said to be "as courtly as his dress." Another Negro musician, known as "London Brigs," who became Gilliat's assistant after the capital was moved from Williamsburg to Richmond, was reputed to be equally skillful on the flute and the clarinet. According to Samuel Mordecai, "To the music of Gilliat's fiddle and 'London Brigs' flute all sorts of capers were cut. . . . Sometimes a 'congo' was danced and when the music grew fast and furious, a jig would wind up the evening." This mention of the congo as a social dance in colonial Richmond arouses a curiosity that the historian finds difficult to satisfy. Unfortunately this is not a contemporary reference, for Mordecai's book was published in 1860, and his sources are vague. Nevertheless, the fact that he does mention the congo provides a clue that may some day lead to interesting data regarding the influence that Negro music and dancing may have had upon the American upper classes in the eighteenth century.

The congo has been well documented as a Negro dance of the Antilles, found also in Louisiana (it is not to be confused with the Cuban *conga*, of later origin). Lafcadio Hearn, in 1885, described the congo as he saw it danced by Negroes in New Orleans. He said it was "as lascivious as is possible." The women "do not take their feet off the ground," while the men "dance very differently, like savages leaping in the air." We are not to assume that the ladies and gentlemen of old Virginia carried on in this uninhibited manner. But the history of social dancing is full of instances in which a dance existed simultaneously on two levels, assuming a decorous form in polite society and manifesting a licentious character among the populace. It is quite possible that the congo, a primitive Negro dance of African origin, flourished in the slave quarters of the plantations, while at the same time a dance of the same name, though certainly not with the identical choreography, was admitted to the ballrooms of the ruling class.

In considering the plausibility of this hypothesis, it is important to bear in mind that in many cases the musicians who played for these society balls were Negroes. And if the music they played "grew fast and furious," cannot we suppose that it reverted to some wild and primitive strain, however modified and restrained by imposed conventions? We know that in Latin America many dances adopted by polite society had their origin in Negro dances which would be regarded as objectionable by the standards of this same society. Albert Friedenthal, a musician who traveled widely in Latin America during the nineteenth century, has some interesting comments to make on the influence that the music and dancing of the Negroes exerted upon their white masters:

> Every day in their hours of rest they [the whites] had opportunities to see the partly sensual, partly grotesque and wild dances of their black slaves, and to hear their peculiar songs. . . . Added to this the strange instruments of percussion which, while marking the rhythm, exerted an almost uncanny effect.[9]

Although the slaves in Latin America, on the whole, had wider opportunities to express themselves musically than those of North America, the conditions described by Friedenthal are largely applicable

[9] Friedenthal, *Musik, Tanz und Dichtung bei den Kreolen Amerikas*, p. 95.

also to the United States. The songs and dances of the plantation Negroes provided first a source of amusement for the landowners and their families; and later, imitated by white entertainers with their faces blackened, the "coon songs," "plantation melodies," and "cakewalks" provided amusement for the whole country through the immensely popular minstrel shows. Ragtime, blues, and jazz were other and still later manifestations of the fascination and influence that Negro music exerted upon the white population. In another chapter we shall observe the influx of Latin American songs and dance rhythms from the Caribbean area, dominated by African influences, into the region of Louisiana and New Orleans in particular. There, in the nineteenth century, the Negro folk music of the American South and the Afro-Hispanic music of the Caribbean were to converge in the creation of jazz.

After this glimpse into the future, we must return to the Atlantic seaboard and the plantations of the South in the eighteenth century to trace the spread of Christianity and of evangelical hymnody among the Negroes, which provide the background for the development of that important body of American folk song known as the Negro spirituals.

The Negroes and the Gospel

In 1675 John Eliott, the Puritan "apostle of the Indians," speaking of the slave trade, said, "to sell souls for money seemeth to me a dangerous enterprise." He meant, of course, dangerous for one's spiritual welfare. But the majority of slaveowners were untroubled by such scruples. A writer in the *Athenian Oracle* of London, in 1705, expressed what was probably a prevalent attitude:

> Talk to a planter of the soul of a Negro, and he'll be apt to tell you (or at least his actions speak loudly), that the Body of one of them may be worth twenty Pounds, but the Souls of an hundred of them would not yield him one farthing.

A plantation owner of Barbados voiced the opinion that one "might as well baptize puppies as Negroes." The vested interests of colonial society, as represented by their official bodies, clothed similar sentiments in the more pretentious verbiage of moral self-justification.

Samuel Davies, the eighteenth-century evangelist and champion of religious tolerance, deplored "the almost universal neglect of the many thousands of slaves . . . who generally continue Heathens in a Christian country." In the course of time these conditions were to change gradually, thanks to the efforts of many zealous missionaries and to a more enlightened attitude on the part of the slaveowners.

It is true that some masters insisted upon having their slaves attend religious services and that special galleries were set apart for this purpose in colonial churches, such as the one in Bruton Parish, Williamsburg, where several hundred Negroes were baptized. Yet the formality of an established religion like the Episcopalian could exert no strong appeal, nor affirm a deep hold, upon the emotions of the Negro slaves. Much more effective was the fervor and freedom, the ecstasy and exuberance, of revivalism as represented by the dissenting sects and the evangelical denominations. The Methodists and the Baptists, to say nothing of the numerous minor sects, far outdid in popular appeal the Episcopalians, the Presbyterians, and the Catholics.

The Rev. John Davies of Virginia was one of the most active preachers of the gospel among the Negroes. John Wesley, the famous founder of Methodism, tells in his journal of receiving a letter "sent from a gentleman in Virginia," who was probably Davies, since he is mentioned later as the writer of a similar letter which Wesley quotes at length. As these letters are among the very few firsthand accounts we have of Christianization among the slaves, and as they contain significant references to music, I quote extensive passages from them. The first letter runs, in part, as follows:

> The poor Negro slaves here never heard of Jesus or his religion till they arrived at the land of their slavery in America, whom their masters generally neglect, as though immortality was not the privilege of their souls, in common with their own. These poor Africans are the principal objects of my compassion, and, I think, the most proper subject of your charity. . . .
>
> The number of these [Negroes] who attend on my ministry is uncertain; but I think there are about 300 who give a stated attendance. And never have I been so much struck with the appearance of an assembly, as when I have glanced on one part of the house, adorned (so it appeared to me) with so many black countenances, eagerly attentive to every word they heard, and some of them covered with tears. . . . As they are not sufficiently polished to dissemble with a good grace, they express the sensations of their hearts so much in

the language of simple nature, and with such genuine indications of artless sincerity, that it is impossible to suspect their professions. . . .

I have supplied them to the utmost of my ability [with books]. They are exceedingly delighted with Watt's [*sic*] Songs. And I cannot but observe, that the Negroes, above all of the human species I ever knew, have the nicest ear for music. They have a kind of ecstatic delight in psalmody; nor are there any books they so soon learn, or take so much pleasure in, as those used in that heavenly part of divine worship.[10]

This emphatic corroboration of the Negro's musical aptitude is impressive; and it seems to me that these paragraphs from the pen of an eyewitness tell us more about the genesis of the Negro spirituals than any amount of *a posteriori* theorizing. Our imaginations can easily reconstruct the atmosphere of emotionalism and fervor, the tears, the heartfelt outpourings in simple language not devoid of striking imagery, the delight in the *Hymns and Spiritual Songs* of Dr. Watts with their direct appeal to the common feelings of plain people, the ecstatic pleasure in the surge of communal song, and the sense of spiritual and physical satisfaction at expressing themselves freely through an innate talent that not even the conditions of slavery could repress.

Further details of the picture may be filled in from another letter quoted in John Wesley's journal, which he specifically states is "from the Rev. Mr. Davies, in Virginia":

When the books arrived, I gave public notice after sermon, and desired such Negroes as could read, and such white people as would make good use of them . . . to come to my house. For some time after, the poor slaves, whenever they could get an hour's leisure, hurried away to me, and received them with all the genuine indication of passionate gratitude. All the books were very acceptable, but none more so, than the Psalms and Hymns, which enabled them to gratify their peculiar taste for psalmody. Sundry of them lodged all night in my kitchen; and sometimes when I have awaked at two or three in the morning, a torrent of sacred psalmody has poured into my chamber. In this exercise some of them spend the whole night.[11]

Extremely illuminating, and bearing even richer stuff for the imagination to work on, is this vivid picture of Negroes spending the whole

[10] *The Journal of the Rev. John Wesley, A.M.*, vol. 2, p. 303.
[11] *Ibid.*, p. 320.

night in the singing of psalms and hymns, producing a veritable "torrent" of sacred song. Lacking a direct detailed description of this "torrent of psalmody," we must draw upon analogy and inference. At this point it will be helpful if the reader goes back to Chapter 2 and rereads the description of the Early New England Folk Style of psalmody, noting that its main characteristics are singing by ear rather than by note or "rule"; the raising or lowering of notes at will; the adding of grace notes, turns, and other embellishments; the "sliding" from one note to another; the adding of parts at the intervals of a fourth, a fifth, and an octave; and the practice of "lining-out," with the leader reading or chanting the verses of the psalm, one or two lines at a time, and the congregation singing them afterward. Now compare the description of African singing earlier in the present chapter, and ask whether the two styles do not possess sufficient elements in common to produce a natural fusion or syncretism. Compare, again, the following description of the singing of a so-called "long meter" hymn (also significantly known as "Doctor Watt") as heard among Southern Negroes some years ago by George Pullen Jackson:

> A deacon or the elder "lines out" a couplet of the text in a sing-song voice and at a fair speaking pace ending on a definite tone. This "tones" the tune. The deacon then starts singing, and by the time he has sung through the elaborately ornamented first syllable the whole congregation has joined in on the second syllable with a volume of florid sound which ebbs and flows slowly, powerfully and at times majestically in successive surges until the lined-out words have been sung. Without pause the deacon sing-songs the next couplet, and the second half of the four-line tune is sung in the same manner. No instrument is ever used. No harmony is indulged in excepting here and there a bit, hit upon by accident as it would seem, and sometimes a one-singer attempt at bass. The women and the men sing, with these exceptions, the same notes an octave apart.[12]

As this type of singing corresponds in its essential aspects to a well-established popular tradition of eighteenth-century psalmody, I venture the hypothesis that something of this sort assailed the ears of the Rev. Mr. Davies when he awoke in the small hours of the morning and heard "a torrent of sacred psalmody" pouring from the throats of the Negroes assembled in his kitchen.

[12] Jackson, *White and Negro Spirituals,* p. 248.

In the same letter to John Wesley from which we quoted above, John Davies wrote: "There are thousands of Negroes in this Colony [Virginia], who still continue in the grossest ignorance, and are as rank Pagans now, as they were in the wilds of Africa." In other words, while a certain percentage of Negroes was exposed to the doctrines of Christianity, and some of them were converted and baptized, the large majority continued to live, spiritually, as though they were still "in the wilds of Africa," which in the eyes of the missionaries meant they were "rank Pagans" clinging to barbarous beliefs.

It is important to keep these proportions in mind as we trace the growth of Afro-American music, observing that there was no uniform development, no general conformity of conditions, but rather a variety of social and cultural conditions, ranging from the comparative sophistication of urbanized Negroes to the primitive plantation life of the Georgia Sea Islands, where slaves living in relative isolation retained definite Africanisms of speech and customs for generation after generation. If we look at Afro-American music as it exists today, we can see that it contains elements derived from these various levels of culture and experience and what the sociologists call "acculturation" (the results of continuous firsthand contact between different cultural groups): there are the highly self-conscious and artistically "correct" arrangements of spirituals, closely conforming to traditional standards of European art music; there are the relatively primitive work songs, shouts, hollers, and blues, strongly marked by African retentions; there are the "Dr. Watt" hymns and "surge songs," survivals of eighteenth-century psalmody and hymnody; and there is jazz and its derivative styles, stemming from the Negro's contact, in urban environments, with the dances and instruments of the dominant white culture fused with the ancestral African heritage. Even within the frame of American musical culture as a whole, Afro-American music is in itself a complex whose diverse strands need to be traced individually as well as in their mutual interaction.

Our minds tend to reject all complexes in favor of simplified stereotypes. It is thus that there emerges the image of the "plantation darkie" as a stock figure of our stage and popular-song literature, leading to a whole musico-theatrical production ranging from the grotesque to the sentimental. From the eighteenth-century sentimental songs about the poor Negro boy, to the "Mammy" songs of twentieth-century tin-pan alley, there is a continuous popular tradition. We shall in due course trace this tradition and its tenuous connection with the actual life of the plantation Negroes. For the moment we simply point to it as one of the phases of America's music that stemmed from the backgrounds of Negro slavery in the United States.

All generalities tend to be misleading through oversimplification. But if we must carry in our minds a composite picture of plantation life in the early days of slavery, then let it be one drawn by a master hand, the informal but authoritative sketch of a great scholar in this field, Ulrich B. Phillips:

> The plantation was a pageant and a variety show in alternation. The procession of plowmen at evening, slouched crosswise on their mules; the dance in the new sugarhouse, preceded by prayer; the bonfire in the quarter with contests in clogs, cakewalks and Charlestons whose fascinations were as yet undiscovered by the great world; the work songs in solo and refrain, with not too fast a rhythm; the baptizing in the creek, with lively demonstrations from the "sisters" as they came dripping out; the torchlight pursuit of 'possum and 'coon, with full-voiced halloo to baying houn' dawg and yelping cur; the rabbit hunt, the log-rolling, the house-raising, the husking-bee, the quilting party, the wedding, the cock fight, the crap game, the children's play, all punctuated plantation life—and most of them were highly vocal. A funeral now and then of some prominent slave would bring festive sorrowing, or the death of a beloved master an outburst of emotion.[13]

And intertwined with the frolic and the fun, the sorrow and the mourning, the work and the prayer, there was always music, not music of one kind, but of many kinds, changing and taking to itself melodies and harmonies and rhythms from here and there, but always based on the bedrock of the black man's intense love and great gift for the solace and beauty and excitement of music.

It is only natural that Thomas Jefferson should have been the first prominent American to recognize and to proclaim publicly the exceptional musicality of the Negro. For Jefferson was not only one of the most perceptive and enlightened men of his time, he was also a keen and discriminating music lover. In the next chapter we shall learn something about the musical tastes of Jefferson, as well as about the interests and activities of other American gentlemen of the eighteenth century who cultivated music as amateurs.

[13] Phillips, *Life and Labor in the Old South*, pp. 202–203.

chapter five

Gentlemen amateurs

They would talk of nothing but high life, and high-lived company; with other fashionable topics, such as pictures, taste, Shakespeare and the musical glasses.

OLIVER GOLDSMITH, THE VICAR OF WAKEFIELD.

On October 11, 1760, the *South Carolina Gazette* carried the announcement of "A Concert of Vocal and Instrumental Music" to be given in Charleston with the assistance of "the Gentlemen who are the best performers, both in Town and Country." In the eighteenth century professional musicians were not considered gentlemen. Hence this announcement, like many others of similar tenor that appeared in newspapers throughout the colonies, refers to the participation of those "gentlemen amateurs" who practiced music because they loved it and who played in public because there were not in those days enough professional musicians in any American community to make up a "full band." As a rule they played in semiprivate subscription concerts such as those sponsored by the St. Cecilia Society of Charleston, but when a worthy member of the musical profession gave a public "benefit" concert—that is, according to the custom of those times, a concert for his own benefit—then the Gentlemen from Town and Country rallied gallantly to his assistance with their fiddles, flutes, and hautboys. French horns, clarinets, and even an occasional bassoon, were not unknown; but these were not regarded as particularly genteel instruments.

That the gentlemen amateurs had no prejudice against performing in the theater is indicated by the following announcement in the *Pennsylvania Gazette* of Philadelphia for November 30, 1769: "The Orchestra, on Opera Nights, will be assisted by some musical Persons, who as they have no View but to contribute to the Entertainment of the Public, certainly claim a Protection from any Manner of Insult." This implies that the professionals, being paid for their pains, had no recourse save to suffer the abuse of the public if their efforts failed to please, while the amateurs claimed immunity from criticism by virtue of their voluntary service. Besides, *they* were Gentlemen.

As a typical gentleman amateur of colonial America, let me introduce Councillor Robert Carter of Nomini Hall in Virginia. Philip Vickers Fithian, a tutor in his household, wrote of him: "He has a good ear for Music, a vastly delicate Taste and keeps good instruments; he has here at Home a Harpsichord, Forte Piano, Harmonica, Guitar & German Flute, and at Williamsburg has a good Organ; he himself also is indefatigable in the Practice." [1] Lest the mention of "Harmonica" evoke an unseemly image of Mr. Carter playing the mouth organ, let me explain that this was, according to a description in the Councillor's own notebook, an instrument invented by Mr. B. Franklin of Philadelphia, "being the musical glasses without water, framed into a complete instrument capable of thorough bass and never out of tune." We shall hear more presently about this wonderful invention. For the moment simply pause to contemplate the edifying spectacle of a country squire who keeps good instruments as one might keep good horses, and who is as familiar with a thorough bass as with a thoroughbred. He, moreover, is reputed to have "a vastly delicate Taste"—than which there could be no higher compliment to a gentleman of the eighteenth century. Good taste was the touchstone of the age.

We take for granted the good taste of our colonial ancestors in architecture and interior decoration because we are familiar with the incontestable beauty of the homes, churches, and public buildings of that period. But we are sadly ignorant concerning the musical taste of our eighteenth-century forebears because it is attested only by musty newspaper files, library inventories, and documental archives. Recently, however, the Williamsburg Festival Concerts have revived the musical elegance and sophistication of that colonial capital, which knew the music of the best European composers, such as Handel, Hasse, Vivaldi, Corelli, Galuppi, Pugnani, Boccherini, Rameau, Arne, Stamitz, the "London" Bach, and many others.

Young Thomas Jefferson, while studying law at the College of William and Mary in Williamsburg, belonged to the intimate circle of Governor Francis Fauquier, of whom he later wrote: "The Gov-

[1] Fithian, *Journal and Letters*, p. 77.

ernor was musical also, being a good performer, and associated me with two or three other amateurs in his weekly concerts." Jefferson himself played the violin; he and Patrick Henry often played duets together. Do not imagine that this sort of thing pertained exclusively to the Cavalier tradition of the South. While there may have been more gentlemen of leisure in the Southern colonies, there were musical amateurs everywhere. Take, for example, Lieutenant Governor John Penn of Pennsylvania, a keen music lover and a good violinist who gave private chamber-music concerts at his home in Philadelphia every Sunday evening during the season, and who, together with his friend Francis Hopkinson, was one of the chief promoters of musical activity in the Quaker City. In all our cities, from Charleston in the South to Boston in the North, the gentlemen of high degree were paying their respects to the heavenly Muse.

The sage of Monticello

Among the devotees of music none was more ardent in his devotion than Thomas Jefferson. Consequently none felt more keenly than he the deterioration in American musical activity that took place during the Revolutionary War. Patriot though he was, he must have looked back wistfully on those halcyon days when, as a crony of Francis Fauquier, he joined in the governor's chamber-music concerts. We know by his own confession that he gazed with intense longing upon the greener pastures of European musical life. In 1778 he wrote to a friend whose name we do not know, probably a Frenchman, saying: "If there is a gratification which I envy any people in this world, it is your country its music." Years later, when his diplomatic mission to France had enabled him to savor this gratification at firsthand, he repeated the same thought in a letter to Charles Bellini, a professor at the College of William and Mary, dated Paris, September 30, 1785: "Were I to proceed to tell you how much I enjoy their architecture, sculpture, painting, music, I should want words. It is in these arts they shine. The last of them, particularly, is an enjoyment, the deprivation of which, with us, cannot be calculated. I am about ready to say it is the only thing which from my heart I envy them, and which in spite of all the authority of the Decalogue, I do covet."

Can this passage be reconciled with the thesis that early musical life in America was not as crude and primitive as it has generally been depicted? I think it can. The concert programs so painstakingly unearthed and assembled by Sonneck prove that the music of the best European composers of that time was known and performed in America. But it would be absurd to pretend that the performances were on a par with the best that could be heard in Europe. Jefferson was thinking of Europe's finest: the Paris Opéra, the "Concert Spirituel," the English oratorio performances. Only the best, and a great deal of it, would satisfy his passion for music. Moreover, after the Revolution the Northern cities took the lead in our musical life, while the South, where Jefferson lived, lagged behind.

Had Jefferson been able to carry out a cherished idea, he would have created a small musical world of his own at Monticello. In the letter of 1778 from which I have already quoted, he outlined an ingenious scheme for providing himself with a private musical establishment somewhat after the manner of the European nobility:

> The bounds of an American fortune will not admit the indulgence of a domestic band of musicians, yet I have thought that a passion for music might be reconciled with that economy which we are obliged to observe. I retain, for instance, among my domestic servants a gardener, a weaver, a cabinet maker and a stone cutter, to which I would add a *vigneron*. In a country where like yours music is cultivated and practised by every class I suppose there might be found persons of those trades who could perform on the French horn, clarinet or hautboy & bassoon, so that one might have a band of two French horns, two clarinets & hautboys and a bassoon, without enlarging their domestic expenses.[2]

Nothing seems to have come of the scheme, but the letter leaves no doubt that Jefferson knew what he wanted. He was not exaggerating when, in this same letter, he referred to music as "this favorite passion of my soul." The truth is that the father of American democracy was an aristocrat in his musical tastes. He courted the Muse like a *grand seigneur*.

The eminent Dr. Franklin

Among Jefferson's letters from Paris there is one to Francis Hopkinson of Philadelphia, dated July 6, 1785, which casts a curious side-

[2] Quoted in *The Writings of Thomas Jefferson*, ed. by P. L. Ford (New York, 1892–1899), vol. 2, p. 159.

light on the musical inclinations of another famous Philadelphian: "I communicated to Doctr. Franklin your idea of Mesmerising the Harpsichord. He has not tried it, probably because his affairs have been long packed & packing; as I do not play on that instrument I cannot try it myself. The Doctr. carries with him a pretty little instrument. It is the sticcado, with glass bars instead of wooden ones, and with keys applied to it. It's principle [*sic*] defect is the want of extent, having but three octaves. I wish you would exercise your ingenuity to give it an upper and lower octave. . . ." [3] These men of the eighteenth century were always exercising their ingenuity on something or other! The reference in the first sentence is to Hopkinson's improved method for quilling the harpsichord, a very ingenious device. As for the "pretty little instrument" that Dr. Franklin carried about with him, it was a sort of glass dulcimer, usually called the "Sticcado-Pastorale." James Woodforde, in his *Diary of a Country Parson*, said that it looked, "when covered, like a working box for ladies." So, what Dr. Franklin carried around in Paris was not necessarily a dispatch box full of state papers.

Benjamin Franklin's musical accomplishments were by no means limited to playing the Sticcado-Pastorale. He played the guitar and the harp, both fashionable instruments at that time. While living in London he offered his services as guitar teacher to the mother of Leigh Hunt, the English poet and essayist. And Franklin was also somewhat of a virtuoso on the instrument that he himself invented, the so-called "Glass Harmonica." He was fond of singing in congenial company and was especially partial to Scotch songs. He tells us of one called "The Old Man's Wish" that he sang "a thousand times in his singing days." In his seventieth year he wrote to the Abbé de la Roche recalling "a little drinking song which I wrote thirty years ago" and quoted from it the following verse and chorus:

SINGER: Fair Venus calls: Her voice obey.
In beauty's arms spend night and day.
The joys of love all joys excell
And loving's certainly doing well.

CHORUS: Oh! No!
Not so!
For honest souls know
Friends and a bottle still bear the bell.

[3] Sonneck, *Francis Hopkinson and James Lyon*, p. 67.

Some biographers have conjectured that Franklin composed music for this and other songs, but it is more probable that he simply set the verses to well-known tunes, as was the custom in those days. The evidence that he might have tried his hand at composing rests chiefly on a passage in a letter from Mme. Brillon, addressed to Franklin, in which she mentions receiving "your music engraved in America." This may refer to music engraved, rather than composed, by Franklin. A manuscript recently discovered in the library of the Paris Conservatory and published in 1946 bears the inscription: *Quartetto a 3 violini con violoncello del Sigre* [Signore] *Benjamin Francklin* (*sic*). This is a kind of suite consisting of five short movements, each bearing a conventional title (*Menuetto*, *Siciliano*, etc.). The music is written for the open strings only and employs an unusual type of tuning known as *scordatura*. The manuscript is not in Franklin's hand, nor is there any further evidence to substantiate his authorship of this string quartet, which has been called "a mathematical tour de force."

The celebrated Glassychord

It was primarily as a musical inventor that Benjamin Franklin made the greatest impression on musical circles both in Europe and America. According to the *Musikalischer Almanach für Deutschland* for the year 1782, "Of all musical inventions, the one of Mr. Franklin of Philadelphia has created perhaps the greatest excitement." By this time the instrument in question had been enjoying a widespread vogue for some twenty years, as indicated by the following news item from the *Bristol Gazette*, dated January 12, 1762:

> The celebrated Glassy-chord, invented by Mr. Franklin of Philadelphia; who has greatly improved the Musical Glasses, and formed them into a compleat Instrument to accompany the voice. . . . Miss Davies, from London, was to perform in the Month of January, several favorite Airs, English, Scotch and Italian, on the Glassychord (being the only one of the kind that has yet been produced) accompanied occasionally with the Voice and German Flute.

From this it appears that Franklin invented his improved version of the musical glasses in 1761 and that the novel instrument was originally called Glassychord (hyphen apparently optional!), a rather clumsy appellation soon dropped in favor of "Armonica," the name that

Franklin himself gave it, in honor, as he said, of the musical Italian language. With the addition of a superfluous but persistent aspirate, it became generally anglicized as Harmonica.

The use of musical glasses was known to the Persians and Arabs at least as early as the fourteenth century and may possibly have spread to Europe from the Near East. A work published at Nuremberg in 1677 mentions "making a cheerful wine-music" by stroking the rims of partially filled glasses with a moistened finger. The same volume also describes a musical experiment with four glasses, filled with brandy, wine, water, and salt water or oil.

No less a personage than the Chevalier Gluck, already crowned with the laurels of operatic success, performed on the musical glasses in London in 1746 and claimed them to be, with some exaggeration, "a new instrument of his own Invention." Gluck's claim could not be taken too seriously, for an Irish adventurer named Richard Pockrich had been giving concerts on the musical glasses since 1743 and continued to win popular acclaim as a performer until both he and his "angelick organ," as he called it, perished in a fire at London in 1759. Something of Pockrich's reputation can be gathered from these verses from "The Pockreiad," an epic poem by Brockhill Newburgh:

> Old Pock no more, still lives in deathless fame,
> He blazed when young, when old expired in flame. . .
> Be silent, dumb, ye late harmonious glasses:
> Free from surprise securely sleep ye lasses.

The musical glasses did not long remain dumb, for one E. H. Delaval made a set modeled after Pockrich's and played on it in London, where among his enraptured listeners was Benjamin Franklin. In his letter to Padre Beccaria describing the Armonica (written from London under date of July 1, 1762),[4] Franklin states that Delaval's instrument was "the first I saw or heard." And he continues: "Being charmed by the sweetness of its tones, and the music he produced from it, I wished only to see the glasses disposed in a more convenient form, and brought together in a narrower compass, so as to admit of a greater number of tones, and all within reach of hand to a person sitting before the instrument. . . ." This, then, was the origin of Dr. Franklin's celebrated Glassychord or Armonica.

[4] This letter is printed in *The Complete Works of Benjamin Franklin*, ed. by Bigelow, vol. 3, pp. 198–204; also in Sonneck, *Suum Cuique*, pp. 60–62.

Instead of having the glasses filled with varying quantities of water to obtain variety of pitch, Franklin had the glasses made of different sizes and used only the bowls, without the stems. He placed the glasses on a horizontal rod or spindle which was rotated by foot action, like a spinning wheel. The instrument, wrote Franklin, "is played upon, by sitting before the middle of the set of glasses as before the keys of a harpsichord, turning them with the foot, and wetting them now and then with a sponge and clean water."

This simple yet ingenious mechanism made the musical glasses infinitely more practical and led to their immediate and widespread success both as a domestic and a concert instrument. Miss Marianne Davies—the young lady mentioned in the item from the *Bristol Gazette*—undertook an extensive concert tour of the Continent in 1768, together with her sister Cecilia, a well-known singer. Paris, Florence, Turin, Milan, and Vienna acclaimed the charming Misses Davies and the novel instrument with the celestial tones "*inventato del celebre dottore Franklin.*" Marianne Davies was especially appreciated in Vienna. The court poet Metastasio wrote an "Ode" which was set to music (for soprano and harmonica) by the fashionable operatic composer Johann Adolph Hasse and performed by the Misses Davies at the wedding of the Archduchess of Austria to the Duke of Parma. Leopold Mozart and his brilliant young son, Wolfgang, were well acquainted with Miss Davies and her harmonica. In the summer of 1773 Leopold wrote from Vienna: "Do you know that Herr von Mesmer plays Miss Davies's harmonica unusually well? He is the only person in Vienna who has learned it and he possesses a much finer instrument than Miss Davies does. Wolfgang too has played upon it. How I should love to have one!"

The Herr von Mesmer mentioned in this letter was Franz Anton Mesmer, the exponent of "animal magnetism" or hypnotism. According to A. Hyatt King, "there seems little doubt that Mesmer used his mastery of the highly emotional tones of the harmonica to induce a receptive state in his patients." The harmonica seems to have had an extraordinary physiological effect. Its tones could unnerve the strongest man and cause women to faint. Most of those who played it frequently, including Marianne Davies, ended by having their nerves shattered. Franklin himself was an exception: he must have had nerves of iron.

In 1791, the year following Franklin's death and the last year of his own life, Mozart, inspired by the playing of a blind girl named Marianne Kirchgässner, composed a remarkable piece of music for the instrument that had so delighted him and his father when he was a boy. This was the lovely Quintet (Adagio and Rondo) for harmonica, flute, oboe, viola, and cello (Köchel 617). Mozart also composed an Adagio for harmonica solo (K. 356). Other more or less celebrated European composers who wrote music for the harmonica were Hasse, Martini, Jommelli, Galuppi, J. G. Naumann, K. L. Röllig, W. L. Tomaschek, and Beethoven. The unearthly tone quality of the harmonica appealed strongly to the Romantic imagination, and inspired the enthusiastic praise of such poets as Goethe, Schiller, Wieland, and Jean Paul Richter. Robert Schumann also succumbed to its spell.

As a musical inventor Benjamin Franklin was not without honor in his own country. To show what impression the harmonica made on his countrymen, let us return to Nomini Hall, the home of Councillor Robert Carter in Virginia, and read Philip Vickers Fithian's description of a certain winter evening in that gentleman's household, in the year 1773: "Evening. Mr. Carter spent in playing on the Harmonica; it is the first time I have heard the Instrument. The Music is charming! The notes are clear and inexpressibly soft, they swell, and are inexpressibly grand; and either it is because the sounds are new, and therefore pleased me, or it is the most captivating Instrument I have ever heard."

Franklin as music critic

Franklin, though many-sided, was no mere dabbler. His interest in music was neither casual nor superficial. Proof of his profound and original thinking on musical subjects is afforded by two of his letters, one to the philosopher Lord Kames of Edinburgh, the other to his brother Peter Franklin, both written from London in 1765. These documents speak for themselves, and in view of their remarkable contents I make no apology for quoting from them at length. In his letter to Lord Kames, Franklin writes as follows:

> In my passage to America I read your excellent work, "The Elements of Criticism," in which I found great entertainment. I only wish that you had examined more carefully the subject of music, and demonstrated that the pleasure artists feel in hearing much of

that composed in the modern taste is not the natural pleasure arising from melody or harmony of sounds, but of the same kind with the pleasure we feel on seeing the surprising feats of tumblers and rope-dancers, who execute difficult things. For my part, I take this really to be the case, and suppose it to be the reason why those who are unpracticed in music, and therefore unacquainted with those difficulties, have little or no pleasure in hearing this music. I have sometimes, at a concert, attended by a common audience, placed myself so as to see all their faces, and observed no signs of pleasure in them during the performance of a great part that was admired by the performers themselves; while a plain old Scotch tune, which they disdained, and could scarcely be prevailed upon to play, gave manifest and general delight.

Give me leave, on this occasion, to extend a little the sense of your position, that "melody and harmony are separately agreeable and in union delightful," and to give it as my opinion that the reason why the Scotch tunes have lived so long, and will probably live forever (if they escape being stifled in modern affected ornament), is merely this, that they are really compositions of melody and harmony united, or rather that their melody is harmony. I mean the simple tunes sung by a single voice. As this will appear paradoxical, I must explain my meaning.

In common acceptation, indeed, only an agreeable *succession* of sounds is called *melody*, and only the *coexistence* of agreeable sounds *harmony*. But, since the memory is capable of retaining for some moments a perfect idea of the pitch of a past sound, so as to compare it with the pitch of a succeeding sound, and judge truly of their agreement or disagreement, there may be and does arise from thence a sense of harmony between the present and past sounds equally pleasing with that between two present sounds.

Now, the construction of the old Scotch tunes is this, that almost every succeeding emphatical note is a third, a fifth, an octave, or, in short, some note that is in concord with the preceding note. Thirds are chiefly used, which are very pleasing concords. I used the word *emphatical* to distinguish those notes which have a stress laid on them in singing the tune, from the lighter connecting notes that serve merely, like grammar articles in common speech, to tack the whole thing together.

[Franklin here puts forth several arguments to demonstrate that the mind can retain "a most perfect idea of sound just passed."]

Farther, when we consider by whom these ancient tunes were composed and how they were first performed, we shall see that such harmonical succession of sounds were natural, and even necessary, in their construction. They were composed by the minstrels of those days to be played on the harp, accompanied by the voice. The harp was strung with wire, which gives a sound of long continuance, and had no contrivance like that in the modern harpsichord, by which the sound of the preceding could be stopped the moment a succeeding note began. To avoid actual discord it was therefore necessary that the succeeding emphatical note should be a chord with the preceding, as their sounds must exist at the same time. Hence arose that beauty in those tunes that has so long pleased, and will please forever, though men scarce know why. That they were originally composed for the harp, and of the most simple kind, I mean a harp without any half notes but those in the natural scale and with no more than two octaves of strings, from C to C, I conjecture from another circumstance, which is, that not one of those tunes, really ancient, has a single artificial half note in it, and that in tunes where it was most convenient for the voice to use the middle notes of the harp and place the key in F, then the B, which, if used, should be a B flat, is always omitted by passing over it with a third. The connoisseurs in modern music will say I have no taste, but I cannot help adding that I believe our ancestors, in hearing a good song, distinctly articulated, sung to one of those tunes and accompanied by the harp, felt more real pleasure that is communicated by the generality of modern operas, exclusive of that arising from the scenery and dancing. Most tunes of late composition, not having this natural harmony united with their melody, have recourse to the artificial harmony of a bass and other accompanying parts. This support, in my opinion, the old tunes do not need, and are rather confused than aided by it. Whoever has heard James Oswald play these on his violoncello will be less inclined to dispute this with me. I have more than once seen tears of pleasure in the eyes of his auditors; and yet, I think, even *his* playing those tunes would please more, if he gave them less modern ornament.[5]

Notice that Franklin, in standing up for his convictions, has the supreme courage to risk being regarded as a person of no taste by "the connoisseurs in modern music."

Now here is the letter to Peter Franklin, which tells something

[5] *Ibid.*

about Benjamin Franklin's own attitude to that "modern music" whose artificialities he deplored and attacked. He writes:

Dear Brother: I like your ballad, and I think it well adapted for your purpose of discountenancing expensive foppery and encouraging industry and frugality. If you can get it generally sung in your country, it may probably have a good deal of the effect you hope and expect from it. But as you aimed at making it general, I wonder you chose so uncommon a measure in poetry that none of the tunes in common use will suit it. Had you fitted it to an old one, well known, it must have spread much faster than I doubt it will do from the best new tune we can get composed for it. I think, too, that if you had given it to some country girl in the heart of Massachusetts, who has never heard any other than psalm tunes or "Chevy Chase," the "Children in the Woods," the "Spanish Lady," and such old, simple ditties, but has naturally a good ear, she might more probably have made a pleasing popular tune for you than any of our masters here, and more proper to the purpose, which would best be answered if every word could, as it is sung, be understood by all that hear it, and if the emphasis you intend for particular words could be given by the singer as well as by the reader; much of the force and impression of the song depending on those circumstances. I will, however, get it as well done for you as I can.

Do not imagine that I mean to depreciate the skill of our composers of music here; they are admirable at pleasing practiced ears and know how to delight one another, but in composing for songs the reigning taste seems to be quite out of nature, or rather the reverse of nature, and yet, like a torrent, hurries them all away with it; one or two, perhaps, only excepted.

You, in the spirit of some ancient legislators, would influence the manners of your country by the united powers of poetry and music. By what I can learn of their songs, the music was simple, conformed itself to the usual pronunciation of words, as to measure, cadence or emphasis, etc., never disguised and confounded the language by making a long syllable short, or a short one long, when sung; their singing was only a more pleasing because a melodious manner of speaking, it was capable of all the graces of prose oratory, while it added the pleasure of harmony. A modern song, on the contrary, neglects all the proprieties and beauties of common speech, and in their place introduces its *defects* and *absurdities* as so many graces. I am afraid you will hardly take my word for this, and therefore I must endeavour to support it by proof. Here is the first song I lay my hand on. It happens to be a composition of one of our greatest masters, the ever famous Handel. It is not one of his juvenile performances, before his taste could be improved and formed; it appeared when his reputation was at the highest, is greatly admired by all his admirers, and is really excellent in its kind. It is called, "The additional favorite Song in Judas Maccabeus." Now I reckon among the defects and improprieties of common speech the following, viz.:

1. *Wrong placing the accent or emphasis* by laying it on words of no importance or on wrong syllables.
2. *Drawling;* or extending the sound of words or syllables beyond their natural length.
3. *Stuttering;* or making many syllables of one.
4. *Unintelligibleness;* the result of the three foregoing united.
5. *Tautology;* and
6. *Screaming* without cause.

Franklin, like an exact and conscientious critic, then quotes musical examples from Handel's song to illustrate each one of these defects. In a postscript he adds that he might have mentioned *inarticulation* among the defects in common speech that are assumed as beauties in modern singing. And he concludes with these two trenchant sentences: "If ever it was the ambition of musicians to make instruments that should imitate the human voice, that ambition seems now reversed, the voice aiming to be like an instrument. Thus wigs were first made to imitate a good natural head of hair; but when they became fashionable, though in unnatural forms, we have seen natural hair dressed to look like wigs."

Though it undoubtedly belongs among the London letters of 1765, this extraordinary document was first published in the *Massachusetts Magazine* for July, 1790, with the title "Criticism on Musick." [6] And excellent musical criticism it is, too, for it reveals wit, exactness, originality, sound judgment, and independence of thought. Franklin is not cowed by the enormous reputation of a composer like Handel; at the same time, he recognizes Handel's greatness and admits his music "is really excellent in its kind."

Franklin was one of the first to recognize the beauty, the power, and the integrity of folk tunes in their pristine state. His contention

[6] *Ibid.*

that these melodies should not be cluttered with new-fangled accompaniments and incongruous harmonizations anticipates the modern aesthetic position derived from the scientific study of folklore, which began fifty years after his death. In his musical ideas, as in everything else, Franklin was the most modern American of his times, the man who, in the words of Ibsen, was "most closely in league with the future."

In a letter to Mary Stevenson written from Philadelphia in 1763, Franklin wrote: "After the first cares of the necessaries of life are over, we shall come to think of the embellishments. Already some of our young geniuses begin to lisp attempts at painting, poetry and music." We shall now meet one of these "young geniuses" who lisped elegantly in all three arts.

"The sacred flame"

In the month of September, 1766, a young lawyer from Philadelphia named Francis Hopkinson, on a visit to relatives in England, attended a performance of Handel's *Messiah* at Gloucester. He had the misfortune of being afflicted by a large and painful boil, which just then was at the height of tension and inflammation. Listening to the music, he no longer felt any pain. The boil even broke while he was at the concert, without his perceiving it. Yet, as he told his friend Thomas Jefferson long afterward, had he been alone in his chamber he "should have cried out with Anguish." And, in a characteristic speculative vein, he added: "May not the Firmness of Martyrs be accounted for on the same principle?"

Whatever Francis Hopkinson may have thought about the Firmness of Martyrs, there can be no question about his belief in the Power of Music, for he repeatedly proved it both by word and deed. Some seven years before his English journey he had written a "Prologue in Praise of Music," in which these lines occur:

> Such pow'r hath music o'er the human soul,
> Music the fiercest passions can controul,
> Touch the nice springs that sway a feeling heart,
> Sooth ev'ry grief, and joy to joy impart.
> Sure virtue's friends and music are the same,
> And blest that person is that owns the sacred flame.

If "the sacred flame" be taken to symbolize devotion to music rather than creative genius, then Francis Hopkinson was abundantly blessed with that gift. At the age of seventeen, when he began to take up the study of the harpsichord, he wrote an "Ode to Music" that fully reveals his enthusiasm for the divine art:

> Hark! Hark! the sweet vibrating lyre
> Sets my attentive soul on fire;
> Thro' all my frame what pleasures thrill,
> Whilst the loud treble warbles shrill,
> And the more slow and solemn bass,
> Adds charms to charm and grace to grace.

And so on for four more stanzas, rising to a grand pæan of praise for "th' admir'd celestial art." To demonstrate Hopkinson's fidelity to the Muse, we need only quote the concluding lines of his poem titled "Description of a Church," in which he describes the effect made upon his sensibilities by the sound of the organ:

> Hail heav'n born music! by thy pow'r we raise
> Th' uplifted soul to arts of highest praise:
> Oh! I would die with music melting round,
> And float to bliss upon a sea of sound.

The final couplet almost matches the emotional mysticism of Fray Luis de León—and this from the pen of an eighteenth-century American lawyer, businessman, and public official!

This was the Age of Reason and of Good Taste, but it was also the Age of Sentiment and of Enthusiasm. A "rational" man like Francis Hopkinson could indulge his sensibilities to the full while keeping a firm hand on practical matters. Although as a poet he wrote about music like an enthusiast (which in eighteenth-century parlance meant a "crackpot"), he could also class it with "reading, walking, riding, drawing &ca." as agreeable pastimes that "season the Hours with calm and rational Pleasure." [7] If Hopkinson let himself go in his feelings toward music, it was precisely because he considered it a "calm and rational pleasure" that even in its most ecstatic moments would not lead him from the path of Virtue and Reason. It thus contrasted with those moral dangers that he mentions in a letter to his mother from London: "You can have no Idea of the many Powerful Tempta-

[7] Letter to Benjamin Franklin from Hartlebury Castle, England, 1767.

tions, that are continually thrown out here to decoy unwary Youth into Extravagance and Immorality."

Being by this time fairly well acquainted with the habits of the gentleman amateur, the reader will not be too surprised at finding a Philadelphia lawyer playing the harpsichord and dabbling in verse, or even trying his hand at painting, which was Hopkinson's third avocation. Born in Philadelphia on September 21, 1737, son of a distinguished father and a pious mother, Francis Hopkinson graduated from the College of Philadelphia, was admitted to the bar, and became prominent in the political, religious, educational, and artistic life of his native city. A staunch patriot, he cast his fortune and the power of his pen with the cause of the American Revolution, was a delegate to the Continental Congress and a signer of the Declaration of Independence. In 1779 he was appointed Judge of the Admiralty from Pennsylvania, and he took an active part in the Constitutional Convention of 1787, influencing its decisions with a humorous political pamphlet titled "The History of a New Roof." During the war he wrote his famous satirical poem, "The Battle of the Kegs," which became immensely popular. It was set to music and widely sung.

John Adams met Hopkinson in the studio of the artist Charles Willson Peale at Philadelphia in 1776 and wrote about the meeting to his wife: "He is one of your pretty, little, curious, ingenious men. His head is not bigger than a large apple. . . . I have not met with anything in natural history more amusing and entertaining than his personal appearance; yet he is genteel and well-bred, and is very social." Adams envied the leisure and tranquillity of mind that enabled Hopkinson to "amuse" himself with "those elegant and ingenious arts of painting, sculpture, statuary, architecture, and music."

Hopkinson as composer

Besides playing the harpsichord and the organ, which many other gentlemen amateurs also did, Francis Hopkinson composed a number of songs, which was a less common accomplishment. That Hopkinson himself was fully aware of the distinction to be derived from this achievement is indicated by the dedication (to George Washington) of his *Seven Songs for the Harpsichord* (1788), in which he says: "However small the Reputation may be that I shall derive from this Work I cannot, I believe, be refused the Credit of being the first

Native of the United States who has produced a Musical Composition." Let us see on what grounds he rested his claim to be regarded as America's first native-born composer.

It is not known for certain whether Hopkinson was self-taught in composition or whether he took lessons from one of the professional musicians who were active in Philadelphia. There is a strong probability that he studied with the English organist James Bremner, with whom he long maintained ties of friendship and upon whose death he wrote a touchingly sincere elegy. During his college days, young Hopkinson had already distinguished himself as a poet, as a performer, and, it would seem, as a composer. In the winter of 1756–1757 the students at the College of Philadelphia produced an adaptation of *The Masque of Alfred the Great* which, according to a newspaper report, included "an excellent Piece of new Music by one of the performers." The piece of music in question was a song, "Alfred, Father of the State," and in all likelihood Francis Hopkinson was its composer.

In 1759 Hopkinson began to copy out in a large book, in his neat and methodical manner, a collection of songs, operatic airs, cantatas, anthems, hymns, and duets, by various celebrated European composers, including Handel, Pergolesi, Purcell, and Arne. The completed collection contained over a hundred pieces in a volume of more than two hundred pages, and scattered among them were six songs signed with the initials "F. H." The first of these is "My Days Have Been So Wondrous Free" (a setting of Thomas Parnell's "Love and Innocence"), which has attained a somewhat unwarranted notoriety as the first known secular song composed by an American. The others are "The Garland," "Oh! Come to Mason Borough's Grove," "With Pleasures Have I Past [*sic*] My Days," "The Twenty-Third Psalm," and "An Anthem from the 114th Psalm." All of them are written in two parts—the ubiquitous eighteenth-century "treble and bass." The common procedure was for the accompanist to fill in the harmony at the harpsichord. It is curious to notice that the anthem includes a figured bass, a rarity in early American music.

The inclusion of the psalm and anthem in this collection points to Hopkinson's lifelong interest in church music. There is strong evidence to indicate that he was the compiler of *A Collection of Psalm Tunes, with a few Anthems and Hymns* . . . published at Philadelphia in 1763 for the United Churches of Christ Church and St.

Peter's Church. Hopkinson served as organist at Christ Church during the absence of James Bremner, and he also instructed the children of the two churches in "the art of psalmody." In 1786 he wrote *A Letter to the Rev. Dr. White on the Conduct of a Church Organ*, which contains some interesting observations on "the application of instrumental music to purposes of piety." Arguing for the dignity of church music, he writes: "It is as offensive to hear lilts and jigs from a church organ, as it would be to see a venerable matron frisking through the public street with all the fantastic airs of a *Columbine*."

During the 1780s, pro-French sentiment was at its height in Philadelphia. Hence we are not surprised to find the following notice in the *Freeman's Journal* for December 19, 1781:

> On Tuesday evening of the 11th inst. his Excellency the Minister of France, who embraces every opportunity to manifest his respect to the worthies of America, and politeness to its inhabitants, entertained his Excellency General Washington, and his lady, the lady of General Greene, and a very polite circle of gentlemen and ladies, with an elegant Concert, in which the following ORATORIO, composed and set to music by a gentleman whose taste in the polite arts is well known, was introduced and afforded the most sensible pleasure. The Temple of Minerva: An ORATORICAL ENTERTAINMENT.

The gentleman whose taste in the polite arts was so well known was, of course, our friend Francis Hopkinson.

A few weeks after this performance, the *Royal Gazette* of New York published the libretto of *The Temple of Minerva*, together with a grossly indecent parody by a Philadelphia correspondent, titled *The Temple of Cloacina*. Hopkinson's reply, published in the *Pennsylvania Gazette*, described the circumstances under which he first saw the parody, in thoroughly Rabelaisian terms. Such was the obverse of eighteenth-century elegance and taste!

On October 25, 1788, Hopkinson wrote to his friend Thomas Jefferson:

> I have amused myself with composing Six easy & simple Songs for the Harpsichord–Words & Music all my own. The Music is now engraving. When finished, I will do myself the Pleasure of sending a Copy to Miss Jefferson. The best of them is that they are so easy that any Person who can play at all may perform them with-

out much Trouble, & I have endeavour'd to make the Melodies pleasing to the untutored Ear.[8]

The work was published before the end of the year and was advertised as follows in the *Pennsylvania Packet:* "These songs are composed in an easy, familiar style, intended for young Practioners on the Harpsichord or Forte-Piano, and is the first work of this kind attempted in the United States."

The letter to Jefferson mentions six songs, the title of the book is *Seven Songs,* and the collection actually contains eight, with the last song bearing a note to the effect that it was added after the title page was engraved. Here is the complete contents, which consists of first lines:

Come, fair Rosina, come away
My Love is gone to the sea
Beneath a weeping willow's shade
Enraptur'd I gaze when my Delia is by
See down Maria's blushing cheek
O'er the hills far away, at the birth of the morn
My gen'rous heart disdains
The traveller benighted and lost

Hopkinson dedicated the volume to George Washington in a letter from which we quoted the passage in which he claims credit for being the first native American composer. He expresses the hope that "others may be encouraged to venture on a path, yet untrodden in America, and the Arts in succession will take root and flourish amongst us." Washington, who was fond of music though he played no instrument, replied in an amiable and humorous letter in which he laments his inability to do anything in support of the music, for "I can neither sing one of the songs, nor raise a single note on any instrument to convince the unbelieving." [9]

There is no point in attempting a detailed analysis and critique of Hopkinson's music. His songs are typical of hundreds written during the eighteenth century and show no creative individuality whatever. However quaint and innocuous they seem to us now, we must not

[8] Quoted in Hastings, *Life and Works of Francis Hopkinson,* pp. 436–437.

[9] The complete dedication and Washington's reply are printed in Hastings, *op. cit.,* pp. 441–444.

assume that they were without emotional effect either for Hopkinson or his listeners. Writing to Jefferson about the collection, Hopkinson said: "The last Song, if play'd very slow, and sung with Expression, is forcibly Pathetic—at least in my Fancy. Both Words & Music were the Work of an hour in the Height of a Storm. But the Imagination of an Author who composes from his Heart, rather than his Head, is always more heated than he can expect his Readers to be."

That at least one listener found this song "forcibly Pathetic" is indicated by Jefferson's reply: "Accept my thanks . . . and my daughter's for the book of songs. I will not tell you how much they have pleased us, nor how well the last of them merits praise for its pathos, but relate a fact only, which is that while my elder daughter was playing it on the harpsichord, I happened to look toward the fire, & saw the younger one all in tears. I asked her if she was sick? She said 'no; but the tune was so mournful.'" So that the reader may compare his or her own reactions with those of Jefferson and his daughter, we quote a portion of this song, *The Traveller Benighted and Lost.*

I - ci - cle hangs on the Spray He
wan - ders in hope some kind shel - ter to find, whilst
thro' the Sharp Haw - thorne still blows the cold wind; He
wan - ders in hope some kind shel - ter to find, whilst
thro' the Sharp Haw - thorne still blows the cold wind.
3

Hopkinson composed only one more song before his death in 1791. Titled "A New Song," it was a gay love lyric in which the poet asks, "What's life without the Joys of Love?"

Francis Hopkinson was correct in assuming that his historical priority would secure him a permanent place in the annals of America's music. It is not so much for his music that we value him, as for his attitude toward music. He represented the Golden Age of American culture, in which men of affairs, successful in business and in the conduct of government, thought it no shame not only to love music and practice it in private, but also to make public their love of the "Divine Art." Men like Jefferson, Franklin, and Hopkinson, in helping to create a nation that recognized man's inalienable right to the pursuit of happiness, did not overlook the aid and comfort that music can give in this unceasing quest.

Each of these three great American music lovers might be taken as a representative figure. Jefferson is the prototype of the patron of music, who, if he had been wealthy enough, would have endowed orchestras and formed rare collections of manuscripts and printed scores. Such patrons, backed by the wealth of the country's industrial development, were eventually to play an important role in the growth of our musical institutions. Franklin was the practical man with a strong inclination toward philosophical speculation: our first music critic, and one of the rare individuals of the eighteenth century who appreciated the strength and character of the musical vernacular. Hopkinson was the ancestor of a long line of amateur composers in the United States, from William Henry Fry in the nineteenth century to John Alden Carpenter in the twentieth. After all, most of our early American composers were amateurs, though few enjoyed such social and political prominence as Hopkinson. Our first professional musicians were those who came from Europe, and it is to these professional emigrants that we turn in the next chapter.

chapter six

Professional emigrants

The promptness of this young country in those sciences which were once thought peculiar only to a riper age, has already brought upon her the eyes of the world.

WILLIAM SELBY, ADVERTISEMENT FOR THE NEW MINSTREL (1782).

On the last Sunday of August in the year 1757, a tall, thin man, about sixty years of age, mounted on a small, white horse, rode rapidly along a road in Westmoreland County, Virginia. A glance inside his saddlebags would have revealed an assortment of musical instruments, including a violin, a German flute, an oboe, and a bassoon. A glimpse into his mind would have revealed that his chief concerns were, first, to place as much distance as possible between himself and Stratford, the home of Philipp Ludwell Lee, Esquire; and secondly, to reach a town whose inhabitants would appreciate the talents of a versatile fellow like himself, skilled in the polite arts of music, fencing, and dancing.

Meanwhile, the master of Stratford was fuming in anger over the loss of his prized bassoon. To relieve his feelings, he sat down and wrote an advertisement to appear in the leading colonial newspapers: "Runaway from the subscriber, at Stratford, in Westmoreland County . . . Charles Love . . . he professes Musick, Dancing, Fencing, and plays exceedingly well on the Violin and all Wind Instruments; he stole when he went away, a very good Bassoon, made by Schuchart, which he carried with him. . . . It is supposed he will make towards Charlestown in South Carolina." This, together with a description of the said Love, and the offer of a generous reward for his apprehension, drew public attention to Mr. Lee's loss.

The interesting point about all this is not that Charles Love stole a bassoon, but that, among the tidewater estates of colonial Virginia, there was a bassoon for him to steal, and a very good one, "made by Schuchart."

Apart from his larcenous propensities, which we may regard as a personal idiosyncrasy, Charles Love was in many ways typical of the professional musician who emigrated to the American colonies: a symbol of those hundreds of humble musicians, more adventurous than their stay-at-home colleagues, who took their luck, for better or worse, in the New World. Versatile and resourceful they had to be in order to survive in a pioneer society in which the "polite arts" had yet to win a secure place. Few of them could earn a living solely by music, even with dancing and fencing as more remunerative sidelines. Some of them were obliged to become Jacks-of-all-trades. Herman Zedwitz, "violin teacher just from Europe," ran a chimney-sweeping business in New York. Giovanni Gualdo of Philadelphia was wine merchant as well as music teacher, concert manager, composer, and performer. William Selby, the organist and composer, sold groceries and liquor in Boston during the Revolution. Many of them found it difficult to keep one step ahead of their creditors. The English flutist and composer William Young, who settled in Philadelphia, was made so desperate by mounting debts that in a fit of rage he killed the constable sent by his creditors to arrest him.

In spite of all hazards and uncertainties, musical emigrants kept coming to America in steadily growing numbers. Before the Revolution, Charleston, South Carolina, was the chief point of attraction for professional musicians. This was because Charleston, in the words of Edmund Burke, "approached more nearly to the social refinement of a great European capital" than any other American city. And music was, of course, an indispensable ingredient of this "social refinement."

French horns and macaronis

The oldest musical society in the United States, the St. Cecilia Society, was founded at Charleston in 1762. It combined private subscription concerts with the most elegant and exclusive social amenities. The activities of the Society are mentioned in the journal of Josiah Quincy of Boston, who visited the Southern metropolis in 1772. Describing a dinner with the Sons of St. Patrick, Quincy writes:

"While at dinner six violins, two hautboys, etc. After dinner, six French horns in concert:—most surpassing music. Two solos on the French horn, by one who is said to blow the finest horn in the world. He has fifty guineas for the season from the St. Cecilia Society." Not bad!

To Josiah Quincy's journal we turn again for a priceless vignette of eighteenth-century music and manners. He recounts his impressions of a concert in Charleston:

> The music was good—the two base viols and French horns were grand. One Abercrombie, a Frenchman just arrived, played the first violin, and a solo incomparably better than any one I ever heard. He cannot speak a word of English, and has a salary of five hundred guineas a year from the St. Cecilia Society. There were upwards of two hundred and fifty ladies present, and it was called no great number. In loftiness of headdress, these ladies stoop to the daughters of the north,—in richness of dress, surpass them,—in health and floridity of countenance, vail to them. In taciturnity during the performance, greatly before our ladies; in noise and flirtation after the music is over, pretty much on a par. The gentlemen, many of them dressed with richness and elegance, uncommon with us: many with swords on. We had two macaronis present, just arrived from London.

As a revelation of the colonial mind, the key to this passage is in the final sentence, and especially the last phrase. Why should a serious and sensible man like Josiah Quincy bother to mention a couple of mincing fops—the two "macaronis"—in his description of a concert? Simply because they had "just arrived from London" and therefore set the ultimate note of fashionable bon ton upon the event he was describing. They brought the latest gossip from the Pall Mall coffee houses, reports of the latest hit at the Drury Lane Theatre, news of the latest Court scandal—just as Monsieur Abercrombie (queer name for a Frenchman!) brought the latest musical fashions from Paris. It was all part of the general pattern of eighteenth-century American urban culture (which the Revolution did not destroy): the imitation of European standards of taste. Though it could be carried to foolish extremes, the tendency at bottom sprang from a desire to get the "best" of everything, from fiddlers to fops. No cultivated American was naïve enough to believe that his youthful country could produce overnight musicians to equal the best of Europe. Yet their partiality to the sons of Bach, to Haydn, Stamitz, and other European celebrities, did not blind them to the merits of local talent. In the liberal-minded eighteenth-century attitude there was room for all: famous masters and local lights, professionals and amateurs, immigrants and native-born. The important thing was to have music, a lot of it, and the best that could be had. The fact that they preferred music by living composers is an amiable eccentricity, difficult for the twentieth-century music lover to understand, since for us the only "great" composers are the dead ones.

To get back to colonial Charleston, concerts had been given there long before the founding of the St. Cecilia Society. In 1737 a concert was announced "for the Benefit of Mr. Theodore Pachelbel," with the following significant notice: "N.B. As this is the first time the said Mr. Pachelbel has attempted anything of this kind in a publick manner in this Province, he thinks it proper to give Notice that there will be sung a Cantata suitable to the occasion." No further details are given regarding this cantata, but it is quite possible that it may have been composed by Pachelbel himself. There exists an admirable Magnificat of his, for eight voices with organ accompaniment, which reveals him as a well-schooled composer of superior ability.[1] This is not surprising in view of his background.

Charles Theodore Pachelbel was the son of the famous Nuremberg organist and composer Johann Pachelbel, one of the notable masters of the South German organ school and a precursor of J. S. Bach. Born in 1690, he migrated to America at the age of forty-three and became organist at Trinity Church in Newport, Rhode Island. In January, 1736, Pachelbel gave the first concert in New York of which a definite record exists. The following year he was in Charleston, where he died in 1750. His career indicates that even in the early decades of the eighteenth century America was attracting distinguished musicians from the Old World.

After the Revolution, musicians began to drift away from Charleston, to New York, Boston, and Philadelphia. The trend of musical progress swung northward. Philadelphia, in particular, became the leading cultural center of the young Republic and the chief center of musical activity.

[1] Published in the New York Public Library Music Series, ed. by H. T. David.

The general attends a benefit

A French observer, Moreau de Saint-Mery, declared that there were more beautiful women in Philadelphia than anywhere else in the world. This feminine pulchritude was matched by an impressive array of professional talent: the city was full of teachers, lawyers, physicians, scientists, philosophers, authors, and artists. In spite of the Quakers, the city was gay. A few cranks tried to clamp down on theatrical amusements but were eventually overridden by the more liberal majority. The pleasure-loving ranks received strong support from the example of General Washington, who never missed an opportunity to attend a play or a concert.

In June, 1787, the General was in Philadelphia as a delegate to the Constitutional Convention. His diary reveals that on June 12 he attended a concert for the benefit of a certain Mr. Alexander Reinagle, a musician from England who had recently established himself in Philadelphia. The program began with an Overture by Johann Christian (the "London") Bach, and ended with two compositions by Reinagle: a Sonata for the Pianoforte, and a new Overture (in which is introduced a Scotch strathspey). Whatever Washington thought of the music—and he probably enjoyed it, for his taste was good—he must have been impressed by Reinagle's skill and commanding presence at the pianoforte.

Alexander Reinagle was then about thirty years old, a handsome and vigorous man with firm features and the air of being a gentleman as well as a musician (a difficult combination to achieve in those days). Regarding his distinctive style of playing the pianoforte, a contemporary wrote: "He never aimed at excessive execution, but there was a sweetness of manner—nay, in the way he touched the instrument I might add, there was a sweetness of tone which, combined with exquisite taste and neatness, produced unusual feelings of delight." [2] The fact is that on this occasion George Washington, whether he knew it or not, was hearing the finest piano playing and the finest piano music produced in America up to that time. That Washington had high regard for Reinagle is indicated by his having engaged the latter to give music lessons to his adopted daughter, Nellie Custis. These two men, the soldier and the musician, had much in common, for each was

[2] John R. Parker, in *The Euterpeiad.*

a leader in his own field, a man of character and integrity who commanded respect from all. Reinagle before his orchestra was a counterpart of Washington before his army. And sometimes an eighteenth-century theater could be almost as dangerous as a battle field.

When General Washington, as President of the United States, attended the theater in Philadelphia (which was the nation's capital from 1790 to 1800), some measure of decorum was preserved by a special military guard, with a soldier posted at each door and four in the gallery—where trouble was most likely to break out. That part of the house was always crowded, and the rowdy element found safety in numbers. The "gods" of the galleries, as they were called, would hurl bottles and glasses, as well as apples, nuts, and vegetables, onto the stage and into the orchestra. No one obeyed the no-smoking signs, hence sensitive nostrils were continually assailed by the stench of cigars. In spite of regulations to the contrary, liquor was brought into the house and freely imbibed during the performance. The gay ladies of the town used the best boxes in the theater as their professional headquarters, until, in 1795, the managers decreed that "no persons of notorious ill fame will be suffered to occupy any seat in a box where places are already taken." When political feeling ran high, riots sometimes broke out in the theater.

As musical director of the New Theatre in Chestnut Street, Alexander Reinagle reigned over this unruly mob like a monarch over his court. This is the picture we get of him from a contemporary historian of the theater:

> Who that only once saw old manager Reinagle in his official capacity, could ever forget his dignified *personne*. He presided at the pianoforte, looking the very personification of the patriarch of music—investing the science of harmonic sounds, as well as the dramatic school, with a moral influence reflecting and adorning its salutary uses with high respectability and polished manners. His appearance was of the reverend and impressive kind, which at once inspired the universal respect of the audience. Such was Reinagle's imposing appearance that it awed the disorderly of the galleries, or the fop of annoying propensities and impertinent criticism of the box lobby, into decorum. . . . It was truly inspiring to behold the polished Reinagle saluting from his seat (before the grand square pianoforte in the orchestra) the highest respectability of the city, as it entered into the boxes to take seats. It was a scene before the

curtain that suggested a picture of the master of private ceremonies receiving his invited guests at the fashionable drawing-room. Mr. Reinagle was a gentleman and a musician.[3]

The admirable Mr. Reinagle

If Reinagle was not a "gentleman" in the strict meaning of the term as understood in the eighteenth century, he undoubtedly had qualities and accomplishments that led his contemporaries to bestow this title upon him *honoris causa.* The only false note we can detect in the description quoted above is that Reinagle was not actually "old" at the time. He was in his forties, and the fact is that he died at the age of fifty-three. He spent slightly less than half of his life in America, and he was unquestionably the most gifted and the most distinguished of the professional musicians who emigrated to this country before 1800.

Alexander Reinagle was born in the busy English seaport and naval base of Portsmouth, in April, 1756—just a few months after the birth of Mozart. His father was an Austrian musician, a fine trumpet player, who had settled in England. When Alexander was in his late teens, the family moved to Edinburgh, where the youngster seems to have received some lessons from the organist and composer Raynor Taylor, who later followed him to America. Young Reinagle became an excellent pianist as well as a violinist of considerable skill. He plunged into the brilliant and cosmopolitan musical life of London and came under the spell of the man who dominated the English musical scene between the death of Handel and the coming of Haydn—the clever and fashionable Johann Christian Bach, "Music Master in the Queen's Household" and chief arbiter of musical taste. The "London" Bach specialized in composing keyboard pieces "such as ladies can execute with little trouble," and in graceful sonatas for piano or harpsichord with violin accompaniment. Reinagle commenced his career as a composer along both of these lines, publishing first two collections of "short and easy pieces" for the pianoforte, followed by Six Sonatas for the Pianoforte or Harpsichord, with an accompaniment for Violin.

In the autumn of 1784 Reinagle went to Lisbon together with his younger brother Hugh, a cellist. They gave a concert there and also played for the Royal Family. Hugh was ill of consumption and died

[3] Durang, *History of the Stage in Philadelphia.*

during their sojourn in Lisbon. It was probably about this time that Reinagle paid a visit to Carl Philipp Emanuel Bach in Hamburg, who wrote him a cordial letter dated February 25, 1785, in which such a visit is mentioned. The "great" Bach expressed a desire to have a portrait of Reinagle to place in his cabinet or gallery of celebrities. The younger man no doubt fully appreciated the honor of such a request, coming from a master who was recognized as the greatest organist of the age. Bach's art and personality made a deep and lasting impression on Reinagle. Like all his contemporaries, Reinagle knew nothing of the art of Johann Sebastian Bach, for the old Cantor of Leipzig had enjoyed only a local reputation and his "difficult" style of composition was entirely out of fashion. The sons of Johann Sebastian were the men of the day.

In the spring of 1785 Alexander Reinagle found himself back in Portsmouth, saddened by the death of his brother. He was nearing thirty and must have felt that he stood at a turning point in his life. He was a member of the Society of Musicians of London and enjoyed good professional standing. Yet he did not take up again the old round of music-making in London. Instead he turned his thoughts to the New World. Was it the sight of the ships in Portsmouth harbor that directed his thoughts to America? Whatever the impulse that drove him, within a year he found himself sailing across the ocean, bound for the port of New York, facing an uncertain future in an unknown land.

Shortly after his arrival in the summer of 1786, Reinagle gave a concert in New York. He also announced that he was prepared to give lessons on the pianoforte, harpsichord, and violin. The response was far from encouraging, for New York, thriving commercially, had yet to develop a demand for musical culture. Hearing about the more favorable prospects offered by Philadelphia, Reinagle soon betook himself there. In Philadelphia he found three of his ex-European colleagues—Henry Capron, William Brown, and John Bentley—engaged in a professional quarrel, as a result of which the "City Concerts" had been discontinued. Reinagle immediately took the situation in hand. Effecting a reconciliation between Capron and Brown (Bentley conveniently left for New York), he revived the City Concerts with himself as principal manager and featured performer. His superior ability was at once apparent, and he forthwith assumed a decisive role in the musical affairs of the Quaker City.

Reinagle as composer

When the actor Thomas Wignell, in 1792, formed a new theatrical company in Philadelphia, Reinagle was appointed musical manager of the enterprise. His first task, however, was to supervise the building of the New Theatre in Chestnut Street, a large and handsome structure that came to be regarded as one of the seven wonders of America, while Wignell went abroad to recruit a company of actors and singers. In those days it was customary for theatrical companies to include musical works—chiefly "ballad operas" like *The Beggar's Opera*—as well as spoken drama in their repertoire. After a long delay caused by the terrible epidemic of yellow fever that ravaged Philadelphia, the New Theatre was formally opened on February 17, 1794, with a performance of Samuel Arnold's opera *The Castle of Andalusia.*

Wignell and Reinagle aimed to give equal importance to music and drama in their repertoire. Hence Reinagle was kept busy arranging and adapting musical works for the theater, and composing the music for several so-called "operas" and pantomimes. We qualify the term "opera" because most of these works were simply plays with incidental music and vocal numbers interspersed at suitable intervals. Among the plays for which Reinagle composed music were *Columbus, or The Discovery of America; Pizarro, or The Spaniards in Peru* (in collaboration with Raynor Taylor); *Slaves in Algiers, or A Struggle for Freedom* (described as "a play, interspersed with songs"); the *Savoyard, or The Repentant Seducer* ("musical farce"); and *The Volunteers*, "comic opera in two acts." This list gives a good idea of the sort of musical fare served up by American theaters in the eighteenth century, ranging from an historical tragedy in five acts (*Pizarro*) to a frothy two-act farce.

Very little of Reinagle's music for the theater has been preserved. The music for *Columbus*, arranged for piano, was copyrighted at Philadelphia in 1799, but no copy has been located. There are, however, two known copies of an *Indian March* "of the much admired play called *Columbus*," which may very likely be one of the numbers composed by Reinagle. The Library of Congress has a score of *The Volunteers*, the text of which was written by Mrs. Susanna Rowson, author of one of the earliest American novels, *Charlotte Temple* (1791). The following song from *The Volunteers* is typical:

When I've got the rea - dy rhi - no wounds I'll dress_ so_
mor - tal fine O I'll keep_ a _ horse_ to_ run_ at_ rac - es
peep through a glass at_ La-dies fa - ces peep through a glass at_
La-dies fa-ces I'll spend_ the_ night in_
ad lib.
gam-ing drink-ing nor e'er_ go_ home till mel-low then
sleep all day to ban - ish think-ing & be_ a_ dash-ing_

Reinagle earned a living and exerted wide influence through his theatrical activities, but as a composer he makes his strongest appeal to us in a more intimate type of music, namely, his sonatas for piano. Some time after his arrival in Philadelphia, Reinagle composed four sonatas for piano, which were never published. The manuscript was found in the music collection of the composer's daughter Georgianna, and is now in the Library of Congress. We have already seen that Reinagle's early sonatas and piano pieces, published in London, were written under the influence of Johann Christian Bach. Those early works reveal no marked individuality, for Reinagle had not yet fully found himself as a composer. Evidently his meeting with another and greater Bach—Carl Philipp Emanuel of Hamburg—shortly before his departure for America, was the beginning of a new phase in Reinagle's creative development, which found its complete fruition in the four Philadelphia sonatas. While the double influence of C. P. E. Bach and Haydn—where could he have found better models?—is apparent in these works, they are by no means mere imitations. They reveal a fresh and lively invention, resourcefulness in development and figuration, a fine feeling for structure and proportion, and a capacity for sustained lyrical expression in the Adagios.

All but the first of these sonatas are in three movements (fast-slow-fast), following the pattern established by Emanuel Bach. In the first sonata the slow movement is missing. Bound together with it in the manuscript, however, are two pieces, both in the form of theme with variations. The second of these, an Andante in A major, is particularly attractive and might well serve as a middle movement for this sonata.

During his last years, which he spent in Baltimore, Reinagle worked enthusiastically on composing a kind of secular oratorio based on selections from Milton's *Paradise Lost.* The original feature of the work was that spoken narrative replaced the usual recitatives. We can only guess at its musical contents, for the manuscript—left incomplete at his death—mysteriously disappeared from the library of the composer's grandson, and has not been recovered.

Reinagle was twice married. By his first wife he had two sons, Hugh and Thomas. His second wife, to whom he was married in 1803, was Anna Duport, daughter of the celebrated dancing master Pierre Landrin Duport of Philadelphia and Baltimore. The offspring of this marriage was a daughter, Georgianna, born several months after her father's death in 1809. Alexander Reinagle was deeply mourned, for, in the words of a contemporary eulogist, he possessed "a heart formed for tenderness and the charities of the world."

A rare character

Frequently associated with Reinagle as a composer for the New Theatre was his older friend, colleague, and former teacher, Raynor Taylor, who outlived him by many years. Trained in the King's singing school as one of the boys of the Chapel Royal, Taylor was for a time musical director of the Saddler's Wells Theatre in London. He came to America in 1792 and appeared in Baltimore as "music professor, organist and teacher of music in general." He also appeared in the less dignified role of theatrical entertainer, specializing in a type of musical skit called "olio," very similar to a modern vaudeville sketch. Moving to Philadelphia soon afterward, he became organist at St. Peter's Church, without renouncing his theatrical high jinks—which is further proof of the eighteenth century's tolerant attitude toward such matters.

Raynor Taylor seems to have been a rare blend of erudition and clownishness. He had the reputation of being the finest organist in America, famous for his masterly improvisations. Reinagle declared that he considered Taylor's extemporizing on the organ "to be equal to the skill and powers of Bach himself"—by whom, of course, he meant C. P. E. Bach of Hamburg. John R. Parker, who often heard him play, wrote of his "never failing strain of harmony and science. . . . His ideas flowed with wonderful freedom in all the varieties of plain chant, imitation and fugue." The same writer mentions the composer's "shelves groaning under manuscript files of overtures, operas, anthems, glees, &c." In spite of his extraordinary skill and industry, Raynor Taylor achieved no other material recompense than "the drudgery of teaching and a scanty organ salary."

But lack of the world's goods did not dampen Taylor's sense of humor. His hilarious parodies of Italian opera were highly appreciated by a select circle. Let Parker, an eyewitness, be once again our chronicler: "Sometimes among particular friends he would in perfect playfulness sit down to the pianoforte and extemporise an Italian opera. . . . The overtures, recitatives, songs and dialogue, by singing alternately in the natural and falsetto voice, were all the thought of the moment, as well as the words, which were nothing but a sort of gibberish with Italian terminations. Thus would he often in sportive mood throw away ideas sufficient to establish a musical fame." [4] Raynor Taylor was potentially the Alec Templeton of his day—all he lacked was a radio audience.

Many of Taylor's compositions have been preserved, but they are mostly comic skits, light songs, and incidental pieces that give little idea of his real stature as a composer. Yet, bearing in mind the importance that the "olio" was to acquire in the minstrel show of the mid-nineteenth century, we may look upon Raynor Taylor, the erudite church organist, as a significant precursor of the popular American lyric theater. He has also another claim to fame, for before his death in 1825 he was active in founding the Musical Fund Society of Philadelphia, one of the most important musical organizations in America.

The versatile Mr. Carr

Associated with Raynor Taylor in founding the Musical Fund Society was Benjamin Carr, one of the most versatile, most energetic, and most successful of the post-Revolutionary musical emigrants. Arriving at New York in 1793, he was soon followed by his brother Thomas, and his father, Joseph Carr. The three of them became very successful as music publishers and dealers, with stores in Philadelphia, Baltimore, and New York. Benjamin Carr made his American debut as a singer and quickly won popular favor in ballad operas. But his most important contributions to America's musical life were made as composer, arranger, organist, pianist, and, above all, as publisher and editor. He edited the *Musical Journal* founded by his father and published *Carr's Musical Miscellany in Occasional Numbers.*

The Carrs imported the best vocal and instrumental music from Europe, but did not neglect local talent. The first issue of *The Gentle-*

[4] Parker, *Musical Biography.*

man's Amusement, a periodical musical collection published by Carr in Philadelphia, contained *The President's March* by Philip Phile. This is of special interest to us because later this march was used for the tune of "Hail Columbia," the famous patriotic song written by Joseph Hopkinson, son of our friend Francis Hopkinson. Hopkinson wrote the words of this song at the request of the actor Gilbert Fox, who sang it for the first time with immense success at the New Theatre on the night of April 25, 1798. Two days later, Carr brought out the old tune in a new edition, advertising it as "the very favorite New Federal Song." And as "Hail Columbia" it soon became established as one of our first national songs.

Also published in *The Gentleman's Amusement* was Carr's *Federal Overture*, arranged as a "duetto for two German flutes," consisting of a medley of patriotic airs, including the highly popular "Yankee Doodle"—this being the first time that this famous tune was printed in America, though it had been widely known since pre-Revolutionary days.

In launching his weekly *Musical Journal* (1800), Carr announced that for his selections of vocal and instrumental music he would draw on "a regular supply of new music from Europe and the assistance of Men of Genius in the Country" (that is, in the United States). This sums up Carr's sound and constructive policy of striking a fair balance between foreign importations and native products. And he recognizes that there are already "Men of Genius" in the country. Of course, the eighteenth century did not attach exactly the same meaning to "genius" that we do: it meant talent and skill rather than supreme inspiration.

That Benjamin Carr was a musician of exceptional talent, if not precisely a "genius," is proved by his extant compositions, including some of the music of his opera, *The Archers; or, the Mountaineers of Switzerland*, produced at New York in 1796. The libretto deals with the story of William Tell. The only two musical numbers from this opera that have been preserved are a graceful Rondo from the overture and the song, "Why, Huntress, Why?" which Carr published in his *Musical Journal*.

Benjamin Carr was born in London in 1768 and died in Philadelphia in 1831. Widely esteemed for his personal and professional qualities, his influence on every phase of musical life in America was strong and far-reaching.

New York and Boston

The presence of such distinguished musicians as Reinagle, Taylor, and Carr, gave to Philadelphia a musical supremacy lasting for several decades. Yet musical talent was not lacking in other cities, particularly Boston and New York. The leading professional musician in New York during the post-Revolutionary period was James Hewitt (1770–1827), violinist, composer, manager, and publisher. He was one of a group of musicians who arrived in New York in 1792, announcing themselves as "professors of music from the Operahouse, Hanoversquare, and Professional Concerts under the direction of Haydn, Pleyel, etc., London." Among them was the ill-fated flutist William Young, and the Belgian violinist Jean Gehot. The first New York concert given by the group included Gehot's Overture in twelve movements, expressive of a voyage from England to America, and Hewitt's Overture in nine movements, expressive of a battle. Presumably Gehot's overture had the advantage of being based on personal experience. This sort of descriptive music was very popular at that time. In New England the blind English organist and pianist John L. Berkenhead used to bring the house down with his powerful and realistic rendition of a piece called *The Demolition of the Bastille*. The classical example of this type of thing was Kotzwara's *Battle of Prague*, introduced to America by Benjamin Carr, which continually cropped up on programs, to say nothing of being thundered out on countless parlor pianos by several generations of amateur keyboard thumpers.

James Hewitt made another contribution to the repertory of battle pieces—this time also making an appeal to American patriotism—with his sonata for piano titled *The Battle of Trenton*, published in 1797 and dedicated to General Washington, whose portrait embellishes the cover. In this quaint period piece, Hewitt undertook to depict musically such episodes as The Army in motion—Attack—cannons—bombs—Flight of the Hessians—General Confusion—Articles of Capitulation signed—Trumpets of Victory—General Rejoicing. Nor did he omit to introduce the ever-popular "Yankee Doodle." Hewitt was obviously catering to a current fad, but he was a thoroughly trained and capable musician, hence this sonata sounds much better than its absurdly literal "program" would lead us to suppose.

Hewitt's position in New York was very similar to that of Reinagle in Philadelphia. He was the leading composer and arranger of operas for the Old American Company, his social standing was high, and his sentimental songs enjoyed wide favor. His three Sonatas for the Pianoforte are attractive period pieces. His opera *Tammany* combined American Indian lore with political implications, for it was produced under the auspices of the Tammany Society of New York, then a center of anti-Federalist feeling. The Federalist faction denounced the opera as "a wretched thing," but this may have been simply due to political prejudice. Since the music has been lost, we have no means of forming our own opinion. Hewitt's song "The Wampum Belt" apparently had no connection with Tammany, though an ousted political boss might well bewail that "The wampum belt can charm no more."

James Hewitt married twice and had six children, several of whom became prominent musicians. His descendants, in fact, are still active in the musical profession.

Next to Hewitt, the principal New York composers were Victor Pelissier, and John Christopher Moller. Pelissier was the most prominent of the French musical emigrants. He composed several operas for the Old American Company, including *Edwin and Angelina* (1796), based on Goldsmith's novel, which had the doubtful distinction of receiving only one performance. Moller, who appeared frequently as a performer on Franklin's harmonica, composed a pleasing *Sinfonia,* a String Quartet, and a Rondo for piano.

Among the foreign musicians who settled in Charleston before the Revolution was Peter Albrecht van Hagen, lately "organist and director of the City's Concert in Rotterdam." In 1789, van Hagen moved with his family to New York—his wife, daughter, and son were all musicians—and later settled in Boston, where he opened a music store, conducted the orchestra at the Haymarket Theatre, and served as organist at the Stone Chapel. He belonged to a distinguished German musical family that had long been active in Holland, and his case is one more proof of the high professional caliber of the early musical emigrants. Van Hagen's compositions include a *Federal Overture* and a *Funeral Dirge on the Death of General Washington*—one of many such musical tributes to the Father of our Country. His son, Peter Albrecht Junior, followed in the paternal footsteps by composing "a new patriotic song" titled "Adams & Jefferson," which rode the current wave of anti-French feeling:

Columbia's brave friends with alertness advance
Her rights to support in defiance of France. . .
To volatile fribbles we never will yield,
While John's at the helm, and George rules the field.

The professional emigrants never lagged behind in musical flag waving.

The pioneer among Boston's professional musicians was the English-born but American-spirited organist, harpischordist, and composer, William Selby (1738–1798), who came to America around 1771. During the lean years of the Revolution he kept a grocery store in Boston, but even before the end of the war, in 1782, he issued proposals for the publication of a musical collection in monthly installments, to be titled *The New Minstrel.* His advertisement indicates that he was more of an enthusiast than a business promoter. Here is a sample of his eloquence:

> At this age of civilization, at this area [*sic*] of the acquaintance with a nation far gone in politeness and fine arts—even the stern patriot and lover of his country's glory, might be addressed on the present subject with not less propriety than the man of elegance and taste.
>
> The promptness of this young country in those sciences which were once thought peculiar only to a riper age, has already brought upon her the eyes of the world.
>
> And shall those arts which make her happy, be less courted than those arts which have made her great? Why may she not be "In song unequall'd as unmatch'd in war"? [5]

Why not, indeed, when such brave fellows as William Selby, and his fellow musicians throughout the land, labored so valiantly and perseveringly, in the face of so many obstacles and discouragements, to the end that their adopted country might truly become "In song unequall'd as unmatch'd in war."

[5] This advertisement appeared in the *Boston Evening Post,* Feb. 2, 1782. Quoted by Sonneck and Upton, *A Bibliography of Early American Secular Music,* p. 293.

chapter seven

Native pioneers

Our Country is made up of the small fry. Give me a Seine of small meshes.
MASON L. ("PARSON") WEEMS, LETTER TO MATHEW CAREY (MARCH 25, 1809).

The native-born American musician in the eighteenth century occupied a sort of no man's land between the privileged security of the gentleman amateur and the acknowledged competence of the professional emigrant. Salaried positions in church or theater were almost invariably filled by the foreign musicians. Our native musical pioneers, being self-taught empiricists with more zeal than skill, could not at this early stage hope to compete with the imported professionals on their own ground. Nevertheless, by their energy and enthusiasm, and the frequent success of a good hymn tune, they managed to stake out an area for themselves which, if it seldom provided them with a living, yet enabled them to supply with considerable effectiveness a large portion of the country's rapidly growing musical needs. Being mostly "small fry" themselves, they knew how to make a seine of small meshes to catch their own kind. They could not boast of having performed before the crowned heads of Europe, but they knew what the farmers and artisans and tradesmen of America wanted. Being of the people, they made music for the people.

As Balzac remarked in a conversation, "To live in a material way one must work—one must be a sower, a reaper, a spinner, a weaver, a carpenter, a mason, a blacksmith, a wheelright. . . . The rest is luxury—luxury of the mind, of genius, of reason." True enough; yet even a mason or a blacksmith may aspire to a taste of that luxury of mind or spirit. The question is, if touched by "the sacred flame," how far shall he let it carry him from the material realities of life—to what heights, or to what depths? Take the case of Jacob Kimball, a blacksmith of Topsfield, Massachusetts. Old Jake had some musical ability; no doubt he sang at his forge; and surely it was a proud day for him when he was "chosen to set ye psalms, and to sit in ye elder's seat" in the local church. Thus on the Sabbath and on meeting days he enjoyed the mild luxury of setting ye psalms—but the rest of the time he stuck to his smithy. Now, the blacksmith of Topsfield had a son, Jacob Kimball, Jr., who was fortunate enough to attend Harvard College, where he prepared himself for the practice of law. What an opportunity, in this democratic land, for the second generation to advance in wealth and social prestige! But what had been a mild infection in the father became virulent in the son. On December 7, 1795, the Rev. William Bentley of Salem wrote in his diary: "Found Mr. Kimball, the celebrated musician, at his father's. It is his purpose to establish himself in the law in Maine." So Jacob Junior, promising young lawyer, is already known as a "celebrated musician." He had, in fact, compiled and published in 1793 *The Rural Harmony*, containing original compositions by himself "for the use of singing schools and singing assemblies." Whatever intention he may have had of establishing himself in the law was soon abandoned in favor of music. Kimball went about teaching singing schools in New England and promoting his own collections of psalms and hymns. He finally died at the almshouse in Topsfield.

Let us glance for a moment at the career of the most popular American composer of his generation, William Billings. He gave up the trade of tanner to devote himself entirely to music. He published many collections, and his music was known and sung all over the country. He managed to buy a house in Boston, but at his death he left his family in poverty. They could not even afford to buy a tombstone for his grave in Boston Common. In the official record of his decease his occupation was given as "tanner." For the American pioneer, music had not yet become either a trade or a profession.

Let us call the roll of these native musical pioneers, for names convey something of the character and background and even perhaps the history of the men who bear them. Here they are: Supply Belcher, Asahel Benham, William Billings, Bartholomew Brown, Amos Bull, Amos Doolittle, Josiah Flagg, Ezekiel Goodale, Oliver Holden, Jeremiah Ingalls, Stephen Jenks, Thomas Loud, Justin Morgan, Daniel Read, Timothy Swan, Abraham Wood. These are not all, but they are enough to give the feel of the breed: solid yeoman names, smacking of the humbler trades and occupations. The records confirm this: Belcher was a tavernkeeper; Billings a tanner; Bull a storekeeper; Doolittle a silversmith; Holden a carpenter; Ingalls a cooper; Morgan a horse breeder; Read a combmaker; Swan a hatter; Wood a fuller, or dresser, of cloth.

Not all of them remained poor and humble. Being Americans in a free society, they were entitled to climb as high on the social and economic ladder as their enterprise and energy could take them. While none of them attained to remarkable wealth or eminence, several became substantial and influential citizens in their communities. Oliver Holden, starting as a carpenter in Charlestown, Massachusetts, became a large-scale real-estate operator and a member of the Massachusetts House of Representatives. Daniel Read set himself up as a manufacturer of ivory combs, and also established a business as publisher and bookseller. Supply Belcher settled in Farmington, Maine, where he became a justice of the peace and a representative in the legislature. These were typical figures in our early musical life, men in close touch with the little people of our country. It will be the purpose of this chapter to relate something of their lives, their achievements, and their lasting influence in shaping America's music.

Almost our first composer

Although the New England group of composers and compilers of sacred music dominates this period, it so happens that the first American book of psalmody to appear after the publications of Tufts and Walter in the 1720s was a work entitled *Urania*, printed at Philadelphia in 1762. Its author was James Lyon (1735–1794), a native of Newark, New Jersey, where his father was "yeoman of the town." Orphaned at an early age, Lyon was sent by his guardians to the College of New Jersey, which until 1756 was located in Newark. In that year the College (later Princeton University) was moved to Princeton, where Lyon received his Bachelor of Arts degree in 1759. The commencement exercises for that year included the singing of an Ode "set to music by Mr. James Lyon, one of the students." Thus we find him already appearing as a composer, without knowing when or how he acquired a musical education. The music of Lyon's commencement ode has not been preserved.

It will be recalled that Francis Hopkinson's earliest extant song dates from 1759, the same year in which Lyon's Ode was sung at Princeton. How, then, does Hopkinson claim precedence over Lyon as "America's first native-born composer"? The fact is that the assignment of such a title to Hopkinson is rather arbitrary and meaningless, because in all probability there were earlier amateur composers of whom we know nothing. Hopkinson is simply the first American composer whose identified works have been preserved. Though Lyon's collection of psalms and hymns was not published until 1762, it is probable that some of his compositions included in that volume were composed somewhat earlier. It is, in any case, futile and pointless to attempt to establish an absolute priority in such matters.

Curiously enough, Hopkinson and Lyon shared the musical honors at a public commencement program given by the College of Pennsylvania in Philadelphia on May 23, 1761. According to a notice in the *Pennsylvania Gazette* the event took place "before a vast Concourse of People of all Ranks," and "there was performed in the Forenoon an elegant *Anthem* composed by James LYON, of New Jersey College, and in the Afternoon an *Ode* . . . written and set to music in a very grand and masterly Taste by Francis Hopkinson, Esq. A.M. of the College of this City." Note that Hopkinson, a "favorite son," is given abundant praise, while Lyon, an outsider who had only recently come to Philadelphia, has to be satisfied with the trite adjective "elegant." Anyway, Lyon's music was publicly performed in the cultured stronghold of Brotherly Love, and this was an important steppingstone to fame.

Shortly after his arrival in Philadelphia in 1760, Lyon issued proposals for the publication by subscription of a collection of psalms, hymns, and anthems, which appeared two years later with the following title:

> *URANIA, or a choice Collection of Psalm-Tunes, Anthems and Hymns from the most approved Authors, with some entirely new; in two, three and four Parts, the whole adapted to the Use of Churches and Private Families; to which are prefixed the plainest and most necessary Rules of Psalmody.*

A new edition was published at Philadelphia in 1767, and another in 1773, indicating the continued demand for Lyon's collection. The author's avowed purpose was "to spread the art of Psalmody, in its perfection, thro' our American colonies." The work was liberally dedicated to "the Clergy of every Denomination in America."

Lyon himself was ordained to the Presbyterian ministry in 1764 (he had taken his M.A. at Princeton in 1762), and the following year was sent to Nova Scotia, where he had a hard struggle to support himself and his family. In 1771 he became pastor in the newly settled town of Machias, Maine, remaining there, except for two brief intervals, until his death. During the Revolution he was an ardent supporter of the American cause, and in 1775 he wrote a long letter to George Washington outlining a plan for conquering Nova Scotia, which he proposed to carry out himself. Washington replied politely, but nothing came of the scheme.

These practical interests and activities apparently did not prevent Lyon from continuing to compose music, judging by an entry in the diary of Philip Vickers Fithian, whom we met previously as a tutor in the home of Councillor Carter of Virginia. In 1774 Fithian spent his vacation at Cohansie, New Jersey, where Lyon also happened to be visiting at the time. Under date of Friday, April 22, 1774, Fithian wrote:

> Rode to the Stage early for the Papers thence I went to Mr. Hunters where I met with that great master of music, Mr. Lyon.—He sung at my request, & sings with his usual softness and accuracy —He is about publishing a new Book of Tunes which are to be chiefly of his own Composition. . . .[1]

Besides confirming Lyon's reputation as a composer, this passage offers our only clue to the possible existence of another book by him. No trace of this "new Book of Tunes" has been found, and for all we know it may never have been published. In the 1930s an old hymnbook with the title page missing was found in a barn in Newburyport, Massachusetts. The first composition in this book is an *Anthem on Friendship* by James Lyon. This has led to the conjecture that the unidentified Newburyport volume might be Lyon's "new Book of Tunes."[2]

The collection titled *Urania* contains six compositions by Lyon: settings of the 8th, the 18th, the 23d and the 95th Psalms; an Anthem taken from the 150th Psalm; and the 104th Psalm "imitated" by Dr. Watts. Other compositions by Lyon appeared in various collections: *A Marriage Hymn* in Daniel Bayley's *New Universal Harmony* (1775), the 17th Psalm in *The Chorister's Companion* (1788) compiled by Simeon Jocelyn, the 19th Psalm in the fourth edition of Andrew Law's *The Rudiments of Music* (1792). The *Anthem on Friendship*, already mentioned, was published in Stickney's *Gentlemen's and Ladies' Musical Companion* (1774) and, as late as 1807, in

[1] Fithian, *Journal and Letters.*

[2] See *Notes* of the Music Library Association, IV, 3, p. 293.

Elias Mann's *Massachusetts Collection of Sacred Harmony.* This makes a total of ten compositions that can definitely be ascribed to James Lyon.

Today we can discover little intrinsic merit in Lyon's music, but we should note his considerable reputation among his contemporaries, who obviously considered his music worthy of praise, publication, and public performance. At one of Andrew Adgate's "Uranian Concerts" at Philadelphia in 1786, an anthem by Lyon was performed on the same program with music by Handel—an indication that our ancestors managed to combine recognition of native talent with admiration for the great European masters. Lacking such encouragement and recognition, the path of our musical pioneers would have been drear and difficult indeed.

"Better music" booster

When *The Psalms of David, imitated in the language of the New Testament,* by Dr. Isaac Watts, was issued in one of several American editions at Philadelphia in 1781, the volume contained an appendix of sixteen pages with "A select number of plain tunes adapted to congregational worship. By Andrew Law, A.B." Law had first published his *Plain Tunes* at Boston in 1767, and they went through four editions up to 1785. Andrew Law (1748–1821) stood somewhat higher in the social scale than most of his fellow pioneers in American music.

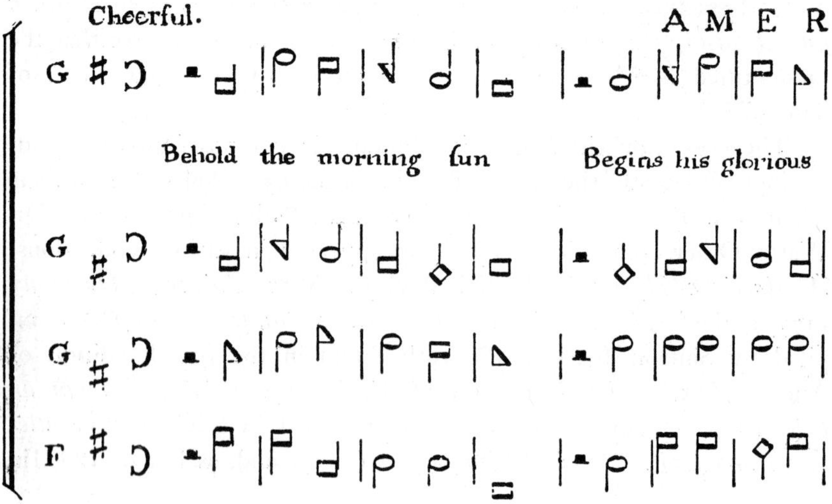

A grandson of Governor Law of Connecticut, he received a master's degree from Brown University, studied divinity privately, began preaching in 1777, and was ordained to the ministry ten years later at Hartford. According to his obituary notice, he was for forty years "an assiduous cultivator and teacher of sacred music." He was also a composer who prided himself on his good taste, but he wrote only one tune that became widely used: the one known as "Archdale."

Law's second publication was *The Select Harmony* (New Haven, 1779), containing, "in a plain and concise manner, the rules of singing." In 1780 appeared *The Musical Primer,* also printed at New Haven. It was apparently in the fourth edition of this work, issued at Cambridge, Massachusetts, in 1803, that Law introduced what he termed "a new plan of printing music." This innovation consisted of using, in place of the customary round notes, characters of four different shapes: diamond, square, round, and triangular. No staff lines were employed, the pitch of the notes being indicated by the relative position of the "shape-note" characters. As Law described this method, the characters "are situated between the single bars that divide the time, in the same manner as if they were on lines, and in every instance where two characters of the same figure occur their situations mark perfectly the height and distance of their sounds." Below is the hymn tune "America" as it appears in *The Musical Primer* in Andrew Law's shape-note system with the music in four parts.

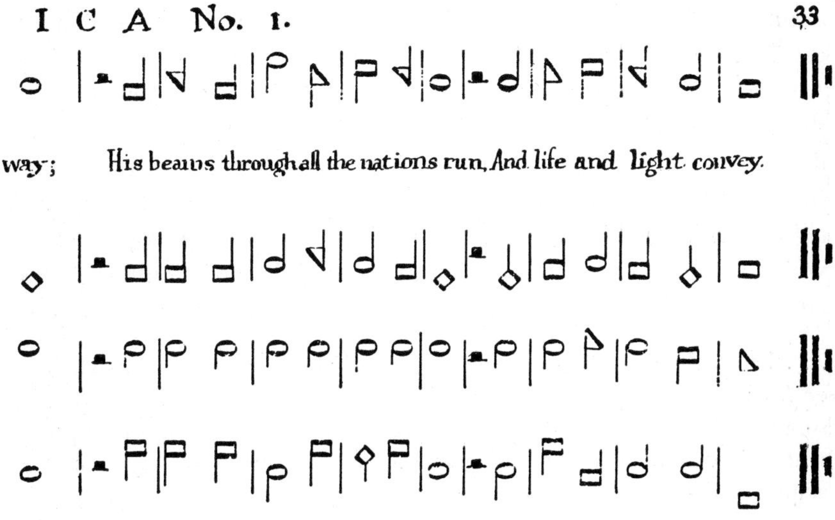
I C A No. 1.
33
way;
His beams through all the nations run, And life and light convey.

It may be asked why only four shape notes were needed, since we are accustomed to use seven different names, or rather, syllables, for designating the notes of the diatonic scale (do, re, mi, fa, sol, la, si, or ti). The early American settlers brought over from England the so-called "fasola" system, which employed only the four syllables: fa, sol, la, mi. The first three were repeated, and "mi" was inserted for the seventh note, the complete scale appearing thus: fa, sol, la, fa, sol, la, mi.

We shall have more to say about the shape-note singing books, and the people who sang from them, in the second part of this book, when we deal with the musical customs and traditions of the American frontier.

Andrew Law energetically promoted this "new plan" of musical notation, and got several prominent persons, including John Hubbard of Dartmouth, to write recommendations for it. To the objection that the system was new and not in general use, he replied that if this argument were accepted there would be an end of all improvement in the arts. It is strange that Law should have been an innovator in this respect, for on the whole his attitude was conservative as opposed to the radical individualism of such a man as Billings. This is attested by a sentence in a newspaper article that appeared after his death: "To his correct taste and scientific improvements may be ascribed much of that decent, solemn and chaste style of singing so noticeable in so many of the American churches." He was, in effect, a staunch upholder of the genteel tradition and one of the first advocates of the "better music" movement that was soon to dominate American hymnody through the influence of Lowell Mason. From the vantage point of his superior education and "correct taste," Andrew Law looked down with disdain upon the antics of the musical small fry that were overrunning our land. In the preface to *The Musical Primer* he deplored the frivolity of the singing in many churches, which resembled more the singing of "songs" than of dignified hymns, and castigated the creative efforts of the American musical pioneers:

> . . . hence the dignity and the ever varying productions of Handel, or Madan, and of others, alike meritorious, are, in a great measure, supplanted by the pitiful productions of numerous composuists, whom it would be doing too much honor to name. Let any one acquainted with the sublime and beautiful compositions of the great

Masters of Music, but look round within the circle of his own acquaintance, and he will find abundant reason for these remarks.

This curious piece of snobbism is interesting on several counts. Students of musical taste and the vagaries of fame will find it instructive that the names of Madan and Handel are coupled as twin luminaries of sacred music. The Rev. Martin Madan, founder and chaplain of Lock Hospital in London, was one of the prime movers in the development of Anglican hymnody. In 1760 he published a *Collection of Psalms and Hymns*, known as the *Lock Hospital Collection*, which had considerable influence in America (it was reprinted in Boston). He composed the tune "Denmark," used for the setting of "Before Jehovah's awful throne"; one must admit that it is a strong and stirring anthem.

From Law's quotation we extract that curious word "composuist," doubtless derived from the obsolete use of "composure" to mean "composition." But Law obviously uses it with disdain—and it *does* have a certain contemptuous ring. It is, in any case, a useful word to have at hand; for there are "composuists" in every age. Whether we call them composers or composuists, Law's remarks make it clear that persons addicted to the writing of music abounded in eighteenth-century America. How did it happen that in the second half of the eighteenth century one had only to look around within the circle of one's acquaintance in order to find a "composer," whereas in the first half of the century the existence of any such creature is not attested by any documentary evidence? There is no valid historical reason why composers should suddenly flourish in America after 1750, where none existed before. Bear in mind that these "composers" were simply men who made up hymn tunes and harmonized them with varying degrees of skill and knowledge. My belief is that individuals in America had been "composing," that is, making up tunes for psalms and hymns, long before the first printed collections began to appear. The rise of popular hymnody gave a strong impetus to these native attempts at musical self-expression, and the spread of book publishing in America —as Parson Weems said, the country was hungry for books—provided a means for the tunes and arrangements to circulate widely in print.

Some Yankee music makers

When Francis Hopkinson, in one of his letters, was describing some of the differences in American and European ways of living, he remarked that in Europe one could get any kind of work done by a specialist, but the average American, in those days, was accustomed to doing everything for himself, from building a house to pulling a tooth. Music was no exception to this rule. Our early music makers belonged to that self-reliant breed of men who built our first towns, established farms, schools, banks, and stores, and yet who believed that music was no less essential than the more mundane needs of life.

Now we meet another of this sturdy breed, Supply Belcher of Stoughton and points north, robust, prolific, sire of ten offspring, hailed by his contemporaries as "the Handel of Maine." For several years Belcher kept a tavern in his native town, where the singing-school movement flourished, but his pioneer spirit urged him on to the northern frontier. He moved with his wife and family to Maine, settling first in Hallowell and later in Farmington, where he remained until his death in 1836 at the age of eighty-five. He taught the first school in Farmington, became choir leader, justice of the peace, and representative in the Massachusetts legislature (Maine was a part of Massachusetts until 1820). In his leisure time he composed music that he hoped would "be ornamental to civilization."

Supply Belcher published *The Harmony of Maine* at Boston in 1794, containing psalms, hymns, fuguing pieces, and anthems of his own composition. He was partial to the "fuging tunes" that Billings had made popular, and aimed at a lively, expressive style of writing. He alternated between extreme simplicity and an elaborate imitative texture. Sometimes the transition from simple to complex texture was made in the same composition, as in his setting of the Christmas hymn, "While shepherds watch'd," which begins in a homophonic style and then repeats the last line in extended imitative passages which Belcher's contemporaries called "fuging" (probably pronounced "fudging").

Elaborations of this type doubtless caused Belcher to be dubbed the Handel of Maine, but he perhaps appeals more to us in his simpler moments, and if our minds run to comparisons we would be inclined to regard him as a precursor of Stephen Foster. Like Foster, he had the gift to be simple and close to the folk; he could be tenderly lyrical or contagiously vivacious. The fact that some of his liveliest tunes were written for hymns need not cause us to deny that they would be equally suitable for a minstrel show. Imagine what a lift the farmers and villagers of the rural singing schools must have got in singing a hymn to Belcher's sprightly tune "Omega":

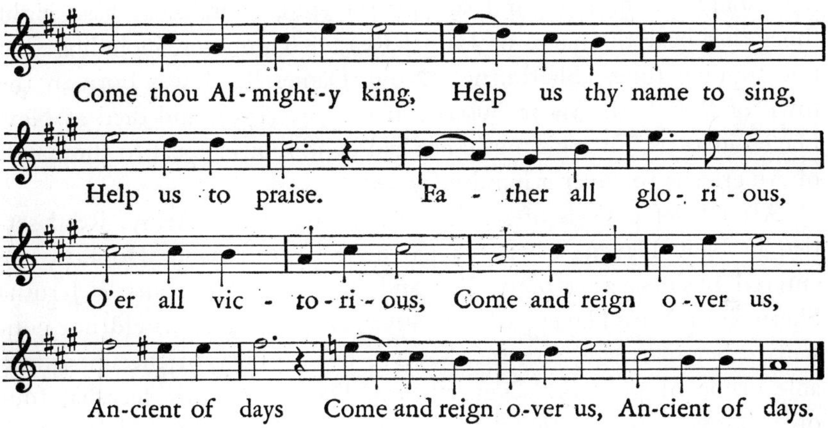

Scarcely less lively is the skipping and leaping tune, known as "York," that Belcher wrote for the hymn "So let our lips and lives express." Here we have the forerunner of the gospel hymn of later days. That Belcher could also write in a more dignified style of hymnody is proved by his fine setting of Isaac Watts's "He reigns! the Lord, the Saviour reigns!" for which he composed the tune called "Cumberland."

There is charm, freshness, and expressiveness in Belcher's three-part setting of "Invitation" ("Child of the summer, charming rose"). The same qualities are also evident in the four-part "Spring," of which we quote the beginning of the air (placed, according to the old custom, in the tenor part):

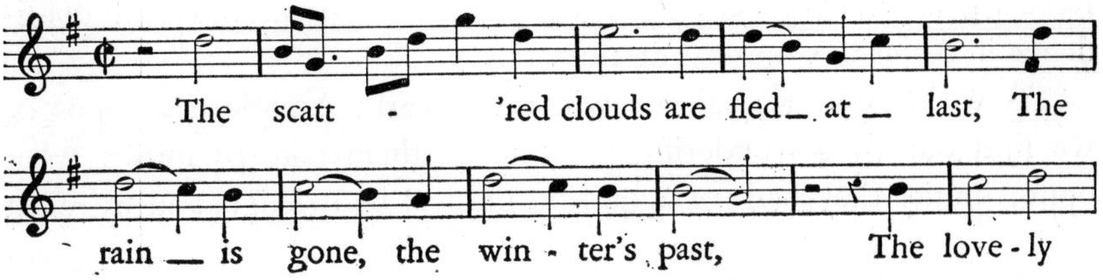

ver - nal flow'rs ap - pear, The feath-er'd choir, de-light our ear.

Both for his music and his personality, Supply Belcher is one of the most engaging figures among the primitives of American music.

The 1936 edition of the *Original Sacred Harp,* the modern shape-note songbook of our rural singing societies, contains at least eight tunes that bear the name of Daniel Read as composer, including that fine fuguing tune, "Sherburne." Now, Daniel Read was born in the town of Rehoboth, Massachusetts, in the year 1757, and died at New Haven in 1836. Thus his music has had continuous appeal to thousands of Americans for over a hundred years.

After brief periods of service in the Continental Army, Read settled in New Haven, where, in partnership with Amos Doolittle, he entered business as a bookseller and publisher. He courted Jerusha Sherman of New Haven, whose father, wrote Read, "would not consent to her marriage with me, because I was guilty of the unpardonable crime of poverty." Nevertheless, Daniel wed his Jerusha, four offspring were born—one of them christened George Frederick Handel—and the *pater familias* proceeded to overcome the crime of poverty. He became a manufacturer of ivory combs, a stockholder in one of the New Haven banks, and a director of the library—also a composer, compiler, and publisher of sacred music.

Read published *The American Singing Book* in 1785, *An Introduction to Psalmody* in 1790, and *The Columbian Harmonist* in 1793 (fourth edition, 1810). In 1786 he began to publish, as a monthly periodical, *The American Musical Magazine,* "intended to contain a great variety of approved music carefully selected from the works of the best American and European masters." Note that Read takes for granted the presence of "American masters" worthy to be included side by side with "the best . . . European masters." The American inferiority complex in music was a later development. The men of Read's generation proceeded with sublime self-assurance and confidence in America's musical destiny.

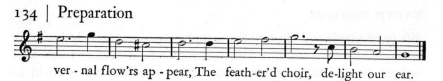

As we become acquainted with these early American composers, we find ourselves wondering what made them take to music, what opportunities they had for acquiring musical knowledge, and by what steps they established a reputation as composers. Something of a pattern has already emerged from the lives touched on thus far: the generally humble beginnings, the versatility, the determination, the enthusiasm. The case of Timothy Swan will fill in further details of the picture. He was born in 1758 at Worcester, Massachusetts, the eighth of thirteen children. Upon the death of his father, he was apprenticed to a merchant, and at sixteen went to live with a brother in Groton. There he attended a singing school, and it was this that awakened his musical interest. It also provided him with his meager musical education and started him on the road to composing. Apprenticed to a hatter in Northfield, he began to jot down tunes at odd moments, writing a few notes at a time. Thus while still very young he composed several hymn tunes that at first circulated in manuscript. He was an enthusiastic admirer of Billings—twelve years his senior—to whom he doubtless looked up as an "American master."

Swan married the daughter of a pastor in Suffield, where he lived for nearly thirty years. In 1807 he moved to Northfield, and died there on his eighty-fourth birthday. It is difficult to understand how he made a living, and it is reported that his neighbors said he was "Poor, proud, and indolent." He was fond of poetry, trees, and birds. He read widely, and wrote verse as well as music.

Like Read, Swan cultivated the fuguing style. His major compilation was *The New England Harmony* (Suffield, 1801). Another collection, *The Songster's Assistant*, published about a year earlier, contained a number of secular songs by Swan. *The Federal Harmony* (Boston, 1785) has also been attributed to him. His best-known hymn tune is "China," said to have been composed in 1790. Others are "London," "Ocean," "Poland," Quincy," "Spring," and "Montague."

Oliver Holden (1765–1844) is remembered chiefly as the composer of the tune "Coronation," used for Edward Perronet's hymn "All Hail the Power of Jesus' Name." In his day he was an influential and successful composer and compiler of sacred music, though he stood somewhat aside from the popular tradition of Billings and his school. His aim, in his own words, was to compose "music in a style suited to the solemnity of sacred devotion." In 1792 he brought out *The American Harmony*, followed by *The Union Harmony*, and *The Massachusetts Compiler*, the latter in collaboration with Samuel

Holyoke and Hans Gram. Holden was also engaged to edit the sixth and later editions of *The Worcester Collection of Sacred Harmony*, first published in 1786, which was one of the most widely used books of that period. Holden seems to have shared Andrew Law's attitude toward American composers of his time, for in the preface to the eighth edition of the *Worcester Collection* he wrote: "It is to be lamented that among so many American authors so little can be found well written or well adapted to sacred purposes, but it is disingenuous and impolitic to throw that little away while our country is in a state of progressive improvement."

In addition to running a music store, directing a choir, conducting singing schools, and composing music, Holden was a real-estate operator, a prominent Mason, a preacher, and a member of the Massachusetts House of Representatives. He wrote the words and music of an *Ode to Columbia's Favorite Son*, which was sung when General Washington was given a triumphal reception at Boston in 1789. This ode was first published in *The Massachusetts Magazine* for October, 1789.

Besides the familiar "Coronation," included in most hymnals, another tune by Holden, titled "Concord," is found in the latest edition of the *Sacred Harp* (1936), proving that his music could survive several generations of "progressive improvement."

Justin Morgan (1747–1798) of West Springfield, Massachusetts, earned a living by teaching school, keeping a tavern, and breeding horses. Among his stallions, by which he bred the "Morgan horse," were Sportsman, Diamond, and True Briton (this was in 1783!). In 1788 Morgan moved with his family to Randolph, Vermont, where he became town clerk. Much of his time was given to teaching singing schools, to which he used to ride on "the original Morgan horse."

Unlike most of his fellow singing teachers, Morgan did not publish any collections of music, though he left such a book in manuscript. Among his more ambitious compositions is a "Judgment Anthem," but his best-known tune is "Montgomery," a fuguing piece that has remained popular with American rural hymn singers up to the present day. Yet the historian Frank J. Metcalf wrote in 1925 that the music of Justin Morgan "has now passed entirely out of use, and is of interest only to the historian." Such statements, all too frequent in our historical writing, can be made only by persons acquainted with but a small segment of America's musical culture. Besides, a good tune never passes entirely out of use; it simply passes into a different cultural environment. We shall see this process at work in a later section of this book, when we deal with the rural singing tradition of the fasola folk in the South and West.

Jeremiah Ingalls (1764–1828) was another native of Massachusetts (he was born in Andover) who moved to Vermont, though he did this when he was much younger than Morgan. Ingalls was in his early twenties when he settled in Newbury, Vermont, where in 1800 he built a house that he kept as a tavern for about ten years. In 1819 he moved to Rochester, Vermont, and later to Hancock, where he died. In addition to keeping a tavern, being deacon of the Congregational Church, leading the choir, teaching singing school, composing and compiling music, Ingalls worked also, at various times, as a farmer and as a cooper.

Jeremiah Ingalls was married to Mary Bigelow in 1791, and they had several children. The following anecdote, quoted by Metcalf without indication of source, depicts music in the Ingalls's family circle:

> His children were musical and his sons could play clarinet, bassoon, flute, and violin, and they would often practice for hours, the old man leading the band with his bass viol. One Sunday they were having an excellent time performing anthems, and after a while the youngsters started a secular piece, the father with composure joining in. From that they went on until they found themselves furiously engaged in a boisterous march, in the midst of which the old gentleman stopped short, exclaiming, "Boys, this won't do. Put away these corrupt things and take your Bibles." [3]

This anecdote is pointed up by the fact that Ingalls's collection, *The Christian Harmony; or, Songster's Companion,* printed at Exeter, New Hampshire, in 1805, contains a large number of very lively tunes, obviously taken from secular songs or dances, as settings for sacred texts. Ingalls may have objected to his boys getting overboisterous on Sunday, but he certainly had no objections to making use of good tunes wherever he found them. One of the songs in *The Christian Harmony*, titled "Innocent Sounds," is a plea for the use of secular tunes for religious purposes:

[3] Metcalf, *American Writers and Compilers of Sacred Music.*

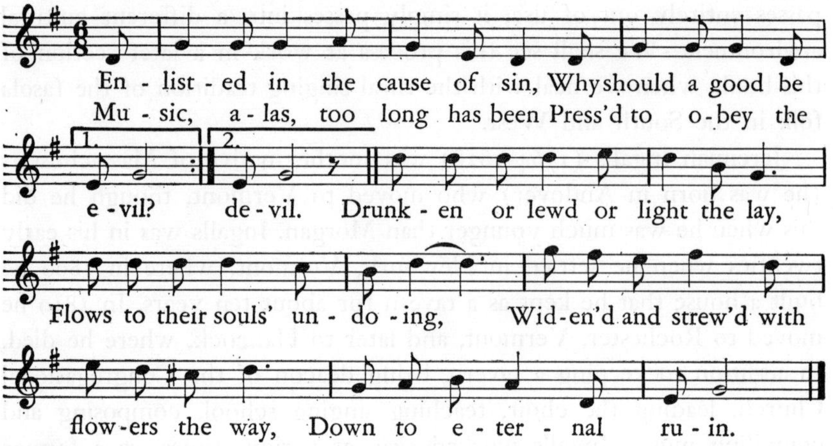
1.
2.
En - list - ed in the cause of sin, Why should a good be
Mu - sic, a - las, too long has been Press'd to o - bey the
e - vil? de - vil. Drunk - en or lewd or light the lay,
Flows to their souls' un - do - ing, Wid - en'd and strew'd with
flow - ers the way, Down to e - ter - nal ru - in.

The second stanza goes on to develop the idea of recovering the "innocent sounds" that have been misused for carnal pleasures:

> Who, on the part of God, will rise,
> Innocent sounds recover;
> Fly on the prey and seize the prize,
> Plunder the carnal lover;
> Strip him of every moving strain,
> Of every melting measure;
> Music in virtue's cause retain,
> Risk the holy pleasure.

Ingalls himself did a rather effective job of "plundering the carnal lover," judging by the large number of tunes in *The Christian Harmony* that are strongly reminiscent of English, Scottish, and Irish popular tunes. A typical example is the anonymous "Redeeming Love." Other tunes in *The Christian Harmony* that have a marked secular character, recalling British dance tunes, are "Angels' Song," "Clamanda," "Mecklinburg," "Rose Tree," and "Separation." Ingalls evidently was very close to the folk hymnody of his day. As we shall see later, he was the first compiler to include in his collection the revival camp-meeting songs that began to be so popular from around 1800.

Ingalls's most popular tune is "Northfield," a fuguing piece that has remained a favorite with the rural hymn singers for nearly one hundred and fifty years. Frederic P. Wells recounts the following anecdote about the origin of "Northfield":

Returning from fishing one day, he [Ingalls] laid [*sic*] down before the fire to get dry and, impatient at the slow progress of dinner, began to sing a parody to a well-known hymn [by Dr. Watts]:

How long, my people, Oh! how long
Shall dinner hour delay?
Fly swifter round, ye idle maids,
And bring a dish of tea.

"Why, Jerry," said his wife, "that's a grand tune."

"So it is," replied the man of song: "I'll write it down." And dinner waited the completion of "Northfield." [4]

Jeremiah Ingalls's famous fuguing piece passed from *The Christian Harmony* to one songbook after another, including the 1854 edition of *The Southern Harmony* and the 1936 revision of *The Original Sacred Harp*. A recording of it, as sung by the Sacred Harp Singers of Alabama, has been issued by the Library of Congress. So that Jerry Ingalls and his music are still very much alive today, and not merely of "historical interest."

Billings of Boston

William Billings was born in Boston on October 7, 1746. As a youth he was apprenticed to learn the tanner's trade, and as far as the official records are concerned, a tanner he remained to the end of his days. But, like so many others around him, he caught the contagion of music, and before long he was devoting all of his remarkable energy and promotional ability to teaching, conducting, composing, and publishing music. Unlike his colleagues, he engaged in no business side lines, but devoted himself completely, recklessly, tirelessly, to the art that he loved above all else. "Great art thou O Music!"—he exclaimed in one of his frequent outbursts of enthusiasm—"and with thee there is no competitor. . . ."

His natural gifts, his energy and industry, and his force of character, all concentrated without deviation on his life's one ambition—the composition, performance, and promotion of music—gave Billings a unique position among his fellow Americans. Great must have been his force of character, for his personal appearance, to judge by the

[4] Cited by Metcalf, *op. cit.*

account of a contemporary, was not prepossessing. The Rev. William Bentley of Salem wrote of him just after his death: "He was a singular man, of moderate size, short of one leg, with one eye, without any address, and with an uncommon negligence of person. Still he spake and sang and thought as a man above the common abilities." Billings knew his own worth.

Billings probably received no formal schooling after the age of fourteen, when his father, a shopkeeper, died. He is said to have received some music lessons from a local choirmaster, and he evidently studied Tans'ur's *Musical Grammar*. He was only twenty-four when he published his first book, *The New England Psalm Singer, or American Chorister* (Boston, 1770), containing psalm tunes, anthems, and canons of his own composition. His other collections were: *The Singing Master's Assistant* (1778; popularly known as "Billings's Best"); *Music in Miniature* (1779); *The Psalm Singer's Amusement* (1781); *The Suffolk Harmony* (1786); and *The Continental Harmony* (1794). He died in Boston on September 26, 1800.

Billings was not in the least disconcerted by his lack of scientific knowledge. On the contrary, he gloried in his musical independence. In *The New England Psalm Singer* he aired his views in words that may be taken as his own musical credo:

> Perhaps it may be expected by some, that I should say something concerning Rules for Composition; to these I answer that Nature is the best Dictator, for all the hard, dry, studied rules that ever was prescribed, will not enable any person to form an air. . . . It must be Nature, Nature must lay the Foundation, Nature must inspire the Thought. . . . For my own Part, as I don't think myself confin'd to any Rules for composition, laid down by any that went before me, neither should I think (were I to pretend to lay down Rules) that any one who came after me were any ways obligated to adhere to them, any further than they should think proper; so in fact, I think it best for every *Composer* to be his own *Carver.*

In justice to Billings, it must be pointed out that he sought to strike a happy balance between nature and art. In the same essay from which we have just quoted, he writes:

> But perhaps some may think I mean and intend to throw Art entirely out of the Question. I answer by no Means, for the more

Art is displayed, the more Nature is decorated. And in some forms of Composition, there is dry Study required, and Art very requisite. For instance, in a *Fuge* [*sic*], where the parts come in after each other, with the same notes; but even there, Art is subservient to Genius, for Fancy goes first, and strikes out the Work roughly, and Art comes after, and polishes it over.

By the term "Fuge," Billings did not, of course, mean what we understand by the term "fugue," in the sense of a formal composition in contrapuntal texture. His "fuges" were imitative vocal passages in which, as he says, "the parts come after each other, with the same notes." Although he did not create the "fuging tune," which was known in England and had earlier antecedents in the old psalm tunes called "Rapports," Billings's name is popularly associated with this type of composition because of his success in exploiting it.

In his *Thoughts on Music,* Billings tells us something about the way in which he thinks his music should be sung:

> Suppose a Company of Forty People, Twenty of them should sing the Bass, the other Twenty should be divided according to the discretion of the Company into the upper Parts, six or seven of the deepest voices should sing the Ground Bass . . . which if well sung together with the upper Parts, is most Majestic; and so exceeding Grand as to cause the floor to tremble, as I myself have often experienced. . . . Much caution should be used in singing a Solo, in my opinion Two or Three at most are enough to sing it well, it should be sung as soft as an echo, in order to keep the Hearers in an agreeable suspense till all the parts join together in a full chorus, as smart and strong as possible.

This reveals the effects at which Billings aimed, and his manner of achieving them. He wanted to produce a strong, powerful, majestic impression, with startling contrasts between the soft "solo" passages and the full chorus. We cannot measure the effect his music had upon his first hearers unless we hear it sung that way, by large groups of powerful voices, and the floor trembling with the reverberation of the booming basses.

In *The New England Psalm Singer,* Billings printed a poem by the Rev. Mather Byles of Boston, which gives us an idea of the impression that the "fuging tunes" made upon listeners and singers of that time:

On Music
Down steers the Bass with grave Majestic Air,
And up the Treble mounts with shrill Career;
With softer Sounds, in mild Melodious Maze,
Warbling between the *Tenor* gently Plays:
But if th' aspiring *Altus* joins its Force,
See, like the Lark, it Wings its tow'ring Course;
Thro Harmony's sublimest Sphere it flies,
And to Angelic Accents seems to rise;
From the bold Height it hails the echoing Bass,
Which swells to meet, and mix in close Embrace.
Tho' diff'rent Systems all the Parts divide,
With Music's Chords the distant Notes are ty'd;
And Sympathetic Strains enchanting winde
Their restless Race, till all the Parts are join'd:
Then rolls the Rapture thro' the Air around
In the full Magic Melody of Sound.

Incidentally, according to the pronunciation of that time, "winde" and "join'd" formed a perfect rhyme. There can be no question that those who sang or heard Billings's music, especially under his dynamic direction, experienced "the full Magic Melody of Sound."

The continued effectiveness of Billings's famous hymn tune "Majesty" is attested by a passage in one of the stories of Harriet Beecher Stowe, who was born in 1811 and as a girl in Litchfield, Connecticut, frequently heard the old fuguing tunes sung by the village choir. The story is called *Poganuc People* and deals with New England life in the early years of the nineteenth century. This is the passage:

> . . . there was a grand, wild freedom, an energy of motion in the old 'fuging tunes' of that day that well expressed the heart of the people courageous in combat and unshaken in endurance. . . . Whatever the trained musician might say of such a tune as old Majesty, no person of imagination or sensibility could hear it well rendered by a large choir without deep emotion. And when back and forth from every side of the church came the different parts shouting—
>
> On cherubim and seraphim
> Full royally He rode,
> And on the wings of mighty winds
> Came flying all abroad,

there went a stir and thrill through many a stern and hard nature, until the tempest cleared off in the words—

He sat serene upon the floods
  Their fury to restrain,
And He as Soverign Lord and King
  For evermore shall reign.

Mrs. Stowe's reference to the singing coming from "every side of the church" would seem to indicate the practice of having a "dispersed choir," with the various sections located in different parts of the church and "answering" one another, which of course would increase the effectiveness of the fuguing tunes. The words to which "Majesty" was sung were from the Sternhold and Hopkins version of the 18th Psalm, beginning, "The Lord descended from above." Billings's setting first appeared in *The Singing Master's Assistant.*

To take the measure of the man, let us run through some of his compositions. Observe how he always identifies himself completely with the subject or the mood that his music portrays. Is the subject Creation? Then Billings strikes the note of grandeur and—as in the hymn of Dr. Watts beginning "When I with pleasing wonder stand"—when he reaches the last line, "Strange that a harp of a thousand strings should keep in tune so long," he brings in his "Fuge" *con spirito,* first the basses, then the tenors, next the altos and sopranos, and so they go flying along fortissimo, one after the other, until they meet in the broad, impressive climax of the final phrase.

Now it is Jesus weeping, and our composer gives us a beautiful, tender melody, cast in the form of a canon or round for four voices, a melody that for sheer inspiration marks the culminating point of American musical primitivism (the term "primitive" is used stylistically, with no connotation of inferiority). Here it is, "When Jesus Wept," from Billings's first book, *The New England Psalm Singer:*

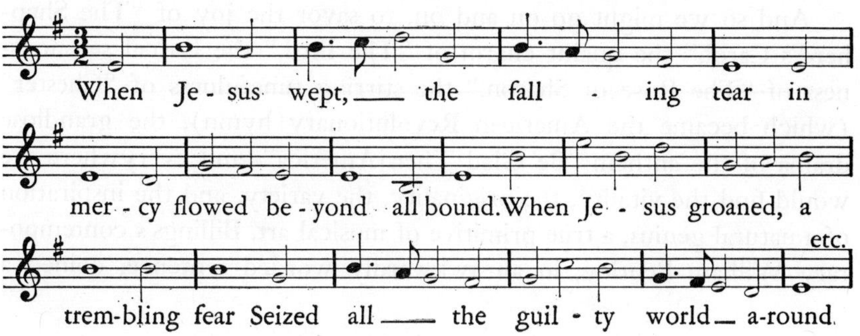

Now it is an old English Christmas carol, "A Virgin Unspotted" ("Judea"), to which Billings has provided one of his most delightful and spirited tunes. When he comes to the refrain, "Then let us be merry, put sorrow away, Our Saviour Christ Jesus was born on this day," his tune becomes as lively as a jig—which no doubt offended the Doctors of Divinity no less than it pleased the people for whom Billings wrote.

We turn next to the Easter anthem, "The Lord is Risen Indeed," in which a strong, surging rhythm contributes to the general effect of jubilant exultation, heightened by the recurrent ejaculation, "Hallelujah." Rhetorically, the anthem employs the device of interrogation and affirmation. One after another the sections of the choir fling forth the interrogation, "And did He rise?" And the full choir peals out affirmatively, "Hear ye, O ye nations, Hear it, O ye dead, He rose, He rose, He rose, He burst the bars of death." Then it is the risen Christ who speaks, affirming His Ascension, and when we reach the lines, "Then first humanity triumphant past [passed] the crystal ports of light," Billings achieves one of his most striking, most original, and most apt effects, using a succession of fourteen open fifths and sixths that convey the image of "the crystal ports of light" with surprising vividness.

Turning to the Old Testament, we have Billings's version of David's lamentation, which reveals his power of pathos achieved through stark, simple means. When David laments, "Would to God I had died for thee, O Absalom, my son!" the music compels us to share his grief, as Billings himself undoubtedly felt it and partook of it, and embodied it in the austere yet deeply expressive texture of his composition. The "incorrect" consecutive octaves and fifths in this passage are precisely what is needed to achieve the desired result. This lament has the strength and simplicity of the ancient ballads, and indeed Billings at his best was a bard of the folk.

And so we might go on and on, to savor the joy of "The Shepherd's Carol," the quaint charm of "The Bird," the lyrical sensuousness of "The Rose of Sharon," the stirring tunefulness of "Chester" (which became the American Revolutionary hymn), the grandiose drama of the anthem "Be Glad Then America"—and everywhere we would find the vitality, the originality, the variety, and the inspiration of a natural genius, a true primitive of musical art. Billings's contemporary William Bentley, in an awkwardly worded sentence, coined a phrase that perhaps conceals more than a grain of truth: "His late attempts, and without a proper education, were the cause of his inferior excellence." *Inferior excellence!* Yes, the queer contradictory term is good. Inferior in education, in knowledge, in technical skill. Excellent in the gifts of nature, in intuition and imagination and emotive power. It seems to me that Billings is an example of that spiritual self-reliance that Emerson had in mind when he wrote (in *Spiritual Laws*): "No man need be perplexed in his speculations. Let him do and say what strictly belongs to him, and though very ignorant of books, his nature shall not yield him any intellectual obstructions and doubts." [5] The kind of integrity and natural force that found expression in Billings's music is well summed up in the words of a writer who was himself far from primitive, William James: "I don't care how incorrect language may be if it only has fitness of epithet, energy and clearness."

We have seen that during the second half of the eighteenth century American composers sprang up in profusion, though within a limited field; numerous American collections of music were published, reflecting the transition from metrical psalmody to free hymnody; the elaborated anthem and the fuguing tune came into vogue; and the institution of the singing school became firmly implanted. Many of the men whom we have discussed in this chapter lived on well into the nineteenth century: the books, the music, the traditions with which they are identified lived on too, and survived them. But they lived on chiefly in the hinterlands, gradually ousted from the dominant urban centers by the pressure of progress and the imposition of more sophisticated standards. In the course of this narrative we shall encounter again and again the tunes of Billings and his contemporaries as a living element in American music. It is therefore only temporarily that we take leave of them now, as the scene changes to another setting in the vast panorama of America's music.

[5] Emerson, *Complete Works: Essays, First Series,* vol. 2, p. 126.

two | Expansion

The frontier is the line of most rapid and effective Americanization.

FREDERICK J. TURNER, THE FRONTIER IN AMERICAN LIFE.

chapter eight

Progress and profit

A line of demarcation between the Musical Art and that other and more worldly pursuit known as the Musical Business . . . is difficult to trace.
PAUL S. CARPENTER, MUSIC, AN ART AND A BUSINESS.

We have seen how the combined efforts of gentlemen amateurs and professionally trained musical emigrants, reinforced by the energy and enthusiasm of some native pioneers, led to the establishment during the eighteenth century of orchestral concerts, operatic performances, choral societies, and similar types of organized musical activity requiring group participation and public support. This organized musical activity at first inevitably concentrated in the cities that formed a sort of fringe along the Atlantic seaboard, from Boston in the North to Charleston in the South. As the nineteenth century advanced, these cities, particularly those of the North, grew in wealth and size due to the effects of a steadily expanding commerce and a rapidly increasing rate of immigration. Thus there were gradually created the three conditions propitious for the regular consumption of art: population, wealth, and leisure. When these three factors assume large proportions in any given society, the consumption of art tends to increase, and may indeed become itself a major economic enterprise.[1]

It was during the first half of the nineteenth century that this pattern of music as big business began to take shape in the United States. For the first time, musicians began to make real money from their art. They profited from American methods of mass production and distribution. They were among the first to use high-pressure pro-

[1] For two recent studies of this phase of music in America, the reader may consult *Music, An Art and a Business*, by Paul S. Carpenter (Norman, Oklahoma, 1950), and *Worlds of Music*, by Cecil Smith (Philadelphia, 1952).

motion and sensational advertising. When the ex-blacksmith Isaac Baker Woodbury wanted to tell the public about his collection of sacred music called *The Dulcimer,* he, or his advertising manager, ran an advertisement in Dwight's *Journal of Music* which screamingly proclaimed:

125,000 Copies in Two Seasons!
Live Music Book!
The Dulcimer

The sacred-music collections of Lowell Mason topped them all. His *Carmina Sacra,* in various editions, sold 500,000 copies between 1841 and 1858. Another of Mason's collections, *The Hallelujah,* sold 150,000 copies in five years! This may not seem impressive in comparison with sales of popular sheet music in later times, but remember that this was "sacred" music, that the unit cost was greater, and that the music industry was still in its infancy. To our early struggling musical pioneers, such as Billings, Lyon, and Kimball, who were likely to end in the poorhouse or a pauper's grave, the idea of making $100,000 from a collection of sacred music, as Mason did, would surely have appeared fantastic.

In the musical activity of the United States during the first half of the nineteenth century, it seems to me that two things stand out as most typical of the age. One is that the leading musical impresario of that period was also the creator of the American circus, the great master of ballyhoo, the exploiter of Tom Thumb and Joice Heth—that incomparable and sensational showman, Phineas Taylor Barnum. The other symbolically significant phenomenon is that the leading musical figure of that mid-century period, Lowell Mason, was in his career and his character the prototype of the self-made, successful American business magnate. The one succeeded by appealing to the frivolity of the public. The other succeeded by "uplifting" the public. The common meeting point is that both were excellent promoters and both were highly successful in a practical and tangible way.

Here are some impressions of Lowell Mason by various persons who knew him. He was very handsome and finely dignified in appearance. He had a "commanding personality." He had "a remarkable degree of personal magnetism." He was "a manager of men, an organizer of movements. . . ." He had "huge industry," "great ability, penetrating foresight, splendid ideas." He was "a clear-sighted, practical man, just the leader the American people could then understand,

and be willing to follow." He was shrewd and successful in business. He was "a man of strong and impressive individuality, a virile nature in which an iron will was coupled with a gentle and tender heart." Discounting the tender heart as sheer sentimentality, would not these characterizations convey the impression that the man in question was one of America's "empire builders," a railroad baron, a real-estate operator, or a shipping magnate? And in effect, Lowell Mason *was* an "empire builder": he opened up vast new areas for musical exploitation, and he did it through industry, energy, determination, and organization. Of all musicians active in the United States during the nineteenth century, Lowell Mason has left the strongest, the widest, and the most lasting impress on our musical culture. This is not a tribute of praise: it is merely an objective statement of fact. Let us examine the record.

The rise of Lowell Mason

Lowell Mason was born in Medfield, Massachusetts, on January 8, 1792. His father was town treasurer and a member of the state legislature; he also sang in the church choir and played several musical instruments. His grandfather, Barachias Mason, had been a singing-school teacher as well as a schoolmaster. Lowell Mason, therefore, inherited a traditional New England musical background. As a boy he attended for a time the singing school of Amos Albee, compiler of *The Norfolk Collection of Sacred Harmony*, and later received musical instruction from Oliver Shaw, a prominent musician of Dedham. He learned to play the organ, the piano, the flute, the clarinet, and various other instruments. In 1812 he accompanied the Medford organ builder George Whitefield Adams to Savannah, where he took a job as clerk in a bank. In Savannah, Mason met a recently arrived German musician named F. L. Abel, from whom he received competent musical instruction. This Abel was the forerunner of many professional German musical immigrants who were to exert a far-reaching influence on America's musical development as the nineteenth century progressed.

Mason became organist and choirmaster of the Independent Presbyterian Church in Savannah, began to compose hymns and anthems, and in 1817 married Abigail Gregory of Westboro, Massachusetts. Though not yet intent on making music his career, Mason, like many of his predecessors and contemporaries, decided to compile and publish a collection of sacred music. In it he included some of his own tunes, as well as melodies from instrumental compositions by Handel, Mozart, Beethoven, and other European masters, adapted to familiar hymns and arranged "for three and four voices with a figured base [*sic*] for the organ or pianoforte." Completing this work in 1819–1820, Mason sought a publisher in Philadelphia and other large cities, but without success. Then he met Dr. George K. Jackson, organist of the Handel and Haydn Society of Boston, who took an interest in the compilation and recommended that the Society sponsor its publication—with several of his compositions incorporated in it. Dr. Jackson, whose opinion carried much prestige, endorsed it as "much the best book of the kind I have seen published in this country." Thus was born the famous *Boston Handel and Haydn Society Collection of Church Music*, which went to press in 1821 and was copyrighted the following year. Lowell Mason's name did not appear as editor, though he was mentioned in the preface. In later years, Mason gave this explanation for the omission of his name: "I was then a bank officer in Savannah and did not wish to be known as a musical man, and I had not the least thought of making music my profession." [2] The success of this collection soon caused Mason to change his mind. The book went through twenty-two editions and brought handsome profits both to its compiler and to the Handel and Haydn Society, to which it gave financial stability and permanent security.

Mason returned to Savannah after the publication of his collection, but in 1826 he was in Boston to deliver a lecture on church music (later printed), and in July, 1827, he was persuaded to settle in Boston as choirmaster of Dr. Lyman Beecher's church on Hanover Street.[3] Being a prudent man, for a while he also took a position as teller in a bank: he was not yet fully convinced that music could be made to pay. In 1827 he was elected president of the Handel and Haydn Society, holding this office until 1832. One of the reasons for his resignation was that he wished to devote more time to teaching music and singing to children, a line of activity that he had begun in Savannah and that was to occupy his attention increasingly as time went on. In 1829 Mason brought out his *Juvenile Psalmist, or The Child's Intro-*

[2] Quoted by Rich, *Lowell Mason*, p. 9.

[3] This church was burned down shortly after Mason's arrival in Boston, and a new one was built on Bowdoin Street, where he continued to conduct the choir.

duction to Sacred Music, followed in 1830–1831 by the *Juvenile Lyre*, which he claimed was "the first school song book published in this country." Mason's work in public-school music is so important that it will be advisable to treat this subject separately in another section of this chapter. Meanwhile, let us briefly summarize the rest of his career.

In 1832, together with George J. Webb and other Boston musicians, Mason founded the Boston Academy of Music for the purpose of applying the Pestalozzian method to the teaching of music to children. The Academy, which had as many as 1,500 pupils in its first year, continued in existence until 1847. The instruction was "free to all children, no other condition being required of the pupils than that they be over seven years of age, and engaged to continue in the school one year." Classes for adults were also given. The Academy was apparently responsible for the beginnings of "music appreciation" in this country, for it sponsored a translation of Fétis's *Music Explained to the World; or, How to Understand Music and Enjoy its Performance*. This work has long been obsolete, but the title still has a familiar ring!

In the summer of 1837, Mason went to Europe to study the Pestalozzian methods of instruction in Switzerland and Germany. At the end of 1851 he again sailed for Europe, this time remaining there fifteen months and spending much of his time in England. After his return to America in 1853, Mason made his headquarters in New York. He died at his home in Orange, New Jersey, on August 11, 1872, at the age of eighty. Of his four sons, the youngest, William, became an influential pianist and teacher. Lowell, junior, with his brother Henry, founded the firm of Mason & Hamlin, manufacturers first of organs and later of pianos. A grandson, Daniel Gregory Mason, was to become a prominent composer.

The age of progress

As the eighteenth century stood for improvement through reason, so the nineteenth century stood for progress through science. One still heard the words "good taste" and "correctness" used occasionally, but they were generally coupled with the words "science" and "progress," and gradually one heard less and less of good taste and more and more of progress. Nowhere was this belief in improvement through progress more firmly entrenched than in the United States. It runs through the thought and the career of Lowell Mason like a leading motive, marking him once again as a highly typical American of his time.

In order to succeed in his ventures, Mason had to strike a balance between lack of novelty and an excess of innovation. The public was conservative in its tastes, strongly attached to the accustomed and the familiar. Yet a certain amount of novelty, if skillfully administered and prepared, could prove attractive, especially if associated with the notion of being "up to date," of keeping up with the times. The manner in which Lowell Mason handled this delicate problem is illustrated in the various editions of *The Boston Handel and Haydn Society Collection of Church Music*, in which the older hymns and psalm tunes were gradually supplanted, in large part, by more "modern" compositions from the pen of celebrated European composers, and of course from the pen of Mason himself. Let us take, for example, the tenth edition of this famous collection, published in 1831. The following passages from the preface are illuminating:

> The several later editions of this work have presented an almost uniform appearance. . . . It is obvious, however, from the progressive nature of science and taste, in respect to music as well as other subjects, that this uniformity cannot be, and ought not to be perpetual. Within the last few years, much attention has been directed to the subject, and, as was to be expected, great improvement has been made, not only in the manner of performing psalm and hymn tunes, but also in their composition.
>
> Is it to be supposed that in psalmody, science and taste have accomplished all that they can accomplish? and is it desirable that all attempts at improvement should be checked? This is impracticable if it were desirable. . . .
>
> Unless, therefore, it be maintained that the present psalm and hymn tunes cannot be improved, and that no better can be substituted in their stead, or else, that bad tunes are as valuable as good ones, there may be as valid reasons, founded in public utility, for introducing alterations into text books of psalmody, as for introducing alterations into text books on arithmetic or grammar. [Another good reason: new editions promote sales].

All this, and considerably more to the same effect, is by way of justifying a "thorough revision" of the *Handel and Haydn Collection.* Mason gives some indication of what he means by "bad" tunes, when he states that he has reduced the number of "imitative and fugueing [*sic*] pieces," kept down the proportion of "light music" in the collection in deference to "the good sense and improved taste of the public." Certainly the public that would show its good sense and improved taste by preferring Mason to Billings would be thoroughly in line with "scientific progress"! In reviewing this collection, the New Haven *Chronicle* wrote: "A book so valuable must become the standard of music in our churches, since its harmony and style are fixed on the immovable basis of science and correct taste." Here the drive toward standardization is clearly manifested. The assumption is that earlier tune writers, not having benefited by "the immovable basis of science" (happily a nineteenth-century discovery) could only write inferior music that needed improvement, correction, or complete elimination by the products of modern science. According to this criterion, Mason's "From Greenland's Icy Mountains" is inevitably a better hymn than Madan's "Before Jehovah's Awful Throne." People who persisted in singing the old-fashioned anthems could be made to feel that they were failing to take advantage of modern improvements, and not many Americans liked to admit that they were behind the times. Hence the sweeping success of the "better music" movement led by Lowell Mason.

As a typical product of this movement, let us glance at a collection of church music edited by Mason entitled *The New Carmina Sacra*, published "under the sanction of the Boston Academy of Music" in 1853. According to the customarily elaborate descriptive title, this collection comprised "the most popular Psalm and Hymn Tunes in General Use, together with a great variety of New Tunes, Chants, Sentences, Motetts, and Anthems; *principally by distinguished European Composers* . . ." (the italics are mine). Once again, "made in Europe" was being stressed as the trade-mark of distinction in music for American consumption, as it had been in the days of the thirteen colonies. Looking through the table of contents of this collection, we come across the names of Arne, Beethoven, Cherubini, Giardini, Handel, Josef and Michael Haydn, Mozart, Palestrina, Pleyel, J. J. Rousseau, Schubert, Vogler, Weber—certainly an impressive and eclectic choice of "distinguished European composers." Perhaps the first question that strikes the reader is, "What are these composers doing in a collection of American church music?" The answer is: "They were providing tunes." The procedure of plundering secular music for making hymn tunes was not, as we have seen in earlier chapters, something new. The Wesleys, among others, had done it. The main difference is that Lowell Mason and his associates did it more systematically and more successfully than any of their predecessors. And as their movement coincided with the era of mass production and standardization, its effects were more widely felt.

At this point the reader should begin to perceive that the emphasis on church music in America during the mid-portion of the nineteenth century was by no means as "churchly" as might appear at first sight. The trend toward secularization was accelerated by two factors. One was the increasing use of tunes from secular compositions: in fact, any tune that appealed to the taste of the day, whatever its origin, was likely to be adapted for a hymn. The second factor was the increasing emphasis on quality of performance: *how* one sang was becoming almost more important than *what* one sang. Here, too, Lowell Mason was an influential leader. He zealously trained his choir at Dr. Lyman Beecher's Bowdoin Street Church in Boston to such a point of excellence that it drew nationwide attention and admiration. According to T. F. Seward:

> Pilgrimages were made from all parts of the land to hear the wonderful singing. Clergymen who attended ministerial gatherings in Boston carried home with them oftentimes quite as much musical as spiritual inspiration. . . .[4]

With the general shift from religious to secular emphasis that took place in American life during the latter part of the nineteenth century, this striving for technical virtuosity and impressive perfection in choral singing was transferred to the schools, resulting eventually in the wonderfully trained public-school choirs that dot the land today.

Returning for a moment to the *New Carmina Sacra*, it should be observed that this collection made a bow to the older traditions of psalmody by including some of the most famous tunes of Tallis, Playford, Tans'ur, and Aaron Williams. Even a few native American pioneers were included: Daniel Read, Isaac Tucker, Oliver Holden. Mason could not afford to alienate completely that portion of the public that clung somewhat stubbornly to its old-fashioned tastes.

One of the most curious features of Mason's musical arrangements

[4] Quoted by Rich, *Lowell Mason*, p. 12.

is the introduction of what might be called "ejaculatory codas." In his Preface to the *New Carmina Sacra,* Mason writes:

> The Codas added to many of the tunes form quite a new feature in a book of this kind, and it is hoped they may add interest to the performance of psalmody. Although they are called codas, yet they are not designed for the close, merely, but may be introduced before the first stanza, or between the stanzas of a hymn as may be appropriate. In the singing schools and choir meetings, they may be always sung, but in public worship the propriety of singing them must depend upon the circumstances of the occasion, hymn, &c. The hymns in which these Hallelujahs may with propriety be introduced, are more numerous than may at first be supposed; for under what circumstances does not the devout heart say, "Praise the Lord?"

Herewith is an example of Mason's "coda," showing only the rhythmic pattern:

Hal - le - lu - jah!
Hal - le - lu - jah!

Mason says that these "codas" constitute "quite a new feature" in collections of sacred music. That such ejaculations were not in themselves a new feature of hymn singing, will be apparent from the account of the beginning of revival hymnody given in Chapter 11. The interjection of "Hallelujah!" sometimes after each line, sometimes after each stanza, was a characteristic of popular hymnody. Sometimes the "Hallelujah" was inserted before the first stanza, which, as Mason suggests, may be done in his collection. Mason claimed this as a novelty which he hoped might "add interest to the performance of psalmody" (here this word is evidently used as synonymous with hymnody). Yet it was a practice that had been prevalent among certain sections of the populace for some fifty years before the publication of Mason's collection. Many examples of the "Hallelujah" refrain and its variants can be found in popular collections of hymns and "spiritual songs" printed before 1850. The evidence seems to indicate that Mason borrowed a feature from popular hymnody in the hope that it would add spice to his collection and perhaps also with the thought that it might keep his followers from straying into the camp of the revivalists. It would never do to let his competitors have a monopoly of the more obvious joys in hymn singing. Let it be noted, in passing, that one of Mason's most successful collections was called *The Hallelujah*.

Mason and the schools

Mason believed and preached that all school children should be taught to sing, just as they were taught to read. He advocated this policy as early as 1826, and after settling in Boston he directed a major portion of his activities toward the introduction and development of music teaching in the public schools of that city. The achievement of this goal was a long and difficult process because the idea was new and had to overcome both inertia and opposition. Finally, in 1838, the Boston School Committee authorized the introduction of music as a branch of instruction in the city schools. Lowell Mason was given charge of this musical instruction, becoming the first Superintendent of Music in an American public-school system. He continued in this post until 1845, when he was forced out by some political intrigue, though the official reason given was "the principle of rotation in office."

In 1851, referring to the Boston school program of music instruction, the first to be officially established in this country, Mason wrote:

> The result already is, that a multitude of young persons have been raised up who . . . are much better able to appreciate and to perform music than were their fathers; and experience proves that large classes of young persons, capable of reading music with much accuracy, may be easily gathered in almost any part of the New-England, or indeed of the United States.[5]

Moreover, Mason pointed out that an increasing number of persons who had received their first musical instruction in the public schools were devoting themselves to the profession of music, particularly as choral conductors, church musicians, and organists.

Mason stressed vocal instruction as the basis of the musical education in the schools. His course of instruction consisted of four main phases: (1) rote singing, (2) the song approach to note reading, (3) note reading, (4) part singing and choral singing. Mason's theory and practice of education were based on the methods of the Swiss reformer Pestalozzi, which in turn were influenced by the theories of Jean Jacques Rousseau. As Mason summed it up: "The teacher in pur-

[5] Mason, *An Address on Church Music*, p. 16.

suance of the right method, is guided by nature; he looks . . . to the intuitions, instincts, and opening faculties or active powers of his pupils. . . ." He stated that music "should be cultivated and taught . . . as a sure means of improving the affections, and of ennobling, purifying and elevating the whole man." Hence, he declared, "the chief value of music . . . in schools or families, will be social and moral." His method of music instruction is embodied in the *Manual of the Boston Academy of Music, for Instruction in the Elements of Vocal Music, on the System of Pestalozzi* (Boston, 1834), and in *The Pestalozzian Music Teacher* (New York, 1871).

Mason was also a pioneer in the teacher-training movement in America. In 1834 he established at the Boston Academy of Music an annual summer class for music teachers. Out of this was formed, in 1836, a Convention "for the discussion of questions relating to the general subject of Musical Education, Church Music, and Musical Performances. . . ." In 1840 the teachers organized themselves into a National Music Convention, which later was reorganized as the American Musical Convention. The idea of holding musical conventions spread rapidly to other cities throughout the country, and, in the words of A. L. Rich, "they were a power in American musical life and musical education," though "often dominated by commercial interests." The latter feature was perhaps inevitable, for music education in America was fast becoming "big business." Today the national music conventions are mammoth affairs involving many thousands of persons, many thousands of dollars, and an impressive array of commercial exhibits ranging from band instruments to television sets. All this has grown from the seeds sown by Lowell Mason.

Among the numerous collections of music compiled by Mason were: *Choral Harmony* (1830), *Spiritual Songs for Social Worship* (with Thomas Hastings, 1831), *Lyra Sacra* (1832), *The Choir; or Union Collection of Church Music* ("including many beautiful subjects from the works of Haydn, Mozart, Cherubini, Naumann, Marcello, Méhul, Himmel, Winter, Weber, Rossini, and other eminent composers, harmonized and arranged expressly for this work," 1832; seven more editions by 1839), *Manual of Christian Psalmody* (with David Greene, 1832), *Sacred Melodies* (with G. J. Webb, 1833), *Sabbath School Songs* (1833), *The Boston Academy's Collection of Church Music* (1835), *The Sacred Harp or Eclectic Harmony* (with Timothy Mason, 1835), *The Boston Academy's Collection of*

Choruses (1836), *The Odeon: a collection of secular melodies, arranged and harmonized for four voices* (with G. J. Webb, 1837), *The Boston Glee Book* (1838), *The Boston Anthem Book* (1839), *The Modern Psalmist* (1839), *Carmina Sacra* (1841; twelve more editions by 1860), *The Psaltery* (with G. J. Webb, 1845), *The Choralist* (1847), *The National Psalmist* (1848, with G. J. Webb), *Mason's Handbook of Psalmody* (1852), *The Hallelujah* (1854), *The People's Tune Book* (1860), *Carmina Sacra Enlarged: The American Tune Book* (1869).

This list, by no means complete, will serve to give an idea, not only of Mason's industry but also of the demand that existed in the United States for vocal music of every kind. When we bear in mind that Mason and his Boston associates, such as Webb (his chief collaborator in the work of the Boston Academy of Music), were not the only ones compiling and publishing collections of music for the American public, we begin to realize that the songbooks of the early American pioneers were producing an enormous progeny. And this, as we shall see later, is only part of the picture. In addition to the urban songbook production dominated by European importations and imitations, the rural and frontier songbook production flourished simultaneously and independently (it will be discussed fully in a later chapter).

As a composer, Lowell Mason wrote mostly hymns, anthems, and school songs. His best-known tune is the so-called "missionary" hymn, "From Greenland's Icy Mountains," written between 1824 and 1827, when Mason was a bank clerk in Savannah, where this hymn was first sung. Scarcely less familiar are the hymns "Nearer My God to Thee" and "My Faith Looks Up to Thee." He attempted some more ambitious anthems, without rising above mediocrity. It is not as a composer but as an organizer, a musical empire builder, that Lowell Mason claims our attention. He exerted a decisive and lasting influence on the course of musical activity in the United States. On the negative side, he was instrumental in thrusting the native American musical tradition, as represented by our early New England music makers, into the background, while opening the gates for a flood of colorless imitations of the "European masters." On the positive side, he brought systematic musical education into our public schools, raised the standards of choral performance, and paved the way for professional music schools. And he was the first American musician to make a fortune out of music. That in itself was no mean accomplishment. He believed in "scientific improvement," and he made progress pay.

Lowell Mason collected a large and valuable musical library, which after his death was presented by his family to Yale University. When the library of Professor Dehn of Berlin was placed on sale, Mason sent an agent to purchase it. According to Metcalf, "It is said that he was unable to read one of the books that were thus acquired, but he wanted them to add value to his growing collection." [6]

The eminent Dr. Hastings and others

Outdoing Lowell Mason in longevity, rivaling him in productivity, success, influence, and mediocrity, was his older contemporary and colleague Thomas Hastings (1784–1872). Metcalf, usually a reliable writer, credits Hastings with having written six hundred hymns, composed over one thousand hymn tunes, published fifty volumes of music, and "many articles on his favorite subject." Out of this huge production, what remains musically alive are about four hymn tunes, of which the most familiar is "Toplady," sung to the words, "Rock of Ages, cleft for me." Other tunes frequently used are "Ortonville," "Retreat," and "Zion."

Thomas Hastings was the son of a country physician and farmer of Washington, Connecticut. When he was twelve years old, the family moved to Clinton, New York, where at eighteen young Hastings became choir leader. In 1828 he settled in Utica, New York, where he edited a religious paper, *The Western Recorder*, in which he aired his musical opinions. From 1832 he was choirmaster at various churches in New York, including the Bleecker Street Presbyterian Church. In 1858, New York University conferred upon him the honorary degree of Doctor of Music. He died in New York City.

One of Hastings's most popular collections was *Musica Sacra*, first issued in 1816 and subsequently republished in numerous editions up to 1836. (For an account of the use of this publication in a Connecticut singing school, see Chapter 10.) Other collections were *The Juvenile Psalmody* (1827), *The Manhattan Collection* (1837), *The Sacred Lyre* (1840), *The Selah* (1856), and *The Songs of the Church* (1862). The *Mendelssohn Collection* of 1849—clearly indicating in its title the Europeanizing trend of the "better music" school—he edited

[6] Metcalf, *American Writers and Compilers of Sacred Music*, p. 215.

in collaboration with William B. Bradbury, the third member of this triumvirate of sacred music in the United States.

William Batchelder Bradbury turned out an average of more than two music books a year from 1841 to 1867. One of his most popular collections was *The Jubilee,* which sold over 250,000 copies. Another collection, *The Golden Chain* (1861), was so successful that it drew severe attacks from his competitors, who claimed that it was full of errors. Doctored up by Bradbury's friend Doctor Hastings, *The Golden Chain* went on selling and brought its compiler a golden harvest. It is estimated that over two million copies of Bradbury's music books were sold.

Bradbury was born in York, Maine, in 1816, and inherited his musical talent from his parents, who were good singers. As a young man he lived in the home of a Boston musician, Sumner Hill, from whom he received lessons in harmony. He entered the Boston Academy of Music, becoming associated with Webb and Lowell Mason. The latter recommended him to teach singing school in Machias, Maine, where James Lyon, the eighteenth-century American composer, had been active for twenty-three years. After a few years, Bradbury went to New York as church organist and choir leader. In 1847 he went to Europe, remaining two years in Germany, where he studied music at Leipzig. He was thus one of the first American musicians to study in Germany, a trend that was soon to become general.

Together with Lowell Mason, Thomas Hastings, and George F. Root, Bradbury taught in the recently established Normal Institutes—a scientifically improved version of the old singing schools—that were organized in the Northeastern states for the training of music teachers. Not satisfied with manufacturing music books, Bradbury entered the piano business with his brother, manufacturing and selling pianos and other musical supplies.

As a composer of hymns, Bradbury is remembered chiefly for "He Leadeth Me," and a Sunday-school song, "Sweet Hour of Prayer."

Another composer of this group who managed to study in Europe for a year was Isaac Baker Woodbury (1819–1858), a native of Beverly, Massachusetts. He began the study of music in Boston at the age of thirteen, learning to play the violin. After a sojourn in London and Paris, he taught music in Boston for six years and later traveled throughout New England with the Bay State Glee Club. He organized the New Hampshire and Vermont Musical Association and became its conductor. Later he went to New York as choirmaster and was also editor of the *New York Musical Review*. Plagued by ill-health, he went to Europe again, hoping to recuperate, and while there gathered music for publication in his magazine. In 1858 he left New York to spend the winter in the South and got as far as Columbia, South Carolina, where he fell mortally ill and died after three days, leaving a wife and six small children.

Among Woodbury's most successful collections were *The Dulcimer* (1850), *The Cytherea* (1854), and *The Lute of Zion* (1856). He also brought out *Woodbury's Self-Instructor in Musical Composition and Thorough Bass*, catering to the American appetite for self-instruction. It is interesting to note that he attempted to gain a following in the South by publishing two collections especially designed for Southern use, *The Harp of the South* (1853) and *The Casket* (1855), the latter sponsored by the Southern Baptist Society and published in Charleston, South Carolina. Woodbury's secular songs, extremely popular in their day, are now forgotten.

In the next chapter we shall discuss the music of another member of this group, George Frederick Root, compiler of *The Young Ladies' Choir* and other church collections, but whose reputation rests more firmly upon his secular songs.

chapter nine

The genteel tradition

I would ask if there are not words in the Anglo-Saxon language that can be associated so as to express what is, in the supreme affectation of fashionable parlance, termed "soirée musicale"?
JOHN HILL HEWITT, SHADOWS ON THE WALL (1877).

Nothing could be more elegant than to refer to a public concert as a *soirée musicale*. These two words were fragrant with the aristocratic aroma of a Paris salon, redolent of an elite society in which artistic celebrities mingled with the representatives of rank and wealth. They disguised the crude fact that the performing musicians were professional entertainers who hoped to make money from their public appearances. Could such a distinguished personage as the Baron Rudolph de Fleur, pianist to His Majesty the Emperor of Russia, be concerned with vulgar pecuniary considerations when, in the year 1839, he gave a recital that attracted the elite of New York society? Or could one place on a mere level of commercial entertainment the elegant series of *soirées musicales* given in New York on alternate Thursdays during February and March of the same year by the eminent maestro Charles Edward Horn and his accomplished wife? The programs offered by Mr. and Mrs. Horn featured vocal selections by the most celebrated European composers of the day, among whom Mr. Horn might be justified in including himself, for he had achieved some success both as composer and singer in England before coming to the United States in 1833, at the age of forty-seven. Moreover, some of these *soirées* were graced by the participation of two of the most successful English ballad composers and singers of that time, Mr. Joseph Knight and Mr. Henry Russell, both of whom were then intent upon elevating the musical taste of the American people.

These gentlemen were not alone in this endeavor. Two distinguished opera singers from England, Anna and Arthur Seguin, who had come to the United States in 1838, offered New York music lovers a series of ten recitals featuring selections from Italian opera. Those who favored this truly fashionable type of musical entertainment were also regaled with Italian operatic selections by such visiting artistes as Madame Albini, Madame Vellani, Signora Maroncelli, and Signor Rapetti.

About this time the Irish composer William Vincent Wallace, author of the opera *Maritana,* was also in New York. It was Wallace who, some years later, made a gallant musical offering to the ladies of America in the form of *Six Valses Elegantes*—six elegant waltzes for piano—further described and pictorially represented on the cover as a bouquet of "*Fleurs Musicales, Offertes aux Dames d'Amérique.*" The elegance of the French language, the exquisite gallantry of the gesture, the beautiful bouquet of flowers on the cover, the polite banality of the music—everything about this musical offering bespoke the influence of the genteel tradition that was being imposed like a veneer on American society.

To savor fully the tone and character of the genteel tradition, one should see the elaborately illustrated sheet-music editions published in the United States during the mid-portion of the nineteenth century, in which sentimental songs and elegant piano pieces are adorned with ornate covers depicting fashionable ladies in refined or poetic attitudes, in domestic or pastoral settings untouched by sordid reality. In 1868, William A. Pond & Co. of New York issued a piece titled *The Grecian Bend,* described as "The Latest Sensation in the Fashionable World." On the cover is shown a young lady of fashion, carrying a ridiculously small parasol and bending over in what is presumably an authentic demonstration of "the Grecian bend." Figuratively speaking, large sections of American society were engaged in doing the Grecian bend, preferably with a Parisian dip and an Italian twist.

The genteel tradition is characterized by the cult of the fashionable, the worship of the conventional, the emulation of the elegant, the cultivation of the trite and artificial, the indulgence of sentimentality, and the predominance of superficiality. Its musical manifestations are found chiefly in a flood of vocal literature that presumably drew tears or sobs from its original listeners or filled them with chills and thrills in its more dramatic moments, but that in the cold light of the twentieth century seem to us more silly than pathetic, more ludicrous than impressive. Nevertheless, we cannot afford to neglect these songs in the chronicle of America's music: some of them continue to appeal to the sentimental streak that is in all of us, and even those that are forgotten once appealed to millions of people and struck deep into the heart of our musical consciousness.

Henry Russell, who composed the music for "Woodman, Spare That Tree," tells an anecdote that is revealing in this respect. He writes:

> A very dear friend of mine, now well-known as a public man . . . has often told me that he dates the birth of his sentimental nature to the fact that an old nurse used to sing *Woodman, Spare That Tree,* at his bedside, and that scores of times as a child he cried himself to sleep over the simple song.

Well, this is not the worst of the sentimental ballads; but it is not really a "simple" song: it is an artificial song, a concocted song, inflated with a synthetic sentimentality; it does not have the genuine emotion, the organic vitality, the timeless and impersonal quality of, for example, the old folk ballads. There is no point in comparing unlike elements, and this contrast is made simply to emphasize the vitiating effect of pseudosimple, artificially sentimental songs in forming adult musical tastes through childhood experiences.

During the nineteenth century the people of the United States as a whole were in this state of aesthetic immaturity. Hence the success of any music that made a blatant appeal to the feelings of the listeners, and the success of musical performers who stressed the elements of exhibitionism and showmanship, like the pianist who played while balancing a glass of water on his head. Aesthetic appreciation—that is, the quality that permits an artistic experience to be received and enjoyed as such—was almost entirely lacking. People were continually crossing the line that separates art from reality; indeed, most of them were not aware that such a dividing line existed. Henry Russell, in his memoirs, tells several anecdotes regarding the reactions of his listeners that illustrate this attitude. One of them concerns the song "Woodman, Spare That Tree," with which Russell never failed to work on the emotions of his audience. One night when he had sung this number at a concert, a dignified gentleman in the audience stood up, and in a very excited voice called out, "Was the tree spared, sir?"

To which Russell replied, "It was." With a sigh of heartfelt relief, the man said: "Thank God for that."

Because he spent nine years in the United States, because he was a shrewd and sympathetic observer of the American scene—"I doubt whether I am not a little more than half American in thought and sentiment," he wrote of himself—because he exerted considerable influence on American musical taste, and because he is such a typical representative of the genteel tradition, Henry Russell deserves more than casual mention in these pages. He began his musical career as a boy singer in England, then went to Italy for further study at Bologna and Milan, becoming acquainted there with Rossini, Donizetti, and Bellini. From Bellini he received some lessons in composition and orchestration. He then went to Paris, where he met Meyerbeer and other celebrities. He thus received the double accolade of Italy and Paris, indispensable for admission to the ranks of fashionable gentility.

Back in England, Russell found no immediate means of turning his fashionable assets into concrete financial returns. He decided to try his fortune in a less crowded portion of the world. Going first to Canada, he was disappointed in that dominion's potentiality for cultural exploitation. A friend persuaded him to visit Rochester, New York, whither he traveled by cart. In Rochester he was offered the position of organist and choirmaster at the Presbyterian church, which he accepted. And it was in Rochester that he began his career as a composer of songs.

According to Russell's own account, "the orator Clay was the direct cause of my taking to the composition of descriptive songs." It seems that Henry Clay delivered a speech in Rochester and made a deep impression on Russell by the musical quality of his voice. "Why," Russell asked himself, "if Henry Clay could create such an impression by his distinct enunciation of every word, should it not be possible for me to make music the vehicle of grand thoughts and noble sentiments, to speak to the world through the power of poetry and song!" Why not, indeed! Then and there Henry Russell set to music a poem by his friend Charles Mackay, "Wind of the Winter Night, Whence Comest Thou?" In the composer's own words, which have a vaguely familiar ring, "Success followed success." The songs "which leapt quickest into popularity" were "Woodman, Spare That Tree," "A Life on the Ocean Wave," "The Gambler's Wife," and "The Maniac."

When Russell went on to New York, he met there his old London friends, the Seguins, and the composer Vincent Wallace. Uniting their forces, they gave "six concerts at New York, Brooklyn, Jersey City, and several other towns in the United States." This proves that even at that time Brooklyn was avid for culture. These concerts, according to Russell, "proved an immense success, both financially and artistically." Thereafter Russell at various times toured all over the United States, singing his own songs and accompanying himself on the piano. Dwight called him a "charlatan" but this did not interfere with his success. After all, Dwight had only five hundred readers for his *Journal*, whereas the songs of Henry Russell sold in the hundreds of thousands.

But it was not through the sale of his songs that Russell made money. As he wrote in his memoirs:

> I have composed and published in my life over eight hundred songs, but it was by singing these songs and not by the sale of the copyrights that I made money. There was no such thing as a royalty in those days, and when a song was sold it was sold outright. My songs brought me an average price of ten shillings each . . . though they have made the fortune of several publishers. Had it not been that I sang my songs myself . . . the payment for their composition would have meant simple starvation.[1]

This bears out my theory that the only way Stephen Foster could have been assured of a lucrative living would have been to appear in public as the interpreter of his own songs, if he could have trained his voice sufficiently for that purpose. Later we shall see that Russell's contemporary, John H. Hewitt, most popular American ballad composer of this period, also found it impossible to make money from his songs and turned to various other occupations for a living.

One of Russell's most dramatic songs was "The Ship on Fire," text by Charles Mackay. It has an elaborate piano accompaniment, full of runs, tremolos, octaves, and arpeggios. The piano begins with a two-page introduction, opening quietly, sweeping up and down in a tremendous run in sixths, crescendo, followed by tremolo chords and crashing octaves. Then the voice enters, *Quasi ad lib: ma Largamento:*

> The storm o'er the ocean flew furious and fast,
> And the waves rose in foam at the voice of the blast,
> And heavily labour'd the gale-beaten Ship. . . .

[1] Russell, *Cheer! Boys, Cheer!*, p. 198.

After further description of the ship, the poet paints this pathetic picture:

> A young mother knelt in the cabin below,
> And pressing her babe to her bosom of snow,
> She pray'd to her God 'mid the hurricane wild,
> Oh Father have mercy, look down on my child.

The storm passes away and terror is succeeded by joy; the mother sings a sweet song to her babe as she rocks it to rest; the husband sits beside her, and they dream of the cottage where they will live when their roaming is finished.

> Ah, gently the ship glided over the sea. . . .

(here the music fades to a pianissimo cadence). But now thunderous octaves strike an ominous warning of impending disaster. "Hark! what was that—Hark, hark to the shout,—FIRE!" The young wife is shaken with terror:

> She flew to her husband, she clung to his side,
> Oh there was her refuge what e'er might betide.

Fire! Fire! Raging above and below. The smoke, in thick wreaths, mounts higher and higher (furious octave runs in the piano accompaniment, fortissimo). There's no remedy save to lower the boat.

> Cold, cold was the night as they drifted away,
> And mistily dawn'd o'er the pathway the day.

Then suddenly, oh joy!

> Ho, a sail, ho! a sail! cried the man on the lee.

The chords of the accompaniment take on a solemn and joyous grandiosity. "Thank God, thank God, we're sav'd."

This is the genteel tradition's equivalent of purging the spirit through pity and terror, running the gamut from bombast to bathos. There are eleven pages to this opus—far too much to quote in full. And it is the sort of thing one has to enjoy *in toto* or not at all (there *are* ways of enjoying such a masterpiece of banality). The reader whose curiosity has been irresistibly whetted by the above résumé may find the complete song, music and words, in the collection titled

Songs of Yesterday, edited by Jordan and Kessler (see bibliography for this chapter).

It is a curious fact, and one that needs to be considered in appraising the "social significance" of the vocal literature of this period, that Henry Russell did not regard himself solely as an artist or an entertainer, but also as a social reformer. Toward the end of his life Russell wrote: "Slavery was one of the evils I helped to abolish through the medium of my songs." Developing this theme, he goes on to give himself credit for promoting other social reforms:

> When I commenced my Anti-Slavery Crusade, I did not stop at seeking to relieve the distresses of the unfortunate coloured race, but, to a certain extent, I happened to forestall the good work that is being done by "The Early Closing Association," by the publication of a song, written in the interests of the overworked shop assistants, and entitled: TIME IS A BLESSING. . . . The private lunatic asylum, another sore in our social system, was attacked . . . by my song, "The Maniac," which was written with the object of exposing the horrors of the iniquitous system.

One may be permitted to wonder whether "The Maniac" was not actually composed for the purpose of making an effect on paying audiences rather than in the interests of social reform. Nevertheless, the fact remains that the espousal of "Causes" was characteristic of this period, and that the trend is amply illustrated in the song literature, as well as in the writings and activities of leading singers, such as Russell and the Hutchinson Family, whom we shall meet presently. In addition to Abolition, a favorite cause was Temperance. Russell did his bit for this cause with his song "Let's Be Gay," which begins:

> Let's be gay, let's be gay, let's be gay, boys,
> We'll quaff, we'll quaff from this cup, ha, ha!

And ends with this anticlimax, followed by two solid lines of "ha, ha" that must indeed have rung out gaily around the flowing bowl:

> But let the draught, but let the draught, be water, water!

Perhaps the most astonishing aspect of Henry Russell's connection with American music is his claim to have composed virtually all of the most popular Negro minstrel or blackface "Ethiopian" songs, from

"Coal Black Rose" to "Old Dan Tucker." No less surprising is his account of the manner in which he composed these songs:

> One hot summer afternoon, when I was playing the organ at the Presbyterian Church, Rochester, I made a discovery. It was that sacred music played quickly makes the best kind of secular music. It was quite by accident that playing the "Old Hundredth" very fast, I produced the air of "get out o' de way, Old Dan Tucker." This was the first of a good many minstrel songs that I composed or rather adopted, from hymn tunes played quickly. Among them are "Lucy Long," "Ober de Mountain" and "Buffalo Girls." . . . Afterwards, when giving my entertainments about the country, I would occasionally illustrate this principle to my audiences by playing slowly and pathetically the "Vesper Hymn," and then repeat it, gradually quickening the time till it became a humerous plantation song, "Oh! take your time, Miss Lucy," or "Coal Black Rose." [2]

Although Russell's claim to these songs cannot be substantiated, his description of the "speed up" method of producing popular tunes out of hymns has fascinating implications. He seems to be describing a sort of rudimentary method for "jazzing the classics"; although this actually requires more than a speed-up in tempo. A few off-beat accents and syncopations would help to produce the desired effect. The reader might find it instructive and amusing to put Russell's formula to the test.

In New York, Henry Russell formed a friendship with a man who played an important role in the genteel tradition. This was George Pope Morris (1802–1864), journalist and poet, founder of the *New York Mirror and Ladies' Literary Gazette*, to which the leading contributors were William Cullen Bryant, Nathaniel Parker Willis, Fitz-Greene Halleck, and Morris himself. A contemporary satirist referred to Morris as,

> A household poet, whose domestic muse
> Is soft as milk, and sage as Mother Goose.

It was Morris who wrote the text of the first published song of Stephen Foster, "Open Thy Lattice, Love." He wrote the words of "Woodman, Spare That Tree" and of "On the Lake, Where Droop'd

[2] Russell, *Cheer! Boys, Cheer!*, p. 68.

the Willow," the latter set to music by his friend Charles Edward Horn, who simply lifted the tune from a popular minstrel song, "Long Time Ago." This is the first stanza of Morris's poem, with the melody as arranged by Horn:

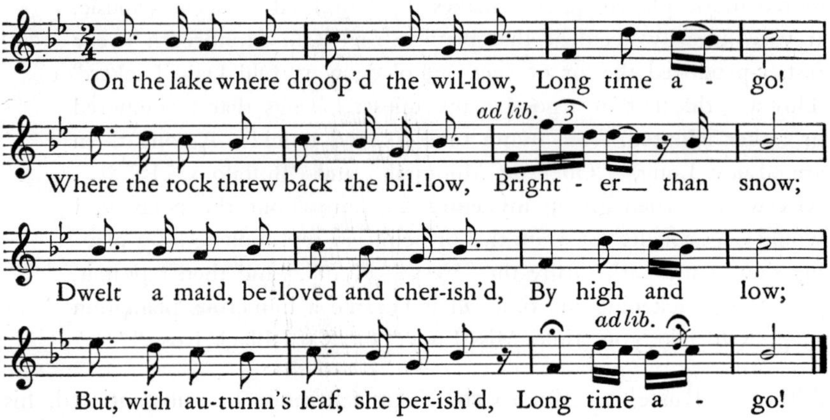
On the lake where droop'd the wil-low, Long time a - go!
ad lib.
3
Where the rock threw back the bil-low, Bright - er— than snow;
Dwelt a maid, be-loved and cher-ish'd, By high and low;
ad lib.
But, with au-tumn's leaf, she per-ish'd, Long time a - go!

In later editions the title was changed to "Near the Lake," perhaps to counteract the impression that the heroine was a mermaid or a water sprite. This song, completely typical of the genteel tradition, enjoyed a great vogue in its time.

Morris wrote the libretto of an opera in three acts, *The Maid of Saxony*, which was set to music by C. E. Horn and in 1842 had a run of about two weeks in New York City. Charles Edward Horn (1786–1849), the son of a German musician who had settled in London, was active in New York from 1833 to 1843. After four years in England he went to Boston as conductor of the Handel and Haydn Society, and died in that city. Together with two other foreign-born musicians, Henry Christian Timm (1811–1892) and William Scharfenberg (1819–1895), and the "Connecticut Yankee" Ureli Corelli Hill (1802–1875), Horn participated in the founding of the New York Philharmonic Society in 1842. He also established a music-publishing business. As a composer he is interesting to us chiefly for his attempts to inject local color into his musical settings of a cycle of poems by G. P. Morris, published collectively as *National Melodies of America.* Besides "On the Lake" the series included a song called "Meeta," "adapted from a negro air," and "Northern Refrain," based on the "carol of the sweeps of the city of New York."

The singing Hutchinsons

It was not only in New York that the year 1839 proved eventful in the annals of American music. On Thanksgiving Day of that year, in the town of Milford, New Hampshire, the eleven sons and two daughters of the Hutchinson family ("the tribe of Jesse") gave a vocal concert in the Baptist meetinghouse. The building was packed with sympathetic listeners who applauded the program of hymns, anthems, and glees. The Hutchinsons felt that they had started something with their first public concert. And they were right. They gave another concert in Lynn and then decided that they needed more scope. Said John Hutchinson to his brothers, "We need more discipline and more culture." So they went to Boston in search of culture. Instinct or foreknowledge guided them straight to the fountainhead of musical culture in the City of Culture: the office of Professor Lowell Mason. Humbly they requested his advice. The eminent musical magnate gave them impeccable advice: he recommended that they acquire and use his latest singing book.

The Hutchinson brothers (only four of them had gone to Boston) thereupon betook themselves to that other eminent apostle of musical culture in Boston, Professor George James Webb, president of the Handel and Haydn Society, composer of such genteel ballads as "Art Thou Happy, Lovely Lady?" "I'll Meet Thee, Sweet Maid," "When I Seek my Pillow," and of the tune used as a setting for the hymn "Stand Up, Stand Up for Jesus." Professor Webb received the Hutchinson brothers most courteously—and invited them to join the Handel and Haydn Society.

At this point the New Hampshire lads probably decided that what they really needed was less culture and more discipline. Renting a room, they settled down to systematic practice. John Hutchinson spent his last dollar to acquire a copy of Henry Russell's cantata, "The Maniac." It was an investment that paid off, for they made a tremendous hit with this number on their concert tours, singing it even more effectively than Russell himself. John was the star performer in this number. While his brothers played a prelude on the violin and the cello, John would sit in a chair behind them, raising the hair on his head with the fingers of each hand. Then he would rise, suitably disheveled, "with the expression of vacancy inseparable from mania," and proceed with the gruesome performance, to the horror and delight of the audience. We shall spare the reader further details of this excruciating opus, though it might still be good for a few laughs.

By 1843, after several successful concerts in Boston and elsewhere, the Hutchinsons were able to have several of the songs in their repertoire published by Oliver Ditson of Boston. These were "The Snow Storm," "Jamie's on the Stormy Sea," "The Grave of Bonaparte," and a temperance song, "King Alcohol." The music for the first of these songs was written by Lyman Heath, a composer and singer of Nashua, New Hampshire; the words by Seba Smith. "The Snow Storm," with its pathetic portrayal of a young mother struggling through the snow drifts, carrying her little babe, is indeed a classic of the genteel tradition.

Armed with a New England reputation and such sure-fire numbers as the above, the Singing Hutchinsons ventured to New York in May, 1843. They were delighted with the metropolis on the Hudson. In his diary Asa Hutchinson wrote:

> O! New York is all that I have had it represented to be; Boston does not compare with it for life and business. The Splendid Street "Broad Way" is the most splendid street that I ever saw, and then the Grand Park, and the splendid water works where the water is thrown into the air to the height of 25 or 30 feet and then falls into the Pool again in the most majestic style.

At their concert in the Broadway Tabernacle, the Hutchinsons were introduced by the celebrated Dr. Lyman Beecher. They sang four of their favorite numbers: "King Alcohol," "We Are Happy and Free," "We Have Come From the Mountains," and their theme song, "The Old Granite State," for which they used the tune of that rousing revival song, "The Old Churchyard." The program was announced as one that had pleased "fashionable audiences in Boston." Though they were country boys themselves, the Hutchinsons aspired to receive the accolade of fashion and of gentility, and they succeeded. In New York they met George P. Morris, who became "their dear friend" and several of whose poems they set to music and featured in their programs. Among these was "My Mother's Bible," thoroughly typical of the Morris output:

This book is all that's left me now,
Tears will unbidden start;
With faltering lip and throbbing brow,
I press it to my heart.

Through Morris, the Hutchinsons met Henry Russell, who said to them: "I think you are the best singers in America." With such friends and admirers, the New Hampshire lads—and their sister Abby, who formed part of the concert group—were definitely established in the genteel tradition. Russell's song "The Gambler's Wife" gave Abby Hutchinson a chance to shine as soloist and wring tears from the audience with her description of the poor, lonely, deserted wife.

The Hutchinsons made a four-part vocal setting of Longfellow's "Excelsior" and then called on the poet to request a few words of explanation of the poem's meaning, which they might append to the sheet music. The poet obligingly complied, and the Hutchinsons had another feather in their cap as well as another successful number in their repertoire. This musical setting of "Excelsior," too long to quote here, will be found in the collection *Songs of Yesterday*.

In 1845 the Singing Hutchinsons made a tour of England and Ireland. Returning to America, they toured widely in this country, not only entertaining large audiences but also espousing such causes as Temperance, Women's Suffrage, and especially Abolition, to which they were enthusiastically devoted. It would be plausible to claim that the Hutchinsons were concerned with bringing music to ordinary people, to "the masses" rather than "the classes," and that therefore they did not really represent the genteel tradition. My view is that they allied themselves with the genteel tradition as far as repertoire is concerned and in their desire to obtain the approval of fashionable urban audiences. Compared with the repertoire of Italian opera, that appealed only to the initiated or the snobbish, their programs were popular and designed for mass appeal. They therefore represented what might be called the "left wing" of the genteel tradition, approaching the popular tradition while retaining the prestige of elegance and refinement associated with such names as Morris and Longfellow and with the accolade of urban culture acquired in Boston and New York. They had, it is true, some humorous songs in their repertoire; but these avoided vulgarity. To the raucous banjo and bones of minstrelsy they opposed the gentle tones of the violin and violoncello, and in dress and manner they emulated a discreet and genteel respectability.

There were numerous other singing families in America, of which the most prominent, after the Hutchinsons, were the Bakers of New Hampshire. Their repertoire included such numbers as "The Happiest Time Is Now," "Where Can the Soul Find Rest?" "The Inebriate's Lament," and "The Burman Lover," all composed by the leader of the group, John C. Baker.

Poet and composer

When Edgar Allan Poe formulated his famous dictum that the most poetic subject was the death of a beautiful young woman, he voiced an aesthetic principle that was a fundamental tenet of the genteel tradition. The maid who dwelt on the lake, or near the lake, and who perish'd with the autumn's leaf, was first cousin to Poe's rare and radiant maiden whom the angels named Lenore. To the same family, and more popular though not so *distinguée*, belonged sweet Lilly Dale, immortalized in verse and music by H. S. Thompson, in a song copyrighted in 1852, which in turn inspired many other musical mementos for the departed maiden, including Sigmund Thalberg's *Lilly Dale, Air Américain varié pour le Piano*—one of the numerous variations on favorite airs with which pianists of that period regaled the public. In Thompson's song the vocal solo is followed by a chorus for four mixed voices.

Poe himself, notwithstanding his superior genius, exhibited at times a surprising indulgence toward the productions of the genteel tradition. Many are the now forgotten female poets upon whom he bestowed flattering praise. Of George Pope Morris's poems, "Woodman, Spare That Tree" and "Near the Lake," he wrote in the *Southern Literary Messenger* (April, 1849) that they were "compositions of which any poet, living or dead, might justly be proud."

While composers such as Henry Russell and Charles E. Horn turned to successful poetasters such as Morris and Mackay for the texts of their songs, the American musician John Hill Hewitt (1801–1890) enjoyed the advantage, if such it was, of being both poet and composer. His accomplishments as a poet, in fact, gained him quite a reputation in his day. In 1833 Hewitt submitted his poem "The

Song of the Wind" in a poetry contest sponsored by the publisher of the Baltimore *Saturday Visitor*, of which Hewitt himself was at that time editor. Among the contestants was Edgar Allan Poe, whose poem "The Coliseum" vied for the first prize with Hewitt's entry. The prize for the best short story, under the same sponsorship, had just been awarded to Poe's *A Manuscript Found in a Bottle*. According to Hewitt, the judges hesitated to bestow the poetry prize upon the author who had also carried off the honors, and the cash, for prose. Hence the first prize for poetry—fifty dollars in cash—was awarded to Hewitt. "This decision," wrote Hewitt, "did not please Poe, hence the 'little unpleasantness' between us."

Poetry and journalism were, together with music, the chief but not the only activities to which John H. Hewitt turned in his varied career. He was a son of the English musician James Hewitt who had emigrated to America in 1792 and had become a prominent leader in the musical life of New York and Boston. John was born in New York, but in 1812 the family moved to Boston, where he attended public school. Hewitt *père* did not favor a musical career for his son. After leaving school the boy was apprenticed to a sign painter, an arrangement not at all to his liking. He ran away and led an adventurous existence for the next few years. In 1818 he received an appointment to the military academy at West Point. During his four years there he studied music with the band leader, and when he was not permitted to graduate with his class because of deficiency in his studies, he decided to take up a musical career.

Joining a theatrical troupe directed by his father, young Hewitt traveled to the South and soon found himself stranded in Augusta, Georgia, when the company failed. He spent the ensuing years in Georgia and South Carolina, reading for the law, publishing a newspaper, and also composing and teaching music. His first song, "The Minstrel's Return from the War," was written at this period and proved widely successful; but as it was not copyrighted, it brought him no money. He fared somewhat better, financially, with his next song, "The Knight of the Raven Black Plume."

The death of his father in 1827 brought Hewitt north to Boston, but a year later he was in Baltimore, which he regarded henceforth as his home city, though he continued to be rather restless. In Baltimore he was active as editor and publisher, and for a time was a political supporter of Henry Clay in Washington. In 1861 he was living in Richmond, and at the outbreak of the Civil War offered his services to the Confederacy. He was assigned the dreary task of drilling recruits. Two years later he was active in Augusta as manager of a theater troupe for which he wrote or adapted numerous plays and operettas. His song "All Quiet Along the Potomac To-Night" was one of the hit tunes of the Civil War.

In the 1870s Hewitt returned to Baltimore and remained there till his death at an advanced age. He had been twice married. By his first wife he had seven children, and four by his second. He composed over three hundred songs, which earned him the title of "Father of the American Ballad," a considerable number of stage works with music, and some oratorios, of which the best known is *Jephtha*, performed in New York, Washington, Baltimore, and Norfolk. In spite of the wide popularity of his songs, Hewitt found that music as a profession did not pay. "The publisher pockets all," he wrote, "and gets rich on the brains of the poor fool who is chasing that *ignis fatuus*, reputation." In his volume of recollections, *Shadows on the Wall*, he summed up his attitude toward music:

> Music has always been, and still is, my frailty. Since my earliest youth I have sought its gentle influence . . . and it finally became my profession, though my parents were solicitous that I should adopt any other honorable calling but that. I studied it as an art and a science; but only for the sake of the accomplishment, never thinking that I should use it as the means of support. . . . Whenever I failed in any enterprise I fell back on music; it was my sheet-anchor.[3]

It is curious that Hewitt's father, a musician himself, should not have wished his son to adopt music as a profession. But his mother, the elder Hewitt's second wife, was the daughter of Sir John King of the British Army, and it is probable that social prejudice, as well as economic motives, may have been behind their desire to have their son adopt "any other honorable calling" but music. Hewitt himself was resentful of being regarded as a professional musician. When he was invited to the homes of wealthy or prominent persons, he wished to be received as an equal, to converse on intellectual or political matters like the other gentlemen, and not to be kept in reserve as an entertainer when the company requested some music. Although he was an outstanding representative of the genteel tradition, he resented

[3] Hewitt, *Shadows on the Wall*, pp. 65–66.

and ridiculed the mania for foreign fashions that was a hallmark of that tradition. He particularly detested the affectation which caused people in society to admire, or pretend to admire, Italian vocal music. His resentment may have been due in large part to his dislike of the foreign musicians—Italian, French, and German—who were becoming increasingly prominent in the musical life of the United States, and whose success hindered the acceptance of native-born musicians like himself. It may be conceded that Hewitt was not an important composer, but he was certainly a representative figure in this transitional period of America's music.

Some Civil War songs

George Frederick Root (1825–1895) was so many-sided in his musical activities that his work might well be distributed among several chapters. He was associated with Mason, Webb, and Bradbury in the "better music" movement radiating from Boston, and wrote hymns that were suitably sentimental, such as "The Shining Shore" ("My days are gliding swiftly by"). Born in Sheffield, Massachusetts, he had from childhood the ambition to be a musician. In Boston he became a pupil of Benjamin Franklin Baker and later assisted Lowell Mason at the Academy of Music. Around 1845 he went to New York, assuming the position of music teacher at Abbot's Institute for Young Ladies. In 1850 a trip to Europe for further musical study gave him the foreign finish needed to uphold the genteel tradition with distinction. Three years later he collaborated with Mason in organizing the Normal Institute for music teachers in New York. One of the interesting aspects of Root's career, however, is that he did not remain in the cultural strongholds of the East, but followed the westward trend of expansion. His brother had opened a music store in Chicago with C. M. Cady as partner, under the firm name of Root & Cady, which became an important publishing house. Root joined his brother in 1859, making Chicago his headquarters henceforth. The business was ruined by the fire of 1871, but recovered rapidly. In 1872 Root attained to the peak of eminent respectability by receiving the degree of Doctor of Music from the University of Chicago.

Root definitely belongs to the genteel tradition through his sentimental ballads. The words for some of these were written by his former pupil, the blind poetess Fanny Crosby, who provided the verses for "Hazel Dell," "There's Music in the Air," and "Rosalie the Prairie Flower." Rosalie proved to be a popular girl, bringing the composer $3,000 in royalties. During the Civil War, Root turned out some of the most successful songs associated with that struggle: "Just Before the Battle, Mother," "The Vacant Chair," "The Battle Cry of Freedom," and "Tramp! Tramp! Tramp!" or "The Prisoner's Hope." It was through these war songs that Root achieved his most lasting reputation. "The Battle Cry of Freedom" was included in the repertoire of the Hutchinson Family and stirred audiences throughout the Northern states. Root also composed several cantatas that are now forgotten.

Henry Clay Work (1832–1884) is best known for his Civil War songs—"Kingdom Coming," "Babylon is Falling," "Marching Through Georgia"—and he was also associated with American minstrelsy through such songs as "We're Coming, Sister Mary" (which he sold to E. P. Christy) and "Wake, Nicodemus," which many people know without being aware that Work composed it. Work was a native of Connecticut but spent part of his boyhood in Illinois, where his father, an ardent abolitionist, had migrated. In 1845 the family returned to Connecticut. At the age of twenty-three, Work, who had learned the printer's trade, went to Chicago and combined the occupations of printer and composer. Like his father, he was an active abolitionist. He also championed the cause of temperance and produced that classic of temperance songs, "Come Home, Father." Work belongs to the genteel tradition through such songs as "The Lost Letter," "The Ship that Never Returned," "Phantom Footsteps," and "Grandfather's Clock."

Expansion and transition

The period that marked the rise of the genteel tradition was also the period of westward expansion. Though most of the songs associated with the genteel tradition deal with romantic or sentimental subjects, there was also a certain type of song written by "armchair pioneers"—musicians and writers who lived comfortably in large cities while turning out jolly songs urging the delights of life on the ocean waves or the allurements of existence on the wild open prairie. Henry Russell actually prided himself on having promoted the westward movement of population through some of his songs. An American song of this type was written and composed by Ossian E. Dodge, voicing the theme of "manifest destiny." The song is titled "Ho, Westward, Ho!" and lauds the virtues of the West as a glorious source of health and wealth.[4] The refrain, "Ho, Westward, Ho!" occurs after each line, following a familiar pattern of revival songs and of Negro work songs, such as the one quoted in Chapter 13, with the refrain, "Ho, meleety, ho!" The song continues for six stanzas, lauding the virtues of the West as a glorious source of health and wealth.

It seems to me that we can get a rather good perspective on musical life in the United States during this era of transition and expansion by listening to the conversation of two foreign musicians, each of whom had contrasting experiences in this country in the antebellum period. One of these musicians is our friend Henry Russell, the other is the Norwegian violinist Ole Bull (1810–1880), who made five visits to America, the first in 1843, and who eventually married an American woman. The scene is New Orleans, and the conversation is reported by Russell in his autobiography. The English musician had gone to pay a professional visit of courtesy to his Norwegian colleague.

B.–I have heard a great deal of you, Mr. Russell,–I am glad to see you; pray sit down. You have been some considerable time in this country; how do you like it?

R.–Very much, but I fear the reception accorded to you has not been worthy of your great talent.

B.–I regret to say that is so. I have encountered, since I have been there nothing but jealousy and rivalry, with but little sympathy from those I most expected it from.

R.–You must not lose sight of the fact that, until the beginning of this century, musical culture was a thing practically unknown outside such towns as New York, Philadelphia, and Boston. It is only now the denizens of the smaller towns are beginning to take an interest in things musical, therefore do not be downhearted. I need hardly say that those people who know anything whatever of music, are charmed with your exquisite playing. Tell me, sir, how do you like New Orleans?

B.–Not a great deal. The people here prefer the nigger's violin to mine. I have travelled from New York to play to people who do not understand me.

[4] This song will be found in *Songs of Yesterday*, edited by Jordan and Kessler.

R.–Yes, the generality of the nation are young in scientific music; their idea of fine music consists of simple song. My dear Mr. Bull, you must have patience. It is only time and perseverance that will teach the uneducated to appreciate your marvellous performance.[5]

Henry Russell was right; in time America would learn to appreciate the playing not only of Ole Bull, but of every other visiting virtuoso with a foreign accent and a European reputation. The Age of Innocence, the Era of Simple Song, would soon be over. Enter then the Age of Scientific Music, the Triumph of Progress, the Era of Big Business. But before we reach those dizzy heights of progress and appreciation, of standardized production and mass consumption, there are other phases of the Era of Simple Song to be explored.

[5] Russell, *op. cit.*, pp. 146–148.

chapter ten

The fasola folk

'Ask for the old paths and walk therein.'

BENJAMIN FRANKLIN WHITE, PREFACE TO 1869 EDITION OF THE SACRED HARP.

In the year 1848 a certain Miss Augusta Brown wrote an article which appeared in *The Musician and Intelligencer* of Cincinnati. Pointing to the musical superiority of Europe, Miss Brown voiced her opinion as to the causes of America's inferiority in this field:

> The most mortifying feature and grand cause of the low estate of scientific music among us, is the presence of common Yankee singing schools, so called. We of course can have no allusion to the educated professors of vocal music, from New England, but to the genuine Yankee singing masters, who profess to make an accomplished amateur in one month, and a regular professor of music (not in seven years, but) in one quarter, and at the expense, to the initiated person, usually one dollar. Hundreds of country idlers, too lazy or too stupid for farmers or mechanics, "go to singing school for a spell," get diplomas from others scarcely better qualified than themselves, and then with their brethren, the far famed "Yankee Peddlars," itinerate to all parts of the land, to corrupt the taste and pervert the judgment of the unfortunate people who, for want of better, have to put up with them.

This outburst of snobbishness, so typical of the genteel tradition, not only confirms the widespread influence and popularity of the singing schools but also reveals the radiating influence of New England's pioneer folk tradition throughout the expanding frontier country. The "genuine Yankee singing masters" were keeping alive throughout the land the spirit of old Bill Billings of Boston. After 1800 many singing-school teachers and compilers of songbooks sprang up in the South and in what was then the West: Kentucky and Tennessee and the valley of the Mississippi. This chapter is the story of these frontier singing folk, their songbooks, and their tunes, which are so vital a part of America's music.

In the eighteenth century the singing school was an urban as well as a rural institution. It was patronized by city idlers as well as country idlers, by ladies and gentlemen as well as country yokels. This is made clear in an advertisement that appeared in the *Pennsylvania Gazette* of 1760:

> Notice is hereby given that the Singing-School, lately kept in the Rooms over Mr. William's School in Second Street [Philadelphia], will again be opened on Monday Evening, the 3d of November next, at the same Place; where the ART OF PSALMODY will be taught, as usual, in the best Manner, on Monday and Friday Evenings, from Six to Eight. And that, if any Number of Ladies and Gentlemen incline to make up an exclusive Set, to Sing on two other Nights, they may be gratified by making Application in time.

So that, if Miss Augusta Brown had lived a couple of generations earlier, she might have joined a singing school in Boston or Philadelphia in the company of an exclusive Set of Ladies and Gentlemen. But under the impact of the "progressive improvement" described in the previous chapter, the singing schools, considered old-fashioned and backward because they refused to adopt the latest European musical fashions, were driven out from the cities to the hinterlands, and the vast new territories opened up for musical cultivation by the expanding frontier. For a while the singing schools lingered as an anachronism in small towns of New England. The most complete description of a singing school in the genuine Yankee tradition was written by the Rev. E. Wentworth in his old age, referring to a period sixty years earlier, probably around 1820, when he attended his first singing school as a lad. His account contains so many curious details that it is worth quoting almost in full:

> Time, sixty years ago; place, south-eastern Connecticut; locality, a suburban school-house; *personelle*, the choir of a Congregational church, and two dozen young aspirants, thirsting for musical knowledge; teacher, a peripatetic Faw-sol-law-sol, who went from town to town during the winter months, holding two schools a week in each place; wages, two dollars a night and board for himself and horse, distributed from house to house among his patrons, according to hospitality or ability; instrument, none but pitch-pipe or tuning-fork; qualifications of teacher, a knowledge of plain psalmody,

ability to lead an old style "set piece" or anthem, a light, sweet, tenor voice, and a winning manner. . . .

For beginners, the first ordeal was trial of voice. The master made the circuit of the room, and sounded a note or two for each separate neophyte to imitate. The youth who failed in ability to "sound the notes" was banished to the back benches to play listener, and go home with the girls when school was out. The book put into our hands was Thomas Hastings' *Musica Sacra,* published in Utica in 1819, in shape like a modern hymnal. There were four pages of elements and two hundred tunes, half of them written in three parts, wanting the alto or confounding it with the tenor. The elements were given out as a lesson to be memorized, studied by question and answer for a couple of evenings or so, and then we were supposed to be initiated into all the mysteries of staff, signature, clef, flats, sharps, and naturals, notes, rests, scales, and, above all, ability to find the place of the "mi." Only four notes were in use—faw, sol, law, mi; and the scale ran faw, sol, law, faw, sol, law, mi, faw. The table for the "mi" had to be recited as glibly as the catechism, and was about as intelligible as some of its theology:—

> The natural place for mi is B;
> If B be flat, the mi is in E;
> If B and E, the mi is in A and C;
> If F be sharp, the mi is in G;
> If F and C, the mi is in C and C.

The Continental scale, do, re, mi, had not yet been imported. The key-note was called the "pitch," and preliminary to singing, even in church, was taking the key from the leader, and sounding the "pitch" of the respective parts, bass, tenor, and treble, in the notes of the common chord. A few simple elements mastered, or supposed to be, the school plunged at once into the heart of the book, and began to psalmodize by note in the second week of the brief term. . . .

The rest of the winter's work comprehended "Barby," "St. Ann's," "St. Martin's," "Colchester," "Portugal," "Tallis," "Winchester," "Shirland," "Silver Street," "Easter Hymn," "Amsterdam," and many others now forgotten. The favorite fugues [i.e., fuguing tunes] of the preceding century had passed out of fashion, and the leading church airs of this were not yet. A few anthems of the simpler sort we tackled, such as "Denmark," "Dying Christian," and "Lord of all Power and Might." . . . That, reader, was sixty years ago. Germany and Italy have since been transported to America, and, musically, we live in a new earth and a new heaven. Yet the simple strains of those days were as perfectly adapted to those who made them as Wagner, Liszt, Mendelssohn, and Chopin are to us today! [1]

What a tremendous segment of America's musical history is enclosed in that passage! The last stand of a popular musical institution against the rising tide of urban domination, the lingering anachronism of the fa-sol-la system of solmization, brought to America by the early English colonists; the falling out of fashion of the fuguing tunes in the urbanized communities of the Eastern seaboard; the oblivion into which many of the old hymns fell among educated music lovers brought up on the latest European importations, "Germany and Italy . . . transported to America." But this shows only one half of the picture. For Reverend Wentworth and other educated city dwellers, the old order may have passed away, but it was not dead. It may have been thrust out of sight and hearing by "progressive improvement," but it was thriving and flourishing, and becoming more American all the time, under the influence of the frontier and of the rural South, where folks preferred to go their own way rather than to take up newfangled notions and "scientific" innovations.

Take, for example, the fa-sol-la system, mentioned by Reverend Wentworth as not yet having been superseded by the imported Continental do-re-mi scale. If the fa-sol-la system was good enough for the first American settlers, it was good enough for the rural singing-school teachers and singing folk of the South and West. So they kept the four-syllable solmization, used it in their singing schools, singing conventions, and songbooks, for generation after generation, even to the present day. That is why we call them the "fasola folk," for the old-time syllables are a symbol of the unchanging folkways of a large body of rural singers who have kept alive the tunes and the traditions of the American pioneers.

Along with the fa-sol-la system, the rural singing folk clung to another device that was considered backward and unprogressive by the advocates of scientific improvement. This was the device of having each of the four notes represented by a character of different shape. In an earlier chapter we mentioned this shape-note system as it was used by Andrew Law in his *Musical Primer* (1803). Law claimed this as a "new plan of printing music," but there is evidence that two singing-school teachers named William Little and William Smith

[1] From Curwen, *Studies in Music Worship*, pp. 115ff.

anticipated the system in a work titled *The Easy Instructor*. There is extant a copyright entry for this book dated 1798, which indicates possible publication at Philadelphia in that year; but the earliest known edition was apparently published at New York in 1802.[2] Little and Smith used the same shape characters as Law, though they arranged them in a different order. Fa (or *faw*) is represented by a right-angled triangle, sol by a circle or round note, la (*law*) by a square, and mi by a diamond, each with a stem appended to it, thus:

In their system, Smith and Little retained the staff lines, which Law had eliminated. Perhaps this was one of the factors that caused singing teachers and compilers in the South and West to adopt the system of Smith and Little rather than that of Law.

In the 1830s Timothy Mason, brother of Lowell Mason, went to Cincinnati and prepared for publication a work called *The Ohio Sacred Harp*. The Masons attempted to do away with the fasola singing and the shape notes (also called "patent" or "buckwheat" notes), and wrote a preface to the above collection in which they attacked the use of these old-fashioned methods. "By pursuing the common method of only *four* syllables," they wrote, "singers are almost always superficial. It is therefore recommended to all who wish to be thorough, to pursue the system of seven syllables, disregarding the different forms of the notes." Perhaps they would have been more successful in their campaign if they had used the homely argument of William Walker, when the latter decided to switch to the seven-character system in 1866: "Would any parent having seven children, ever think of calling them by only four names?" As it was, the publishers of *The Ohio Sacred Harp* were the first to disregard the Masons' advice, for they issued the collection with shape notes, explaining that this was done "under the belief that it will prove much more acceptable to a majority of singers in the West and South."

Thus the two sets of syllables, fa-sol-la and do-re-mi, came to represent two conflicting cultural trends. The do-re-mi system, with

[2] See the bibliographical study by Frank J. Metcalf, "The Easy Instructor," in *The Musical Quarterly*, XXIII (1937), 89–97. Further research on this subject has been done by Allen P. Britton of the University of Michigan.

all that it implied in the way of "scientific improvement," was victorious in the cities and those areas, chiefly of the Eastern seaboard, dominated by urban culture. But the fasola folk held their own in the hinterland.

Fasola leaders and songbooks

The main path of the singing-school movement appears to have been from New England to Pennsylvania, thence southward and westward. Frédéric Ritter, writing of Andrew Law in his book *Music in America*, says: "He did good pioneer work in the New England States and in the South." Since this statement is unconfirmed by documentary evidence, the extent of Law's activity and influence in the South must remain a matter of conjecture. There was, however, another advocate of the shape-note system, a New Englander by the name of John Wyeth (1770–1858), who settled in Harrisburg, Pennsylvania, and who published there in 1810 a collection titled *Repository of Sacred Music*, which went through seven editions up to 1834 and had an extremely wide circulation for those times. In this collection, Wyeth used the shape-note system of Little and Smith.

John Wyeth was born in Cambridge, Massachusetts, learned the printer's trade, and at twenty-one went to Santo Domingo to superintend a printing establishment in that island, from which he was soon afterward driven away by the Negro insurrection, escaping with great difficulty and danger, disguised as a sailor. He reached Philadelphia, worked there as a printer, and in 1792 moved to Harrisburg, where he purchased a newspaper, established a bookstore and a publishing house. President Washington appointed him postmaster of Harrisburg in 1793. The hymn tune "Nettleton" ("Come, Thou Fount of Every Blessing") is attributed to Wyeth.

The *Repository of Sacred Music* contains numerous pieces by the early New England composers, such as Billings, Holyoke, Read, and Swan, whose music was falling into neglect in the North but was to continue flourishing in the songbooks and singing conventions of the South and West. In 1813 Wyeth issued a supplement to the *Repository*, as Part II, intended particularly for Methodists, which includes the hymn "Come, Thou Fount of Every Blessing" followed by the refrain, "Hallelujah, Hallelujah, We are on our journey home." This is a typical camp-meeting chorus, of which more will be said in the next chapter.

Here it is necessary to emphasize the importance of Wyeth's *Repository of Sacred Music, Part Second,* as a primary source of American folk hymnody. It was intended especially for use at revivals and camp meetings and, as such, contained a large proportion of tunes that may properly be classified as "folk hymns," that is, basically "a secular folk tune which happens to be sung to a religious text." [3] Most of the southern tune-book compilers of the early nineteenth century, beginning with Ananias Davisson, borrowed extensively from *Part Second* of Wyeth's collection (which in spite of the misleading title, was entirely different in character from the original *Repository of Sacred Music*).

According to Irving Lowens, the "musical brains" behind Wyeth's influential tunebook was the Rev. Elkanah Kelsay Dare (1782–1826), author of a theoretical work on music (which seems never to have been published: Wyeth quotes from it as a "Manuscript work"), who is named as the composer of thirteen tunes in this collection. Reverend Dare must therefore take his place as one of the initiators of the important Southern folk-hymn movement.

The next singing book in the four-shape system was compiled by Ananias Davisson of Virginia around 1815, and thereafter we find the chief concentration of the fasola movement in the South. Virginia, North and South Carolina, Kentucky, Tennessee, Alabama, and Georgia, were the homegrounds of several generations of rural singing-school teachers and songbook compilers who carried on the tradition of the native New England pioneers. Let us make the acquaintance of some of these fasola leaders.

Not much is known of Ananias Davisson (1780–1857), except that he was an elder of the Presbyterian Church, that he was active in northwestern Virginia, and that he acquired "a practical knowledge as a teacher of sacred Music." His *Kentucky Harmony* was copyrighted in 1817, but there is evidence that it may have been in circulation a couple of years earlier. This collection contains 144 tunes in four-part harmony, the parts being bass, tenor, counter, and treble. In his instructions on singing, Davisson writes: "The bass stave is assigned to the gravest voices of men, and the tenor to the highest. The counter to the lowest voices of the Ladies, and the treble to the highest of Ladies' voices." What this means is that the principal melody

[3] The definition is by Irving Lowens, who has done extensive research in the history of early American vocal music and has in preparation a definitive work on the subject. (See the bibliography for this chapter.)

or "air" was carried by high male voices in the tenor part, while the women sang subordinate parts. This practice of having men sing the melody was another heritage from colonial times and was opposed to the "improved" urban practice of having the women sing the melody in the soprano. The custom of the tenor melody continued to prevail in the fasola tradition, although it should be pointed out that the arrangers of these tunes tried to make each voice melodically interesting and independent. Their conception of voice-leading was "horizontal" rather than "vertical": they aimed at real part singing rather than at harmonized melody.

The reader must not suppose, however, that the voice-leading and the resultant harmonies were "correct" according to the academic tradition. On the contrary, the violation of conventional "rules" was so persistent, and generally so consistent, as to constitute a well-defined style. In the first place, it should be pointed out that in the most authentic fasola tradition the vocal settings were for three voices rather than four. Although Davisson arranged his tunes for four voices in the *Kentucky Harmony*, many other tune books, including the *Harp of Columbia*, the *Southern Harmony*, the *Missouri Harmony*, and the *Sacred Harp*, employed the more characteristic three-part arrangement (with the "tune" in the middle part). Charles Seeger, who has made the most thorough study of the contrapuntal style of these three-voiced shape-note hymns, found that they systematically violated most of the established rules, such as those forbidding parallel fifths, octaves, and unisons; parallel fourths between outer voices or between upper voices without a third in the bass; unprepared and unresolved dissonances; and crossing of voices.[4] It is not *because* the rules are violated that this type of authentic American music is interesting to us, but rather because, in seeking their own style of expression, these early composers created a kind of choral writing that has a "rigorous, spare, disciplined beauty" of its own. And it is also interesting to observe that a similar rigorous and spare quality, avoiding harmonic lushness and padding, has characterized some of the most significant "new" music of our own times. It is no wonder that modern composers like Cowell and Thomson have drawn inspiration from the texture and the spirit of the American folk hymns. But let us return now to Ananias Davisson and his companions of the shape-note tradition.

In compiling the *Kentucky Harmony*, Davisson drew on the col-

[4] For musical examples of the three-voiced shape-note style, see the article by Charles Seeger listed in the bibliography for this chapter.

lections of Billings, Holyoke, Andrew Adgate, Smith and Little, Wyeth, and others. Among the New England composers represented are Billings, Justin Morgan, and Timothy Swan. Fifteen tunes were claimed as his own by Davisson. Of these, the best-known is "Idumea," a pentatonic melody, used with a text by Charles Wesley:

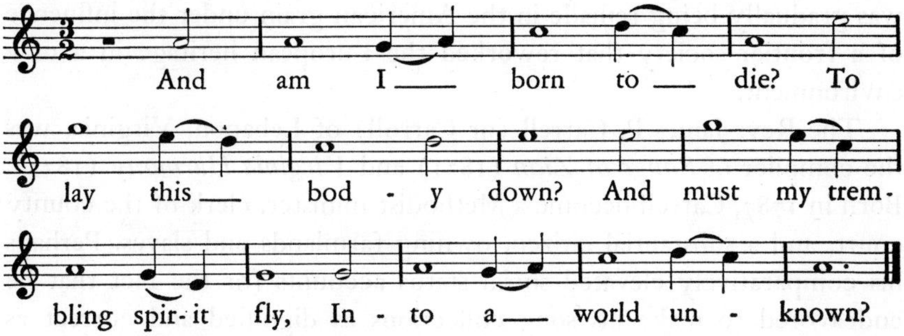
And am I — born to — die? To
lay this — bod - y down? And must my trembling spir-it fly, In - to a — world un - known?

In 1820 Davisson brought out the *Supplement to the Kentucky Harmony*, proudly placing after his name the initials A. K. H.—"Author of Kentucky Harmony." Davisson claimed authorship of eleven tunes in this collection, besides six written in collaboration with others. It is difficult to say with certainty whether any of the tunes in these collections were actually composed by the musicians whose names are affixed to them. In some cases the compilers frankly acknowledged that they had merely harmonized or arranged the tunes, and therefore considered them as their own. In other cases they expressly state that some of the tunes were taken from oral tradition. And in some instances the same tune was claimed by several different "composers." The whole question of individual authorship is not of prime importance in the fasola singing-school tradition. These poorly educated rural musicians were not composers in any professional sense of the term. They inherited a large body of traditional music, derived mainly from the British Isles. This, together with the techniques and rules of the early New England music teachers and compilers, was their musical stock-in-trade. Sometimes they took over these tunes in their natural state; sometimes they altered them, or constructed new tunes with the same melodic elements. They were craftsmen rather than creators. The tradition was more important than the individual.

Whatever hand Davisson may have had, therefore, in the composition of the twenty-six tunes that he claimed as his own, the real significance of his work lies in his having compiled and published two extensive collections that served as a reservoir of American rural hymnody, upon which later compilers drew freely. Through his work we can observe the beginnings of a widespread regional movement in America's music, the true homespun music of the American people. Certainly, if we look only at the notes of this music, at its metrical and modal patterns, we find that it is of British or Celtic origin. But it was gradually being remade in the American grain under the influence of a frontier society that reworked the European heritage in a new environment.

The Rev. James P. Carrell (or Carroll) of Lebanon, Virginia, was the compiler of *Songs of Zion* (1821) and *Virginia Harmony* (1831). Born in 1787, Carrell become a Methodist minister, clerk of the county court, and a substantial citizen, owning farmlands and slaves. Perhaps his comparatively elevated social status accounts for the fact that he endeavored to make his song collections as dignified and correct as possible. The preface of the *Virginia Harmony* states that the editors "have passed by many of the light airs to be found in several of the recent publications . . . and have confined themselves to the plain psalmody of the most eminent composers." This means, for example, that he snubbed his colleague Ananias Davisson, using only two of the latter's tunes. It is curious to observe these nuances of caste and decorum in the popular tradition. Lowell Mason would have looked down his nose at Carrell as a rustic singing teacher, but Carrell in turn deprecated the "light airs" composed or arranged by his less dignified associates. Yet Carrell was entirely loyal to the fasola system itself, extolling in his *Rudiments* the advantages of the four-shape notes, which he calls "patent" notes, "on account of their author's having obtained a patent for the invention."

Carrell affixed his name as composer to seventeen tunes in the *Virginia Harmony*. In spite of his ministerial dignity, he was very close to the folk tradition in his music. This is demonstrated, for instance, in his "Dying Penitent," a characteristic specimen of the American religious ballad stemming directly from British folk music:

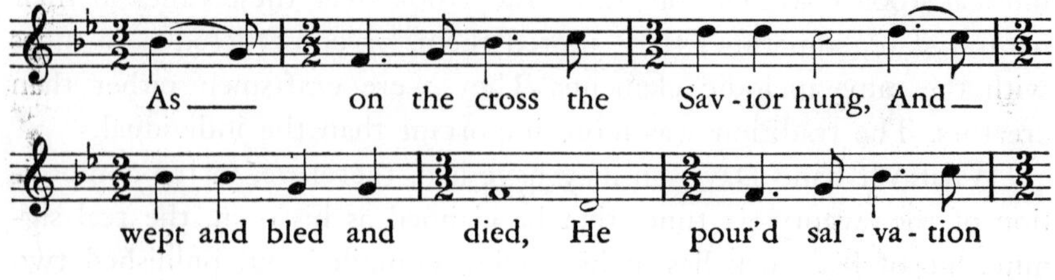

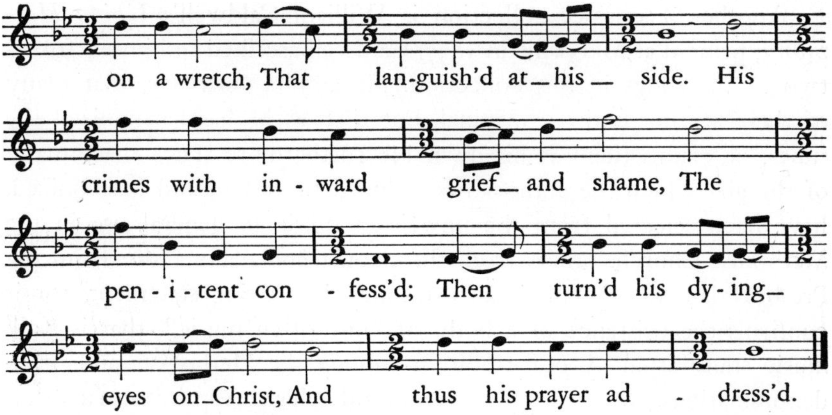
on a wretch, That lan-guish'd at his side. His
crimes with in - ward grief and shame, The
pen - i - tent con - fess'd; Then turn'd his dy - ing
eyes on Christ, And thus his prayer ad - dress'd.

Eight other religious songs signed by Carrell were reprinted in later collections by other compilers, indicating that he continued to enjoy some regional reputation as a composer. Carrell died in 1854.

In 1825 William Moore, of Wilson County, Tennessee, brought out his *Columbian Harmony*, printed in Cincinnati. In his "General Observations" Moore gives some rather amusing admonitions to singers: "Nothing is more disgusting in singers than affected quirks and ostentatious parade, endeavoring to overpower other voices by the strength of their own, or officiously assisting other parts while theirs is silent." Much of his material is taken from Ananias Davisson, thirteen of whose songs are included in Moore's collection.

Moore himself claimed authorship of eighteen songs in the *Columbian Harmony*. One of these songs, "Sweet Rivers," is interesting as containing one of the early examples of the "crossing over Jordan" theme that is so frequent in American folk hymnody. The tune also is typical of this tradition.

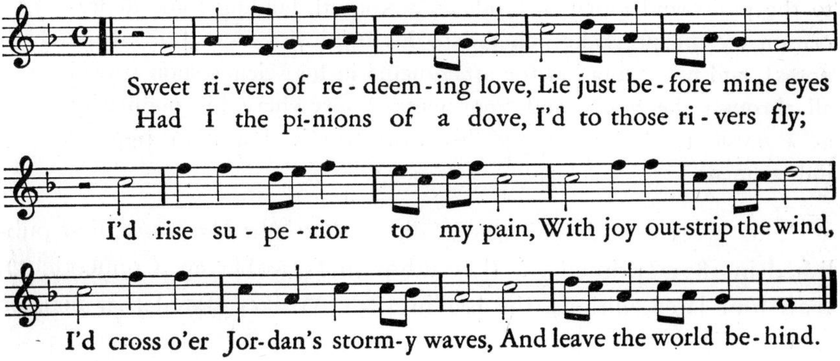
Sweet ri - vers of re - deem - ing love, Lie just be - fore mine eyes
Had I the pi-nions of a dove, I'd to those ri - vers fly;
I'd rise su - pe - rior to my pain, With joy out-strip the wind,
I'd cross o'er Jor-dan's storm-y waves, And leave the world be - hind.

Another Tennessee collection is William Caldwell's *Union Harmony*, printed at Maryville in 1837. Caldwell ascribed to himself forty-two of the songs in this collection. He admits, however, that many of these are not entirely original, but that, as he has harmonized the tunes, he claims them as his own. He furthermore states that "many of the airs which the authors has reduced to system and harmonized, have been selected from the unwritten music in general use in the Methodist Church, others from the Baptist and many more from the Presbyterian taste." This is an extremely interesting statement, for it confirms the existence of a body of "unwritten music"—that is, folk music transmitted by oral tradition—among the Methodists and other denominations, and through William Caldwell's enterprise actual specimens of this early American folk music have been preserved on the printed page.

"A wonderful book"

Passing over John B. Jackson's *Knoxville Harmony*, printed at Madisonville, Tennessee, in 1838, we turn to a book of exceptional interest and importance: William Walker's *Southern Harmony*. "Singin' Billy" Walker, as he was familiarly called, was the son of poor parents who settled in Spartanburg, South Carolina, when he was eighteen years old (he was born in 1809). He received only a rudimentary education, but early in life was filled with the ambition "to perfect the vocal modes of praise." According to a quaint account in Landrum's *History of Spartanburg County* (Atlanta, 1900):

> From the deep minstrels of his own bosom he gathered and arranged into meter and melody a wonderful book suitably adapted to the praise and glory of God. . . . Notwithstanding some depreciation by the press, he adhered to his original system [i.e., shape notes], and his reputation for attainments in his science soon spread all through the South and Southwest. Everywhere his popularity as a music teacher went and his work received a most popular indorsement.

The "wonderful book" was Walker's *Southern Harmony*, first published in 1835 (printed for the author in New Haven, Connecticut), with four later editions, the last in 1854. Walker stated that 600,000 copies of *Southern Harmony* were sold. In the 1930s Walker's book was still being used by fasola singers in Benton, Kentucky—eighty years after the publication of the last edition!

The original edition of *Southern Harmony* contained 209 songs, of which twenty-five were claimed by Walker as composer. In later editions he ascribed other songs to himself, making a total of forty songs to which he claimed authorship. Before me is a reproduction of the 1854 edition of *Southern Harmony*, which carries us right into the heart of the fasola singing movement. The title page is worth reproducing in full, for in itself it tells us much about this aspect of America's musical culture:

THE
SOUTHERN HARMONY, AND MUSICAL COMPANION:
CONTAINING A CHOICE COLLECTION OF
TUNES, HYMNS, PSALMS, ODES, AND ANTHEMS:
SELECTED FROM THE MOST EMINENT AUTHORS IN THE UNITED STATES:
TOGETHER WITH
NEARLY ONE HUNDRED NEW TUNES, WHICH HAVE NEVER BEFORE BEEN PUBLISHED:

SUITED TO MOST OF THE METRES CONTAINED IN WATTS'S HYMNS AND PSALMS, MERCER'S CLUSTER, DOSSEY'S CHOICE, DOVER SELECTION, METHODIST HYMN BOOK, AND BAPTIST HARMONY:
And Well Adapted To
CHRISTIAN CHURCHES OF EVERY DENOMINATION, SINGING SCHOOLS, AND PRIVATE SOCIETIES: ALSO, AN EASY INTRODUCTION TO THE GROUNDS OF MUSIC, THE RUDIMENTS OF MUSIC, AND PLAIN RULES FOR BEGINNERS

BY WILLIAM WALKER

Sing unto God, ye kingdoms of the earth; O sing praises unto the Lord.—DAVID
Speaking to yourselves in psalms, and hymns, and spiritual songs and making melody in your hearts to the Lord.—PAUL

NEW EDITION, THOROUGHLY REVISED AND MUCH ENLARGED
PHILADELPHIA:
PUBLISHED BY E. W. MILLER, 1102 and 1104 SANSOM STREET
and for sale by
J. B. LIPPINCOTT & CO., AND BOOKSELLERS, GENERALLY, THROUGHOUT THE UNITED STATES

Outwardly, this title page, which is typical of other shape-note collections, is not much different from the title pages of collections published by Lowell Mason and his associates. And, in effect, we actually find in Walker's collection a tune "arranged from Handel," taken from Mason's *Carmina Sacra,* as well as a few tunes by Mason himself. Just as we find in Mason's collections a few tunes by the old New England pioneer school. The urban and the rural traditions had certain points of contact, but the *emphasis* was entirely different. What was occasional and peripheral in one was predominant in the other. The fasola books gave much place to fuguing pieces, to pentatonic and other "gapped scale" melodies of folk character, and to revival "spiritual songs" used at camp meetings. In spite of an occasional bow to progress and elegance, folk hymns, religious ballads, revival spirituals, and fuguing pieces formed the bulk of the fasola repertory.

Another important collection is the *Sacred Harp* (1844), compiled by B. F. White and E. J. King, both active in Georgia. Not much is known of King, but Benjamin Franklin White (1800–1879) was one of the most prominent figures in the fasola movement. White was born in Spartanburg, South Carolina, the youngest of fourteen children. He attended school for a few months only, but inherited a musical inclination from his father. Like most of these singing-school teachers, he was self-taught in music. Around 1840, White moved to Harris County, Georgia, where he published a newspaper called *The Organ,* in which many of his sacred songs first appeared. He was also clerk of the superior court of Harris County. The teaching of singing he considered his life's work, but, says his biographer Joe James, "he never used his talent as a musician to make money." He gave instruction free to those who could not afford to pay for it, and lodged many of his pupils in his home without charge. "He was gentle in his nature, lovable in disposition and treated everyone with universal kindness." In religious matters he was remarkably liberal, for while himself a Missionary Baptist, he worshipped also in the churches of other denominations: the Primitive Baptist, Presbyterian, Lutheran, Methodist, Christian, etc. He had fourteen children, of whom nine lived to adulthood. Several of them carried on the family's musical tradition.

White became president of the Southern Musical Convention, organized in 1845, which, together with the Chattahoochee Musical Convention, founded in 1852, was the chief center of *Sacred Harp* activity and influence. These conventions brought fasola singers together for annual "singings" lasting several days—a custom still kept up in some sections of the Deep South, notably Georgia, Alabama, and Texas. The *Sacred Harp* has had the longest continuous history of any of the shape-note singing books, for in various editions and revisions, it has been in print and in use from 1844 to the present day (1954). Revised editions appeared in 1850, 1859, 1869, 1911, and 1936 (Denson Revision).

The Rev. William Hauser, M.D.—he was doctor, preacher, editor, teacher, composer, and singer—was one of the most remarkable figures in the Southern fasola movement, and indeed in all the annals of American music. Born in Forsyth County, North Carolina, in 1812, the youngest son of eleven children, he lost his father when he was two years old, and his mother was able to provide him with only a meager education. But Hauser had a strong thirst for knowledge, plus the determination and perseverance to acquire it. Joining the Methodist Church in 1827, he was licensed to preach seven years later. He then traveled a circuit for two years, "preaching, praying, and singing wherever he went." In 1837 he married, and in 1839 went to Emory and Henry College, Virginia, to study Greek and Latin. In 1841 he settled in Richmond County, Georgia, where he taught school and began the study of medicine, which he commenced to practice in 1843, becoming a highly successful and respected member of the profession. He was appointed professor of physiology and pathology in the Oglethorpe Medical College, Savannah (1859–1860) and was assistant editor of the *Oglethorpe Medical Journal.*

It is interesting to note that Hauser was of Moravian stock, his grandfather, Martin Hauser, having emigrated to North Carolina about the year 1750. As we mentioned in an earlier chapter, the Moravians gave exceptional importance to music not only in their religious observances but also in their community life. It will be recalled also that Winston-Salem, North Carolina, was the center of a Moravian settlement in that state.

Such was the man, versatile, hard-working, practical, with a genius for self-improvement and a strong, simple, religious faith, who in 1848 brought out the work that has been called "the rural South's biggest and best song book," the *Hesperian Harp,* printed in Philadelphia, filled with over 550 pages of music ranging from "standard" hymns of urban or European provenience to pure folk melodies recorded from oral tradition. Hauser's name stands as composer of thirty-six songs in this colossal collection, and as arranger of numerous others. Well represented are his Southern colleagues: Ananias Davisson, William Walker, and William Caldwell.

As a "composer" William Hauser was very close to the folk tradition. Let this pentatonic tune, "Hope Hull," taken from Hauser's *Hesperian Harp,* serve to confirm the foregoing statement:

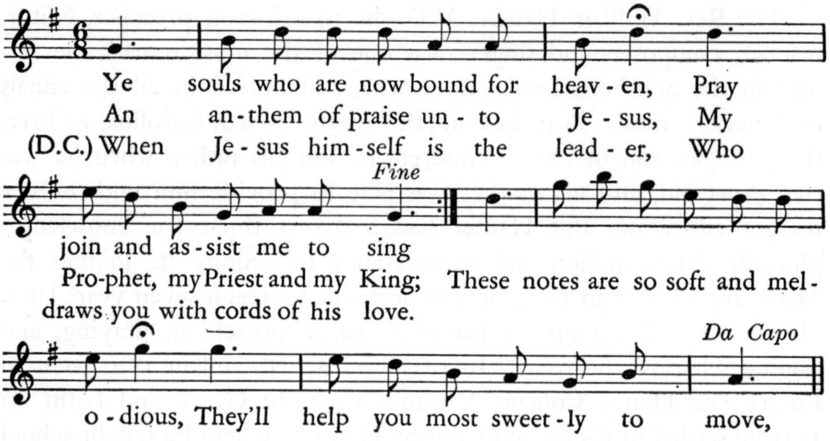
Ye souls who are now bound for heav - en, Pray
An an-them of praise un - to Je - sus, My
(D.C.) When Je - sus him - self is the lead - er, Who
Fine
join and as - sist me to sing
Pro-phet, my Priest and my King; These notes are so soft and mel -
draws you with cords of his love.
Da Capo
o - dious, They'll help you most sweet - ly to move,

Like their New England predecessors, these Southern singing leaders and music makers were practical, hard-working men, taking a full part in the tasks and the affairs of daily life, closely identified with the people for whom they made their music. John Gordon McCurry (1821–1886), of Hart County, Georgia, was a farmer and a tailor as well as a singing-school teacher. He was also a Missionary Baptist and a Royal Arch Mason. He compiled the *Social Harp* (Philadelphia, 1859), which is exceptionally rich in songs of indigenous flavor, including "revival spirituals" (which will be discussed in a later chapter). Forty-nine songs in this collection were claimed by McCurry as composer. One of these is "John Adkins' Farewell," typical of the religious or moral ballad in which a repentant wrongdoer bids other people to take warning by his example and avoid the pitfalls of sin and crime. John Adkins, it seems, was a drunkard who killed his wife and was hanged for it. This is his farewell message, which consists of nine doleful stanzas, culminating in a final plea for the mercy "That pardons poor drunkards, and crowns them above."

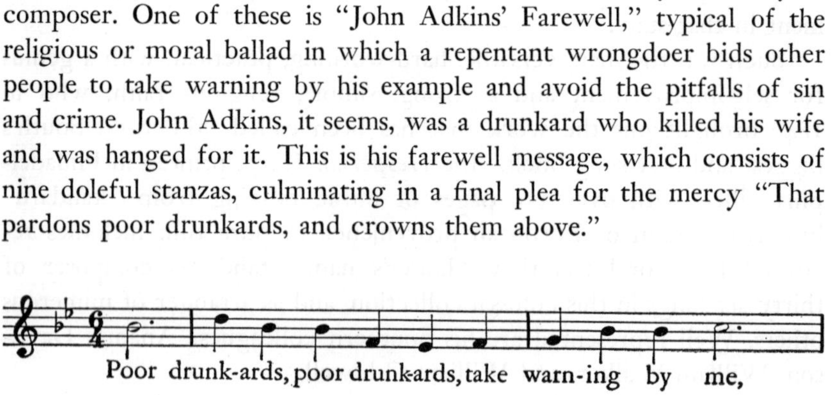
Poor drunk-ards, poor drunkards, take warn-ing by me,

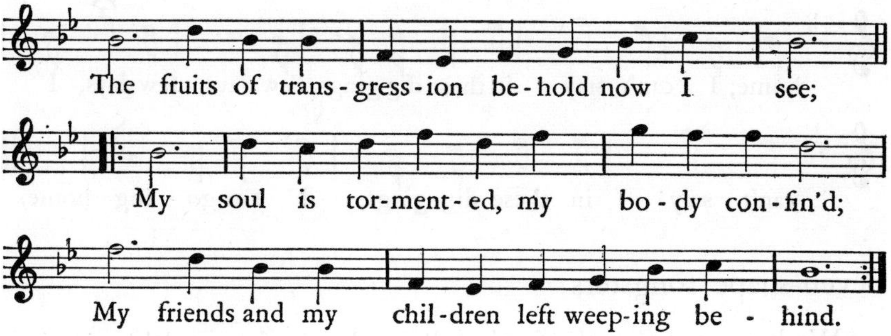
The fruits of trans - gress - ion be - hold now I see;
My soul is tor - ment - ed, my bo - dy con - fin'd;
My friends and my chil - dren left weep - ing be - hind.

Dr. George Pullen Jackson has pointed out that this tune is identical with that of the folk song "When Boys Go A-Courting," recorded in the Appalachians by Cecil Sharp. There is a Negro version of the tune adapted to the ballad of the fabulous race horse "Noble Skewball."

As a "composer" McCurry was partial to lively tunes. Among the songs which he ascribed to himself, many will be found of the kind that was anathema to the "better music" boys. Thoroughly typical of this trend is the camp-meeting song "Few Days," with its syncopations that savor more of minstrelsy than of hymnody. As a matter of fact, a song embodying the same idea ("I am going home") and the identical refrain, appeared in the *Negro Singer's Own Book* (1846), though without any tune. A variant of McCurry's tune and text, with the interpolation of two lines about Jonah and the whale, has been recorded among the mountain whites of Tennessee sometime in the 1920s. It is clear, therefore, that this song, like many others of its kind, has had a long life in America's music; how long, we cannot exactly tell, for it may have existed in oral tradition before McCurry caught it up and put his name to it. A song with such a history, and so characteristic of the American popular tradition, deserves quotation. Here is "Few Days," from McCurry's *Social Harp,* dated 1855:

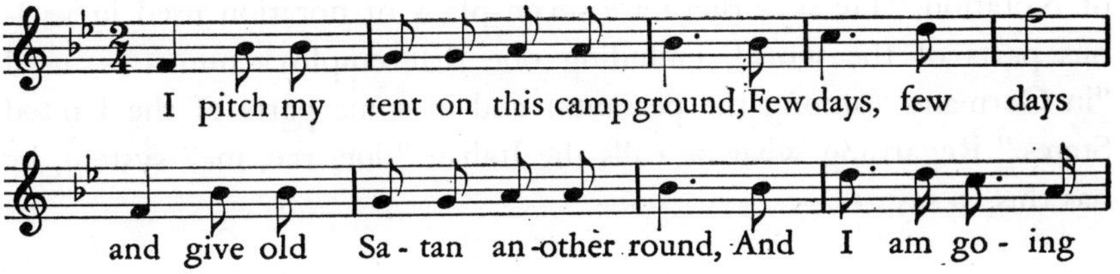
I pitch my tent on this camp ground, Few days, few days
and give old Sa - tan an - other round, And I am go - ing

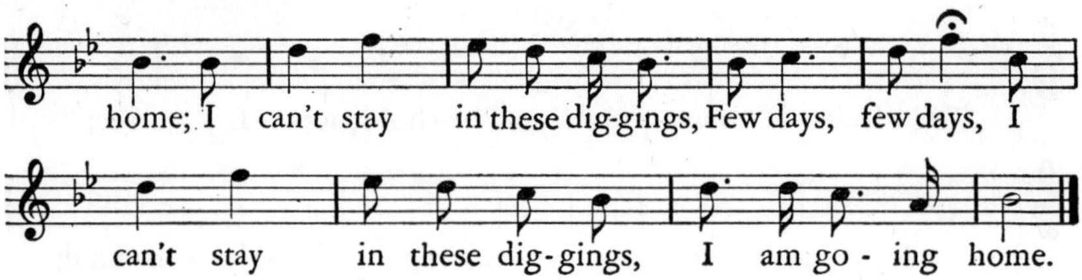
home; I can't stay in these dig-gings, Few days, few days, I
can't stay in these dig-gings, I am go - ing home.

Seven-shape songsters

We have seen that the fasola folk used only four syllables in singing the notes of the scale: fa-sol-la-fa-sol-la-mi. We also remarked that the newer European system of solmization, using a different syllable for each note (do-re-mi-fa-sol-la-si) was rapidly gaining ground in America during the first half of the nineteenth century and soon became firmly entrenched in the urban and urban-dominated singing tradition as exemplified by Lowell Mason and his followers. From 1832 attempts were made to combine the do-re-mi system with the shape notes or patent notes to which the vast majority of rural singers were stubbornly attached. The most successful manipulator of this combined system was Jesse B. Aikin of Philadelphia, whose collection, the *Christian Minstrel* (Philadelphia, 1846), went into 171 editions by 1873. Aiken simply added three more shape notes to the four that had been in general use, so that his complete scale appeared as follows:

At least six other seven-shape systems were introduced by various compilers up to 1866, but Aiken's was the one that proved most popular and that was accepted as standard by the numerous seven-shape songbook publishers of the South.

William Walker, in the introduction to the 1854 edition of his *Southern Harmony*, devoted a page to discussing "The Different Plans of Notation." He says there are seven plans of notation used in various parts of the world, including one that employs numerals, used "in Germany (among the peasants) and in some parts of the United States." Regarding what he calls the Italian "doe, rae, me" system, he has this to say:

> Some contend that no one can learn to sing correctly without using the seven syllables. Although I have no objections to the seven syllable plan, I differ a little with such in opinion, for I have taught the four syllable patent notes, the Italian seven syllables, and the numerals also, and in twenty-five years' experience, have always found my patent note pupils to learn as fast, and sing as correct [*sic*] as any.

Nevertheless, William Walker was wavering. The seven-shape practitioners seemed to be aligned with progress. Walker decided to switch to the Italian system. When he published his *Christian Harmony*, printed at Philadelphia in 1866, it appeared with a seven-shape system of his own invention. Now he was convinced that the "seven-syllable character-note singing" was "the quickest and most desirable method known."

A certain aspiration toward "scientific improvement" accompanied the spread of the seven-shape do-re-mi system. Its principal champion, Jesse Aiken, expressed the hope that his *Christian Minstrel* would supplant the "trashy publications" so widely used in the South and West. Even "Singin' Billy" Walker endeavored to include in his *Christian Harmony* "more music suitable to church use," and in the edition of 1873 he incorporated "the most beautiful and desirable of modern tunes." The editors of another important seven-shape book, the *New Harp of Columbia* (1867), stated that many tunes originally published in the first edition of their collection (1848) had been discarded "and their places filled by others of superior merit." This is the language of Lowell Mason and progressive improvement.

The process of urbanization, accelerated in recent times by the radio and the phonograph, has been undermining the old, indigenous, rural folk tradition of the fasola singers. This trend has been going on for a long time. Leaders of the "better music" movement in the South were two brothers, L. C. Everett (1818–1867) and A. B. Everett (1828–1875), who, having received an excellent musical education, including a period of European study, established their headquarters in Richmond, Virginia, and spread the gospel of scientific improvement as widely as they could. They were ably seconded by Rigdon McCoy McIntosh (1836–1899) of Tennessee and Georgia, one of the most active propagators of the "Everett Method" and of urbanized church music. These men aspired to be the Lowell Masons and the

Thomas Hastings of the South. If they did not succeed on such a large scale, it is because the South is primarily a rural area, hence strongly conservative and traditional in its culture. The "better music" advocates took over the official church hymnals, but the rural folk continued in large measure to cling to their old fuguing tunes, folk hymns, religious ballads, and revival spirituals.

Since the fuguing tune is essentially an eighteenth-century product, and as the revival songs will be discussed in the next chapter, it will be appropriate now to give one or two more examples of the religious ballad and folk hymn. From a song literature so abundant and so rich in traditional values, it is difficult to make such a limited selection. Perhaps a good example of the religious ballad would be "Weeping Mary," of which the earliest printed version appeared in Ingall's *Christian Harmony* of 1805. The version reproduced here is from William Walker's *Southern and Western Pocket Harmonist*, published in 1846. The tune belongs to a large family of English secular folk songs.

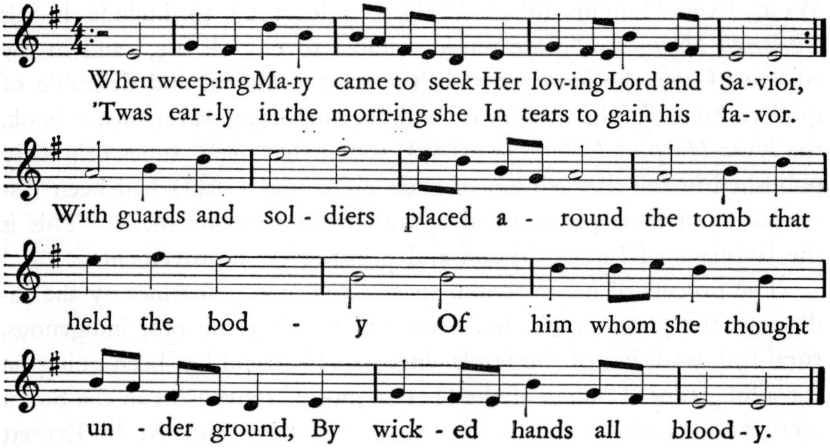
When weep-ing Ma-ry came to seek Her lov-ing Lord and Sa-vior,
'Twas ear-ly in the morn-ing she In tears to gain his fa-vor.
With guards and sol - diers placed a - round the tomb that
held the bod - y Of him whom she thought
un - der ground, By wick - ed hands all blood - y.

For an example of the folk hymn, we may take one that has had a long history in the American oral tradition, "Amazing Grace," with text by the English evangelist John Newton, whose colorful career was described in an earlier chapter. The tune, under various names, is found in numerous fasola songbooks without any composer's name affixed to it. Numerous versions have also been recorded from oral tradition by modern folk-song collectors. In William Walker's *South-*

ern Harmony it appears under the title "New Britain." The melody is pentatonic. It is this version (from the edition of 1854) which we quote here:

A - maz - ing — grace! (how sweet the sound) That
saved a — wretch like — me! I — once was — lost, but —
now am — found, Was blind, but — now I see.

Dr. George Pullen Jackson recorded in 1936 an ornamented version of this tune, sung very slowly and with numerous grace notes, which he describes as "an excellent illustration of the widespread southern folk-manner in the singing of hymns of this sort." Thus we have here a continuation of the tradition of ornamented psalmody that flourished in the eighteenth century and that caused such consternation and condemnation among the New England divines. This is the ornamented version as printed by Dr. Jackson in *Spiritual Folk-Songs of Early America:*

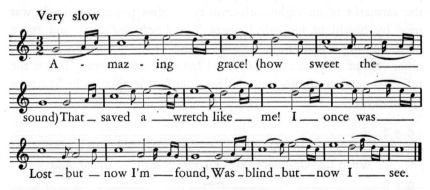

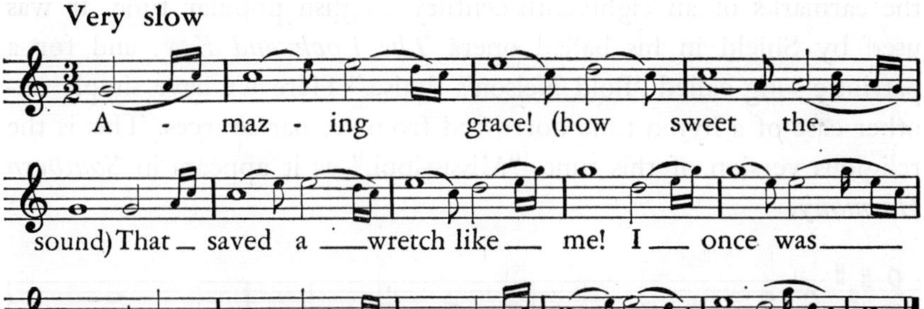

A - maz - ing grace! (how sweet the —
sound) That — saved a — wretch like — me! I — once was —
Lost — but — now I'm — found, Was — blind — but — now I — see.

The fasola singing leaders and compilers did not, of course, think of their songs according to the classifications mentioned above. We need to bear in mind the cultural law that "folklore does not exist for the folk." These people did not regard themselves as quaint or backward or as followers of an archaic tradition. Conservative they were, yes; and believers in the tried-and-true values of their ancestors. When a revision of the *Sacred Harp* was being discussed in 1879, and the question of adopting the seven-shape notation was raised, Benjamin Franklin White held out firmly for the old four-shape system. "The four-note scheme," he declared, "has had the sanction of the musical world for more than four hundred years [!]; and we scarcely think that we can do better than to abide by the advice . . . 'Ask for the old paths and walk therein.' " Preserve the past, yes; but as something alive and useful for the present. The fasola leaders considered themselves as supplying the musical needs of their communities according to methods and values that they thought were suitable and acceptable to the people around them.

When Ananias Davisson published his *Kentucky Harmony* in 1817 he divided the contents into two main classifications: (1) "Plain and easy tunes commonly used in time of divine worship" and (2) "More lengthy and elegant pieces, commonly used at concerts, or singing societies." The same classification was adopted by other fasola compilers. William Walker, in his *Southern Harmony*, for instance, includes in Part II the more dignified or elaborate hymns, the fuguing pieces, and anthems. One of the hymns in this section, taken probably from the *Supplement to the Kentucky Harmony*, is titled "Mississippi," the composer's name being given as "Bradshaw." In spite of the composer's name and the imposingly grandiose text, the melody bears all the earmarks of an eighteenth-century English popular tune. It was used by Shield in his ballad opera *The Lock and Key*, and for a patriotic song called "Bold Nelson's Praise." Here we have simply another case of a hymn tune borrowed from secular sources. This is the religious version of this tune, "Mississippi," as it appears in *Southern Harmony:*

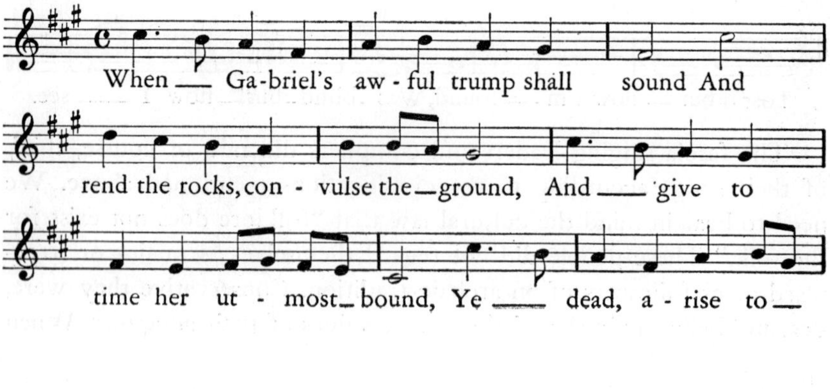

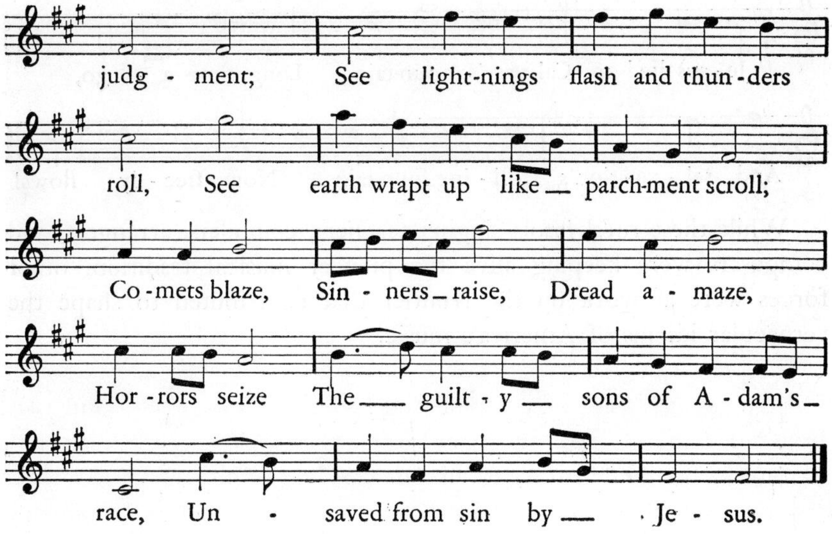
judg - ment; See light-nings flash and thun-ders
roll, See earth wrapt up like parch-ment scroll;
Co-mets blaze, Sin - ners raise, Dread a - maze,
Hor-rors seize The guilt - y sons of A-dam's
race, Un - saved from sin by Je - sus.

William Walker included in his *Southern Harmony*, with no indication of the author or composer, another tune that has an exceptionally curious history. This is "Long Time Ago," obviously borrowed from an old Negro song that was already widely known by the time the first edition of *Southern Harmony* appeared in 1835. According to the editors of *Slave Songs of the United States* (1867), the original Negro melody was sung to words beginning, "Way down in Raccoon Hollow." An arrangement by William Clifton, beginning, "O I was born down ole Varginee," was published in 1836 and described as "A Favorite Comic Song and Chorus" (see musical example on page 279). As we have seen, a "refined" version, in the high-flown sentimental fashion of the genteel tradition, was made by the composer Charles E. Horn with words by George P. Morris (see musical example on page 172). This is a striking illustration of the borrowing of material among different cultural traditions. Although the original Negro version has not been located, we can assume that it existed; thus we have four different traditions represented in the various versions of this song: (1) Negro folk tradition, (2) urban popular tradition (blackface minstrelsy), (3) white rural folk tradition, (4) urban cultivated tradition. The religious version of "Long Time Ago," as printed by William Walker, is given below:

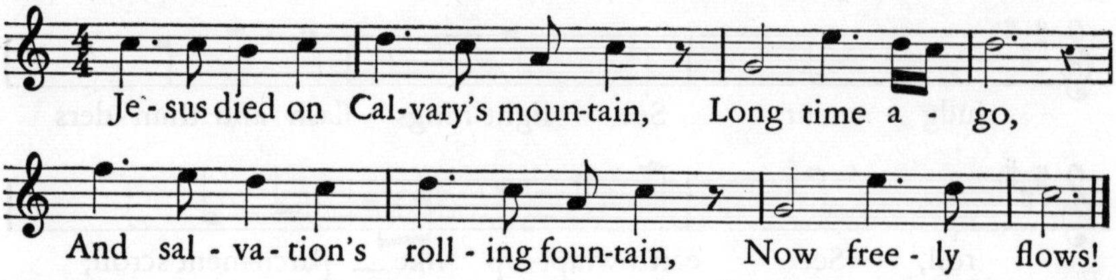
Je-sus died on Cal-vary's moun-tain, Long time a - go,
And sal - va - tion's roll - ing foun-tain, Now free - ly flows!

While these rural fasola singing teachers, compilers, arrangers, and composers were keeping alive the pioneer musical tradition, other forces were at work on the frontier that contributed to shape the vernacular idioms of America's music.

chapter eleven

Revivals and camp meetings

Shout, shout, we're gaining ground,
Halle, hallelujah!
Satan's kingdom is tumbling down,
Glory hallelujah!
REVIVAL HYMNS (BOSTON, 1842).

It has been said that "to the American frontier Methodism gave the circuit rider and to Methodism the frontier gave the camp meeting." The circuit rider was an itinerant preacher who traveled up and down the countryside on horseback, preaching, praying, singing, and bringing the gospel to the widely scattered rural population. Francis Asbury, the first American circuit rider, is credited with having ridden a total of 275,000 miles. But no matter how many miles the preacher on horseback traveled, he could bring the gospel only to as many people as were gathered together within reach of his voice at a single time. Hence it was a natural development for the people of a certain territory to come together at a specified time and place to hear the itinerant preacher, whose arrival had been announced in advance; and since these rural people often had to travel long distances to the meeting ground, they came prepared to stay several days. This was the origin of the American camp meetings, of which the first was held in Logan County, Kentucky, near the Gaspar River Church, in July of the year 1800.

The immediate instigator of the camp-meeting movement appears to have been the Rev. James McGready, a Presbyterian minister. Hence the movement was not exclusively Methodist. In fact, it was customary for preachers of several denominations to get together and arrange for a camp meeting jointly. The crowds were so large, ranging anywhere from two thousand to twenty thousand, that several preachers were needed to conduct the activities. If the Methodists soon gained the ascendancy in the camp meetings that quickly spread from Kentucky to the rest of the United States, it was partly because they had a large stock of popular hymnody that could readily be thrown into the emotionally boiling caldron out of which was to emerge the revival spiritual. Speaking of the Methodist invasion of the early camp meetings, a historian of the Presbyterian Church writes:

> They succeeded in introducing their own stirring hymns, familiarly, though incorrectly, entitled "Wesley's Hymns"; and as books were scarce, the few that were attainable were cut up, and the leaves distributed, so that all in turn might learn them by heart.[1]

The book so roughly handled at these first camp meetings was probably *The Pocket Hymn Book* (Philadelphia, 1797), which was rapidly going through one edition after another in response to the eager demand for revival hymns. This book, like many others published in the next few decades to supply the revivalist movement, contained only the words of the hymns or spiritual songs, not the music. The tunes were either familiar ones that everybody already knew, or of such a simple and catchy nature that they could quickly be picked up from the singing of the preacher, who was also the song leader. As Benson remarks, "Of the tunes to which the Camp Meeting Hymns were sung the leaders demanded nothing more than contagiousness and effectiveness." [2]

In a previous chapter, tracing the development of evangelical hymnody in England under the influence of the Wesleys and their followers, with particular reference to the intensely emotional and folksy hymns of Cennick and Newton, we described the background out of which grew the popular religious songs of the American camp meetings. We should recall the use of the term "spiritual songs" in many of the collections of evangelical hymnody, including the *Hymns and Spiritual Songs* of Isaac Watts in 1709. This term was taken over in American collections, such as Joshua Smith's *Divine Hymns or Spiritual Songs* (Portsmouth, New Hampshire, 1794), Henry Alline's *Hymns and Spiritual Songs* (Stoningtonport, Connecticut, 1802), David Mintz's *Spiritual Song Book* (Halifax, North Carolina, 1805), and John C. Totten's *A Collection of the most admired hymns and spiritual songs, with the choruses affixed as usually sung at camp-meet-*

[1] Davidson, *History of the Presbyterian Church in Kentucky*, p. 134.
[2] Benson, *The English Hymn*, p. 294.

ings (New York, 1809). Many such books (a total of over fifty) were published up to the time of the Civil War. Totten's collection is particularly interesting as making specific mention of camp meetings and of the choruses that, as we shall presently see, constituted the most striking feature of revival hymnody.

Since the compilers speak of hymns *and* spiritual songs, it is obvious that some distinction between the two categories was intended. For our purpose it will be convenient to treat of revival hymnody as a whole, in relation to the camp-meeting movement; but we shall place the emphasis on those songs that were most specifically and organically a product of the revivalist fervor, and it is to these that the term "spiritual songs" may be especially applied. In its shortened form, "spirituals," the term has come to be generally associated in America with the religious songs of the Negroes. But the term is clearly of English evangelical origin, and in this chapter we shall refer to the camp-meeting songs either as "revival spirituals" or as "spirituals." Since both Negroes and whites attended the same camp meetings and sang the same songs, there is no need, at this stage at least, to make any kind of racial distinction. Amid the sometimes unedifying features of the revivalist frenzy, we have to put down in the credit column that the camp meetings broke through rigid denominational barriers and encouraged both religious and racial tolerance.

Traveling the circuit

Perhaps the best way to share the spirit of the camp meetings is to travel the circuit with one of the Methodist riders who was most fervently engaged in the revivalist movement. Lorenzo Dow (1777–1834) of Connecticut early in life felt the call to preach, and in spite of much opposition and many difficulties, caused in part by his eccentric and extravagant character, he succeeded in carrying the gospel throughout most of the United States, and even brought the camp-meeting movement to England, where he aroused large crowds with his fervor and enthusiasm. He married a person as enthusiastic and eccentric as himself, Peggy Dow, who in 1816 brought out *A Collection of Camp-meeting Hymns*, printed in Philadelphia (words only). Dow left a voluminous journal of his travels and experiences in America and the British Isles.

According to a footnote in Dow's journal, "Camp meetings *began* in Kentucky—next N. Carolina—attended them in Georgia—introduced them in the centre of Virginia, N. York, Connecticut, Massachusetts and Mississippi Territory!—1803–4–5." Thus within five years the camp-meeting craze had spread all over the United States, from North to South, and westward to the frontier territory. In 1804, Lorenzo Dow attended a camp meeting at Liberty, Tennessee, and wrote in his journal:

> Friday 19th. Camp-meeting commenced at Liberty: here I saw the *jerks;* and some danced: a strange exercise indeed; however it is involuntary, yet requires the consent of the will: i.e., the people are taken *jerking* irresistibly, and if they strive to resist it, it worries them much, yet is attended with no bodily pain, and those who are exercised to dance (which in the pious seems an antidote to the jerks) if they resist, it brings deadness and barrenness over the mind; but when they yield to it they feel happy, although it is a great cross, there is a heavenly smile and solemnity on the countenance, which carries great conviction to the minds of the beholders; their eyes when dancing seem to be fixed upwards as if upon an invisible object, and they lost to all below.[3]

The question of dancing, so closely related to the jerks, was evidently a matter of some theological concern. On Sunday the 21st, writes Dow,

> I heard Doctor Tooley, a man of liberal education, preach on the subject of the *jerks* and the *dancing exercise:* He brought ten passages of scripture to prove that dancing was once a religious exercise, but corrupted at Aaron's calf, and from thence young people got it for amusement. I believe the congregation and preachers were generally satisfied with his remarks.

Lorenzo Dow found that the jerks had no respect for denominations. In Tennessee he met some Quakers who said, "the Methodists and Presbyterians have the *jerks* because they *sing* and *pray* so much, but we are still a peaceable people, wherefore we do not have them." But later, at a meeting, he found that about a dozen Quakers "had the *jerks* as keen and as powerful as any I have ever seen, so as to occasion a kind of grunt or groan when they would jerk." Summing it all up, Lorenzo wrote:

[3] Dow, *Journal*, p. 213.

> I have seen Presbyterians, Methodists, Quakers, Baptists, Church of England, and Independents, exercised with the *jerks;* Gentleman and Lady, black and white, the aged and the youth, rich and poor, without exception. . . .[4]

So much for the universal democracy of the jerks.

Back in his native Connecticut, Lorenzo gives us a brief picture of the general atmosphere of a camp meeting:

> About three thousand people appeared on the ground, and the rejoicing of old saints, the shouts of young converts, and the cries of the distressed for mercy, caused the meeting to continue all night.[5]

It was at night that the revival frenzy reached its greatest intensity. As the campfires blazed around the grounds, preachers went through the crowds exhorting the sinners to repent and be saved from the fires of Hell. The volume of song rose to a mighty roar, the sound of shouting shook the earth; men and women jerked, leaped, or rolled on the ground until they swooned and had to be carried away. Amid sobs and groans and shouts, men and women shook hands all around and released all their frustrations and emotions in great bursts of song that culminated in "the singing ecstasy."

> Jesus, grant us all a blessing,
> Shouting, singing, send it down;
> Lord, above may we go praying,
> And rejoicing in Thy love.
> Shout, O Glory! sing glory, hallelujah!
> I'm going where pleasure never dies.

The typical revivalist is a pilgrim traveling through the wilderness, burdened with the sins of the world but rejoicing in the vision of the promised land, which is in sight just on the other side of Jordan, and when he gets there he'll be able to lay his burdens down, his troubles will be over.

A well-known hymn by the English dissenting divine, Samuel Stennett,

> On Jordan's stormy banks I stand, and cast a wishful eye
> To Canaan's happy land, where my possessions lie,

[4] *Ibid.*, p. 184.
[5] *Ibid.*, p. 187.

was taken up by the revivalists and appears with a variety of typical camp-meeting choruses appended to it. Here is one, first printed in the *Southern Harmony* of 1835, that is thoroughly typical:

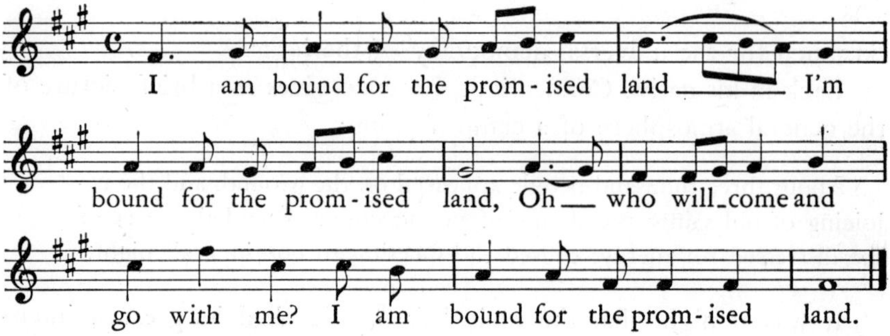
I am bound for the prom - ised land ___ I'm
bound for the prom - ised land, Oh ___ who will_come and
go with me? I am bound for the prom - ised land.

Here on earth life is full of woe and trouble, of trials and tribulations; but just ahead lies the prospect of the promised land—O, glory, hallelujah!

We have ___ our ___ tri - als here ___ be - low, O
glo - ry, hal - le - lu - jah! We have_ our_ tri - als
here ___ be - low, O glo - ry hal - le - lu - jah!
There's a bet - ter day a - com-ing, Hal - le - lu -
jah! There's a bet - ter day a-com-ing, Hal - le - lu - jah!

This revival spiritual is also from William Walker's *Southern Harmony*, where it is entitled "Christian Prospect." It belongs to the pattern that has a refrain interpolated after each line. This was a very popular pattern in revival singing, because it was easy to "compose" a song in this manner on the spot, and because it gave an effective opportunity for mass participation and all-out shouting.

One of the earliest recorded songs of this type is "Satan's Kingdom Is Tumbling Down," which was printed in *Revival Hymns*, compiled by H. W. Day (Boston, 1842). In a headnote to this spiritual song, the compiler writes:

> This hymn and the original melody, *which have been so useful in revival seasons, for more than half a century*, and which, it is believed, have never before been published together, were lately procured after considerable search, from the diary of an aged servant of Christ, bearing the date 1810.

I have italicized the passage above simply to emphasize that many of these spirituals had circulated in oral tradition long before they were published in books; this applied particularly to the music, for it was not until after 1840 that the music of the camp-meeting spirituals began to be included to any extent in the songbooks with notation, and then they found a place chiefly in the shape-note books described in the preceding chapter.

Another interesting feature of "Satan's Kingdom" is that the text is pieced together by an accumulation of "wandering verses" that formed the stock-in-trade of revivalism. It was by having a large reserve of such material, usually in the form of rhymed couplets, to draw upon that the camp-meetings spiritual could proliferate so rapidly and so abundantly. "Satan's Kingdom" has the refrain after each line of the quatrain, and this in turn is followed by a typical camp-meeting chorus of four lines:

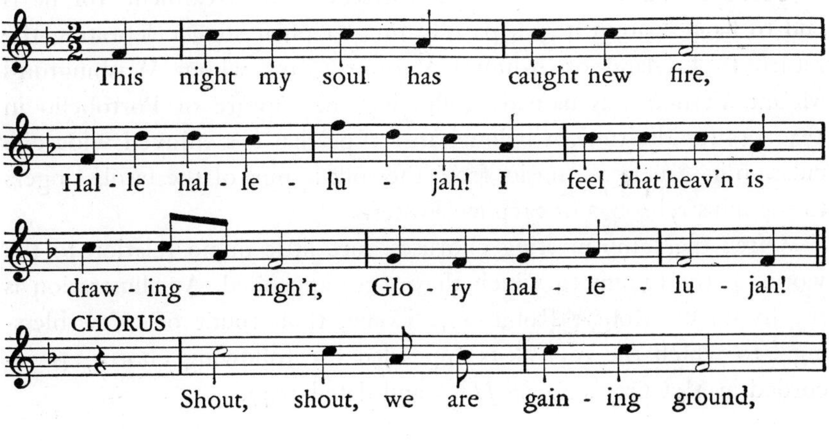

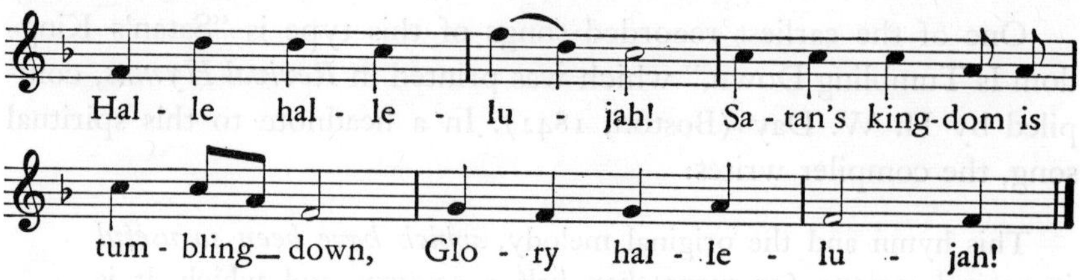
Hal - le hal - le - lu - jah! Sa - tan's king-dom is
tum - bling— down, Glo - ry hal - le - lu - jah!

By inserting a familiar tag line after each verse, and singing the whole to a rollicking tune, it was easy to transform a Wesleyan hymn into a camp-meeting spiritual. This is what happened to Charles Wesley's hymn, "He comes, he comes, the Judge severe." The revivalists tacked on the refrain, "Roll, Jordan, roll," after each line, and added a characteristic "I want to go to heaven" chorus.

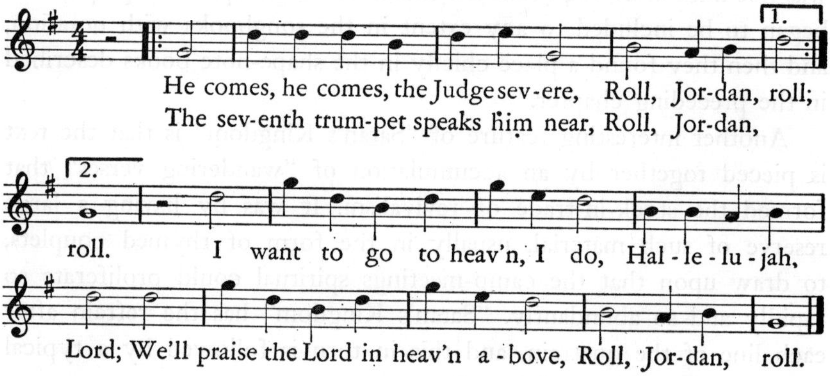
1.
He comes, he comes, the Judge sev-ere, Roll, Jor-dan, roll;
The sev-enth trum-pet speaks him near, Roll, Jor-dan,
2.
roll. I want to go to heav'n, I do, Hal - le - lu - jah,
Lord; We'll praise the Lord in heav'n a - bove, Roll, Jor-dan, roll.

Perhaps Charles Wesley's hymn deserved this treatment, for he is said to have written it as a parody on a popular song celebrating the return to England of Admiral Vernon (after whom Washington's Mount Vernon was named) following the capture of Portobello in 1739. As for the tune, it belongs to a type that has enjoyed wide circulation in America's music, from the folk hymns of the fasola singers to the minstrel songs of Stephen Foster.

Often the camp-meeting choruses bore little or no relation to the words of the hymns to which they were appended. An illustration is the hymn by Robert Robinson, "Come, thou fount of ev'ry blessing," to which the revivalists appended the following chorus, as recorded in McCurry's *Social Harp* and dated 1849:

And I hope to gain the prom-is'd land, O
hal-le, hal-le - lu - jah; And I hope to gain the prom-is'd
land, yes I do; Glo - ry, glo - ry,
How I love my Sav - ior, Glo-ry, glo - ry, yes I do.

Also included in McCurry's *Social Harp* (1855) is a version of John Cennick's popular hymn, "Jesus, my all, to heaven is gone," with a "Jordan" chorus added to it, and the refrain "Happy, O happy" after each line. The chorus goes like this:

> We'll cross the river of Jordan
> Happy, O happy,
> We'll cross the river of Jordan,
> Happy, in the Lord.

Another one of Cennick's hymns, "Children of the heavenly King," was printed in the *Social Harp* with McCurry's name as composer and with the following "happy" chorus of camp-meeting origin:

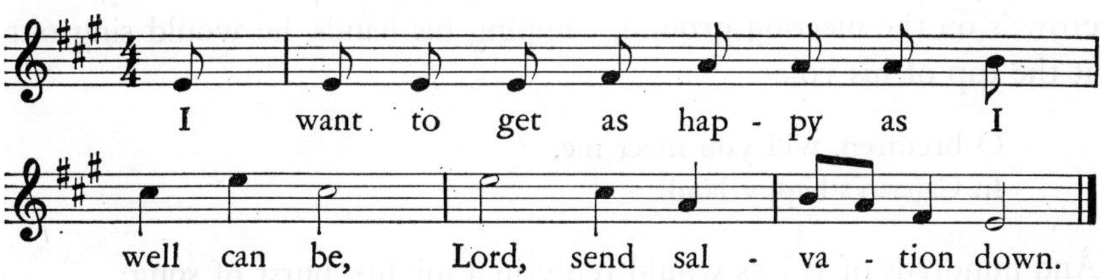
I want to get as hap - py as I
well can be, Lord, send sal - va - tion down.

In the following revival spiritual from William Hauser's *Hesperian Harp* (1848), the Jordan theme is combined with the highly popular and widespread theme of the "Old Ship of Zion," of which numerous versions are found in various songbooks. In Hauser's version the Ship of Zion does not make its appearance until the second stanza.

Come a - long, come a - long and let us go
home; O glo - ry hal - le - lu - jah!
Our home is o - ver Jor - dan, hal - le - lu -
jah! Our home is o - ver Jor - dan, hal - le - lu - jah!

Then the second stanza:

What ship is this that will take us all home?
O glory hallelujah!
'Tis the old ship of Zion,
O glory hallelujah!

And in the fifth stanza we find another familiar theme of the revival spirituals:

If you get there before I do,
You may tell them that I'm coming.

It is part of the larger "traveling to Canaan" theme that recurs in so many spirituals. As the revivalist preacher passed through the crowds on the meeting ground, clapping his hands, he would sing out at the top of his voice:

O brethren, will you meet me,
In Canaan's happy land?

And hundreds of voices would reply in a mighty burst of song:

By the grace of God, we'll meet you,
In Canaan's happy land.

Another time the preacher would sing out:

I feel the work reviving, I feel the work reviving,
Reviving in my soul.

And the camp-meeting crowd would respond:

We'll shout and give him glory,
We'll shout and give him glory,
We'll shout and give him glory,
For glory is his own.

It was possible to keep a song going almost indefinitely, merely by changing one word in the stanza. For instance, in the line "O brothers will you meet me," the word "brothers" could be replaced in subsequent repetitions by "sisters," "mourners," "sinners," and so on. In the same manner, "We have fathers in the promised land" could be followed by "We have brothers, sisters, mothers, etc."

We do not know exactly how the early revival spirituals were sung because when the music appeared in the songbooks it was modified by harmonized arrangements that followed the singing-school tradition, with three or four voice parts blending together in more or less correct harmony. From the patterns of the song texts, and from descriptive accounts left by some witnesses and participants in the camp meetings, such as Lucius Bellinger of South Carolina, active as a revivalist from around 1825, we can be fairly certain that many of the songs, though not all, were sung according to the leader and chorus pattern indicated above. This is, in any case, a common practice in mass group singing, where the crowd is always ready to come in on a familiar chorus.

Then there were the "dialogue songs," in which one phrase was sung by men and another by women. An example of this is the "Mariner's Hymn," from the *Millennial Harp* (1843):

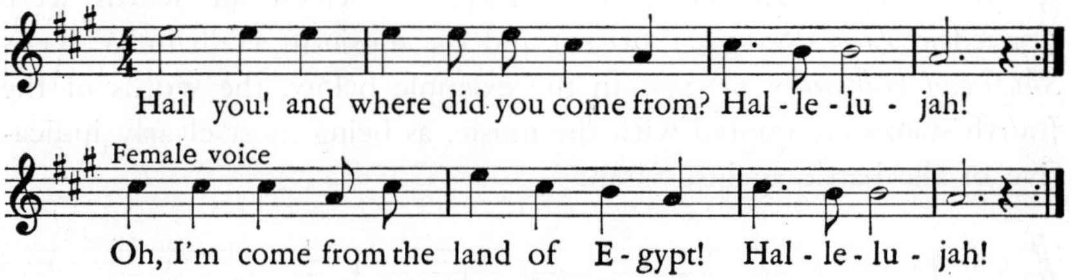
Hail you! and where did you come from? Hal - le - lu - jah!
Female voice
Oh, I'm come from the land of E - gypt! Hal - le - lu - jah!

The dialogue continues:

Hail you! and where are you bound for?
Hallelujah!
Oh, I'm bound for the land of Canaan,
Hallelujah!

Hail you! and what is your cargo?
  Hallelujah!
Oh, religion is my cargo.
  Hallelujah!

And so on, for several more stanzas. Dr. Guy B. Johnson believes that the pentatonic tune of this revival spiritual came from some sailor song, and points to its similarity to the hoisting chantey "Blow, Boys, Blow."

The idea of gaining ground against sin is another basic theme of the revival spirituals. We find it in a camp-meeting chorus affixed to the eighteenth-century hymn "I know that my Redeemer lives," in the following song which appeared originally in the *Social Harp* (1855), attributed to F. C. Wood of Georgia, and which is here reproduced from the Denson Revision of the *Original Sacred Harp:*

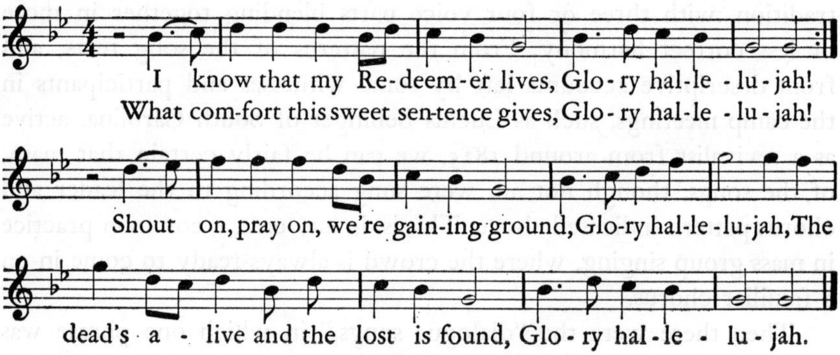
I know that my Re-deem-er lives, Glo-ry hal-le-lu-jah!
What com-fort this sweet sen-tence gives, Glo-ry hal-le-lu-jah!
Shout on, pray on, we're gain-ing ground, Glo-ry hal-le-lu-jah, The
dead's a-live and the lost is found, Glo-ry hal-le-lu-jah.

The same theme of conflict and victory is embodied in a revival spiritual called "The Good Old Way," of which the words were printed in *Zion's Songster* (1832) and the music in William Walker's *Southern Harmony* (1835). In the example below, the words of the fourth stanza are quoted with the music, as being most clearly indicative of the battle against Satan:

Though Sa-tan may his power em ploy, O
Our peace and com-fort to de-stroy, O
hal-le, hal-le-lu-jah, Yet
hal-le, hal-le-lu-jah.

nev - er fear, we'll gain the day,— O hal - le, hal - le -
lu - jah; And — tri - umph in — the good old
way, O hal - le, hal le - lu jah.

A characteristic example of the way in which a text by Dr. Watts could be made to serve as the nucleus of a camp-meeting spiritual is "Sweet Canaan," in which the refrain "I am bound for the land of Canaan" is inserted after each line. The tune, of unknown origin, though attributed by the editors of the *Original Sacred Harp* to "Rev. John Moffitt, 1829," is probably traditional and bears a resemblance to some of Stephen Foster's minstrel songs.

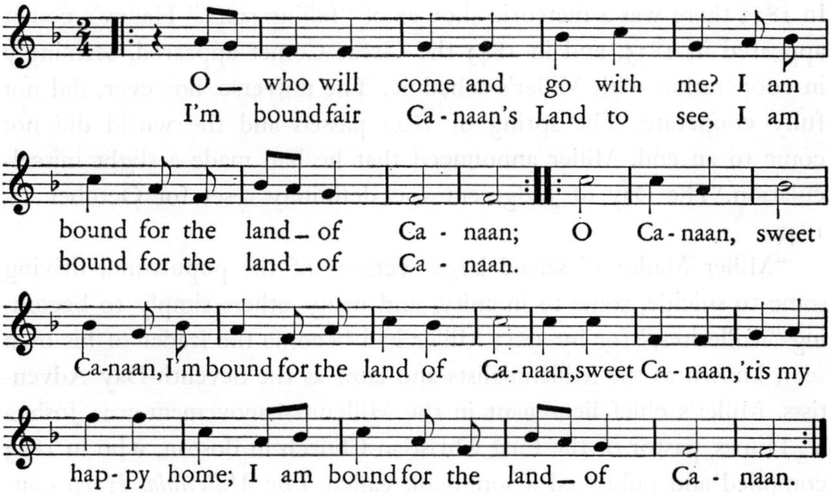
O — who will come and go with me? I am
I'm bound fair Ca - naan's Land to see, I am
bound for the land — of Ca - naan; O Ca - naan, sweet
bound for the land — of Ca - naan.
Ca-naan, I'm bound for the land of Ca - naan, sweet Ca - naan, 'tis my
hap - py home; I am bound for the land — of Ca - naan.

A well-known hymn by Dr. Watts, beginning "When I can read my title clear to mansions in the skies," was given the revival treatment and emerged as "I Want to Go" in McCurry's *Social Harp*, where it is dated 1851. McCurry ascribed it to himself as composer, but in all probability he merely arranged or harmonized a tune that had circulated in oral tradition. The chorus goes like this:

I want to go, I want to go,
I want to go to glory;
There's so many trials here below,
They say there's none in glory.

The revival movement reached its peak in the 1830s and 1840s, owing largely to the preaching of a Vermont farmer by the name of William Miller (1782–1849), who predicted that the end of the world would come in the spring of the year 1843:

In eighteen hundred forty-three
Will be the Year of Jubilee.

Obtaining a Baptist license to preach, Miller traveled around the country carrying his message of the coming Day of Wrath, distributing tracts, hymnbooks, and printed propaganda of every kind. His message of impending doom was reinforced by the portents of Nature. In 1833 there was a meteoric shower of "falling stars." Halley's comet appeared in 1835, and in 1843 the Great Comet appeared, seemingly in cooperation with Miller's schedule. The universe, however, did not fully cooperate. The spring of 1843 passed and the world did not come to an end. Miller announced that he had made a slight miscalculation. The Day of Judgment was definitely reset for October 22, 1844.

"Miller Madness" seized large sections of the population, driving some to suicide, some to insanity, and many others simply to becoming "Millerites," for by 1843 Miller had become the leader of his own sect, known as the Millennialists and later as the Seventh-Day Adventists. Miller's chief lieutenant in the Millennial movement was Joshua V. Himes, pastor of the First Christian Church in Boston, who in 1843 compiled and published a songbook called *The Millennial Harp* containing over two hundred songs, mostly in the tradition of revival spirituals, written or adapted especially for conveying the message of the Second Advent. Himes took, for example, a popular and widely used revival chorus, "I will be in this band, hallelujah!" and adapted it to the Millerite message by adding "In the Second Advent Band, hallelujah!" Appropriate stanzas were also added, such as:

O bless the Lord, we need not fear,
For Daniel says he'll come this year.

Here is the first stanza and chorus of "Christian Band," with the music, as published in the *Millennial Harp:*

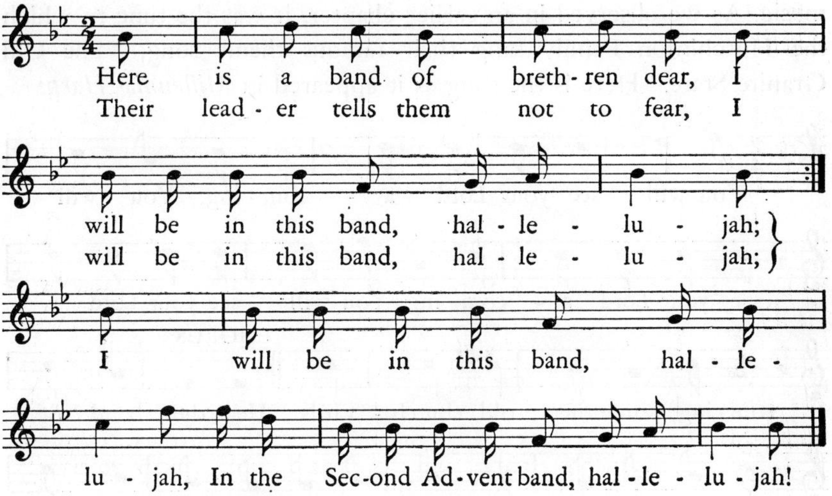
Here is a band of breth - ren dear, I
Their lead - er tells them not to fear, I
will be in this band, hal - le - lu - jah;
will be in this band, hal - le - lu - jah;
I will be in this band, hal - le -
lu - jah, In the Sec-ond Ad-vent band, hal - le - lu - jah!

Another Millennial song, evidently prepared especially for the "tarrying season" that began in the spring of 1844, had the following text:

Now we feel the Advent Glory
While the Savior seems to tarry,
We will comfort one another
And be trusting in his name.
Are your lamps all burning?
Are your vessels filled with oil?

By some unaccountable obstinacy of Nature, the world survived the fateful day of October 22, 1844. Miller himself survived his disappointment by five years, dying in 1849; his followers did not lose faith, for a few years later they were singing:

O praise the Lord, we do not fear
To tell the world he'll come next year.
In eighteen hundred fifty-four
The saints will shout their suff'frings o'er.
(*Pilgrim's Songster*, 1853)

One of the most stirring songs in the *Millennial Harp* was "Old Churchyard," sung especially at meetings in the cemeteries, for many of the Millerites "sought the graveyards where friends were buried, so as to join them as they arose from their earthly resting places and ascend with them." The tune has been widely used in American folk music. As we observed in an earlier chapter, it was the tune to which the Hutchinson Family sang their famous theme song, "The Old Granite State." Here is the song as it appeared in *Millennial Harp:*

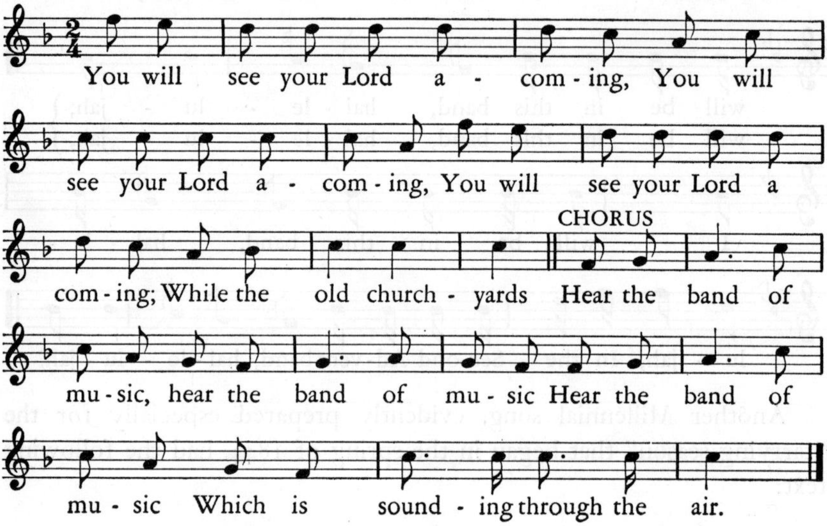
You will see your Lord a - com - ing, You will
see your Lord a - com - ing, You will see your Lord a
CHORUS
com - ing; While the old church - yards Hear the band of
mu - sic, hear the band of mu - sic Hear the band of
mu - sic Which is sound - ing through the air.

Now we have learned something about the revival spirit, the atmosphere of the camp meetings, and various types of revival spirituals and camp-meeting hymns. The question remains—and it is an important one—how did the singing sound? Unfortunately, those who witnessed the early camp meetings have left us more detailed accounts of the sensational manifestations of religious hysteria than of the exact nature of the singing that went on. We have to pick up clues here and there, and then rely largely on our imagination to project the old-time tunes as they were actually sung at camp meetings. The Southern revivalist Lucius Bellinger has some references to revival singing strewn among his autobiographical *Stray Leaves from the Portfolio of a Local Methodist Preacher* (1870). Writing of a preacher who led the singing: "He was a man with a sharp, strong, piercing voice. We now have old-time singing—clear, loud, and ringing." All accounts agree that the singing was loud.

Samuel E. Asbury, a descendant of the Rev. Henry Asbury who was America's pioneer circuit rider, recalling the old-time revival singing of his youth, said: "The immediate din was tremendous; at a hundred yards it was beautiful; and at a distance of a half mile it was magnificent." No musical instruments at all were used, not even a tuning fork. Some brass-lunged male pitched the tune. A lot of other brass-lunged males took it up and carried it along. It was the men, not the women, who sang the "tune." The women sang their subordinate part an octave higher, often, says Mr. Asbury, "singing around high C with perfect unconcern because they didn't realize their feat." They may have enjoyed themselves, but they were not singing for the sake of singing. "What they were there for was to hammer on the sinner's heart and bring him to the mourner's bench." There was no thought of art; the singing was like a force of nature, an uncontrollable torrent of sound.

But the tunes were beautiful and stirring. To hear them sung at the height of the revival fervor must have been a thrilling experience. Bearing in mind the remarks quoted above—the clear, loud, ringing voices, the high male voices carrying the tune, the basses below, and the female voices soaring above—let the reader give full scope to his or her imagination in recreating the sonorous texture of this wonderful revival spiritual, one of the glories of America's music: "Morning Trumpet," words by John Leland, music attributed to Benjamin Franklin White, compiler of the *Sacred Harp* (1844):

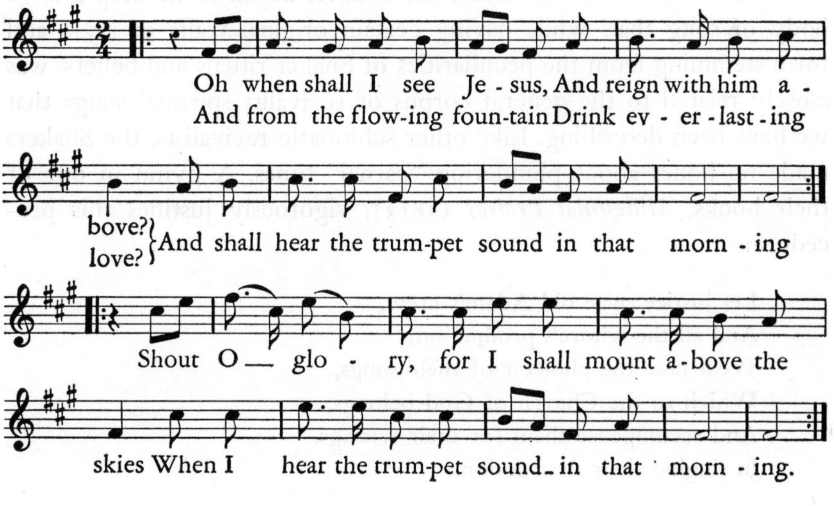

There is one aspect of revival singing that cannot be reconstructed from the printed music and that can be but inadequately described with words. That is the practice of taking familiar, conventional hymns and ornamenting the melodies with what Mr. Asbury calls "numberless little slurs and melodic variations." He mentions "Jesus, Lover of My Soul" and "How Firm a Foundation" as hymns that were sung in this manner. References to this ornamented style of folk singing were made in the second chapter of this book and also in Chapter 10, where an example was given of "Amazing Grace" with melodic ornamentation. The best way to become acquainted with this style, which was not limited to revival meetings but is widespread in folk tradition, is to listen to some of the recordings of Southern folk singers issued by the Library of Congress. Though these were recorded comparatively recently, the old tradition remains essentially unchanged, because conservatism, in its literal sense of preserving the values of the past, is the very essence of folklore.

Shakers defy the devil

When the Shakers—officially the United Society of Believers in Christ's Second Appearing—spread their activities westward in the early years of the nineteenth century, they swelled their ranks with converts from various schismatic sects that had been prominent in promoting the spirit of revivalism. Under the influence of frontier revivalism in Kentucky and Ohio, the Shakers began to develop a large body of song that, while having certain original traits of style and form stemming from the peculiarities of Shaker rituals and beliefs, was closely related to the general corpus of revivalist spiritual songs that we have been describing. Like other schismatic revivalists, the Shakers made no bones about plundering "carnal" tunes. A hymn in one of their books, *Millennial Praises* (1813), vigorously justifies this procedure:

> Let justice seize old Adam's crew,
> And all the whore's production;
> We'll take the choicest of their songs,
> Which to the Church of God belongs,
> And recompense them for their wrongs,
> In singing their destruction.

Since the Shakers' religion brought them joy and holy mirth, they saw no reason for avoiding gay and lively tunes:

We love to sing and dance we will
Because we surely, *surely* feel
It does our thankful spirits fill
With heavenly joy and pleasure.

In 1807 the Shaker community at Watervliet, New York, produced a song called "The Happy Journey," of which one line might easily be misconstrued by the evil-minded as indicating that the Shakers went in for nudism:

O the happy journey that we are pursuing,
Come brethren and sisters let's all strip to run.

While the act of stripping to run was no doubt symbolic, in many instances the Shakers interpreted literally and realistically the actions described in their songs. When they sang of their faithful brethren,

I love to see them *stamp* and *grin*,
And curse the flesh, the seat of sin,

they actually stamped and grimaced.

In warring against the flesh and the devil, the Shakers found a perpetual source of excitement and of realistic ritual:

> The act of chasing or shooting the devil was a revival ritual. In one account, as some one spies the devil coming into the meeting, he gives the alarm, whereupon every true believer "opens the battery at once." This was done "by drawing the right knee nearly to the chin, placing the arm in the position of a sportsman, then straightening themselves out with a jerk, and a stamp of the foot, accompanied by a quick bursting yelp, in imitation of a gun. . . ." As the devil starts to flee, cries arise: "See him dart!" "Shoot him!" "Kill him!" All rush for spiritual weapons from the "spiritual Arsenal." The fight then commences.[6]

As "Old Ugly" was driven away, the victory of the faithful might be celebrated with a song: [7]

[6] Andrews, *The Gift to Be Simple.*

[7] The Shaker songs in this chapter are quoted from *The Gift to Be Simple,* by permission of the author, Edward D. Andrews.

Be joy-ful, be joy-ful, be joy-ful, be joy-
ful, For Old Ug-ly is go-ing.
Good rid-dance, good rid-dance, good rid-dance we say,
And don't you nev-er come here a-gain.

Even though "Old Ugly" did not always appear in person, it was necessary to wage continual battle against the flesh. The process of "shaking" was a powerful weapon in this fight, as described in the following song, "Shake Off the Flesh":

Come, let us all u-nite To purge out this
filth-y, flesh-y, car-nal sense, And la-bor for the
pow-er of God To mor-ti-fy and stain our pride.
We'll raise our glitt-'ring swords and fight And war the
flesh with all our might, All car-nal ties we now will break And
1.
2.
in the pow'r of God we'll shake. God we'll shake.

In the autumn of 1837 the Shakers experienced a great revival that lasted for more than ten years and that produced a large quantity of songs. Many of these were "gift" or "vision" songs, revealed to the faithful in dreams or visions, sometimes by the spirit of Mother Ann, sometimes by angels, and other times by the spirits of famous persons whose relation to the Shaker religion is not readily explicable: Alexander the Great, Queen Elizabeth, George Washington, William Penn, Christopher Columbus, Thomas Jefferson, Napoleon, and many others. "Native" songs were received from the spirits of American Indians, Eskimos, Chinese, Hottentots, and other heathen races. When the Shakers were possessed by the spirits of Indians, they behaved like Indians themselves. An eyewitness described a "dancing night" at which "eight or nine of the Sisters became possessed of the Spirits of Indian Squaws and about six of the Brothers became Indians: then ensued a regular 'Pow Wow,' with whooping, yelling, and strange antics. . . ." Here is an example of an Indian "vision song" received in 1838:

One of the Shaker exercises consisted of a sort of lively whirling dance, "during which the worshippers constantly turned or whirled" (Andrews), at the same time singing an appropriate song. Many of the Shaker songs were "action songs," that is, songs that described an action which was performed during the singing. They had, for instance, "bowing songs," such as the following:

I will bow and be simple
I will bow and be free
I will bow and be humble
Yea bow like the willow tree.

Then there was a "hopping and jumping" song which is quite graphic in its description of movement:

Hop up and jump up and whirl round, whirl round,
Gather love, here it is, all round, all round.
Here is love flowing round, catch it as you whirl round,
Reach up and reach down, here it is all round.

In a ritual song of mortification, the faithful "scour and scrub" to take away the stains of sin:

Bow down low, bow down low,
Wash, wash, clean, clean, clean, clean.
Scour and scrub, scour and scrub
From this floor the stains of sin.

Another time the ritual might be that of sweeping the floor clean:

Sweep, sweep and cleanse your floor,
Mother's standing at the door,
She'll give us good and precious wheat,
With which there is no chaff nor cheat.

The imaginary drinking of "spiritual wine" was another Shaker ritual that had its appropriate songs. "The Gift of spiritual wine," wrote Isaac N. Youngs, "carried a great evidence of its reality, by the paroxysms of intoxication which it produced, causing those who drank it to stagger and reel like drunken people." This realistic imitation of drunkenness is reflected in such drinking songs as the following:

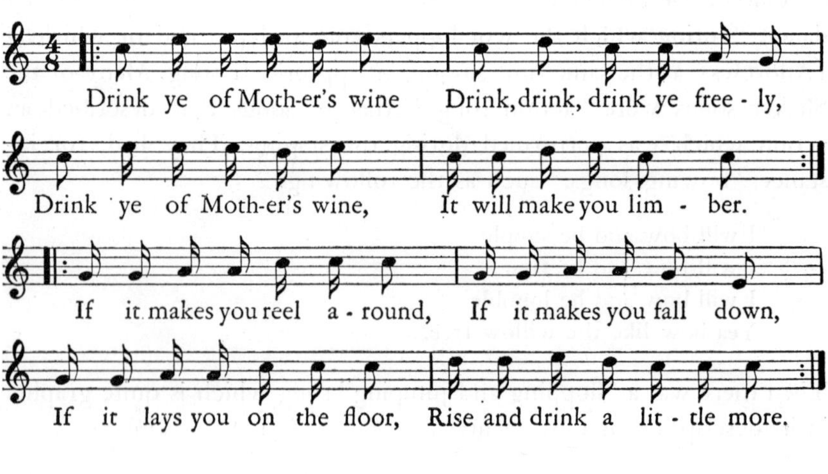
Drink ye of Moth-er's wine Drink, drink, drink ye free - ly,
Drink ye of Moth-er's wine, It will make you lim - ber.
If it makes you reel a - round, If it makes you fall down,
If it lays you on the floor, Rise and drink a lit - tle more.

It is easy to laugh at the antics of the Shakers and to ridicule the crude and naïve manifestations of their religious fervor. But they contributed something vital and genuine to American folkways, both in their songs and in their dances. They had what one of their most famous songs describes as "the gift to be simple." In their best songs and rituals there is a spirit of play, a sense of the dramatic, and a feeling for plastic movement that can readily be transferred to the aesthetic realm of choreographic art, as Martha Graham has done in the ballet *Appalachian Spring*, with music by Aaron Copland based partly on traditional Shaker tunes.

No song more fully embodies the Shaker spirit than does the one titled "Simple Gifts," a favorite among all Shaker communities in the United States. It is said to have been composed in 1848. The tempo is allegro:

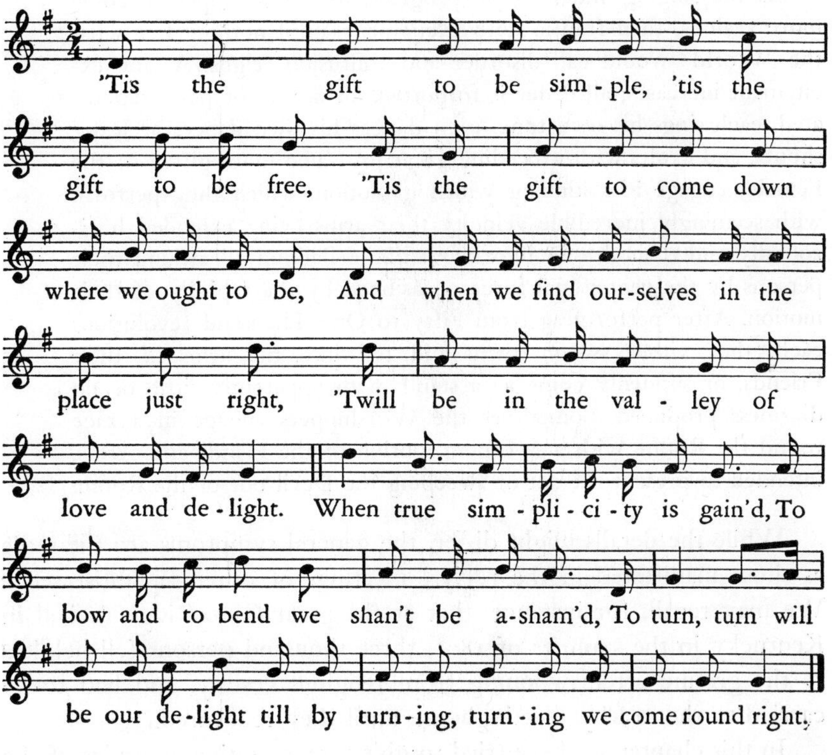

When fully under control, the exercises of the Shakers, including elaborate marching formations and ritual dances of various kinds, were well ordered and disciplined. But under the effect of revival frenzy, decorum was often destroyed and unrestrained freedom prevailed in the expression of religious emotion through song and dance. A meeting at West Union, Indiana, in 1851, was thus described by an eyewitness:

> The Sound is like mighty thunderings, Some a Stamping with all their might and Roaring out against the nasty stinking beast. . . . Others turning with great Power and warring against the flesh, and at the same time a number Speaking with new tongues with such Majestic Signs and motions that it makes the powers of Darkness tremble. . . .

Another eyewitness account, by A. J. Macdonald, describes a meeting in the grip of extreme revival frenzy:

> As the singing and dancing progress, the Worshippers become more zealous, then frantic with excitement—until nothing but what the "World" would call disorder and confusion reigns. As the excitement increases, all order is forgotten, all unison of parts repudiated, each sings his own tune, each dances his own dance, or leaps, shouts, and exults with exceeding great joy—The more gifted of the Females engage in a kind of whirling motion, which they perform with seemingly incredible velocity their arms being extended horizontally and their dresses blown out like a Balloon all around their persons by the centrifugal force occasioned by the rapidity of their motion. After performing from Fifty to One Thousand revolutions each, they either swoon away and fall into the arms of their Friends, or suddenly come to a stand, with apparently little or no dizziness produced. Sometimes the Worshippers engage in a race round the Room, with a sweeping motion of the Hands and Arms, intended to present the act of sweeping the Devil out of the Room.

While the details might differ, the general symptoms are the same as those manifested in the revival meetings of other separatist sects. We may recall, for instance, that at the great Cane Ridge revival in Kentucky in the summer of 1801, three thousand persons fell helpless to the ground after swooning from religious ecstasy, and had to be carried to the nearby meetinghouse until they recovered.

In this chapter we have tried to give representative examples of the songs that came out of the great revivals and camp meetings that swept the country from about 1800 to the eve of the Civil War, reaching their apogee in the 1830s and 1840s. The music, as we have observed, came from many sources and could not, in its constituent elements, be regarded as a product of American revivalism. But the songs as a whole were shaped by the environment and emerged remade as manifestations of the American frontier.

If anyone doubts that these revival songs are woven deep in the fabric of America's music, deep in the strands of our national culture, let him recall a song that all Americans know, that they have sung for generations, and that each rising generation inherits anew—the song that we know as "The Battle Hymn of the Republic," but that, years before Julia Ward Howe wrote the words beginning "Mine eyes have seen the glory of the coming of the Lord," was a rousing camp-meeting spiritual, with a typical repetitive stanza and a swinging hallelujah chorus.

While the revivalist movement and the camp-meeting tradition were developing this large body of popular hymnody, a closely related but distinctive body of religious folk song was taking shape among the Negroes of the United States. The growth of the Negro spirituals, and their "discovery" by the country at large at the time of the Civil War, will be the subject of the next chapter.

chapter twelve

The Negro spirituals

Ole Satan is a busy ole man,
He roll stones in my way;
Mass' Jesus is my bosom friend,
He roll 'em out o' my way.
NEGRO SPIRITUAL.

There are very few accounts of the singing of the Negroes on Southern plantations previous to the Civil War. One of the earliest and most detailed accounts is that of Frances Anne (Fanny) Kemble, the English actress and writer who was married to Pierce Butler and spent some time on his plantations on the coast of Georgia. In her *Journal of a Residence on a Georgia Plantation in 1838–1839,* Fanny Kemble writes of a Negro funeral that she attended in the evening, by torchlight: "Presently the whole congregation uplifted their voices in a hymn, the first high wailing notes of which—sung all in unison . . . — sent a thrill through all my nerves." Here is Mrs. Kemble's description of the singing of the Negroes who rowed to St. Simon's, one of the Georgia Sea Islands at the entrance of the Altamaha on which her husband's rice and cotton plantations were located: [1]

> . . . As the boat pushed off, and the steersman took her into the stream, the men at the oars set up a chorus, which they continued to chant in unison with each other, and in time with their stroke, till their voices were heard no more from the distance. I believe I have mentioned . . . the peculiar characteristics of this veritable negro minstrelsy—how they all sing in unison, having never, it appears, attempted or heard anything like part-singing. Their voices seem oftener tenor than any other quality, and the tune and time they

[1] Kemble, *Journal of a Residence on a Georgia Plantation in 1838–1839,* pp. 128–129.

keep something quite wonderful; such truth of intonation and accent would make almost any music agreeable. That which I have heard these people sing is often plaintive and pretty, but almost always has some resemblance to tunes with which they must have become acquainted through the instrumentality of white men; their overseers or masters whistling Scotch or Irish airs, of which they have produced by ear these *rifacciamenti.* The note for note reproduction of "Ah! vous dirai-je, maman?" in one of the most popular of the so-called negro melodies with which all America and England are familiar, is an example of this very transparent plagiarism; and the tune with which Mr. —'s rowers started him down the Altamaha, as I stood at the steps to see him off, was a very distinct descendant of "Coming Through the Rye." The words, however, were astonishingly primitive, especially the first line, which, when it bursts from their eight throats in high unison, sent me into fits of laughter:

> Jenny shake her toe at me,
>   Jenny gone away.
> (*bis*)
> Hurrah! Miss Susy, oh!
>   Jenny gone away.
> (*bis*)

Elsewhere Mrs. Kemble speaks of "an extremely pretty, plaintive, and original air," to which "there was but one line, which was repeated with a sort of wailing chorus—'Oh! my massa told me, there's no grass in Georgia.' Upon inquiring the meaning of which, I was told it was supposed to be the lamentation of a slave from one of the more northerly states, Virginia or Carolina, where the labor of hoeing the weeds, or grass as they call it, is not nearly so severe as here, in the rice and cotton lands of Georgia."

Later in her journal, Mrs. Kemble confesses that in her daily voyages up and down the river she has encountered a number of Negro songs that seemed to her "extraordinarily wild and unaccountable," and for which she could recall no counterpart in any European melodies familiar to her. Of these songs she writes: "The way in which the chorus strikes in with the burden, between each phrase of the melody chanted by a single voice, is very curious and effective. . . ." What she describes here is the leader-and-chorus or call-and-response pattern that we have noted as characteristic of African singing.

Mrs. Kemble refers repeatedly to the "strangeness" of the words of the Negro songs, most of which made no sense to her. She was struck by the oddness of one song whose burden was the line "God made man, and man makes money!" Truly, as she remarks, "a peculiar poetical proposition." She mentions "another ditty . . . they call Caesar's song: it is an extremely spirited war-song, beginning, 'The trumpets blow, the bugles blow—Oh, stand your ground!'" It would be strange indeed to hear the slaves sing a "war-song," and there is a strong suspicion that this may be an early example of a Negro spiritual.

Apparently no sharp distinction was made, either in the occasion or the manner, between the singing of purely secular songs and those having some sacred or spiritual import. Sir Charles Lyell, writing about a visit to a Southern plantation in 1849, remarks of some Negro boatmen: "Occasionally they struck up a hymn, taught them by the Methodists, in which the most sacred subjects were handled with a strange familiarity." [2] Just such a rowing song as Lyell describes, from the Port Royal Islands of South Carolina, is included in the first collection of Negro spirituals to be published, *Slave Songs of the United States* (1867). In it the Archangel Michael is made to row the boat ashore:

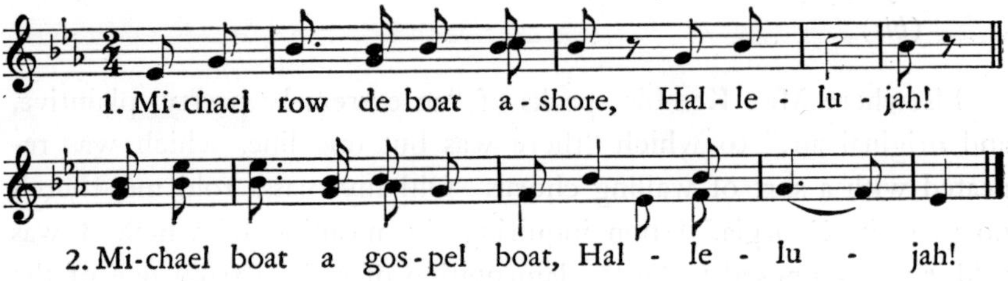
1. Mi-chael row de boat a-shore, Hal-le-lu-jah!
2. Mi-chael boat a gos-pel boat, Hal-le-lu-jah!

Each line of this spiritual that was used as a rowing song is followed by the refrain, "Hallelujah!" Additional verses of this song, "Michael Row the Boat Ashore," are quoted below to illustrate the making of a Negro spiritual:

On de rock gwine home in Jesus' name.
Gabriel blow de trumpet horn.
Jordan stream is wide and deep.
Jesus stand on t'oder side.
O de Lord he plant his garden deh.
He raise de fruit for you to eat.

[2] Lyell, *A Second Visit to the United States of North America*, New York, 1849, p. 244.

He dat eat shall neber die.
Sinner row to save your soul.

In addition to the repeated hallelujah refrain, the reader will recognize in these verses some of the basic themes or tag lines of the revival hymns discussed in the previous chapter. What is distinctive about the Negro song, besides the manner of singing, is the adaptation of the imagery and vocabulary of evangelical hymnody to concrete situations related to his own environment and experience. For instance, in the last verse the idea of the sinner saving his soul is fused with the necessity of performing a given task (rowing) and attaining a practical objective (the shore). The crossing over Jordan is identified with the immediate task of rowing across a body of water. The line "Michael boat a music boat" probably an improvised variant on the line "Michael boat a gospel boat," takes one by surprise; yet it leads naturally to the mention of Gabriel's trumpet in the next line. This in turn suggests the Last Judgment and the need to care for one's soul:

O you mind your boastin' talk.
Boastin' talk will sink your soul.

There the soul, like the boat, is in possible danger of *sinking*—a bold and appropriate metaphor. The danger incurred by the sinner is assimilated into the prospect of danger that could beset the boat in landing if overtaken by darkness and rising waters:

When de ribber overflo,
O poor sinner, how you land?
Ribber run and darkness comin'.
Sinner row to save your soul.

The more one lingers over this Negro spiritual, the more one becomes aware of how beautifully its seemingly disparate elements are bound together by an imaginative fusion of themes and images.

The English musician Henry Russell, who was in the United States from 1833 to 1841, writes in his memoirs about a Negro service that he attended:

> I had long taken a deep interest in negro life, and I often wondered whether it was possible that negroes could originate melody. I was desirous of testing this, and I made up my mind to visit many negro meetings throughout several of the States. On my entering the

> chapel at Vicksburg [then a slave town] there was a restlessness about the little congregation—whether it emanated from one or two white people being present I cannot say. There was one peculiarity that struck me very forcibly. When the minister gave out his own version of the Psalm, the choir commenced singing so rapidly that the original tune absolutely ceased to exist—in fact, the fine old psalm tune became thoroughly transformed into a kind of negro melody; and so sudden was the transformation, by accelerating the time, that, for a moment, I fancied that not only the choir but the little congregation intended to get up a dance as part of the service.[3]

Russell was not far wrong in this last supposition. Had white persons not been present it is very likely that the Negroes at that service would have taken up that peculiar type of religious dancing and singing known as "shout," which will be described later in this chapter. It should be remarked that when Russell speaks of "negro melody" he means that of blackface minstrelsy, the only kind with which he was familiar. We may assume therefore that the old psalm tune which he heard was not only greatly accelerated but also strongly syncopated, in the manner of most minstrel melodies.

It is important to observe that hymns and spirituals were sung not only in church and at religious meetings but also as accompaniment to all kinds of labor. The singing of spirituals by rowers among the Georgia Sea Islands has already been noted. In an account written by William Cullen Bryant, who visited a tobacco factory in Richmond, Virginia, in 1843, we learn of Negroes singing while performing sedentary work. The owner of the factory, noticing that Bryant's attention was caught by the singing, offered some comments on it:

> What is remarkable [he continued], their tunes are all psalm tunes and the words are from hymn books; their taste is exclusively for sacred music; they will sing nothing else. Almost all these persons are church members; we have not a dozen about the factory who are not so. Most of them are of the Baptist persuasion; a few are Methodists.[4]

If we compare this with the description of Negro singing given by Samuel Davies in 1755 (see p. 80), we are at once impressed by the

[3] Henry Russell, *Cheer! Boys, Cheer!*, pp. 84–85.

[4] Bryant, quoted in *DeBow's Review*, n.s., I (1850), p. 326. Cited by Johnson, *Folk Culture on St. Helena Island*, p. 85.

similarity, for Davies wrote that the Negroes "are exceedingly delighted with Watts' Song" and "they have a kind of ecstatic delight in psalmody." Behind the Negro spirituals, then, was a century-long tradition "of ecstatic delight in psalmody." And what, indeed, is more characteristic of the spirituals than that quality of ecstatic delight in the glories of Heaven, the visions of the Promised Land, the mercy of Jesus, and the salvation of the sinner?

Although the religious instruction of the Negroes left much to be desired, they had ample opportunity to become familiar with English hymnody. In 1833 the Rev. Samuel J. Bryan of Savannah issued *A Plain and Easy Catechism: designed for the benefit of colored children, with several verses and hymns.* Charles C. Jones, in his work *The Religious Instruction of the Negroes,* published in 1842, states that the period from 1820 to 1842 was "a period of revival of religion in respect to this particular duty, throughout the Southern states; more especially between the years 1829 and 1835. This revival came silently, extensively, and powerfully; affecting masters, mistresses, ministers, members of the church, and ecclesiastical bodies of all the different evangelical denominations." [5] The author's statement that the revival "came silently" is not, we suppose, to be taken literally; for it gave a further impetus to the singing of hymns among the colored population.

The spread of religious instruction among the Negroes coincided with the rise of the camp-meeting movement. As we know from the journals of Lorenzo Dow and other contemporary sources, Negroes as well as whites took part in the early camp meetings. How long this practice continued is uncertain, but in any case there is no doubt that the same songs were sung by both races. In a book published in 1860 there is an account of revival singing that implies a sort of rivalry in this respect: ". . . the loudest and most fervent camp-meeting singers amongst the whites are constrained to surrender to the darkeys in *The Old Ship of Zion* or *I Want to go to Glory*." [6] The Southern evangelist Lucius Bellinger wrote of one of his camp meetings: "The negroes are out in great crowds, and sing with voices that make the woods ring." [7]

Some early writers are struck by the "wildness" of the Negroes'

[5] Jones, *The Religious Instruction of the Negroes,* pp. 96–97.

[6] Dr. R. Hundley, *Social Relations in Our Southern States.* New York, 1860, p. 348. Cited by Johnson, *loc. cit.*

[7] Bellinger, *Stray Leaves,* p. 17.

singing, others are impressed by its musicality and "correctness." An English journalist, William Howard Russell, writing in 1863, speaks of "those wild Baptist chants about the Jordan in which they delight." [8] Another Englishman, the Rev. William W. Malet, writing about the same time (1862), has this to say about the Negroes' singing:

> Just before bed-time more solemn sounds are heard: the negro is demonstrative in his religion, and loud and musical were heard every evening the hymns. . . . Remarkable for correctness are their songs, and both men's and women's voices mingled in soft though far-sounding harmony. Some old church tunes I recognized.[9]

It is a question as to whether Reverend Malet is using the term "harmony" in its literal or in a figurative sense. If the former, it would mean that the singing was in parts, something which no other account mentions. It is likely that the writer refers simply to the blending of voices of different *tessitura*, especially as he mentions the blending of men's and women's voices. In any case, the manner of Negro singing cannot be accurately described in terms either of "unison" or "harmony." It is more complex than that, a style *sui generis*. A clue to the style is contained in Emily Hallowell's remark that the "harmonies seem to arise from each [singer] holding to their own version of the melodies or from limitation of compass." A fairly comprehensive description is given by William Francis Allen in his preface to *Slave Songs of the United States*, based on singing heard in the Port Royal Islands (South Carolina) in the early 1860s:

> There is no singing in *parts*, as we understand it, and yet no two appear to be singing the same thing; the leading singer starts the words of each verse, often improvising, and the others, who "base" him, as it is called, strike in with the refrain, or even join in the solo when the words are familiar. When the "base" begins the leader often stops, leaving the rest of the words to be guessed at, or it may be they are taken up by one of the other singers. And the "basers" themselves seem to follow their own whims, beginning when they please and leaving off when they please, striking an octave above or below (in case they have pitched the tune too high), or hitting some other note that "chords," so as to produce the

[8] W. H. Russell, *My Diary, North and South*, Boston, 1863, p. 143.

[9] Malet, *An Errand to the South in the Summer of 1862*, p. 49. Cited by Johnson, *loc. cit.*

effect of a marvellous complication and variety and yet with the most perfect time and rarely with any discord. And what makes it all the harder to unravel a thread of melody out of this strange network is that, like birds, they seem not infrequently to strike sounds that cannot be precisely represented by the gamut and abound in "slides from one note to another and turns and cadences not in articulated notes."

Surely the reader who still bears in mind the account of early New England popular psalmody cannot fail to recognize the analogies between that style and the manner of singing described above: "no two appear to be singing the same thing" . . . "seem to follow their own whims" . . . "striking an octave above or below" . . . "hard to unravel a thread of melody" . . . abounding in "slides from one note to another and turns and cadences not in articulated notes." There is practically the whole catalogue of indictments drawn up against the followers of the folk tradition by the New England reformers. That Negro singing in America developed as the result of the blending of several cultural traditions is certain; and it seems equally certain that one of these traditions was the folk style of early New England psalmody and hymnody, carried southward in the late eighteenth and early nineteenth centuries.

From Allen's description of Negro singing, apart from the specific details, it is important to retain the impression of "a marvellous complication and variety," for it is this complication and variety, fused together by a powerful musical impulse (basically rhythmic), that gives to the spirituals, and to other types of American Negro song, their original and fascinating quality, most of which has been distorted or destroyed in the standardized arrangements made to conform with conventional European musical practice.

Discovery of the spirituals

As we have seen, the singing of the Negroes attracted the attention of an isolated writer here and there in the period before the Civil War. But it was only during and after the war that the songs of the Negro, and the spirituals in particular, began to arouse widespread interest and to receive general attention. The impulse to the "discovery" of the spirituals came, as might be expected, from the North. The immediate occasion was the sending of an educational mission to the

Port Royal Islands in 1861. In the words of the editors of *Slave Songs of the United States:*

> The agents of the mission were not long in discovering the rich vein of music that existed in these half-barbarous people, and when visitors from the North were on the islands, there was nothing that seemed better worth their while than to see a "shout" or hear the people sing their "sperichils."

Listed as "established favorites" in those days were "Roll, Jordan, Roll," "I Hear from Heaven Today," "Blow Your Trumpet, Gabriel," "Praise, Member," "Wrestle On, Jacob," "The Lonesome Valley."

The first American Negro spiritual to appear in print with its music is believed to be "Roll, Jordan, Roll," published by Miss Lucy McKim of Philadelphia in 1862. The second spiritual to be printed was probably "Done Wid Driber's Dribin," which appeared in an article by H. G. Spaulding titled "Under the Palmetto," published in *The Continental Monthly* for August, 1863. This song has the familiar revival refrain, "Roll, Jordan, Roll":

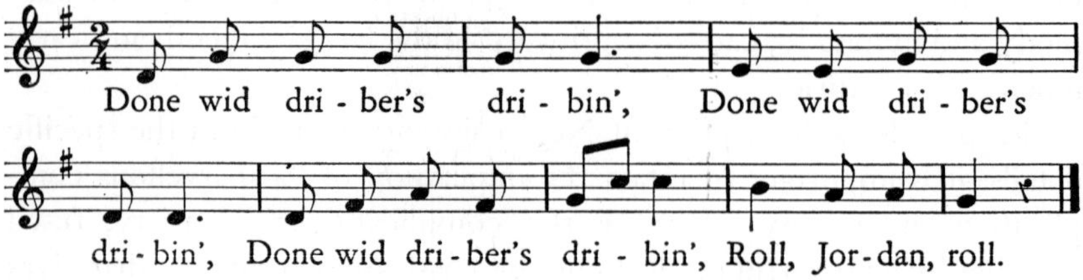

The verses continue with "Done wid Massa's hollerin' " and "Done wid Missus' scoldin'." This is one of the very few spirituals that make direct reference to emancipation.

Another emancipation song was published by Colonel Thomas Wentworth Higginson in his interesting essay, "Negro Spirituals," in *The Atlantic Monthly* for June, 1867. This was "No More Peck o' Corn for Me," also known, from its refrain, as "Many Thousands Go." Other verses are: "No more driver's lash for me,"—"No more pint o' salt for me,"—"No more hundred lash for me," etc. According to Higginson, the peck of corn and pint of salt were slavery's rations. It is said to have been first sung when Beauregard took the slaves to the islands to build the fortifications at Hilton Head and Bay Point:

No more peck o' corn for me, No more, no more;
No more peck o' corn for me, Man - y tou - sand go.

Colonel Higginson speculated on the origin of the spirituals and recounted an incident that enabled him actually to witness the "birth" of one of these songs. This occurred when he was being rowed across from Beaufort to Ladies' Island:

> One of the oarsmen, a brisk young fellow . . . on being asked for his theory of the matter, dropped out a coy confession. "Some good speritual s," he said, "are start jest out o' curiosity. I bin a-raise a sing myself once." . . . I implored him to proceed.
>
> "Once we boys went for tote some rice, and de nigger driver, he keep a-callin' on us: and I say, "O, de ole nigger driver!" Den anudder said, "Fust t'ing my mammy tole me was not'in so bad as a nigger driver." Den I made a sing, just puttin' a word and den anudder word."
>
> Then he began singing and the men, after listening a moment, joined in the chorus as if it were an old acquaintance, though they evidently had never heard it before. I saw how easily a new "sing" took root among them.

O' de ole nigger driver!
  O, gwine away!
Fust t'ing my mammy tell me.
  O, gwine away!
Tell me 'bout de nigger driver,
  O, gwine away!
Nigger driver second devil,
  O, gwine away!
Best t'ing for do he driver,
  O, gwine away!
Knock he down and spoil he labor—
  O, gwine away!

One reason, of course, that the Negroes could so readily improvise a song was that the metrical pattern was pretty well established beforehand. The above arrangement conforms to the general pattern of Negro songs with which the reader is already familiar. In the same manner, a poet can readily turn out a sonnet, because the form has already been determined for him.

In an address delivered in Philadelphia on July 9, 1862, J. Miller McKim told of a somewhat similar experience, except that he was given only an explanation, not a specimen of the product:

> I asked one of these blacks, one of the most intelligent of them, where they got these songs.
>
> "Dey make 'em, sah."
>
> "How do they make them?"
>
> After a pause, evidently casting about for an explanation, he said:
>
> "I'll tell you; it's dis way: My master call me up an' order me a short peck of corn and a hundred lash. My friends see it and is sorry for me. When dey come to de praise meeting dat night dey sing about it. Some's very good singers and know how; and dey work it in, work it in, you know, till dey get it right; and dat's de way."[10]

Although this anecdote savors of abolitionist propaganda, we may accept the hypothesis that many of the spirituals (and other songs too, for that matter) were "made" in this spontaneous manner, while reiterating the proviso that they were made largely out of pre-existing elements, both as regards the words and the music. That the factor of invention, as well as of accretion and transformation, entered into the process, is not to be denied. But it was probably invention of detail rather than of a whole: some felicitous phrase or contagious tag line thought up and caught up on the spur of the moment and incorporated into the ever-changing content of a traditionally established form. We have already observed something of this "spontaneous generation" of song in connection with the revival hymns, and the principle underlying the creation of the Negro spirituals is the same; as it is, indeed, for all folk music.

This seems an appropriate place to quote the definition of a spiritual —rather ironic, but realistic—attributed by R. W. Gordon to "a learned colleague":

> A Spiritual is nothing but a tune—never twice the same—accompanied by not over two standard verses—not the same—followed by

[10] Quoted in Allen, *Slave Songs of the United States.*

as many other verses from different songs as the singer happens to remember.[11]

It is salutary to quote this definition here because it will serve to warn the reader against assuming that there is ever one and only one version of a Negro spiritual. There is, for example, no fixed, definite, and unvarying musicopoetic entity known as "Nobody Knows the Trouble I See." Any particular printed version or arrangement is arbitrary and artificially static. The spiritual itself is a composite and infinitely varied creation that exists with its own genuine being only in that moment of time during which it is actually sung. Captured on a phonograph recording, that experience can be repeated at will, but the song itself goes on having its own independent existence, so that another recording made a year later will not be exactly the same song. We may be able to record a hundred different versions of a song to which we give the same title; but we cannot say that any *one* of these versions is *the* song. The song is all of them together and none of them individually.

The first collection of Negro spirituals

As a result of the activities of the United States Educational Mission to the Port Royal Islands, the first collection of American Negro spirituals was published in 1867 under the title, *Slave Songs of the United States*, edited by William Francis Allen, Charles Pickard Ware, and Lucy McKim Garrison. Though this collection contains many errors and bears slight evidence of musical scholarship, it yet retains its importance as a primary source. Only the words and the tunes are printed, without harmonization. Some representative spirituals from this collection will be quoted. The editors were at least aware of the difficulties of their undertaking. They had heard these spirituals sung in their pristine state by the Negroes on these isolated rice and cotton plantations: they knew it was different from any other kind of singing with which they were familiar, and they made it clear in their prefatory remarks that their notations could only approximate, not accurately reproduce, the characteristic traits of the music in actual performance:

[11] Gordon, "The Negro Spiritual," in *The Carolina Low Country*, p. 193.

> It is difficult to express the entire character of these negro ballads by mere musical notes and signs. The odd turns made in the throat and the curious rhythmic effect produced by single voices chiming in at different irregular intervals seem almost as impossible to place on the score as the singing of birds or the tones of an aeolian harp.

Only the advent of the phonograph could solve this problem of reproducing folk music as it actually sounds.

Most of the early writers refer to the spirituals as being in the "minor," probably because the unusual intervals and the manner of singing gave in many cases an impression of "melancholy" or "plaintiveness." In spite of this impression, it has been established that the majority of spirituals are in the major mode. Of 527 Negro songs examined by H. E. Krehbiel, 331 were found to be in the major mode. In addition, 111 songs were pentatonic. Furthermore, according to Krehbiel's data:

> Of the 331 major songs twenty . . . have a flat seventh; seventy-eight—that is, one fourth—have no seventh, and forty-five, or nearly one-seventh, have no fourth. Fourth and seventh are the tones which are lacking in the pentatonic scale, and the songs without one or the other of them approach the pentatonic songs in what may be called their psychological effect.

On the whole, Krehbiel interprets the musical data "as emphasizing the essentially energetic and contented character of Afro-American music, notwithstanding that it is the fruit of slavery." [12]

One of the most characteristic spirituals, both musically and poetically, that appeared in this pioneer collection, is the one called "O'er the Crossing," concerning which the editors printed the following note: "This 'infinitely quaint description of the length of the heavenly road,' as Col. Higginson styles it, is one of the most peculiar and widespread of the spirituals. It was sung as given [here] in Caroline Co., Virginia, and probably spread southward from this state variously modified in different localities." What is especially to be remarked in this song is the rhythmic pattern of the melody at the phrase beginning, "Keep prayin'." This rhythmic figure, , is characteristic

[12] Krehbiel, *Afro-American Folk Songs*, p. 70. Copyright 1914 by G. Schirmer, Inc.

of all types of Afro-American music, from spirituals to ragtime. Here is the song:

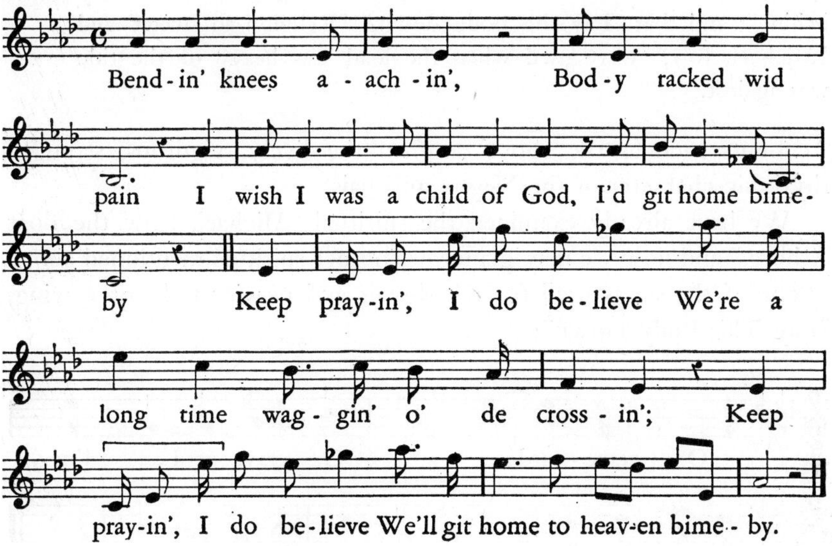
Bend - in' knees a - ach - in', Bod - y racked wid
pain I wish I was a child of God, I'd git home bime -
by Keep pray - in', I do be - lieve We're a
long time wag - gin' o' de cross - in'; Keep
pray-in', I do be - lieve We'll git home to heav-en bime - by.

It is not clear what is meant by the line "We're a long time waggin' o' de crossin'." It has been suggested that "waggin' " may be a corruption of "lagging." Another possibility is "Waggoning o'er de crossin'," which would relate to a familiar experience in fording rivers. The fourth stanza of this spiritual contains some striking imagery:

> O see dat forked lightnin'
>   A-jump from cloud to cloud,
> A-pickin' up God's chil'n;
>   Dey'll git home bime-by.
> Pray, mourner, I do believe, etc.

The use of spirituals as working songs has already been mentioned. Of the spirituals included in *Slaves Songs of the United States*, twelve were most commonly used for rowing. One of the editors, Charles P. Ware, writes as follows about these songs:

> As I have written these tunes, two measures are to be sung to each stroke, the first measure being accented by the beginning of the stroke, the second by the rattle of the oars in the rowlocks. On the passenger boat at the [Beaufort] ferry they rowed from sixteen to

thirty strokes a minute; twenty-four was the average. Of the tunes I heard I should say that the most lively were "Heaven bell a-ring," "Jine 'em," "Rain fall," "No man," "Bell da ring" and "Can't stay behin' "; and that "Lay this body down," "Religion so sweet" and "Michael, row," were used when the load was heavy or the tide was against.

Accounts such as the above confirm the lively, vigorous, strongly rhythmic character of the Negro spirituals.

We have already examined the spiritual "Michael, Row the Boat Ashore," and now we may glance at another spiritual mentioned above as one of the songs used for the slower and heavier tasks of rowing, "Lay This Body Down":

This may have been the same song that W. H. Russell heard when he was being rowed from Pocotaligo to Barnwell Island by some Negro boatmen at midnight:

> The oarsmen, as they bent to their task, beguiled the way singing in unison a real negro melody, which was unlike the works of the Ethiopian Serenaders as anything in song could be unlike another. It was a barbaric sort of madrigal, in which one singer beginning was followed by the others in unison, repeating the refrain in chorus, and full of quaint expression and melancholy:—
>
> Oh your soul! oh my soul! I'm going to the churchyard
> To lay this body down;
> Oh my soul! oh your soul! We're going to the churchyard
> To lay this nigger down.
>
> And then some appeal to the difficulty of passing the "Jawdam" constituted the whole of the song, which continued with unabated energy during the whole of the little voyage. To me it was a strange scene. The stream, dark as Lethe, flowing between the silent, houseless, rugged banks, lighted up near the landing by the fire in the

woods, which reddened the sky—the wild strain, and the unearthly adjurations to the singers' souls, as though they were palpable, put me in mind of the fancied voyage across the Styx.[13]

Apart from its picturesque quality, this account from a book published in 1863 confirms the description given by Mrs. Kemble of the manner in which the spirituals were sung: the singing in unison, the beginning of each verse by the leader alone, the repeating of the refrain in chorus, and a certain wild and barbaric effect that these writers are able to feel but not to define.

Russell states that the Negro melodies he heard in the Port Royal Islands were completely unlike those of the "Ethiopian Serenaders," that is, the blackface minstrels. H. G. Spaulding, in the article previously cited, wrote that the melodies of the Negro spirituals "bear as little resemblance to the popular Ethiopian melodies of the day as twilight to noonday." Both writers are contradicted by the musical facts. Doubtless they received an impression of hearing something completely different because of the manner of singing and the circumstances under which they heard the spirituals. But the tunes themselves in many cases reveal a close kinship with those made familiar by the blackface minstrels. The editors of *Slave Songs of the United States* were sometimes aware of these similarities. Regarding the spiritual "Gwine Follow," William Allen observes: "The second part of this tune is evidently 'Buffalo' (variously known also as 'Charleston' or 'Baltimore') 'Gals.' "—

Tit - ty Ma - ry, you know I gwine
fol-low, I gwine fol-low, gwine fol-low, Brud-der
Wil-liam, you know I gwine to fol-low, For to
do my Fa-der will. 'Tis well and good I'm a -

[13] W. H. Russell, *op. cit.*, chap. 18.

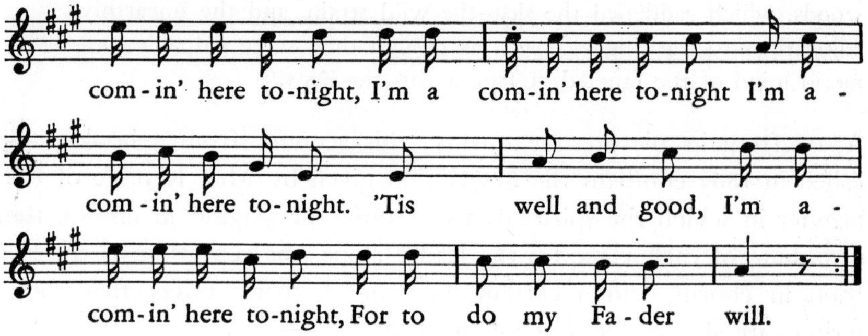
com - in' here to-night, I'm a com-in' here to-night I'm a -
com - in' here to- night. 'Tis well and good, I'm a -
com-in' here to-night, For to do my Fa - der will.

Additional similarities were noted by H. E. Krehbiel in his work, *Afro-American Folk Songs.* He observed particularly "a palpable likeness" between "Lord, Remember Me" and "Camptown Races," the latter composed by Stephen Foster in 1850. He believes that the tune was invented by Foster and borrowed by the Negroes for their spiritual. This is entirely plausible; yet the possibility of a common ancestor for both should not be discounted. The exact process of tune borrowing, conscious and unconscious, that went on during this period will in all probability never be fully known nor completely traced. What matters most, perhaps, is to recognize, in addition to definite borrowings (whatever their direction), a general family resemblance in the basic melodic materials of the three main popular traditions of vocal music that developed in the United States during the first half of the nineteenth century: the revival hymns of the whites, the Negro spirituals and work songs, and the so-called "plantation" or "Ethiopian" melodies. What gave to each current or branch its peculiar character was the "working over" of the material, the transformation of basic elements through the shaping spirit and the prevailing trend of each tradition, each with its concomitant cultural factors, ranging from ancestral African patterns to vulgarized commercial entertainment. None of these traditions was particular about the kind of materials it used, provided these could be made effective for the purpose at hand. And the force of the tradition, in each case, generally brought about the transformation required for its needs. There are examples of old British ballads, for instance, so "worked over" by the tradition of Negro folk singing that they are scarcely recognizable.

Regarding the spiritual "Oh, Freedom Over Me," Krehbiel remarks that it "challenges no interest for its musical contents, since it is a compound of two white men's tunes—"Lily Dale," a sentimental ditty, and "The Battle Cry of Freedom," a patriotic song composed by George F. Root. . . ."[14] The challenge, however, would lie in hearing what the Negroes might do with this composite, borrowed tune after they had worked it over for a generation or two. Folk music is made, not born.

As a final selection from *Slave Songs of the United States*, we quote the spiritual "Good-bye, Brother," which thoroughly resembles a typical "Ethiopian" melody, or, if you prefer, a Stephen Foster tune:

Good-bye, bro-ther, good-bye, bro-ther, If I don't see you more;
Now God bless you, now God bless you, If I don't see you more.

The folk tradition of the spirituals

Mention has previously been made of the survival of lining-out among the Negroes. This practice is found in connection with the slow-paced and embellished singing of old hymns, undoubtedly derived from the eighteenth-century tradition. Since this procedure conforms perfectly to the leader-and-chorus or call-and-response pattern of African song, its adoption by the Negroes in America is a natural instance of musical syncretism or blending. Mary Allen Grissom, in *The Negro Sings a New Heaven*, recorded some examples of Negro hymns sung and chanted with lining-out by the leader. Regarding these she writes:

> This type of singing is used particularly at funerals and very solemn occasions. It is rarely heard now. It probably had its origin in the old type of hymn-singing, used in the early church, in which the hymn was "lined" by a leader. When given with the Negro's peculiar style of chanting and sliding to and from the main melody note, it is distinctly a thing apart. The example given here is purely Negro both in tune and words, but frequently one hears a well-known

[14] Krehbiel, *op. cit.*, p. 17.

hymn chanted. The entire congregation sings in unison with each line of the verse chanted by the leader.[15]

FULL CHORUS
Very slowly
I — stood out - side — thay — gate They —
would — not — let — me — in — me —
CHANT (LEADER)
in. I prayed to my good lawd. I — prayed — to —
my — good — Lawd
CHANT
to cleanse me from all sin To —
cleanse — me — from — all — sin uh all — sin.

We have now brought the history of the religious songs of the American Negro—including the African backgrounds discussed in an earlier chapter—up to the time of their general "discovery" and initial diffusion through the printed page shortly after the close of the Civil War. It would be well at this point to summarize the data that we have been able to assemble from the various contemporary accounts to which reference has been made.

1. The spirituals were sung with a freedom, independence, and individuality in the vocal lines that conveyed the effect of a sort of unconventional polyphony, attaining to "a marvellous complication and variety."

2. There was a prevalence of the leader-and-chorus (or call-and-response) pattern, the melody sung or chanted by a single voice, the chorus joining in with the refrain.

3. Spirituals were used as working songs, e.g., for rowing and for field tasks, as well as at religious meetings.

4. Some of the melodies resembled familiar European tunes, while others were "extraordinarily wild and unaccountable."

[15] Descriptive note and musical example used by permission of the publisher, The University of North Carolina Press.

5. There was much singing of standard hymns, especialy Methodist and Baptist, among the Negro population of the South.

6. The Negroes participated in camp-meetings and often sang the same revival songs as the whites did.

7. At some Negro services, psalms and long-meter hymns were sung according to the old practice of lining-out (which could be readily assimilated into the call-and-response pattern).

8. The singing of the Negroes was characterized by peculiar vocal effects, difficult if not impossible to indicate by regular notation.

In the remainder of this chapter an attempt will be made to throw further light on these aspects of Negro song, with a view to establishing its true nature and its present status.

It is necessary to recognize the existence of two main currents in the history of the Negro spiritual after the Civil War. One current tended to assimilate the spirituals into the forms and techniques of European art music. The other tended to conserve their traditional folk character with retention of primitive and archaic survivals. The first spread rapidly and widely through the publication of harmonized arrangements, the tours of trained Negro choirs at home and abroad, concert performances by celebrated artists, the vogue of choral arrangements used by choirs and glee clubs everywhere, and instrumental transcriptions or stylizations of every sort. The second followed a kind of undercover existence, somewhat as the original Negro spirituals did during the ante-bellum period; that is, cultivated by the folk, chiefly in rural areas or small communities, and attracting little attention from outsiders. It is to this second current that we shall direct our attention, not because we deprecate the pleasure that may be derived from listening to artistic arrangements of Negro spirituals beautifully sung by trained artists but because it seems more important, from the standpoint of cultural history, to try to know and understand a musical tradition in its unique and essential nature rather than in its secondary derivations. The spirituals are a folk product, and their true character must therefore be sought in a folk tradition.

The folklorist should be our guide in any folk tradition. It is to the folklorists of the twentieth century that we owe the "rediscovery" of the Negro spirituals, and indeed of virtually the whole body of Negro folk music, including the remarkable wealth of secular songs of which very little was known previously. In several current collections of American folk music, there can now be found numerous Negro songs carefully and faithfully notated with the most scrupulous regard for authenticity and accuracy. Better still, in recordings issued by Ethnic Folkways Records and by the Library of Congress, the singing itself can be heard in all the "marvellous complication and variety" that astonished and delighted the first Northern visitors to the Port Royal Islands.

One of the earliest and most detailed descriptions of authentic Negro folk singing was given by Jeannette R. Murphy in an article published in *Popular Science Monthly* for September, 1899. Speaking of the difficulty that a white person has in singing Negro spirituals, she points out that "he must break every law of musical phrasing and notation." Furthermore:

> . . . around every prominent note he must place a variety of small notes, called "trimmings," and he must sing tones not found in our scale; he must on no account leave one note until he has the next one well under control. . . . He must often drop from a high note to a very low one; he must be very careful to divide many of his monosyllabic words in two syllables, placing a forcible accent on the last one, so that "dead" will be "da-*ade*," "back" becomes "ba-*ack*," "chain" becomes "cha-*ain*."

To illustrate some of these points, Mrs. Murphy printed her notation of a spiritual, which is of exceptional interest both textually and musically: [16]

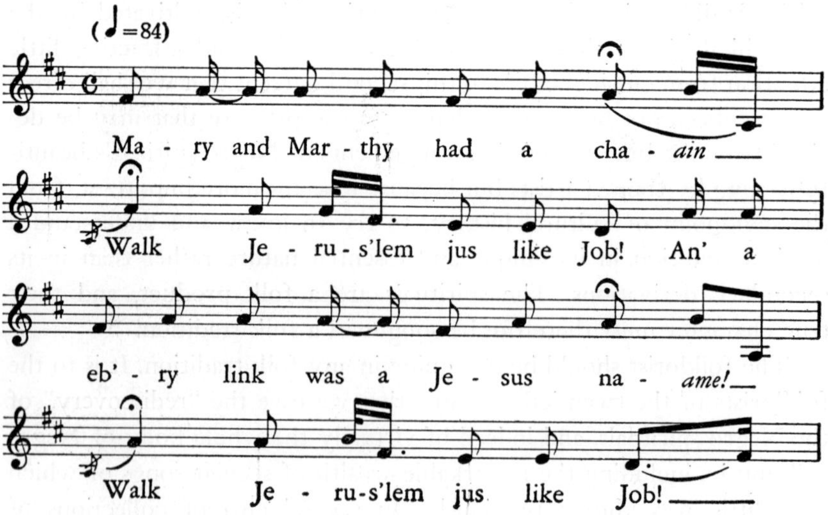

[16] *Popular Science Monthly*, Sept. 1899, p. 665.

REFRAIN
When I comes ter die I
want ter be read - y
When I comes ter die gwine ter
walk Je - ru - s'lem jus like Job!

It should be added that the difficulties mentioned above apply chiefly to persons accustomed to standard or conventional musical practice; there are white folk singers who sing spirituals in this same style, with "trimmings" and all the other characteristics of the tradition.

Natalie Curtis Burlin, in an article titled "Negro Music at Birth," published in 1919, caught the mood of Negro singing with real sympathy and understanding; she is describing a group of Negroes in a meeting at the Calhoun Industrial School in Alabama:

> Seated in rows, reverent and silent, they waited for something to happen. And as they sat, patient in the early warmth of the April sun, suddenly a rhythmic tremor seemed to sway over the group . . . there arose a vibration, an almost inaudible hum . . . and then the sound seemed to mold itself into form, rhythmic, melodic, taking shape in the air . . . till soon the entire gathering was rocking in time to one of the old plantation melodies. Men, women and children sang, and the whole group swung to and fro, from side to side, with the rhythm of the song, while many of the older people snapped their fingers in emphasis like the sharp click of an African gourd rattle. . . .
>
> And as usual with Negroes, this was extemporaneous part-singing—women making up alto, men improvising tenor or bass, the music as a whole possessed so completely by them all (or so utterly possessing them!) that they were free to abandon themselves to the inspiration of their creative instinct.[17]

[17] *Musical Quarterly*, I, 1 (Jan. 1919), 87–88.

Elsewhere in the same article, the author tells of hearing a group of Negro workers in a tobacco factory and of being impressed by "their brilliant unmodulated grouping of diatonic chords, their sudden interlocking of unrelated majors and minors, and their unconscious defiance of all man-made laws of 'voice progressions.' "

The transition from unison to part singing in the Negro spirituals evidently took place in the decades following the Civil War and was probably due to increased contact with white persons and to the influence of the schools in particular. The educated Negro grew to be ashamed of the "barbaric" elements in his music. Institutions for the education of Negroes, such as Fisk University, and the Hampton and Tuskegee Institutes, attempted to "improve" the musical quality of Negro singing by making it conform to the standards of "refined" practice. "Wrong" notes and "incorrect" harmonies had to be changed in the name of "progress." Nevertheless, the folk tradition persisted, as we have remarked, with its own style of singing, its own harmonies and progressions.

The question remains: what were the sources of this tradition? Did it originate with the Negro or did he adopt it from the white man? In recent years much controversy has surrounded this question. Some investigators, notably George Pullen Jackson, Guy B. Johnson, and Newman White, maintain that the Negro spirituals were copied from the white spirituals, that is, the religious folk songs of the rural Southern white population. Guy B. Johnson found pentatonic scales, flat sevenths, and "neutral" thirds in the folk songs of the whites as well as the Negroes, and concluded from this evidence that the songs of the latter were imitations of the former. The melodic and textual analogies between white and Negro spirituals compiled by G. P. Jackson are intended to support the same conclusion. What these investigators have done is to establish an incontrovertible correspondence or analogy between the white and Negro spirituals, but they have proved nothing as regards the *direction* of the influences. The fact that the white spirituals were *printed* before the Negro spirituals is not proof that they existed earlier in the oral tradition.

The opposite theory, upheld by Krehbiel, by Kolinski, by Herzog, and by Waterman, is that the Negro spirituals, and all Afro-American music in general, embodies traits that are fundamentally of African origin, though blended with Anglo-American elements. Waterman stresses the concept of "hot" rhythm as the essential characteristic of African and Afro-American music, and states:

> The religious songs the Negroes learned from the missionaries were soon given the "hot" treatment. Known today as "Spirituals," they are found, in their folk setting . . . to employ hand-clapping and foot-stamping in lieu of drumming, and to make consistent use of off-beat phrasing in a manner directly in line with African musical thought-patterns. The concept of "hot" religious music had been communicated to Southern whites by the close of the revivalistic period, during which heavily rhythmic hymns were useful in inducing camp-meeting "possession."[18]

More will be said regarding the concept of "hot" rhythm and its influence on American music in the chapter dealing with the rise of jazz. Waterman's thesis that Negro "hot" rhythm, as exemplified in the spirituals, may have influenced the camp-meeting hymns of Southern whites, is plausible and extremely interesting.

The musicologist M. Kolinski made a comparative study of Negro spirituals and West African songs, which has not been published, but which Waterman summarizes as follows:[19] Thirty-six spirituals are either identical or closely related in tonal structure (scale and mode) to West African songs. The spiritual "Cyan' Ride" has an almost exact counterpart in a Nigerian song, and "No More Auction Block" is clearly the same as one of the Ashanti songs. Certain features of melodic progressions such as "pendular thirds," sequences of at least three intervals of a third moving in the same direction, and both linear and pendular combinations of fourths, are common in both the spirituals and the West African songs. Duple or binary meters are predominant in both groups of songs. Syncopated and rubato figures, triplets, off-beat phrases, and sequences of several notes of equal time value, appear in the same forms in both bodies of music. The beginning rhythms of thirty-four spirituals are almost exactly like those of several songs of Dahomey and the Gold Coast. Regarding the leader-chorus pattern, generally admitted to be an African survival in the spirituals, Kolinski found that in many cases the overlapping of parts produced identical polyphonic patterns in the two types of songs.

[18] Waterman, *Journal of the American Musicological Society*, I, 1 (1948), 30.
[19] See bibliography for Chapter 4.

Fifty spirituals were discovered, in this respect, to have the identical formal structure of certain West African songs.

Kolinski concludes, according to Waterman, that while many of the spirituals are evidently patterned after European tunes, some without *apparent* distortion, they are all either altered so as to conform, or selected for adoption because they already did conform, to West African musical patterns. It is in this connection that he indicates the role of a "common musical base" of European and West African music, which facilitated this musical syncretism.

The theory of musical syncretism of West African and European elements in the American Negro spiritual—whether or not the hypothesis of a "common musical base" be accepted—seems the soundest conclusion that can be reached in the light of the available evidence.

There remains to speak of a highly important custom in connection with Negro religious practice, one having a direct and vital bearing on the preservation of the spirituals in their traditional form. We refer to the "shout" or "holy dance" of the Negroes. This ceremony was described in *The Nation* of May 30, 1867, by a writer who had witnessed it on a Southern plantation:

> . . . The true "shout" takes place on Sundays, or on "praise" nights through the week, and either in the praise-house or in some cabin in which a regular religious meeting has been held. Very likely more than half the population of a plantation is gathered together. . . . The benches are pushed back to the wall when the formal meeting is over, and old and young, men and women . . . all stand up in the middle of the floor, and when the "sperichil" is struck up begin first walking and by and by shuffling around, one after another, in a ring. The foot is hardly taken from the floor, and the progression is mainly due to a jerking, hitching motion which agitates the entire shouter and soon brings out streams of perspiration. Sometimes they dance silently, sometimes as they shuffle they sing the chorus of the spiritual, and sometimes the song itself is also sung by the dancers. But more frequently a band, composed of some of the best singers and of tired shouters, stand at the side of the room to "base" the others, singing the body of the song and clapping their hands together or on the knees. Song and dance are alike extremely energetic, and often, when the shout lasts into the middle of the night, the monotonous thud, thud of the feet prevents sleep within half a mile of the praise-house.[20]

[20] Quoted in Allen, *op. cit.*

It is above all through the rhythmic ecstasy of the shout that the "hot" element in the spirituals has been kept alive.

The association of the shout or holy dance with the spiritual seems natural indeed, for in the words of Robert W. Gordon, "Anyone who has heard the spiritual properly sung has found it practically impossible to keep still while listening. The rhythm demands bodily movement. The feet insist on tapping, the body sways in time, or the hands pat. There is an almost uncontrollable desire to rise and throw the whole body into the rhythm." [21]

The sentence, "The rhythm demands bodily movement," links the spirituals and shouts to the tradition of African music on the one hand, and on the other to some of the most distinctive manifestations of America's music from blackface minstrelsy to ragtime and jazz. We have seen that Henry Russell, when he attended the Negro church service in Vicksburg, momentarily expected the congregation "to get up and dance." Had they done so, Russell would doubtless have found the spectacle "quaint," or "barbaric," or "amusing." These were the terms most often applied by white observers to Negro singing and dancing. The dancing, in particular, was always regarded as amusing by white people. It exerted a peculiar and powerful fascination, whether in the plantation "walk-arounds" or in the "ring shouts." The division of secular or secular usage made little difference as far as the basic facts are concerned. The prancing walk-arounds and the shuffling shouts were motivated by an identical impulse and resulted from the same traditional concept of "hot" rhythm in the indissoluble union of song and dance.

The Northern abolitionists and educational uplifters who "discovered" and publicized the Negro spirituals during and after the Civil War were intent upon dignifying the Negro and emphasizing what they considered to be his higher, spiritual qualities. Hence they stressed the Negro's religious songs and neglected his secular songs, though they could not in many instances fail to recognize that there was a close connection between the two. The members of the educational mission to the Port Royal Islands prided themselves that they "were not long in discovering the rich vein of music that existed in these half-barbarous people"; but actually this was no discovery at all. At least forty years earlier white musicians and entertainers had

[21] Gordon, "The Negro Spiritual," *op. cit.*, p. 192.

begun to discover "the rich vein of music" that existed among the Negroes. From the early 1820s they began tentatively to exploit that vein, and by the 1840s the exploitation was in full swing. This exploitation of the rich vein of Negro music in the realm of popular entertainment came to be known as the "Ethiopian business," or "Negro minstrelsy," or simply "American minstrelsy." It brought to the whole of America, and to much of the rest of the world, a new type of humor and a new note of pathos that could have come only from the background of American plantation life.

chapter thirteen

The Ethiopian business

The source of Negro minstrelsy is to be found in the soil of the Southland.
CARL WITTKE, TAMBO AND BONES.

One evening in February of the year 1843, four grotesque figures in blackface, wearing white trousers, striped calico shirts, and blue calico coats with long swallowtails, appeared on the stage of the Bowery Amphitheatre in New York City. They proceeded to entertain the delighted audience with a combination of singing, dancing, Negro dialect patter, and instrumental music played on the banjo, violin, bone castanets, and tambourine. Their performance concluded with a general dance and "breakdown."

This was the historic debut of "the novel, grotesque, original and surpassingly melodious Ethiopian Band, entitled, the Virginia Minstrels," as advertised in the New York papers. The Virginia Minstrels had been recently organized in New York City by four friends who possessed a measure of musical and comic talent, and some theatrical experience. These four friends were Daniel Decatur Emmett [1] (violin), Billy Whitlock (banjo), Frank Brower ("bones"), and Dick Pelham (tambourine). All of them were to leave their mark in the American popular theater, and one of them—"Old Dan" Emmett—was to win great and lasting fame as the composer of "Dixie." They advertised their show as "an exclusively minstrel entertainment . . . entirely exempt from the vulgarities and other objectionable features which have hitherto characterized Negro extravaganzas."

From this it appears that "Negro extravaganzas"—blackface entertainment by white performers who blackened their faces with burnt cork—had been familiar to the American public for some time. American entertainers, such as George Washington Dixon and "Daddy"

[1] In his early years on the minstrel stage, he was known as "Old Dan Emmit."

Rice, had been giving blackface performances since the 1820s. How, then, could the Virginia Minstrels claim that their "Ethiopian Band" was a novel and original type of entertainment? The novel feature of the Virginia Minstrels was the association of four entertainers in a coordinated team, dressed in distinctive costumes, each assigned a specific role in the ensemble, each playing a characteristic instrument, and putting on a complete, self-contained show. This four-man team was the classic type of American minstrel show that sprang into enormous popularity in the two decades preceding the Civil War.

The "Ethiopian business" prospered tremendously, much to the chagrin of the upholders of the genteel tradition. As one writer lamented: "How frequently the most eminent in tragedy or comedy, have toiled through the choicest efforts, to scanty listeners; while upon the same evenings, fantazias upon the bones, or banjo, have called forth the plaudits of admiring thousands." It should perhaps be added that among those "admiring thousands" were some of "the most eminent in tragedy or comedy," who by no means disdained the novelty, the exuberant nonsense, the genuine pathos, and even the underlying implications of tragedy, that characterized the best of American minstrelsy. Thackeray was deeply moved by Negro minstrel melodies; the great actor Forrest declared that "he knew no finer piece of tragic acting than the impersonation of Dan Bryant as the hungry Negro in *Old Time Rocks*." (Dan Bryant, like Emmett and E. P. Christy, was one of the famous pioneer figures of minstrelsy.)

The vogue of minstrelsy spread rapidly and far. It reached California with the forty-niners during the gold rush. One minstrel troupe, headed by Henry Whitby, brought the "plantation melodies" to South America when it appeared at Santiago de Chile in 1848, en route to California around Cape Horn. American minstrel troupes went to England in the 1840s and 1850s, achieved resounding acclaim, and succeeded in amusing Queen Victoria. Blackface minstrelsy was a unique and novel type of entertainment, completely a product of the American scene. Often crude, sometimes mawkish, at its best it had an exuberant vitality and an exotic fascination. It brought to birth and kept alive a vast body of American popular song; it remained the mainstay of American popular entertainment for over half a century; and before it expired it ushered in one of the most typical and influential forms of American popular music: ragtime.

The antecedents of American minstrelsy are therefore worth looking into. Without discussing isolated eighteenth-century examples,[2] we may begin with what might be called "the pre-minstrel-show period," with such early nineteenth-century blackface entertainers as G. W. Dixon, George Nichols, Bob Farrell, and "Jim Crow" Rice. George Nichols, for many years a clown in "Purdy Brown's Theatre and Circus of the South and West" (there was a close connection between the circus and minstrelsy), is said to have got the idea of singing in Negro make-up "from a French darky banjo player, known throughout the Mississippi Valley as Picayune Butler, a peripatetic performer who passed the hat and sang, 'Picayune Butler is Going Away.' " The reference to "a French darky"—probably a Louisiana Negro from Saint Domingue or Martinique—is interesting. Nichols was one of those who claimed authorship of that popular minstrel song, "Zip Coon"—a claim disputed by both Dixon and Farrell. According to Wittke, Nichols was the first to sing in public another old-time favorite that enjoyed immense popularity, "Clare de Kitchen," which "he had adapted from a melody which he had heard sung by Negro firemen on the Mississippi River." One frequently comes across statements that this or that minstrel song was adapted from a Negro melody; but since the original source is never given, such statements cannot be corroborated. Whatever may have been the origin of "Clare de Kitchen," it was first copyrighted in 1832 by George Willig, Jr., the Baltimore music publisher, and it was widely popularized (in a somewhat altered version) by "Jim Crow" Rice.

George Washington Dixon was one of the most successful of the early blackface entertainers. He was doing Negro songs in character at Albany as early as 1827, and two years later he appeared at the Bowery Theatre in New York, where he introduced one of the favorite numbers in his repertoire, "Coal Black Rose," which Foster Damon describes as "the first burnt-cork song of comic love." Edward L. Rice, in *Monarchs of Minstrelsy*, states that the tune was "appropriated from an old ballad," which he does not identify. An edition of 1829 attributes the authorship of "Coal Black Rose" to White Snyder. Because of its early date and wide popularity—it was sung at all the theaters from 1829 on—a sample of the words and melody is given

[2] It should nevertheless be mentioned that eighteenth-century English stage impersonations of Negroes had considerable influence on early American minstrelsy, particularly as regards the use of dialect and the type of melody used in certain so-called "plantation melodies."

here, from a sheet-music edition published by Firth & Hall of New York.

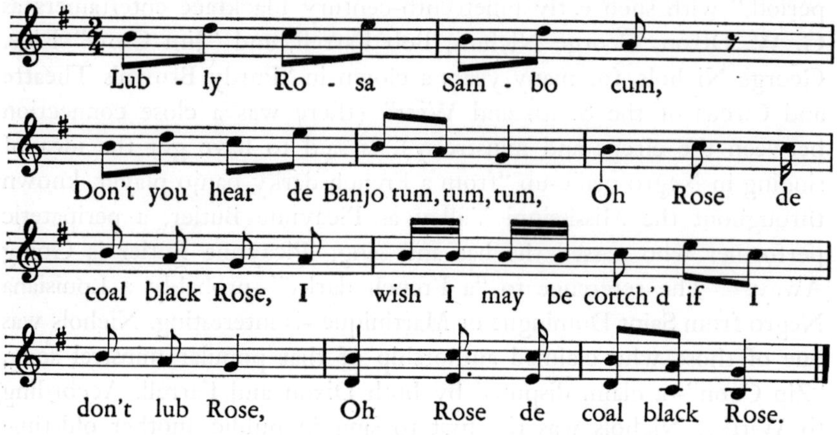

The edition from which this music was quoted has a crude sketch of "Lubly Rosa" and of "Sambo," each playing on the primitive Negro gourd banjo, also known as the "bonja" or "banga." The reader may recall that Thomas Jefferson, in his *Notes on Virginia,* called it the "banjar." This brings to mind one of the earliest of the blackface songs, the "Bonja Song," published in a sheet-music edition sometime between 1818 and 1821. The words, written by R. C. Dallas, show the stilted, artificial style of pseudo-Negro diction.

Since we have mentioned the "bonja" here, we may jump ahead chronologically for a moment to trace its transformation into the "banjo." The man credited with this development is Joel Walker Sweeney (1813–1860), who played the banjo and sang with various minstrel shows and circuses. According to Foster Damon: "Dissatisfied with the four-stringed gourd, he cut an old cheese-box in half, covered it with skin, and strung it with five strings, thus inventing the modern banjo. He is credited with doing this as early as 1830; by 1840 his reputation was secure." In the absence of concrete evidence, one is inclined to regard Mr. Sweeney's "invention" of the five-stringed banjo as rather mythical, like the invention of the lyre by Apollo. In any case, it is the instrument with four strings, not five, that is depicted on the cover of "The celebrated Banjo Song" titled "Whar Did You Cum From?" or "Knock a Nigger Down," advertised as "Sung with great Applause at Broadway Circus by Mr. J. W. Sweeney" (New York, Firth & Hall, 1840). The transition to the five-stringed banjo probably took place around 1845, and there is no proof that Sweeney was responsible for it.

Minstrel music for banjo is an extremely interesting phase of early American popular music that has not yet been sufficiently studied. On this subject Dr. Hans Nathan writes:

> Some of it is fashioned after Irish-Scotch tunes; other tunes are banjo variants of well-known minstrel songs (using typical banjo figuration); and there are original tunes. The latter kind are so primitive (constant repetition of brief motives of small range, with downward trend of the motives, etc.) that these tunes no doubt include many elements of the early plantation music. In many minstrel banjo tunes (though less frequently in those related to the fiddle music of the Old World) there are distinct and tricky syncopations.[3]

The following is an example of such a syncopated banjo tune, taken from one of Emmett's manuscripts but *not* composed by him:

Returning to George Washington Dixon— He claimed the authorship of another early and highly popular minstrel song, "Long Tail Blue," which he featured in his performances from 1827. Other blackface entertainers, such as Barney Burns and William Pennington, helped to popularize this song, which became a standard minstrel number for the next fifty years. The character is that of a Negro dandy out strolling on Sunday dressed in his elegant blue swallowtail coat. As one of the earliest and most successful of the burnt-cork melodies, "Long Tail Blue" deserves quotation; here are the words and tune of the chorus:

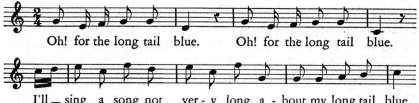

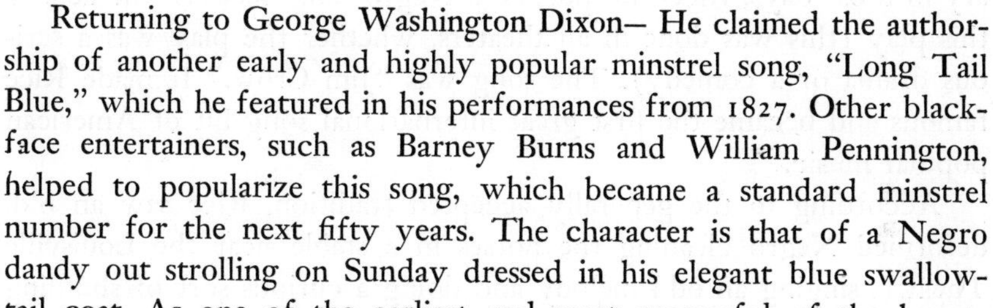

I'll — sing a song not ver - y long a - bout my long tail blue.

[3] In a letter to the author, dated Feb. 26, 1954. Dr. Nathan was kind enough to supply the banjo tune quoted here.

As Foster Damon observes, "Long Tail Blue" was the first comic song of the Negro dandy, a character that was to reappear frequently in our popular entertainment. The "dandy" stood as a contrast to that other stock type of blackface minstrelsy, the ragged "plantation darky."

"The father of minstrelsy"

We come now to the man who has been called "the father of American minstrelsy," known to his contemporaries as "Daddy" or "Jim Crow" Rice, but whose full name was Thomas Dartmouth Rice (1808–1860). He was born of poor parents in New York City and was trained to be a wood carver. Lured by the stage, he obtained occasional jobs as a supernumerary at the Park Theatre, and soon took to the road as an itinerant player, heading for the frontier settlements of the Ohio Valley. He got a job as general handyman in Ludlow and Smith's Southern Theatre in Louisville, Kentucky, and later joined a stock company at the Louisville Theatre, where he played bit parts. This was in 1828. One of the parts he played was that of a Negro field hand in a local drama titled *The Rifle.* As was customary in those days, Rice interpolated a Negro song between the acts of this play (this was done in all theaters, whether the play was a serious drama or a comedy). The song was "Jim Crow." It made Rice famous and became the first great international song hit of American popular music.

According to the generally accepted tradition, Rice saw an old, deformed Negro cleaning the horses in a stable near the Louisville Theatre, singing an odd melody and doing a curious sort of shuffling dance. Every time he reached the chorus of his song, he gave a little jump that set his "heel a-ricken." His right shoulder was drawn up high and his left leg was crooked at the knee and stiff with rheumatism, so that he walked with a limp. Rice decided to imitate this old Negro on the stage, and to copy his song, making up additional stanzas of his own. His impersonation, his shuffling step and jump, and his song, all caught the fancy of the public: in Louisville, in Cincinnati, in Pittsburgh, in Philadelphia, in Baltimore, in Washington, in New York (1832), and finally in London, where "Jim Crow" Rice achieved a sensational success in 1836.

In Pittsburgh, Rice got his friend W. C. Peters (who afterward published Stephen Foster's first minstrel songs) to write down the music of "Jim Crow." Peters opened a music store in Louisville in 1829, and it may have been at that time that Rice became friendly with him. By the end of 1830, however, Peters was back in Pittsburgh, where he went into partnership with Smith and Mellor. Within a short time many editions of "Jim Crow" were published, some of them making no mention at all of Rice. Both words and melody varied considerably in different editions. Here is the tune of "Jim Crow" as it appears in an edition published in Baltimore by George Willig, Jr., with no date, but probably issued around 1828 (the introductory measures and the piano accompaniment are omitted in the example quoted below).

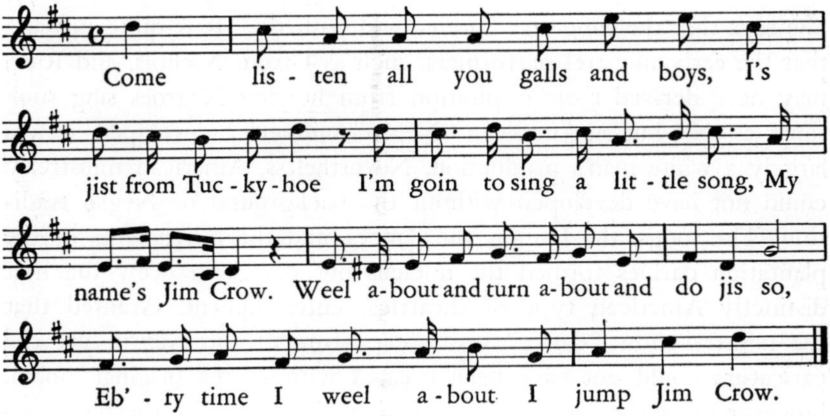
Come lis - ten all you galls and boys, I's
jist from Tuc - ky - hoe I'm goin to sing a lit - tle song, My
name's Jim Crow. Weel a - bout and turn a - bout and do jis so,
Eb' - ry time I weel a - bout I jump Jim Crow.

In the innumerable stanzas of "Jim Crow" that accumulated as the song was put through the paces of minstrelsy, we find echoes from topical events ranging from politics ("I put de veto on de boot/ An nullefy de shoe") to the playing of the celebrated violin virtuoso Paganini:

> I'm a rorer on de fiddle,
>   An down in ole Virginny
> Dey say I play de skientific
>   Like massa Pagganninny.

Verses such as this show clearly the accretion of commercialized theatrical jargon in some of the more obviously concocted "plantation melodies." One may contrast this type of "darky" song with the verses of a genuine Negro song as given by a Southern plantation owner and printed in *Putnam's Monthly*, January, 1855:

De ladies in de parlor,
  Hey, come a rollin' down–
A drinking tea and coffee;
  Good morning, ladies all.

De genmen in de kitchen,
  Hey, come a rollin' down–
A drinking brandy toddy;
  Good morning, ladies all.

This is evidently the same song that Fanny Kemble mentions in *A Journal of a Residence on a Georgia Plantation, 1838–1839* (p. 127). She says that the tune was "pretty and pathetic." It is quite possible that the early minstrel performers, such as Dixon, Nichols, and Rice, may have derived their inspiration from hearing Negroes sing such songs as this; but as American "Negro" minstrelsy developed, it was largely a white man's production. Nevertheless, American minstrelsy could not have developed without the background of Negro tradition. The songs, the humor, the dances, and the instruments of the plantation darkies formed the nucleus out of which grew the first distinctly American type of theatrical entertainment. Granted that the minstrel-show "darky" was a caricature of the Negro; yet the caricature could not have been created without the original model, however great the subsequent distortion. After all, the theater, especially the comic stage, has always created standard "types" that everyone recognizes as caricatures. And the early minstrel performers managed to convey a great deal of pathos and emotion in their presentation of the more serious songs. Once, after attending a minstrel performance, Thackeray wrote: ". . . a vagabond with a corked face and a banjo sings a little song, strikes a wild note, which sets the heart thrilling with happy pity." Something genuine did come through.

Rise of the minstrel show

Wittke, in his book *Tambo and Bones*, states that one of Rice's better-known renditions "contained the idiotic line, 'Kitty-co-dink-a-ho-dink! oh, oh, roley-boley-Good morning, ladies all!'" Now, the line probably is nonsense; or, at least, we have lost the clue to its original meaning, as happens in the case of many of the old Negro songs; but the last four words are identical with the last line of the song quoted above as representing a "genuine" Negro plantation melody. The question is: did Rice copy the song from the Negroes, or did the latter copy it from him? As far as the dates and the documentary evidence are concerned, it could have happened either way.

"Daddy" Rice was not merely an impersonator and singer of blackface songs: he was the creator of numerous farces and burlesques, full of crude, often vulgar, humor, into which he wove his "plantation melodies." Among these farces, which for a time were known as "Ethiopian Operas," may be mentioned *Long Island Juba*, *The Black Cupid*, and *Bone Squash Diavolo*. He also concocted a burlesque of *Othello*. These blackface extravaganzas were the forerunners of the variety acts that were incorporated into the "second part" of the minstrel show after the latter became fully organized. Rice himself was primarily identified with the preminstrel show period. In later life he played the role of Uncle Tom in the dramatization of Harriet Beecher Stowe's antislavery novel. He suffered a stroke of paralysis around 1850, recovered, but was again stricken, fatally, in September, 1860. At the time of his death he was poor and alone, for he had squandered the fortune that his popularity had brought him.

We have seen how Dan Emmett and his associates launched the first organized minstrel show in New York in 1843. There is some controversy as to whether this really was the first minstrel company organized in this country. Claims have been made that E. P. Christy organized the first minstrel troupe in Buffalo in 1842. We need not concern ourselves overmuch with these rival claims. What seems fairly well established is that the Virginia Minstrels set the pattern of the minstrel show in its conventional form: the division into two parts, and the semicircular arrangement of the performers, with a middleman or interlocutor in the center and two endmen, known respectively as "Tambo" and "Bones" because one played the tambourine and the other the bone castanets. Christy organized the routine of songs, jokes, and repartee which made of the first part a lively, continuous, coordinated program. The second part, called an "olio," consisted, as has been said, of variety acts, a farce or burlesque opera, closing with a singing and dancing number for the entire cast.

E. P. Christy was born in Philadelphia in 1815. After organizing the Christy Minstrels in Buffalo, he toured through the West and the South, and in 1846 appeared at Palmo's Opera House in New York. In 1847 Christy leased Mechanics' Hall on Broadway, where his troupe played for almost ten years. In 1854 Christy retired with a fortune, and the company was taken over by his brother, George Christy. The victim of attacks of melancholia, E. P. Christy died as the result of jumping from a second-story window of his home in New York.

Many other minstrel troupes sprang up in the two decades from 1850 to 1870, which was the heyday of American Negro minstrelsy.[4] The blackface minstrel show became an American institution and enjoyed an international vogue, for several companies toured in the British Isles with great success. This is not the place for an account of minstrel companies as such, because our main concern is with the music of minstrelsy, and in particular the songs of its two outstanding composers, Daniel Decatur Emmett and Stephen Collins Foster. Just as Foster's beginnings in minstrelsy are associated with E. P. Christy, so the first notable musical success of Emmett as a composer is associated with Bryant's Minstrels. Dan Bryant (*recte* Daniel Webster O'Brien) was an enterprising Irishman who, after playing with various minstrel troupes, formed his own company in New York in 1857. Among those who joined Bryant's Minstrels in that year was Dan Emmett, who remained with the company until 1865. He was engaged both as performer and composer, it being his task to provide songs for the show.

"Old Dan" Emmett

Daniel Decatur Emmett was born in Mt. Vernon, Ohio, on October 29, 1815, of an Irish-American pioneer family that had followed the path of westward migration from Virginia, first across the Blue Ridge Mountains, then beyond the Alleghenies, and finally to the frontier country of Ohio. The first of four children, he received scant

[4] This refers to the rise of Negro minstrelsy as a widespread type of commercialized popular entertainment. The most authentic or "classical" period of minstrelsy was from 1830 to 1850. After 1870 the minstrel shows became more lavish and spectacular, and in the 1880s it was customary to have as many as 100 performers in a troupe. These shows were designated by such adjectives as "Gigantean," "Mammoth," and "Gargantuan." Thereafter their decline was rapid. By 1896 there were only ten minstrel companies on the road.

schooling, but somehow learned to read and write while helping in his father's blacksmith shop. At thirteen he began to work in a printing office, and at seventeen he joined the Army as a fifer. Emmett's own account of his army experience is worth quoting:

> At the early age of 17, I enlisted in the U.S. Army as a fifer, and was stationed at Newport Barracks, Ky., the then school of practice for the western department. For one year, or more, I practiced the drum incessantly under the tuition of the renowned John J. Clark (better known as "Juba"), and made myself master of the "Duty" and every known "side beat" then in use. Being transferred to the 6th U.S. Infantry, then stationed at Jefferson Barracks, Mo., I was retained as "leading fifer" until discharged. In the meantime I continued my drum practice, which was then taught according to the *School of Ashworth.* In after years I travelled as Small Drummer with the celebrated Edward Kendall while he was leader of Spalding and Rogers' Circus Band.[5]

Whoever "the renowned John J. Clark" may have been, it is interesting to note that he was nicknamed "Juba," for this is the name of a familiar Negro dance song frequently encountered in the folklore of the South.[6] In addition to his competence on the fife and drum, Emmett learned to play other instruments, excelling particularly on the violin and the flute. He was also a good singer. In the summer of 1835 he was discharged from the Army "on account of minority," and it was then that he entered show business via the circus, traveling through the West and South before organizing his own minstrel troupe in New York.

If army and circus bands provided a major portion of Emmett's musical training on the instrumental side, his musical talent and his earliest musical repertoire, were inherited from his mother, who had a nice voice and sang to him often when he was a child. In later years Emmett said:

> As far back almost as I can remember, I took great interest in music. I hummed familiar tunes, arranged words to sing to them and made up tunes to suit words of my own. I paid no especial attention to the poetry and thought little about the literary merit of

[5] Cited by Galbreath, *Daniel Decatur Emmett.*

[6] It is also found as a Negro name in the West Indies as early as the eighteenth century.

what I wrote. I composed *Old Dan Tucker* in 1830 or 1831, when I was fifteen or sixteen years old, before I left Mt. Vernon.[7]

Whenever it may have been written, "Old Dan Tucker" was not published until 1843. An edition copyrighted in that year and published by Millet's Music Saloon, New York, describes it as "A Favorite Original Negro Melody . . . By Dan. Tucker, Jr." As often happened with minstrel songs, the authorship of "Old Dan Tucker" has been disputed. Perhaps the most curious claim is that of the English singer and composer Henry Russell, mentioned in an earlier chapter, who asserted that he composed the tune at Rochester, New York, in 1835, and in the following strange manner: "It was quite by accident that, playing 'Old Hundredth' very fast, I produced the air of 'Get Out o' de Way, Old Dan Tucker.' "

Musically, the most interesting feature of "Old Dan Tucker" is the syncopation in the chorus, at the words, "Get out de way!":

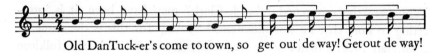

Old Dan Tuck-er's come to town, so get out de way! Get out de way!

Dan Emmett himself was convinced that his "walk-arounds" faithfully reflected the character and the traditions of the Southern plantation Negro. In some preliminary remarks for a manuscript collection of his minstrel "walk-arounds," he wrote:

In the composition of a "Walk 'Round" (by this I mean the style of music and character of the words), I have always strictly confined myself to the habits and crude ideas of the slaves of the South. Their knowledge of the world at large was very limited, often not extending beyond the bounds of the next plantation; they could sing of nothing but everyday life or occurrences, and the scenes by which they were surrounded. This being the undeniable fact, to be true to the Negro peculiarities of song, I have written in accordance.[8]

The whole question of the relationship between the tradition of Negro minstrelsy and the reality of Southern Negro life and character is a

[7] Regarding this passage, Dr. Nathan comments: "Emmett said all kinds of things when he was old. The *tune* of 'Old Dan Tucker' is definitely *not* by him."

[8] Cited by Galbreath, *op. cit.*

complex sociocultural problem that needs to be studied carefully by anyone wishing to get at the truth. The subject has been very ably treated in *The Southern Plantation* by Francis Pendleton Gaines, described as "A Study in the Development and the Accuracy of a Tradition." The interested reader should consult in particular Chapter V, A, "The Plantation in Minstrelsy," and Chapter VIII, "Plantation Characters" (The Conception Compared with the Actual).

Most writers agree that in its beginnings American minstrelsy, in the words of Brander Matthews, "endeavoured to reproduce the life of the plantation darkey. The songs sung by the Ethiopian serenaders were reminiscences of the songs heard where the Negro was at work, on the river steamboat, in the sugar field, or at the camp-meeting. . . ." It is likely that the steamboats of the Mississippi and the Ohio, as well as the Southern plantations, were the direct source of many Negro tunes and songs that found their way into the repertoire of the earliest blackface entertainers, such as Dixon, Rice, and Emmett. The river was a great carrier of songs, and many Negroes worked on the river.

One of Dan Emmett's best songs, "De Boatman's Dance," copyrighted and published in 1843, is a direct reflection of life on the river.[9] Here are a couple of typical stanzas of this song:

When you go to de boatman's ball,
Dance wid my wife, or don't dance at all;
Sky blue jacket and tarpaulin hat,
Look out my boys for de nine tail cat.

De boatman is a thrifty man,
Dars none can do as de boatman can;
I neber see a putty gal in my life
But dat she was a boatman's wife.

As far as we can judge, from internal and external evidence, "De Boatman's Dance" seems to belong in the group of early minstrel songs

[9] The chorus of this song appears to have been sung by Ohio River boatmen one or two decades before the publication of Emmett's version (cf. *The Pioneers of the West*, by W. P. Strickland, New York, 1856, p. 198). According to Nathan, the words of this song, except for the chorus, are by Emmett, and the tune is probably his also, though this is by no means certain. "Boatman's Dance" appears with the remark "Words by old Dan Emmit" in *Songs of the Virginia Minstrels: A Correct Edition of the Celebrated Songs of the Virginia Minstrels* . . . Boston, 1843. (Information from Nathan's bibliography of Emmett's songs.)

that reflect with comparative fidelity the music that the Negro may have actually used. Be that as it may, the song has outlived its vogue on the minstrel stage and passed into the tradition of American folklore. Here, then, are the tune and the words of the first stanza as printed in a sheet-music edition of 1843:

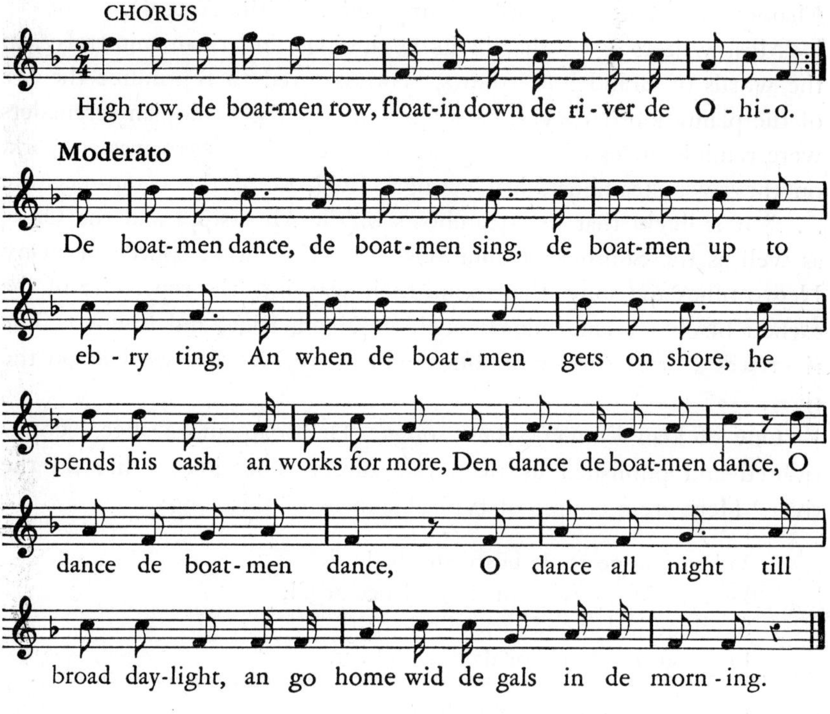

Another song by Emmett, also copyrighted in 1843, is "My Old Aunt Sally." The words are of the stilted, artificial pseudo-darky type that soon became prevalent in minstrelsy; but the tune is of interest as containing examples of the "flattened seventh" (in this case F natural) which is characteristic of much American Negro music.

"In Dixie Land . . ."

To most people Emmett is known, if he is known at all, as the composer of "Dixie," a song which has become more famous than the man who wrote it. This was one of the walk-arounds that Emmett wrote for Bryant's Minstrels in 1859. To give an idea of his output in this field, we print below the list of the walk-arounds composed by Emmett (words and music) from 1859 to 1868, as set forth by his biographer Galbreath:[10]

1859

I ain't got time to tarry
Nigger in de tent
John come down de holler
Road to Georgia
Flat foot Jake
Billy Patterson
Hai, Johnny Roach
Loozyanna low grounds
I wish I was in Dixie's Land
Johnny Gouler
Chaw roast beef
What o'dat?
Turkey in de straw

1860

Darrow Arrow
Old K.Y., Ky.
De Contrack

1862

De Back-log
Bress old Andy Jackson
Mr. Per Coon
Black Brigade

1863

High Daddy
Here we are, or cross ober Jordan
Greenbacks
Goose and Gander
Ober in Jarsey

1864

Foot-falls on de karpet
U.S.G.

1865

Whar ye been so long?
Old times rocks

1868

Burr Grass
Pan-cake Joe
Want any shad?
Sugar in de ground
Whoa, Bally!
Yes or no
Abner Isham Still
I am free

From the foregoing it will be seen that when Emmett joined Bryant's Minstrels in the fall of 1858, he entered upon an extremely productive period as a writer of minstrel melodies. He now had a job that required the full exercise of his talents as a musician and a black-face entertainer. Unlike Stephen Foster, whose association with minstrelsy was marginal, Dan Emmett was thoroughly immersed in the "Ethiopian business"; hence his songs, and the walk-arounds in particular, are an epitome of the minstrel tradition in its heyday. This heyday coincided with the growing tension over the slavery issue, and it is important to realize that political factors, however disguised by humor or sentiment, were increasingly reflected in the minstrel

[10] The list is not complete; it does not, for instance, include variants.

songs of the decade preceding the outbreak of the Civil War. When war came, Dan Emmett's "Dixie" was claimed by both sides; but it was the Confederacy that decisively took it over and made it virtually into a national anthem. The war gave an unforeseen significance to the lines of the carefree chorus: "In Dixie Land I'll take my stand, To lib and die in Dixie."

Emmett's song "Johnny Roach," performed in March 1859 and published in New York the following year, tells of a Negro slave bound for Canada by "de railroad underground," but who wishes "he was back agin." Then he tells why he wishes to be back in the South again:

> Gib me de place called "Dixie's Land,"
> Wid hoe and shubble in my hand;
> Whar fiddles ring an' banjos play,
> I'll dance all night an' work all day.

According to Hans Nathan, who has made the most thorough study to date of Emmett's life and work, this is "the very first occurrence in print of the word 'Dixie' as another name for the South—the black one, to be exact."

There has been much discussion as to the origin of the word "Dixie." A common assumption is that it was derived from the name Dixon and referred to the South as the part of the country below the Mason and Dixon's line. Another theory is that the name was taken from the French bank notes issued in New Orleans, said to be called "dixies"—from the French word "*dix*," meaning "ten." A third version has it that Dixie was the name of a man who kept slaves on Manhattan Island, New York, until the hostility of the abolitionists obliged him to move to the South, taking his slaves with him. The latter allegedly kept wishing they were back in "Dixie's Land." This last version is absurd and has no foundation whatever. The other two theories are more plausible but are unsupported by any valid evidence. Emmett himself, in later life, stated that the phrase "I wish I was in Dixie's Land" was a common expression referring to the South used by people in the entertainment business. The available evidence indicates that the term "Dixie," in any case, was of Northern origin. The earliest use of the name that Nathan was able to discover occurred in 1850 in a Northern minstrel play titled *United States Mail and Dixie in Difficulties*. Here the name "Dixie" is given to a stupid

Negro postboy.[11] Nathan is probably right when he suggests that the name may have been invented by white showmen as an occasional nickname for a Negro character, by phonetic analogy with such Negro stage-types as "Pompey" and "Cuffee."

The whole vexing matter of the origin and significance of the term Dixie has been authoritatively summarized by Dr. Nathan:

> Since Dixie meant the Negro, "Dixie's Land" was obviously the Land of the Negro, that is, according to the consensus of the mid-nineteenth century, the black South. When Emmett in his famous song abbreviated the phrase to Dixie Land and finally to Dixie, there appeared again the original name though not referring to a person but to its habitation. Thus Dixie had five connotations: it was first a synonym for the Negro (probably the Southern Negro); it changed (as a simplified version of Dixie's Land and Dixie Land) to a synonym for the Negro's South, then for the South pure and simple, and finally to a synonym for the South as seen by the Confederates. Parallel to this, Dixie was the popular title by which Emmett's song was known.[12]

Emmett's famous song was originally billed as "Dixie's Land" when it was first performed by Bryant's Minstrels at Mechanics' Hall, New York City, on April 4, 1859. It was announced as a "Plantation Song and Dance . . . Introducing the whole Troupe in the Festival Dance." On that occasion it did not conclude the program, but was next to the last number. According to the custom prevailing in minstrel walk-arounds, "Dixie's Land" was sung in a manner reminiscent of the call-and-response pattern of Afro-American music. The first part of the song (it is divided into two sections of sixteen measures each) was sung alternately by a soloist and by a small chorus in unison which came in at the end of every other line with a brief interjection, "Look away! Look away! Dixie Land!" As performed on the minstrel stage, "Dixie," like other walk-arounds, also had an instrumental section of eight measures, during which the members of the troupe would do a grotesque dance.

"Dixie" became an immediate popular success, and several publishers clashed over the copyright. Emmett gave the song to Firth,

[11] It appears in a playbill of the Sabine Minstrels of Portsmouth [N.H.?], in the possession of the American Antiquarian Society, Worcester, Mass. Cf. Nathan's article, "*Dixie*," cited in the bibliography for this chapter.

[12] In his forthcoming book, *Dan Emmett and Early American Negro Minstrelsy.*

Pond & Co. of New York, who brought it out in June, 1860. In the same year several other editions appeared, without credit to Emmett. One of these editions was published by P. P. Werlein of New Orleans, with the composition accredited to J. C. Viereck! This matter was eventually straightened out, and in subsequent editions Viereck's name appeared as "arranger." Then, in February, 1861, Emmett sold all his rights in the song to Firth, Pond & Co. for the sum of $300. Werlein, on his side, took advantage of the outbreak of hostilities to bring out another edition of "Dixie" in which Emmett's name was omitted as composer and Viereck's restored. The writ of Northern publishers and composers did not run in the Confederacy. Soon there were many unauthorized Southern editions of "Dixie." It was sweeping the South, both as a song (often with words written especially for the war) and as a march arranged for military band. A Confederate band played "Dixie" at the inauguration of President Jefferson Davis, and many Southern regiments marched in quickstep to its enlivening rhythm and jaunty tune. Emmett himself, whose sympathies were with the North, is reported to have said, "If I had known to what use they were going to put my song, I'll be damned if I'd have written it."

The North, for its part, was anxious to claim "Dixie" as its own. During the first year of the war, "Dixie," in spite of its adoption by the Confederacy, was at the peak of its popularity in the North, especially in New York, the city of its origin. The words, of course, were not considered appropriate for Northern usage, but that could easily be remedied. Many "Northern" versions of the song began to appear, among them "Dixie for the Union" and "Dixie Unionized." A "Unionized" text was published in *John Brown and the Union Right or Wrong Songster* (San Francisco, 1863).

At the end of the Civil War—in fact, the day after the surrender of General Lee's army at Appomattox—President Lincoln took steps to restore "Dixie" to the Union. A crowd had assembled at the White House to serenade him with a band. The President made a very brief speech, and then requested the band to play "Dixie," which he said was one of the best tunes he ever heard. Alluding to its quasi-official status as a Confederate song, he remarked dryly: "I had heard that our adversaries over the way had attempted to appropriate it. I insisted yesterday that we had fairly captured it . . . I presented the question to the Attorney-General, and he gave his opinion that it is our lawful prize. . . . I ask the Band to give us a good turn upon it." In this manner "Dixie" was "officially" restored to the North; but since the South never relinquished its claim upon the song, it belongs now to both North and South—it is a truly national song, probably the most genuinely "American" song that we possess.

According to Marius Schneider, "The popularity of a melody is the result of its degree of simplicity and of its conformity to the melodic type current in a given culture." Melodically and harmonically, the music of "Dixie" is simplicity itself. In style it closely resembles other tunes by Emmett, and it has a family kinship with a wide range of popular tunes current in America, stemming from Irish-Scotch sources. "Dixie" is in duple time, in the major mode, does not modulate, and employs syncopation.[13] These traits are common to a vast body of American vernacular music that has been put to various usages, from revival meetings to minstrel shows. Yet "Dixie" itself is unique, for it possesses high individuality within its conformity to type. In spite of its simplicity it is a well-constructed song, both unified and varied.

In 1888 Dan Emmett retired to a small country home near his native town of Mt. Vernon, Ohio. There he was discovered by A. G. Field, who persuaded him to take to the road again with Field's Minstrels.[14] This was in the year 1895. "Old Dan's" tour was triumphant, especially in the South (he never aired his antisecessionist views publicly). On April 11, 1896, he bade farewell to the public for the last time and returned to his rural homestead once more. There he lived on a pension from the Actors' Fund of New York until his death on June 28, 1904, at the age of eighty-eight.

Minstrel medley

Among the hundreds of songs associated with American minstrelsy, let us glance more closely at some that, for one reason or another, seem to merit special attention.

Recalling Jefferson's proposal for the establishment of a Negro "haven" abroad, and remembering that in the 1830s the Negro Republic of Haiti appeared to offer just such a haven, we turn to a blackface song published at Boston in 1833 as "Sambo's Address to He' Bred'rin" and also known as "Ching a Ring Chaw," in which the "bred'rin" are urged to emigrate to "Hettee," where each one will be

[13] The syncopation in "Dixie" is slight but effective. It is used twice in the chorus with a peculiarly characteristic effect.

[14] Apparently all that he did in the performance was to sing "Dixie."

received "gran' as Lafayette," where all will "lib so fine wid our coach and horse," where "we smoke de best segar, fetch from Havanna," where "our wibes be gran', an in dimons shine," and "dar dance at nite jig, what white man call cotillion, in hall so mity big it hole haff a million." In contrast with this life of ease and luxury, the song depicts the hard lot of the Negro in the United States, forced to perform all the menial and unpleasant tasks. Although this is obviously a white man's concoction, and was treated as a comic number, it shows what might be called the "social significance" aspect of Negro minstrelsy.

One of the most widely successful of the early blackface songs was "Jim Along Josey," written and introduced on the stage by Edward Harper around 1838. The tune uses only the five notes of the pentatonic scale. The song itself is followed by a lively "Dance" in which the comic actor had a chance to "do his stuff." The popularity of the song was doubtless due in large measure to the catchy tune of the chorus:

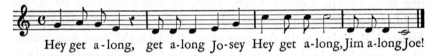

Hey get a-long, get a-long Jo-sey Hey get a-long, Jim a-long Joe!

Apart from its popularity on the minstrel stage, "Jim Along Josey" became widely used as a "Play Party Song" in the Middle West, and, as Foster Damon observes, was admitted as a game even among those stricter sects that prohibited dancing, "although to uncritical eyes the players seemed to be doing something easily mistaken for a Virginia Reel." There are many examples of songs and tunes passing from the minstrel stage into the realm of folklore.

To complete the cycle of borrowings, we should reiterate that many minstrel songs have their origin in anonymous folk tunes, so that they have passed from the domain of folklore and back to it again after the usual process of being modified or "reworked." A case in point is "Zip Coon," one of the most successful of the early minstrel songs, which has persisted in American folklore in numerous versions. As "Turkey in the Straw" it became a favorite fiddle tune for country dances. Bob Farrell, who sang "Zip Coon" in New York in 1834, claimed authorship of the song. His claim was disputed by George Washington Dixon. There is no reason to believe that either of these men actually "composed" the song—certainly not the music (one of them may have written the words). There is strong evidence to indicate that this is one of the many American minstrel songs of Scotch-Irish descent. Hans Nathan has found a Scotch reel that is very similar to parts of "Zip Coon." And Francis O'Neill writes that there is "convincing evidence of its Irish antecedents." [15]

Another old favorite is "Clare de Kitchen," popularized by "Daddy" Rice in the early 1830s, which has the "Old Virginny never tire" refrain. The text of the song is closer to the tradition of Negro humor than are the later minstrel songs. In a succession of nonsense verses we meet various animals: an old blind horse, a jaybird sitting on a hickory limb, a bull frog dressed in soldier's clothes, and "a little Whip poor will" whose sad fate it is to be eaten. In the last stanza of one version, the line occurs, "I wish I was back in old Kentuck"—the first of the "I wish I was . . ." tag lines that became a stock item in the nostalgic type of minstrel song.

Another song popularized by "Daddy" Rice and later by William Clifton, who arranged a version printed in 1836, was "Long Time Ago," in which the refrain is sung at the end of each line. Of interest is the syncopation on the words "Varginee" and "free." The whole structure of this song, in relation to Negro music, is worth noting (my reference is to Clifton's version, copyrighted 1836). The structure of the song is as simple as possible: the verse consists of two lines, each repeated, with an identical metrical pattern in the melody. Letting "C" stand for the chorus, the scheme may be expressed thus: A-C, A-C, B-C, B-C. The music example below is printed so as to show this parallel arrangement:

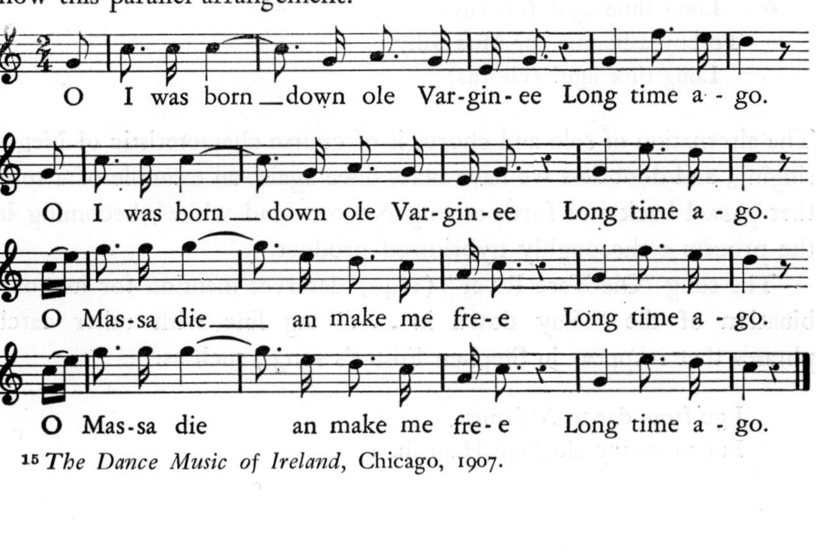

[15] *The Dance Music of Ireland*, Chicago, 1907.

Compare this pattern with that of the following corn-shucking song published in *Putnam's Monthly*, 1855, as an example of a genuine Negro plantation song:

> Cow boy on middle 'e island–
>   Ho, meleety, ho!
> Cow boy on middle 'e island–
>   Ho, meleety, ho!

Mrs. Kemble, in *A Journal of a Residence on a Georgia Plantation, 1838–1839*, quotes the words of a "rowing chant" with an identical pattern:

> Jenny shake her toe at me
>   Jenny gone away
> Jenny shake her toe at me
>   Jenny gone away.

The editors of *Slave Songs of the United States* (1867) state in a footnote in their preface that " 'Long Time Ago' . . . was borrowed from the negroes, by whom it was sung to words beginning 'Way down in Raccoon Hollow.' " This still does not prove that the plantation Negroes originated the melody, which was very likely picked up from a white man's song. A version of "Long Time Ago," published by John Cole of Baltimore in 1833, has the following words:

> As I was gwoin down shinbone alley,
>   Long time ago! (chorus)
> To buy a bonnet for Miss Sally,
>   Long time ago! (chorus)

The alternation of solo and chorus is of course characteristic of Negro singing, and doubtless we have here, once again, an example of a song that passed back and forth among Negroes and whites, becoming in the process a thoroughly hybridized product.

The song "Ole Tare River" (1840) deserves mention for its combination of the "Way down in . . ." tag line with other catch phrases that reappear in Stephen Foster's songs, such as:

> I go from dar to Alabama
> For to see my ole Aunt Hannah.

and

> Now Miss Dinah I'm going to leave you
> And when I'm gone don't let it grieve you.

One thinks also of "Way down upon the Swanee River," and one observes that both melodies are based on the pentatonic scale. Old Aunt Hannah seems to be a close relative of Miss Susanna. Herewith is a portion of "Ole Tare River," omitting the instrumental interludes:

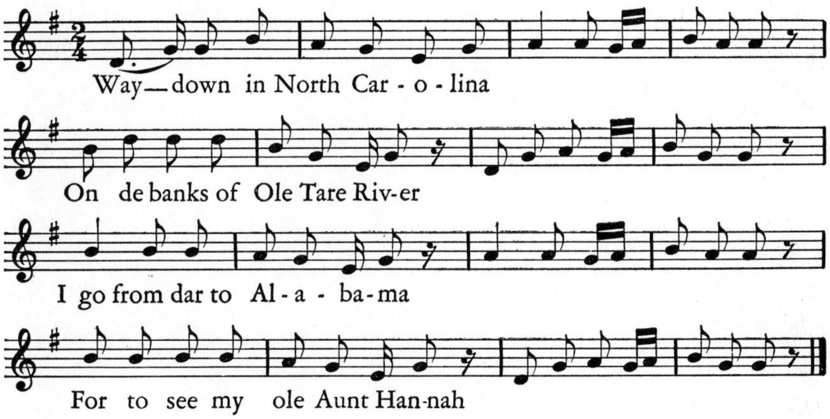

The song "Lubly Fan" (Will You Come Out To Night?), written and copyrighted by Cool White in 1844, has had a varied history. A few years later it was brought out by the Christy Minstrels as "Bowery Gals," and in 1848 it was featured by the Ethiopian Serenaders as "Buffalo Gals." It is with this last title that the song has circulated most widely in the oral tradition, although in the South it was often heard as "Charleston Gals." The tune is so well known that direct quotation may be spared.

These old minstrel songs are so much a part of the American tradition, and have in many cases such wide ramifications in our folklore, that one is tempted to linger over them indefinitely, discussing and quoting one after another. Enough has been given, at least, to show the roots of the tradition and to trace some of its most characteristic manifestations and developments. If we have dwelt almost exclusively on the early period of minstrelsy, from the appearance of the first blackface entertainers to the rise of the original minstrel troupes in the 1840s, it is because this period produced the songs that were most deeply rooted in America's music, and which in turn branched out most widely into the oral tradition of the folk, both black and white. Moreover, we shall have more to say of Negro minstrelsy and its influence on America's music when we discuss the life and work of Stephen Collins Foster.

chapter fourteen

America's minstrel

I have concluded . . . to pursue the Ethiopian business without fear or shame and . . . to establish my name as the best Ethiopian songwriter.
STEPHEN C. FOSTER, LETTER TO E. P. CHRISTY, MAY 25, 1852.

In the spring of 1853 the pious, respectable, and prolific Mr. Thomas Hastings, composer of over a thousand hymn tunes, most of which have been forgotten by almost everybody, took his pen in hand to indite an indignant epistle to the editor of the *Musical Review and Choral Advocate*. The editor of that chaste periodical had recently commented on the deplorable fact that certain "Ethiopian melodies" were being adapted for use in Sunday schools. Mr. Hastings, while carefully protecting his respectability by stating that he was "not very conversant with Ethiopian minstrelsy," disclosed that he had actually discovered a Sunday-school superintendent endeavoring to foist the melody of "Old Folks at Home" on a large class of innocent "infant scholars." The superintendent thought the children would not recognize the tune. So the teacher sang a line or two—with suitably pious words, of course—and then asked, " 'Children, have you ever heard anything like that before?'—*'Old Folks at Home! Old Folks at Home!'* shouted the little urchins with such merry glances and gesticulations as showed them upon the very point of 'cutting up,' when the experiment ended and the piece was abandoned."

Mr. Hastings, in his letter, went on to castigate those responsible for perverting the taste of children by "fishing up something from the lowest dregs of music" by which their minds "are filled with poisonous trash, to forget which in after life would be to them a blessing." The practice he describes, he says, is nothing new. "It is an old trick, which many seem determined to 'play off' every time they have an opportunity." Mr. Hastings fears these abuses will not yet be abandoned, in spite of the fact that there are, he says, plenty of good hymn tunes in circulation. But "Christy has more melodies; and then *Yankee Doodle, Frog and Mouse*, and *Jim Crow*, I believe, have not yet been appropriated." Thus the eminent Mr. Thomas Hastings, soon to receive the degree of Doctor of Music from New York University, vented his sarcasm and his scorn upon "the lowest dregs of music," including the "Ethiopian melodies" of Stephen Collins Foster.[1]

Perhaps the perpetrator of "Old Folks at Home," before his tragic death at the age of thirty-seven, had an opportunity to redeem himself in the eyes—or the ears—of Mr. Hastings and other advocates of the "better music" movement. In 1863, the last year of his life, when he had sunk to his lowest level of physical and spiritual vitality, Foster turned out what his granddaughter calls "about a dozen uninspired expressions of religious hack-writing" that surely were respectable and mediocre enough to satisfy even Mr. Hastings. The latter lived to be eighty-eight; when he finally went to his reward, perhaps his soul had been edified by hearing such masterpieces of bathos as Stephen Foster's "Little Ella's an Angel in the Skies" or "Willie's Gone to Heaven, Praise the Lord." Sad as was the physical and social deterioration of Stephen Foster in the last years of his life, it is still sadder to observe his deterioration as an artist, his surrender to mediocrity. But in his short life, with its unhappy ending, Stephen Foster, in spite of some vacillations and an eventual succumbing to adverse circumstances, succeeded surprisingly well in producing the kind of songs that earned the disapproval of the "better music" advocates.

The pontifical John S. Dwight, in his *Journal of Music*, had to admit—this was in the year 1853—that such tunes as "Old Folks at Home" were whistled and sung by everybody; but he asserted that they had not really taken a deep hold of the popular mind; that their charm was only *skin-deep;* and that such melodies "are not popular in the sense of musically inspiring, but that such and such a melody *breaks out* every now and then, like a morbid irritation of the skin." [2]

The battle lines were clearly drawn, and the worst of it is that Stephen Foster often had to fight the same battle in his own mind. As a member of a solid and highly respectable middle-class family, he did not grow up naturally into show business and the world of popular entertainment as did the poor country lad Dan Emmett. In his circle,

[1] Morneweck, *Chronicles of Stephen Foster's Family*, vol. 2, p. 467.
[2] Quoted by J. T. Howard, *Our American Music*, p. 185.

music was not considered a suitable profession. If one did take up music, it should be of the most respectable kind. Stephen Foster aspired to be a writer of sentimental ballads and elegant songs "rendered" by sentimental and elegant young ladies in the most polite society. In his younger days he omitted his name on the title pages of his Ethiopian melodies because he feared the association would injure his reputation as a composer of refined music—he does not actually use the word "refined" but that is the implication of his meaning when he writes that the prejudice against Ethiopian songs might injure his reputation "as a writer of another style of music." Yet in May, 1852, a few months after the publication of "Old Folks at Home," he writes to E. P. Christy saying that he had decided "to pursue the Ethiopian business without fear or shame." That was Stephen Foster's first and greatest spiritual victory: to overcome the fear of not appearing respectable, to fight off the feeling of shame associated with writing the kind of music that everybody liked and sang and whistled and remembered forever.

Yet the fight went on. The forces of respectability would not let him be himself. He had to be continually tilting against the genteel tradition. The *Musical World and Times* of New York, on January 29, 1853, deplored the talented Mr. Foster's propensity for Ethiopian melodies and expressed the hope that he would turn his attention to a higher type of music. More: it informed the public that Mr. Foster had personally given his assurance to the editor that henceforth he intended to devote himself to composing "white men's music." Here, apparently, we have a bit of race prejudice thrown in to enrich the theme of respectability. When Foster made the statement reported above, "My Old Kentucky Home" had just been published. It was to be followed by "Massa's in de Cold Ground," in July, 1852, and by "The Glendy Burk," "Old Black Joe," and "Down Among the Cane Brakes," the last three all published in the same year, 1860. No, fortunately for us and for America's music, Stephen Foster did not abandon the writing of Ethiopian melodies. He turned out a few more glorious songs before succumbing to drink and the genteel tradition.

Early life in Pittsburgh

Stephen Collins Foster was born on July 4, 1826, in "The White Cottage" on his father's farm overlooking the village of Lawrenceville, near Pittsburgh, Pennsylvania. His father, Colonel William Barclay Foster, had moved from eastern Pennsylvania to Pittsburgh when the latter place was little more than a frontier trading post. He became associated with a firm of local merchants and took charge of their river trade, which obliged him to journey down the Ohio and Mississippi Rivers about twice a year. While on a business trip to Philadelphia, Colonel Foster met Eliza Tomlinson, member of a substantial Eastern family, whom he married in 1807. They had ten children, of whom two died in infancy. Stephen grew up with three sisters—one of whom, Charlotte Susanna, died young—and five brothers—one of whom (William) was an adopted child. Stephen himself was next to the youngest in the family.

Colonel William B. Foster became wealthy, but later suffered financial reverses, which in 1826 led to the loss of his property by foreclosure. The family lived for a while in the village of Harmony, and in the autumn of 1832 moved into a new home in the town of Allegheny. Music in the Foster family was encouraged as a form of recreation and as a polite accomplishment for young ladies. Mrs. Foster, who had been raised in Baltimore and was filled with ideas of gentility, was eager to have her daughters receive the benefits of a "polite education," including the accomplishment of playing the piano and singing sentimental ballads. Opportunities for acquiring the "polite arts" were not lacking in Pittsburgh. Charlotte Foster's music teacher was one Williams Evens, who in 1826 issued the following advertisement: [3]

> Wm. Evens, teacher of the French Horn,
> Trumpet, Bugle, Serpent, Bassoon, Clarionet,
> German Flute, Hautboy, Violin,
> Violoncello, and Tenor Viol—
> at Six Dollars per quarter.
> W. E. professes the Andante stile. Those
> who wish to play Concerto's or become
> Prestissimo Players need not apply.
> Tempo Gusto. [*sic*]

Here, indeed, was every guarantee of sedate respectability, even to the exclusion of *tempo rubato!*

This William Evens was a plane maker by trade, but in 1817 he opened a singing school in his shop, and afterward was very active as

[3] Quoted by Morneweck, *op. cit.*, vol. 1, p. 30.

a choir leader and teacher in Pittsburgh. He formed a manuscript collection of the works of Bach, Haydn, Handel, and Beethoven, copying them out meticulously by hand and employing in the process, we are told, gallons of homemade black ink. To his pupils he offered instruction in the music of "the most celebrated modern composers." It is not true, as some writers have stated, that Stephen Foster grew up in a musical wilderness. Pianos were by no means unknown in Pittsburgh. Some were transported from the East, some were manufactured to order, right in the town, by Charles Rosenbaum, as early as 1815. The Fosters had a piano in their home by 1818; they had to give it up in 1821, but Brother William, hard-working and prosperous, presented the family with a new piano in 1828, two years after Stephen's birth. As his granddaughter writes, "From early childhood, Stephen Foster was always accustomed to music in the home of his parents and their friends." The question, of course, is: what kind of music? The answer, I think, is: many kinds. Popular ballads of the day (that is, currently popular songs, chiefly of a sentimental type) probably held first place. Evelyn Foster Morneweck, in her excellent and valuable *Chronicles of Stephen Foster's Family*, evokes a picture of the little boy Stephen leaning against the piano "whilst his sisters charmed their admiring family circle with 'Come Rest in This Bosom'; 'Go, My Love, Like the Gloom of Night Retiring'; 'Flow on, Thou Shining River'; 'I Have Loved Thee, Mary'; 'Home, Sweet Home'; 'I'd Be a Butterfly,' and 'Susan in the Valley.' " Among the more than two hundred songs that Foster was to compose, there were many of this type, and most of them have been forgotten as completely as most of the songs mentioned above. Undoubtedly, an inescapable portion of Foster's musical heritage was the genteel tradition of his own family circle. But it was not the whole heritage. The children used to be delighted by their father's singing of some jolly old songs, in particular "Good Old Colony Times," with its tale of three rogues: a miller, a weaver, and a little tailor.

The Fosters had a colored servant named Olivia Pise, called "Lieve," said to be the mulatto daughter of a French dancing master from the West Indies. As a boy Stephen loved to attend the services in the Negro church with Lieve and to hear the "shouting" of the people. Later in life, Stephen told his brother Morrison that two of his songs, "Oh! Boys, Carry Me 'Long" and "Hard Times Come Again No More," were based on snatches of Negro melodies that he heard while attending Negro services as a boy with Olivia Pise. Many other snatches of melody may have remained in his memory and been used unconsciously in his plantation melodies. It is also tempting to speculate on the possibility that Lieve may have sung to him some West Indian songs, like those that the French Negroes brought to Louisiana from Martinique and Saint Domingue.

According to Morrison Foster, when Stephen was two years old, he would lay his sister's guitar on the parlor floor and pick out harmonies on the strings of the instruments. When he was about six, he took up a flageolet—an instrument that he had never before handled—in Smith & Mellor's Music Store, and in a few minutes was playing "Hail, Columbia" with perfect correctness. Soon afterward, his mother bought him a clarinet. There was no question of providing systematic music instruction for the boy: music was not a serious occupation for boys or men in the Foster household. Foster's granddaughter believes that all he knew of musical theory was acquired from an older friend and professional musician of German origin named Henry Kleber, from whom he received some lessons. However, Stephen's earliest composition, *The Tioga Waltz,* written at the age of fourteen when he was attending a school at Athens, near Towanda, was apparently produced before he received any instruction from Kleber. Nor does Stephen appear to have taken advantage of the musical instruction that was offered at Athens Academy. He did not like school, and preferred to follow his own inclinations both in study and in music. There must have been a general feeling in the family that Stephen was devoting too much time to music, for once he wrote to his brother William saying "I will also promise not to pay any attention to my music untill after eight Oclock in the evening." He was lonesome and homesick at Athens and in 1841 returned home, somewhat to the distress of his father, who wrote: "He is a very good boy, but I cannot get him to stick at school. He reads a good deal, and writes some in the office with me." William B. Foster was then mayor of Allegheny.

Sometime in 1843, probably after passing his sixteenth birthday, Stephen set to music a poem by George Pope Morris titled "Open Thy Lattice, Love," which was published in the following year by George Willig of Philadelphia. This was his first published song. It was as pretty and polite as anyone could wish. On the back of the original manuscript of this song, Stephen wrote a little waltz for piano, "Dedicated to Miss Maria Bach"—we do not know who she was.

Foster and Negro minstrelsy

But neither the pretty song nor the conventional waltz were indicative of the main road that Stephen Foster was to take as a composer. For an indication of this we must go back to another aspect of his boyhood. Stephen Foster had a keen feeling for fun, a talent for comedy, and a love for lively, zestful song. He and his brothers, together with neighborhood youngsters, formed a "Thespian Company" for the performance of plantation melodies, the popular blackface songs of the 1830s mentioned in the previous chapter: "Coal Black Rose," "Long Tail Blue," "Jim Crow," and "Zip Coon." Stephen was the star performer of the company; his brother writes that his performance was so inimitable and true to nature that he was greeted with uproarious applause and called back again and again. Later the boys made the acquaintance of the celebrated clown Dan Rice, who in 1843 wrote to Morrison Foster: "I am making money pretty fast. . . . A Bout twenty five dollors A Weeke. I am clowning an also my nigero singing an Dancing is drawing good houses."[4] Stephen doubtless thought Rice's spelling was pretty bad, but he was probably intrigued by the "nigero singing." The reader will recall that this was the year, 1843, in which the first organized minstrels shows made their appearance. The result was to be decisive for the budding songwriter Stephen Foster.

About this time Stephen obtained a position in a Pittsburgh warehouse, checking cotton bales as they were rolled up from the steamboat wharf to the building. The work was done by Negro roustabouts who sang cheerfully at their task. We may be sure that Stephen kept his ears open. It may be that the river, and the men who worked on it, were his best music teachers. Echoes not only of his churchgoing experiences with Lieve, but also of the singing of the Negro roustabouts, mingled with the currently popular plantation melodies, must have been in Stephen's mind when, in the year 1845, he began to compose his first Ethiopian songs. In Morrison Foster's biography of his brother, the origin of these songs is described as follows:

> In 1845, a club of young men, friends of his, met twice a week at our house to practice songs in harmony under his leadership. . . . At that time, Negro melodies were very popular. After we had sung over

[4] Morneweck, *op. cit.*, vol. 1, p. 265.

and over again all the songs then in favor, he proposed that he would try and make some for us himself. His first effort was called *The Louisiana Belle.* A week after this, he produced the famous song of *Old Uncle Ned.* . . . At the time he wrote "His fingers were long like de cane in de brake," he had never seen a canebrake, nor even been below the mouth of the Ohio river, but the appropriateness of the simile instantly strikes everyone who has travelled down the Mississippi.

In these songs Stephen followed his usual practice of writing both the words and the melody himself.

Around 1845 Stephen's brother Dunning established himself in business in Cincinnati under the firm name of Irwin & Foster. Either late in 1846 or early the following year Stephen went to Cincinnati to work as a bookkeeper in his brother's office, which was near the largest steamboat landing in the city. He frequented the music store of Peters & Field, of which one of the partners was William C. Peters of Pittsburgh, who published some of Stephen's earliest songs. He met William Roarke, member of a minstrel troupe known as the Sable Harmonists, who introduced his song "Old Uncle Ned" in one of their programs. This was probably Stephen's first professional contact with the minstrel stage.

In September, 1847, the proprietors of The Eagle Saloon in Pittsburgh organized a musical contest for the best Ethiopian melody. Stephen submitted a lively little song called "Away Down Souf," which has a curious geographical juxtaposition in the chorus:

No use talkin' when de darky wants to go
Whar de corntop blossom and de canebrake grow;
Den come along to Cuba, and we'll dance de polka-juba,
  Way down souf, whar de corn grow.

Stephen's song "Away Down Souf" did not win the silver Prize Cup. But Nelson Kneass, musical director of The Eagle Saloon, wrote it down and tried to copyright it under his own name the next day! This Kneass, incidentally, was the author of "Ben Bolt," one of those moribund songs that refuses to die. On September 11, 1847, The Eagle Saloon announced a Grand Gala Concert which featured:

SUSANNA—A new song, never before given to the public.

Once "given to the public"—and, one might say, given to the publishers, because Stephen got only a hundred dollars for it—"Susanna" took the country by storm. Before long, the "forty-niners" had carried it all the way to California. Stephen sold the song to Peters, who had it copyrighted on December 30, 1848. Meanwhile, a pirated edition was issued in New York and copyrighted in February of the same year. Such piratings and copyright imbroglios were not uncommon in those days. Small as was the sum he received, Stephen was pleased at getting paid for his work. He wrote to Robert Nevin:

> Imagine my delight in receiving one hundred dollars in cash! Though this song was not successful, yet the two fifty-dollar bills I received for it had the effect of starting me on my present vocation of song-writer.

Stephen was wrong about the success of his song: Peters made more than ten thousand dollars from it and from "Old Uncle Ned." Within a year both songs were being featured by minstrel troupes throughout the country. Another song of this period, featured by the Sable Harmonists, titled "Way Down South in Alabama," was recently discovered to have been composed by Foster, though the published version was arranged by Frank Spencer.

In spite of the success of these plantation melodies, Stephen felt that he should be composing music of a more genteel character, suitable for the parlor rather than the stage. He turned out a piano piece called *Santa Anna's Retreat from Buena Vista,* full of elegant pianistic effects. Immediately afterward he wrote "Nelly Was a Lady," one of his delightfully simple and effective plantation melodies, with much of that plaintive quality that was to endear his songs to millions of people. Yet Stephen was ashamed of it, called it a "miserable thing," told his brother to take "10$, 5$ or even 1$ for it," and ended by giving all the rights to Firth, Pond & Co., in return for fifty copies of the printed music. He did the same thing with another "darky" song, "My Brudder Gum," and the only benefit he received from this transaction was that it led to signing a contract, in the autumn of 1849, with Firth, Pond & Co., leading music publishers of New York, who brought out most of his songs for the next ten years. The signing of this contract was doubtless one of the major factors that caused Stephen to abandon bookkeeping in favor of a musical career. He was encouraged to believe that he could earn a living as a writer of songs.

Returning to his family's home in Pittsburgh, Stephen began to court Jane McDowell, the daughter of a prominent neighbor, with whom he had fallen in love while she was visiting in Cincinnati. On June 22, 1850, Stephen and Jane were married. His financial assets as a married man had been augmented by the writing and publication of "Dolcy Jones," "Summer Longings," "Oh! Lemuel!", "Mary Loves the Flowers," "Soiree Polka," "Camptown Races," "Dolly Day," "Angelina Baker," "Ah! May the Red Rose Live Alway," "Way Down in Cairo," "Molly! Do You Love Me?", and "The Voice of Bygone Days." Of these, the one that turned out to be most successful was "Camptown Races"—at least from the standpoint of fame and popularity. Financially it did not prove to be a best seller, for in seven years it brought Foster only $101.25 in royalties, representing a sale of some 5,000 copies over that period. This was a bonanza, however, in comparison with "Angelina Baker," which in the same seven-year period earned for the composer a total of $16.87!

It will be noticed that of the songs listed above, half were plantation melodies. Stephen was determined to use the minstrel stage to forward his career as a songwriter. On February 23, 1850, he wrote to E. P. Christy, leader of the famed Christy Minstrels, sending him copies of "Camptown Races" and "Dolly Day," and saying, "I wish to unite with you in every effort to encourage a taste for this style of music so cried down by opera mongers." Stephen was now composing at a great rate. In July, 1851, he rented an office, where he could work without interruption, and installed a piano in it. By this time he had a baby girl, as well as a wife, to support. He was trying to be as businesslike as possible.

It was in the summer of 1851 that Stephen composed the most famous of all his songs, "Old Folks at Home." According to his brother Morrison's account, Stephen asked him, "What is a good name of two syllables for a southern river? I want to use it in this new song, *Old Folks at Home*." With a laugh, Morrison answered, "How would Yazoo do?" referring to a current comic song called "Down on the Old Yazoo." Stephen replied, "Oh, that's been used before," and they both started looking for a suitable river in an atlas that Morrison had on his desk. They hit on Suwannee, a river flowing from Georgia through Florida to the Gulf of Mexico. Stephen, delighted, crossed out the name "Pedee," which he had originally written, and substituted the more euphonious "Suwannee," merely simplifying it to "Swanee"—thus producing the familiar opening line of his song, "Way down upon the Swanee River."

Foster made an arrangement with Christy whereby the latter would have "first performance" rights on his new songs, in advance of publication, in return for a payment of ten dollars on each song. In the case of "Old Folks at Home" this payment was increased to fifteen dollars. Moreover, Stephen agreed to let Christy's name appear on the title page as the composer of this song. It was a foolish thing to do, and Stephen soon realized his mistake, for on May 25, 1852, he wrote a significant letter to Christy, parts of which have already been quoted in this chapter, and which is important enough to reproduce in full: [5]

E. P. Christy, Esq.
Dear Sir:

As I once intimated to you, I had the intention of omitting my name on my Ethiopian songs, owing to a prejudice against them by some, which might injure my reputation as a writer of another style of music, but I find that by my efforts I have done a great deal to build up a taste for the Ethiopian songs among refined people by making the words suitable to their taste, instead of the trashy and really offensive words which belong to some songs of that order. Therefore I have concluded to reinstate my name on my songs and to pursue the Ethiopian business without fear or shame and lend all my energies to making the business *live*, at the same time that I will wish to establish my name as the best Ethiopian song-writer. But I am not encouraged in undertaking this so long as "The Old Folks at Home" stares me in the face with another's name on it. As it was at my own solicitation that you allowed your name to be placed on the song, I hope that the above reasons will be sufficient explanation for my desire to place my own name on it as author and composer, while at the same time I wish to leave the name of your band on the title page. This is a little matter of pride in myself which it will certainly be to your interest to encourage. On the receipt of your free consent to this proposition, I will if you wish, willingly refund you the money which you paid me on that song, though it may have been sent me for other considerations than the one in question, and I promise in addition to write you an opening chorus in my best style, free of charge, and in any other way in my power to advance your interests

[5] Morneweck, *op. cit.*, vol. 2, pp. 395ff.

hereafter. I find I cannot write at all unless I write for public approbation and get credit for what I write. As we may probably have a good deal of business with each other in our lives, it is best to proceed on a sure basis of confidence and good understanding, therefore I hope you will appreciate an author's feelings in the case and deal with me with your usual fairness. Please answer immediately.

Very respectfully yours,
Stephen C. Foster

According to Morrison Foster, who must have had the information from Stephen himself, Christy paid $500 for the privilege of placing his name as author on the title page of "Old Folks at Home." Christy refused to accede to Foster's request. In fact, on the back of Stephen's letter the celebrated minstrel performer wrote down his opinion of the composer as "a vacillating skunk"! Royalties on the song were paid to Stephen, but for the rest of his life he suffered the humiliation of seeing his most famous song appear with the name of another man as author and composer. Not until the copyright was renewed in 1879 did Stephen C. Foster's name appear as the composer of "Old Folks at Home."

In February, 1852, Stephen and Jane and a party of friends took a trip to New Orleans on the steamboat *James Milligan*, of which Stephen's brother Dunning was captain. They were away for a month. This was Stephen's only trip to the deep South.

In that year, 1852, Stephen wrote two of his best-known plantation melodies, "Massa's in de Cold Ground" and "My Old Kentucky Home, Good Night." There is a legend, without foundation in fact, that the latter song was written at Federal Hill, the home of the Rowan family in Bardstown, Kentucky. Stephen wrote the first draft of his song as "Poor Uncle Tom, Good Night," evidently influenced by the vogue of Harriet Beecher Stowe's *Uncle Tom's Cabin*, published in 1851–1852. Later he changed it to its present form, doubtless thinking that there were enough Uncle Toms on the market already. It is also interesting to note that in the first draft, the Uncle Tom version, Stephen used Negro dialect, as he had in his other "darky" songs; but in the revised version he dropped the dialect, and "My Old Kentucky Home" is written in ordinary English. Stephen's taste guided him wisely in this, for the absence of dialect doubtless adds to the universal appeal of the song. He followed the same practice in "Old Black Joe," the last of his great plantation melodies, written in 1860.

The last years

Stephen's marriage was not running smoothly. Quarrels grew more frequent, and in May, 1853, Jane left Stephen, taking baby Marion with her. Stephen went off to New York, but within the year he and Jane were reconciled and began living together again. Their troubles, however, were not over. Stephen's financial situation was not flourishing. John Tasker Howard has calculated that from 1849 to 1857 his average yearly income from royalties was $1425.84, enough for the small family to live on with careful management. But Stephen was not a good manager. He was in debt and overdrawn at his publishers. In 1857, therefore, he sold out all his future rights in the songs published by Firth, Pond & Co., for the sum of $1872.28. He also sold the complete rights to sixteen other songs (including "Camptown Races") to F. D. Benteen for $200. He thus raised immediate cash, but forfeited the future income from royalties, upon which he depended for a living. This, in turn, put him under the necessity of continuing to produce at a rapid rate, regardless of quality or inspiration, in order always to have something to sell. If Stephen Foster had been a good showman and self-promoter like Henry Russell, if he had gone on the stage and presented his own songs in person, surrounded with unlimited ballyhoo, he doubtless would have made money. But as a mere writer of songs he was doomed to an unequal struggle and a losing battle. The performers and the publishers were the ones who made the money.

In 1860 Stephen moved to New York with his wife and daughter. By this time he had practically ceased to write the plantation melodies that were his true vein. "Old Black Joe," "The Glendy Burk," and "Down Among the Cane Brakes" were published in 1860, but these were the last of their kind. Of far different character were the other songs that Foster submitted to his publishers in that year: "Poor Drooping Maiden," "None Shall Weep a Tear for Me," "The Wife; or He'll Come Home," and "Under the Willow She's Weeping." In spite of potboilers, he continued to be seriously overdrawn at Firth, Pond & Co., and was trying to make contracts with other publishers in a desperate effort to improve his situation.

Stephen by this time was drinking heavily. Jane left him in the summer of 1861, though she visited him that September and continued to be anxious about his welfare. They were together again in 1862, but the following year found Jane working as a telegraph operator at Greensburgh, Pennsylvania. Meanwhile, Stephen's relations with Firth, Pond & Co. had deteriorated. His latest songs were not making money. Firth, Pond, refused to take his song, "Our Bright, Bright Summer Days are Gone"; so Stephen gave it to his friend John Mahon, told him to submit it to another publisher, "and take what he will give you." Stephen Foster was reduced to a mere peddler.

After 1862 Stephen Foster was a defeated man. America's greatest songwriter was transformed into a slovenly alcoholic, an ailing and penurious hack. He turned out potboilers at a furious rate: forty-six songs in one year! And only once did any of these songs reveal a gleam of inspiration: "Beautiful Dreamer, Wake Unto Me," composed in 1863. Incidentally, this was not, as William Pond claimed, the "last song" written by Foster before his death.

In New York Stephen lived at the New England Hotel, on the corner of Bayard Street and the Bowery. There, on January 9, 1864, he went to bed ill and weak with fever. The next morning, when he tried to get a drink of water, he fell against the washbowl and cut a severe gash in his face and neck. When his friend George Cooper arrived in response to an emergency call, Stephen gasped, "I'm done for." Cooper took him to Bellevue Hospital and sent a telegram to Henry Foster telling him that his brother Stephen was very sick and wished to see him. He also wrote a letter to Morrison Foster with the same message, adding, "He desires me to ask you to send him some pecuniary assistance as his means are very low."

For a while Stephen seemed to rally, but on Wednesday afternoon he fainted and did not regain consciousness. He died at half past two o'clock on the afternoon of January 13, 1864. No friend or relative was at his bedside. The next day George Cooper telegraphed to Henry and Morrison: "Stephen is dead. Come on."

On January 21, 1864, while an orchestra played "Come Where My Love Lies Dreaming," the remains of Stephen Collins Foster were interred in Allegheny Cemetery, Pittsburgh. His grave is marked by a simple marble tombstone. In Pittsburgh's Highland Park a statue was erected to his memory. There are two figures in the sculptured group: one is that of the composer, seated and writing down a song; the other is that of a Negro strumming a banjo.

A summing-up

Stephen Foster's music may be described as a product of the urbanized frontier. Had he been raised in Boston, New York, or Philadelphia, he would have grown up hearing concerts of music "by the most celebrated European composers"; he would have heard operas, oratorios, symphonies, concertos, and he might have been tempted to try to become a composer in the grand style. He would, in any case, have been entirely an urban, that is to say, a thoroughly Europeanized product, completely cut off from the frontier. In Pittsburgh, and in Cincinnati, he had contact with the frontier, he became a part of the process of Americanization achieved by the frontier. Yet his environment was that of the *urbanized* frontier, which was rapidly ceasing to be a frontier at all as the cities of the then West became more and more Europeanized, aspiring to cultivate the "polite arts" in the same degree as the older cities of the Atlantic seaboard. Stephen Foster's wide appeal lies largely in this cultural dualism of his background, through which he was able to combine the vitality of the frontier and a certain element of primitive simplicity with the genteel tradition of the urban fringe, dominated by sentimentality, conventionalism, and propriety.

To appreciate Stephen Foster's musical output in relation to the cultural context in which it was produced, one needs to go through all of his more than two hundred songs in their original or at least contemporary sheet-music editions, or in nineteenth-century songbooks like *The Love and Sentimental Songster* or *The American Dime Song Book,* to see their illustrated covers with portraits of sentimental maidens and lovers in stilted romantic attitudes, and to realize the overwhelming proportion of merely "pretty" songs that he turned out for the genteel trade. Stephen Foster's preeminence as an American songwriter rests upon some dozen songs, to which may be added another dozen of lesser fame but of evident superiority to the rest of his output or to that of his contemporaries. The "big four" among Foster's songs, the pillars of his universal fame, are "Old Folks at Home," "My Old Kentucky Home," "Massa's in de Cold Ground," and "Old Black Joe." Now, these are not the songs that are closest either to the roots of Negro folksong or to the prevailing style of blackface minstrelsy. Neither are they the closest to the genteel tradition of the Europeanized urban fringe. In terms of Foster's songs, they stand midway between "Oh! Susanna" or "Camptown Races" and "Come Where My Love Lies Dreaming" or "Wilt Thou Be Gone, Love?" In three of the "big four," the Negro dialect has been eliminated, and in the fourth, "Massa's in de Cold Ground" it is somewhat attenuated. Foster himself stated that he intended to make the minstrel melodies or Ethiopian songs palatable to refined tastes, and this is part of the cleaning-up process. Musically, these four songs are in slow tempo: *Moderato con espressione*, *Poco adagio*, *Poco lento*, and again *Poco adagio* for "Old Black Joe." Above all, "*con espressione*"!—that is an indispensable requirement of the genteel tradition. Compare, for example, such an old-time minstrel song as "Long Time Ago" with "Old Folks at Home." The former is really rooted in popular tradition: it is marked Allegro, and the minstrels have their way with it as a comic song. As we saw in the previous chapter, Morris and Horn made a sentimental song out of "Long Time Ago." Their concoction strikes us as ludicrous now because it leans so obviously on a faded tradition. Foster wrote plenty of sentimental songs that seem equally ludicrous—one need only mention "Willie We Have Missed You" as an example. But he was not, like Charles Horn, a hopeless victim of the genteel tradition. Like the Ohio and the Missouri flowing into the Mississippi, two traditions converged in the broad stream of Stephen Foster's best music. It is this that gives him his unique position and significance in American music. How thoroughly he was master of both traditions is proved by the fact that he excelled in the pure minstrel song, he excelled in the sentimental ballad, and he excelled in the combination of both types: the blending of simplicity and pathos with expression and refinement that marks his most famous and most beloved songs.

Stephen Foster's songs may be divided into two broad categories: minstrel songs and nonminstrel songs. Under the latter there are some minor subdivisions, such as religious songs and war songs, which have slight value if any. The best of Foster's Civil War songs is probably "We Are Coming Father Abraham, 300,000 More," published in 1862. As for the "Ethiopian" productions, they fall into two groups: the comic songs and the sentimental songs, the latter represented chiefly by the "big four" already mentioned. Let us glance more closely at a song in each of these groups.

"Oh! Susanna" is a typical example of the comic or nonsense minstrel song. The music consists of four nearly identical periods, each divided into two phrases to correspond with the eight lines of the verse. The same period is used for the last two lines of the chorus, so that the only new material occurs in the first portion of the chorus, which also contains the one instance of syncopation, on the word "Susanna." Having said that the melodic periods are nearly identical, it remains merely to remark that the only difference lies in a slight melodic variation of the second phrase. The first period leads to a semicadence on the dominant, the second to a full cadence. The second phrase of the chorus, "do not cry for me," has exactly the same melodic and metrical pattern as the last phrase of the first line. This unity through repetition, with only slight but effective contrasts, is characteristic of Foster's songs. Harold Vincent Milligan, remarking on this trait, wrote: "The repetitiousness of Foster's melodies is such that one cannot fail to wonder that they exert such an influence upon the listener as they do." [6] But, being such good tunes to begin with, it is precisely through this repetitiousness that they make their unfailing effect. And this, in turn, makes the variation doubly effective when it does occur.

"Old Folks at Home" may be taken as an example of the sentimental plantation melody constructed on the same simple basis. As in the case of "Oh! Susanna," the first introduction of new melodic material occurs in the first two lines of the chorus, and again this is followed by a repetition of the main melody. Again we have four successive repetitions of the principal melody, ending twice on a semicadence and twice on a full cadence. Very characteristic is the rhythmical "snap" which dislocates the accent on words having normally a feminine ending, such as "ribber," "ebber," "plantation," and "weary." Except for the first part of the chorus, the melody of "Old Folks at Home" uses only the five tones of the pentatonic scale.

While recognizing the element of repetition in Foster's melodies, we should nevertheless bear in mind that slight metrical variations in the melody were, in some cases, introduced for different stanzas, as shown by the original editions. For instance, in the original edition of "Old Folks at Home," published by Firth, Pond & Co. in 1851, the following metrical variants occur for the second and third stanzas of the song:

[6] Milligan, *Stephen Collins Foster*, p. 113.

A 

B 

As regards harmony, Foster stays pretty close to the tonic, dominant, and subdominant. A rare example of the use of secondary chords is to be found in the song "Ah! May the Red Rose Live Alway." Modulations are very scarce and confined chiefly to the dominant key, as in "My Old Kentucky Home" and "Old Black Joe."

Among Foster's nonminstrel songs, the best known is, of course, "Jeanie with the Light Brown Hair." It seems that in his original manuscript book Foster wrote the name as "Jennie," definitely indicating that he had his wife Jane in mind, for she was often affectionately addressed as Jennie. But the publishers preferred "Jeanie" and brought the song out with this name. "Jeanie" has not always been so popular. After the composer's death, when the copyright was renewed for the benefit of his widow and daughter, they received, for a nineteen-year period, accumulated royalties of 75 cents! Only fifteen copies had been sold.

We have already observed, according to the dictum of Marius Schneider, that the popularity of a melody depends partly on its degree of simplicity and partly on its conformity "to the melodic type current in a given culture." The melodies of Stephen Foster fulfill these conditions in the highest degree. Simplicity is the essence of his music. His songs conform to melodic types widely current in American folklore. These melodic types and their basic harmonic patterns, in turn, are deeply rooted in age-old folk traditions inherited from Anglo-Celtic civilization transplanted to America. These factors contribute to make Stephen Collins Foster the most beloved composer whom America has produced.

chapter fifteen

The exotic periphery

Existence in a tropical wilderness, in the midst of a voluptuous and half-civilized race, bears no resemblance to that of a London cockney, a Parisian lounger, or an American Quaker.

L. M. GOTTSCHALK, NOTES OF A PIANIST.

In the 1820s, somewhat more than two decades after the Louisiana Purchase, there arrived in the turbulent and colorful city of New Orleans a young Englishman from London named Edward Gottschalk. He had studied medicine at Leipzig, but after emigrating to America in his twenty-fifth year he became a successful broker. Handsome, cultured, and affluent, he was admitted to the best Creole society—that is, the old French and Spanish families—of New Orleans, and in this aristocratic milieu he met, and fell in love with, a young girl of exceptional charm and beauty, Aimée Marie de Bruslé. Her grandfather had been governor of the northern province of the French colony of Saint-Domingue, one of the wealthiest and most luxurious colonies of the New World until its prosperity was shattered by war and civil strife. In that troubled period, Mlle. de Bruslé's father, an army officer, fled to Jamaica, where he married a lady of French and Spanish noble birth. Soon afterward, like many other refugees from the West Indies, they settled in New Orleans, a city congenial to them because of its gay social life and its mixed heritage of French and Spanish culture.

Founded by the Sieur de Bienville in 1718, New Orleans soon became a city of strong contrasts, ranging from the most refined elegance to the most unbridled depravity. While the French royal governor, the Marquis de Vaudreuil, busied himself with creating a little Versailles on the Mississippi and organizing grand balls with court dress *de rigueur*, he at the same time fostered gross corruption and nepotism, while his official laxity made the provincial capital an open city for thieves, prostitutes, gamblers, and lawless adventurers of every description. Negro slaves were brought from Africa in considerable numbers (later they came mostly from the West Indies) and in 1724 the original "Black Code" was promulgated for the regulation of Negroes in Louisiana. It prohibited any mingling of the races, black and white, either through marriage or concubinage, regardless of whether the Negroes were free or slave. To manumitted slaves it granted "the same rights, privileges, and immunities which are enjoyed by free-born persons." This was the basis of the code adopted by the Louisiana legislature after the territory became a part of the United States.

In 1762, by a secret treaty, France ceded Louisiana to Spain, whose colonial empire already included vast sections of what is now the United States, from Florida to California. Not until 1769 did Don Alexander O'Reilly arrive in New Orleans to take possession of the city and the province in the name of the Spanish King. New Orleans then became a Spanish colonial city, with its *cabildo*, its *regidores*, its *alcaldes*. In spite of two disastrous fires, the city grew and prospered under the Spanish regime; in fact, the fires may have done some good, for as a result the Spaniards rebuilt most of the city, thus giving rise to the local saying that they found "a town of hovels and left it a city of palaces."

In 1800 Spain retroceded Louisiana to France, but before the French authorities could take effective possession, the territory was purchased by the United States, and in 1803 New Orleans became officially an American city. Essentially it remained an exotic city within the borders of the United States. The son born to Edward Gottschalk and his Creole wife on May 8, 1829, an American citizen by reason of the Louisiana Purchase, was to become and remain an exotic personality within his native country; and, like the city of his birth, he acted as a link between the progressive, practical civilization of the expanding United States, and the seductive, colorful civilization of Latin America. Louis Moreau Gottschalk—he was named after his mother's uncle, Moreau de l'Islet—whether he lived in Paris or New York, never forgot that he was a child of the tropics; and what we value in his music today is not the glitter of the concert hall or the sophistication of the salon, but the alluring charm of his Caribbean rhythms and melodies.

"Caribbean" is perhaps the best word to describe the musical atmosphere of New Orleans in which Louis Moreau Gottschalk spent his boyhood. I do not, of course, refer to the world of French opera as performed at the Théâtre d'Orléans, attended by fashionable audiences in full dress. Gottschalk knew this world of "cultivated" music, both at home and during his years of study in Europe. What I refer to is that exotic, unconventional, hybrid, exciting blend of musical elements, the product of complex racial and cultural factors in a new society evolving under strange conditions, which finds its most characteristic expression in the Caribbean area. There was an influx of population from the islands of the Caribbean to New Orleans. Negro slaves were brought from the West Indies, but many other persons, both white and colored, came to the city on the Mississippi as refugees from the terrors of revolution in Haiti, or to escape the international strife that afflicted the Caribbean area. In 1809 and 1810, more than ten thousand refugees from the West Indies arrived in New Orleans, most of them originally from Saint-Domingue (or Haiti, as the former French colony was called after it became independent in 1804). Of these, about three thousand were free Negroes, or rather "persons of color," for their racial composition varied greatly. In order to understand the racial background of this emigration, it will be helpful to glance at a breakdown of the population in the French colony of Saint-Domingue in the year 1789:

White	30,826	Free Negroes and Mulattoes	27,548	Slaves	465,429

To be noted in particular are (1) the overwhelming majority of Negro slaves, and (2) the large proportion of free "persons of color." It was the coming of the latter class to New Orleans that gave the city, in large part, its peculiar social structure. The mulatto women—called quadroons or octoroons, according to the proportion of white blood in their veins—were famous for their seductive beauty, as well as for their gay and attractive dress. The gentlemen of Louisiana flocked to the celebrated Quadroon Balls not merely to dance and admire but also to select the mistress of their choice. The free men of color could gain admittance to these balls only in the capacity of musician, to fiddle for the dancers. Thus it was that the "f.m.c."—free male of color—frequently turned to music as a profession; if such it could be called, for the dance musician was little more than a menial.

The persons of color, *gens de couleur*, having even a single drop of white blood, were a class apart from the blacks, the Negroes. Even within the *gens de couleur* there were rigid caste distinctions, according to the proportion of white blood. It might be unnecessary to dwell on this subject, were it not for the importance of the caste-and-color system in New Orleans for the future development of American music, particularly with relation to the origin and growth of jazz. Furthermore, these distinctions have led to a curious confusion in the use of the term "Creole." This word is the French equivalent of the Spanish *criollo,* which was used from early colonial times to designate a person of European parentage born in America. It was during the Spanish regime that this term came into usage in Louisiana. As a noun the term was always applied to white persons of European ancestry, born in the New World. But as an adjective, it was applied also to Negroes born in the New World, as opposed to those brought from Africa. It was also applied to the dialect, or patois, spoken by these Negroes, which was a strongly corrupted variety of French. Hence in popular speech the term "Creole" became associated with Louisiana Negro dialect, songs, customs, and dances. Later the octoroons of New Orleans began to be called Creoles, which added to the confusion. In short, the term "Creole" has become so laden with conflicting connotations that it can be used only when hedged around with definitions.

New Orleans had three colorful, exotic dance rituals that all visitors wanted to see: the Quadroon Balls, the voodoo ceremonial dances, and the dances of the Negroes in Place Congo, or Congo Square. The cult of voodoo (more correctly, *vodoun*) is a form of African religion involving ritualistic drumming and dancing to induce "possession" by the *loa* or supernatural spirits. Because one of the leading deities of the cult is Damballa, the serpent god, voodooism is popularly associated with snake worship. Voodoo probably existed in Louisiana from the earliest colonial period, but it received a marked impetus from the influx of West Indian refugees from 1809 to 1810, for the cult flourished primarily among the free "persons of color." Although basically African in origin, voodoo became mixed with Roman Catholic elements, and therefore, like most Caribbean cultural manifestations, was a hybrid product. In New Orleans the principal public voodoo ceremonies took place on St. John's Eve (June 23) and attracted a multitude of spectators. But there were also secret ceremonies that few if any outsiders ever witnessed. George W. Cable described voodoo dances in New Orleans with a great show of moral indignation and the vividness of an eyewitness:

> . . . the voodoo dance begins. The postulant dances frantically in the middle of the ring, only pausing, from time to time, to receive heavy alcoholic draughts in great haste and return more wildly to his leapings and writhings until he falls in convulsions. He is lifted, restored, and presently conducted to the altar, takes his oath, and by a ceremonial stroke from one of the sovereigns is admitted a full participant. . . . But the dance goes on about the snake. The contortions of the upper part of the body, especially of the neck and shoulders, are such as to threaten to dislocate them. The queen shakes the box and tinkles the bells, the rum bottle gurgles, the chant alternates between king and chorus:
>
> Eh! Eh! Bomba hon, honc!
> Canga bafio tay,
> Canga moon day lay,
> Canga do keelah,
> Canga li!
>
> There are swoonings and ravings, nervous tremblings beyond control, incessant writhings and turnings, tearing of garments, even biting of the flesh—every imaginable invention of the devil.[1]

That gifted writer Lafcadio Hearn, whose book on the West Indies might well serve as background for this chapter, became interested in the music of the Louisiana Negroes, and at one time conceived the idea of writing a book on the subject in collaboration with the music critic H. E. Krehbiel. According to the latter, Hearn proposed to relate the migrations of African music through the ages: "Then I would touch upon the transplantation of Negro melody to the Antilles and the two Americas, where its strangest black flowers are gathered by the alchemists of musical science and the perfume thereof extracted by magicians like Gottschalk." [2]

Dancing in Congo Square

But in Gottschalk's time "the alchemists of musical science" (today more prosaically called comparative musicologists) were not yet busy gathering the "strange black flowers" of Negro music; so Gottschalk had to gather the flowers himself as well as extract the per-

[1] Cable, *The Century Magazine,* Apr. 1886.
[2] Krehbiel, *Afro-American Folksongs,* p. 39.

fume thereof. The question is, under what circumstances did he do it? In his entertaining book on the New Orleans underworld, *The French Quarter,* Herbert Asbury asserts in a footnote: "Louis Moreau Gottschalk . . . based one of his best known compositions, *La Bamboula,* on what he heard and saw in Congo Square as a boy." Now, it is true that the bamboula was one of the Negro dances that could be seen and heard (it was also a song) in Congo Square when Gottschalk was a boy in New Orleans. Whether the boy Moreau—as his family called him—was ever taken to see the dances in Congo Square is a matter of conjecture. But before we attempt to bring him to this exciting spectacle, let us first bring him out of the cradle, where we left him some time ago.

Louis Moreau Gottschalk took only three years to progress from the cradle to the piano. Such, at least, is the family tradition. According to his sister, when Moreau was three years old, one day everyone in the family was startled by a faint but most exquisite melody on the piano. "The tone and touch were perfect." When Mamma rushed into the drawing room, "she found little Moreau standing on a high stool, playing the melody she had sung to him in the morning." After that, Papa lost no time arranging for his small son to take music lessons. He studied both piano and violin, but the piano was his instrument. At the age of eight he gave his first public concert, a benefit for his violin teacher Miolan. Shortly before his twelfth birthday, his father decided to send him to Europe for further study. In May, 1842, after giving a farewell concert, young Moreau sailed for France and was placed in a private school in Paris. Three years later, while convalescing from an attack of typhoid fever in the French provinces, he composed the piano piece that was to become so popular everywhere, *La Bamboula.*

If Gottschalk based that composition on "what he heard and saw in Congo Square," then it is obvious that he must have been taken to see the dancing there before his departure for Europe. Assuming that the sheltered child was taken there, perhaps by a Negro nurse if not by his parents, what would he have seen and heard? Firsthand accounts are lacking, but George W. Cable, in his article *The Dance in Place Congo,* published in 1886, seems to have reconstructed the scene with considerable authenticity. The following is extracted from his article.

The booming of African drums and blast of huge wooden horns called to the gathering. . . . The drums were very long, hollowed, often from a single piece of wood, open at one end and having a sheep or goat skin stretched across the other. . . . The smaller drum was often made from a joint or two of very large bamboo . . . and this is said to be the origin of its name; for it was called the Bamboula.

The drummers bestrode the drums; the other musicians sat about them in an arc, cross-legged on the ground. One important instrument was a gourd partly filled with pebbles or grains of corn, flourished violently at the end of a stout staff with one hand and beaten upon the palm of the other. Other performers rang triangles, and others twanged from jew's-harps an astonishing amount of sound. Another instrument was the jawbone of some ox, horse or mule, and a key rattled rhythmically along its weatherbeaten teeth. . . . But the grand instrument at last, was the banjo. It had but four strings, not six. . . .

And then there was that long-drawn human cry of tremendous volume, richness, and resound, to which no instruments within their reach could make the faintest approach:

Eh! pou' la belle Layotte ma mourri 'nocent,
Oui 'nocent ma mourri!

All the instruments silent while it rises and swells with mighty energy and dies away distantly, "yea-a-a-a-a!"—and then the crash of savage drums, horns, and rattles.

Cable then goes on to describe the dancing of the bamboula:

The singers almost at the first note are many. At the end of the first line every voice is lifted up. The strain is given the second time with growing spirit. Yonder glistening black Hercules, who plants one foot forward, lifts his head and bare, shining chest, rolls out the song from a mouth and throat like a cavern. . . . See his play of restrained enthusiasm catch from one bystander to another. They swing and bow to right and left, in slow time to the piercing treble of the Congo women. . . . Hear that bare foot slap the ground! one sudden stroke only. . . . The musicians warm up at the sound.

A smiting of breasts with open hands begins very softly and becomes vigorous. The women's voices rise to a tremulous intensity. . . . The women clap their hands in time, or standing with arms akimbo receive with faint courtesies and head-liftings the low bows of the men, who deliver them swinging this way and that.

See! Yonder brisk and sinewy fellow has taken one short, nervy step into the ring, chanting with rising energy. . . . He moves off to the farther edge of the circle, still singing, takes the prompt hand of an unsmiling Congo girl, leads her into the ring, and leaving the chant to the throng, stands before her for the dance. . . . A sudden frenzy seizes the musicians. The measure quickens, the swaying, attitudinizing crowd starts into extra activity, the female voices grow sharp and staccato, and suddenly the dance is the furious Bamboula.

Now for the frantic leaps! Now for frenzy! Another pair are in the ring. The man wears a belt of little bells, or, as a substitute, little tin vials of shot, "bram-bram sonnette!" And still another couple enter the circle. What wild—what terrible delight! The ecstasy rises to madness; one—two—three of the dancers fall—*bloucoutoum! boum!* —with foam on their lips and are dragged out by arms and legs from under tumultuous feet of crowding new-comers. The musicians know no fatigue; still the dance rages on:

Quand patate la cuite na va mangé li!
("When that 'tater's cooked don't you eat it up!")

For Cable, the bamboula represented "a frightful triumph of body over the mind," and he adds: "Only the music deserved to survive, and does survive. . . . The one just given, Gottschalk first drew from oblivion." The second musical example quoted above is one of several tunes included in a supplement to Cable's article. It is titled *The Bamboula,* the arrangement is credited to Miss M. L. Bartlett, but no source for the music is given. Actually this tune bears little resemblance to a West Indian dance; so it is not surprising to find Cable remarking, "I have never heard another to know it as a bamboula."

But he goes on to remark that in *Slave Songs of the United States* there is a bamboula from Louisiana, "whose characteristics resemble the bamboula reclaimed by Gottschalk in so many points that here is the best place for it." He then quotes the music of this song, under the title "Miché Banjo," in an arrangement by H. E. Krehbiel (who, incidentally, calls attention to what he describes as "the particularly propulsive effect of the African 'snap' at the beginning"). I quote the music as it appears on page 113 of *Slave Songs of the United States* (New York, 1867), where it is titled "Musieu Bainjo": the song is about a mulatto who puts on airs, with his hat on one side, his cane, and his new boots that creak. The spice of the text is in the double meaning between *mulet* (mule) and *mulatre* (mulatto).

Creole songs and dances: the background

The editors of the collection from which this song was taken, state that, along with six others in the same volume, it was obtained from a lady who heard them sung, before the Civil War, on the Good Hope plantation, St. Charles Parish, Louisiana. According to them, it represents "the attempt of some enterprising Negro to write a French song." There is perhaps no need to take this information literally, but they were undoubtedly correct in recognizing this song as the product of French music plus Negro "enterprise." Its West Indian character is unmistakable. When the French *contredanse* was transplanted to Haiti in the eighteenth century, it began to undergo rhythmic modifications under Negro influence, particularly by the introduction of the "habanera rhythm" in the bass. This rhythm became the basis of the *contradanza* of the Antilles, as well as of the habanera, the tango, and numerous other Latin American dances. Further modifications occurred when Negro musicians altered this fundamental rhythm by transferring the accent to a weak beat. This may be seen in the bass of a *contradanza* titled *Los Merengazos:*[3]

The alert reader will at once notice that this metrical pattern corresponds exactly to that of the first and third measures of "Musieu Bainjo." It is, moreover, identical with the so-called "cakewalk" figure that forms the rhythmic basis of American ragtime music.

Let us now seek a Caribbean counterpart for the metrical pattern of the second and sixth measures of "Musieu Bainjo." Among many examples that could be quoted, we shall choose a Cuban *contradanza* from the early nineteenth century, which also shows the habanera rhythm in the bass.[4] The metrical pattern that concerns us particularly is marked with a bracket.

The foregoing, among numerous other illustrations that might be cited, should serve to indicate concretely the extremely close relationship between the music of the "Creole" Negroes of Louisiana and the music of the Caribbean islands, with its mixture of Spanish, French, and African elements. It is worth noting that the editors of *Slave Songs of the United States* speak of these tunes as "peculiar . . . difficult to write down, or to sing correctly." Their notation is probably only an approximation of what the Louisiana Negroes actually played and sang when they made their music "hot" for Place Congo.

The supposition that Gottschalk "lifted" his *Bamboula* from Congo Square seems farfetched. A more likely explanation is that, like the anonymous lady who supplied the Creole tunes for *Slave Songs of the United States*, he heard this, and other similar tunes, sung by Negroes in his household or on nearby plantations. Cable is correct

[3] From Carpentier, *La Música en Cuba*, p. 119.
[4] *Ibid.*, p. 112.

in remarking the traits that Gottschalk's *Bamboula* has in common with "Miché Banjo" (or "Musieu Bainjo"). The points of resemblance have to do chiefly with the use of two characteristic rhythmic figures: that of the habanera and that of the cakewalk. Gottschalk uses the former in the treble over a heavily accented first beat in the bass: [5]

The cakewalk figure appears in the following measures in combination with a typical pattern of the *contradanza:*

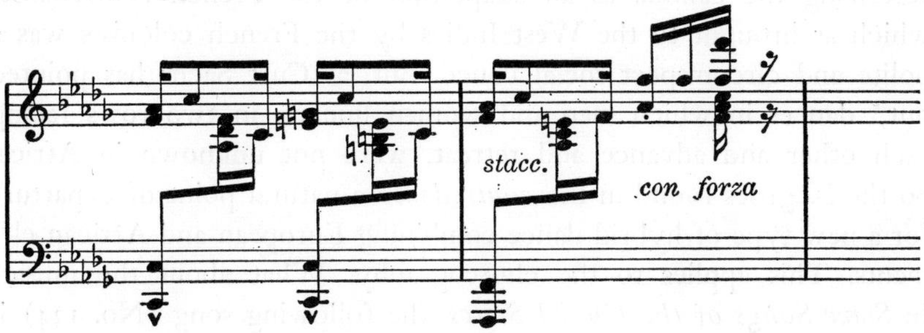

Elsewhere in this piece, he uses the *contradanza* rhythm with the characteristic accent on the weak beats.

In his Cuban dance titled *Ojos Criollos,* there is an interesting juxtaposition of the cakewalk and the habanera rhythms, with syncopation in the bass. In another Cuban dance, *Dí que si* (also known by its French title, *Réponds-moi*), the cakewalk figure appears systematically over a bass that repeatedly stresses the weak beat of the measure (in 2/4 time).

Although Gottschalk adapted his Creole and Caribbean compositions to the prevailing style of mid-nineteenth-century piano writing in the virtuoso manner, he was highly sensitive to the nuances of local color and extremely perceptive of the rhythmic intricacies of this New World music.

[5] This and the following example copyrighted in 1908 by G. Schirmer.

Among other dances of the Louisiana Negroes, all reported by various writers as found in the West Indies also, were the *babouille*, the *cata* (or *chacta*), the *counjaille* (or *counjai*), the *voudou*, the *calinda*, and the *congo*. According to Cable, the congo ("to describe which would not be pleasant") was known as the *chica* in Santo Domingo, and in the Windward Islands was confused under one name with the calinda. It is indeed difficult to unravel the nomenclature of these dances. Probably the most widespread of all was the calinda, which Cable says was the favorite dance all the way from New Orleans to Trinidad.

The editors of *Slave Songs of the United States* wrote that the calinda "was a sort of contra-dance." They quote the description of a French writer, Bescherelle, who mentions the two lines of dancers as "advancing and retreating in cadence, and making very strange contortions and highly lascivious gestures."[6] They were right in characterizing the calinda as an adaptation of the French *contredanse*, which as brought to the West Indies by the French colonists was a polite and circumspect social dance. But, as Curt Sachs has pointed out,[7] dances in which men and women line up in two rows facing each other and advance and retreat, were not unknown in Africa. So the Negroes found in the *contredanse* a natural point of departure for a new type of hybrid dance combining European and African elements. This applies to the choreography. What about the music? In *Slave Songs of the United States*, the following song (No. 134) is given as an example of the calinda:

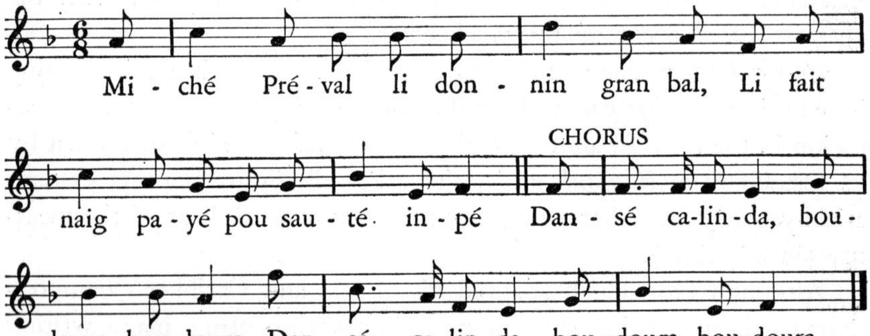
Mi - ché Pré - val li don - nin gran bal, Li fait
CHORUS
naig pa - yé pou sau - té in - pé Dan - sé ca-lin-da, bou -
doum, bou-doum, Dan - sé . ca-lin-da, bou - doum, bou-doum.

[6] I have been unable to identify the work from which this quotation is taken. Compare, however, the quotation from Père Labat given on p. 314. It would not be surprising if this were the source of the description attributed to Bescherelle.

[7] Sachs, *World History of the Dance*.

The first thing that strikes one about this tune is its completely European character; it is clearly a tune of French origin, which has undergone little or no modification by the Caribbean milieu. In this connection we observe also that of seven Creole tunes included in the collection, this is the only one in 6/8 meter. Of the others, four are in 2/4 and two in common time. This distinction is significant, for, although 6/8 meter is not foreign to Caribbean music, the 2/4 meter is by far the more prevalent, not only in Caribbean music, but in Afro-American music as a whole. In short, this calinda is obviously a tune that has scarcely been "worked over" at all by the Negroes, and one cannot but be struck by the incongruity between this pleasant little tune and the wild orgies which Cable describes as taking place in the Congo Square. Of course, it no doubt sounded wilder when the Negroes played and sang it to the accompaniment of drums, gourd rattles, triangles, jew's-harps, jawbone and key, quils (Pan's pipe made of three cane reeds), and banjos.

The songs of the calinda are satirical and often personally abusive. The calinda quoted above is about a certain Monsieur Préval who gave a ball in New Orleans, using a stable as the ballroom—much to the astonishment of the horses, says the song—and neglecting to obtain the necessary license. Krehbiel, in his book *Afro-American Folksongs*, gives a composite text for this song, in which he includes several stanzas that he says were supplied to him by Lafcadio Hearn. One of these is particularly interesting: "Black and white both danced the bamboula; never again will you see such a fine time." Two points are significant here: one, that the bamboula was a ballroom dance; two, that it may have been danced by both blacks and whites. Let the reader return for a moment to what was said in Chapter 4 of this book, where mention was made of the congo as a ballroom dance in Colonial Virginia. Cable and other writers describe the congo and the bamboula as wild, lascivious, primitive dances. Yet it is likely that they also existed as more or less restrained social dances, performed to such European instruments as the violin and the clarinet.

Mention of the calinda as a favorite dance of the Antilles goes back as far as the early part of the eighteenth century. Père Labat, in *Nouveau Voyage . . .* (The Hague, 1724), mentions it as an "African" dance, which he saw in Santo Domingo around the year 1698. According to this author, the Spaniards learned the "calenda," as he calls it, from the Negroes, who brought it over from the Coast of Guinea in Africa. His description follows:

> The calenda is danced to the sound of instruments and of voices. The participants are arranged in two lines, one in front of the other, the men facing the women. The spectators form a circle around the dancers and the musicians. One of the participants sings a song, of which the refrain is repeated by the spectators, with clapping of hands. All the dancers then hold their arms half-raised, leap, turn, make contortions with their posteriors, approach within two feet of each other, and retreat in cadence, until the sound of an instrument or the tone of the voices, signals them to approach again. Then they strike their bellies together two or three times in succession, after which they separate and pirouette, to begin the same movement again, with highly lascivious gestures, as many times as the instrument or the voice gives the signal. From time to time they go arm in arm, and circle around two or three times, while continuing to strike their bellies together and exchanging kisses, but without losing the cadence.

This description, which was copied (without acknowledgment) by several later writers, supplies the realistic details omitted by Cable in his account of the dance in Place Congo. It would not be at all surprising to find that this passage was also one of the major sources for Cable's article. Cable was born in 1844, a year after the dancing in Place Congo was suppressed; he had to reconstruct the scene from earlier accounts of writers who had actually witnessed the West Indian dances that were transplanted to New Orleans. As for the music, he took most of the tunes from the Creole songs included in *Slave Songs of the United States.* These songs evidently circulated widely in Louisiana, and Gottschalk must have had ample opportunity to hear them elsewhere than in Congo Square.

Gottschalk in Europe

There is sufficient evidence that Moreau Gottschalk carried with him to Europe, deeply impressed in his mind, the Creole songs of his native Louisiana. Besides his *Bamboula,* there is his Ballade Creole (Opus 3 *de la Louisiane*) titled *La Savane,* dating from his first years in Europe, in which he uses the theme of a song called "Lolotte" (No. 135 in *Slave Songs of the United States*):

Gottschalk used only a portion of the original melody, which is one of the most attractive of the Creole songs. Poor Lolotte, says the song, has only a heartache, while Calalou has an embroidered petticoat and a Madras kerchief. Pointing out that *calalou* was originally the term for a West Indian dish, a noted ragout, Cable thinks that in this song "Calalou" is a derisive nickname "intended to apply here to the quadroon women who swarmed into New Orleans in 1809 as refugees from Cuba, Guadeloupe, and other islands. . . ." A composite version of "Pov' piti Lolotte," with the music arranged by H. T. Burleigh, is given in Krehbiel's *Afro-American Folksongs.*

One more remark may be made about this song, and that is the strong resemblance it bears to the familiar American play-party song, "Skip to my Lou." Numerous versions of this old play-party song are available in collections of American folk music, so that the reader can easily verify this similarity—if indeed the familiar tune be not remembered from one's own childhood. Are the two songs related? Do the words "Skip to my Lou" indicate some connection with Louisiana? Is the play-party song derived from the Creole song? I do not know the answers.

La Savane was among the pieces that Gottschalk composed while he was in France, at the age of fifteen or sixteen. *La Bamboula*, as previously stated, was another; and a third was *Le Bananier* ("The Banana Tree"), subtitled "*Chanson nègre.*" These youthful compositions might be called a Louisiana trilogy and were to become and remain favorites with the public, along with that other characteristic and brilliant showpiece, *The Banjo*, subtitled "*Fantaisie grotesque*" and probably composed in Spain in 1851. (According to Gottschalk's Cuban biographer Fors, there was an earlier version of *The Banjo*, published by Espadero; but I have not located a copy of it.)

Gottschalk's first piano teacher in Paris was Charles Hallé, with whom he worked for six months. He then studied piano with Camille Stamaty and harmony with Maledan. Through his mother's family connections he was received and feted in the *salons* of the French nobility. In April, 1845, just after his sixteenth birthday, he gave his first public concert in the Salle Pleyel and attracted the attention of Chopin, who saluted him as a future "king of pianists." He became the pupil and friend of Hector Berlioz, with whom he gave a series of concerts at the Théâtre des Italiens during the season of 1846–1847. Concerning Gottschalk as a pianist, Berlioz wrote:

> Gottschalk is one of the very small number who possess all the different elements of a consummate pianist—all the faculties which surround him with an irresistible prestige, and give him a sovereign power. He is an accomplished musician—he knows just how far fancy may be indulged in expression. . . . There is an exquisite grace in his manner of phrasing sweet melodies and throwing light touches from the higher keys. The boldness, the brilliancy, and the originality of his playing at once dazzles and astonishes. . . .

In 1850 Gottschalk made a concert tour of the French provinces, Savoy, and Switzerland. The following year he went to Spain, where his success was enormous. The Queen entertained him in the royal palace and bestowed upon him the diamond cross of the Order of Isabel la Católica. He remained in Spain nearly two years, concertizing, composing, and basking in adulation. Among the compositions that recall his Spanish sojourn are *Midnight in Seville*, *Manchega* (*Etude de Concert*), *The Siege of Saragossa*, and *Jota Aragonesa*.

In the autumn of 1852 Gottschalk returned to Paris, where he took leave of his mother and his sisters, who had been living there since the end of 1847. He then embarked for New York, where he was met by his father and where his formal American debut as a mature pianist took place on February 11, 1853, in the ballroom of Niblo's Garden. The success of the concert may be judged by the fact that P. T. Barnum immediately offered him a contract for $20,000, plus expenses, for a concert tour of one year. Gottschalk refused, on the advice, it is said, of his father, whose dignity was doubtless offended at the thought of having his son exhibited in public like a side show. Nevertheless, under the management of Max Strakosch, Gottschalk embarked on a tremendously successful concert career. In the winter of 1855–1856 he gave eighty concerts in New York alone, and in 1862–1863 he gave more than eleven hundred concerts in the United States and Canada. In the intervening years he was far otherwise engaged: the lure of the tropics, the spell of the Caribbean, held him in thrall.

Caribbean vagabondage

Gottschalk seems to have visited Cuba for the first time in 1853. In his *Notes of a Pianist* he wrote:

> I shall never forget the two months which I passed at Caymito, in the interior of Cuba. The house which I inhabited was at an hour's distance from the first cabins of Caymito. . . . Unfortunately, the only company of my Eden was a very ugly negress, who, every evening, after having roasted the coffee, bruised her corn in a hollow piece of wood, and recited the Ave Maria before an old coloured image of the Virgin, came and squatted down at my feet on the veranda, and there, in the darkness, sung to me with a piercing and wild voice, but full of strange charm, the *canciones* of the country. I would light my cigar, extend myself in my *butaca,* and plunge, surrounded by this silent and primitive nature, into a contemplative reverie, which those in the midst of the everyday world can never understand. The moon rose over the Sierra de Anafe. . . . The distant noises of the savanna, borne softly by the breeze, struck on my ear in drawn-out murmurs. The cadenced chant of some negroes belated in the fields added one more attraction to all this poesy, which no one can ever imagine.

What a pity that Gottschalk did not write down for us the notation of these Afro-Cuban songs and chants. He did, however, try to capture some of this atmosphere in his own music. Meanwhile, the atmosphere of the tropics captured him. In 1856 he returned to Havana and then began a period of vagabondage in the Caribbean that lasted nearly six years: ". . . six years madly squandered, scattered to the winds"—so he wrote of this period afterward. About these irresponsible years he tells us in his *Notes of a Pianist:*

> I have wandered at random, yielding myself up indolently to the caprice of Fortune, giving a concert wherever I happened to find a piano, sleeping wherever night overtook me,—on the green grass of the savanna, or under the palm-leaf roof of a *veguero* [caretaker of a tobacco plantation], who shared with me his corn-tortilla, coffee, and bananas. . . . And when, at last, I became weary of the same horizon, I crossed an arm of the sea, and landed on some neighbor-

ing isle, or on the Spanish Main. Thus, in succession, I have visited all the Antilles,—Spanish, French, English, Dutch, Swedish, and Danish; the Guianas, and the coasts of Pará [Brazil]. At times, having become the idol of some obscure *pueblo,* whose untutored ears I had charmed with its own simple ballads, I would pitch my tent for five, six, eight months, deferring my departure from day to day, until finally I began seriously to entertain the idea of remaining there for evermore. Abandoning myself to such influences, I lived without care, as the bird sings, as the flower expands, as the brook flows; oblivious of the past, reckless of the future, and sowed both my heart and my purse with the ardor of a husbandman who hopes to reap a hundred ears for every grain he confides to the earth. But, alas! . . . the result of my prodigality was, that, one fine morning, I found myself a bankrupt in heart, with my purse at ebb-tide. Suddenly disgusted with the world and myself, weary, discouraged, mistrusting men (ay, and women too), I fled to a desert on the extinct volcano of M— [in Guadeloupe], where, for several months, I lived the life of a cenobite. . . .

My hut, perched on the verge of the crater, at the very summit of the mountain, commanded a view of all the surrounding country. . . . Every evening I rolled my piano out upon the terrace; and there, facing the most incomparably beautiful landscape, all bathed in the soft and limpid atmosphere of the tropics, I poured forth on the instrument, and for myself alone, the thoughts with which the scene inspired me. . . .

Amid such scenes I composed "Réponds-moi," "La Marche des Gibaros," "Polonia," "Columbia," "Pastorella e Cavaliere," "Jeunesse," and many other unpublished works. . . . My despair was soothed; and soon the sun of the tropics . . . restored me with new confidence and vigor to my wanderings.

I relapsed into the manners and life of these primitive countries: if not strictly virtuous, they are, at all events, terribly attractive. . . . The mere thought of re-appearing before a polished audience struck me as superlatively absurd. . . . It was at this period that Strakosch wrote to me, offering an engagement for a tour of concerts through the United States. . . .

Gottschalk hesitated, breathed a sigh of regret—and accepted. He felt morally rescued: ". . . but who could say, if, in the rescue, youth and poetry had not perished?" Meanwhile, thousands of America's youth were perishing in the Civil War; but this did not diminish the brilliant success of Gottschalk's concert tour. Actually, Gottschalk did not remain indifferent to the issues of the Civil War. His sympathies were with the North, perhaps in part because—as John Kirkpatrick surmises—he was conscious of his musical debt to the Negroes. In 1862 or 1863 he composed a piece called *The Union*, an allegory prophesying the rescue of the Union by the Northern armies.

From his sojourn in Cuba, Gottschalk drew material for a number of his most effective piano pieces. These include *Souvenir de la Havane* (Opus 39), *Souvenir de Cuba* (Mazurka), *Dí que sí* (*Réponds-moi!*), *Suis-moi!*, *Ojos Criollos*, and *La Gallina* ("The Hen"). John Kirkpatrick, the pianist who frequently features Gottschalk's pieces on his programs of American music, tells me that he thinks the piece titled *Suis-moi!* ("Follow Me!") shows the composer "at his very best." Kirkpatrick has made a two-piano arrangement of Gottschalk's symphony in two movements, *La Noche de los Trópicos* ("The Night of the Tropics"). Another large work inspired by tropical atmosphere is the *Escenas Campestres Cubanas* ("Cuban Country Scenes") for vocal soloists (soprano, tenor, baritone, and bass) and orchestra.

In all his travels Gottschalk never forgot that he was an American. Whenever the occasion arose, he was ready to talk on American subjects, and in his concerts he also recalled his native land. At a concert in Havana in 1854, he performed a fantasia for piano on "Old Folks at Home," which he titled *Recuerdos de mi Patria* ("Memories of my Homeland"). Wherever he went in Latin America, he was highly esteemed and honored, both as a person and as an artist.

It is ironic that American musicians had to wait until 1893 for Antonin Dvořák to tell them about the possibilities of utilizing American Negro music to achieve "local color," when Gottschalk began doing just that as early as 1845.

South American triumphs

In June, 1865, Gottschalk sailed for California, where he spent the summer concertizing. Then he embarked on a ship bound for Chile, beginning what was to be his life's last journey. In Peru, en route, he remained long enough to give about sixty concerts and to receive "a gold, diamond, and pearl decoration." Gottschalk was always ready to place his talent at the disposal of charity and other worthy causes. Hence it is not surprising that in Valparaiso, Chile, the board of public schools, the common council, the board of visitors of the hospitals, and the municipal government, each presented him with a gold medal. The government of Chile voted him a special grand gold medal. In Montevideo, Republic of Uruguay, Gottschalk gave a benefit concert for the "Society of the Friends of Education," which warmly thanked "this noble American citizen." In a letter to the society, Gottschalk expressed himself eloquently and with apparent conviction on the subject of democracy and education in the United States. He pointed out that "The popular system of education in the United States . . . which, of a child, makes successively a man, and later a citizen, has, for its principal object, to prepare him for the use of liberty. . . ." The United States has seldom if ever had a more effective cultural ambassador in South America than Louis Moreau Gottschalk.

In Buenos Aires he gave other charity concerts and in November, 1868, organized a great music festival at the Teatro Solis, with over three hundred participants (orchestra, chorus, and soloists). After compositions by Verdi, Meyerbeer, and Rossini, the concert ended with two works by Gottschalk: *Marche Solennelle* and *Montevideo*, the latter a descriptive symphony. In the spring of 1869, Gottschalk went to Rio de Janeiro, where his triumphs exceeded anything previously experienced. Brazil was then ruled by the Emperor Dom Pedro II, a benevolent and liberal monarch. Gottschalk's success in Brazil is best described in his own words, from a letter to a friend in Boston:

> My Dear Old Friend,–My concerts here are a perfect *furore*. All my houses are sold eight days in advance. . . . The emperor, imperial family, and court never missed yet one of my entertainments.
>
> His Majesty received me frequently at palace. . . . The *Grand Orient* of the masonry of Brazil gave me a solemn reception. . . .
>
> The enthusiasm with which I have been received here is indescribable. At the last concert, I was crowned on the stage by the artists of Rio. . . .
>
> The emperor is very fond of my compositions, especially "Printemps d'Amour" and "Ossian."
>
> My "Morte" (she is dead!) has had here, the same as in the Rio de la Plata, *un succès de larmes*, as several of my fair listeners wept at listening to that rather sad and disconsolate of my last effusions, which is my favorite now, and which I consider as being neither better nor worse than old "Last Hope."

My fantaisie on the national anthem of Brazil, of course, pleased the emperor, and tickled the national pride of my public. Every time I appear I must play it.

In great haste, yours as ever,
GOTTSCHALK

Of the compositions mentioned in this letter, *Ossian* was one of his earliest piano pieces, written for his mother's birthday when he was a young student in Paris (from the same period dates his *Danse Ossianique*, originally called *Danse des Ombres*). The piece titled *Morte* is mentioned again in a letter to the music publishers Hall & Son of New York, dated Rio, October 24, 1869:

Herewith I send you a new piece ("Morte,"–"She is Dead"),– a lamentation. I do not know whether it will be successful or not, but I believe it to be my best effort for years. Ever since I have played it, it has been encored; and a great many women have hysterics and weep over it–maybe owing to the romantic title. . . .

For once, Gottschalk appears to have been too modest. If anything could make women weep and swoon, it was his own playing and the romantic aura of his personality. And if *Morte* did not become as famous as his earlier sentimental effusions, *The Last Hope* and *The Dying Poet*, it was probably because Gottschalk did not live long enough to play it himself for the American public in his own inimitable manner.

On July 24, 1869, Gottschalk wrote to his Boston friend F. G. Hill, saying, among other things: "On the 30th, the emperor gives a grand fête at the palace, at which I am to play. I see his Majesty very often. He is a very kind and liberal-minded man. He is fond of inquiring about the States; and we have long talks together, alone in his private apartments." Soon after this, Gottschalk was stricken with yellow fever. On August 5 he was so low that the physicians gave him up. Yet by the latter part of September he had recovered sufficiently to resume his concerts. He was preparing "three grand festivals, with eight hundred performers, at which I will produce my symphonies, and the grand 'Marche Triomphale' I dedicated to the emperor. He is very anxious to have those festivals organized, and has offered me the means to muster in Rio all the musicians that can be had within the province." In another letter he exclaimed: "Just think of eight hundred performers and eighty drums to lead!" There speaks the disciple of Berlioz. Gottschalk burned up all his energy, expended the last ounce of his depleted strength, to organize and conduct this mammoth festival, which took place on November 26, 1869, at the Opera House of Rio de Janeiro.

The *Marche Triomphale*, which closed the first program, and into which the composer had woven the strains of the Brazilian national anthem, aroused tremendous enthusiasm, the excited audience rising to its feet and cheering. Gottschalk was called to the stage again and again to receive the ovations of the public. It was his last triumph. The next day he felt very weak, drove to the Opera House in his carriage, but was unable to conduct the orchestra in the second program of the festival. About two weeks later he was taken to the suburb of Tijuca, where, after much suffering, he died at four o'clock on the morning of December 18, 1869. The next day his embalmed body was exposed in state in the hall of the Philharmonic Society of Rio de Janeiro, and there the orchestra of the society played Gottschalk's *Morte* before the coffin was removed to the cemetery of St. John the Baptist, several miles outside the city. The newspapers of Brazil printed glowing eulogies of the dead musician. The following year Gottschalk's remains were taken to New York and placed in Greenwood Cemetery (October, 1870).

While admitting that he was no more than a *petit maître*, it seems to me that Gottschalk is a significant figure in America's music, not merely a historical effigy. Apart from the fact that his best music still has power to delight and charm the listener, his significance lies in his capacity for fully absorbing the atmosphere of the New World in some of its most characteristic aspects. As far as most American composers of the nineteenth century were concerned, Columbus might just as well have never discovered the New World. Our national folkloristic movement in music did not acquire definite momentum until the arrival of Dvořák, half a century after Gottschalk had composed his characteristic Creole pieces. Under more favorable circumstances, Gottschalk might have been the Glinka of America's music, the initiator of an impulse toward exploring and exploiting a new world of musical impressions. As it was, he remains an isolated, exotic figure, his music marked by a curious ambivalence. On the one hand he produced elegant *salon* pieces that stand as slightly tarnished gems of the genteel tradition. And on the other hand he ventured into exotic realms of personal and musical experience, projecting, however tentatively and incompletely, something of that untrammeled eclecticism, that reaching out for, and eager acceptance of, unprecedented sensations and impressions, that should characterize the artist who feels himself privileged to be born in a new world.

chapter sixteen

Europe versus America

Shun the lures of Europe.
TIMOTHY DWIGHT, GREENFIELD HILL (1794).

Americans of the eighteenth century were as confident of America's artistic glory as they were of her political, military, and material success. This confidence extended to all the arts, including music. Billings was hailed as a man of extraordinary genius, whom Nature had made "just such a musician, as she made Shakespeare a poet." Supply Belcher was called "the Handel of Maine." There was a general belief that the American, "the new man" saluted by Crèvecœur as one "who acts upon new principles," would manifest his freedom and his newness in powerful and individual works of the imagination, whether in literature, painting, or music. Yet, in 1838, Emerson had to admit: "This country has not fulfilled what seemed the reasonable expectation of mankind." In his address at Dartmouth, he went on to say:

> Men looked, when all feudal straps and bandages were snapped asunder, that nature, too long the mother of dwarfs, should reimburse itself by a brood of Titans, who should laugh and leap in the continent, and run up the mountains of the West with the errand of genius and of love. But the mark of American merit in painting, in sculpture, in poetry, in fiction, in eloquence, seems to be a certain grace without grandeur, and is itself not new, but derivative, a vase of fair outline, but empty. . . .[1]

Emerson might have included music in his catalogue, had he deigned to consider music seriously as an art. In any event, his remarks apply to American art music of the nineteenth century, and continued to

[1] "Literary Ethics, An Oration Delivered before the Literary Societies of Dartmouth College," July 24, 1838.

apply long after they ceased to be applicable to literature, since American music had to wait much longer for the equivalent of a Melville or a Walt Whitman.

The post-Revolutionary self-confidence was succeeded by an attitude of condescension toward American culture. In their obsession with good taste, with elegance, with gentility, cultivated Americans sought, like the colonial gentry, to imitate or import the products of European culture. While folk and popular music (also derived in the main from Europe) became gradually transformed by the American environment, fine art music, on the contrary, developed for several generations with scarcely any organic relationship to that environment.

It was inevitable that European musicians, both immigrants and those who came to America temporarily, should endeavor to exploit the American musical market. True, an American showman, P. T. Barnum, did the same thing, but he did it with European talent. And an American musician, Lowell Mason, made a fortune out of selling hymn books, but these, too, offered a thinly disguised European product. What actually happened was that European musical culture, with much of its apparatus and its standard repertoire, was transported to the United States and superimposed upon our social structure. In a sense, however, it is incorrect to say that European *culture* was brought to America, because culture, strictly speaking, is inseparable from its environment. It would be more accurate to say that the products, the techniques, and the carriers of European musical culture were transported to America.

And it was precisely because these products, these techniques, and these carriers had no organic—that is, no true cultural—relationship to the structure of American society, that they proved sterile, that they failed to provide the American composer with "a usable past," an operative tradition. Not until the end of the nineteenth century did a composer in the larger forms arise who carried within him the living tradition of "a usable past" in America's music. Most of the nineteenth century is merely an extended parenthesis in the history of American art music. Take it out and nothing vital is lost in the cultural continuity. (I am speaking, be it understood, of the cultivated fine-art tradition, not of our popular composers such as Emmett and Foster.) Nevertheless, in the discourse of history, we cannot ignore that long parenthesis, since history imposes itself upon us not only by its significance but also by its existence as preterit fact. We cannot change what has happened, however strongly we may be convinced that it should have happened differently.

A champion of American music

The musician who may be taken as the typical professional composer of art music in the United States during the nineteenth century was the son of an English organist—a circumstance that may not be pleasing to everyone. On the other hand, he was born in Brooklyn, which entitles him to some sort of consideration as a native son. George Frederick Bristow was born in Brooklyn, New York, on December 19, 1825. His life spanned nearly the whole of the remaining three-quarters of the century, for he died in 1898. If we view the American musical scene through his eyes, we will encounter most of the major developments in the panorama of musical art in the United States during the nineteenth century. He was the first American composer to handle successfully the traditional forms of European art music, including opera and symphony. Not that his treatment of these forms was in any way remarkable, but he did display sufficient competence and industry to establish his reputation as a professional composer and to get his works publicly performed during a period of some fifty years. He showed an interest in American subjects for his stage works, he endeavored to be inspired by the natural wonders of America (viz., in the symphony *Niagara*, his last work), and he showed himself to be properly patriotic in his symphonic ode, *The Great Republic*. Moreover, he championed the "cause" of the American composer.

Apparently there was no question about Bristow's taking up a musical career. He learned the violin and at the age of eleven played in the orchestra of the Olympic Theatre in New York. He studied theory and composition with Henry Christian Timm, a native of Hamburg, Germany, who had settled in New York in 1835, and who later was one of the founders of the New York Philharmonic Society and its president from 1847 to 1864. Bristow also had some lessons from the English composer G. A. MacFarren. When the New York Philharmonic was founded in 1842, Bristow joined the violin section of the orchestra, an activity which he continued for some forty years. One of his earliest compositions, a Concert Overture (Opus 3), was performed by the New York Philharmonic in November, 1847. Two years earlier Bristow had composed his First Symphony, in E flat. His cantata *Eleutheria* was written in 1849. In 1851 he became conductor of the Harmonic Society of New York, a choral association, holding this position until 1862.

In 1850, when P. T. Barnum brought Jenny Lind, "the Swedish Nightingale," to the United States for her first sensational concert tour —he offered her a guarantee of $150,000 plus expenses—Bristow was in the orchestra that played for her opening concert in New York's Castle Garden. Three years later Bristow was among the sixty American musicians engaged by the no less sensational French conductor Jullien to augment the band of forty players he had brought from Europe. Jullien was a Frenchman who specialized in giving popular concerts heralded by high-powered publicity and presented with elaborate showmanship. He boasted of having twelve hundred pieces in his repertoire, including an *American Quadrille* "which will contain all the NATIONAL AIRS and embrace no less than TWENTY SOLOS AND VARIATIONS." The New York *Courier and Enquirer* declared roundly that "Monsieur Jullien is a humbug," but admitted that "the discipline of his orchestra is marvellous" and concluded that both the humbug and the music were magnificent. Along with his quadrilles, polkas, schottisches, galops, and so forth, Jullien occasionally played some "classical" music—a movement from a symphony by Mozart, Beethoven, or Mendelssohn—and, what is more to the point, he included in his programs the music of American composers.

This matter of performing the works of native American composers was one upon which Bristow felt strongly. When the New York Philharmonic Society was founded, a clause in its constitution formulated the policy in regard to the performance of American works:

> If any grand orchestral compositions such as overtures, or symphonies, shall be presented to the society, they being composed in this country, the society shall perform one every season, provided a committee of five appointed by the government shall have approved and recommended the composition.

Actually, the phrase "composed in this country" left the door wide open for visiting musicians or recent immigrants, so that the native-born American composer was really given no special consideration at all. The attitude of the New York Philharmonic toward American music was made into a public issue in 1853 by a letter written by William Henry Fry and published in the *Musical World*, in which he declared that ". . . the Philharmonic Society of this city is an incubus on Art, never having asked for or performed a single American composition during the eleven years of its existence."

Henry C. Timm, president of the Philharmonic Society, published an answer to Fry's letter in which he said that the society had performed "several American compositions by either native or adopted citizens of this country." However, of the ten works mentioned, only three were by native Americans: a Duetto for two cornets by Dodworth, a Serenade by William Mason, and an Overture by George F. Bristow.

At this point Bristow himself jumped into the controversy. In a letter to the *Musical World* he wrote:

> As it is possible to miss a needle in a hay-stack, I am not surprised that Mr. Fry has missed the fact, that during the eleven years the Philharmonic Society has been in operation in this city, it played once, either by mistake or accident, one single American composition, an overture of mine. As one exception makes a rule stronger, so this single stray fact shows that the Philharmonic Society has been as anti-American as if it had been located in London during the Revolutionary War, and composed of native-born British tories. . . .
>
> It appears the society's eleven years of promoting American art have embraced one whole performance of one whole American overture, one whole rehearsal of one whole American symphony, and the performance of an overture by an Englishman stopping here. . . .[2]

The "American symphony" to which Bristow refers was his own First Symphony which, according to Timm, had been "performed twice at public rehearsal." Bristow evidently chose to overlook the two small pieces by Dodworth and Mason. Under the circumstances, it is not surprising that Bristow's resignation from the Philharmonic Society was announced two weeks later.

Yet the breach was not permanent. Bristow soon returned to his desk at the Philharmonic, and on March 1, 1856, the Society per-

[2] Quoted in Howard, *Our American Music*, p. 247.

formed his Second Symphony, in D minor. This was followed, on March 26, 1859, by a performance of his Third Symphony, in F sharp minor. Finally, to complete the tale, Bristow's Fourth (*Arcadian*) Symphony, in E minor, was played by the Philharmonic Society on February 14, 1874. Perhaps his letter had done some good, after all! The Overture to Bristow's unfinished opera, *Columbus*, was performed at the first concert given by the Philharmonic Society in Steinway Hall (then located at Fourteenth Street), November 17, 1866.

In March, 1861, the New York Harmonic Society, the choral group of which Bristow was director, performed his oratorio *Praise to God.* Another oratorio, *Daniel,* was performed by the Mendelssohn Union on December 30, 1867. As conductor of the Harmonic Society, Bristow made it a policy to perform the works of American composers—when he could find them.

"American" grand opera

"Sebastopol has fallen, and a new American opera has succeeded in New York!"—thus began an article by the critic Richard Storrs Willis published in the New York *Musical World* in the autumn of 1855. The opera was *Rip Van Winkle,* the composer was George F. Bristow, and the première took place at Niblo's Theatre on September 27, 1855. It ran for four weeks. The box-office receipts compared favorably with those of other New York attractions. They were better, for example, than those of the Italian opera at the Academy of Music.

Rip Van Winkle was the second grand opera composed by a native American (the first was Fry's *Leonora*). In adapting Washington Irving's tale for the operatic stage, Bristow's librettist introduced a love affair between Rip's daughter Alice and a British officer, which provided opportunity for the indispensable love duets.

Richard S. Willis found something to praise in Bristow's work, though not without reservations:

> The opera of Rip Van Winkle exhibits an easy flow of melody. This melody is free from effort and spontaneous—an important quality in a dramatic composer. But in none of the arias of Mr. Bristow do we meet with large conception or rich development of

ideas; none of them is shaped after a large pattern. The same remark will apply to the choruses. . . .

Willis criticized most severely the instrumentation of the opera: "The orchestra of Rip Van Winkle is in general inanimate and lifeless, and devoid of that brilliancy which we must meet with in modern opera."

In spite of these shortcomings, *Rip Van Winkle* showed some vitality, for in 1870 it was revived. Today it stands on the shelf of musical antiques as the first specimen of American grand opera dealing with a "native" subject, a subject taken from American legend and literature. Before taking leave of Bristow we should remark that from 1854 until the year of his death he was a supervisor of music in the public schools of New York. Thus, as composer, as executant, as conductor, as church organist, as educator, and as champion of American music, his career reflected virtually every phase of organized musical activity in the United States during the second half of the nineteenth century.

We mentioned William Henry Fry as the man who protested publicly about the New York Philharmonic Society's neglect of the American composer. Fry was born in Philadelphia in 1815, the son of a newspaper publisher, and received a good education, with the emphasis on literature rather than music. He learned to play the piano, composed an overture at the age of fourteen, and then studied theory and composition with Leopold Meignen, a graduate of the Paris Conservatory who had settled in Philadelphia. Fry turned out three more overtures before he was twenty, and one of them was locally performed. But it was not his intention to take up music as a profession. He embarked on a journalistic career by entering his father's office in 1839, became editor of the Philadelphia *Public Ledger* in 1844, and from 1846 to 1852 was in Europe as correspondent for this and other newspapers, including the New York *Tribune*, for which he served as music editor after returning to the United States. In 1861 he received a diplomatic appointment at Turin, but his health was poor, and in 1864 he died of tuberculosis at Santa Cruz, in the West Indies.

Like his Russian contemporary Glinka, Fry was an amateur, and like Glinka he tried his hand at opera. But unlike the Russian composer, Fry did not draw upon his country's folk music for his material, or upon its history and legend for his subject matter. The libretto of Fry's opera *Leonora* was adapted from Bulwer-Lytton's novel *The Lady of Lyons*. It was "grand opera" according to the most approved Italian recipe, complete with coloratura arias, recitatives, choruses, and ensemble numbers. The initial production, at the Chestnut Street Theatre in Philadelphia, on June 4, 1845, was given by the Seguin opera troupe, and paid for by the composer. The opera was sung in English and ran for twelve nights.

During his sojourn in Europe, Fry tried unsuccessfully to have *Leonora* produced in Paris, at his own expense. According to Fry's account, the director of the Paris Opera told him: "In Europe we look upon America as an industrial country—excellent for electric telegraphs, but not for art . . . they would think me crazy to produce an opera by an American."

After his return to America, Fry succeeded in having his opera performed by an Italian company at the Academy of Music in New York (1858), this time sung in Italian. The New York critics were not impressed by *Leonora*. The critic of the *Express* wrote:

> The opera seems to us a study in the school of Bellini. It is full of delicious, sweet music, but constantly recalls the Sonnambula and Norma. It is marked by skill in instrumentation. . . . It has many flowing melodies, many pretty effects, much that should encourage its author to renewed efforts. . . . The peculiarities which most strongly distinguish his production are sweetness of melody and lack of dramatic characterization.

The *Times* praised the fertility of melodic invention but pointed out that some of the melodies carried the memory "to past pleasures afforded by other composers." The *Musical Review and Gazette* was condemnatory: "Almost everything is poorly shaped and put together, and what is still worse, worked closely after the most common pattern."

In May, 1929, a concert of excerpts from *Leonora* was presented by the Pro Musica Society in New York, with the metropolitan music critics present. Oscar Thompson of the *Post* made a good point when he wrote: ". . . at least one tenor-soprano duet in mellifluous thirds would not have been laughed at, it is fair to assume, if it had been heard in a performance of Norma, Puritani or Sonnambula at the opera." If Fry, as Herbert Peyser said, "played the sedulous ape to Bellini, Donizetti, and Auber," he seems to have done it rather well.

However, one can scarcely blame the American public for preferring the genuine article, imported from Italy, to an American imitation made in Philadelphia. There is no suggestion that Fry *improved* on Rossini, Bellini, or Donizetti.

The ambitious Mr. Fry also tried his hand at writing symphonies. He composed four, each with an appropriate title indicating the programmatic content: *Childe Harold*, *A Day in the Country*, *The Breaking Heart*, and *Santa Claus*. These concoctions were actually performed, thanks to the enterprising Monsieur Jullien, who thought they would be effective "novelties" on his American programs. Willis, writing in the *Musical World*, refused to take the *Santa Claus Symphony* seriously as a work of art. He called it "a kind of extravaganza which moves the audience to laughter, entertaining them seasonably with imitated snow-storms, trotting horses, sleighbells, cracking whips, etc." This made Fry furious. He dashed off a spirited reply to Willis, saying among other things: "I think that the American who writes for the mere dignity of musical art, as I understand it, without recompense, deserves better treatment at the hands of his countrymen at least." It was in this letter that Fry made his attack on the New York Philharmonic Society, previously quoted.

One of Fry's most ambitious undertakings was a series of lectures on the forms and history of musical art, illustrated with selections performed by a chorus and orchestra of eighty players. The series started on November 30, 1852, in the Metropolitan Hall, New York. We are told that the second part of the first lecture opened with some specimens of Chinese music. "This was followed by the overture to *Der Freyschutz* [*sic*] which marked all the advance of Christian upon Pagan civilization.

In the last lecture of his series, Fry voiced his opinions on musical art in the United States. He called for a Declaration of Independence in Art on the part of American composers. Let them cease to bow down to a Handel, a Mozart, or a Beethoven. Let them strike out into untrodden realms, guided only by nature and their own inspirations. Let them discard their European liveries and found an American school of composition. Only then shall we cease to be provincial in Art. Brave words, yet strange from the lips of one who "played the sedulous ape" to Bellini and Donizetti, who cultivated the form of "grand opera" which lies entirely outside the tradition of American culture. It is not the last time that we shall encounter this strange dichotomy in American music: the case of the composer who pleads for artistic independence while (perhaps unconsciously?) imitating European models in his own work.

The true worshipers

Fry's plea for nonworship of European composers did not meet with much response. In the same year that he gave his New York lectures, an item in Dwight's *Journal of Music*, sent in by a correspondent from Newport, Rhode Island, expressed the prevailing atmosphere of musical incense burning:

> The lover of music has great privileges here. . . . In Mr. Scharfenberg's little cozy parlor, Beethoven, Chopin and Mendelssohn, Spohr, and other worthy associates, are daily worshipped by a few of the true worshippers. . . .

In this atmosphere, most American musicians found it advisable to become "true worshippers" themselves, in the hope that at least a little of the incense might eventually be wafted in their direction.

Take, for example, the case of William Mason (1829–1908), son of the eminent Doctor Lowell Mason of Boston. After preliminary study with Henry Schmidt in Boston, young Mason sailed for Europe in 1849. There he studied with Moscheles and Hauptmann in Leipzig, with Dreyschock in Prague, and with Liszt in Weimar. To Liszt, Mason dedicated one of his first piano pieces, elegantly titled *Les Perles de Rosée*. After five years of soaking up this superrefined musical atmosphere, Mason returned to America to spread the gospel of good music. On one occasion, when giving a piano recital on tour, he was asked by a member of the audience to improvise by playing "Old Hundred" with one hand and "Yankee Doodle" with the other. By offering to improvise on any themes that might be suggested, he had placed himself in the position of a showman bound to please the public. Later Mason became more austere. He formed a string quartet with which he appeared as pianist in concerts of chamber music, not precisely a popular form of entertainment. Much of Mason's time was devoted to teaching the piano, a field in which he was extremely successful and influential.

We mention William Mason chiefly because he and his family are so typical of the prevailing trend in American musical life. His great-grandfather, Barachias Mason, conducted singing schools in his spare time. His grandfather, Johnson Mason, found time, among more important civic duties, to play the cello and sing in the parish choir. His father, Lowell Mason, as we know, passed from the banking business to a full-time, lucrative career in music. But Lowell Mason was still partly bound by the tradition of hymnody and the singing-school movement. He did not fully penetrate the inner circle of those who worshiped at the shrine of Liszt, Mendelssohn, and Brahms. To his son William was vouchsafed the privilege of entering this arcanum: the culmination of four generations of progressive improvement. The fruits: some piano pieces, such as *Les Perles de Rosée* and *Amitié pour Amitié*. The latter, we are told, was a favorite with Liszt. *Summum bonum!*

We turn now to two American musicians who were born in the same year, 1839, and whose life span extended into the first decade of the twentieth century. Each was highly successful and widely honored in his lifetime. (We must go far to find that mythical creature, the "neglected American composer.") Their names were Dudley Buck and John Knowles Paine, and both were New Englanders. Dudley Buck's background is interesting as showing the transition from mercantile to artistic interests in an American family of the upper middle class. His father was a shipping merchant of Hartford, Connecticut, and the son was intended for a commercial career. Not until he was sixteen did he begin to receive music lessons. His progress was then so impressive that Buck senior gave his consent to a musical career and decided that the youngster should have the best musical education that money could buy. This meant, of course, packing him off to Germany. In Leipzig, Buck became a pupil of Hauptmann, Moscheles, Plaidy, and Richter. He studied the organ in Dresden and then spent a year in Paris before returning to the United States in 1862. He had been abroad four years.

After holding positions as church organist in Hartford, Chicago, and Boston, Buck in 1875 settled in New York in a similar capacity. As a composer he devoted himself chiefly to choral works, including a series of short cantatas for church use. Among his more ambitious works are the *Centennial Meditation of Columbus* (1876, with words by Sidney Lanier), *Scenes from the Golden Legend* (1880, after Longfellow), *King Olaf's Christmas* (1881, also after Longfellow), *The*

Light of Asia (dramatic cantata), and *The Voyage of Columbus* (another dramatic cantata, adapted from Irving's *Life of Columbus*).

Some remarks on *The Golden Legend* will serve to illustrate Buck's style. The legend tells of Prince Henry of Hoheneck, who is afflicted with an incurable malady that can be cured only by the blood of a maiden who will freely consent to die for his sake. He finds such a maiden, but refuses to let her make the supreme sacrifice. Instead, the prince is miraculously healed and marries the willing maiden. The music employs the Wagnerian device of the leitmotiv—melodic themes to identify characters, emotions, and the forces of Nature. Here, for example, is one of the storm motives:

There is a suitably sentimental solo for "Elsie's Prayer," a Pilgrims' Chorus, a Bacchanalian Monks' Song, a scene of Revel, a Drinking Song, an orchestral Barcarolle, a Chorus of Sailors, a solemn Cathedral motive (with Gregorian reminiscences), and a grand finale with a Hymn of Praise by full chorus and orchestra. In short, there is all the conventional paraphernalia of pseudo-Wagnerian claptrap, chords of the diminished seventh included.

Buck enjoyed some reputation abroad. His cantatas were performed in England and Germany. At home he wrote for the taste of the day and for a ready market. He supplied the demand for church music that was mellifluous and not difficult to perform. He died in 1909.

The composer as professor

John Knowles Paine was born in Portland, Maine, on January 9, 1839. His family was musical. His grandfather had built the first organ in Maine. In Portland young Paine studied with a local musician, Hermann Kotzschmer, and in 1857 went to Germany, becoming a pupil of Haupt in Berlin. He concentrated on the organ and gave numerous recitals in Germany before returning to America in 1861. The following year he was appointed director of music at Harvard College, where he remained until a year before his death. Beginning as an instructor, he attained full professorship in 1875, not without opposition from those who felt that music was not a subject to be taken seriously in the college curriculum. It seems that Francis Parkman, the historian, was one of the most stubborn opponents of music at Harvard. As a member of the Corporation, he is said to have ended every meeting of that body with the words "musica delenda est."[3] Whenever the question of raising funds came up, Parkman was ready with a motion to abolish the music department in the interests of economy.

In 1867 Paine revisited Germany, where his Mass was performed under his direction at the Berlin Singakademie. At home he lacked neither recognition nor public performance. In 1873 he conducted the first performance of his oratorio *St. Peter* in his native city, Portland. In 1876 Theodore Thomas conducted the première of Paine's First Symphony in Boston. In the same year Paine set to music Whittier's "Hymn" for the Centennial Exposition at Philadelphia. The first performance of his Second Symphony, a programmatic work titled *Im Frühling* ("In the Spring"), given at Boston in 1880, was received with unprecedented enthusiasm. According to contemporary accounts, ladies waved handkerchiefs, men shouted their approval, and the dignified John S. Dwight, arbiter of musical taste in Boston, "stood in his seat, frantically opening and shutting his umbrella as an expression of uncontrollable enthusiasm."[4] This was the same man who dismissed Stephen Foster's songs as cheap trash.

As we look at Paine's *Spring Symphony*, we may well wonder what all the shouting was about. The first movement portrays the departure of winter and the awakening of Nature. Here is the winter theme, given out by the cellos:

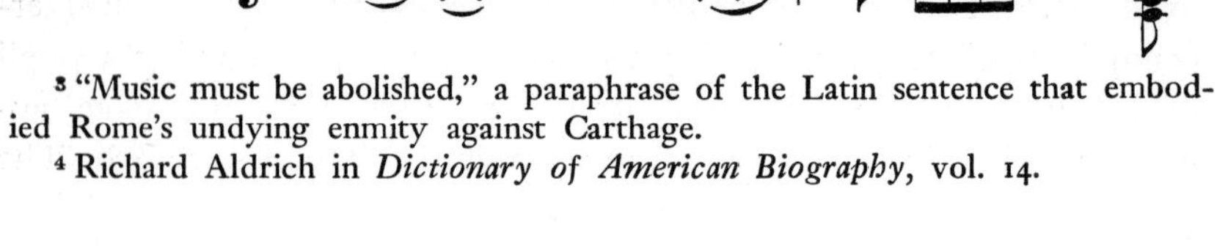

[3] "Music must be abolished," a paraphrase of the Latin sentence that embodied Rome's undying enmity against Carthage.

[4] Richard Aldrich in *Dictionary of American Biography*, vol. 14.

The second movement, "May-night Fantasy," is a scherzo. Then comes the slow movement, "A Romance of Springtime" (Adagio), which is in the form of a rondo. The final movement, Allegro giocoso, depicts "The Glory of Nature" and is in sonata form. The musical idiom is that of academic postromanticism, stemming from the school of Raff. It is a coincidence that Raff composed a *Spring Symphony* in 1878, the year before Paine's symphony was completed. The plan of both symphonies is remarkably similar. No doubt it was mere coincidence, but a coincidence that serves to emphasize to what an extent American composers were simply echoing the current clichés of German postromanticism.

Paine wrote what is probably his best and most enduring music for a performance of Sophocles' *Oedipus Tyrannus* given at Cambridge, Massachusetts, in 1881. The music consists of a Prelude, six Choruses, and a Postlude. This is one of the few examples of Paine's music with which the listener of today may become acquainted, for the Prelude has been recorded under the direction of Howard Hanson in the album "American Music for Orchestra." A comment made by Rupert Hughes on the opening chorus is worth noting. After remarking that the second strophe has a few good moments, he adds "but soon [it] falls back into what is impudent enough to be actually catchy!" Fortunately for his reputation as our leading academic composer, Paine seldom succumbed to the temptation of writing catchy tunes.

Among other compositions of Paine are the *Columbus March and Hymn* for the Chicago World's Fair, *Hymn to the West* for the St. Louis World's Fair, several symphonic poems (*The Tempest*, *Poseidon and Aphrodite*, *Island Fantasy*), and an opera, *Azara*, based on the medieval story of Aucassin and Nicolette, for which Paine himself wrote the libretto and which never had a stage performance (it was performed twice in concert form, in 1903 and 1907). From this score he extracted three *Moorish Dances* and some ballet music, which were frequently performed—as was, indeed, nearly all of Paine's music during his lifetime.

Paine's music has some qualities of workmanship and invention that raise it above work previously attempted by American composers in the symphonic field. Nevertheless, it remains primarily of historical interest. Paine has a place as our first notable academic composer in the larger forms, and as the teacher of others who were to carry on the academic tradition with some distinction. Among his pupils were

Arthur Foote, Frederick S. Converse, Daniel Gregory Mason, and John Alden Carpenter.

Gilchrist and Gleason

Two composers born in the 1840s may be mentioned as having attained a considerable reputation in their time. They were William Wallace Gilchrist (1846–1916) and Frederick Grant Gleason (1848–1903). The latter was born in Middletown, Connecticut, where his father was a banker. Like many another well-to-do gentleman, Gleason senior was an amateur flutist. He considered music a pleasant pastime but not a serious occupation. He wanted his son to enter the ministry—a good old New England tradition. But the son insisted on becoming a composer, and the father yielded. Young Gleason studied with another Connecticut Yankee who had gone musical: Dudley Buck. He then made the inevitable pilgrimage to Europe, studying with a long list of musicians in Germany. After six years in Europe he returned to America, and in 1877 went to Chicago, where he was active as a teacher and music critic. In 1897 he became president of an organization titled the "American Patriotic Musical League" (!).

Gleason's compositions include a *Processional of the Holy Grail* written for the Chicago World's Fair; a symphonic poem, *Edris,* based on a novel by Marie Corelli; the tone poem *Song of Life;* a Piano Concerto; a cantata with orchestra, *The Culprit Fay;* and two operas: *Otho Visconti* and *Montezuma.* The former was produced at Chicago in 1907. He left other scores in manuscript, with instructions that they were not to be publicly performed until fifty years after his death. W. S. B. Mathews describes Gleason's operatic style as an attempt "to combine the melodic element of Italian opera with the richness of harmonization characteristic of the modern German school and the leit-motif idea of Richard Wagner." [5] At least, in fifty years American grand opera had "progressed" from Bellini to Wagner.

Gleason applied the leitmotiv principle to his setting for solos, chorus, and orchestra of Joseph Rodman Drake's poem *The Culprit Fay*, described as "A Fairy Cantata." The poem is a coyly romantic concoction that tells about a "fay" (a river sprite) who "has loved an earthly maid" and who in punishment therefor is assigned the accom-

[5] Mathews, *The Great in Music* (1900), p. 188.

plishment of two difficult tasks, one of which is to catch a drop of brine from the brow of a leaping sturgeon on the shore of elfin land, the other to follow a shooting star and light the elfin lamp from a spark of its burning train. Gleason's music is developed from the following themes: summer-night motive, mystery motive, gathering of the fays, fairy life, the fay's love, penalty motive, night on the Hudson, water sprites' motive, task motive, and sylphid queen's love motive. A quotation of the motive of the fay's love will serve to illustrate Gleason's style. The theme is begun by the clarinets, taken up by the oboes, and continued by the flutes.

Gleason's contemporary William Wallace Gilchrist was born in Jersey City in 1846 and at the age of eleven moved with his family to Philadelphia, where he studied music with H. A. Clarke. His father's business having been ruined during the Civil War, young Gilchrist turned to the law and to business for his own living, but finally decided to take up music as a career. With the exception of a short period in Cincinnati (1871–1872), he lived in Philadelphia, where he was active as church organist, teacher, and leader of musical clubs. He founded the Mendelssohn Club of Philadelphia.

In 1882 Gilchrist won the Cincinnati Festival Prize for his setting of the 46th Psalm, for soprano solo, chorus, and orchestra. Among his other choral works are *Ode to the Sun*, *Journey of Life*, *The Uplifted Gates,* and *Legend of the Bended Bow*. He composed two nonprogrammatic symphonies, and some chamber music, including a nonet for piano, strings, flute, clarinet, and horn.

Although Gilchrist was one of the very few American composers of this period who did not study in Europe, his style is no less imitative and conventional than that of his Europeanized colleagues.

The self-made man in music

No account of American music in the nineteenth century would be complete without an example of that typically American product, the self-made man. A perfect specimen of the type is to be found in the person of Silas Gamaliel Pratt (1846–1916), a native of Vermont whose family moved to Illinois while he was still a boy. His father's business failed and he was obliged to start working at the age of twelve. His liking for music induced him to get employment as clerk in several Chicago music stores. Determined to take up a musical career, he saved enough money to go to Europe (i.e., Germany) in 1868, remaining there three years while studying piano and composition. An injury to his wrist from overstrenuous practice prevented him from becoming a concert pianist. Returning to Chicago in 1871, he had his First Symphony performed there. But he felt the need for another touch of Germany, whither he returned in 1875 for further study with Liszt and Heinrich Dorn. It was in Germany that he composed his *Centennial Overture*, performed in Berlin on July 4, 1876, and later played in the Crystal Palace, London, in the presence of General Grant, to whom the piece was dedicated. In 1885, Pratt visited London again for a performance of his Second Symphony (*The Prodigal Son*) at the Crystal Palace. Meanwhile his opera *Zenobia* had been produced in Chicago and New York (1883). Another opera, *Lucille* (originally called *Antonio*), was performed in Chicago in 1887. From 1888 to 1902 Pratt taught at the Metropolitan School of Music in New York, and in 1906 he founded the Pratt Institute of Music and Art in Pittsburgh.

Pratt aspired to be the great national composer of the United States, a sort of grand exalted tonal commentator on national events, past and present. His dramatic cantata, *The Triumph of Columbus* (1892), celebrated the discovery of America. The list of his symphonic works includes *Paul Revere's Ride*, a *Fantasy* depicting the struggle between the North and the South, a *Lincoln* Symphony, *The Battle of Manila*, and *A Tragedy of the Deep* (on the sinking of the *Titanic*).

The remarks on Pratt's career made by F. L. Gwinner Cole in the *Dictionary of American Biography* deserve to be quoted not only as a comment on this composer's life but also as a priceless recipe for success from which all aspiring composers may profit:

Throughout his life he had been industrious and persevering and had succeeded in bringing his name before the public as a composer of rank. In this he was greatly aided by his exaggerated opinion of the worth of his own compositions.

In contrast to these practical men who succeeded in becoming known as composers by dint of application and imitation, the man to whom we shall now dedicate a page or two was a stifled genius, perhaps the most magnificent and tragic failure in the annals of American music. He was born in 1842 and died in 1881. His name was Sidney Lanier.

Poet-Musician of the South

One of Lanier's best biographers, Edwin Mims, remarked: "It is unfortunate that he left no compositions to indicate a musical power sufficient to give him a place in the history of American music." True, Sidney Lanier, dying of tuberculosis at the age of thirty-nine, did not live to complete the larger musical compositions that he was planning: a *Choral Symphony* for chorus and orchestra (being a setting of his "Psalm of the West"), and a *Symphony of the Plantation* ("being the old and the new life of the negro, in music"). It may be doubted whether, if he had lived to finish these works, he could have risen above the limitations of his training and his background. The tragedy of Sidney Lanier as a creative musician depends not so much on his premature death as on his premature existence. He was born too soon, too early in America's cultural development.

Sidney Lanier's father was a lawyer in Macon, Georgia, his mother the daughter of a Virginia planter. From early childhood the boy could play any musical instrument on which he happened to lay hands; his favorites were the violin and the flute. Music as recreation was a good old Southern tradition, but music as a profession was not to be considered by a gentleman or the son of a gentleman. Yet Lanier was fully conscious of his musical capacities and inclinations. In a notebook written while he was at college, probably before the age of eighteen, he inquired earnestly of himself regarding "God's will" for his future life:

I am more than all perplexed by this fact, that the prime inclination, that is, natural bent (which I have checked, though) of my nature is to music; and for that I have the greatest talent; indeed, not boasting, for God gave it me, I have an extraordinary musical talent, and feel it within me plainly that I could rise as high as any composer. But I cannot bring myself to believe that I was intended for a musician, because it seems so small a business in comparison with other things which, it seems to me, I might do. Question here, What is the province of music in the economy of the world? [6]

In later years Lanier was to answer that last question to his own satisfaction and on a lofty mystical plane: "Music is Love in search of a word." Whether he could have persuaded his father to let him study composition professionally is a moot question. Well-to-do New England parents encouraged their sons to enter the ministry or take up business; but if the sons insisted on music the fathers usually yielded and sent the sons to Boston or to Europe for musical training. In New England there was a practical (economic) rather than a social (aristocratic) prejudice against music as a profession. Young Lanier probably shared his father's conviction that music was not a fit profession for a gentleman. We know, at any rate, that he felt himself to be endowed with remarkable musical powers, sufficient to carry him to the pinnacle of creative music. Yet he was reluctant to take the plunge, to commit himself fully to the hazard of art.

Whatever his plans at the moment may have been, they were interrupted by the outbreak of the Civil War, into which Lanier threw himself with high spirit and confidence. He believed that "the new Confederacy was to enter upon an era of prosperity such as no other nation, ancient or modern, had ever enjoyed," and that "the city of Macon, his birthplace and home, was to become a great art-centre." And perhaps he dreamed that in this great art center he, Sidney Lanier, might become the great composer of a new nation. The impact of reality was harsh and bitter. After serving in the Confederate Army for four years he was captured and imprisoned at Point Lookout, Maryland. Released at the end of the war, he made his way painfully on foot to his home city and fell dangerously ill for two months. Thereafter it was a struggle for existence, for mere survival. He clerked in a hotel, he worked in his father's law office, he did some teaching. In 1867 he married and soon there was the burden of a family to support. During these years poetry as well as music had attracted his

[6] Quoted in Mims, *Sidney Lanier.*

latent creative talents. His father wanted him to settle in Macon and share his law practice, with a comfortable assured income. But Lanier was now ready to commit himself to art, to his twin stars of music and poetry. From Baltimore, where he had moved with his family, he wrote to his father, in 1873, a letter from which I quote the following passages:

> Then, as to business, why should I, nay, how *can* I, settle myself down to be a third-rate struggling lawyer for the balance of my life, as long as there is a certainty almost absolute that I can do some other things so much better? . . . My dear father, think how, for twenty years, through poverty, through pain, through weariness, through sickness, through the uncongenial atmosphere of a farcical college and of a bare army and then of an exacting business life . . . I say, think how, in spite of all these depressing circumstances, and of a thousand more which I could enumerate, these two figures of music and of poetry have steadily kept in my heart so that I could not banish them. Does it not seem to you as to me, that I begin to have the right to enroll myself among the devotees of these two sublime arts, after having followed them so long and so humbly, and through so much bitterness?

The father was won over by this plea, and thenceforth did what he could to help his son. But Lanier's great enemy now was tuberculosis. He went to San Antonio, Texas, for his health, and while there composed a piece for flute, *Field-larks and Blackbirds*. It was about this time that he wrote in a letter, "I am now pumping myself full of music and poetry, with which I propose to water the dry world. . . . God has cut me off inexorably from any other life than this. . . . So St. Cecilia to the rescue! and I hope *God* will like my music."

Mere mortals, in any case, liked Lanier's music, and praised it enthusiastically. In Baltimore he played his *Field-larks and Blackbirds* for the conductor Asger Hamerik, who was in the process of organizing the Peabody Symphony Orchestra. Hamerik "declared the composition to be that of an artist, and the playing to be almost perfect." Lanier was engaged as first flutist of the Peabody Symphony: he was now a professional musician. He kept on studying and practicing, striving always to perfect himself in his art. His playing had an extraordinary effect on those who heard him. The opinion of Hamerik, a highly competent professional musician, is worth quoting:

> In his hands the flute no longer remained a mere material instrument, but was transformed into a voice that set heavenly harmonies into vibration. Its tones developed colors, warmth, and a low sweetness of unspeakable poetry. . . . His playing appealed alike to the musically learned and to the unlearned—for he would magnetize the listener: but the artist felt in his performance the superiority of the momentary living inspiration to all the rules and shifts of mere technical scholarship. His art was not only the art of art, but an art above art.

Miss Alice Fletcher indulged in feminine hyperbole when she declared that Lanier "was not only the founder of a school of music, but the founder of American music." [7] What I would venture to say is that Sidney Lanier was the truest artist among American musicians of the nineteenth century, the only one to whom the term "genius" might be applied.

Lanier's known compositions are the following: *Sacred Melodies* for flute solo (performed in Macon, July, 1868); *Field-larks and Blackbirds,* for flute solo (composed in 1873); *Swamp Robin,* flute solo (same year); *Danse des Moucherons,* for flute and piano (probably composed in December, 1873; three manuscripts are at The Johns Hopkins University); *Longing,* flute solo (composed early in 1874); *Wind-song,* flute solo (1874); songs for voice with piano: *The Song of Love and Death* (Tennyson, "Lancelot and Elaine"), *Love That Hath Us in the Net* (Tennyson, "The Miller's Daughter"), *Little Ella* ("A Beautiful Ballad"; words and music by Sidney Lanier; composed in 1866; published in 1888), and *My Life Is Like a Summer Rose* (poem by Richard Henry Wilde). He left unfinished a Choral Symphony, Symphony of Life, and Symphony of the Plantation.

This is, of course, a pitifully slight output with which to impress posterity, and it is overbalanced by the weight of Lanier's literary reputation and his poetic production. Nevertheless, the music he left is the work of a gifted musician and a true artist. It has been my privilege to hear Lanier's *Wind-song* admirably played by that modern "gentleman amateur" of American musicians, Carleton Sprague Smith, and the piece is certainly worthy of being included in the permanent repertoire of American music for flute. Perhaps Sidney Lanier was right when he felt in his soul that he could become a great com-

[7] Quoted by Starke, *Musical Quarterly,* XX, 4 (1934), p. 389.

poser. The fact that circumstances did not permit him to develop his creative genius to the full is one of the major tragedies of America's music.

Lanier's ideas on music, his system of prosody based on the identity of music and poetry, his remarkable poem titled "The Symphony"—these and other aspects of his work and thought might well claim our attention, did space permit. Here we must content ourselves with giving to Sidney Lanier, the musician, the place that he deserves as a precursor in the long struggle for the recognition and encouragement of native musical talent in the United States. The light of his tragic glory illumines the fulfillment of America's music that he did not live to see.

Very different was the fate of the American composer whose life and work will be discussed in the next chapter. Though Edward MacDowell was struck down by illness at the height of his powers, his musical talents were carefully nurtured from an early age, and he had full opportunity to develop his natural talents and to receive the proud acclaim of his country during his lifetime.

chapter seventeen

A romantic bard

Music . . . is a language, but a language of the intangible, a kind of soul-language.
EDWARD MACDOWELL, CRITICAL AND HISTORICAL ESSAYS.

In a book published in 1900,[1] Rupert Hughes wrote of Edward MacDowell that "an almost unanimous vote would grant him the rank of the greatest of American composers." One is mildly surprised at the intrusion of the qualifying adverb "almost." Who was there to cast a dissenting vote? Perhaps some admirer of John Knowles Paine or of Ethelbert Nevin. The opposition, indeed, was not strong. Now, half a century later, if such a hypothetical plebiscite were held among American music lovers, it would be rash to predict that MacDowell would be kept in top place by an electoral landslide. To the present generation his name is more familiar than his music. We have more or less agreed to let the handsome effigy of Edward MacDowell stand on the pedestal where our admiring parents placed him, to gaze respectfully on the statue labeled "America's greatest composer," and to write *tacet* over most of his musical scores. Amateur pianists doubtless continue to delight in the smaller piano pieces, but the larger works —the sonatas, the concertos, the orchestral suites—are heard infrequently in our concert halls.

No such neglect afflicted the composer during his lifetime. MacDowell was fully, even fulsomely, appreciated by his contemporaries; his music was played, published, applauded, and praised without stint. Americans of the *fin de siècle* were so pleased at finding an authentic composer in their midst that they heaped superlatives upon him. When MacDowell was offered the professorship of music at Columbia Uni-

[1] Hughes, *American Composers.*

versity, the nominating committee cited him as "the greatest musical genius America has produced." For Rupert Hughes, the piano sonatas of MacDowell were "far the best since Beethoven."

MacDowell found his most eloquent panegyrist in the person of the critic Lawrence Gilman, who, in 1905, three years before the composer's death, contributed an enthusiastically appreciative volume to the "Living Masters of Music" series; a volume which he later brought out, revised and enlarged, as *Edward MacDowell: A Study* (1908). Gilman, who became music critic of the New York *Herald Tribune*, and the author of many other books, may have lived to regret some of his more unabashed outbursts, such as the statement that MacDowell's name "is the one name in our music which . . . one would venture to pair with that of Whitman in poetry." This is Gilman's summing up of the American composer's art:

> He was one of the most individual writers who ever made music—as individual as Chopin, or Debussy, or Brahms, or Grieg. His manner of speech was utterly untrammelled, and wholly his own. Vitality—an abounding freshness, a perpetual youthfulness—was one of his prime traits; nobility—nobility of style and impulse—was another. The morning freshness, the welling spontaneity of his music, even in moments of exalted or passionate utterance, was continually surprising: it was music not unworthy of the golden ages of the world.

Twenty years later, Paul Rosenfeld, adventurous "voyager among the arts," impressionistic critic of music, art, and literature, wrote in *An Hour With American Music* (1929):

> The music of Edward MacDowell . . . amounts more to an assimilation of European motives, figures and ideas than to an original expression. In any case, the original elements are small and of minor importance. . . . The ideas of the main romantic composers, particularly Wagner, continued to haunt MacDowell even in his later, more personal phase. . . . He was badly equipped in polyphonic technique; and where . . . he attempted canonic imitation, we find him essaying it clumsily, and with all the obsessive rapture of a child in possession of a new and dazzling toy. . . . Even where he is most individual, even in the personal, characteristically dainty and tender little piano pieces, he frequently appears fixed and rigid in invention.

It might be wise to steer a middle course between these poles of affirmation and negation; to put aside the issue of MacDowell's greatness, to avoid adulation and deprecation, and to regard him, sympathetically but objectively, in his historical role as one of the first Americans to acquire fame as a composer of "serious" music.

The lure of Europe

Edward Alexander MacDowell (he dropped the middle name in later life) was born in New York City on December 18, 1861, of Irish-Scotch descent. His father was a prosperous businessman with artistic inclinations which had been thwarted by Quaker parents. There is no mention of a musical heritage in the family, but Edward early manifested musical aptitude and around the age of eight began to receive piano lessons from a family friend, a Colombian by the name of Juan Buitrago. His next piano teacher was a professional musician, Paul Desvernine, with whom he studied until the age of fifteen. It was then decided that Edward should go abroad for further study. Accompanied by his mother, he sailed for Europe in April, 1867, and in the following autumn was admitted to the Paris Conservatory as a pupil of Marmontel (piano) and of Savard (theory).

The methods and atmosphere of the Conservatory appear to have been uncongenial for the young American student. After hearing Nicholas Rubinstein play in the summer of 1878—the year of the Paris Exposition—Edward exclaimed to his mother, "I can never learn to play like that if I stay here." His ambition then was to become a pianist rather than a composer. Leaving Paris, mother and son went first to Stuttgart, which proved to be even more unsatisfactory, and then to Wiesbaden, where Edward took some lessons in theory and composition from Louis Ehlert, whose informal approach "rather staggered" the American because, as he said later, his idea in leaving Paris "was to get a severe and regenerating overhauling." Edward worked hard all winter and heard lots of new music, which, he tells us, "was like manna in the desert after my long French famine." This is an early example of MacDowell's persistent Francophobia. The primary purpose in coming to Wiesbaden was to meet the pianist Karl Heyman, who was visiting there at the time. Heyman taught at the Frankfort Conservatory, and it was there that MacDowell decided to go in the autumn of 1879, his mother having meanwhile returned to America.

The director of the Frankfort Conservatory was Joachim Raff (1822–1882), whom Alfred Einstein characterizes as a composer of "mostly Romantic routine works, none of which have shown lasting vitality," and whose music Adolfo Salazar describes as being "of a Mendelssohnian and picturesque Romanticism and of weak pulsation." When Raff was told that MacDowell had studied for several years the "French school" of composition, he flared up and declared that there was no such thing nowadays as "schools"—that if some French writers wrote flimsy music it arose simply from flimsy attainments, and such stuff could never form a "school." [2] This was the man with whom MacDowell studied composition, and in whom, according to Gilman, he encountered "an influence at once potent and engrossing—a force which was to direct the currents of his own temperament into definite artistic channels."

MacDowell felt thoroughly at home in Germany. "His keen and very blue eyes, his pink and white skin, reddish mustache and imperial and jet black hair, brushed straight up in the prevalent German fashion, caused him to be known as 'the handsome American.' " MacDowell had now been five years in Europe, but apparently he had no intention of returning to his native land. His studies were finished and he had embarked on his professional career as pianist, teacher, and composer. In 1881 he applied for, and obtained, the position of head piano teacher at the nearby Darmstadt Conservatory. He commuted between Frankfort and Darmstadt, composing on the train. He also read a great deal, especially Goethe, Heine, Byron, Shelley, and—his favorite—Tennyson.

After a year the Darmstadt duties proved burdensome, and MacDowell resigned. In the spring of 1882 he went to visit Liszt at Weimar, taking with him the score of his First Piano Concerto, which Liszt heard and praised. It was upon Liszt's recommendation that MacDowell's Second Modern Suite, Opus 14, was published at Leipzig by Breitkopf & Härtel. Meanwhile, in the summer of 1882, Joachim Raff died. His death was felt as a deep personal loss by MacDowell.

It was Raff who had persuaded MacDowell that his real path lay in composition, and during the next two years he gave an increasing amount of time to composing. In June, 1884, MacDowell returned to America to marry his former pupil, Marian Nevins. A few days after

[2] Cited by Gilman, *Edward MacDowell: A Study*, p. 9.

the wedding the couple sailed for Europe, going first to England and then to Frankfort, which by this time must have seemed like home to MacDowell. He applied, unsuccessfully, for a position at the Würzburg Conservatory (as he had done previously at the Frankfort Conservatory). During this period he wrote the two-part symphonic poem, *Hamlet and Ophelia.* In 1885 he applied, again unsuccessfully, for the position of examiner at the Royal Academy of Music in Edinburgh. The following winter was spent in Wiesbaden, and in the summer of 1886 the MacDowells visited London again. Returning to Wiesbaden, they made their home in a small cottage in the woods, where MacDowell worked at his composition. But, according to Gilman, "Musicians from America began coming to the little Wiesbaden retreat to visit the composer and his wife, and he was repeatedly urged to return to America and assume his share in the development of the musical art of his country."

The Boston years

In September, 1888, MacDowell and his wife sailed for the United States. It would be incorrect to say that he left Germany behind, because actually he brought it along with him. Furthermore, Boston, where the MacDowells settled, was musically a sort of German province. With the exception of the brief trip in 1884, MacDowell had lived in Europe from his fifteenth to his twenty-seventh year. Most of these twelve years were spent in Germany, warming his hands in the embers of a dying Romanticism.

In Boston, before his arrival, MacDowell was already known as a successful composer—that is, one who had received the accolade of European performance and publication. The celebrated pianist Teresa Carreño had included some of his pieces on her programs. In April, 1888, MacDowell's First Piano Concerto was performed in Boston, and, wrote W. F. Apthorp in the *Transcript*, "The effect upon all present was simply electric." After his return to America, MacDowell further consolidated his position both as composer and executant. His first great success was when he played his Second Piano Concerto in New York in March, 1889; a success repeated soon afterward in Boston. In the summer of that year he appeared as soloist in this concerto at a concert of American music conducted by Van der Stucken in Paris (July 12, 1889). Other composers represented on this historic program were Dudley Buck, George W. Chadwick, Arthur Foote, Henry Holden Huss, Margaret Ruthven Lang, John K. Paine, and Frank Van der Stucken.

In Boston, where he remained for eight years, MacDowell taught privately and composed industriously. The more important works composed during this period include the Concert Study for piano (Opus 36), the Twelve Studies for piano (Opus 39), the Six Love Songs (Opus 40), the Sonata *Tragica* (Opus 45), the twelve Virtuoso Studies (Opus 46), the Eight Songs (Opus 47), the Second (*Indian*) Suite for orchestra, the Sonata *Eroica* (Opus 50), and the *Woodland Sketches* (Opus 51). This last collection contained some of his best-known pieces, such as *To a Wild Rose*, *From an Indian Lodge*, and *To a Water Lily*. Several of his larger works—the symphonic poem *Lancelot and Elaine*, the Orchestral Suite in A Minor, *The Saracens* and *The Lovely Alda* (episodes from *The Song of Roland*), *Hamlet and Ophelia*—were performed by the Boston Symphony Orchestra. The public applauded, the critics praised him. James Huneker wrote of the D minor Piano Concerto that "it easily ranks with any modern work in this form." W. J. Henderson called the same work "a strong, wholesome, beautiful work of art, vital with imagination, and made with masterly skill."

Teaching at Columbia

In May, 1896, the trustees of Columbia University in New York offered MacDowell the newly created professorship of music at that institution. After some hesitation, he accepted. He seems to have been fired by the vision of accomplishing great things in music education. This was his program of instruction: "First, to teach music scientifically and technically, with a view to training musicians who shall be competent to teach and to compose. Second, to treat music historically and aesthetically as an element of liberal culture." [3] This program was to be carried out in five courses of study. For the first two years MacDowell bore the entire burden of teaching by himself, after which an assistant was appointed. As a teacher, MacDowell worked hard and conscientiously, shirking none of the drudgery associated with this

[3] W. J. Batzell, in Preface to MacDowell's *Critical and Historical Essays*.

task. He was an inspiration to his students and his courses were well attended. His lectures ranged over the entire field of musical history, from the ancient Greeks and Romans, and included a survey of Oriental and primitive music. He was outspoken in his opinions, independent in his ideas, and repeatedly urged his students to think for themselves rather than to accept ready-made judgments from others. As a lecturer he was fluent, dynamic, and, on occasion, humorous.

During the academic year 1902–1903, MacDowell took his sabbatical vacation, making first an extended concert tour in the United States and then spending the spring and summer in Europe. It was in 1902 that Nicholas Murray Butler succeeded Seth Low as president of Columbia University, and while MacDowell was absent Butler undertook to reorganize the teaching of the fine arts at the university. Now, this was a subject very near to MacDowell's heart; he had definite ideas on the scope and nature of a department of fine arts that would embrace music, painting, sculpture, architecture, and belles-lettres. These ideas, according to MacDowell, were rejected as impractical by President Butler. Feeling dissatisfied with the situation, MacDowell, early in January of 1904, presented his resignation. Indiscreetly, he talked to two student reporters who came to interview him, and the next day the story of his resignation was featured in the New York papers, with such tendentious headlines as "No Idealism Left in Columbia." Thus "the MacDowell affair" became overnight a *cause célèbre* in the annals of America's music. Butler issued a statement to the press in which he stated that MacDowell's resignation had been prompted by the latter's wish to devote all his time and strength to composition. MacDowell countered with another statement for the press, in which he said:

> President Butler has evidently misunderstood my interview with him when he affirms that my sole object in resigning from Columbia was to have more time to write: he failed to explain the circumstances which led to my resignation. . . . There is certainly individual idealism in all universities, but the general tendency of modern education is toward materialism.

Thus, for MacDowell the fundamental issue was one between idealism and materialism. In his report to the trustees he made his position fully clear. He was opposed to Butler's plan for a Division of Fine Arts with "the inclusion of Belles Lettres and Music, including kindergarten, etc., at Teachers College. . . . The Division of Fine Arts thus acquires somewhat the nature of a co-educational department store, and tends toward materialism rather than idealism. . . . For seven years I have put all my energy and enthusiasm in the cause of art at Columbia, and now at last, recognizing the futility of my efforts, I have resigned the chair of music in order to resume my own belated vocation."

There is no point in attempting to follow further the details of the controversy. The important thing to emphasize is that in MacDowell's mind it was a question of idealism versus materialism: whether art should be dispensed as in "a co-educational department store" or whether it should be considered on a high aesthetic and technical level. The issue is a vital one, and by no means dead in American higher education. The only footnote that it seems necessary to add to this affair is that the chief professorship of music at Columbia University now bears the name of the Edward MacDowell Chair of Music.

During the years at Columbia, MacDowell continued to compose and to develop as a creative artist. He wrote the admirable *Sea Pieces* (Opus 55), the Third Piano Sonata (called *Norse,* Opus 57), the *Keltic* Sonata (Opus 59), the *Fireside Tales* (Opus 61), the *New England Idyls,* and some of his best songs. In 1896 he had acquired a farmhouse and some arable and wooded land near Peterboro, New Hampshire, where he and his wife thenceforth spent their vacations. In a log cabin that he built in the woods he did most of his composing, during the summer months. It was an ideal spot for both work and relaxation, but MacDowell, after his resignation from Columbia, was not long to enjoy the satisfaction of creative work. In the spring of 1905 his health began to deteriorate. He showed signs of nervous exhaustion, but the malady proved to be malignant and incurable: it soon left him helpless and mentally impotent. Tended by his faithful wife, he dragged out his existence for many months and finally passed away in New York City on the evening of January 23, 1908. His remains were taken to Peterboro for burial. Today the artists' colony at Peterboro, established by his widow as a summer haven for creative workers in the arts, stands as a tribute to MacDowell's memory.

To understand the personality, the background, and the art of Edward MacDowell is to understand a large segment of our musical culture. To arrive at this understanding, we should consider Mac-

Dowell's attitude toward America, his relation to Europe, and his conception of the art of music.

MacDowell and America

Writing sympathetically of MacDowell in the *Dictionary of American Biography*, John Erskine remarked that "undoubtedly he missed some of the contacts with national life which are helpful to creative art." This is an understatement. The composer spent his boyhood in New York City, in the sheltered circle of an upper middle-class family. At fifteen he went to Europe and stayed there until he was twenty-seven. Upon his return he lived in Boston and New York. It was a narrowly circumscribed cultural orbit, bounded on all sides by the conventions of the urban genteel tradition. As we have pointed out, the prevailing weakness of the genteel tradition was sentimentality, and from this weakness the music of MacDowell suffered grievously. In the words of Paul Rosenfeld:

> The feelings entertained about life by him seem to have remained uncertain; and while fumbling for them he seems regularly to have succumbed to "nice" and "respectable" emotions, conventional, accepted by and welcome to, the best people. It is shocking to find how full of vague poesy he is. . . . His mind dwells fondly on old-fashioned New England gardens, old lavender, smouldering logs, sunsets, "a fairy sail with a fairy boat," little log cabins of dreams, the romance of German forests and the sexual sternness of Puritan days.[4]

Apropos of this last phrase, it is interesting to compare Gilman's remark about MacDowell's music: "It is music curiously free from the fevers of sex." And he says of the composer that "his sensuousness is never luscious." Shall we then speak of subconscious puritan inhibitions in the music of MacDowell? That is scarcely necessary; it is enough to observe the ravages of a sentimentality which turns the artist away from life into a private dreamworld, where even the erotic becomes sublimated into "vague poesy." In paying tribute to MacDowell, Philip Hale said he was one "who in his art kept himself pure and unspotted." We may connect this with Howard's statement that in his latter years MacDowell "often told his friends that he

[4] Rosenfeld, *An Hour with American Music.*

avoided hearing music, so that he would not be in danger of showing its influence." This I construe as a sort of aesthetic sterilization.

Erskine claims that MacDowell's "interest in America was genuine and deep, reaching far beyond the field of music." Even within the field of music, he concerned himself with the problem of an American "national" school. Opposing the ideas of Dvořák, he rejected the concept of musical nationalism based on folklore. His views on this subject are worth quoting in full:

> So-called Russian, Bohemian, or any other purely national music has no place in art, for its characteristics may be duplicated by anyone who takes the fancy to do so. On the other hand, the vital element in music—personality—stands alone. . . . We have here in America been offered a pattern for an "American" national musical costume by the Bohemian Dvořák—though what the Negro melodies have to do with Americanism in art still remains a mystery. Music that can be made by "recipe" is not music, but "tailoring." To be sure, this tailoring may serve to cover a beautiful thought; but—why cover it? . . . The means of "creating" a national school to which I have alluded are childish. No: before a people can find a musical writer to echo its genius it must first possess men who truly represent it—that is to say, men who, being part of the people, love the country for itself: men who put into their music what the nation has put into its life; and in the case of America it needs above all, both on the part of the public and on the part of the writer, absolute freedom from the restraint that an almost unlimited deference to European thought and prejudice has imposed upon us. Masquerading in the so-called nationalism of Negro clothes cut in Bohemia will not help us. What we must arrive at is the youthful optimistic vitality and the undaunted tenacity of spirit that characterizes the American man. That is what I hope to see echoed in American music.[5]

This passage, taken from one of his lectures at Columbia University, seems amazing, almost incredible, coming from MacDowell. Is it this bard of the Celtic twilight, this worshiper of Arthurian flummeries, who cries for the expression of "youthful optimistic vitality" in American music? Is his the prophetic voice that summons American composers to put into their music what the nation has put into its life? The phrases are there, and we can only wonder at this dichotomy of

[5] MacDowell, *Critical and Historical Essays.*

word and deed, repeating the query of the apostle: "What *doth it* profit, . . . though a man say he hath faith, and have not works? . . ."

As we shall see in the next chapter, it was Dvořák, and not MacDowell, who proved to be the man of the hour, the man who felt the historical need of the moment in American music. This does not mean that MacDowell was entirely wrong in theory and Dvořák entirely right. MacDowell was right in maintaining that folklore and nationalism are not permanent, absolute values in artistic creation. Art is the product of a personality multiplied by a cultural tradition, or by the sum of several traditions, depending on the complexity of the artist's heritage and equipment. MacDowell inherited the genteel tradition of American urban culture, which in turn was a derivation of conventional European modes. In so far as the American imitation failed to reproduce the authentic atmosphere of the European original, by that much was MacDowell a spiritual expatriate from Europe. As Erskine writes:

> The deep emotions of his early manhood were bound up with Europe, with a tradition and an atmosphere not to be found on this side the ocean. Perhaps he was always looking for it here, wistfully and tragically. He gave the impression, against his will, of being a visitor in his own land, trying to establish himself in alien conditions.

Perhaps this explains his remarks on American music previously quoted: he was trying desperately, trying too hard, to say what he thought he should say as an American composer; but the lack of conviction—or, rather, the lack of an operative American tradition in his cultural heritage—prevented him from embodying a bold, independent speech in his own creative work. He was in love with Europe, and the worst of it is that, in the words of Erskine, "the Europe he loved was a dream country, suggested by the great poets and artists and by ancient monuments, by folk-lore, by enchanting forests." Even after he transferred his *décor* to New England, it was this dream country that continued to inspire him. His music was a bridge from reality to that dream.

Music as a "soul-language"

What, then, was MacDowell's conception of music, of its nature and meaning? This is what he said in one of his lectures:

> The high mission of music . . . is neither to be an agent for expressing material things; nor to utter pretty sounds to amuse the ear; nor a sensuous excitant to fire the blood, or a sedative to lull the senses; it is a *language,* but a language of the intangible, a kind of soul-language. It appeals directly to the *Seelenzustände* it springs from, for it is the natural expression of it, rather than, like words, a translation of it into stereotyped symbols which may or may not be accepted for what they were intended to denote by the writer.[6]

For MacDowell, then, music is a language in which one soul speaks to another. He states plainly that "*music is not an art,* but psychological utterance" (my italics). He denies that music can be compared with architecture, painting, or poetry. "Painting is primarily an art of externals . . . for that art must touch its audience through a palpable delineation of something more or less material; whereas *music is of the stuff dreams are made of.*" (Again the italics are mine.) Speaking of the type of music that "suggests," as contrasted with music that "paints," he says:

> The successful recognition of this depends not only upon the susceptibility of the hearer to delicate shades of sensation, but also upon the receptivity of the hearer and his power to accept freely and unrestrictedly the mood shadowed by the composer. *Such music cannot be looked upon objectively.* To those who would analyze it in such a manner it must remain an unknown language; its potency depends entirely upon a state of willing subjectivity on the part of the hearer.[7]

This passage, particularly the sentence italicized (by me), is crucial in relation to MacDowell's own music. If we do not voluntarily place ourselves in a state of willing subjectivity to the "mood shadowed by the composer," if we do not lay aside an objective awareness of the musical substance, the sonorous structure as such, then his music remains for us "an unknown language"—that is, it does not communicate —and thereby loses its potency.

Perhaps the key to MacDowell's limitations in his attitude toward music as a medium of artistic expression has been unwittingly provided for us by Gilman in the following sentence:

[6] MacDowell, *Critical and Historical Essays.*
[7] *Ibid.*, p. 259.

> His standpoint is, in the last analysis, that of the poet rather than that of the typical musician: the standpoint of the poet intent mainly upon a vivid embodiment of the quintessence of personal vision and emotion, who has elected to utter that truth and that emotion in terms of musical beauty.

What this means, in effect, is that MacDowell did not think in terms of musical expression. Therefore, if we find ourselves unable or unwilling to share a priori his moods and emotions, we are apt to find his musical expression inadequate. He will have the listener abjure "that objective state which accepts with the ears what is intended for the spirit." He considers that a higher order of music which "aims at causing the hearer to go beyond the actual sounds heard, in pursuance of a train of thought primarily suggested by this music."

In contrast to this superior type of soulful music is "mere beauty of sound," which is, in itself, "purely sensuous." Developing this thought, MacDowell writes: "It is the Chinese conception of music that *the texture of a sound is to be valued;* the long, trembling tone-tint of a bronze gong, or the high, thin streams of sound from the pipes are enjoyed for their ear-filling qualities. . . ." Thus the concept that the texture of sound is to be valued is regarded as an outlandish notion, the mark of an inferior civilization, for, says MacDowell, this is "sound without music." One wonders why he does not simply advocate music without sound, since that is the surest way of eliminating the "purely sensuous" element of sonorous beauty. The following passage is extremely revealing: "If we could eliminate from our minds all thoughts of music and bring ourselves to listen only to the *texture* of sounds, we could better understand the Chinese ideal of musical art." [8] This is truly an amazing dichotomy, which draws a line between *music* and *the texture of sounds.* Further on this subject: "For instance, if in listening to the deep, slow vibrations of a large gong we ignore completely all thought of pitch, fixing our attention only upon the roundness and fullness of the sound and the way it gradually diminishes in volume without losing any of its pulsating colour we should then realize what the Chinese call music." In other words, if we listen to a musical sound with full aesthetic awareness of its properties and effects as sound, we should then realize what the Chinese call music but what is not music for MacDowell. The significance of all this, apart from its revelation of MacDowell's atti-

[8] *Ibid.,* p. 60.

tude toward music, is that many people are still prevented from appreciating, for instance, twentieth-century music, because of this concept of music as a "soul-language" divorced from consideration of the actual texture of sounds in the musical artwork. Conversely, no amount of insistence upon the "nobility" of the message contained in the "soul-language" of MacDowell's music will arouse a response in those of us who find that his sonorous texture lacks interest and structural vitality.

MacDowell spoke disparagingly of counterpoint: "*Per se*, counterpoint is a puerile juggling with themes, which may be likened to high-school mathematics. In my opinion, J. S. Bach . . . accomplished his mission, not by means of the contrapuntal fashion of his age, but in spite of it. . . . Neither pure tonal beauty, so-called 'form,' nor what is termed the intellectual side of music (the art of counterpoint, canon, and fugue), constitutes a really vital factor in music." [9]

Writing of the music of Schumann, which he admired, MacDowell said: "It represents . . . the rhapsodical reverie of a great poet to whom nothing seems strange, and who has the faculty of relating his visions, never attempting to give them coherence, until, perhaps, when awakened from his dream, he naïvely wonders what they may have meant." This passage tells us much more about MacDowell than it does about Schumann. Many of MacDowell's smaller pieces are musical reveries, or moods expressed in tone, while his larger works, particularly the four piano sonatas, tend toward the rhapsodical. Even in the sonatas, however, as Rosenfeld remarks, "we are never very far from the little old rendezvous" represented by echoes of such pieces as *At an Old Trysting-place* or *An Old Garden*. Here, for example, is a passage from the second movement of the Fourth (*Keltic*) Sonata, which is supposed to be a musical portrait of the enchanting Deirdre: [10]

[9] *Ibid.*, p. 265.
[10] By permission of the copyright owners, The Arthur P. Schmidt Co., Inc.

The music for piano

Most of MacDowell's piano pieces may be divided into two categories: the "quaint" (sentimental) and the "frisky" (lively). In the former class belong *To a Wild Rose, At an Old Trysting-place, To a Water Lily, A Deserted Farm, Told at Sunset, An Old Garden, With Sweet Lavender, Starlight,* and *Nautilus.* The second class includes *Will o' the Wisp, In Autumn, From Uncle Remus, By a Meadow Brook, The Joy of Autumn*—to mention only pieces from *Woodland Sketches* and *New England Idyls.* There is a third category, in which the descriptive or emotional content tends toward the "dramatic," with contrasting moods of emotional emphasis and lyrical tenderness. The prototype of this category is *From Puritan Days,* in which the musical message is underlined by such directions as "pleadingly" and "despairingly." In this class also belong *In Deep Woods, To an Old White Pine, From a Log Cabin, From an Indian Lodge, A.D. MDCXX, Song* (from *Sea Pieces*), and *In Mid-Ocean.* The first of the *Sea Pieces,* titled *To the Sea,* might also be placed in this category, though it is more of a single mood, to be played throughout "with dignity and breadth."

It seems unnecessary to dwell at length on the four piano sonatas. The first, Sonata *Tragica* in G minor (Opus 45), is said to have been composed while MacDowell "was moved by the memory of his grief over the death of his master Raff." The work attempts "to heighten the darkness of tragedy by making it follow closely on the heels of triumph." As for the music, on the evidence of its facile romanticism, one can truly believe that the composer was moved by memories of Raff.

The Sonata *Eroica* in G minor (Opus 50), published in 1895, bears the motto *Flos regum Arthurus*. It has a programmatic content, as explained by the composer: "While not exactly programme music, I had in mind the Arthurian legend when writing this work. The first movement typifies the coming of Arthur. The scherzo was suggested by a picture of Doré showing a knight in the woods surrounded by elves. The third movement was suggested by my idea of Guinevere. That following represents the passing of Arthur." Gilman called this work "the noblest musical incarnation of the Arthurian legend which we have."

The Third Sonata, called *Norse* (Opus 57), published in 1900, bears the following verses at the head of the score:

Night had fallen on a day of deeds.
The great rafters in the red-ribbed hall
Flashed crimson in the fitful flame
Of smouldering logs;
And from the stealthy shadows
That crept 'round Harald's throne,
Rang out a Skald's strong voice,
With tales of battles won;
  Of Gudrun's love
  And Sigurd, Siegmund's son.

Along with the crashing chords and sweeping figurations of this music, we find such passages of chromatic tenderness as the following, marked to be played "Very dreamily, almost vague." [11]

[11] By permission of the copyright owners, The Arthur P. Schmidt Co., Inc.

The Fourth (*Keltic*) Sonata (Opus 59), was published in 1901 and, like the third, was dedicated to Edvard Grieg. Like the third also it has only three movements. Four lines of MacDowell's own verse stand at the head of the score:

> Who minds now Keltic tales of yore,
> Dark Druid rhymes that thrall,
> Deirdre's song and wizard lore
> of great Cuchullin's fall.

Hedging, as usual, on the matter of programmatic content, MacDowell wrote that "the music is more a commentary on the subject than an actual depiction of it." He wrote of this sonata that it was "more of a 'bardic' rhapsody on the subject than an attempt at actual presentation of it, although I have made use of all the suggestion of tone-painting in my power." It is as "bardic rhapsodies" that the sonatas of MacDowell, particularly the last two, may best be appreciated.

Orchestral works: *Indian Suite*

MacDowell did not compose symphonies, overtures, or string quartets. For orchestra he wrote symphonic poems, suites, and two piano concertos. The Second Piano Concerto, in D minor (Opus 23), completed in 1885, remains one of MacDowell's most viable works, probably because it purports to carry no solemn "soul message" but is simply a good, workable concerto in neo-romantic style. Of his orchestral works, the best is the Second or *Indian* Suite (Opus 48), first performed in 1896, which consists of five movements: (1) "Legend," (2) "Love Song," (3) "In War Time," (4) "Dirge," (5) "Festival." According to Henry F. Gilbert, who was at one time a pupil of MacDowell, the genesis of the *Indian Suite* was as follows:

> MacDowell became somewhat interested in Indian lore and curious to see some real Indian music. He asked me to look up some for him, so I brought him Theodore Baker's book, *Die Musik der Nordamerikanischen Wilden.* "Oh, yes," he said, "I knew of this book, but had forgotten about it." From Baker's book the main themes of his Indian Suite are taken. . . . Although all the themes have been changed, more or less, the changes have always been in the direction of musical beauty, and enough of the original tune has been retained to leave no doubt as to its barbaric flavor.

The theme of the first movement ("Legend") occurs in a sacred ceremony of the Iroquois. A love song of the Iowas is used as the theme of the second movement ("Love Song"). A Kiowa tune, a chant of mourning, provides the theme for the fourth movement ("Dirge"), which is considered by many to be the most beautiful and effective orchestral music written by MacDowell. The last movement ("Festival") utilizes a women's dance and a war song of the Iroquois. Gilman quotes MacDowell as having said, in 1903: "Of all my music, the 'Dirge' in the Indian Suite pleases me most. It affects me deeply and did when I was writing it. In it an Indian woman laments the death of her son; but to me, as I wrote it, it seemed to express a world-sorrow rather than a particularized grief."

We have already seen that MacDowell frowned upon musical nationalism based on folklore. To Hamlin Garland he said: "I do not believe in 'lifting' a Navajo theme and furbishing it into some kind of musical composition and calling it American music. Our problem is not so simple as that." Certainly not. Yet there is something curiously ironic in the fact that MacDowell should have drawn from American Indian music the material and the inspiration for some of his best and most effective pages. It represents at least an attempt to get away from secondhand romanticism and genteel sentimentality. If we are now in considerable doubt as to "its barbaric flavor," and if we have no delusions regarding its significance as "American music," we at least are ready to acknowledge that it is rather good music, and to be thankful that MacDowell turned for a moment from Teutonic forests, New England nooks, and Celtic legends, to look into a book on American Indian music.

Something should be said about MacDowell's songs, though his production in this field was not large: he wrote forty-two songs for single voice with piano. He believed that "song writing should follow declamation," and that "the accompaniment should be merely a background for the words." MacDowell had literary aspirations and wrote the words for many of his own songs. He felt that much of the finest poetry, including that of Whitman, was unsuitable for musical setting. Among his more effective songs are "Fair Springtide," "Confidence," "Constancy, "The Swan Bent Low to the Lily," "A Maid Sings Light," "Long Ago," "To the Golden Rod," and "As the Gloaming Shadows Creep."

When Edward MacDowell appeared on the scene, many Americans felt that here at last was "the great American composer" awaited by the nation. But MacDowell was not a great composer. At his best he was a gifted miniaturist with an individual manner. Creatively, he looked toward the past, not toward the future. He does not mark the beginning of a new epoch in American music, but the closing of a fading era, the *fin de siècle* decline of the genteel tradition which had dominated American art music since the days of Hopkinson and Hewitt. This does not mean that the genteel tradition died with MacDowell: it survived in countless other composers of lesser reputation. But MacDowell was the last to endow it with glamour and prestige, the last important figure to live and work entirely within its orbit. After him the tradition either becomes identified with academic dignity, as in the composers of the so-called "Boston Group," or simply peters out in inconsequential drivel. Since we shall not concern ourselves with the latter, we may turn now to the group of composers sometimes called the "Boston Classicists," among whom MacDowell lived for a time and whose ideals he shared in large measure.

chapter eighteen

The Boston classicists

One truth you taught us outlived all the rest:
Music hath Brahms to soothe the savage breast.

D. G. MASON, LINES TO PERCY GOETSCHIUS, ON HIS EIGHTY-SECOND BIRTHDAY.

On Thanksgiving Day in the year 1895 a young American composer wrote in his journal: "Thank God Wagner is dead and Brahms is alive. And here's to the great classical revival of the 20th century in America." The name of this ardent young classicist—he was then only twenty-two—was Daniel Gregory Mason.[1] The reader is familiar with the name of Mason and what it stands for in American music: the transition from the pioneer singing-school tradition of early New England to the imitative provincialism of such Europeanizers as William Mason. Daniel Gregory was the nephew of William, and with him this New England musical dynasty reaches its culmination in an almost ecstatic surrender to the potent spell of the classical-romantic European tradition. In a volume of reminiscences, *Music in My Time*, Daniel Gregory Mason has described both the musical background of his boyhood in Massachusetts and his own musical credo as a mature individual. Describing the musical atmosphere of the family circle, he writes:

> The truth is, our whole view of music was based on the style of classic and romantic symphonists, beginning with Haydn and Mozart and ending with Mendelssohn and Schumann. Even Bach was rather on the edge of the music we recognized, and the rhythmic freedom or unmetricality of say, Gregorian chant, was decidedly beyond our horizon.[2]

[1] Mason died on Dec. 4, 1953, at the age of eighty. For an account of his compositions, see p. 380.

[2] Mason, *Music in My Time*, p. 14.

In speaking of rhythmic freedom and unmetricality, Mason need not have gone as far afield as Gregorian chant: he might have cited American folk music as an example; but that, of course, was also a closed book in this highly restricted musical circle. As regards his own views of musical art, Mason says:

> . . . one of my deepest convictions has always been a sense of the supreme value in art of balance, restraint, proportion—in a word, of classic beauty. Hence my lifelong adoration of men like Bach, Mozart, Schubert, Beethoven, Brahms, in whom this ideal is supremely realized. Contrariwise I have always felt an instinctive antipathy toward excess, unbalance, romantic exaggeration, sensationalism, typified for me in such composers, great artists though they be, as Wagner, Tschaikowsky, Liszt, Strauss.[3]

As we shall see, Mason also felt, and expressed, "an instinctive antipathy" toward everything in American music that did not conform to this classic ideal of balance and restraint. And his antipathy crystallized around an element in American music that came to symbolize for him the "excess" and "exaggeration" that he hated. This element was the Jewish influence. But of that we shall speak later. For the moment we must attempt to define the prevailing New England attitude toward musical art, that is to say, the attitude that dominated the musical thinking of those New England composers who, in the final decades of the nineteenth century and the first of the twentieth, succeeded in forming a rather impressive school variously known as the "Boston Classicists" or the "New England Academicians." It might be denied that they formed a "school" in the strict sense of the term, but, like all New England cultural manifestations, this musical movement that centered in Boston and that flourished from about 1880 to World War I assumed rather definite characteristics, and I think it can be shown that it stemmed from a fairly homogeneous cultural and aesthetic background.

If we look at American art music as a whole during the period covered by the activity of this Boston group, we must admit that their achievement was notable. With such men as Chadwick, Foote, and Parker, American art music certainly had a group of composers who counted for something. At the same time, we may bear in mind R. H. Shryock's observation that "New England once excelled in cultural

[3] *Ibid.*, p. 101.

achievement, by the simple device of defining culture in terms of those things in which New England excelled." [4] Translated into musical terms this means, for example, that if you arbitrarily set up Brahms as the ideal of musical art, then all music reflecting Brahmsian influence must *ipso facto* be considered superior to any other type of music.

We have already dealt with John Knowles Paine, who may be regarded as the ancestor of the Boston academicians. Among his pupils was Arthur W. Foote (1853–1937). In one respect, Foote's musical education was not typical of the New England group: he did not study in Europe. Born in Salem, Massachusetts, he was allowed by his parents to take piano lessons when he was fourteen, but with no thought that he would take up music as a profession. At Harvard he became conductor of the Glee Club and studied music with Paine, yet still had a business career in sight when he graduated. It was B. J. Lang, to whom he had gone for some lessons on the organ, who persuaded young Foote that his future lay in music rather than business. So Foote became an organist and a pianist, opened a teaching studio in 1876, began to compose, and settled down to a quiet, productive existence in Boston. Like most of his contemporaries he was a Brahmsian, but, with exceptional adroitness, managed to be simultaneously a devotee of Wagner.

The Brahmsian influence is apparent chiefly in Foote's chamber music: Piano Quartet (Opus 23, 1891), String Quartet in E (1894); Quintet for piano and strings (1898), Piano Trio in B flat (1909). He followed the lead of Liszt in his ambitious symphonic poem called, after Dante, *Francesca da Rimini* (1893), in which he attempted some moderately realistic programmatic effects. He had a predilection for strings: his compositions for string orchestra include a pseudoclassical Serenade in E and Suite in D, and a rather austere Suite in E, composed in 1910. He also composed a mildly evocative *Night Piece* for flute and strings. Among his works for full orchestra are an overture, *In the Mountains* (1887), a Cello Concerto (1894), and *Four Character Pieces after Omar Khayyám* (1912).

Foote's Serenade for string orchestra, Opus 25, consists of Prelude, Air, Intermezzo, Romance, Gavotte. It was this sort of thing that Rupert Hughes had in mind when he wrote of Foote: "I know of no modern composer who has come nearer to relighting the fires that

[4] Shryock, in *The Cultural Approach to History*, ed. by Caroline F. Ware (New York, 1940), p. 267.

beam in the old gavottes and fugues and preludes."[5] This remark is quoted because it seems so typical of what the Bostonians were trying to do: relighting the fires of old forms and calling it a classical revival. Unfortunately, Hughes let the skeleton out of the closet (and also made a quick change of metaphor) when he went on to add that the gavottes of Foote "are an example of what it is to be academic without being only a rattle with dry bones." This gives us another characterization of the so-called "classical" revival: dry bones rattling in the academic closet. One could at least hope to cover the bones attractively. Or, as Louis Elson put it, "Foote uses the classical forces with most admirable ease and fluency."[6]

Foote left a large body of vocal music, both sacred and secular. His major choral works are *The Farewell of Hiawatha*, for men's voices (1886), *The Wreck of the Hesperus* (1888), and *The Skeleton in Armor*, with orchestra (1893). In these two latter works, Wagnerism is rampant, particularly in the storm scenes. A prolific composer, Foote wrote a quantity of church music, about one hundred and fifty songs (with a preference for Elizabethan lyrics), numerous piano pieces, and some thirty works for organ.

Among the adjectives that have been applied to the music of Arthur Foote by various writers are "noble," "pure," "refined," "dignified," "earnest," and "agreeable." These adjectives seem to me not only to delimit an individual production but also to epitomize an era and an aspiration that converged in Boston of the *fin de siècle*.

A Boston blend

In examining the antecedents of modern New England composers, time and again we find them emerging from a family background whose pattern repeats that of the native musical pioneers of the eighteenth century. Such is the case, for example, with George W. Chadwick, born in Lowell, Massachusetts, November 13, 1854. His father was one of those versatile, self-reliant Yankees who managed to combine the love and cultivation of music with success in practical matters. Beginning as a farmer, he became a machinist, and in 1860 established an insurance company, which prospered. Like the old New England singing-school masters, he taught a singing class in his

[5] Hughes, *Contemporary American Composers*, p. 227.
[6] Elson, *The History of American Music*, p. 479.

spare time, and organized a chorus in his community. His sons were encouraged to study music, and there were frequent musical gatherings in the family. In this scheme of things, music was not supposed to take the place of business, but to provide a wholesome and "uplifting" leisure-time occupation. So it was that George Chadwick, after learning to play the organ and the piano, entered his father's business according to the prescribed procedure. Before long, however, he decided that music was more important to him than business, left the paternal firm, and became a student at the New England Conservatory, of which many years later he was to be director. After a brief period of teaching music at Olivet College, young Chadwick decided to go to Europe to complete his musical education, to learn the art of orchestration, and to master the complexities of composing in the larger forms. It was then that he met with parental opposition: music as a full-time profession was still a heretical idea to the elder Chadwick. But it was too late for his opposition to be effective: music as a career was becoming a reality in America, and George Chadwick was moving with the times. He went to Europe.

Inevitably, for a Bostonian of that time, his destination was Germany. He first studied with Haupt in Berlin but soon went to work with the celebrated Jadassohn in Leipzig, after which he received a final polishing from Rheinberger in Munich. By 1880 he was back in Boston, thoroughly imbued with the laws of counterpoint and strict composition, a knowledge which he offered to impart to others for a moderate fee. Among his earliest pupils were three destined to achieve some prominence in American music: Horatio Parker, Sidney Homer, and Arthur Whiting. In 1882 he began teaching at the New England Conservatory and gradually ascended the pedagogic ladder until, fifteen years later, he was appointed director of that institution, holding this position until his death in 1931. Meanwhile, he had conducted choral societies, served as church organist, and composed industriously. His was indeed an exemplary musical career, pursued with tenacity and crowned with success.

Unlike some of his contemporaries, Chadwick did not have the benefit of a Harvard education, for he went to work after finishing high school. But, perhaps to compensate for his lack of a higher education, he continually turned to "high-brow" subjects, setting Latin texts to music, as in his *Phoenix Expirans* for mixed chorus

(1892), or alluding to ancient Greek legend and mythology, as in his overtures *Thalia* (the Muse of Comedy, 1883), *Melpomene* (the Muse of Tragedy, 1887), *Euterpe* (the Muse of Music, 1906), *Adonais* (1899), and the symphonic poem *Aphrodite* (1913). The programmatic content of the last-mentioned composition has been described as follows:

> The idea of the work was suggested by a beautiful head of the goddess, found on the island of Cnidos, and now in the Boston Art Museum. The composition endeavors to portray the scenes that might have taken place before such a statue when worshipped in its temple by the sea. There are festal dances; a storm at sea; the thanks of rescued mariners to their patron goddess; religious services in the temple; and other similar suggestions of suitable nature.[7]

The score itself is headed by the following verses:

> In a dim vision of the long ago
> Wandering by a far-off Grecian shore
> Where streaming moonlight shone on golden sands
> And melting stars knelt at Aphrodite's shrine,
> Imploring her with many a fervid prayer
> To tell the secret of her beauty's power
> And of the depths of ocean whence she sprang.
> At last the wave-born goddess raised her hand
> And smiling said: "O mortal youth behold!"
> And all these mysteries passed before mine eyes.[8]

These quotations are given in full because they are so revealing of the cult for the past—especially a remote and legendary past that could be conceived only "in a dim vision of the long ago" and enveloped in vague reveries and fantasies—which characterized the artistic aspirations of Chadwick and, to a greater or lesser degree, the whole group of Boston classicists. It should also be observed that the sequence of scenes described in the program note to this symphonic poem—the feast, the dances, the storm, the shipwreck, the rescue, the thanksgiving—is of such a stereotyped pattern that it could serve for any descriptive seapiece. This indicates what is confirmed by the music itself: that the whole work is conceived on a plane of academic

[7] Hughes, *op. cit.*, p. 479.
[8] Score published by The A. P. Schmidt Co., Inc.

conventionality. It is no more than a proper Bostonian flirtation with the shade of Aphrodite.

Chadwick had a preference for descriptive music, either in the form of orchestral program pieces or of choral settings of narrative poems. His setting of *The Viking's Last Voyage* (1881) for baritone solo, male chorus, and orchestra, reminds one of Rupert Hughes's query, "What would part-song writers do if the Vikings had never been invented? Where would they get their wild choruses for men, with a prize to the singer that makes the most noise?" [9] Other choral works by Chadwick include *Dedication Ode*, *Lovely Rosabelle*, *The Pilgrims*, and *Phoenix Expirans*. Though he wrote smoothly and correctly for voices, his choral output "dates" more than his instrumental music, partly because the Victorian cantata as a genre has "dated," and partly because he was less original in his vocal writing than in his best instrumental works. Chadwick tried his hand at opera, both serious and light, without much success, his most ambitious effort being the music drama *Judith*, which achieved a concert performance in 1901. Of his numerous songs (over a hundred), the best-known is his setting of Sidney Lanier's "Ballad of Trees and the Master."

Chadwick's instrumental works, in addition to those already mentioned, include five string quartets, a piano quintet, three symphonies, the early program overtures *Rip Van Winkle* (1879) and *The Miller's Daughter* (1884), and a set of four orchestral pieces which he called *Symphonic Sketches* (1895–1907), consisting of "Jubilee," "Noël," "Hobgoblin," and "A Vagrom Ballad." It is these symphonic sketches that make of Chadwick a figure of more than historical interest in America's music. Heard today, they have a vitality, a genuineness, a human and emotional quality that takes them out of the category of museum pieces. We may not feel that "Jubilee" and "A Vagrom Ballad" are entirely successful in expressing, as Philip Hale said, "the frankness, swagger and recklessness that Europeans commonly associate with Americans"—nor do we necessarily feel that there is any particular virtue in the musical expression of these traits, assuming that we do indeed possess them. But we do feel that this music is *alive*, and that Chadwick was at least on the right track when he broke away from his pseudoclassical preoccupations and gave vent to the Yankee humor and humanity that was in him. At the head of the score of "Jubilee," the composer placed the following verses:

[9] Hughes, *op. cit.*, p. 213.

No cool gray tones for me!
  Give me the warmest red and green,
  A cornet and a tambourine,
To paint *my* jubilee!
  For when the flutes and oboes play,
    To sadness I become a prey;
    Give me the violets and the May,
But no gray skies for me!

To establish this mood, the sketch (Allegro molto vivace) opens with a jovial theme proclaimed by the whole orchestra, fortissimo, followed soon by another striking theme stated by bass clarinet, bassoons, violas, and cellos, in unison. Then the horns announce a phrase in C major, which Philip Hale describes as a "patting Juba horn call," referring to some verses from Richard Hovey's *More Songs From Vagabondia:* [10]

When the wind comes up from Cuba
And the birds are on the wing,
And our hearts are patting Juba
To the banjo of the spring . . .

After a lyrical episode for wood winds and horns, the piece ends excitingly with a coda marked presto.

Of the three remaining *Symphonic Sketches*, the one titled "A Vagrom Ballad" is probably the most effective. Its atmosphere is evoked in these lines:

A tale of tramps and railway ties,
Of old clay pipes and rum,
Of broken heads and blackened eyes
And the "thirty days" to come.

While this sort of toying with the seamy side of life is still conceived on a conventional plane—a sort of Boston blend of the pastoral and picaresque traditions—the attempt to grasp some kind of earthy reality, rather than to dwell on remote legends and misty myths, marks a wholesome departure from the mood of high-minded imaginings and dreamy escapism that dominates so much of the music produced by the Bostonians of this period. Not that there is any

[10] Boston, 1896.

specific musical virtue in railway ties and old clay pipes as compared with the fabulous phoenix or the beautiful Aphrodite; and it would in any case be fallacious to judge the value of music by its associative connotations rather than by its intrinsic substance. But there is a danger in the artist's completely losing contact with his environment and having no real roots in the cultural traditions of his own land. Edward MacDowell was an artist of this type, as were most of the New England neoclassicists. We come now to a composer who deliberately cut himself off from direct contact with his environment, enclosing himself, as with a medieval moat, in a refuge of exquisitely elaborate sonorities.

An exquisite artificer

Charles Martin Loeffler was born in Alsace on January 30, 1861, and died at his farm in Medfield, Massachusetts, on May 20, 1935. A violin pupil of Joachim and Massart, he spent some time in Russia as a youth, then joined the Pasdeloup Orchestra in Paris. Had he remained in Paris, he would have become identified with the French impressionists, setting to music the poems of Baudelaire and Verlaine, indulging his taste for delicate nuances and his passion for polished workmanship. There would then have been no reason for including him in this book, or for raising the question as to whether or not he can really be considered an American composer. The late Carl Engel, in a disconcerting outburst of hyperbole, apparently settled that question to his own satisfaction by declaring that Loeffler was the greatest of American composers.[11] For a dissenting opinion, we may turn, as usual, to the iconoclastic Rosenfeld, who characterized Loeffler as a correct and inhibited New Englander (though he was only that by geographical proximity) who produced music that was sterile and stiff with the dead weight of tradition. And the truth, as usual, would seem to rest midway between these extremes. I do not think that Loeffler can be regarded as an American composer in anything but a literal sense of that term, that is, a composer who lived and worked for most of his life in America.

Loeffler came to the United States in 1881, spent about a year in New York, and then, upon the invitation of Major Higginson, joined

[11] Engel, in *The International Cyclopedia of Music and Musicians,* ed. by Oscar Thompson.

the recently founded Boston Symphony Orchestra as first violin. He continued in this capacity until 1903, when he resigned and retired to a farm that he had acquired in Medfield. He had been composing for a number of years, and the Boston Symphony had performed several of his works from manuscript, notably a Suite for violin and orchestra (after Gogol), *Les Veillées de l'Ukraine* (1891), a *Fantastic Concerto* for cello and orchestra (1894), and a Divertimento for violin and orchestra (1895). After his retirement he began to publish some large works, such as the symphonic poem *La Mort de Tintagiles* (after Maeterlinck) and a *Symphonic Fantasy* (after a poem by Rollinat), both published in 1905. In 1901 he had written a work titled *A Pagan Poem* for chamber orchestra with piano. This he later rewrote for full orchestra, with piano obbligato, in which form it was played by the Boston Symphony in 1907. It remains Loeffler's best-known work. *A Pagan Poem* is based on the eighth Eclogue of Virgil, which tells of a Thessalian girl who tries to use sorcery to win back her errant lover Daphnis, repeating the magical refrain: *Ducite ab urbe domum, mea carmina, ducite Daphnim* ("Draw from the city, my songs, draw Daphnis home"). Three trumpets obbligati, heard at first off-stage and then gradually drawing nearer, finally merging with the orchestra on-stage, suggest the incantation of the sorceress, gaining in passion and potency as she weaves her spell.

Of Loeffler's numerous compositions, only three others need be mentioned here. These are Music for Four Stringed Instruments (published in 1923), *Canticum Fratris Solis* for voice and chamber orchestra (1925), and *Evocation* for orchestra, women's chorus, and speaking voice (1931). All of these compositions display Loeffler's penchant for the archaic and the impressionistic, for the evocation of past ages and idioms. His setting of St. Francis's "Canticle of the Sun," commissioned by the Elizabeth Sprague Coolidge Foundation and first performed at the Library of Congress in 1925, is another example of his musical preciosity and technical refinement.

Loeffler's work forms a sort of parenthesis in the history of America's music. He drew nothing from the American environment and contributed nothing to it in the way of immediate influence or directions for others to follow. Unlike other musical immigrants, he did not throw himself into the main stream of America's musical life. Spiritually remote and physically isolated, he created a dreamworld of lovingly wrought sounds, capable, indeed, of affording us delight, but in the end perhaps palling by its very exquisiteness.

It will be appropriate here to mention briefly another member of the Boston group, Arthur B. Whiting (1861–1936), not because his music is important (he outlived its reputation) but because it is so highly symptomatic of the Boston coterie which we are discussing. A native of Cambridge, Massachusetts, Whiting studied composition with Chadwick at the New England Conservatory of Music, then betook himself to Germany for the customary academic polishing, exposing himself to the teachings of Abel and Rheinberger, two eminent Teutonic pedagogues, at the Munich Conservatory. He returned to Boston brimful of enthusiasm for Brahms and imbued with what his friend and admirer Mason calls "the classic spirit," sternly opposed to anything "slipshod or mawkish or inept." In this mood of idealistic austerity he proceeded to produce a series of works, including a Concert Overture, a Suite for horn and strings, some chamber music and songs, and a Fantasy for piano and orchestra (Opus 11), which drew from the irrepressible Philip Hale the following choice bit of critical sarcasm:

> Mr. Whiting had, and no doubt has, high ideals. Sensuousness in music seemed to him as something intolerable, something against public morals, something that should be suppressed by the selectmen. Perhaps he never went so far as to petition for an injunction against sex in music; but rigorous intellectuality was his one aim. He might have written A Serious Call to Devout and Holy Composition, or A Practical Treatise upon Musical Perfection, to which is now added, by the same author, The Absolute Unlawfulness of the State Entertainment Fully Demonstrated.[12]

Mr. Hale obviously knew his early New England tracts. He did, however, concede that Whiting had put somewhat more of warmth and humanity into his Fantasy than he had permitted to appear in his earlier works. If there is any possibility at all of reviving interest in Whiting's music, it will probably be through this Fantasy for piano and orchestra.

Some cantatas and an opera

Horatio Parker is a composer who stands very near the top of the Boston group. Born in Auburndale, Massachusetts, on September 15, 1853, he came of a highly cultured New England family. His father

[12] Quoted by Hughes, *op. cit.*, p. 289.

was an architect and his mother an amateur organist and a lover of literature who knew Greek and Latin. Not until he was fourteen did Parker begin to take any interest in music, and then his mother became his first teacher, in piano and organ. Within two years the boy had made such progress that he was appointed church organist in Dedham and began to compose hymns and anthems, just as any of his early New England forebears might have done. When Chadwick returned from Europe in 1880 and opened a teaching studio in Boston, young Parker became one of his first pupils. The next step, of course, was for him to follow in Chadwick's footsteps and make his own pilgrimage to Germany, which he did in 1882, electing to sit at the feet of Rheinberger in Munich, from whom he absorbed with exemplary thoroughness the rules of counterpoint. While in Germany, Parker composed several large works—concert overtures, a Symphony, cantatas—some of which were performed in Munich. After three years abroad he settled in New York, as church organist, teacher at the National Conservatory, and music director at St. Paul's School, Garden City. In 1893 he transferred his activities to Boston, and a year later accepted the Battell Professorship of Music at Yale University, where he remained until his death in 1919. He was also very active as a choral conductor, which kept him busily commuting between New Haven and New York. Although his position at Yale and his choral conducting removed him physically from the Boston scene, Parker definitely belongs with the Boston group because of his background, his training, his associations, and his aesthetic tendencies.

Although he wrote nine orchestral works, some chamber music, and pieces for piano and for organ, it is as a composer of choral music that he made his reputation. His first conspicuous success came with the performance in New York in 1893 of his sacred cantata *Hora Novissima*, for mixed chorus and orchestra, a setting of 210 lines from the twelfth-century Latin poem by Bernard of Cluny, "De Contemptu Mundi." This was the work that established Parker's fame in England, when it was performed at the Three Choirs Festival, Worcester, in 1899. As a result, he was commissioned to write two choral works for English festivals: *Wanderer's Psalm* and *Star Song*. Another ambitious sacred cantata, dramatic in conception and Wagnerian in style, *The Legend of St. Christopher*, was performed in Bristol and led to the culmination of Parker's English fame when he received the degree of Doctor of Music from Cambridge University in 1902. An earlier cantata, *The Dream King and His Love,* had won the prize in a contest sponsored by the National Conservatory of Music in New York in 1892. Thus both abroad and at home Parker was honored and acclaimed.

Parker had a capacity for winning important prizes. When the Metropolitan Opera House of New York offered a prize of $10,000 for an opera by an American composer, Parker entered the competition and won the prize for his opera *Mona,* with a libretto by Brian Hooker. The story deals with the well-worn theme of love versus patriotism, for Mona is a princess of Britain at the time of the Roman conquest who falls in love with the son of the Roman governor and yet cannot stifle her hatred for the haughty invaders of her country. *Mona* was produced at the Metropolitan Opera House on March 14, 1912, being the third opera by an American to be performed by that institution (the other two were Converse's *Pipe of Desire* and Herbert's *Natoma,* produced, respectively, in 1910 and 1911). It received only a few performances that season and was never revived. Arguments as to the merits of the opera *Mona* seem rather futile. That it contains some well-written academic music is undeniable, but this does not establish it as a viable dramatic work for the lyric theater. As a footnote to Parker's operatic ventures, it should be remarked that in 1913 he won another $10,000 prize, this time offered by the National Federation of Music Clubs, with an opera titled *Fairyland,* also having a libretto by Brian Hooker. This opera received six performances in Los Angeles in 1915 and has not been heard since then.

The cantata *Hora Novissima* is generally acknowledged to be Parker's masterpiece. Yet even the admiring Philip Hale admitted that its most eloquent moments are "expressed in the language of Palestrina and Bach," while the enthusiastic W. J. Henderson spoke of an *a cappella* chorus that "might have been written by Hobrecht, Brumel, or even Josquin des Près." Other critics remarked on its Mendelssohnian mannerisms and Handelian repetitiousness, all of which adds up to a rather disconcerting hodgepodge of influences. Philip Hale, in what was meant to be high praise, wrote that *Hora Novissima* was a work to which "an acknowledged master of composition in Europe would gladly sign his name." The point is that several European masters could have legitimately signed their names to it. Perhaps this sort of accomplishment was important while America's music was coming of age. It meant that, judged by European standards, American music had no need to be ashamed of itself: the imitation was getting to be practically as good as the model. But what we really needed was some American music to which no European master of composition could sign his name and get away with it. This the Boston classicists were incapable of giving us.

A lady and two professors

The Boston group had a feminine representative in the person of Amy Marcy Cheney (1867–1944), who later became Mrs. H. H. A. Beach. A native of Henniker, New Hampshire, she belonged to one of those long-settled New England families who cultivated music and learning in their leisure and passed on this cultural heritage from generation to generation. She received her first musical lessons from her mother, continued with various teachers when the family moved to Boston, and at sixteen made her debut as a professional pianist. Meanwhile she had been composing since early childhood, and it was not long before she established a reputation as the most prominent American woman composer of her time. Official commissions confirmed her success as a career woman in musical composition: a *Festival Jubilate* for the dedication of the Woman's Building at the Chicago World's Fair in 1893; a *Song of Welcome* for the Trans-Mississippi Exposition at Omaha in 1898; and a *Panama Hymn* for the Panama-Pacific Exposition at San Francisco in 1915.

Of Mrs. Beach's larger works, the best-known are the *Gaelic Symphony*, based on Gaelic folk tunes, and a Piano Concerto. A quantity of church music, some chamber music, many piano pieces, and over one hundred and fifty songs—her most popular output—constitutes the bulk of the work that she produced in her long and busy life. She achieved considerable recognition, particularly in Germany, in the years immediately preceding World War I. While a place must always be reserved for her in the history of American music, the public will doubtless remember her best for such songs as "Ah, Love, But a Day" and "The Year's at the Spring."

Few composers have been more closely identified with the Boston tradition than has Edward Burlingame Hill, born in Cambridge in 1872, of old New England ancestry, grandson of a president of Harvard University, son of a professor there, and himself on the staff of Harvard from 1908 until his retirement in 1940. Inevitably he attended Harvard as a youth and was a pupil in music of John Knowles Paine. He also studied with Chadwick and Whiting in Boston, and with Widor in Paris. Where he differs most sharply from the Boston classicists is in his preference for French music, of which he made a special study. He lectured on this subject at the universities of Lyon and Strasbourg, and published a book titled *Modern French Music.*

Hill has written instrumental music almost exclusively. His orchestral works include three symphonies, several suites, the symphonic poems *Launcelot and Guinevere* and *Lilacs,* two sinfoniettas, a Concertino for piano and orchestra, a Violin Concerto, and Music for English Horn and Orchestra. His two *Stevensoniana* suites are based on poems from Stevenson's *A Child's Garden of Verses.* Hill's chamber music consists of a Sextet for wind instruments and piano, a Quintet for clarinet and strings, a String Quartet, a Sonata for flute and piano, and a Sonata for clarinet and piano.

When Hill's Symphony No. 3 in G major received its first performance by the Boston Symphony Orchestra on December 3, 1937, the composer wrote that the work had "no descriptive background, aiming merely to present musical ideas according to the traditional forms." As he said much the same thing about his First Symphony, this may be taken as a statement of his aesthetic position as an academic traditionalist. He aims to maintain interest by deft instrumentation and skillful organization of his material in accepted forms. In this he is a precursor of Walter Piston and heralds the new generation of Boston traditionalists who adhere to the fundamental triad of form, style, and craftsmanship, as conceived and regulated by academic canons.

At the beginning of this chapter we mentioned the late Daniel Gregory Mason (1873–1953), who as a young man in Boston hailed "the great classical revival of the 20th century in America." Mason's classical ideal was defined by what he himself spoke of as "an instinctive antipathy toward excess, unbalance, romantic exaggeration, sensationalism, typified for me in such composers, great artists though they be, as Wagner, Tschaikowsky, Liszt, Strauss." Among European contemporaries he had little use for Debussy and Ravel, but felt a profound admiration for Vincent d'Indy, with whom he studied in Paris and from whom he learned the value of "the unbroken stream of tradition." Although Mason eventually left Boston for New York, it seems fitting to write of his life and work here because, stemming from a long line of New Englanders and imbued with a stern sense of what was fitting and proper in musical expression, he embodied throughout his long career both the virtues and the limitations that we associate with the Boston Classicists.

Born in Brookline, Massachusetts, Mason attended Harvard University and was for a time a pupil there of J. K. Paine, whom, however, he found unsatisfactory as a teacher. Later he studied composition with Chadwick in Boston and with Goetschius in New York. From 1910 he was a member of the music faculty at Columbia University, where he was appointed MacDowell Professor of Music in 1929. He retired from the chairmanship of the Music Department in 1940.

Among Mason's orchestral works are three symphonies, of which the Third (1936) is the *Lincoln Symphony*, a tone-portrait of the "Great Emancipator." His best-known orchestral composition is the *Chanticleer Overture* (1928), inspired by passages from Thoreau's *Walden*, as quoted in the score: "All climates agree with brave Chanticleer. He is more indigenous than the natives. His health is ever good, his lungs, his spirits never flag."

Mason's interest in Anglo-American folk material is revealed in his *Suite After English Folk Songs* for orchestra (1924) and his *Folk Song Fantasy* (*Fanny Blair*) for string quartet (1929). His numerous chamber-music works include an attractive String Quartet on Negro Themes, first performed in 1919. The first movement is based on the spiritual "You May Bury Me in the East," while the second movement develops the theme of "Deep River," with a contrastingly energetic theme in the middle section. The third movement uses three spirituals: "O What Do You Say, Seekers?" "Shine, Shine, I'll Meet You in the Morning," and "Oh, Holy Lord!"

Other chamber-music works by Mason are a Violin Sonata; Three Pieces for flute, harp, and string quartet; Sonata for clarinet and piano; Variations on a theme of John Powell for string quartet; *Divertimento* for five wind instruments; *Sentimental Sketches* for violin, cello, and piano; and Variations on a Quiet Theme for string quartet.

Mason thought of himself as "a musical humanist." But his humanism tended to be scholastic and restrictive, and caused him to balk at our "heterogeneous national character." For his views on this subject, the reader is referred to page 402. Here we may mention two of Mason's books, dealing with the contemporary scene in American music: *Tune In, America* and *The Dilemma of American Music*. Perhaps the most perceptive comment on Mason's music is that made by Randall Thompson, when he wrote: "A certain sinister and foreboding pessimism, a dour and bitter irony in Mason's music has not been fully appreciated." [13] It may be that this dour quality will endure longer than the lusty bravado of Chanticleer.

In summing up the achievements of the Boston Classicists we may say that they gave to the American composer a professional dignity, a social and artistic prestige, and a degree of recognition both at home and abroad, such as he had not previously enjoyed. In a sense their mission was similar to that accomplished in France by Vincent d'Indy and his associates of the Schola Cantorum: the affirmation of idealism combined with technical discipline. If they were stronger in idealism than in technique, and stronger in technique than in originality, that was partly the consequence of historical factors. They were epigoni rather than originators, and they almost succeeded in making Boston a musical suburb of Munich. They were not moving with the main stream of America's music, nor were they able to recognize and cherish their native musical heritage.

While many of the Boston group were still flourishing, a reaction took place among another group of American musicians, stimulated by a famous visitor from abroad and led by a composer from the Middle West, which resulted in greater awareness of American values, freedom from the musical hegemony of Germany, and a keen interest in the folk, popular, and primitive music of the United States, including Anglo-American folk songs and ballads, Negro spirituals, minstrel tunes, ragtime, and the tribal melodies of the Indians. In the next chapter, with which Part III of this book commences, we turn to the beginnings of what is generally known as "musical nationalism." Actually, the outlook of the composers who participated in this movement was widely international. They sought stimulation and fresh ideas from many sources; many of them were attracted by the folk music of far-off countries. But as Americans aware of their own cultural heritage they felt that America's native or popular music was worth looking at and listening to and using in their compositions. Thus, with the third part of this book, a new era begins in America's music. We become conscious of our musical heritage, we explore it in all its

[13] In *The Musical Quarterly*, XVIII, 1, p. 13.

aspects, we feel the excitement of new popular currents in the rise of ragtime and jazz, our vernacular musical theater develops, our composers achieve mastery of the larger forms, and we witness a tremendous expansion of all our musical resources and activities. Such, in brief, are the developments that form the subject matter of the third and concluding section of this work.

three | Fulfillment

The real America is not to be found either in the order of the long-settled communities or in the disorder of the frontier, but in that area of dynamic and expanding life which is born of the union of the two.

FLOYD STOVALL, AMERICAN IDEALISM.

chapter nineteen

Nationalism and folklore

I get a great kick out of a rip-snorting development of a good old American tune.
ARTHUR FARWELL.

In his *History of American Music*, Louis C. Elson recounts that Massenet once spoke enthusiastically to him about the inspiration that ought to come to the American composer. "Were I in America," said he, "I should be exalted by the glories of your scenery, your Niagara, your prairies; I should be inspired by the Western and Southern life; I should be intoxicated by the beauty of your American women; national surroundings always inspire national music!" [1] The last phrase might be supplemented by adding: "Especially if one is a foreigner." Until recently, for instance, the most effective "Spanish" music was written by foreigners: Glinka, Bizet, Lalo, Rimsky-Korsakoff, Ravel. Turning for a moment to poetic inspiration, one thinks of the Cuban, José María Heredia, spending two years of exile in the United States (1823–1825), gazing spellbound at Niagara Falls, and producing under this overwhelming impression one of the famous poems of the Spanish language, "Niágara."

Shortly before Heredia's sojourn in the United States another foreigner arrived in this country, an eccentric amateur musician from Bohemia named Anton Philip Heinrich (1781–1861), who became enthusiastic about creating an "American" music inspired by the natural scenery, the history, and the native Indian music of the United States. Formerly a banker in Hamburg, Heinrich came to America around 1818, was active first in Philadelphia as musical director of the Southwark Theatre and then went to Louisville, Kentucky, where he taught violin. He spent some time among the Indians in Bardstown and was

[1] Elson, *History of American Music*, p. 337.

fascinated by the possibility of using Indian themes in his compositions. In 1820 Heinrich published *Dawning of Music in Kentucky, or the Pleasures of Harmony in the Solitudes of Nature*, in which he declared that "no one would ever be more proud than himself, to be called an *American Musician*." This "*American production*" was recommended to the favorable notice of the public in the pages of Parker's *Euterpeiad*, which hailed the composer as "the *Beethoven* of America." Heinrich tried hard to play the role of great American composer. He turned out such works as *The Columbiad, Grand American national chivalrous symphony, Jubilee* ("a grand national song of triumph, composed and arranged for a full orchestra and a vocal chorus—in two parts, commemorative of events from the landing of the Pilgrim fathers to the consummation of American liberty"), *Yankee Doodliad, The New England Feast of Shells* ("Divertimento Pastorale Oceanico"), and numerous works "inspired" by his interest in Indian music: *Indian Carnival, Indian Fanfares, The Mastodon, Manitou Mysteries,* and *Pushmataha.*

Certainly old "Father" Heinrich, as he was called, found plenty of "inspiration" in the national surroundings of America; the only drawback was that he lacked talent and technique as a composer. But his enthusiasm for all things American, his aspiration to be known as an *American* musician, his interest in American Indian lore, were symptomatic of things to come. He tried to do, singlehanded and poorly equipped, what it took a whole generation of American musicians to accomplish, collectively and arduously, many decades after Father Heinrich had passed away from the American musical scene on which he made so slight and ephemeral an impression.

Curiously enough, it was another Bohemian—but this time a talented and trained musician—who gave a definite impetus to the formation of a "national" school of composers in the United States. His name was Antonin Dvořák, the composer of the Symphony "From the New World." Before recounting the circumstances of Dvořák's sojourn in the United States from 1892 to 1895, and its effects on the development of American music, it would be well to review briefly the rise of the movement known as "musical nationalism," of which Dvořák was one of the leading representatives.

The spirit of nationalism was rooted in romanticism, which exalted liberty and which recognized the artistic value of folklore. In some cases the use of folk music went hand in hand with a passionate patriotism. Chopin, writing his Polonaises and his Mazurkas, thought of his native land, Poland, enslaved and oppressed. Smetana and Dvořák thought of the political subjugation of Bohemia, a land rich in culture but deprived of independence. Edvard Grieg identified himself with the movement for the independence of Norway. In Russia, on the other hand, the movement was almost exclusively artistic and centered on the exploitation of Russian folk music for the creation of a distinctively "national" school of composition that would assert its independence from the musical hegemony exercised by Germany over Europe.

In the person of Mikhail Glinka (1803–1857), Russian music found its liberator, the creator of a national school with his operas *A Life for the Czar* and *Russlan and Ludmilla.* True, the Russian aristocracy sneered at Glinka for writing "coachmen's music," just as American snobs sneered at composers who used "Negro melodies." But Glinka's music appealed to the people, and what is more, a whole group of composers arose to follow in his footsteps. The group of composers known as the "Mighty Five"—Balakirev, Moussorgsky, Borodin, Cui, Rimsky-Korsakoff—formed the "new school of Russian music" in the 1860s, which soon became widely influential, challenging the supremacy of the Germanic tradition and, later in the century, stimulating the emergence of national schools in such countries as France, Spain, and England. The United States, isolated by the domination of German influence, was one of the few countries that did not feel this stimulating current of liberation and creative vigor until after the turn of the century. Nevertheless, thanks to the presence and the prestige of Antonin Dvořák, some American composers began to be aware of the value of their folk music before the nineteenth century drew to a close.

Dvořák in America

Dvořák had come to America in response to an invitation to be director of the National Conservatory of Music in New York. Among his pupils there were William Arms Fisher (*b.* 1861), Rubin Goldmark (1872–1936), Harvey Worthington Loomis (1865–1930), and Henry Thacker Burleigh (1866–1949). Anyone disposed to minimize Dvořák's influence might point out that none of these men proved to be creative artists of exceptional stature. Fisher, known chiefly as a writer of songs, had the happy thought of adapting the melody of the Largo (slow movement) from Dvořák's *New World Symphony* to the words of "Goin' Home," thus producing a pseudo spiritual that has become widely popular. Goldmark, nephew of the Austrian composer Carl Goldmark and trained at the Vienna Conservatory before studying with Dvořák, became professor of composition at the Juilliard School of Music in New York. His musical Americanism manifested itself in several orchestral works: *Requiem* (suggested by Lincoln's Gettysburg Address), *Hiawatha Overture, Negro Rhapsody,* and *The Call of the Plains.* Loomis became particularly interested in American Indian music, which he studied carefully and arranged effectively in his *Lyrics of the Red-Man* for piano (Opus 76), published in 1903–1904. Burleigh, a Negro, made a career as singer and as arranger of Negro spirituals (his setting of "Deep River" is well known). His association with Dvořák is of special interest to us, for it was through Burleigh's singing that the Bohemian composer became acquainted with many of the Negro spirituals that were to fascinate him. Years later, in 1918, Burleigh wrote as follows regarding the genesis of the *New World Symphony:*

> There is a tendency in these days to ignore the Negro elements in the "New World" Symphony, shown by the fact that many of those who were able in 1893 to find traces of Negro musical color all through the symphony, though the workmanship and treatment of the themes was and is Bohemian, now cannot find anything in the whole four movements that suggests any local or Negro influence, though there is no doubt at all that Dvořák was deeply impressed by the old Negro "spirituals" and also by Foster's songs. It was my privilege to sing repeatedly some of the old plantation songs for him at his house, and one in particular, "Swing Low, Sweet Chariot," greatly pleased him, and part of this old "spiritual" will be found in the 2nd theme of the first movement of the symphony, in G major, first given out by the flute. The similarity is so evident that it doesn't even need to be heard; the eye can see it. Dvořák saturated himself with the spirit of these old tunes and then invented his own themes. There is a subsidiary theme in G minor in the first movement, with a flat 7th, and I feel sure the composer caught this peculiarity of most of the slave songs from some that I sang to him; for he used to stop me and ask if that was the way the slaves sang.[2]

[2] Quoted by M. (Cuney) Hare, *Negro Music and Musicians,* p. 59.

There is a certain inconsistency in Burleigh's insistence on the identity of the "Swing Low, Sweet Chariot" theme and his statement that "Dvořák saturated himself with the spirit of these old tunes and then invented his own themes." The latter statement I believe to be true, and the thematic similarity merely a coincidence. This is confirmed by a declaration attributed to Dvořák regarding the program notes for the *New World Symphony:* "Omit that nonsense about my having made use of 'Indian' and 'American' motives. That is a lie. I tried only to write in the spirit of those national American melodies." Dvořák, then, did not advocate the literal use of folk tunes. In this he differed from Glinka, who said: "We the composers are only arrangers." Glinka, being only a gifted amateur, could afford such modesty, such self-effacement in favor of the collective document, the traditional tune. But Dvořák, the great composer, was angry at the thought of being considered a mere arranger. Fundamentally, these attitudes represent two significantly different points of view: that of the composer who "dresses up" folk tunes in attractive instrumental colors and that of the composer who, assimilating the elements of folk music, seeks to develop its idiosyncratic traits of idiom and expression. To the first group belong such composers as Glinka, Lalo, Rimsky-Korsakoff. Among representatives of the second group are Dvořák, Grieg, Falla, and Bartók. While these last-mentioned composers used folk tunes occasionally, their aim was not to provide attractive window dressing for folk songs, but rather to explore ways of musical thinking based on the characteristic rhythms, modalities, and melodic intervals of the folk tunes of a given culture.

Dvořák, of course, approached the subject much more superficially than did later composers such as Falla and Bartók, who made a profound study of the folk music of their respective countries (Spain and Hungary). The scientific study of folk music was in its infancy in Dvořák's day, and at the period of his sojourn in the United States almost nobody knew or cared anything about American folk music. Elson reflected the general opinion when he wrote: "It must be admitted that in this field [folk music] America is rather barren." [3] And Frederic L. Ritter asked rhetorically: "How are we to account for this utter absence of national people's music and poetry in America?" [4] The trouble was that most city-bred, Europeanized Americans were

[3] Elson, *The History of American Music,* p. 123.

[4] Ritter, *Music in America,* p. 388.

so busy keeping their noses in the air that they never thought of putting their ears to the ground. When they finally got down to earth, they heard the land shaking with music.

As we know, some Americans began to be interested in the Negro spirituals shortly after the Civil War; and the study of Indian music, begun by Catlin and Schoolcraft in the first half of the nineteenth century, was continued by specialists in the latter decades of the century. But MacDowell was asking superciliously what "the Negro melodies" had to do with "Americanism in art," and sneering at the pattern for "an 'American' national musical costume" offered by "the Bohemian Dvořák." The truth is that Dvořák was not offering a pattern. He was pointing to a potential source of inspiration. And more important than any particular source he mentioned—Negro spirituals or Indian melodies—was the attitude of mind, the spiritual message, that he conveyed to American musicians.

Dvořák, in effect, was saying to the American composer, "Look homeward" and "Cultivate your own garden." He was not simply saying, "Play around with folk tunes for a change." His message, translated into its broader and deeper significance, meant that American composers should turn their attention to the indigenous products of American culture, that they should value and cultivate—by assimilation rather than by imitation—the idiosyncratic elements of musical culture in America. The fact that Dvořák was incompletely acquainted with these elements—that he mistook the part for the whole—is of no particular consequence, for with time and increasing knowledge, American musicians obtained a wider perspective of the subject. The important fact is that he issued a challenge, a challenge which was accepted by a small but enthusiastic and determined group of American composers, with significant results for America's music.

Given the circumstances of his time and background, Dvořák can scarcely be blamed for sharing the common fallacy, expressed by Elson in the dictum that "American folk song in its true sense can only be derived from Indian or plantation life." Of these two elements, Dvořák attached more importance to the so-called "plantation melodies." In this connection it is interesting to note his high regard, mentioned by Burleigh, for the songs of Stephen Foster. This admiration is significant, for Foster, frowned upon by the devotees of the genteel tradition, did not at that time occupy the eminent place in our musical pantheon that we have since accorded to him.

In a statement issued before the New York première of the *New World Symphony* in 1893, Dvořák was quoted as having said, referring to the plantation melodies:

> These beautiful and varied themes are the product of the soil. They are American. They are the folk songs of America, and your composers must turn to them. In the Negro melodies of America I discover all that is needed for a great and noble school of music.

Philosophically and ethnographically considered, it would be easy to find fault with this statement. By this time, however, the reader knows much more about the Negro spirituals than did Dvořák; so there is no need to embark on a lengthy critique of his views. He was on safer ground, because simply expressing a personal preference based on taste, when, in an article published in the *Century Magazine* (February, 1895), he said, "The so-called plantation songs are indeed the most striking and appealing melodies that have been found on this side of the water." When we contrast this with the contemptuous attitude of such musical snobs as Hastings and Dwight—the latter died in the same year that the *New World Symphony* was first performed—we can begin to appreciate the wholesome and liberalizing effect of Dvořák's opinions.

Dvořák, who visited various sections of the United States and lived for a while in Spillville, Iowa, became so enthusiastic about this country that he wrote a Cantata to the American flag and even proposed to write a new national anthem for the United States! In addition to his famous Symphony "From the New World" (No. 5, in E minor), he also composed a String Quartet and a Quintet utilizing themes derived from, or suggested by, the Negro spirituals.

Revolt against German hegemony

The significance of Dvořák's American visit does not reside exclusively in his enthusiasm for American folk songs (as far as he knew them), in his call for the formation of an American "national school" of composition, or in his writing of notable works inspired by his experiences in the New World. All these are important factors, but they are transcended by the over-all liberating influence symbolized by his visit in relation to this particular historical moment in the development of musical culture in the United States. To put it in plain language, let us recall MacDowell's contemptuous reference to the nationalistic notions of "the Bohemian Dvořák," quoted in a previous chapter. On the face of it, one might take MacDowell's epithet as signifying a foreigner, one who is not an American and who therefore has no business telling Americans how they shall create their "national" music. But the implication of MacDowell's epithet seems rather to be somewhat as follows: "Here is a composer *who is not German* and who yet presumes to establish values and directions for American music." Translated into its broader implications, this attitude represents the last stand of the German conservatories and their satellites against the "invasion of the barbarians"—that is, the rise and the spread of invigorating musical forces, coming chiefly from Russia, but also from France, from Bohemia, from the Orient, from the New World.

The German domination of American music was so complete that, in the words of Arthur Farwell, only German music sounded natural to concertgoers in the United States. A revolt against this domination was an absolute historical necessity. Dvořák prepared the way, and the movement of liberation found its American spokesman in the person of Arthur Farwell, musician of the Middle West, who in 1903 boldly proclaimed a plan of action:

> The first correction we must bring to our musical vision is to cease to see everything through German spectacles, however wonderful, however sublime those spectacles may be in themselves! The correction is to be effected by making the thorough acquaintance of Russian and French music of the present, by allowing Russia and France not the mere opportunity of occasionally getting a musical word in edgewise, but of engaging, with Germany, equal shares of our musical conversation. . . . Thus fortified, we will no longer fear that the American composer is going to the dogs when he revels in a new and unusual combination of notes; that is, one which differs from the good old German tradition.[5]

Farwell fearlessly proclaimed the heresy that "France and Russia lead the world today in musical invention, in all that makes for greater plasticity of tone as an art medium."

Was this simply advocating a change of masters? By no means. In the first place, Farwell was not proposing to discard German music, whose achievements he respected and valued. His plea was for an enlightened eclecticism, a search for originality resulting from the inter-

[5] Quoted by Waters, *The Wa-Wan Press*, pp. 222-223.

play of multiple influences. Imitation he believed to be a necessary step in acquiring artistic individuality, but let us begin by imitating *all* styles and forms. Eventually, from the factors of our environment, there would result a characteristically American manner of expression, compounded of many styles, in which would be found: "Notably, ragtime, Negro songs, Indian songs, Cowboy songs, and, of the utmost importance, new and daring expressions of our own composers, sound-speech previously unheard." [6] The last half of this statement we shall leave for later consideration in the chapter dealing with our musical experimentalists. Before commenting on the remainder of the statement, let us learn something about the man who made it.

Arthur Farwell was born in St. Paul, Minnesota, in 1872. Although he received violin lessons from the age of nine, he was not groomed for a musical career. He went east to attend the Massachusetts Institute of Technology, from which he was graduated with a degree in engineering in 1893—the year of the *New World Symphony*. It was after going to Boston that he heard a symphony orchestra for the first time. Music soon became his chief interest, and after graduating he studied composition with Norris in Boston. Following the nearly inevitable trend at that time, he went to Germany in 1897 for study with Humperdinck and Pfitzner; but he also went to Paris, where his teacher was Guilmant. Two years later he returned to the United States and became lecturer on musical history at Cornell University, at the same time taking up the study of American Indian music. After founding the Wa-Wan Press, in 1901, for the publication of American music, he undertook, from 1904, a series of transcontinental tours, lecturing on American music and playing his compositions based on Indian themes. During his travels he studied the Indian music of the Southwest and collected the folk songs of Spanish California. He was eager to embrace the entire range of musical expression in America.

From 1909 to 1917, Farwell was active in New York, as staff writer for *Musical America*, as Supervisor of Municipal Music (1910–1913), and finally as director of the Music School Settlement. For one year (1918–1919) he was on the staff of the University of California, and from 1927 to 1939 he taught at Michigan State College in East Lansing. He wrote the music for several pageants and was keenly interested in developing "Community Music Drama" along the lines of *La Prima-*

[6] Quoted by Waters, *loc. cit.*

vera, produced at Santa Barbara in 1920. Through these varied activities he was brought into firsthand association with virtually every aspect of America's musical life. Farwell died in 1951.

The Wa-Wan Press

It was through the Wa-Wan Press, and the movement that centered around it, that Farwell made his most significant contribution to the advancement of America's music. He had been unable to find a publisher for his Indian melodies, and he felt that the American composer simply had no status in his own country. He knew that he was not alone in this feeling. One night, while he was thinking about this problem, there suddenly came to him "the thought of William Blake and William Morris, with their presses, printing their own work and that of colleagues, at least in Morris' case." There, he believed, was the solution. Combining his work with that of others, he would "launch a progressive movement for American music, *including a definite acceptance of Dvořák's challenge to go after our folk music*" (my italics). He talked it over with Edgar Stillman Kelley and others, and they were all for it.

The enterprise was launched without capital and without financial backing of any kind. Farwell engaged a local printer in Newton Center, Massachusetts, borrowed a few dollars for postage, and set out to get subscribers. The music engraving and lithography were done in Boston. The plan was to bring out two books of music each quarter; later the publications were also issued separately, in sheet-music form. During one year the press did receive a modest subsidy from George Foster Peabody, but mostly it was supported by Farwell's lectures, for the subscriptions did not always cover expenses. The enterprise continued for eleven years and the catalogue was then turned over to the firm of G. Schirmer (excepting the compositions of Gilbert and Troyer).

In his preliminary announcement of the Wa-Wan Press, Farwell stated:

> The Wa-Wan Press is a natural outcome of the rapid growth of true musical genius in America, and in proportion to its capacity and growth, will aim to render available hitherto unpublished compositions of the highest order, which because of circumstances which the

art-life of America is rapidly outgrowing, have heretofore been denied the daylight of print.

He also declared:

> We are in earnest. We shall ask of the composer, not that he submit to us work which is likely to be in demand, but that he express himself. We shall do our utmost to foster individuality. Name shall be nothing to us. We shall stand for no particular composer, but for a principle. . . . We shall avoid the trivial, the ephemeral, the merely pretty, and seek the poetic and vitally emotional, striving to produce works of genial fire and enduring worth.

To what extent did the publications of the Wa-Wan Press bear out this ambitious program? As far as catholicity of selection and artistic integrity are concerned, the record is creditable. As regards "genial fire and enduring worth"—which are rare in any place and any age—the results were somewhat less satisfactory. Of the thirty-seven composers represented in the catalogue of the Wa-Wan Press, the most important, besides Farwell himself, are Henry F. B. Gilbert, Arthur Shepherd, Edward B. Hill, Harvey W. Loomis, Frederic Ayres, and Edgar Stillman Kelley. Of these, only Farwell, Gilbert, and Shepherd may be said to have achieved a considerable degree of significance in our national music. Others, however, acquired an estimable reputation in various fields: Arthur Olaf Andersen, John P. Beach, Gena Branscombe, Natalie Curtis Burlin, Rubin Goldmark, Katherine Ruth Heyman, Carlos Troyer, Arne Oldberg, and Louis Campbell Tipton. Let us admit that this is scarcely a roster of flaming genius. Nevertheless, looking at the movement as a whole, there are positive values. One notices a remarkable variety of individual interests and backgrounds. This was not *coterie* music. This was not a *clique* of Indianists and Negrophiles. We have here a group of young artists working in the musical medium, striving to develop their creative capacities and to gain a hearing in a society that had hitherto virtually refused to acknowledge their existence, or even to recognize that, as social beings, they had any rightful relation to the *res publica*. The Wa-Wan Press was intended to establish the identity of the American composer as a free creative artist, independent of commercial interests.

In retrospect, Farwell wrote of his publishing venture: "There were two major departments of our plan. One comprised all American work showing talent or progress along any of the paths of musical tradition. The other comprised all interesting or worthwhile work done with American folk-material as a basis." Let us examine further the second department of this plan. Among those comparatively few composers who turned to folk material in publications issued by the Wa-Wan Press, the main interest centered on American Indian music. Farwell himself brought out *American Indian Melodies* (1901), *The Domain of Hurakan* (1902), *Impressions of the Wa-Wan Ceremony of the Omahas* (1906), *From Mesa and Plain* (Indian, Cowboy, and Negro Sketches, 1905), and *Dawn* (1902), based on Omaha Indian themes. All these were for piano solo. The *Navajo War Dance* (one of the pieces in *From Mesa and Plain*) and *Dawn* were also arranged for orchestra (unpublished). In addition, the catalogue included Farwell's collection, for voice with piano accompaniment, *Folk-Songs of the West and South* (Negro, Cowboy, and Spanish-California). Harvey Worthington Loomis was represented by his *Lyrics of the Red-Man,* already mentioned. Carlos Troyer (1837–1920), who made a special study of Indian music of the Southwest, contributed two series of *Traditional Songs of the Zúñis* for voice and piano (1904), *Hymn to the Sun* ("An ancient jubilee song of the sun-worshippers. With historic account of the ceremony and the derivation of music from the sun's rays"), *Ghost Dance of the Zúñis,* and *Kiowa-Apache War-Dance.*

An eclectic folklorist

In the case of Henry Franklin Belknap Gilbert (1868–1928) we find a composer whose interest in folk music ranged over the world. This interest is only slightly adumbrated in his publications for the Wa-Wan Press, though it is curious to notice the inclusion of *Two South American Gypsy Songs* ("La Montonera" and "Zambulidora" indicating that, after Gottschalk, he was one of our first composers to take an interest in Latin American music (his ethnology, however, was weak: there is no "Gypsy" music in South America). The *Negro Episode* for piano (1902) reflects another phase of Gilbert's concern with American material.

Henry Gilbert had an unorthodox background. Though he was MacDowell's first American pupil in Boston (1889–1892), he led no sheltered academic existence. While studying composition he earned a living playing the violin for dances and in theater orchestras. Later he took up miscellaneous occupations: real-estate agent, factory foreman, silkworm grower, and bread- and pie-cutter in a restaurant at the Chicago World's Fair of 1893. Eager to hear the first performance of Charpentier's opera *Louise* in Paris, he went to Europe on a cattle boat. Soon after the founding of the Wa-Wan Press he and Farwell became close friends, drawn together by a common interest in folklore and in promoting a national musical movement. Gilbert was an eclectic by choice: his nationalism was not narrow. This is how he explained his attitude toward music:

> It has been my ideal not to allow any composer or school of music to influence me to the point of imitating them. I have striven to express my own individuality regardless whether it was good, bad, or indifferent. I prefer my own hat to a borrowed crown. Of course, I have had many admirations and have absorbed musical nutriment from many sources. . . . More than the music of any individual composer; more than the music of any particular school, the folk tunes of the world, of all nationalities, races, and peoples, have been to me a never-failing source of delight, wonder, and inspiration. In them I can hear the spirit of all great music. Through them I can feel the very heart-beat of humanity. Simple as these folk melodies are in structure, they yet speak to me so poignantly, and with such a deep sincerity of expression, as to be (for myself, at least) more pregnant with inspirational suggestion than the music of any *one* composer.[7]

It is important to note that Gilbert's concern with "native" American music went hand in hand with an enthusiasm for music of the folk everywhere, of all nationalities and all races throughout the world. This is a significant point, to which we shall return later. It prepares the way for that eclecticism which I take to be the essence of America's music.

In a foreword printed with the score of his symphonic poem *The Dance in Place Congo,* Gilbert described the basis of his musical nationalism:

> It has been for a long time an ideal of mine to write some music which should be in its inspiration native to America. The efforts of my compatriots, though frequently very fine technically, failed to

[7] Quoted by Farwell, *Music in America,* p. 408.

> satisfy me. To my mind they leaned far too heavily upon the tradition of Europe, and seemed to me to ignore too completely the very genuine touches of inspiration which exist in *our* history, *our* temperament, and *our* national life. I was, therefore, moved to strike out boldly on a different course. . . .

Gilbert furthermore tells us that in casting about for an American subject upon which to base a symphonic poem he was much attracted by the picturesque quality of the life in New Orleans during the antebellum days. Notice that what attracts him is the *picturesque,* and that he is drawn to what I have called "The Exotic Periphery" in America's musical culture. He came across the article by George W. Cable in the *Century Magazine* describing the dancing in Place Congo and decided to use this as a background for a symphonic poem, taking his themes from the tunes published by Cable (quoted in Chapter 15). The first episode is developed from the melody that Cable calls a "bamboula" (see musical example on page 308). Gilbert saw in this material "a strong and romantic picture . . . full of dramatic and colorful suggestion," and he treated it Romantically, that is, descriptively and dramatically. The subject, indeed, struck him as "so picturesque and so full of dramatic possibility" that he decided, after completing the score, to write a scenario for it, thus transforming the work into a ballet-pantomime which was performed at the Metropolitan Opera House, New York, on March 23, 1918. Later it was performed by the Boston Symphony Orchestra as a symphonic poem.

The same orchestra had performed, in 1911, Gilbert's *Comedy Overture on Negro Themes,* the first work that brought him national recognition. It was originally planned as an overture for an opera (never completed) based on the Uncle Remus stories. The overture is based on two short (four-measure) melodies taken from the collection *Bahama Songs and Stories* by Charles L. Edwards, a highly interesting work published in 1895, on part of a Mississippi boat song, "I'se gwine to Alabammy, oh," and on the first four measures of the spiritual "Old Ship of Zion," used as the subject of a fugue.

In his *Negro Rhapsody* (1913) Gilbert attempted to contrast the "barbaric" and the "spiritual" elements in Afro-American culture. Ten years earlier he had turned to tunes of the blackface minstrel tradition —"Zip Coon," "Dearest May," and "Don't Be Foolish, Joe"—in his *Americanesque* for orchestra. A set of three *American Dances in Ragtime Rhythm* was another incursion in the field of musical Americana.

With his five *Indian Scenes* for piano, Gilbert delved into Indian lore. He roamed further afield with his *Celtic Studies* for voice and piano (1905), and various piano pieces, including *The Island of the Fay* (after Poe) and *Two Verlaine Moods* (1903). *Salâmmbo's Invocation to Tanith* (1902), originally for voice with piano, was subsequently orchestrated. The *Fish Wharf Rhapsody* (1909) for voice with piano, is an experiment in musical realism. Finally, we should mention the Symphonic Prelude to Synge's drama, *Riders to the Sea*, originally written for small orchestra (1904), later expanded for full orchestra.

Though Gilbert's music "dates" perceptibly and is often derivative, he deserves to be honored as a forward-looking pioneer. His place in American music has been aptly summed up by Arthur Farwell: "Often rough in technique, though greatly resourceful, and rich in orchestral imagination, it is to the spirit of the time and nation that Gilbert makes his contribution and his appeal." [8]

Of Farwell himself, as a composer, something more must be said, for the reader should not be left with the impression that he was merely an arranger of Indian music. His orchestral works include *Symbolistic Study No. 3* (after Walt Whitman, 1922), *The Gods of the Mountain* (suite, 1927), *Symbolistic Study No. 6: Mountain Vision* (piano concerto in one movement, 1931), *Prelude to a Spiritual Drama* (1932), and *Rudolph Gott Symphony* (1934). His *Mountain Song* (1931) is a symphonic work in five movements with incidental songs by mixed chorus. His chamber music includes a String Quartet (*The Hako*), a Piano Quintet, and a Sonata for Violin and piano. In his later works he experimented with the use of Oriental scales. Farwell was the prototype of the eclectic composer in America.

Other "Indianist" composers

Among other composers who have utilized American Indian material, Charles Wakefield Cadman (1881–1947) achieved wide popularity with his song "The Land of the Sky Blue Water," in which the indigenous elements are so thickly sugar-coated as to be almost imperceptible. Cadman composed two operas dealing with the relation of the Indians to the civilization of the whites. The first of these, *Shanewis*, was produced at the Metropolitan Opera House in 1918;

[8] Farwell, *loc. cit.*

the second, *The Sunset Trail,* received its première at Denver in 1925. His *Thunderbird Suite* for piano (also orchestrated) is based on Omaha themes. After 1925 Cadman began to be less interested in Indian music, and turning to other aspects of Americana, composed the two-act opera *A Witch of Salem* (1926), *Dark Dancers of the Mardi Gras* for piano and orchestra (1933), *American Suite* (1937), and the overture *Huck Finn* (1945). His "abstract" compositions include a Symphony and some chamber music. He was a minor figure in the development of musical nationalism in America; his style is facile and undistinctive.

Charles Sanford Skilton (1868–1941), in spite of his New England background, his education at Yale University, and his musical training in Berlin, became strongly attracted to Indian music after he went to teach at the State University of Kansas in 1915. Like Cadman, he composed "Indian" operas: *Kalopin* (three acts, 1927) and *The Sun Bride* (one act, 1930). For orchestra he wrote *Two Indian Dances* (*Deer Dance, War Dance*), *Suite Primeval, American Indian Fantasie* (with cello solo), and *Sioux Flute Serenade* (chamber orchestra). Widely performed in its day, his Indianizing music, superficial and conventional, has for us now solely the interest of a period piece, demonstrating the "picture postcard" school of "native" music.

Arthur Nevin (1871–1943), brother of Ethelbert Nevin, composed the opera *Poia,* based on the traditional lore of the Blackfeet Indians of Montana. Curiously enough, this work was produced not in America but at the Royal Opera House in Berlin (1909). Two foreign-born musicians who settled in the United States, Alberto Bimboni and Carl Busch, became, like "Father" Heinrich, enamored of American Indian music. Bimboni composed the opera *Winona* (1926), using Indian themes, with the chorus singing in unison. Busch wrote the symphonic poem *Minnehaha's Vision, Four Indian Tribal Melodies* for string orchestra, and *A Chant from the Great Plains* for military band.

The "Indianist" movement in American music may now be recognized as a transitory phase. It attracted a number of composers who were looking for something indigenous, something that could immediately and unmistakably be identified as "American." But the fallacy of attempting to create representative American music out of Indian material soon became apparent. Indian tribal music was not part of the main stream of American culture. It was an interesting but essentially exotic branch that one could follow for a time as a digression, a diversion from the European heritage. But if followed to its source it led to a primitive culture that had nothing in common with prevailing norms and trends of American civilization. It is perhaps fair to say that nowadays we are more interested in the study of Indian tribal music for its own sake, as a manifestation of primitive cultural patterns, than for its possible influence on American art music and its hypothetical contributions to musical "nationalism." Indeed, musical nationalism as it was understood at the beginning of this century appears to have run its course in the United States, and with its decline as a main issue, the interest of our composers in utilizing Indian material rapidly waned. The momentum of the Indianist movement ceased about twenty-five years ago, and it is not likely to be revived.

The Anglo-American heritage

In addition to those American composers who turned to Afro-American and Indian tribal material, there were some who held that the real roots of American national music lay in the tradition of Anglo-American folk song. A leading representative of this school is John Powell, born in Richmond, Virginia, in 1882. A pupil of Leschetizky in Vienna, he appeared frequently as a pianist, often in performances of his own works, such as the *Negro Rhapsody* for piano and orchestra (1918) and *Sonata Virginianesque* for violin and piano (1919). Although Powell used highly stylized Negro material in the two works just mentioned—both of which have programmatic connotations—his abiding concern has been with the cultivation of Anglo-American folk music, of which there exists a rich heritage in his native state of Virginia.

Among Powell's compositions utilizing Anglo-American folk music are the overture *In Old Virginia* (1921); *Natchez on the Hill* (1932) and *A Set of Three* (1935), both for orchestra; *At the Fair*, suite for chamber orchestra (1925); *The Babe of Bethlehem*, folk carol for mixed chorus *a cappella; Soldier, Soldier*, folk song for chorus *a cappella* with soprano and baritone solos; *Five Virginia Folk Songs* for baritone and piano; *Twelve Folk Hymns;* and the Symphony in A, commissioned by the National Federation of Music Clubs and first performed by the Detroit Symphony Orchestra on April 26, 1947. This symphony is a noble, sincere, and ambitious effort to apply the neo-romantic symphonic technique to the development of Anglo-

American folk themes. It comes out of a lifetime of devotion to, and close study of, this aspect of America's music. Yet, impressive though it may be, the Symphony in A leaves one with the suspicion that its aesthetic premise and its technical apparatus are outmoded. It is a grand monument, but one feels that the folk songs from which it derives possess more vitality and a more enduring quality.

John Powell is definitely a composer of the South, one of the few distinctly regional composers of any stature that the United States has produced. For Daniel Gregory Mason, a New England colleague who believes in the absolute and representative value of the Anglo-American tradition in America's music, the significance of Powell's contribution is more than regional. Holding to the conviction that the characteristic musical expression of America must be based on what he calls "Anglo-Saxon reticence," Mason cites Powell's overture *In Old Virginia* as an example of this reticence. According to Mason: "This Anglo-Saxon element in our heterogeneous national character, however quantitatively in the minority nowadays, is qualitatively of crucial significance in determining what we call the American temper."[9] It is difficult to see how the national temper or character can be determined by an element that is quantitatively in the minority. It seems more reasonable to hold that "our heterogeneous national character" itself determines what is "the American temper"—all-embracing, generous, and expansive. That is why we really have no "national" school in American music.

[9] Mason, *Tune In, America*, p. 160. This book, incidentally, offers a striking instance of musical anti-Semitism. The author quotes himself in an earlier magazine article, as follows: "The insidiousness of the Jewish menace to our artistic integrity . . . is due to the speciousness, the superficial charm and persuasiveness of Hebrew art, its violently juxtaposed extremes of passion, its poignant eroticism and pessimism." There is much more to this effect; I quote it merely as a curiosity in our musical literature.

chapter twenty

Indian tribal music

I believe it to be true that among no people, the world over, is music so loved and so generally used as among the North American Indians.
FREDERICK R. BURTON, AMERICAN PRIMITIVE MUSIC, 1909.

The Indians of North America comprise many tribes, each with its own language, customs, and traditions. Even though we limit our study to those regions of North America contained within the present boundaries of the United States, the number of tribes is disconcerting for the purpose of a brief survey. Nevertheless, in spite of these differences, Indian tribal music as a whole possesses certain common traits that permit a degree of generalization. Our method will be to proceed from the general to the particular, giving a résumé of the general characteristics of North American Indian music, and then illustrating its specific manifestations with examples drawn from representative tribes of various regions.

All competent observers agree on the importance of music in Indian culture. In the words of Natalie Curtis Burlin:

> Wellnigh impossible is it for civilized man to conceive of the importance of song in the life of the Indian. To the Indian, song is the breath of the spirit that consecrates the acts of life. Not all songs are religious, but there is scarcely a task, light or grave, scarcely an event, great or small, but has its fitting song.[1]

And Alice C. Fletcher writes:

> Music enveloped the Indian's individual and social life like an atmosphere. There was no important personal experience where it did not bear a part, nor any ceremonial where it was not essential to

[1] Burlin, *The Indians' Book*, p. xxx.

the expression of religious feeling. The songs of a tribe were coextensive with the life of the people.[2]

Passages of similar tenor could be cited from the writings of those who have made the closest study of the Indians and their music.

It is only within the past sixty years or so that Indian tribal music in the United States has been the object of systematic and concentrated investigation by musicians and ethnologists. Earlier writings on Indian life and lore, such as those of Henry Rowe Schoolcraft (1793–1864) and George Catlin (1796–1872) contained only passing references to music in connection with the songs, dances, and ceremonies of the various tribes. The first scientific monograph to be published on North American Indian music was Theodore Baker's *Über die Musik der Nordamerikanischen Wilden* (Leipzig, 1882). Baker was an American musicologist who studied in Leipzig and who chose American Indian music as the subject for his doctoral thesis. He spent the summer of 1880 among the Senecas in western New York and then visited the Training School for Indian Youth in Carlisle, Pennsylvania. His treatise, admirably organized and documented, copiously illustrated with transcriptions of tribal melodies, remains a basic work in its field. Strangely enough, Baker himself never saw fit to translate his work into English; and as no one else has undertaken the task, his book remains comparatively little known and of limited influence. Edward MacDowell, however, used it as the source for the themes in his *Indian Suite* for orchestra.

Indian studies in the United States owe much to Mrs. Mary Hemenway of Boston, who from 1887 until her death in 1894 sponsored the Hemenway Southwestern Expedition. Mrs. Hemenway also commissioned J. Walter Fewkes to study Indian folklore among the Passamaquoddy of Maine, in the winter of 1889–1890. Fewkes, on this occasion, was the first to employ a phonograph in the study of Indian music and speech. In the summer of 1889 Fewkes was appointed director of the Hemenway Expedition (succeeding Frank C. Cushing) and thereupon proceeded to apply the phonograph to the investigation of Zuñi and Hopi tribal music. The melodies thus recorded were transcribed and analyzed, with a wealth of scientific apparatus, by

[2] Fletcher, *Indian Story and Song*, p. 114.

Benjamin Ives Gilman, and published in *A Journal of American Ethnology and Archaeology*, a publication in five volumes containing the reports of the Hemenway Southwestern Expedition. This remains the most valuable source for the study of Zuñi and Hopi tribal music.

The first work on Indian music to attract wide attention was that of Alice C. Fletcher, who began to study the songs of the Omaha Indians around 1882 and whose findings were published in 1893 by the Peabody Museum of Harvard University. She had the assistance of Francis La Flesche, an Omaha Indian, and of John Comfort Fillmore, a trained musician who analyzed and harmonized the tribal melodies. In 1900 she published a small popular book, *Indian Story and Song From North America*, with melodies harmonized by Fillmore.

Frederick R. Burton and Natalie Curtis (later Mrs. Paul Burlin) began to work among the Indians about the same time but independently, around 1901. Burton, a composer, worked chiefly among the Ojibways (Chippewas) in Minnesota and Wisconsin, while Natalie Curtis concentrated on the Southwest area (Hopis and Zuñis), though eventually she extended her field of interest and included songs of many tribes in *The Indians' Book*, which she published in 1907. Burton's book, *American Primitive Music*, appeared two years later, shortly after his death. Miss Curtis printed only the melodies and words of the songs, without accompaniment. Burton, who was interested in using Indian themes in his compositions (he wrote music for *Hiawatha* in 1882), printed the unaccompanied melodies in the body of his book and added an appendix with his harmonizations, some of which are rather elaborately developed as art songs. Natalie Curtis Burlin, a devoted and enthusiastic student of Indian lore, died in Paris in 1921, as the result of being struck by a motor vehicle.

The study of Indian tribal music undertaken by Arthur Farwell and other American composers in the early decades of the present century, and the use made of this material in American art music, have been discussed in the previous chapter. It remains to speak here of the studies of Indian music made over a long period of years by Frances Densmore, who from 1907 worked under the auspices of the Bureau of American Ethnology of the Smithsonian Institution, which published her findings in its Bulletins. These studies, embracing tribal melodies of the Chippewa, Mandan and Hidatsa, Menominee, Northern

Ute, Papago, Pawnee, Teton Sioux, Tule (Panama), and Yuman and Yaqui Indians, constitute the most comprehensive and objective survey and analysis of North American Indian music thus far undertaken. Miss Densmore's monographs, containing hundreds of melodies, many illustrations, and a wealth of background material on Indian lore, have provided the principal source of material for this chapter.

General characteristics of Indian music

Of the three main elements of musical structure—melody, harmony, and rhythm—there is general agreement that rhythm is the most important in Indian tribal music. Miss Densmore's remarks on Chippewa songs are generally applicable to most Indian tribal music. Her analysis shows that the large majority of songs consists of "simple intervals and complicated rhythms." Further:

> The tones comprised in the songs are limited in number, many of the songs containing only three or four tones, except as the number is extended by repetition in a lower octave; the variety of rhythms is great. . . . Accidentals rarely occur in the songs. An accidental in the opening measures of a song is worthy of little consideration, as in many instances the introductory measures are sung only once, and the singer is allowed some freedom in them. The rhythm of the song is determined by noting the accented tones and dividing the song into measures according to them.
>
> By observation we find that in many of the songs the metric unit is the measure, not the individual count in the measure. In these instances the accented measure beginnings are found to conform to a very slow metronome beat, but the intervening tones are irregular in length and can not be accurately indicated by note values. These songs would probably be chants except for the freedom of their melody progressions. . . .
>
> There are other songs in which two or more measures of varying lengths combine to form a rhythmic unit, which is repeated throughout the song. One measure constitutes the rhythmic unit, which is continuously repeated. . . .
>
> The drum and voice are usually independent in metric units, the drum being a rapid unaccented beat and the voice having a rhythm which bears a relation to the mental concept of the song.[3]

[3] Densmore, *Chippewa Music,* part I, p. 18.

This metrical independence of the singing voice and the accompanying drum is strongly characteristic of tribal music and is a feature that has baffled many non-Indian observers.

In her melodic analyses, Miss Densmore makes reference to the five pentatonic or five-toned scales as tabulated by Helmholtz, as follows:

1. The First Scale, without Third or Seventh (Keynote G; sequence of tones G, A, C, D, E).
2. The Second Scale, without Second or Sixth (Keynote A; sequence of tones A, C, D, E, G).
3. The Third Scale, without Third and Sixth (Keynote D; sequence of tones D, E, G, A, C).
4. The Fourth Scale, without Fourth or Seventh (Keynote C; sequence of tones C, D, E, G, A).
5. The Fifth Scale, without Second and Fifth (Keynote E; sequence of tones E, G, A, C, D).

An analysis of 600 Indian melodies (Chippewa and Sioux) revealed that 137 songs used the Fourth Five-toned Scale, and 74 the Second Five-toned Scale. The other pentatonic scales appeared with insignificant frequency. Fifty-four melodies used the octave complete except for the seventh; 49 the minor triad and fourth; 46 the major triad and sixth; 35 the octave complete; 29 the octave complete except for the sixth; 22 the octave except seventh and sixth; and 21 the octave except seventh and second. Approximately half of the songs were found to be in the major tonality and half in the minor tonality. As regards the last note of the song, 371 were found to end on the keynote, 155 on the fifth, and 72 on the third. Eighty-five per cent of the melodies contained no accidentals. As regards structure, 397 songs were classified as melodic (meaning that "contiguous accented tones do not bear a simple chord-relation to each other"), 85 as melodic with harmonic framework, and 116 as harmonic. Miss Densmore's analysis includes many other factors, but the above summary is sufficient to convey a general idea of the structure of Indian tribal melodies.

It should be remembered, of course, that the Indian has no conception of scales, modes, or tonality as such. Analysis simply reveals that his melodies tend to fall into certain basic tonal patterns that are common to large segments of primitive music throughout the world.

The concept of harmony is also foreign to the Indian mind. Indian tribal melodies are sung as solos or in unison.

The manner of singing is very important in Indian music. As described by Alice Fletcher:

> The continual slurring of the voice from one tone to another produces upon us the impression of out-of-tune singing. Then, the custom of singing out of doors, to the accompaniment of the drum, and against the various noises of the camp, and the ever-restless wind, tending to strain the voice and robbing it of sweetness, increases the difficulty of distinguishing the music concealed within the noise,—a difficulty still further aggravated by the habit of pulsating the voice, creating a rhythm within the rhythm of the song.[4]

Miss Densmore observes that the Indian "greatly admires a pronounced vibrato" and that "a falsetto tone is also considered a mark of musical proficiency." She remarks also that "a peculiar nasal tone is always used in the love songs." As regards intonation, considerable variation was found, according to the proficiency of the singer. Indians with a reputation for being good singers "keep the pitch of their tones approximately that of the tones of the diatonic scale." Intervals with accidentals are sung more accurately than those without accidentals. There is considerable accuracy in the repetition of songs. While deviations from correct diatonic pitch occur, there is no evidence of systematic microtonal alteration.

Downward melodic progressions occur with about twice the frequency of upward progressions. The two intervals most frequently found in both downward and upward progressions are the major second and the minor third. In general the line of the melody is descending.

The Indians of the United States have only two types of native musical instruments: pipe and percussion. The pipelike instrument, often referred to as a "flute," is in reality a kind of flageolet, blown at the end instead of at the side. This is about 18 to 24 inches long, pierced with six holes, and capable of playing a complete octave; but the intonation is inaccurate. Love songs are often played on the flageolet, by a lover to his sweetheart, as a form of courtship. There are also small pipes, with three holes, that play up to five tones.

[4] Fletcher, *op. cit.*, p. 117.

The percussion instruments consist of drums and various kinds of rattles. There is a water drum consisting of a small keg partly filled with water and covered with a skin; its pitch may be changed by wetting the cover or by scraping it dry. Drums are of different sizes and facture. Many were made from hollow logs, covered with untanned deerskin, and played with a curved stick. Most songs are accompanied by drums, many by rattles also. The Iroquois use rattles made from gourds, from the horns of steers, and from the carapaces of turtles, with a stick inserted through the head and neck to form a handle.

The Iroquois and the Chippewas

We may begin our survey of tribal melodies with those of the Iroquois, or "The Five Nations"—the Mohawk, Oneida, Onondaga, Cayuga, and Seneca tribes—who occupied the central part of New York State and who still adhere to many of their ancestral traditions. It will be recalled that Theodore Baker spent some time collecting the tribal melodies of the Senecas. He transcribed several songs of the Harvest Festival, celebrated every year at the time of the ripening of the corn. Herewith is the "First Harvest Song," of which the words, according to Baker, mean: "He came from Heaven to us lowly ones and gave us these words."

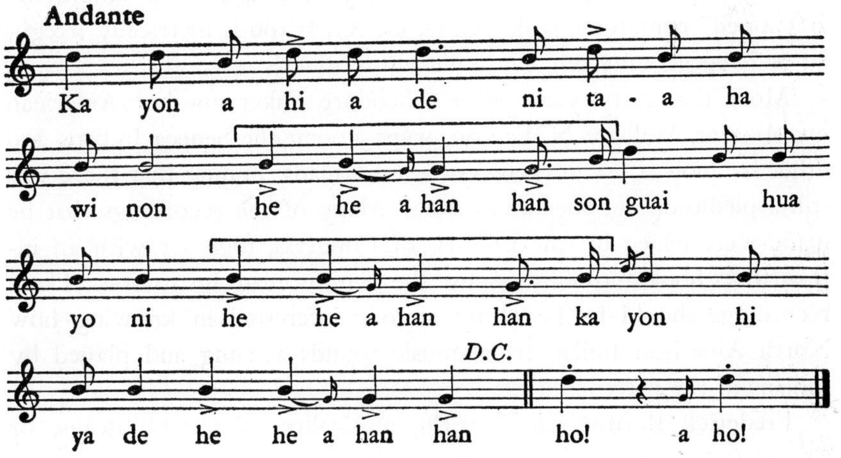

It will be noticed that the melody employs only three tones, that there are many repeated tones, that the melodic line descends a fifth, and that the metrical pattern is irregular, with but one figure repeated (marked with a bracket).

Another Iroquois tribal melody transcribed by Baker is that of the *Women's Dance*, for which the words, he says, have no exact meaning. While the women danced, a chorus of seventeen young men sang this song, fifteen of them accompanying themselves with rattles and two with drums, in unison:

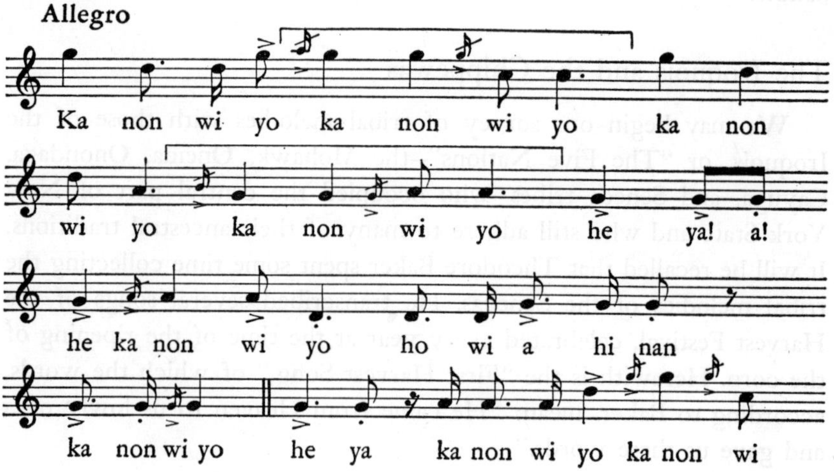
Allegro
Ka non wi yo ka non wi yo ka non
wi yo ka non wi yo he ya! a!
he ka non wi yo ho wi a hi nan
ka non wi yo he ya ka non wi yo ka non wi

Having only four tones, this melody may be considered as employing a "gapped" pentatonic scale (C, D, G, A). It too is metrically irregular and repeats only one rhythmic figure exactly.

More than fifty years after Theodore Baker another American investigator, William N. Fenton, went among the Seneca Indians and other Iroquois tribes in New York and Canada, finding that there was still a plenitude of songs and dances. Many of the recordings that he made were issued by the Library of Congress, together with an informative booklet published by the Smithsonian Institution. These recordings should be heard by anyone interested in knowing how North American Indian tribal music sounds as sung and played by Indians of the present time.

Frederick Burton felt that the musicality of the Ojibways, or Chippewas, the tribe to which he devoted special attention, was superior to that of other North American Indian tribes. While this is doubtless a purely subjective judgment, it is true that he managed to find among the Ojibways of Minnesota a number of attractive tunes, such as "My Bark Canoe" and "The Lake Sheen," which, harmonized and provided with stylized piano accompaniments, caused these songs to become widely and favorably known. These artistic versions, however, belong more to what might be called the "aesthetic projection" of Indian music than to the traditional lore of tribal song. On the other hand, Burton included in his book some unharmonized melodies that reflect more faithfully the character of the traditional music. One of these is a song known to be of considerable antiquity, for Schoolcraft made a versified translation of the words in the 1840s. Of course the music underwent some change during the intervening period, and in fact Burton recorded three different versions of the song, which he believed revealed different stages of development. He found one version that was quite long and involved much repetition. Another version, the one generally current among the Ojibways at that time, was shortened by the omission of several repetitions. Burton was inclined "to believe that the change from the older to the modern version was due to the Ojibway's groping for formal, that is, artistic expression." And he declared: "Musically the song is far better in the modern version because there are fewer repetitions of the leading phrase." Actually, while the compressed version of the song may be "better" according to our artistic standards, it may not be so from the viewpoint of Indian tradition, in which repetition is a fundamental trait. At any rate, Burton transcribed a third version of "The Lake Sheen" (as he called it), sung by an old man who probably adhered rather closely to the traditional pattern of the melody: [5]

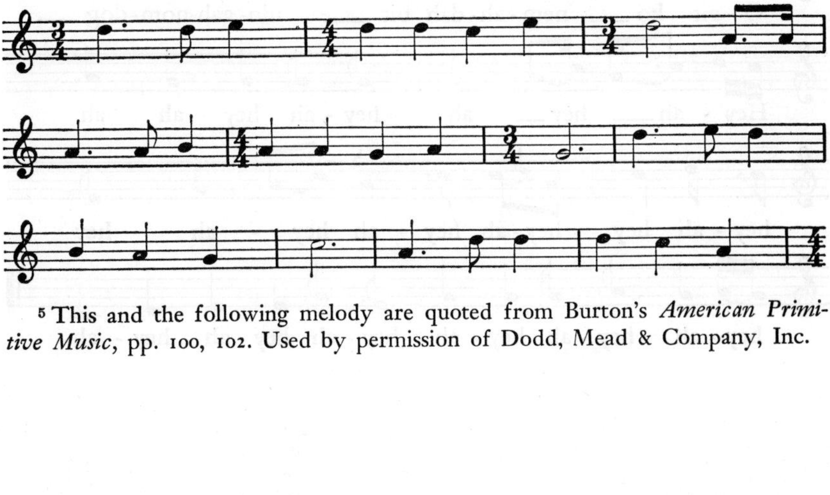

[5] This and the following melody are quoted from Burton's *American Primitive Music,* pp. 100, 102. Used by permission of Dodd, Mead & Company, Inc.

This melody was sung to words meaning: "I have lost my sweetheart, but I will leave no place unsearched and will find her if it takes me all night. As day breaks I think I can see her in the distance, but as I draw near I find that what I saw was the flash of a loon's wing on the water."

A more characteristic tribal melody that Burton recorded among the Ojibways is a "Visiting Song," most of the words of which consist of meaningless syllables, with one phrase signifying, "Who sits on the ice will hear me singing"—which indicates that it was a song used for visiting in winter. The introduction, the descending melodic line, and the conventional ending, are typical:

This melody falls within the structure of the Fourth Five-toned Scale, with the fourth and the seventh omitted and the keynote of C.

In her study of Omaha Indian music (which embraced the linguistically related tribes of the Dakotas, Otos, and Poncas), Alice Fletcher made some significant observations concerning the role of words in Indian tribal songs. She writes:

> Words clearly enunciated in singing break the melody to the Indian ear and mar the music. They say of us that we "talk a great deal as we sing." Comparatively few Indian songs are supplied with words, and when they are so supplied, the words are frequently taken apart or modified so as to make them more melodious; moreover, the selection of the words and their arrangement do not always correspond to that which obtains in ordinary speech. A majority of the songs, however, are furnished almost wholly with syllables which are not parts or even fragments of words but sounds that lend themselves easily to singing and are without definite meaning; yet when a composer has once set syllables to his song, they are never changed or transposed but preserved with as much accuracy as we would observe in maintaining the integrity of a poem.[6]

This passage once more confirms that what is accepted as "good" in one cultural tradition appears to be "bad" in another cultural tradition. It also points to one of the fundamental factors that have to be understood if we are to appreciate the essential qualities of Indian tribal song.

Since the Omaha melodies collected by Miss Fletcher were harmonized by Fillmore, and as it is our policy not to include harmonizations in this chapter because they are alien to the tradition of Indian music, the linguistic family of these Plains Indians will be represented here by a "Night Song" (serenade) of the Dakotas, transcribed by Baker. It was sung by several young men walking through the village, to the accompaniment of a drum.

DRUM RHYTHM (♩=96)

etc.

[6] Fletcher, *A Study of Omaha Indian Music*, p. 12.

Andante con moto

Shi ce shi ce shan te ma shi ca shi
ce la ka shi ce na pi ma yu za - a!

The Ojibways are one of the largest of the North American Indian tribes, a branch of the Algonquins, formerly spread over a vast region from the Great Lakes to the Dakotas, now consisting of some 30,000 people, half of whom live in the United States and half in Canada. Frances Densmore, in reporting extensively on the music of these Indians, preferred to use for them the more widely accepted name Chippewa, rather than Ojibway, used by Burton. Miss Densmore began to study the music of the Chippewas in 1907 and published her findings in *Bulletins Nos. 45* and *53* of the Bureau of American Ethnology. Music, she wrote, "is one of the greatest pleasures of the Chippewa." And: "Every phase of Chippewa life is expressed in music."

The Chippewas were frequently engaged in warfare with the Sioux. An old Chippewa Indian named Odjib'we recounted many of his experiences as a warrior and sang several songs of the warpath, of which the following is a typical example. The words mean: "I will go to the south/ I will bring the south wind." This was sung by the leader of a war party or by the scouts:

(♩=112) (VOICE AND DRUM)

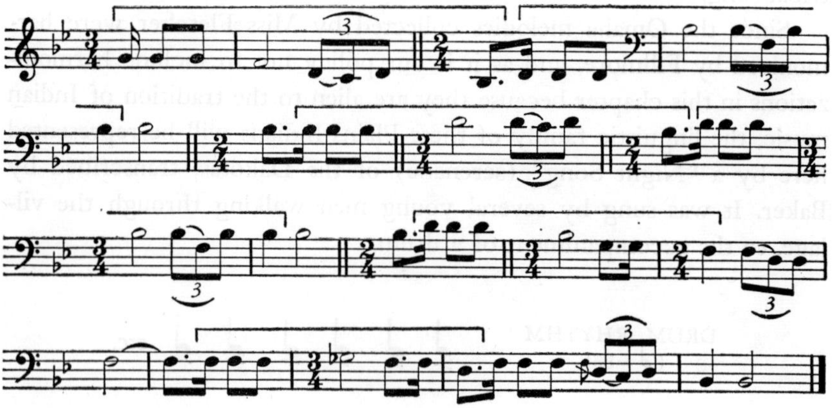

The following drum rhythm was used for the accompaniment of this song.

DRUM RHYTHM

A Chippewa song of more definitely warlike character, the "Arrow Song," also sung by Odjib'we, was used while the warriors dipped the heads of their war arrows in red "medicine." The text is concise: "Scarlet is its head." The song is interesting both for its rhythmic and melodic contours.

VOICE (♩=60)

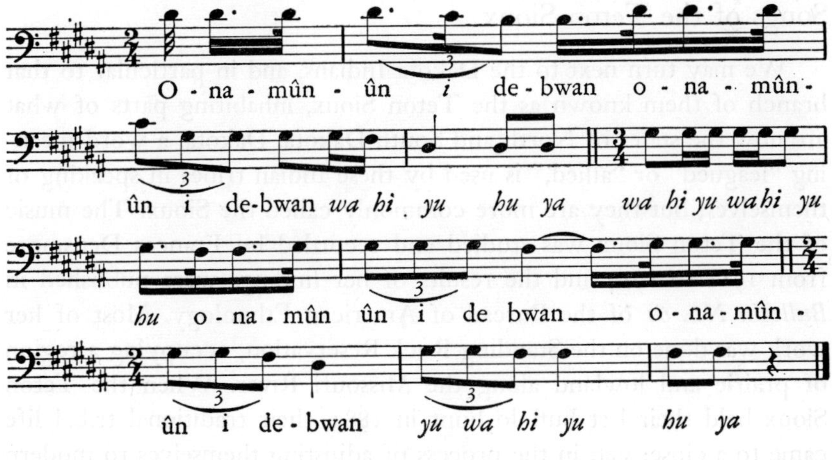

DRUM RHYTHM
(♩=84)

Among the ceremonies of the Chippewa there is one called "Restoring the Mourners," which marks the end of the period of mourning for family deaths. Painting the face is part of the ceremony, and while this is being done the following melody is sung:

As Miss Densmore remarks: "This melody contains a peculiar grace and charm."

Songs of the Teton Sioux

We may turn next to the Dakota Indians, and in particular to that branch of them known as the Teton Sioux, inhabiting parts of what are now the states of North and South Dakota. Dakota, a word meaning "leagued" or "allied," is used by these Indian tribes in speaking of themselves; but they are more commonly called the Sioux. The music of the Teton Sioux was studied and recorded by Frances Densmore from 1911 to 1914 and the results of her findings were published in *Bulletin No. 61* of the Bureau of American Ethnology. Most of her work was done on the Standing Rock Reservation, occupying a region of prairie and lowland along the Missouri River. When the Teton Sioux held their last buffalo hunt in 1883, their traditional tribal life came to a close; yet, in the process of adjusting themselves to modern civilization, these Indians of the plains have preserved many of their old songs and ceremonies. According to Miss Densmore, "Music may perhaps be said to be the last element of native culture remaining in favor among the Sioux." In comparing the older with the newer songs of the Teton Sioux, Miss Densmore found significant changes:

> Summarizing briefly the results of a comparison of the old and the more modern Sioux songs, we find in the percentages a reduction in the compass of the songs with an increase of harmonic form and of accidentals; a more direct attack (shown by the increase of songs beginning on the accented part of the measure); an increase of songs

beginning in 2-4 time; and also in songs without a change in time. We find a change in the drumbeat from a rapid and somewhat tremolo beat to a quarter-note value, with a reduction in the tempo of the drum and an increase in the proportion of songs in which the tempo of voice and drum is the same. We note further a development of the rhythmic sense in song construction, shown by the increase in the number of songs having two or more rhythmic units. These contrasts between the two groups of songs may suggest a connection between the Indians' manner of life and the form of their musical expression, or they may be regarded as an effect of contact with the more conventional music of the white race.[7]

In other words, a process of acculturation has been going on, and the norms of the dominant white civilization appear to be in the ascendancy in the development of American Indian music, which is gradually shedding the traits that characterized it during the period of organized tribal existence.

Many tribal melodies are associated with ceremonies, and these in turn are related to the legends and myths upon which a large measure of Indian tradition reposes. Among the Teton Sioux the principal supernatural being was the White Buffalo Maiden, who appeared to two young men of the tribe as they were out hunting and announced to them that she had something important to present to the tribe. She was a beautiful young maiden, wearing a fringed buckskin dress, leggings, and moccasins, with a tied tuft of shedded buffalo hair on her left side, and her face painted with red vertical stripes. When all preparations had been made to receive her, she appeared in the camp at sunrise, carrying in her hands a pipe. Entering the lodge, she spoke to the assembled people, praising the virtues of the tribe, saying, among other things:

For all these good qualities in the tribe you have been chosen as worthy and deserving of all good gifts. I represent the Buffalo tribe, who have sent you this pipe. . . . Take it, and use it according to my directions. This pipe shall be used as a peacemaker. . . . By this pipe the medicine-man shall be called to administer help to the sick.

After finishing her speech and presenting the pipe to the chief, she went slowly out of the tent and as soon as she was outside she turned into a white buffalo calf.

[7] Densmore, *Teton Sioux Music*, p. 25.

Here is the "Song of the White Buffalo Maiden," which she is said to have sung as she entered the Sioux camp:

The words mean: "With visible breath I am walking/ this nation I walk toward/ and my voice is heard/ I am walking with visible breath I am walking/ this scarlet relic/ [for it] I am walking." The italicized vocables in the song are interpolated between the meaningful words.

The "scarlet relic" mentioned in the above song refers to another Sioux custom, that of "keeping a spirit," which requires the making of a scarlet-wrapped packet containing objects belonging to the dead person whose spirit is being "kept." It was considered highly desirable to place the spirit-bundle upon the robe of a white buffalo in the lodge. When such a robe was used, the "Song of the White Buffalo Maiden" was sung as part of the spirit-keeping ceremony.

One of the most interesting customs of the Sioux was that of forming "dream societies," composed of men who had seen the same animal in their fasting visions. Often the dreams or visions would be acted out in the dances performed by members of these societies. There were buffalo, elk, wolf, and horse societies. The following is a

Horse Society song, which says: "Daybreak appears when a horse neighs."

The drum accompaniment to this song was a rapid tremolo in a rhythm of eighth notes, as follows:

DRUM RHYTHM:
(♩=92)

A song described as a favorite of the Sioux is "Those Hills I Trod Upon," which reveals the Indian's feeling for nature. In another version of the song, the singer mentions the streams instead of the hills, but the evocation of nature and solitude is in the same spirit. The words say: "In the north to those hills I climbed/roaming again I myself come."

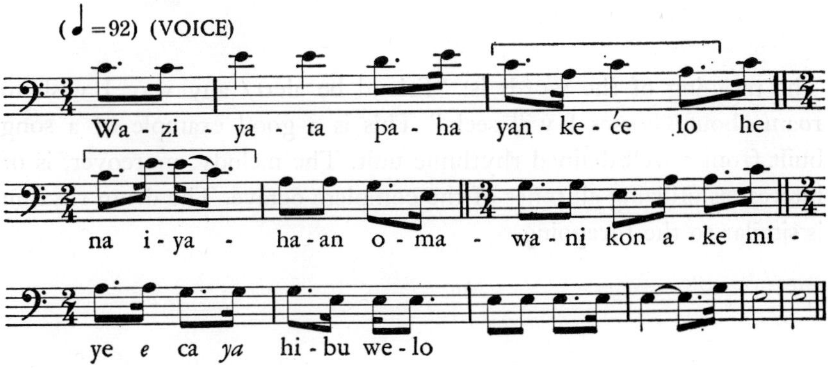

The melody is based on the Fourth Five-toned Scale.

A Sioux Indian named Jaw explained that before any important undertaking (such as a horse-stealing expedition) he offered prayers to Wakan'tanka and smoked a pipe in a certain ritualistic manner, saying: "Wakan'tanka, I will now smoke this pipe in your honor. I ask that no bullet may harm me when I am in battle. I ask that I may get many horses." Upon completing the ceremony, he sang this song, "I Wish to Roam":

The meaning of the words is: "Friend be alert/ any way I wish to roam about/ horses I will seek." This is a good example of a song built from a well-defined rhythmic unit. The melody, moreover, is of interest as utilizing all tones of the complete octave. The drum rhythm is similar to the foregoing.

Pawnee ceremonial songs

The Pawnee, located in Oklahoma, are a small tribe but one with a highly developed mythology and ceremonialism. In the words of Alice C. Fletcher, among the Pawnee,

> . . . religious ceremonies were connected with the cosmic forces and the heavenly bodies. The dominating power was Tirawa, generally spoken of as "father." The heavenly bodies, the winds, thunder, lightning, and rain were his messengers. . . . The mythology of the Pawnee is remarkably rich in symbolism and poetic fancy, and their religious system is elaborate and cogent. The secret societies, of which there were several in each tribe, were connected with the belief in supernatural animals. The functions of these were to call the game, to heal diseases, and to give occult powers. Their rites were elaborate and their ceremonies dramatic.[8]

The Pawnee personified the Evening Star as a woman, placing her next in power to Tirawa. From her garden in the west, with fields of ripening corn and many buffalo, sprang all forms of life. Her consort was the Morning Star, a warrior who drove the other stars before him across the sky. From their union the first human being was created. The second human being was the daughter of the Sun and the Moon. From her marriage to the son of the Morning Star and the Evening Star, sprang the human race.

The Morning Star ceremony was held in the early spring, for the purpose of securing good crops in the coming season. One of the principal songs in this ceremony was sung to the following melody:

[8] Fletcher, *Handbook of American Indians,* Bulletin 30, Bureau of American Ethnology, part II, p. 215. Quoted by Densmore, *Pawnee Music,* p. 4.

Miss Densmore writes that this song was considered too sacred for phonographic recording and was taught to her orally by the singer, Coming Sun. The words of the song signify: "This I did when I became angry, in order that in the future the earth might be formed." In singing this and other ceremonial songs, one voice sang the opening phrase, which was repeated by two or three voices while the first singer held a low tone; then all the voices sang the remainder of the song in unison. This song was found among the Skidi (Wolf Pawnee), one of the bands into which the Pawnee tribe is divided.

A principal ceremony among the Chaui Band of Pawnee is that of Painting the Buffalo Skull, held every spring and including a buffalo dance with various related songs. One of these is connected with an incident that occurred long ago. A great herd of buffalo suddenly appeared near the Indian encampment, to which it threatened destruction. An old Indian named Naru'dapadi rode out toward the herd, shouting and firing his rifle to divert the buffalo; but he was caught in the herd, surrounded by the buffalo, and swept away across the stream. This is the song, "The Herd Passes Through the Village":

we re ri tu-ru kat - ka a a — we re ra hu ka - ta - ta.

DRUM RHYTHM:
(♩=120)

One more Pawnee song will be given here. It is neither a ceremonial song nor a song of the societies, but was sung by the wife of a chief whose infant daughter had died—"Mother's Song for a Dead Baby."

(♩=72)
1.
2.

Drum not recorded

The second half of the fourth measure is described as "a descending wail" in which the tones E-D-B were connected by a glissando. This wailing phrase is all that alters the regular recurrence of the rhythmic unit upon which the song is built.

Music of the Pueblo Indians

The Pueblo Indians, the ruins of whose ancient towns are scattered throughout New Mexico and Arizona, were a peaceful agricultural people skilled in handicrafts and with an elaborate ceremonial ritual. The Spaniards called them *Pueblo* Indians because they lived in towns or villages, in houses made of stone and adobe. Their best-known tribes are the Zuñi and the Hopi.

The Zuñis live near the Little Colorado River, among the buttes and mesas of New Mexico. The occupations of their daily life are reflected in their corn-grinding songs, sung by the women as they grind the corn in stone troughs called "metates" upon which the corn is placed and ground by another stone. One of these corn-grinding songs, recorded by Natalie Curtis, refers to the "sacred mountain" of the Zuñis, the great mesa that they call To'yallanne.

In the words of J. Walter Fewkes: "Almost everything in the life of a Zuñian has a religious side, or is to be met by something which for want of a name we may call a religious observance." In addition to the ceremonial rain dances, and dances connected with the ripening of corn, Fewkes classified the following as semireligious observances among the Zuñis: foot races, rabbit hunts, planting of prayer-plumes, and communal burning of pottery. The periods of the summer and winter solstices have much prominence in the Zuñi ritual and are celebrated with appropriate ceremonies. The Zuñis have primitive altars upon which they regularly make offerings of plumes, sacred meal, and water. Their important summer ceremonies have the prime purpose of securing water for the crops. Featured in these ceremonies are the various rain dances. The most important of these, at least at the time when Fewkes observed them, was the Sacred Dance of the *Ko-ko,* which he described as follows:

> Each *Ko-ko* wore a painted mask with a long horse-hair beard extending down on the breast, while his own hair, carefully dressed, fell down the back. On the top of his head he wore two or three bright yellow feathers, while on a string weighted by a stone, which hung down over the hair, small, white, downy feathers were tied at intervals. The mask was of blue color, with two slits for the eyes, and a third with zigzag bars representing teeth. . . . Around the neck hung numerous chains of shell beads and worsted yarn, from which depended ornaments made of the abalone and other shells. The shoulders and body, down to the loins, were bare, but the shoulders were painted a pinkish color, with zigzag markings, said to be rain symbols. . . . In one hand he held a gourd rattle, and in the other a sprig of cedar. The body was thrown into a slightly stooping position, the elbows bent so that the forearm was thrown forward. Some of the *Ko-ko* dancers carried in the hand a live turtle. . . . Around the loins each *Ko-ko* wore a Moqui (Hopi) dance-blanket, a sash with long, white pendent strings knotted at the ends, and from behind hung a fox-skin, with head uppermost, and tail extending to the ground. Empty turtle shells . . . were tied to the sash behind. The legs and feet were bare, with the exception of a black woolen garter tied on the left leg, and a turtle shell securely fastened on the

right, inside the knee. This turtle shell . . . had small hoofs suspended by buckskin thongs on one side. The rattle of these hoofs on the empty turtle shells could be heard for a considerable distance as the dancers, settling back on one leg, raised their feet and then brought them down to the earth, in accord with the song which they chanted.[9]

This is the Zuñi tribal melody of the Sacred Dance of the *Ko-ko*, as recorded by Fewkes and transcribed by Gilman:

Among the summer ceremonial dances of the Zuñi, one of the most impressive was the Dance of the Hay-a-ma-she-que ("Dancers Who Wear the Masks"), in which thirty-four dancers participated, wearing elaborately painted masks and strings of ornaments similar to those worn by the Ko-ko dancers, and with the upper part of body painted a deep red or copper color. The peculiar feature of this dance was the tablet carried by each dancer. As described by Fewkes:

Their heads were wholly covered by cedar boughs, which formed a helmet with an extensive collar. The tablet which they carried on their head above the cedar was a thin, flat board with three apical

[9] Fewkes, *A Journal of American Ethnology and Archaeology*, vol. 1, pp. 27–28.

projections, each ornamented with a feather. On this tablet, which was about two feet high, there were gaudily painted figures in the form of crescents, birdlike outlines, and variegated circles. . . . In the hands they carried a gourd rattle and a sprig of cedar. . . . The turtle-shell rattle and brass bells also dangled at the knee, making a noise with every movement of the legs.[10]

Here is part of the melody for the Dance of the Hay-a-ma-she-que:

Benjamin Ives Gilman, who transcribed and analyzed the Zuñi and Hopi melodies recorded by Fewkes, was convinced that these were "examples of a music without scale." He formulated his conviction in these terms:

> What we have in these melodies is the musical growths out of which scales are elaborated, and not compositions undertaken in conformity to norms of interval order already fixed in the consciousness of the singers. In this archaic stage of the art, scales are not formed but forming.

This statement stirred up some controversy when it was published, and later investigators have not accepted Gilman's conclusion, as nearly all Indian melodies have been classifiable under some kind of scale. It is true, however, as previously remarked, that the Indian probably did not have a conscious a priori concept of scale. It should be added that Gilman was very thorough in his investigations, and his data deserve to be carefully studied.

Snake songs figure prominently in the tribal melodies of the Hopi (or Moqui) Indians, the cliff dwellers of northern Arizona. For the

[10] *Ibid.*, pp. 38–39.

rest, many of the ceremonial songs, like those of the Zuñis, are connected with invocations for rain and with the planting and ripening of corn. The following is a Hopi snake song as transcribed by Gilman:

Papago tribal melodies

Indian music of the Southwestern desert may be represented by tribal melodies of the Papago Indians, of which six subdivisions live in southern Arizona, the rest in Mexico. The Papago are a Piman tribe, given to agricultural pursuits. Their musical instruments are a gourd rattle, used for songs to bring rain and songs for treating the sick; scraping sticks, used in pairs, a smooth stick being scraped over one that is notched and slightly curved; basket drum, simply a household basket turned upside down and struck with the hands, usually by three or four men at once; and the "flute," made of cane, end-blown, with three finger holes.

Papago songs are characterized by exceptional melodic freedom. For this reason it is often difficult to designate any tone as a keynote. There is a very small percentage of harmonic melodies among the Papago songs. A glissando is frequently used in certain types of songs. In contrast to those of other tribes, the words of Papago songs are always continuous throughout the melody.[11]

Tribal melodies collected by Miss Densmore among the Papago Indians included songs connected with legends; songs for the treat-

[11] Data from Densmore, *Pawnee Music*, from which next three melodies are quoted.

ment of the sick; songs connected with ceremonies; songs connected with expeditions to obtain salt; war songs; songs of the kicking-ball races; songs of the Bat Dance; dream songs; hunting songs; songs for the entertainment of children; and miscellaneous songs, the latter including some humorous songs. The following is an example of a Papago humorous song, of which the words mean: "The pigeon pretended that he was setting up a tiswin lodge. The frog doctor drank his wine, got drunk and shouted, and pulled out his cloud." Tiswin is a wine made from the fruit of the saguaro cactus. It was customary to construct a special lodge for the drinking of tiswin, and the wine was drunk during the ceremony for making rain; hence the reference to the cloud in this song, "The Pigeon and His Tiswin Lodge."

The Papago ceremony for making rain was held early in August and was the occasion for a festival in which a large number of rain-making songs were sung. There were said to be more than a hundred of these songs. The following song, "I Draw the Rain," was supposed to have been first sung by a small boy who wished to be of help to his people. It says: "Here I am sitting and with my power I draw the south wind toward me. After the wind I draw the clouds, and after the clouds I draw the rain that makes the wild flowers grow on our home ground and look so beautiful."

Another Papago ceremony for obtaining rain and good crops was the *Viikita,* held every four years. The ceremony involved fasting and the carrying of an object representing the sun. In some sections the drinking of tiswin was part of the ritual, in others it was not. The following song of the *Viikita* ceremony again emphasizes the importance of clouds in the cosmic economy of these desert dwellers. The translation of the words is: "We see the light that brightens in the east/ it seems to turn to flame/ on the edge of it is something that looks like a white feather/ but we see that it is white clouds."

Indian tribal music today

The tribal melodies of the North American Indians belong largely to the past, intimately bound up as they are with traditions and folkways that in some cases have already disappeared and that in others may soon vanish before the impact of civilization. Nevertheless, the Indian often shows a surprising tenacity in the retention of his ancestral traditions, and this retention is generally strongest in the realm of tribal music. The evidence indicates that the Indians who are in closest contact with civilization tend to assimilate some of the traits of the white man's music, particularly as regards tonality, harmonic feeling, elimination of repetition, and regularity of metrical patterns. The resulting musical syncretization, while combining elements of both cultures, does not necessarily cease to be "Indian," since it expresses the creative personality of the Indian within the context of the new environment to which he has had to adapt himself and his traditions.

The Indians are still making songs that are a blend of the old and the new, that reflect the conditions of today's world in terms of inherited techniques united to recently acquired values and resources. In 1942, after the United States found it necessary to go to war for the second time in the defense of freedom for the world, a Sioux folk poet wrote the words of a song that said:

> The President, the flag, and my country,
> These things I stand for.
> So saying the Sioux boys went as soldiers.

In the summer of 1942 Willard Rhodes visited the Oglala band of the Teton Sioux on the Pine Ridge Indian Reservation in South Dakota and recorded twelve songs dealing with World War II, composed by the Indians within the traditional framework of their tribal melodies. He found them to be based on a tetratonic scale consisting of the following tones: D, F, G, A; and marked by a smaller tonal range than the older war songs recorded by Frances Densmore among the Teton Sioux several decades ago. Here is one of the new war songs as transcribed by Rhodes: [12]

This is the translation of the words:

[12] This song and the remarks by Willard Rhodes are reprinted from the quarterly *Modern Music*, XX, 3 (Mar.–Apr. 1945), 158; by permission of the League of Composers, Inc., copyright 1943.

From across the ocean, my friend,
They come charging.
With airplanes above,
And with submarines under the water
They come charging.
The Sioux boys are brave.
That is what the United States says.

Regarding the manner of singing the song, Rhodes writes:

> At this point [2] the women join in the refrain of the song. While the men continue singing with a "pulsating tone," indicated by dots above or beneath the notes, the women vocalize the phrase very legato with a meaningless syllable, *he.* The sharply timbred voices of the women singers is highly suggestive of the tone quality of a reed instrument.

Concerning intonation and melodic structure, Rhodes remarks:

> A plus or minus sign over a note indicates a slight raising or lowering of the pitch of that particular tone. Inasmuch as the tonic tone, D, is sung consistently flat throughout this song, only the initial appearance of the D is so marked [at the point indicated by the numeral "1"]. In the melodic cadence which occurs at the end of each phrase, F functions as a leading tone in relation to D. This results in an interval that is neither major nor minor, a neutral third which is fairly common in primitive music.

It may be true, as Willard Rhodes suggests, that "the time has arrived when the composer can safely reconsider American Indian music as a source of material"—now that the romantic and picturesque exploitation of the American Indian is a thing of the past, reaching its apogee in the Indianist movement of the early 1900s. There is another approach that may also prove fruitful in a reconsideration of Indian music today: its intimate relationship to the myths and rituals that form the foundation of traditional Indian life. Today we are conscious, as never before in the modern world, of the significance of myth and ritual in the life of mankind and in his arts—whether of music, poetry, or drama—whereby he seeks to express his sense of mystery and of awe, and of participation in a common and unknown destiny. Whatever may be the limitations of the Indian's mode of musical expression, it has always been a deep and indispensable part of his living.

chapter twenty-one

The rise of ragtime

I can shake the earth's foundation wid de Maple Leaf Rag!
SIDNEY BROWN, "MAPLE LEAF RAG SONG" (1903).

During the Gay Nineties, ragtime music swept the country and even made a considerable impression on Europe. It rose rapidly to an immense popularity—became, indeed, a sort of craze—was taken over for commercial exploitation by tin-pan alley, degenerated into unimaginative manipulation of clichés, and fizzled out like a wet firecracker about the time the United States went into World War I.

In the 1940s there was a revival of interest in ragtime. Looking at it in the perspective of time, one discovers that it was no ephemeral fad, but an important phase of America's music, deeply rooted in our folk and popular traditions; not a mere novelty but something strongly original; not wholly a meretricious commercialized output but a movement genuinely creative at the core that produced a permanent body of music and that exerted an enduring influence.

The convergence of ragtime and blues in classic New Orleans jazz, which occurred during the last decades of the nineteenth century, is one of the fundamental developments in the history of American music. Although these three currents of American popular music—ragtime, blues, and jazz—are closely related, it will be convenient, for the sake of clarity, to trace separately the course of each. Ragtime and blues may be considered as important tributaries of jazz, the Mississippi River of American music. These tributaries are of interest for their own sake as well as for what they contribute to the main stream of jazz.

There are direct links between ragtime and American minstrelsy. Two of these links are the so-called "plantation melodies" or "coon songs," generally sung with banjo accompaniment, and the type of dance known as "cakewalk," which became increasingly popular as a feature of minstrel shows from about 1880. We must bear in mind that while in the beginning the blackface minstrel troupes consisted of white performers with their faces blackened—who more or less faithfully imitated what they took to be typical traits of Negro music and dancing—after the Civil War and the emancipation of the slaves, with the consequent incorporation of the Negro into many phases of American life, particularly the entertainment field, Negroes themselves began to take part in the minstrel shows. While the Negro minstrel performer was still more or less bound by the long-established stereotypes of blackface minstrelsy, he nevertheless was able, through details of emphasis and interpretation, to give the songs and dances and instrumental accompaniments an authenticity and an originality that they had not previously possessed.

In an earlier chapter it was pointed out that many of the old minstrel tunes were marked by syncopation. For example, both "Old Zip Coon" and "Old Dan Tucker," among many others, contain the characteristic rhythmic figure, , that became the standard cakewalk formula of ragtime music. Among the songs of Stephen Foster, particularly those in which he was most influenced by the singing and dancing of the Negro roustabouts on the Ohio River, this syncopation is also found. Willis Laurence James has observed that Foster's "The Glendy Burk" (1860) is "a true ragtime song," and that to be convinced of this one need simply pat the hands and feet while singing it, to provide the regular beat of the bass in ragtime.

It is thus a very thin gap that separates the more genuine minstrel songs of the mid-nineteenth century from the authentic ragtime style that emerged a few decades later. That gap was filled by the Negro performers, particularly the banjoists and later the pianists, who began to find an outlet for their musical talents and an expression for their racial heritage in minstrelsy, in vaudeville and variety (which soon replaced the minstrel shows), and in the entertainment world in general. As we shall presently see, some of that "entertainment" was associated with the unrespectable "underworld" that opposed no barriers of convention or prejudice to the Negro musicians and their strangely disconcerting music with its "hot" rhythm and its "blue" notes. It was the musical meeting of these two worlds—that of the honky-tonks and barrel houses, and that of the popular stage and commercial publishing—that made possible the rise of ragtime as a permanent form of American popular music. Before we go on to describe where and in what manner this development took place, we must cast a backward glance at some of the antecedents of ragtime, which are equally applicable to the background of jazz and the blues.

The entire body of Afro-American music is in fact a whole, possessing an organic unity stemming from a common cultural tradition (the basic traits of this tradition were described in Chapter 4). We are aware that Afro-American music absorbed many influences, from folk tunes of the British Isles to the French and Spanish dance music of Louisiana. We also know that it has manifested itself in various directions: the spirituals and shouts, the work and play songs, the children's songs and lullabies, the cornfield "hollers" and the blues, the banjo tunes and the many dances that go with them. In spite of superficial differences, all these manifestations, when one gets to the core of them, disregarding conventional adulteration (such as the "arranged" spirituals sung by trained choirs and concert artists), will reveal their common ancestry and close kinship. This common tie is in the "hot" quality of the music. All true Afro-American music is "hot," whether it be a spiritual, a work song, a blues, a banjo tune, a piano rag, or a jazz piece.

"Hot rhythm" on the levee

That greatly gifted writer and observer of Afro-American folkways, Lafcadio Hearn, spent several years in Cincinnati as a young man, before going to New Orleans. He took a keen interest in the music of the Negro stevedores, and in 1876 published in the Cincinnati *Commercial* an article called "Levee Life,"[1] in which he vividly described the songs and dances of these workers. He also collected the words of many of the songs, but unfortunately not the music. His article was subtitled "Haunts and Pastimes of the Roustabouts, Their Original Songs and Peculiar Dances." His description is worth quoting, for it is one of the basic documents on the folk backgrounds of ragtime and jazz. He begins by setting the scene:

> . . . on a cool spring evening, when the levee is bathed in moonlight, and the torch-basket lights dance redly upon the water, and

[1] Reprinted in *An American Miscellany*, vol. 1.

the clear air vibrates to the sonorous music of the deep-toned steam-whistle, and the sound of wild banjo-thrumming floats out through the open doors of the levee dance-houses. . . .

Then he tells something of their songs and dances in general:

Roustabout life in the truest sense is, then, the life of the colored population of the Rows, and, partly, of Bucktown—blacks and mulattoes from all parts of the States, but chiefly from Kentucky and Eastern Virginia, where most of them appear to have toiled on the plantations before Freedom; and echoes of the old plantation life still live in their songs and their pastimes. You may hear old Kentucky slave songs chanted nightly on the steamboats, in that wild, half-melancholy key peculiar to the natural music of the African race; and you may see the old slave dances nightly performed to the air of some ancient Virginia-reel in the dance-houses of Sausage Row, or the "ballrooms" of Bucktown. . . . Many of their songs, which have never appeared in print, treat of levee life in Cincinnati, of all the popular steamboats running on the "Muddy Water," and of the favorite roustabout haunts on the river bank and in Bucktown.

Finally he takes us into one of these "dance-houses," where on the back of a long bench, placed with its face to the wall, with their feet inwardly reclining upon the seat, sat the musicians:

A well-dressed, neatly-built mulatto picked the banjo, and a somewhat lighter colored musician led the music with a fiddle, which he played remarkably well and with great spirit. A short, stout negress, illy dressed, with a rather good-natured face and a bed shawl tied about her head, played the bass viol, and that with no inexperienced hand.

What Hearn calls a "bass viol" is doubtless the double bass or bull fiddle (generally referred to as string bass, or simply bass, in jazz terminology), which later came to be an important element in the rhythm section of the classic New Orleans jazz band. It is exasperating that Hearn does not tell us *how* this Negro woman played the string bass, instead of how well she played it. If it was used primarily to mark the rhythm, then we have the precursor of a jazz trio.

Hearn then goes on to describe the dancing:

The musicians struck up that weird, wild, lively air, known perhaps to many of our readers as the "Devil's Dream," and in which "the musical ghost of a cat chasing the spectral ghost of a rat" is represented by a succession of "miauls" and "squeaks" on the fiddle. The dancers danced a double quadrille, at first, silently and rapidly; but warming with the wild spirit of the music, leaped and shouted, swinging each other off the floor, and keeping time with a precision which shook the building in time to the music. The women, we noticed, almost invariably embraced the men about the neck in swinging, the man clasping them about the waist. Sometimes the men advancing leaped and crossed legs with a double shuffle, and with almost sightless rapidity.

Then the music changed to an old Virginia reel, and the dancing changing likewise, presented the most grotesque spectacle imaginable. The dancing became wild; men patted juba and shouted, the negro women danced with the most fantastic grace, their bodies describing almost incredible curves forward and backward; limbs intertwined rapidly in a wrestle with each other and with the music; the room presented a tide of swaying bodies and tossing arms, and flying hair. The white female dancers seemed heavy, cumbersome, ungainly by contrast with their dark companions; the spirit of the music was not upon them; they were abnormal to the life about them.

Once more the music changed—to some popular Negro air, with the chorus—

Don't get weary,
I'm goin' home.

The musicians began to sing; the dancers joined in; and the dance terminated with a roar of song, stamping of feet, "patting juba," shouting, laughing, reeling. Even the curious spectators involuntarily kept time with their feet; it was the very drunkenness of music, the intoxication of the dance.

It was something of this "intoxication of the dance," something of this irresistible "hot" rhythm that forced you to keep time with your feet, that the whole country was to feel when ragtime swept across the land. Notice Hearn's remark that the white dancers were not possessed by the spirit of this music, and that only with the Negroes did it appear as a natural, spontaneous outpouring of rhythm and feeling. The rise of ragtime could take place only after the Negro was given an opportunity to express himself musically outside of his own limited milieu: on the stage and in the world of entertainment.

What is important to remember is that the fusion in ragtime of the more or less conventional "coon song" and cakewalk tradition of minstrelsy with the authentic strain of genuine Afro-American syncopated and polyrhythmic "hot" music could not have occurred unless the culturally untamed (i.e., conventionally uneducated) Negro folk had kept alive throughout the South, and more particularly along the vast Mississippi River basin, their uninhibited "hot" style of making music. The cities along the Mississippi and its tributaries were especially significant in this development because they provided employment for the Negroes on the levees and steamboats and created permanent urban communities where the kind of music and dancing described by Hearn could flourish unmolested by the entrenched forces of respectability. What Hearn saw and heard and described in Cincinnati in 1876—in effect a kind of primitive jam session—had obviously been going on for some time before that, and undoubtedly had its replica in other riverside cities. His account reveals the existence of a well-established tradition of "hot" instrumental music flourishing "beyond the pale" in the water-front dance houses of our riparian cities. It is no wonder, then, that the rise of ragtime and blues and jazz was to center around these cities, chiefly New Orleans, Memphis, and St. Louis. Later, of course, Chicago and New York became the inevitable centers of commercial exploitation and mass diffusion.

Thus far we have traced two principal currents as converging in the creation of ragtime: the blackface minstrelsy of the stage, with its concomitant output of "coon songs," and the genuine, "hot" Afro-American folk music. A third contributing current should now be mentioned: the Negro brass bands of the towns and cities, which began to spring up shortly after the Civil War. More will be said about these street bands in the chapter on jazz, in the development of which they had a vital role. Here it is sufficient to mention that Negro brass bands, under the driving impulse of "hot" rhythm, soon began to "rag" many of the marches and tunes they played. This "ragtime" band music was later imitated by such celebrated white bands as Sousa's and Pryor's, and in fact it was Sousa's band that gave Europe its first taste of ragtime. Band music, however, is more important in connection with the history of jazz, because ragtime is essentially music for piano. Ragtime may be described as the application of systematic syncopation to piano playing and composition. More precisely, it consists basically of a syncopated melody played over a regularly accented beat (2/4 time) in the bass. As previously observed, the basic rhythmic formula of ragtime is the so-called "cakewalk" figure, which, as we pointed out in discussing the compositions of L. M. Gottschalk, is also frequently met with in much of Latin American popular music, particularly that which has been strongly influenced by Afro-American elements from the Caribbean area. In view of the close connection between the cakewalk and the rise of ragtime something should be said here about the background of the former.

Cakewalk and "coon songs"

The cakewalk appears to have originated in an actual custom of plantation life in ante-bellum days. Featured in the blackface minstrel shows, it passed over into the variety acts that marked the transition to vaudeville. When the team of Harrigan and Hart presented, in 1877, a number called "Walking for Dat Cake" (music by Dave Braham and words by Harrigan), they billed it as an "Exquisite Picture of Negro Life and Customs." It was a precursor of the many cakewalk songs that flooded the nation around the turn of the century.

According to the testimony of Shephard N. Edmonds, a Negro born in Tennessee of freed slave parents,

> The cakewalk was originally a plantation dance, just a happy movement they (the slaves) did to the banjo music because they couldn't stand still. It was generally on Sundays, when there was little work, that the slaves both young and old would dress up in hand-me-down finery to do a high-kicking, prancing walk-around. They did a take-off on the high manners of the white folks in the "big house," but their masters, who gathered around to watch the fun, missed the point. It's supposed to be that the custom of a prize started with the master giving a cake to the couple that did the proudest movement.[2]

The combination of cakewalk rhythm and banjo technique is a direct forerunner of ragtime.

During the 1890s variety teams such as Smart and Williams, and especially Williams and Walker, popularized the cakewalk, which quickly became a national craze. Cakewalk contests sprang up everywhere, from the biggest cities to the remotest hamlets. That high-

[2] Quoted in Blesh and Janis, *They All Played Ragtime*, p. 96.

kicking step and that tricky rhythm had captivated the country. A large part of the world was also fascinated by this American novelty.

One of the earliest and most perceptive writers on American music, the novelist Rupert Hughes, wrote in 1899:

> Negroes call their clog dancing "ragging" and the dance a "rag," a dance largely shuffling. The dance is a sort of frenzy with frequent yelps of delight from the dancer and spectators and accompanied by the latter with hand clapping and stomping of feet. Banjo figuration is very noticeable in ragtime music and division of one of the beats into two short notes is traceable to the hand clapping.[3]

There can be no question about the importance of the banjo in the genesis of ragtime. This instrument, used by the Negroes from the early days of slavery, and having undoubtedly an African prototype, was the precursor of piano ragtime music. As we observed in an earlier chapter, the original "coon songs" took the banjo as the symbol of the plantation melody, even though they were published in versions for voice and piano. When the "coon songs" were revived and attained a new and wider popularity toward the end of the nineteenth century, they still clung to the banjo as a symbol of the plantation life that was by then very much under the enchantment of distance and ignorance. One of these songs, "New Coon in Town," by J. S. Putnam, published in 1883, was specifically subtitled "Banjo Imitation." This was an adumbration of ragtime before the name itself was applied to popular music. Just as in the early plantation melodies syncopation occurs incidentally, so in the later "coon songs" of the 1880s and 1890s ragtime appears in a few measures here and there, until, by 1897, full-fledged ragtime piano numbers began to be published with a rush. In order to explain this sudden surge of published ragtime, it is necessary to take up the story of the popular pianists who created American ragtime music out of the materials and backgrounds we have been describing.

"King of ragtime"

The most famous name associated with the rise of ragtime is that of Scott Joplin (1869–1917), though there is some dispute as to

[3] Hughes in the Boston *Musical Record*, Apr. 1, 1899.

whether he actually deserves the title of "King of Ragtime." Perhaps such titles are unnecessary anyway. Joplin, a Negro, was born in Texarkana, Texas, and grew up in a household that was full of music. His mother sang and played the banjo, his father played the violin, and his brother the guitar. Scott himself was attracted by the piano (there was one in a neighbor's house). When his father managed to save enough money for the purchase of an old-fashioned square grand, Scott taught himself to play, and attracted the attention of a local German musician who gave him lessons and familiarized him with the music of the great European composers. This orthodox influence was counterbalanced by his wanderings as an itinerant musician while he was still in his teens: an experience that brought him into intimate contact with the folklore and the low-life of the South. In 1885, at the age of seventeen, he arrived in St. Louis, which became his headquarters for the next eight years. He played there in the honky-tonks on Chestnut and Market Streets, where Negro pianists were developing, with freedom and originality, the style of piano music that was soon to be known as ragtime.

In 1893 Joplin, along with many other musicians, went to Chicago for the World's Columbian Exposition, where he met some of the early Chicago ragtime players, such as "Plunk" Henry and Johnny Seymour. He also made the acquaintance of Otis Saunders, who returned with him to St. Louis and soon persuaded him to write down and publish some of the piano pieces that he was playing. The following year he went across the river to Sedalia, Missouri, where he wrote his first compositions. These, however, were sentimental songs, not rags. Joplin nevertheless was still playing ragtime piano, notably at a place called the Maple Leaf Club. There, in the summer of 1899, he was heard by a man who was to become a central figure in the spread of ragtime: the music publisher John Stillwell Stark. The latter was a pioneer and ex-farmer who had settled in Sedalia around 1885 and had taken to cultural pursuits with characteristic vigor and enthusiasm. Although he embraced the genteel tradition on one side (his daughter studied music with Moszkowski in Germany), he was broad-minded enough, and his pioneer instincts were strong enough, to recognize something new and vital in American music when he heard Scott Joplin play at the Maple Leaf Club. The result was the publication, in 1899, of a composition that made history: *Maple Leaf Rag*, with its classic ragtime syncopation over the steady rhythm of the bass.

Joplin's *Maple Leaf Rag* was a huge success. Stark had given him a royalty contract, so that composer as well as publisher profited from the sales, which were enormous for those times. Stark, ready for bigger things, moved over to St. Louis, set up his own printing press, and continued to publish ragtime numbers, by Joplin and others. Later he opened an office in New York, but he was not cut out for the tin-pan-alley type of business. In 1912 he returned to St. Louis, where he continued to champion ragtime, insisting that it was both respectable and valuable. He outlived the vogue of ragtime by some ten years, for he died in 1927. John Stark was a true pioneer, a man of conviction and culture, whose name should be honored in the annals of America's music.

Scott Joplin soon outgrew the "tenderloin" district where he and so many other pianists had found employment and an opportunity to play ragtime. He moved into a large house of his own and set himself up as a music teacher. He went on composing a long succession of rags and other popular pieces, some of them in collaboration with Scott Hayden, Arthur Marshall, and Louis Chauvin. His first published rag was not the *Maple Leaf Rag*, but *Original Rags*, published in March, 1899. In all, Joplin published thirty-nine piano rags, of which seven were written in collaboration with others. There are also a number of unpublished rags in manuscript. Among his rags for piano solo are *Peacherine Rag* (1901), *The Easy Winners* (1901), *Palm Leaf Rag—A Slow Drag* (1903), *Rose Leaf Rag* (1907), *Fig Leaf Rag* (1908), *Euphonic Sounds* (1909), *Stoptime Rag* (1910), *Scott Joplin's New Rag* (1912), and *Reflection Rag—Syncopated Musings* (1917).

In 1903 Joplin wrote the book and music for *A Guest of Honor*, described as "A Ragtime Opera." It received only one concert performance in St. Louis and was never published, though Stark evidently contemplated its publication, judging by an entry in the U.S. Copyright Office. The manuscript has disappeared; so nothing is known concretely of this first attempt at an American ragtime opera.

From about 1909 Joplin lived in New York, and there he tried his hand at opera again. The work was *Treemonisha*, an opera in three acts, which he published at his own expense in 1911, in a piano score. The scene of the opera is laid "on a plantation somewhere in the State of Arkansas," and the action takes places in 1886. Treemonisha is a Negro girl who receives an education and is thus able to overcome the superstitions by which her people are bound. She is acclaimed as their teacher and leader, while the Negroes assemble and dance *A Real Slow Drag*, which forms the climax of the opera:

> Dance slowly, prance slowly,
> While you hear that pretty rag.

The score of *Treemonisha* employs ragtime, but not exclusively. Scott Joplin was trying to create an American folk opera; he deserves credit for pioneering in this direction.

After he had painstakingly orchestrated the work, a single performance was given in Harlem, in a concert version without scenery or costumes, and with piano accompaniment. It did not reach the right audience, obtained no success, and was never heard again. The dashing of his operatic ambitions was a severe blow to Joplin. His mind began to fail, and on April 1, 1917 he died, famous and honored for his rags if not for his operas.

Other ragtime composers

Another important figure in early ragtime was the Negro pianist Thomas M. Turpin, composer of the first published Negro rag that is known, the *Harlem Rag*, which appeared in 1897. This was followed by *The Bowery Buck* (1899), *A Ragtime Nightmare* (1900), *St. Louis Rag* (1903), and *The Buffalo Rag* (1904). Turpin was definitely associated with the St. Louis sporting district and wrote most of his rags in a place called the Rosebud, which he owned and where he played the piano and imparted to other colleagues the secrets of ragtime. He died in 1922, having earned the unofficial title of "Father of St. Louis Ragtime."

James Sylvester Scott (1886–1938) learned to play the piano in his home town of Neosho, Missouri, and later moved to Carthage, Kansas, where he got a job in Dumars's music store and played ragtime in his spare time. Dumars thought his music was good enough to publish; so the next few years saw the publication of several James Scott numbers. Scott visited St. Louis where Stark published his *Climax Rag* in 1914. Other early Scott rags include *Frog Legs Rag*

(1906), *Kansas City Rag* (1907), *Great Scott Rag* (1909), *Sunburst Rag* (1909), *Hilarity Rag* (1910), and *Ophelia Rag* (1910). Altogether he published thirty rags for piano solo, the last of which was *Broadway Rag*, issued in 1922.

From 1914 James Scott lived as a music teacher and performer in Kansas City, continuing to compose and to develop his extraordinary technique as a ragtime pianist. *Honeymoon Rag* and *Prosperity Rag*, both published by Stark in 1916, reveal the increasing complexity of his style.

Louis Chauvin, a Negro pianist of St. Louis, who could neither read nor write music, is credited by some authorities with being one of the pioneer creative figures in ragtime, though only his *Heliotrope Bouquet* (1907) was published with his name (in collaboration with Scott Joplin). Two writers on ragtime, Simms and Borneman, assert that "many of his [Chauvin's] original tunes and syncopations were transcribed by Tom [Turpin] and later by Scott Joplin without any due credit." It is impossible to prove or disprove this statement, but it is a fact that much appropriation of unpublished material was going on in the 1890s, when musicians, both Negro and white, were racing neck-and-neck to get on the ragtime band wagon with compositions that they could call their own once the copyright had been registered. Actually, the first piano rag to be copyrighted was by a white musician, William Krell, and was titled *Mississippi Rag* (January 25, 1897). Not until December of 1897 was the first rag by a Negro composer published; that was, as previously noted, Tom Turpin's *Harlem Rag*.

If one took the date of copyright or of publication as the criterion, then precedence in the ragtime field would go to a white musician named Ben R. Harney, from Middlesboro, Kentucky (*b.* 1871), whose celebrated hit tune, "You've Been a Good Old Wagon but You've Done Broke Down," was published in Louisville in January, 1895. The following year it was brought out by Witmark in New York. This was a song, not a piano rag, but, in the words of Blesh and Janis,[4] "the piano accompaniment and the concluding instrumental 'dance' section are bona fide, if elementary, ragtime. . . . These facts establish Harney's unassailable priority as a pioneer of printed ragtime—if one disregards a mere matter of nomenclature or titling—and amply explain

[4] Blesh and Janis, *op. cit.*, p. 95.

his own staunch conviction that he 'originated ragtime.'" Actually, Harney was a writer of ragtime songs rather than of piano rags. Another famous early ragtime hit of his was *Mr. Johnson (Turn Me Loose)*, published in 1896.

Ben Harney undoubtedly had a lot to do with popularizing ragtime. When he appeared in New York in 1896, at the age of twenty-five, an item in the New York *Clipper* said: "Ben R. Harney . . . jumped into immediate favor through the medium of his genuinely clever plantation Negro imitations and excellent piano playing." When Harney published his *Rag Time Instructor* in 1897, he called himself "Original Instructor to the Stage of the Now Popular Rag Time in Ethiopian Song." Harney certainly did not originate ragtime, but he was a link in the chain that connected the old-time "Ethiopian business" with the folk-rooted novelty called ragtime.

Many other white musicians, nearly all from the South or Middle West, where they had ample opportunity to hear the true ragtime Negro playing and to absorb its characteristic traits at first hand, took a prominent part in the development and diffusion of ragtime. Among the most notable were George Botsford, Charles H. Hunter, Charles L. Johnson, Joseph Lamb, and Percy Wenrich. Botsford began with *The Katy Flyer–Cakewalk Two Step* in 1899 and ended with the *Boomerang Rag* in 1916. Charlie Johnson published about thirty rags, among them *Doc Brown's Cake Walk* (1899), *Dill Pickles* (1906), *Swanee Rag* (1912), *Blue Goose Rag* (1916), and *Fun on the Levee –Cakewalk* (1917). Some of his rags were published under the name of Raymond Birch. Hunter, a native of Nashville, Tennessee, almost totally blind from birth, first appeared in print in 1899 with *Tickled to Death*, followed by *A Tennessee Tantalizer* in 1900, *'Possum and 'Taters* in 1901. Hunter published a few more numbers, but died of tuberculosis in 1907. Joseph Lamb, a protégé of Joplin in New York (he was, exceptionally, an Easterner), was the author of *Excelsior Rag* and *Ethiopia Rag* (both 1909), *American Beauty Rag* (1913), *Cleopatra Rag* (1915), *Contentment Rag* (1915), and numerous others, many of which remain unpublished. Percy Wenrich, born in Joplin, Missouri, in 1880, and known as "The Joplin Kid," began imitating Negro ragtime at the age of twelve and later attended the Chicago Musical College but preferred–to use the title of one of his songs– "Wabash Avenue after Dark." He brought out *Peaches and*

Cream Rag (1905), *Noodles* (1906), *Sweet Meats Rag* (1907), *Memphis Rag* (1908), *Sunflower Rag* (1911), and others. He also wrote many successful songs, among them: "Put on Your Old Grey Bonnet" (1909) and "When You Wore a Tulip and I Wore a Big Red Rose" (1914).

Other ragtime composers who merit at least passing mention are Eubie Blake (*Charleston Rag*, c. 1899), Thomas E. Broady (*Mandy's Broadway Stroll*, 1898), Robert Hampton (*The Dogin' Rag*, 1913), Tony Jackson (*The Naked Dance*, c. 1902), Joe Jordan (*Double Fudge*, 1902), Henry Lodge (*Temptation Rag*, 1909), Arthur Marshall (*Ham and–Rag*, 1908), Artie Matthews (*Pastime Rags*, Nos. 1–5, 1913–1920), Paul Pratt (*Vanity Rag*, 1909), Luckey Roberts (*Junk Man Rag*, 1913), J. Russel Robinson (*Sapho Rag*, 1909; *Dynamite Rag*, 1910). Other prominent ragtime musicians—Ferdinand "Jelly Roll" Morton, Thomas "Fats" Waller, and James P. Johnson—will be discussed later, for their careers run over into the postwar period of ragtime.

Genuine ragtime music was difficult to play. But around 1900, and for several years thereafter, almost everybody in the United States wanted to play it. Harney's *Rag Time Instructor* proved unsatisfactory as a textbook. A more practical method was needed, and this came in 1903 when Axel Christensen of Chicago hired a studio and advertised: "Ragtime Taught in Ten Lessons." Pupils flocked to him, and encouraged by his success he published in 1904 Christensen's *Instruction Book No. 1 for Rag-Time Piano Playing*, which went into several revised and enlarged editions. Admitting that "It takes a skillful musician to play ragtime flawlessly," Christensen nevertheless undertook to impart the rudiments and "to teach the rawest beginner how to play ragtime in twenty lessons" (not *ten* this time!).

Far different was *The School of Ragtime—Six Exercises for Piano*, by Scott Joplin, published by John Stark in 1908. This is not a beginner's school, but a set of *études* for the advanced student. In his preface Joplin wrote:

> What is scurrilously called ragtime is an invention that is here to stay. That is now conceded by all classes of musicians. That all publications masquerading under the name of ragtime are not the genuine article will be better known when these exercises are studied. That real ragtime of the higher class is rather difficult to play is a

painful truth which most pianists have discovered. Syncopations are no indication of light or trashy music, and to shy bricks at "hateful ragtime" no longer passes for musical culture. To assist the amateur players in giving the "Joplin Rags" that weird and intoxicating effect intended by the composer is the object of this work.

Joplin wrote his exercises on three staves, of which the uppermost is a kind of guide and not to be played. This fundamental document of classic ragtime, consisting of the exercises and the composer's comments thereon, demands some quotation here. In his note to Exercise No. 1 the author writes:

It is evident that, by giving each note its proper time and by scrupulously observing the ties, you will get the effect. So many are careless in these respects that we will specify each feature. In this number, strike the first note and hold it through the time belonging to the second note. The upper staff is not syncopated, and is not to be played. The perpendicular dotted lines running from the syncopated note below to the two notes above will show exactly its duration. Play slowly until you catch the swing, and never play ragtime fast at any time.[5]

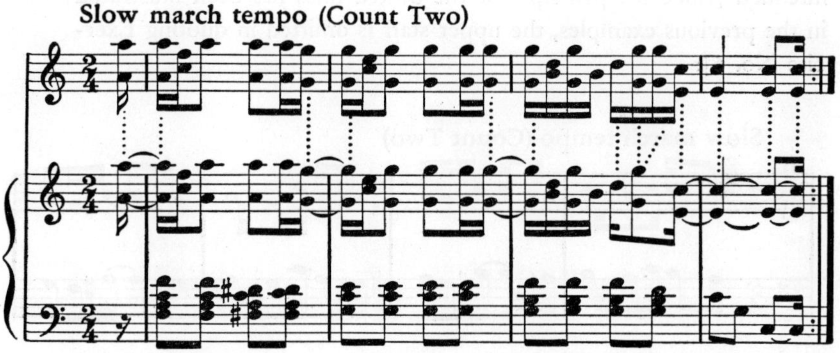

Concerning Exercise No. 3, Joplin made the following comment:

This style is very effective when neatly played. If you have observed the object of the dotted lines they will lead you to a proper rendering of this number and you will find it interesting:

[5] Excerpts from *The School of Ragtime* used by permission of Scott Joplin's estate.

Slow march tempo (Count Two)

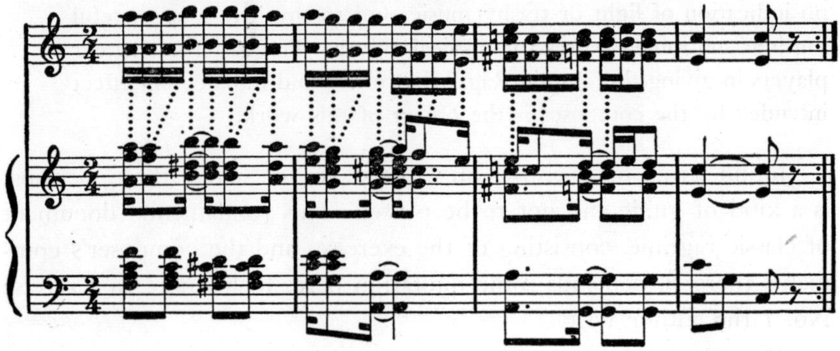

The sixth and final exercise is preceded by the following note:

The instructions given, together with the dotted lines, will enable you to interpret this variety which has very pleasing effects. We wish to say here, that the "Joplin ragtime" is destroyed by careless or imperfect rendering, and very often good players lose the effect entirely, by playing too fast. They are harmonized with the supposition that each note will be played as it is written, as it takes this and also the proper time divisions to complete the sense intended [since the principle of the dotted lines has been illustrated in the previous examples, the upper staff is omitted in quoting Exercise No. 6]:

Slow march tempo (Count Two)

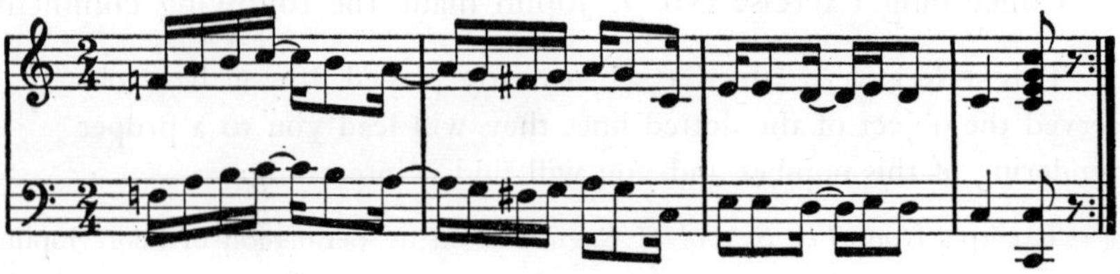

It is significant that Joplin stresses the need of a moderate tempo for ragtime. "Never play ragtime fast," he tells the student. And again, ". . . very often good players lose the effect entirely, by playing too fast." This was the classic St. Louis concept of ragtime, as exemplified by Scott Joplin.

New Orleans and New York

Important as was St. Louis in the rise of ragtime, the contribution of New Orleans must not be overlooked. That was the original center of "ragging" street bands and of the ragtime dance bands that ushered in jazz. It was also a center of ragtime piano, especially in the notorious red-light district of "Storyville," a section of the city set aside for "sporting" purposes. The leading New Orleans ragtime pianists were Antony Jackson (1876–1921) and Ferdinand "Jelly Roll" Morton (1885–1941), both of whom later went to Chicago. Morton's major role in the history of jazz will receive attention in a later chapter. Meanwhile our main concern will be with his piano rags. But first a few words about Tony Jackson.

Tony Jackson was a singer as well as a pianist, and the "composer" of several song hits, though he could not read music. His "Pretty Baby" (in collaboration with Egbert Van Alstyne) was a big hit in 1918. Among other melodies are "Don't Leave Me in the Ice and Snow" and "Miss Samantha Johnson's Wedding Day." As a ragtime player and improviser he is recalled as a fabulous performer by old-timers, but none of his rags was ever published. When queried about this, Jackson is said to have replied that he would burn them before he would give them away for five dollars apiece. The men who made money out of ragtime were not always its genuine creators.

During eight weeks in 1938, Jelly Roll Morton recorded for the Library of Congress, on 116 record sides, the story of his life, with musical illustrations at the piano. Here is a large part of the saga of ragtime, blues, and jazz, requiring the addition of many scholarly footnotes on points of historical fact, but presenting, with vivid and authentic details that otherwise would be lost to history, the background and genesis of a people's music. In Morton's recordings we can follow the transformation of an old French quadrille into the famous *Tiger Rag*, and observe the metamorphosis of *Maple Leaf Rag* into the hot, "stomping" style of New Orleans ragtime, of which Jelly Roll was the great piano exponent.

Morton did not begin to have his piano rags published until 1918, but many of them were written much earlier. The celebrated *King Porter Stomp,* for instance, dates from 1906. Other piano rags by Morton include *Frog-i-more Rag, The Pearls, Kansas City Stomps, Shreveport Stomps, Midnight Mama, Chicago Breakdown, Black Bottom Stomp, Ham and Eggs, Bugaboo, Mister Joe, Crazy Chord Rag, Buddy Carter's Rag, The Perfect Rag* (some unpublished). Through the many recordings that Jelly Roll Morton made, we can appreciate both the individual brilliancy of his style and the development of the typical New Orleans "hot" idiom.

With James P. Johnson (*b.* 1894) and Thomas "Fats" Waller, the scene shifts to New York. Johnson received lessons in harmony and counterpoint from a "long hair" professor and has worked ambitiously at compositions in the larger forms, such as the *Jasmine* (*Jazz-o-Mine*) *Concerto* for piano and orchestra and the *Harlem Symphony,* in four movements (1932), which includes a syncopated passacaglia on the hymn tune "I Want Jesus to Walk with Me." Looking upon Scott Joplin as a great forerunner, Johnson has endeavored to continue the tradition of classic ragtime with such piano pieces as *Caprice Rag* (1914), *Harlem Strut* (1917), *Carolina Shout* (1925), and many others. Mention should also be made of his syncopated *Eccentricity Waltz* (1926).

Thomas "Fats" Waller (1904–1943), a Negro born in New York, was the son of a pastor; his mother, who was musical, provided him with a high-class musical training under Carl Bohm and Leopold Godowsky. But he took to ragtime as to his natural element, composing his first rag at the age of fifteen. A man of huge bulk, irrepressible humor, and prodigious energy, he turned out over four hundred compositions in his relatively brief lifetime. In addition to his popular songs and scores for Broadway shows (*Keep Shufflin', Hot Chocolates, Early to Bed*), Waller composed many piano rags, among them: *Handful of Keys, Smashing Thirds, Fractious Fingering, Bach Up to Me,* and *Black Raspberry Jam.*

The heyday of ragtime was from about 1897 to 1910. It was in 1897 that Kerry Mills, white composer of sentimental songs, brought out, in an inspired moment, his stirring and immensely popular ragtime tune, *At a Georgia Camp Meeting,* based on the Civil War song

"Our Boys Will Shine Tonight." Contrary to a popular notion, Irving Berlin's much-publicized *Alexander's Ragtime Band* (1911) did not usher in the great age of ragtime. By that time ragtime was on the way out. Berlin's tune caught the public fancy and gave a fillip to the waning vogue of ragtime. But overexploitation by commercial interests, the high-pressure promotion of pseudo ragtime, and the mechanical repetition of routine formulas, soon brought about the decline of ragtime as a vital form of American music.

That this decline was under the circumstances inevitable may now be clearly perceived. What may also be now perceived and proclaimed is that ragtime, in its most authentic manifestations, as played and as written by both Negro and white musicians who were closest to its traditional origins, with its spurious elements sifted out by time and critical appraisal, remains as a permanent, important, and original contribution to America's music.

chapter twenty-two

Singin' the blues

Got de blues, but too dam' mean to cry.
(TRADITIONAL.)

The spirituals are the manifestation of Afro-American folk music in choral singing. The blues are the manifestation of Afro-American folk music in solo singing. When "a lonely Negro man plowing out in some hot, silent river bottom," raised his voice in a wailing "cornfield holler," he was singing the birth of the blues.[1] When a roustabout resting on the levee sang,

> Gwine down de river befo' long,
> Gwine down de river befo' long,
> Gwine down de river befo' long,

as if strengthening his lazy resolve by reiteration, he was singing the birth of the blues, with its three-line, twelve-bar pattern.

The three-line stanza seemed to develop naturally by repetition. Since the singer was giving relief to his feelings—of lonesomeness, or longing, or resentment, or sorrow—there was consolation in repeating the sentiment that he wanted to express. He began by telling what was on his mind, repeated it once for emphasis, and finished it off with a second repetition for good measure. This pattern was certainly no strain upon the singer's powers of improvisation. When the latter sought more scope, a variation in the third line resulted:

> I've never seen such real hard times before
> I've never seen such real hard times before
> The wolf keeps walkin' all 'round my door.

[1] See John and Alan Lomax, *American Ballads and Folk Songs,* p. 191.

This three-line stanza, consisting of statement, repetition, and "response," is the classic verse form of the blues. There are other patterns, for the blues are not stereotyped; but the above may be regarded as the norm.

Within their compact form the blues conveyed a complete mood and situation:

> Railroad blues
>
> I'm gonna lay my head on some lonesome railroad line
> I'm gonna lay my head on some lonesome railroad line
> An' let that two-nineteen train pacify my min'.

Often the verses of the blues, like those of the spirituals, were made up of current tag lines strung together in the moment of improvisation.

Although most blues have the burden of lament associated with the expression "feeling blue," they have an undertone of humor, not so much stressed as implied, that gives them a character utterly different from that of the ordinary sentimental song. Indeed, they are not sentimental at all, but combine realism and fantasy in a straightforward projection of mood and feeling.

The origin of the blues is lost in obscurity. Conjecturally, we can say that they developed concurrently with the rest of Afro-American folk song in the South of the United States. By 1870 they were probably widespread throughout that region, though assuredly not known by the name of "blues" until considerably later.

Besides being a type of folk song in their own right, and later a form of American popular music, the blues were a means of effecting the transition of Afro-American "hot" music from the vocal to the instrumental realm through the medium of piano blues and the jazz band. The blues are therefore of far-reaching significance in the development of American music.

The musical structure of the blues

Abbe Niles was unquestionably right when he remarked that "the blues architecture is admirably adapted to impromptu song and versification alike"—except that the term "architecture" is a bit pretentious for folk music. Since we have already seen something of the versification, let us now glance at the musical structure of the blues. First, as regards harmony: the harmonic scheme of the blues is merely a foundation upon which the melodic structure rests; its function is important—for without it the whole structure would collapse—but it does not constitute the creative element in the blues. It is like the form of the sonnet in poetry, providing a definite framework, capable of being varied within limits but needing the skill and inspiration of the poet to result in something creative. Keats and Hunt could not have improvised sonnets on the spur of the moment unless they had been thoroughly familiar with the sonnet as a traditional form.

To be suited to "impromptu" song, a harmonic scheme must be simple and stable, and at the same time provide scope for sufficient variation to avoid absolute sameness. The harmonic scheme of the blues fulfills these conditions. Normally only three chords are used: tonic, subdominant, and dominant seventh. The usual progression consists of the common chord of the tonic, the same on the subdominant, the chord of the dominant seventh, and back to the tonic chord. There are several variants, such as the introduction of the dominant seventh at the beginning, but essentially the harmonic foundation is "solid" enough to offer a firm base for the melodic inspiration of the singer or instrumentalist.

The usual structure of the blues consists of a twelve-bar pattern. Each line of the verse corresponds to four measures of the music. To express it in another way, there are two complete melodic statements (corresponding to the verse statement and its repetition), each ending on the tonic (or the third or fifth of the tonic chord), followed by the melodic "response" (corresponding to the third line of the verse), which also ends on the tonic. Here is an example in the widely diffused folk blues, "Joe Turner": [2]

Dey tell me Joe Tur-ner's come and gone— Dey tell me Joe
Tur-ner's come and gone— Got my man an' gone—

[2] From *A Treasury of the Blues*, p. 12. Copyright 1926, 1929, by W. C. Handy and Edward Abbe Niles. Published by Charles Boni, New York. Used by permission of the copyright owners.

It will be noticed that there is a considerable gap between the end of one melodic phrase and the beginning of the next. Each statement actually occupies three rather than four measures. Abbe Niles has ably described the significance of this time interval in the melodic structure of the blues:

> This is typical, and important. It affords to the improviser, for one thing, a space in which his next idea may go through its period of gestation,—and this is important to him. But to us it is of far greater interest that, assuming he isn't compelled to concentrate on what is to follow, he can utilize this space, not as a hold, but as a *playground* in which his voice or instrument may be allowed to wander in such fantastic musical paths as he pleases, returning (not necessarily but usually) to the keynote, third, or fifth, yet again before vacation is over. Regularly in folk-blues the last syllable of each line thus coincides, not only with the keynote or another element of the tonic major triad, *but with the first beat, third bar, of its corresponding four bars of music*, leaving seven quick beats or three slow ones (according to the time-signature) before the melody proper resumes its motion.[3]

This pattern can be verified by reference to the melody of "Joe Turner" quoted above. The space between the end of one melodic statement and the beginning of the next was often filled in with a simple ejaculation sung on a few interpolated notes, such as *oh, Lawdy!* As we have previously noticed, the interpolation of a brief ejaculatory refrain after each line is a common trait of Negro folk song, being frequently found both in spirituals and work songs. In the blues, the interpolated notes, whether sung or played instrumentally, came to be known as the "break" or the "jazz"; but this was after the blues had passed their archaic or folk stage. All these folk-born forms—blues, ragtime, jazz—existed in practice long before they were tagged with a name, classified, imitated, and exploited.

The "break" might be very simple or very elaborate, according to the impulse and skill of the singer or player. From the very beginning of our chronicle of America's music we have been familiar—recall the early folk psalmody of New England—with the traditional practice of melodic ornamentation. Handy says that as a child he heard Negro congregations singing "baptisin'" and "death-and-burial" songs with

[3] *Ibid.*, p. 14. From the introductory text by Abbe Niles.

all the voices weaving their own melodic threads around the notes of the tune. He transcribed one of these melodic improvisations, as recalled by him: [4]

This is interesting (though much more so would be the combination of many voices in this improvised embellishment); but Niles, who quotes this transcription, is mistaken when he writes that these hymns, in their ornamented versions, were "sung as they never were except by Negroes." The Negroes undoubtedly had their peculiar intonation, rhythm, and intervals; but the singing of tunes with improvised melodic embellishments, and the filling-in of "gaps" or holds with interpolated notes, was a firmly established practice in Anglo-American folk music long before the development of the Negro spirituals and the blues. The *manner* of jazz improvisation may be unique, but the principle has a long tradition in both the folk and the art music of Europe.

Many of the folk blues use the pentatonic scale (it will be found in "Joe Turner," above, with the addition of a minor third), but this scale, so widespread in folk music, is not what gives to the blues their peculiar melodic quality. The characteristic trait is rather the flatting of the third and seventh degrees of the diatonic scale. These are the so-called "blue notes" that have been of such significance in modern

[4] *Ibid.*, p. 23. Arranged by W. C. Handy. Copyright 1926 by W. C. Handy. Used by permission.

music. Frequently, in singing the blues, a Negro will return to the third of the tonic chord; and as Niles remarks, this is "a fact of the first importance to the blues because of the tendency of the untrained Negro voice when singing the latter tone at an important point, to *worry* it, slurring or wavering between flat and natural." [5] Strictly speaking, therefore, it is not the flatted third as such, but rather this ambivalent, this *worried* or slurred tone, that constitutes the true "blue note."

The blues scale (diatonic, with microtonally flatted third and seventh) lies at the very core of Afro-American folk song, and its influence has permeated large sectors of American music, both in the popular and in the fine-art idioms. To demonstrate the widespread use of the blues tetrachord in every type of Afro-American vocal expression, Winthrop Sargeant cites the "chanting sermon" of a Negro preacher in Alabama who in his declamation employed just two notes: a tonic, and the "blue" third above it.[6] And the congregation would echo him in similar fashion.

All the evidence indicates that the blues scale, and the blues intonation that goes with it, are an original and unique contribution of the Negro race to America's music.

The primitive or archaic blues, as we have remarked, were probably sung at first without accompaniment. But as the possession of musical instruments became more common among the Negroes, instrumental accompaniments, usually on the banjo or the guitar, later on the piano, were added. This instrumental participation was of immense importance in the development of the blues and their transition into jazz. The incorporation of the blues scale, blues harmony, and melodic improvisation, into the idiom of instrumental music, from the piano to the emergent jazz band, was an epoch-making development in the history of American music. The accompanying instrument, or instruments—for there might be several—not only provided the basic harmony but imitated, and in a manner competed with, the voice in melodic improvisation. The solo voice is the "leader"; the instruments "follow the leader" but also weave semi-independent melodic lines, while at the same time filling in the harmony and marking the beat of the rhythm. When the voice ceases at the end of a melodic statement (i.e., a line of the verse), it is "answered" by the

[5] *Ibid.*, p. 14.
[6] Sargeant, *Jazz: Hot and Hybrid*, p. 183.

instruments, which then find themselves "on their own," free to assert their individuality boldly before the voice assumes its ascendancy again in the next vocal statement. And at the end, when the voice has finished with its third line, it is the instruments that have the final say. Since each vocal statement is answered by an instrumental statement, there is a perfect antiphonal pattern that corresponds to a fundamental device of Afro-American music.

Since the instruments, in addition to "answering" the voice, also weave their melodic lines along with it, we get the element of polyphony in the blues, with a more or less complex contrapuntal texture, depending on the number of instruments involved. And since the singer will sometimes follow a melodic line independent of the underlying harmony, we also get the element of polytonality (or more accurately, bitonality), that is, the simultaneous use of two or more keys. Thus the vocal and instrumental blues, within their deceptively simple framework, are capable of considerable complexity and variety.

It is important to stress the interplay between the vocal and instrumental elements in the blues. As we shall see later, jazz developed largely from the attempt to render the effects of Afro-American vocal intonation on modern musical instruments. When, toward the end of the nineteenth century, the piano began to be widely used for accompanying the blues, Negro pianists employed the so-called "blues tone-cluster," played by simultaneously sounding the flat and natural keys of the third and seventh, as follows:

These piano "blue notes" were the keyboard equivalent of the "slurred" or microtonal pitch used in singing.

To summarize: the blues developed originally as a form of Afro-American folk song, probably took shape gradually after the Civil War, were widely sung throughout the rural South in the final decades of the nineteenth century, and soon emerged as a (normally) twelve-bar song form with instrumental accompaniment, basically antiphonal in structure. Taken up by the Negro musicians who converged on the cities of the South and Middle West in the 1890s in search of employment, legitimate or otherwise, the *urbanized* blues branched off from the archaic or folk blues (which continued on their own course) and took a line of development that in turn branched off into two distinct channels: the blues as popular song and the blues as jazz. Both of these currents eventually converged in the productions of tin-pan alley, where the blues became less blue and the jazz less hot.

Composer of "St. Louis Blues"

Many musicians and many singers, some anonymous, some legendary, some obscure, some famous, many now dead, some still living, were responsible for the transition of the blues from a folk song of one region and one group to a type of song known throughout the land, widely imitated, often changed, frequently distorted, occasionally cheapened, but generally asserting its essential integrity and individuality as a musical form and as a nonsentimental expression of feeling. Among these musicians, there is one whose name has been particularly associated with the rise of the blues as a type of popular music: W. C. Handy, known above all as the composer of "St. Louis Blues."

William Christopher Handy was born in Florence, Alabama, on November 16, 1873. His father, a Methodist preacher, was strongly opposed to the boy's musical inclinations. "Son," he said one time, "I'd rather follow you to the graveyard than to hear you had become a musician." Nevertheless, young Handy managed to acquire the rudiments of music in school—and out of it also, though scarcely in an orthodox fashion. In his own words:

> We Handy's Hill kids made rhythm by scraping a twenty-penny nail across the teeth of the jawbone of a horse that had died in the woods near by. By drawing a broom handle across our first finger lying on a table we imitated the bass. We sang through fine-tooth combs. With the thumb of the right hand interlocked with the little finger of the left, we placed the thumb of the left hand under our chin and made rhythmic sounds by rattling our teeth. We would put the thumb of our right hand on our goozle or Adam's apple, yelling at the same time:
>
> Went down the river,
> Couldn't get across,
> Paid five dollars for an old gray horse.
>
> . . . For drums we wore out our mother's tin pans and milk pails, singing:

Cornstalk fiddle and shoestring bow
Broke in the middle, jumped up Joe.[7]

Then there was the eighty-year-old fiddler called Uncle Whit Walker, who not only fiddled but sang and "stomped" at the same time. "Uncle Whit could stomp the left heel and the right forefoot and alternate this with the right heel and the left forefoot, making four beats to the bar. That was real stomping." And it was real musical training for young Handy.

Later, having learned to play an old-fashioned rotary-valve cornet, Handy took to the road with a minstrel show. In 1903 he formed his own dance band in Clarksdale, Mississippi, and in 1905 transferred his activities to Memphis, where he formed a new band. In the 1909 campaign for mayor of Memphis, Handy's Band was hired by the supporters of a candidate named E. H. Crump. Handy set out to write a campaign song that would not only help elect Mr. Crump but also provide a hit tune for his own band. The result was a piece originally called "Mister Crump," but published three years later as "Memphis Blues." Regarding this composition, Handy wrote in his autobiography:

> The melody of *Mister Crump* was mine throughout. On the other hand, the twelve-bar, three-line form of the first and last strains, with its three-chord basic harmonic structure (tonic, subdominant, dominant seventh) was that already used by Negro roustabouts, honky-tonk piano players, wanderers and others of their underprivileged but undaunted class from Missouri to the Gulf, and had become a common medium through which any such individual might express his personal feelings in a sort of musical soliloquy.[8]

Handy, therefore, did not claim to have originated the blues, but merely to have developed and exploited the vein of Negro folk music with which he had become familiar in his boyhood and youth. The lyrics he mostly pieced together from snatches of folk song that he picked up here and there.

In the "Memphis Blues," Handy introduced a rhythmic figure in the bass, which is that of the habanera or tango rhythm, widely dif-

[7] Handy, *Father of the Blues*, p. 15.
[8] *Ibid.*, p. 99.

fused in the music of the Caribbean and the east coast of South America: 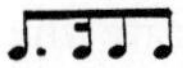. He called it the "tangana" rhythm. A variant of this pattern, by the way, produces the rhythm of the once-popular American dance called the Charleston (). Handy also introduced the tangana rhythm into his famous "St. Louis Blues," composed in 1914. He used it in the instrumental introduction and in part of the accompaniment (middle strain).

Handy used both three- and four-line verses in "St. Louis Blues." The first two strains consist of the typical three-line verse of the folk blues, so that the first part is made up of two twelve-bar strains. But the second part consists of a four-line unit, so that we get the sixteen-bar strain that is standard for most American popular songs. This procedure of using the sixteen-bar strain in the blues was continued as a regular practice by most of the commercial composers who turned out the pseudo blues of tin-pan alley.

Handy himself stood about midway between the tradition of Negro folk music and that of tin-pan alley. He claimed that in his blues he "aimed to use all that is characteristic of the Negro from Africa to Alabama." Nevertheless, he also confesses that he took up with the "low forms" of Negro folk music hesitantly and approached them "with a certain fear and trembling" because they were not considered respectable and they did not come from books, which were the symbol and source of education. So Handy was to a certain extent another victim of the genteel tradition, which functions on many levels. Whatever strength he has as a musician, he owes entirely to the tradition of Negro folk music, some of which he absorbed in spite of himself.

From Memphis, Handy moved to Chicago and later to New York, where he formed his own music publishing company. He eventually became blind, but continued to carry on courageously with his work. In addition to those already mentioned, Handy's published blues include "Joe Turner Blues" (1915), "The Hesitating Blues" (1915), "John Henry Blues" (1922), and "Blue Gummed Blues" (1926). In spite of the much-publicized title, "Father of the Blues," W. C. Handy did not create the blues any more than Ben Harney created ragtime. But he was indubitably a pioneer of the *composed* blues as a type of American popular song.

The following blues cadences and connecting passages (examples furnished by W. C. Handy [9]) will serve to demonstrate the harmonic style as developed in the popular idiom:

Numerous white composers began to cultivate the blues as a type of popular song, among them Cliff Hess ("Homesickness Blues," 1916), Jerome Kern ("Left-All-Alone-Again Blues," 1920), Irving Berlin ("School-House Blues," 1921), and George Gershwin ("The Half of It, Dearie, Blues," 1924). The use of the blues idiom in the symphonic music of Gershwin and other composers of "serious" music will be discussed in the chapter titled "The Americanists." It is time now to return to the folk roots of the blues and to say something about those who in a sense were and are the real creators of the blues: the Negro singers and players through whose interpretations are heard the deep ancestral strains of this traditional song, containing the quintessence of the Afro-American spirit in music.

The great blues singers

Listening to recordings of the great blues singers is the only way that one can learn to know the real spirit and texture of these unique songs. As a word of caution, it should be remarked that many of the blues do not conform to the three-line twelve-bar pattern that was de-

[9] From *A Treasury of the Blues*, p. 21.

scribed as the norm. Folk music is not standardized, and form in the sense of pattern is not the prime factor in the blues. The intonation, the rhythm, the harmonic progression and melodic inflection, the style and the spirit: these are what make the blues be really the blues. And these qualities have to be embodied in a real blues singer before they come alive in all their power and authenticity.

We began this chapter by saying that the spirituals were the manifestation of Afro-American folk music in choral singing, and the blues in solo singing. This is true in the main, but on occasion a man or a woman alone might sing a spiritual for his or her own solace, perhaps even humming or chanting it without words; and very likely it was out of this kind of lonesome singing, just for consolation, just for the pleasure and beauty of the music, that the blues were born. An example of Negro song with guitar accompaniment, chanted without words, in which the spiritual blends into the blues, is heard in the haunting singing and playing of "Blind Willie" Johnson in "Dark Was the Night." To hear this beautiful and somber chant is to feel the folk roots of the blues entwined very deeply indeed in the heart of the Negro race.

Another example of the organic relationship between the spiritual and the blues is to be found in "Blind Willie" Johnson's singing of "Lord, I Just Can't Keep From Crying," with guitar accompaniment and female "helpers" (women's voices as background). This is, strictly speaking, a spiritual, but its mood of lament is very close to the origin of the blues. Furthermore, this is an extraordinary number that should be heard by anyone interested in either the spirituals or the blues. The rhythm of the guitar, the husky, moving quality of Blind Willie's voice, and the graceful weaving of the women's voices in the background, create an unforgettable impression.

The true minstrels of American music were not those of the stage, but those itinerant Negro singers and players, sometimes blind like the bards of old and led by a boy, who wandered through the Southland, singing the songs learned in their childhood and others that came from later and more bitter experience of life, like the blues that were so often a lament for betrayal in love:

> Ain't got no mama now, ain't got no mama now.
> She told me late las' night, you don' need no mama no how.

"Blind Lemon" Jefferson sings this "Black Snake Moan" (the snake is an age-old sexual symbol) with guitar accompaniment and some wordless chanting in between the verses.

With Gertrude "Ma" Rainey (1886–1939) we come to the greatest personality in blues singing. She was in show business all her life, and at fifteen was already married and traveling with her husband's minstrel troupe. Ma Rainey's rich and powerful voice, and the classic line of her blues singing, may be heard in "Traveling Blues," accompanied by her own tub, jug, and washboard band (Folkways Records, Album FP 59). Other fine recordings made by Ma Rainey include "Counting the Blues," "Jelly Bean Blues," "Levee Camp Moan," "Moonshine Blues," "Stack O'Lee Blues," and "Slow Driving Moan." Here it will be appropriate to quote Rudi Blesh's fine appreciation of Ma Rainey's qualities as a blues singer:

> Ma Rainey's singing, monumental and simple, is by no means primitive. It is extremely conscious in its use of her full expressive means, definitely classic in purity of line and its rigid avoidance of the decorative. . . . Rainey's voice is somber, but never harsh, and its sad and mellow richness strikes to the heart. Her vibrato, slow, controlled and broad, is one of the important and characteristic elements in her tone production, and her tones are projected by sheer power with an organlike fullness and ease. The deepest and most genuine feeling fills her every note and phrase with gusty humor or with an elegiac and sometimes almost gentle sadness.[10]

Bessie Smith (*d.* 1937) continued the tradition of Ma Rainey and became known as "Empress of the Blues." Before succumbing to commercialism in her later years, she produced many excellent recordings of the blues, of which one of the most beautiful and best-known is her singing of "Careless Love," an Anglo-American folk song made over into a blues. Other notable recordings are "You've Been a Good Ole Wagon," "Empty Bed Blues," "Spider Man's Blues," "Poor Man's Blues," "Back Water Blues," "Mean Old Bed Bug Blues," and "A Good Man is Hard to Find."

An interesting combination of instruments–guitar, piano, and tuba –accompanies the singing of Gertrude Perkins in "No Easy Rider Blues," recorded in New York in 1928 but couched in traditional folk style, with interpolated humming and chanting, and a generally un-

[10] Blesh, *Shining Trumpets,* p. 124.

sophisticated delivery. This may be compared with Bessie Smith's earlier recording of "Yellow Dog Blues," which also deals with the familiar theme of the "easy rider" (lover).

One of the most picaresque, and also most gifted, figures in the field of American Negro folk music was Huddie Leadbetter (1885–1949), more familiarly known as "Leadbelly." He was born in Louisiana, acquired a vast repertoire of folk songs that he never forgot, and became a masterly performer on the twelve-string guitar, as well as a folk singer of extraordinary qualities.

As a youth, Leadbelly was "lead man" for Blind Lemon Jefferson and accompanied the latter on many of his wanderings through the South, learning from him much of the authentic blues tradition. As a recollection of those days, Leadbelly used to sing a number that he called "Blind Lemon Blues."

Along with Ma Rainey and Bessie Smith, Bertha "Chippie" Hill must be mentioned as one of the great blues singers. Her recordings of "How Long Blues" (close to the spiritual tradition), "Careless Love," and "Trouble in Mind," are masterpieces in the classic blues style. In her original recording of "Trouble in Mind" she is accompanied by Louis Armstrong on the trumpet and Richard M. Jones on the piano (recorded in 1926; another recording was made in 1946 with Lee Collins, trumpet; Lovie Austin, piano; John Lindsay, bass; and "Baby" Dodds, drums). The lyrical quality of Armstrong's trumpet in the earlier recording is a thing of wondrous beauty, and the blending of voice, piano, and trumpet in warm, vibrant tone colors is a joy to hear.

The same instrumental combination—Armstrong on trumpet and Jones on piano—accompanies Nolan Welsh's singing of "Bridwell [*recte* Bridewell] Blues," in a recording also made in 1926. But the term "accompaniment" is misleading in connection with such a performance. After each vocal statement, Armstrong's eloquent trumpet answers with lyrical phrases that not merely match but surpass the expressive power of the voice, especially in rhythmic flexibility and variety of tone. This is a perfect example of the antiphonal form of the blues at its best.

Ferdinand "Jelly Roll" Morton was a blues singer of the very first order as well as a truly creative figure of instrumental jazz. The lyrical quality of his style is demonstrated in such recordings as "Winin' Boy" and "Mamie's Blues," in both of which he accompanies himself on the piano (a partial scoring of the latter number will be found in the appendix of Blesh's *Shining Trumpets,* Example 24, and will repay careful study). In the "shouting" type of blues he performs effectively in "Michigan Water Blues" and "Doctor Jazz." Transposition of the blues from vocal to instrumental performance is exemplified in the recording of "Mr. Jelly Lord" and "Wolverine Blues," which Jelly Roll made together with Johnny Dodds on clarinet and "Baby" Dodds on drums. This recording brings us straight into the heart of jazz. The clarinet takes the place of the voice. It *sings.*

The merging of ragtime and blues in piano solo may be observed in Jelly Roll Morton's playing of "Tom Cat Blues," recorded in 1924 (Folkways Jazz Anthology, vol. 9), which is in the New Orleans style of "hot" piano that Morton himself did more than anyone else to develop and perpetuate.

Piano blues and "boogiewoogie"

The "boogiewoogie" school of piano blues playing was launched by Jimmy Yancey (1898–1951), whose wife, "Mama" Yancey was also a remarkable blues singer (cf. the recordings of "Pallet on the Floor" and "How Long Blues" made by Mama and Jimmy Yancey). Boogiewoogie transfers to the piano the twelve-bar pattern of the blues with its basic harmonic structure and is characterized by a persistent percussive rhythmic figure in the left hand, which continues unchanged while the right hand embroiders its own rhythmic-melodic configurations. The resulting cross-rhythms are complex and exciting. The typical Yancey bass, said to have been derived from locomotive rhythms, has a powerful drive and moves ahead with gathering momentum.

Among the recorded piano blues of Jimmy Yancey are "The Fives or Five O'Clock Blues" (also recorded as "Yancey Stomp"), "Midnight Stomp" (fast blues), and "How Long Blues." This last is a slow blues in which the perfection of Yancey's art can be fully appreciated; it is full of the genuine mood of the blues.

Continuators of the boogiewoogie style were Clarence "Pine Top" Smith (1900–1928), who first popularized the term "boogiewoogie"; and Meade Lux Lewis (*b.* 1905). Pine Top Smith, whose checkered career ended when he was shot by a stray bullet during a brawl in a night club—an institution where he spent most of his waking hours—composed "Pine Top's Boogie Woogie," "Pine Top's Blues," "Now I Ain't Got Nothin' At All," and "Jump Steady Blues." Meade Lux Lewis's masterpiece is "Honky-Tonk Train Blues," noteworthy for its chromatic harmonies and compelling cross-rhythms.

The transformation of the vocal blues into the "hot" idiom of boogiewoogie piano may be further demonstrated in the playing of another Yancey follower, Albert Ammons (1903–1949), whose solo version of the "St. Louis Blues," executed with tremendous virtuosity, is an impressive example of this trend.

James P. Johnson, mentioned in the chapter on ragtime, is also an outstanding performer and composer of blues for the piano. His "Snowy Morning Blues," dating from 1927 (recorded in 1943 for Folkways Records), reveals him as a masterly continuator of the classic blues tradition. One should also recall his fine accompaniments for various blues singers, especially for Bessie Smith in "Back Water Blues."

The evolution of the blues has been traced from the primitive solo chant, sung alone or with guitar, to the blues with instrumental jazz accompaniment, or played by a jazz ensemble without singing, and finally to the boogiewoogie blues for piano solo. None of these manifestations or transformations of the basic form known as "blues" is, of course, a substitute for any other. The archaic folk blues are as beautiful and powerful today as they ever were. The blues of classic New Orleans jazz cannot be bettered. The interpretations of the great blues singers of the past remain as models of style and expression. The blues will go on changing and evolving and engendering new forms of American music. They have had, and will continue to have, their influence upon the art music as well as the popular music of the United States, and of other countries also.

chapter twenty-three

The growth of jazz

Jazz has contributed an enduring value to America in the sense that it has expressed ourselves.

GEORGE GERSHWIN, IN REVOLT IN THE ARTS.

In 1917 the now defunct but then widely read *Literary Digest* observed that "a strange word has gained widespread use in the ranks of our producers of popular music. It is 'jazz,' used mainly as an adjective descriptive of a band." That is rather vague, but at least it offers testimony that the term "jazz" was established as a musical term in the United States before the end of World War I. No one knew just where the word came from, and hardly anybody knew exactly what it meant, except that it had something to do with dance bands. Today we know considerably more about jazz, but we are still somewhat uncertain as to the origin of the word itself.

There are many theories concerning the etymology of the word "jazz." Most of them are fanciful, especially those that allege a derivation from the name of some Negro musician, such as Jess, or Chaz (abbreviated from Charles). More plausible is the derivation from the Negro patois of Louisiana, though whether the root is of French or African origin remains in doubt. One theory asserts that the root is in the French verb *jaser*, meaning to babble or cackle; another affirms that such forms as *jas*, *jass*, *jazz*, and *jasz* originated in an African dialect. The first appearance of the word "jass" (as it was then spelled) to designate a certain type of music, appears to have been in 1915, when a band from New Orleans was billed at Lamb's Café in Chicago as "Brown's Dixieland Jass Band." But according to the testimony of Lafcadio Hearn, the word was known much earlier in New Orleans, and certainly the music that came to be called jazz existed for several decades before the Chicago episode.[1]

[1] According to Charles Edward Smith, author of *The Jazz Record Book* (p. 4), "This word jazz is a corruption of the Elizabethan *jass* which had survived in the vernacular of bawdy-houses."

New Orleans was the birthplace of jazz music. In our chapter titled "The Exotic Periphery" we traced the racial, cultural, and musical currents that converged and mingled in "The Crescent City," where French, Spanish, African, Caribbean, and American influences created a cultural climate uniquely propitious for the emergence of an urban folk music such as jazz. Many strands went into the making of jazz. There were the traditional patterns and impulses of native African music, remote but potent in survival (see Chapter 4). There was the whole body of Afro-American folk song, the spirituals, the work songs, the ballads, the blues. There were the blackface minstrel tunes, which in turn had drawn upon the storehouse of Irish, Scottish, and British folk melody. Closely related to minstrel music, and forming a principal link with jazz, was ragtime, the syncopated piano music of the 1890s. Important, too, was the heritage of Creole folk songs and dance tunes, which gave such a gay and brittle character to the popular music of New Orleans. It remains to show how these diverse and apparently heterogeneous elements entered the blood stream of jazz.

Jazz resulted, essentially, from the Negro's opportunity to obtain, and to use in his own fashion, the conventional manufactured musical instruments of European origin, such as the trumpet or cornet, the clarinet, the trombone, the snare and bass drums, as well as the piano. This opportunity occurred because of the special situation of band music in New Orleans. In the colorful, spectacular, exuberant life of the city, with its annual Mardi Gras processions, its frequent parades and celebrations of all kinds, brass bands occupied an important place. Brass bands were needed not only for parades and celebrations, but also for weddings and funerals, for picnics and excursions, in short, for every occasion that was either festive or solemn—and often the solemn was turned into the festive through the music of the marchings bands, playing such gay tunes as *Gettysburg March*, *High Society*, and *Panama* (Robert Goffin has identified the last two as derived from traditional marches played by village bands in France and Belgium).

In a city abounding with bands, there was no scarcity of musical instruments. After the Civil War, dispersed Confederate military bands provided a source of secondhand instruments. These became so plentiful and cheap that they were within the reach of everyone. There were many Negro, as well as white, bands in New Orleans during the nineteenth century. Negro fraternal and benevolent associations, and various labor organizations, had their own bands. More than a dozen Negro brass bands took part in the mammoth funeral procession for President Garfield in 1881.

We do not know *exactly* how these Negro bands played in the second half of the nineteenth century. That is, we do not know to what extent they conformed to the conventional standards of the white bands, or to what extent they made the music "hot" in accordance with their own traditional musical values. In view of the strong tradition of Afro-American music that existed in New Orleans, and the freedom of cultural expression that the Negro had long enjoyed there, it is reasonable to suppose that, in some cases at least, the old popular tunes were played more or less "hot" by these early Negro bands. Furthermore, these proletarian street bands were made up of workers who played in their spare time and who were probably influenced little or not at all by the trend toward conventional education that succeeded in denaturing and distorting the Negro spirituals after they were "discovered" and arranged by cultivated musicians. The "hot" qualities that went into the singing of work songs and of spirituals in their pristine state were carried over into instrumental music by the Negro bandsmen of New Orleans who were the precursors of classic jazz, which therefore emerges as an organic growth from the traditional roots of Afro-American folk music, and as a natural development from the sociocultural conditions of the city in which jazz was born.

The "hot" band music that developed through the New Orleans Negro street bands during this early period, roughly from about 1870 to 1890, has been termed "archaic jazz." It was mostly for street parades and funerals. The street bands would accompany the funeral cortege to the cemetery (interment is always aboveground in New Orleans), playing slow dirges, perhaps an adaptation of some old hymn or sentimental song. After the interment, on the way back, the band would begin to play gayer tunes, and the music would soon get "hot," in some familiar "leaving the cemetery" tune, such as "Oh, Didn't He Ramble." Meanwhile, there would be a "second line" of players walking along beside the band. This consisted of children, fascinated by the music and the shining instruments, whistling or singing the tunes, and trying to imitate a brass band with all kinds of improvised or homemade instruments. In this "second line," absorbing the elements of "hot" band music, there were assuredly many boys who grew up to be the makers and leaders of New Orleans jazz.

When "hot" brass bands began to be used for dancing, the era of jazz was definitely ushered in. It had been the custom previously, in Louisiana, to use string orchestras, sometimes with a piano, for dancing indoors, and the music they played was "sweet." When the powerful impetus of the street bands, with their contagious "hot" style, was unleashed on the dance floor, it was the beginning of a revolution in American popular music. This development took place in the 1890s.

Pioneers of jazz

The most colorful figure associated with the beginnings of classic jazz in New Orleans was Charles "Buddy" Bolden (1868–1931), a barber with his own shop, and publisher of a scandal sheet called *The Cricket*. He learned to play the cornet in his spare time, and in the early 1890s formed a band that was in wide demand both for parades and dances. It was a small band, consisting of from five to seven pieces. This was the norm for classic New Orleans jazz. It included cornet, clarinet, valve trombone (alternating with slide trombone, the latter used for glissandi), guitar, bass, and drums. Later a second clarinet was added. During the twelve years or more of its existence, the personnel of Bolden's Band included many of the great pioneers of hot jazz.

There is a difference of opinion as to the extent of Bolden's musical training and knowledge. "Bunk" Johnson, who played second cornet in Bolden's band in 1895–1897, wrote years later: "Buddy could not read a note, but he surely played a good stiff lead and would have you in maybe six sharps before you finished, but I could always go anywhere the King went. We played parades and advertising wagons and, excuse me for the expression, honky tonks, and together we made many famous blues." [2] Bolden was called "King" after his skill, his personality, and his enterprise had given him the ascendancy over other pioneer trumpet players in New Orleans. Johnson insists on Bolden's musical illiteracy as a prime factor in the success of his band:

> Here is the thing that made King Bolden Band be the first band that played jazz. It was because it did not Read at all. I could fake like 500 myself; so you tell them that Bunk and King Bolden's Band was the first ones that started Jazz in the City or any place else.

[2] Letter to Frederic Ramsey, Jr., quoted in Ramsey and Smith's *Jazzmen*.

A recent historian of jazz, Paul Eduard Miller, while conceding that Bolden "undoubtedly was one of those rare natural, instinctive musicians who had a flair for the right jazz phrasing and intonation," nevertheless adds that, "judging from the overwhelming consensus of reports from old-time New Orleans musicians, he was a reasonably good musician too and not all his playing was sheer spontaneity or so-called improvisation. His technique too, was good and was acquired by a natural bent for the medium rather than protracted study, although there is little question that he was given considerable instruction on the cornet before he approached the zenith of his career as a jazz virtuoso." [3] The fact remains that collective improvisation and the remaking or reworking of the traditional New Orleans marches and dance tunes in "hot" rhythm and intonation, were at the core of the style developed, though not created (he had precursors in this field) by King Bolden and his band.

Of course, there were many other bands, active in New Orleans about the same time, which must share the credit for the growth of jazz. One of the earliest was The Excelsior Band, led by the clarinetist T. V. Baquet, which came to include such outstanding "hot" players as Alphonse Picou (clarinetist), Manuel Perez (cornet), and John Robichaux (bass drum)—note the preponderance of French and Spanish names. Perez and Robichaux also had bands of their own. The latter's first band, formed in 1885, was, like Bolden's, a small hot group, though later he formed bigger bands. Perez, considered by some to be the greatest of the pioneer jazz trumpeters, played with the Onward Brass Band from the 1880s, and continued with it during its various transformations (becoming continually hotter) until 1917.

Associated with The Olympia Band from 1900 to 1912 was another legendary figure of early jazz, Freddie Keppard (1883–1932), who first learned to play the violin but switched to cornet and formed his own band at the age of sixteen. When King Bolden was struck with insanity in 1909 and had to be committed to an asylum, where he spent the rest of his life, Keppard became the leading figure of New Orleans jazz, and his Olympia Band reigned supreme. With such hot players as Louis "Big Eye" Nelson (clarinet), Sidney Bechet (clarinet), Willy Santiago (guitar), Zue Robertson (trombone), and King Oliver (cornet), this combination was unbeatable. Keppard was one of the first

[3] From "Fifty Years of New Orleans Jazz," in *Esquire's 1945 Jazz Book*, p. 7. Reprinted by permission of Esquire, Inc.

to spread jazz to other parts of the country, when he toured with his band from 1912 to 1917, going as far as the Pacific Coast.

Many people are under the impression that jazz originated in the red-light district of New Orleans, popularly known as "Storyville," named after the alderman who initiated the city ordinance to have this section of the city set aside for organized vice. Storyville flourished from 1887 to 1917, at which time it was abolished owing to pressure from the War and Navy Departments. This period coincided with the rise of jazz, and it is true that many jazz musicians—pianists, singers, and some bands—found employment in Storyville, where cash was plentiful, prejudice rare, and liberty unrestrained. However, our account should have made it clear that jazz went through its formative period before the establishment of Storyville, that it was originally a music of the streets and later the dance floor, and that what it got from Storyville was the encouragement and support long denied to it by the more respectable elements of society. Not until 1925 did the voice of a courageous preacher arise in the land to proclaim that "Jazz is not necessarily the gateway to hell." And it was many years before "nice" people were willing to admit that its early associations did not necessarily make jazz immoral.

Joseph "King" Oliver (1885–1938), who became leader of the famous Olympia Band in 1916, was one of the numerous New Orleans jazz musicians who migrated northward after the closing of Storyville. He was a great trumpeter and a gifted leader, and his recordings constitute one of the basic documents of classic jazz. From 1918 to 1920, and again from 1922 to 1928, he led his celebrated Creole Jazz Band in Chicago, and afterward went to New York. Before taking up the migrations of the various bands that spread jazz throughout the United States, it would be well to give an account of the white musicians from New Orleans who popularized the style known as "Dixieland jazz."

Rise of "Dixieland jazz"

Dixieland music is jazz played by white musicians in a style closely approximating that of classic New Orleans jazz as developed by Negro players. In Dixieland jazz, the white musicians of New Orleans paid the compliment of imitation to their Negro confreres who had created this new and original type of American music.

The father of white or Dixieland jazz was Jack "Papa" Laine (*b.* 1873), leader of several bands, including the Reliance Brass Band, dating from about 1892–1893, and Jack Laine's Ragtime Band. The latter set the style for Dixieland jazz and is therefore of considerable historical importance. Laine himself played the drums in his Ragtime Band; the other instruments consisted of cornet, clarinet, trombone, guitar, and string bass. It should be pointed out that before the term "jazz" came into general usage, this type of hot music, whether for band or piano, was called "ragtime" in New Orleans. Hence the title of Laine's band.

Another white New Orleans outfit was the Tom Brown Band, which was discovered by a promoter in 1914 and brought to Chicago the following year, opening an engagement at Lamb's Café in June, 1915, and thereby launching the vogue of Dixieland jazz that soon would sweep the country. As already noted, the billing of Brown's Band as "Brown's Dixieland Jass Band" initiated the currency of the term "jazz" (as it later came to be spelled). The word "jass" is allegedly a vulgar and derisive term with sexual connotations.

The success of Brown's Band stimulated the search for more New Orleans talent. In 1916 a promoter from Chicago contracted Alcide "Yellow" Núñez, the clarinetist, and a group of four other players: Eddie Edwards (trombone), Dominique "Nick" La Rocca (cornet), Henry Ragas (piano), and Tony Sbarbaro (drums). This band opened at Schiller's Café under the name of Dixieland Jass Band. With somewhat different personnel, and calling itself the Original Dixieland Jass Band, this outfit went to New York in 1917 and began a sensational engagement at Reisenweber's Restaurant. It was this band that made the first recordings, in 1917, of Dixieland jazz. Among these pioneer recordings were *Tiger Rag*, *Reisenweber Rag*, *Barnyard Blues*, *At the Jazz Band Ball*, *Ostrich Walk*, *Bluin' the Blues*, and *Clarinet Marmalade*. The Original Dixieland Jass Band went to England in 1919, and gave a big impulse to European interest in jazz.

Although Negro jazz was not unknown in Chicago prior to the invasion of the white Dixieland bands, it did not make much impression on the general public until after the arrival, in 1917 or 1918, of King Oliver. After playing with other bands for two years, Oliver obtained an engagement at the Dreamland Café and organized his famous Creole Jazz Band, whose personnel included Jimmy Noone on the clarinet (soon replaced by Johnny Dodds); Honore Dutrey on trombone; Ed Garland, string bass; Lillian Hardin, piano; and Minor "Ram" Hall, drums. In 1921 Oliver took his band to California, where Hall was replaced on the drums by Edward "Baby" Dodds. Returning to Chicago the following year, Oliver added a second cornet to his band: a young player from New Orleans by the name of Louis Armstrong.

Oliver continued to play at various spots in Chicago, where, from 1922, he made a series of recordings that are fundamental for the understanding of New Orleans classic jazz. He made about thirty-five sides, among which may be mentioned *Canal Street Blues, Mandy Lee, Snake Rag, Riverside Blues,* and *High Society Rag.* In 1928 Oliver went to New York, where he continued to record. From 1931 to 1937 he toured in the Southeast.

Ferdinand "Jelly Roll" Morton was another of the pioneer New Orleans jazzmen who went to Chicago in search of wider opportunities. He was active there from 1923 to 1928, forming a small group called the Red Hot Peppers, with which, from 1926, he made a series of recordings that are likewise of crucial importance for the appreciation of the New Orleans style. Besides Morton at the piano, this group included George Mitchell on cornet, Omer Simeon on clarinet, Kid Ory on trombone, Johnny St. Cyr on guitar and banjo, John Lindsay on string bass, and Andrew Hilaire on the drums—a distinguished roster of jazz players. Among the records made by Morton's Red Hot Peppers are *Black Bottom Stomp, Smoke House Blues, Steamboat Stomp, Sidewalk Blues, Original Jelly Roll Blues, Doctor Jazz,* and *Cannon Ball Blues.* Each is a historic document of jazz.

Further backgrounds of jazz

Before continuing the story of jazz in Chicago and thereafter, it will be desirable to return to its original birthplace, New Orleans, and to attempt a description of New Orleans jazz as it developed in that city. Unlike other fields of musical history, where written sources exist, the phonograph record is the basic document for the history of jazz. In the words of Jelly Roll Morton: "Jazz music is a style not a composition." One might modify that by saying that it is not a *written* composition; but assuredly, in the act of performance, the style creates a *composition,* that is, a piece of music with a definite form and texture. In any case, the style and the music must be heard to be known, and the history of jazz means nothing without the phonograph recordings that give it life and substance. Fortunately, there is available a recorded historical anthology of jazz, issued by Folkways Records, which the reader will find of immense value in tracing the antecedents, the genesis, and the growth of jazz. Most of the recordings discussed in this chapter will be found in this series.

We have no recordings by Negro bands from the early classic New Orleans period. Our knowledge of what New Orleans jazz was like during this period comes partly from collateral sources (personal recollections and descriptions) and partly from later recorded performances of players who were active in New Orleans during the classic period, such as King Oliver, Sidney Bechet, Jelly Roll Morton, Bunk Johnson, and others. These recordings, in turn, fall into two categories: those made when the New Orleans bands first began to record, in the 1920s, and those made after the revival of interest in jazz history, initiated by the publication of the book *Jazzmen*, by Ramsey and Smith, in 1939. The latter recordings were made in the 1940s, utilizing as far as possible old-timers from New Orleans, and resulted in what is generally called the "New Orleans Renaissance." With this as background, we may proceed to discuss (and for the reader, it is hoped, to hear) some of the recordings, old and new, that will help us to reconstruct the growth of jazz and, what is more valuable, to understand and enjoy its qualities as music.

The instrumental and vocal antecedents of jazz were rather extensively covered in the preceding chapters on ragtime and blues. In view of the importance of the New Orleans street bands in the emergence of jazz, it may be well to note what Jelly Roll Morton says about the early Negro street bands:

> All we had in a band, as a rule, was bass horn, trombone, trumpet, an alto horn and maybe a baritone horn, bass, and snare drum—just seven pieces, but, talking about noise, you never heard a sixty-piece band make as much noise as we did.

In spite of Morton, these bands often included clarinet also, which, together with the trumpet and trombone, became one of the principal melody instruments of the jazz band. Alphonse Picou, a clarinetist who played in the street bands, became one of the most famous pioneers of jazz. Together with other old-time jazzmen—Henry "Kid" Rena (trumpet), Louis Nelson (clarinet), Jim Robinson (trombone), Willie Santiago (guitar), Albert Gleny (bass), Joe Rena (drums)—Picou took part in a recording, made in New Orleans in 1940, of the *Gettysburg March,* which demonstrates the early jazz treatment of a slow march tune. Each of the three melody instruments plays its solo over the steady beat of the percussion (guitar, bass, drums), with that *singing* quality that is vital to jazz, and also play together in characteristic three-voiced polyphony.

The term "tailgate trombone" is often heard in connection with jazz. This arose from the custom of using bands for advertising in New Orleans. Often these bands, when hired for an advertising job, would ride around the city in a wagon, making as much noise as possible (see Jelly Roll's comments on this subject above), and the trombonist would sit at the back, with his instrument projecting over the tailgate. Frequently, when two "band wagons" met, there would be a competition, or "cutting contest," between the rival groups.

The influence of ragtime

Let us consider next the influence of ragtime on early jazz. According to Louis Armstrong, the influence of Scott Joplin's piano rags was "great" among the pioneer jazzmen. Said Armstrong: "If you played his music and phrased it right, you was *swinging* way back there!" [4] Armstrong asserts that King Oliver is credited with the composition of *Snake Rag,* which he recorded with his *Creole Jazz Band* in Chicago in 1923, but this may be one of the pieces that owed much to Scott Joplin and his piano rags.

Ragtime was played in the South not only by honky-tonk pianists but also by small instrumental groups that might include, in addition to guitar, banjo, and mandolin, such unorthodox instruments as washboard and jug. A recording of *Dallas Rag* for jug, guitar, mandolin, and banjo, demonstrates the old ragtime style which in New Orleans was taken over by the instruments most favored in that city: cornet, clarinet, trombone, guitar, string bass, and drums (the classic New Orleans ensemble). Here is Jelly Roll Morton reminiscing about the old "spasm" bands that played for "any jobs they could get in the streets":

[4] Quoted in *The Record Changer.*

They did a lot of ad-libbing in ragtime style with different solos in succession, not in a regular routine, but just as one guy would get tired and let another musician have the lead.

Morton claimed to have created the famous *Tiger Rag* from a French quadrille. In his own picturesque language:

The Tiger Rag I happened to transform from an old quadrille, which was originally in many different tempos. First there was an introduction, "Everybody get your partners!" and the people would go rushing around the hall getting their partners. After five minutes lapse of time, the next strain would be the waltz strain. . . . Then another strain that comes right beside the waltz strain in mazooka time. . . . We had two other strains in two-four time. Then I transformed these strains into the tiger rag which I also named, from the way I made the "Tiger" roar with my elbow.[5]

Whether or not Jelly Roll portrayed his personal role with strict accuracy and impartiality (which he seldom did), the fact remains that *Tiger Rag* was derived from a French quadrille. The influence of French dances, marches, and songs was widespread in New Orleans jazz.

There was also what Jelly Roll calls the "Spanish" influence, though it was more specifically a Caribbean influence, and still more precisely, an Afro-American influence. It is the Negro influence that gives to the popular music of the Caribbean, and thence of Latin America, the traits that distinguish it from European music. Let us hear, in any event, what Jelly Roll has to say on this subject:

Now in one of my earliest tunes, *New Orleans Blues*, you can notice the Spanish tinge. In fact, if you can't manage to put tinges of Spanish in your tunes, you will never be able to get the right seasoning, I call it, for jazz. This *New Orleans Blues* comes from around 1902. I wrote it with the help of Frank Richards, a great piano player in the ragtime style. All the bands in the city played it at that time.[6]

Jelly Roll's comments on the "New Orleans Blues" also serves to confirm the direct influence of early piano ragtime on New Orleans jazz: a pianist like Frank Richards would compose or arrange a piano rag, and all the bands in the city would take it up and play

[5] Quoted by Alan Lomax, *Mr. Jelly Roll.*
[6] *Ibid.*

it in jazz style. As already noted, the first bands that played this music were called "ragtime bands," before the term "jazz" came into general use.

Classic New Orleans jazz

In the previous chapter we observed how the instrumental accompaniments to blues singing gradually acquired more importance and independence, leading to the full development of the call-and-response or antiphonal pattern that jazz carried over from the blues. A good blues singer working together with a New Orleans clarinet and cornet, and a rhythm instrument (guitar or piano) keeping the beat, gives us that perfect coordination and teamwork that is the heart of jazz. Such a performance is to be found in a recording of Margaret Johnson singing "When a 'Gaitor Hollers," accompanied by clarinet, cornet, and piano. The players are unidentified, but it is possible that the cornet may be none other than King Oliver himself. The two melody instruments, playing discreetly under the voice, come up with assertive solos or piquantly discordant duets in the "breaks," the clarinet answering with a real "dirty" intonation, and the cornet stridently singing its own version of the blues.

Blues singer, clarinet, and cornet, make three "voices" singing over the steady beat of the rhythm section. Take the singer away, add a trombone as the third melody instrument of the classic jazz band, and you still have three "voices" that "sing" the blues over the throbbing bass. These three instruments—cornet (or trumpet), clarinet, and trombone—were the ones chosen by the Negro jazzmen as the most expressive and most flexible to constitute the melody section of the band. The trumpet takes the place of the solo singer. It is the "leader," playing the principal melodic part. The clarinet (high voice) and the trombone (low voice) complete the three-part harmony, embroider around the trumpet's melody, and take their own breaks in turn.

Originally, and as a general rule, the rhythm section of the classic New Orleans jazz band was composed of guitar, bass, and drums (bass drum and snare drum). A few early bands included piano and banjo in the rhythm section; the piano was considered a rhythm instrument, though it had a dual role, being associated with the melody section through the melodic embroiderings of the right hand. The banjo was rare until about 1918, when it often began to replace the guitar. The rhythm section of King Oliver's Creole Jazz Band in 1923 consisted of banjo, piano, bass, and drums. The melody section consisted of two cornets, clarinet, and trombone. It was this combination, including some of the greatest players ever known, that recorded, in 1923, such masterpieces as "Dippermouth Blues" and "High Society." The latter demonstrates to perfection the jazz treatment of a modern march, originally written by Porter Steele and published in 1901. In addition to Oliver and Armstrong on trumpets, the personnel includes Honore Dutrey, trombone; Johnny Dodds, clarinet; Lillian Hardin, piano; Bud Scott, banjo; Bill Johnson, bass; and Baby Dodds, drums. In these recordings, the phrasing, the timing, the tone color, the dissonant polyphony, the coordination between the two sections of the band, and the completely relaxed yet wonderfully controlled style of playing, provide a paradigm of classic jazz.

The full flowering of the blues idiom in jazz, the complete transposition from vocal to instrumental performance, may be observed in a recording of "Working Man's Blues" by King Oliver and his Creole Jazz Band made in 1923 with the same personnel as above, except that Johnny St. Cyr plays banjo, and Charlie Johnson on bass saxophone replaces Bill Johnson on string bass. (In this case, the bass saxophone, like the tuba in some early bands, is used as a rhythm instrument.) King Oliver was very close to the folk tradition of the blues as developed in their second or urbanized phase. He and his gifted arranger, Lillian Hardin, have caught the full spirit and the authentic idiom of the blues in this instrumental version, which, more than a whole book on the subject, reveals what jazz really is. The melody instruments sing with all the expressiveness of genuine Afro-American vocalization, the King does what he calls "a real low-down solo" on the cornet, and the call-and-response pattern is beautifully exemplified.

Men who played with King Oliver, among them Louis Armstrong and Barney Bigard, imbibed the blues tradition from him, carried it to other bands, and diffused it throughout the land. Armstrong is a gifted singer of the "low-down" blues as well as a very great trumpet player and leader. Both individual and traditional elements in his treatment of the blues are present in his recording of "Keyhole Blues," made in 1927 with several of the same performers who had played in King Oliver's band, except that Kid Ory plays trombone and Pete

Briggs tuba (taking the place of string bass). Armstrong sings like his trumpet, and his trumpet sounds like his singing. The group with which he recorded in 1927 was called Louis Armstrong and his Hot Seven.

Armstrong and Chicago

Louis Armstrong was born in New Orleans in 1900. At the age of thirteen, after having fired his father's pistol while celebrating New Year's Eve, he was arrested as a wayward boy and placed in the Waifs Home, where he learned to play the trumpet. In 1918 he joined Kid Ory's Brown Skinned Babies, and the following year he was playing in riverboat bands on the Mississippi. In 1922, as we know, he was called to Chicago by Joe Oliver. There he married the pianist Lil Hardin, with whom he went to New York in 1924, joining Fletcher Henderson's big band. He was soon back in Chicago, playing with his wife's Dreamland Syncopators and then with his own groups, the Hot Five and the Hot Seven. From 1929, his fame as a jazz player fully established, he was in New York again, and from 1932 to 1935 he toured in Europe with the band that he had formed in Chicago in 1931. In 1940 he recorded in New York with a small New Orleans type of band, proving again his mastery of the classic style. Before taking up the vogue of swing, with which Armstrong's name became associated, we must trace the course of jazz in Chicago after the initial success of New Orleans jazz there, as played by both white and Negro bands.

After the Original Dixieland Jass Band, the most important white band in Chicago was the New Orleans Rhythm Kings, which opened in 1920, led by Paul Mares (1900–1949) on trumpet, and including Leon Rappolo on clarinet and George Brunies on trombone. This group adhered very closely to the New Orleans style, with its smooth, relaxed rhythm. When it began to record in 1923, Jelly Roll Morton acted as musical director and also played piano in several numbers, including his own composition, *Milneburg Joys.* The New Orleans Rhythm Kings included a saxophone in the melody section, setting a fashion that was to be widely followed. Their recordings of *Tiger Rag* and *Milneburg Joys* demonstrate the pure Dixieland style and its affinity with the traditional sources of New Orleans jazz. Both the ensemble and the solo work are brilliant and typical.

New Orleans jazz flourished in Chicago in the decade from 1920 to 1930, played by both white and Negro musicians. There were many bands and players that we do not have space to mention. Suffice it to say that youngsters growing up in the tough Chicago of the 1920s had ample opportunity to acquaint themselves with New Orleans jazz by listening to its pioneer practitioners. A group of white boys, fascinated with this new music that seemed so thoroughly to express the spirit of the age, abandoned the path of respectability and took up the torch of jazz. There was Charles Pierce and his Orchestra, in which Pierce played saxophone, Muggsy Spanier cornet, Frank Teschemacher clarinet, and Jack Read trombone. Recordings made by this orchestra in 1927, including "Sister Kate," "Bull Frog Blues," "China Boy," and "Nobody's Sweetheart," display a tendency toward a more "tricky" style of playing, whose characteristics have been summed up by Mezz Mezzrow under the following headings: (1) the flare-up, (2) the explosion, (3) the shuffle rhythm, and (4) the break.[7]

Frank Teschemacher's Chicago Rhythm Kings, with which Mezzrow played tenor saxophone, Muggsy Spanier cornet, Eddie Condon banjo, and Gene Krupa drums, continued the development of what came to be known as Chicago-style jazz. Condon himself, together with the vocalist and comb player Red McKenzie, formed a group called the "Chicagoans," which featured the cornetist Jimmy McPartland who was leader of a band called the "Wolverines" in Detroit in 1925–1926. But the most celebrated and influential Wolverine Orchestra was that organized by Leon "Bix" Beiderbecke in Chicago in 1923, in which he played the cornet. Beiderbecke's much-imitated playing and leadership accelerated the trend toward "sweet" jazz with romantic tendencies. During the 1930s the sweet orchestra trend, featuring violins, soft saxophones, and sentimentality, almost crowded jazz out of the picture.

The acme of the sweet trend was reached in Paul Whiteman's overstuffed orchestra, which did have some fine players in it, but which was lush with violins and saxophones and played saccharine orchestrations written out in advance. Whiteman was a violinist who had been fired from a jazz band at Tait's in San Francisco because "he couldn't jazz it up." (That is his own account of the episode.[8]) In

[7] Mezzrow and Wolfe, *Really the Blues.*
[8] Whiteman and McBride, *Jazz,* p. 36.

his autobiography, Whiteman wrote: "It is a relief to be able to prove at last that I did not invent jazz. . . . All I did was to orchestrate it." [9] It is an astounding revelation of the widespread ignorance that prevailed about jazz that Whiteman could have acquired the reputation of having invented it, when what he actually did was to denature it.

Jazz in New York

Many jazz musicians flocked to New York in the 1920s and 1930s, but there was not much chance to keep alive the real jazz in the face of the slick commercial competition. Eddie Condon summed it up by saying: "The only place we could play was in our rooms, at our own request." A white musician from Texas who really knew the blues, by the name of Jack Teagarden, was one of the men who did most to keep alive the spirit of jazz. His authentic singing and expressive trombone are heard in recordings of "Basin Street Blues" (1929), in which he plays with Red Nichols on trumpet and Pee Wee Russell on clarinet; and "Beale Street Blues" (1931), in which Charlie Teagarden plays trumpet and Benny Goodman is heard on clarinet and saxes. In the recording of "Junk Man" (1934), Jack Teagarden and Benny Goodman are joined by another famous name in jazz: Art Tatum at the piano.

Fletcher Henderson, a Negro pianist and arranger from Georgia, was an influential leader in New York jazz. He formed a large orchestra which played at the Roseland dance hall from 1919 and which included Louis Armstrong as one of the trumpets and Coleman Hawkins on tenor saxophone. The large orchestra brought with it the necessity of orchestral arrangements written out in advance and thoroughly rehearsed, because groups of more than nine players could not achieve in performance the spontaneous cohesion and smooth coordination possible in the classic New Orleans ensemble. It was thus that the art of the arranger came to assume prime importance and ushered in a new phase of jazz music.

The significant fact to retain in connection with the large-band-cum-written-arrangement phase of jazz is that this brought with it an inevitable subservience to conventional standards. More exactly, it increased the influence of European orthodoxy on both the texture

[9] *Ibid.*, p. 20.

and style of jazz music. However much there may have been of anticipated effect in New Orleans classic jazz, it was clearly a different type of music from that obtained by strictly following the indications of a complete blueprint, which is what the orchestral arranger provides.

Among the jazz arrangers who influenced large-band style, in addition to Fletcher Henderson, mention should be made of Don Redman, who was with the McKinney Cotton Pickers in Detroit from 1926 and who formed his own orchestra in 1931; Benny Carter, who organized the recording group known as the Chocolate Dandies; Jimmie Lunceford (1902–1948), a band leader with an academic background who relied upon a "team" of arrangers that included Sy Oliver, Willy Smith, and Edwin Wilcox; and, top figure among them all, Edward "Duke" Ellington.

Ellington, born in Washington in 1899, studied music at the Pratt Institute of that city and formed his first band, a small one, in 1918. From the outset he endeavored to impose his personal style upon his orchestra and to produce his own type of music. Collective improvisation was not in his credo, though he tolerated it temporarily. Like the European composers of the Romantic tradition, he aimed at individual expression.

Following his engagement at the Kentucky Club in 1927, Ellington rose rapidly to national and international fame, touring Europe with immense success in 1933. He began to make recordings from 1926, with "East St. Louis Toodle-oo" (composed by Bubber Miley), continuing with such well-known productions as "Black and Tan Fantasy," "Hot and Bothered," "Tishomongo Blues," "The Mooche" (all 1928), "Saratoga Swing" (1929), "Mood Indigo" (1930; may be regarded as his theme song), "Rockin' in Rhythm," "Limehouse Blues," "Echoes of the Jungle" (all 1931), "Delta Serenade" (1933), "Clarinet Lament," "Echoes of Harlem" (both 1936), and "Blue Goose" (1940).

Duke Ellington has aspired to be the man of distinction in jazz. And he has succeeded, at the price of turning jazz away from its traditional channels. Sophistication, cleverness, mechanical smoothness are the marks of his music. This trend has become increasingly accentuated in the course of his career as leader, arranger, and composer. In this last capacity he has gained enviable laurels. Constant Lambert called him "the first jazz composer of distinction." His most ambitious creative effort is the orchestral suite titled *Black, Brown and Beige*, in four movements purporting to portray the development of jazz: (1) "Work Song," (2) "Come Sunday" (spiritual), (3) "The Blues," (4) "West Indian Dance: Emancipation Celebration: Sugar Hill Penthouse." Pretentious in its aping of modern European composers and the conventional tone poem, this work is more contrived than creative. The same may be said of other compositions by Ellington in the larger forms, such as *Reminiscing in Tempo* and *Diminuendo and Crescendo in Blue*. There are critics who maintain that Ellington is outside the tradition of jazz entirely. It would perhaps be more just to say that he is on its periphery. He is an extremely talented arranger and composer in the field of popular music. He has a place in America's music, wherever that place may be.

Attention must be called to a significant development in jazz performance that occurred in New York during the 1930s. This was the growth of "mixed" recording sessions, with the participation of white and Negro musicians. With the exception of Jelly Roll Morton's sessions with the Rhythm Kings in Chicago in 1923, this type of recording had not hitherto taken place, owing to the timorous attitude of the recording companies rather than to any feeling among the players. Notable examples of mixed recording sessions were those made in 1929 by Fats Waller and His Buddies and Louis Armstrong and His Orchestra. Eddie Condon played banjo with the former, and Jack Teagarden trombone with the latter. After that, the Negro musicians from the South who had come to New York bringing some of the spirit and technique of real jazz, and the white musicians from all over the country who had a genuine interest in this style of music, could sit down together and revive the traditions of New Orleans and Dixieland jazz. Of course, times were changing, and jazz was changing with the times. The real renaissance of New Orleans jazz did not occur until the 1940s. Meanwhile, something called "swing" was in the air.

The rise of "swing"

In 1936 Louis Armstrong published a book titled *Swing That Music*, in which he claimed that swing was the basic principle of New Orleans jazz. The main difference between jazz and swing, he maintained, was that the latter incorporated some of the orthodox techniques of European music, using scored orchestrations and musically trained players (i.e., those who could read music). Early New Orleans jazz he regarded as "the Daddy of swing." Conversely, and by implication, swing might be described as jazz with a college education.

What actually happened was that large dance bands were commercially successful during the depression of the 1930s, and the small hot jazz groups were not. Certain large Negro bands, such as those of Fletcher Henderson, Duke Ellington, Louis Russell, and Chick Webb, with their slick arrangements and written orchestrations, were already playing, during the 1920s, the type of music that came to be known as swing, which may be briefly defined as streamlined jazz for the modern mechanical age. It relied heavily on the *riff*, a reiterated phrase that builds up tension; on the sensational solo characterized by trick playing; on a strident tone color in the wind instruments; and on a powerful, driving rhythm which was insistent rather than complex.

A ragtime pianist named Bennie Moten (1894–1935) had formed a band in his native Kansas City in the 1920s, whose playing, according to Charles Edward Smith, was characterized by "a rolling rhythm, arrived at with the help of banjo and tuba, and a loose adaptation of New Orleans style." By the 1930s Moten's Band had developed a four-beat rhythm (in contrast to New Orleans two-beat) which came to be known as "jump" or "Kansas City Style." When Moten died his band was taken over by the pianist William "Count" Basie, whose musical credo is thus summed up: "I don't go for that two-beat jive the New Orleans cats play, because my boys and I got to have four heavy beats to a bar and no cheating." [10] William Russell suggests that this emphasis on four heavy beats to the bar may have come about through the influence of boogiewoogie piano playing, especially that of the Kansas City pianist Pete Johnson (*b.* 1905). Be this as it may, the potent influence of Count Basie and his Kansas City jump style made itself widely and powerfully felt. He became the leading exponent of what is called "Kansas City jazz." In the 1930s, Basie's Orchestra carried this style to New York, where it gave a further impetus to so-called powerhouse performance.

Another of the many "kings" elevated to an illusory throne by American popular music is Benny Goodman (*b.* 1909), the "King of Swing," who played a sensational clarinet in his native Chicago from the age of sixteen. He played with Ben Pollack's Chicago Band from

[10] Quoted by Frederic Ramsey, Jr., in Notes for Jazz Vol. 10, Folkways Records No. FP73.

1926 to 1931, and with Red Nichol's Five Pennies and other groups in New York until 1934, when he formed his own band, a large swing ensemble that won immediate acclaim. Fletcher Henderson made some fine arrangements for Goodman's band, including those of *King Porter Stomp* and *When Buddha Smiles*. Goodman is a phenomenal clarinetist who plays "classical" (standard European) as well as swing with equal mastery.

Other names associated with swing music are those of Harry James, Gene Krupa, Tommy Dorsey, Woody Herman, Glenn Miller, Artie Shaw, and Lionel Hampton. According to Rudi Blesh: "Swing is completely anti-jazz . . . opposed to the real musical values which jazz represents." [11] That is one man's opinion, though it is shared by other adherents of New Orleans jazz. Certainly, "classic" jazz and swing are different in spirit, in form, and in technique. They may start from the same basis, as Armstrong maintained, but they proceed in different directions. Classic New Orleans jazz was a special genre that arose from unique and definitely circumscribed cultural conditions. Swing is a type of popular music; more accurately, a manner of arranging and playing that music. Each has its place in America's music, and each listener has the privilege, as well as the responsibility, of determining their relative values.

[11] Blesh, *Shining Trumpets*, p. 290.

chapter twenty-four

The Americanists

I was anxious to write a work that would immediately be recognized as American in character.
AARON COPLAND, OUR NEW MUSIC.

In the 1920s many composers in the United States were trying very hard to be "American." Some composers turned to the tribal chants of the Indians, some were attracted by the Negro spirituals, others drew on the tradition of Anglo-American folk music, and others found material in the songs of the cowboys. A few composers, among them Antheil, Carpenter, and Copland, were tapping the resources of current popular music. Gershwin, by profession a highly successful composer of popular songs, was making the transition from tin-pan alley to Carnegie Hall through the medium of so-called "symphonic jazz." That term, like everything else connected with jazz, is controversial. In no other field of American music does one have to tread more warily than in that of jazz and its manifold ramifications. Our concern in this chapter is not so much with jazz itself as with some of its by-products, particularly in the realm of symphonic music.

In a symposium entitled *American Composers on American Music*, published in 1933, Gershwin made a statement on "The Relation of Jazz to American Music" (his words were set down by the editor, Henry Cowell). He summed up his views as follows:

> Jazz I regard as an American folk-music; not the only one, but a very powerful one which is probably in the blood and feeling of the American people more than any other style of folk-music. I believe that it can be made the basis of serious symphonic works of lasting value, in the hands of a composer with talent for both jazz and symphonic music.[1]

[1] Reprinted from *American Composers on American Music*, edited by Henry Cowell, with permission of the publishers, Stanford University Press. Copyright 1933 by the Board of Trustees of Leland Stanford Junior University.

When Gershwin made that statement, he had already composed the *Rhapsody in Blue* (1924), the Piano Concerto (1925), *An American in Paris* (1928), and the *Second Rhapsody* (1932)—compositions which the consensus would today regard as "serious symphonic works of lasting value." The world at large considers these works not only as typically American, but also as classical examples of jazz composition. Through countless performances, through records, radio programs, and films such as *Rhapsody in Blue* and *An American in Paris*, millions of people the world over have received from these compositions their most vivid impressions of "the American idiom" in symphonic music.

But to the question: is it jazz? the experts reply with a round No! Here is the opinion of jazz enthusiast Robert Goffin:

> Jazz has not made any important contribution to serious American music. Composers like Gershwin and Ferde Grofé made a mistake in trying to develop a concert jazz, since they were trying to intellectualize a phenomenon of sensibility. Behind their musical constructions one senses the mind rather than the heart. That isn't and can never be jazz.[2]

Perhaps only a European critic of jazz—than whom none are more fanatic on the subject—could characterize such a work as the *Rhapsody in Blue* as an attempt "to intellectualize a phenomenon of sensibility!" Most people simply think of it as a very agreeable piece of music, in which the "heart" (call it sentiment, if you wish) has its full share. As for the use of the mind in musical composition, Bach, Beethoven, and Brahms, to mention only the three B's, established a fairly good precedent along that line. However, Mr. Goffin may still be right when he asserts that the compositions of Gershwin are not jazz. It all depends on what one understands by the term. Let us see what Gershwin himself had to say on this subject. In a statement for the volume *Revolt in the Arts*, edited by Oliver M. Saylor, he wrote:

> It is difficult to determine what enduring values, aesthetically, jazz has contributed, because "jazz" is a word which has been used for at least five or six different types of music. It is really a conglomeration of many things. It has a little bit of ragtime, the blues, classicism, and spirituals. Basically, it is a matter of rhythm. After rhythm

[2] Goffin, *Jazz: From the Congo to the Metropolitan*, p. 83.

in importance come intervals, music intervals which are peculiar to the rhythm. . . . Jazz is music; it uses the same notes that Bach used. When jazz is played in another nation, it is called American. When it is played in another country, it sounds false. Jazz is the result of the energy stored up in America. It is a very energetic kind of music. One thing is certain. Jazz has contributed an enduring value to America in the sense that it has expressed ourselves. It is an original American achievement which will endure, not as jazz perhaps, but which will leave its mark on future music in one form or another. The only kinds of music which endure are those which possess form in the universal sense and folk-music. All else dies. But unquestionably folk-songs are being written and have been written which contain enduring elements of jazz. To be sure, that is only an element; it is not the whole. An entire composition written in jazz could not live.

To this last statement, the jazz experts would counter by saying that an entire composition written in jazz could not exist, because jazz is essentially improvisation. As stated by Goffin, "What is important in jazz is not the written text, but the way it is expressed by the musician." However, what we are primarily concerned with now is Gershwin's conception of jazz. Granted that, in the light of modern "dogmatic" jazz criticism, Gershwin's views are erroneous. The fact remains that Gershwin seized upon certain traits of American popular music—which he loosely called "jazz"—and embodied these traits in compositions based, as regards form, on nineteenth-century European models. He was never close to the folk roots of jazz or to its purest improvisatory manifestations. His primary field was that of commercialized popular music. He was a product of tin-pan alley. As a writer of musical comedies and hit tunes, he used certain elements of what he conceived to be jazz. When he turned his attention to the symphonic field, and to the field of opera, he followed the same procedure, except that he put the ingredients into larger forms. He was not trying to write jazz. He was trying to use some traits of jazz in symphonic music, as Liszt had used Hungarian *tzigany* music in his Rhapsodies. The verdict of time seems to be that he was eminently successful.

Success in the field of popular music came quickly to George Gershwin, who was born in Brooklyn, New York, on September 26, 1898. He studied piano with Charles Hambitzer and Ernest Hutcheson, harmony and composition with Edward Kilenyi and Rubin Goldmark. But as a youth he was not reaching for symphonic laurels. At the age of fourteen he had written his first popular song, and before he was twenty he had composed his first musical comedy, *La, La, Lucille*. Meanwhile, at sixteen, he had taken a job as pianist and "song plugger" for the house of Remick, continuing to write tunes on the side. After three years of this employment, he was commissioned to write the music for *George White's Scandals* (1920–1924). The immense popularity of his song hit, "Swanee," interpreted by Al Jolson, brought him into national prominence. He continued to write scores for musical comedies, including *Lady, Be Good* (1924), *Tip Toes* (1925), *Oh, Kay* (1926), *Strike Up the Band* (1927), *Funny Face* (1927), *Girl Crazy* (1930), and *Of Thee I Sing* (1931), this last a political satire which was awarded a Pulitzer Prize.

Meanwhile, Paul Whiteman, who was having wide success with a conventionalized type of orchestral arrangement that he called "jazz," decided to give a concert in Aeolian Hall, New York, under the pretentious title, "Experiment in Modern Music." For this concert he commissioned Gershwin to write a piece embodying jazz elements in symphonic form. Gershwin set to work and in three weeks completed the piano score of his *Rhapsody in Blue*, which was then orchestrated by Ferde Grofé in time for Whiteman's concert, which took place on February 12, 1924. Whiteman conducted and Gershwin was the piano soloist. Thus was the Broadway tunesmith launched on his career as a composer of "serious" music. Thereafter he continued, musically, to lead a double life. Carnegie Hall opened its doors to him, but he did not shut up shop in tin-pan alley.

The *Rhapsody in Blue* is unquestionably Lisztian in style, with strong reminiscences of Tchaikovsky in the slow section. It represents the fusion of two traditions that already had much in common, because the stock-in-trade of tin-pan alley consists largely of stereotyped procedures borrowed from nineteenth-century musical idioms. Gershwin, saturated with both traditions by temperament and by experience, was able to combine elements of popular style and of conventional art form with remarkable felicity and with an effect of novelty because these elements had not previously been brought together in such an intimate manner. To be sure, several European composers, notably Stravinsky and Milhaud, had envisaged the possibilities of jazz and had used some of its effects with considerable success. But this was for them an exotic venture, whereas Gershwin was working *within* the tradition of American popular music. It was not he, but the European musicians, who were "trying to intellectualize a phenomenon of sensibility."

The year after the première of *Rhapsody in Blue,* Walter Damrosch, at that time conductor of the New York Symphony, commissioned Gershwin to write a work of symphonic proportions for that orchestra. The result was the Concerto in F for piano and orchestra, first performed in New York on December 3, 1925, with Gershwin as soloist. For this work Gershwin himself did the orchestration: he was now a "serious" composer, and *noblesse oblige!* In presenting the Concerto, Dr. Damrosch made a short speech in which he contributed to the current fallacy that Gershwin had taken jazz and dressed it up "in the classic garb of a concerto," thereby making it presentable to concert audiences. What Gershwin actually had done was to write a conventional piano concerto utilizing some traits of American popular music, including the standardized or commercialized type of jazz, while the real jazz went on its own way, eventually making its entry into Carnegie Hall without benefit of any "classic garb."

The Concerto in F is in three movements: Allegro, Andante con moto, and Allegro con brio. John Tasker Howard was of the opinion that Gershwin's attempt to be formally correct in the Concerto "took away much of the natural charm that had been found in his previous *Rhapsody in Blue*." But a concerto for piano and orchestra is a work of art, not a work of nature, and the Concerto in F is a better work of art than the *Rhapsody in Blue*. When the English conductor Albert Coates, in 1930, named Gershwin's Concerto in F as one of the best musical compositions of all time—and the only one by an American to figure on his list—he displayed remarkable acumen as well as exceptional courage. Today, more than a quarter of a century after its première, Gershwin's Concerto is firmly entrenched as the first work in that form by an American composer to have entered the permanent repertoire of symphonic music.

Gershwin's next symphonic work was the orchestral tone poem *An American in Paris,* first performed in New York on December 13, 1928. This is a gay and brash composition, colorfully and realistically orchestrated (the score includes taxi horns), not without its moments of sentimentality, mixed with mockery. The work has an especially effective blues section. In this tone poem the composer caught the spirit of a decade and produced the difficult paradox of a period piece that "dates" without fading.

In 1931 Gershwin wrote the music for a film comedy called *Delicious*, in which there was a sequence of New York street scenes. For this sequence he devised a "rivet theme" to express the dynamic energy of the city and its skyscrapers. Around this theme he composed a rhapsody for piano and orchestra that originally bore the title *Rhapsody in Rivets*. Renamed *Second Rhapsody* (perhaps in order not to frighten prospective listeners), it was first performed by the Boston Symphony Orchestra under the direction of Serge Koussevitzky on January 29, 1932. Mechanistic effects, dance rhythms, and tunes of the Broadway type are utilized in this orchestral impression of a modern metropolis.

The *Cuban Overture*, written in 1934, was the last orchestral work that Gershwin lived to complete. His next major effort was in the lyric theater, with his opera *Porgy and Bess*, produced in 1935, which constitutes a landmark in American operatic history. (It is discussed in another chapter of this book.) Before writing *finis* to Gershwin's tragically brief career, we must mention his three Preludes for piano (orchestrated by Arnold Schoenberg), which rank high in their field for authentic qualities of style and effective pianism.

In 1937 Gershwin was living in Hollywood, California, writing music for films. While working on a score for the *Goldwyn Follies* he was suddenly taken ill and had to undergo an operation on the brain, which proved unsuccessful. He died on July 11, 1937.

Gershwin's place in American music is secure. His popular songs will last as long as any music of this type, and his work in the larger forms of art music mark the triumph of the popular spirit in the art music of the United States. Gershwin was a composer of the people and for the people, and his music will be kept alive by the people.

Composer from Brooklyn—no. 2

Aaron Copland, like Gershwin, was born in Brooklyn (on November 14, 1900), and took harmony lessons from the same teacher, Rubin Goldmark. All the Copland children—there were five of them—had music lessons, but only Aaron thought of taking up music seriously as a career. The idea occurred to him when he was about thirteen, and some two years later he definitely decided that he would like to become a composer. After an unsatisfactory attempt to learn harmony by correspondence, he began to study with Goldmark, an excellent teacher but very conservative in his tastes. Goldmark warned his pupil against the "moderns," which of course immediately set him on their track. Young Copland reveled in the music of Scriabin, Debussy, and Ravel, and quickly acquired the reputation of a musical radical.

Copland's next objective was Paris. Reading of the establishment of a summer music school for Americans at Fontainebleau, in 1921, he was the first to apply for admission. At the Fontainebleau School he studied composition with Paul Vidal, whom he describes as "a French version of Rubin Goldmark," only more difficult to understand. But there was another teacher at Fontainebleau, the brilliant Nadia Boulanger, whose acquaintance Copland soon made. This encounter marked a decisive moment in his career. He decided to stay in Paris as long as possible in order to continue studying with Nadia Boulanger. He was the first American pupil in composition of this remarkable woman whose teaching and personality have exerted such a profound influence on contemporary American music. Copland remained in Paris for three years, studying, becoming familiar with new music, and composing several vocal and instrumental works, including the score of a one-act ballet, *Grohg*. In June, 1924, he returned to the United States.

Nadia Boulanger had commissioned him to write a symphony for organ and orchestra, in which she was to appear as soloist. The work received its first performance by the New York Symphony on January 11, 1925, with Walter Damrosch conducting. According to Copland, Damrosch made a little speech in which he declared, "If a young man at the age of 23 can write a symphony like that, in five years he will be ready to commit murder." On the other hand, Koussevitzky, who conducted it in Boston, liked the symphony and remained thenceforth a strong champion of Copland's music.

In his autobiographical sketch, *Composer from Brooklyn*, Copland tells us that at this time he "was anxious to write a work that would immediately be recognized as American in character." He does not explain why he had this desire, except to say that it was symptomatic of the period. The interesting point is that in trying to write music that would immediately be recognized as American in character he turned to the idioms of our popular music, and specifically to jazz, or what he conceived to be such. The award of a Guggenheim Fellowship in 1925 (the first given to a composer) gave him freedom to compose as he pleased. His first important experiment "in the American idiom" was a suite for small orchestra and piano titled *Music for the Theatre*, composed at the MacDowell Colony in New Hampshire during the summer of 1925. This suite consists of five movements: "Prologue," "Dance," "Interlude," "Burlesque," "Epilogue." Neoclassical in form and spirit, influenced by Stravinsky, it is in the movement titled "Dance" that the traces of jazz technique are most apparent.

In his Concerto for Piano and Orchestra, which he played for the first time with the Boston Symphony on January 28, 1927, Copland continued to develop the use of jazzlike rhythms, particularly in the second movement. Referring to the Piano Concerto, he afterward wrote:

> This proved to be the last of my "experiments" with symphonic jazz. With the Concerto I felt I had done all I could with the idiom, considering its limited emotional scope. True, it was an easy way to be American in musical terms, but all American music could not possibly be confined to two dominant jazz moods: the "blues" and the snappy number.[3]

This limitation of jazz to two moods is rather arbitrary. Students of jazz have found it to contain at least five well-defined moods or emotional attitudes, as follows: (1) The Blues ("simple, direct, personal sadness"), (2) The Romantic (expansive, buoyant, dramatic, imaginative), (3) The Lyric ("a highly personal expression—a singing, a brilliant soaring of the spirit . . ."), (4) The Decadent (veering between plaintive resignation and intense maladjustment), (5) The Protest ("an angry, sometimes vicious, attack on life").[4] Objectively, it would be difficult to sustain Copland's statement that "these two moods [the blues and the snappy number] encompass the whole gamut of jazz emotion."

In any case, Copland confesses that he was more interested in the letter than in the spirit of jazz. "What interested composers," he writes, "was not so much the spirit . . . as the more technical side of jazz—the rhythm, melody, harmony, timbre through which that spirit was expressed."[5] And he adds that "By far the most potent influence

[3] Copland, *Our New Music*, p. 227.

[4] See "The Main Currents of Jazz" by Miller and Crenshaw in *Esquire's 1945 Jazz Book*, pp. 25–26.

[5] Copland, *op. cit.*, p. 88.

on the technical side was that of rhythm." He concludes, therefore, that only the technical procedures of jazz were of permanent value to the composer, since these "might be applied to any number of different musical styles." Referring to the polyrhythms of jazz, he writes: "The peculiar excitement they produce by clashing two definitely and regularly marked rhythms is unprecedented in occidental music. Its polyrhythm is the real contribution of jazz." This at least makes clear Copland's position as a composer with regard to jazz and its influence.

In 1929 Copland entered a competition sponsored by the RCA Victor Company, which offered an award of $25,000 for a symphonic work. He wished to submit a one-movement symphony, which he called *Symphonic Ode,* but was unable to complete it in time to meet the deadline. He therefore extracted three movements from the score of his early ballet, *Grohg,* and submitted them under the title of *Dance Symphony.* None of the works submitted won the full award, which was divided among five contestants, Copland receiving $5,000 for his symphony. No one would ever guess from the *Dance Symphony* that its composer was born in Brooklyn, but it contains ample evidence of his sojourn in Paris. It fluctuates between the impressionism of Debussy and the primitivism of Stravinsky, with more than passing recognition to Ravel. While these influences indicate the musical climate of Copland's formative years, the *Dance Symphony* nevertheless bears the mark of his individuality both in mood and texture. It is derivative but not imitative.

Here it should be mentioned that in 1928 Copland made a version for orchestra alone of his Symphony for Organ and Orchestra. This revised version, for large orchestra, became his First Symphony. It is in three movements: Prelude, Scherzo, Finale (Lento). Characteristic of Copland is the placing of a slow movement at the end of the work; he does this also in the Piano Sonata and the Piano Quartet. The First Symphony is interesting for its rhythmic complexity and its contrapuntal texture.

At about the same time (1928–1929), Copland completed his *Symphonic Ode,* which was first performed by the Boston Symphony Orchestra on February 19, 1932. Copland himself refers to this work as "fulsome" and observes that it "marks the end of a certain period in my development as a composer." He was now interested in writing music of a more austere character, more intellectual in conception and expression.

Austerity and imposed simplicity

To this "period of austerity" belong the Piano Variations (1930), the *Short Symphony* (1933) and *Statements* for orchestra (1934). To these should be added another work of similar tendency, the Piano Sonata, which, though not completed until 1941, was begun, according to Arthur Berger, in 1935. The trio titled *Vitebsk*, "Study on a Jewish Theme," for violin, cello and piano (1929), may also be regarded as related to this period. This work is significant also as Copland's only deliberate attempt to treat Jewish material in his music, though critics have found reflections of his Jewish background in other phases of his work, particularly in his early compositions.

Copland remarks of his compositions of this period that "They are difficult to perform and difficult for an audience to comprehend." That is undoubtedly why they represent the least-known portion of his output. On the other hand, difficulty is relative, and in the second half of the twentieth century more listeners may be prepared to assimilate what seemed difficult two decades ago. There is therefore hope that Copland's music of this period may receive wider recognition as time goes on.

The Piano Variations is a work of ingenious and masterly construction, forceful in utterance, concise in expression, modern not only in manner but in essence. Conciseness is also a quality of the *Short Symphony*, which takes barely fifteen minutes to perform. For originality, for inventiveness, for vitality and expressiveness, for workmanship and beauty of detail, the *Short Symphony* is one of Copland's finest works. In 1937 the composer made an arrangement of the *Short Symphony* for sextet (string quartet, clarinet, piano).

Whatever the artistic qualities of these works, there were comparatively few listeners for this type of music. Copland felt the urge to reach a larger public. In his own words:

> During these years I began to feel an increasing dissatisfaction with the relations of the music-loving public and the living composer. The old "special" public of the modern music concerts had fallen away, and the conventional concert public continued apathetic or indifferent to anything but the established classics. It seemed to me that we composers were in danger of working in a vacuum. Moreover, an entirely new public for music had grown up around the radio and the phonograph. It made no sense to ignore them and

to continue writing as if they did not exist. I felt that it was worth the effort to see if I couldn't say what I had to say in the simplest possible terms."[6]

Thus began what Copland describes as his "tendency toward an imposed simplicity."

The works representing this tendency range from *El Salón México* (1936) to *Appalachian Spring* (1944). The prevailing trend is toward the utilization of folk material. But there is also the phase of writing occasional or "workaday" music for special purposes, such as the "play-opera" for high-school performance titled *The Second Hurricane* (1937); the *Music for Radio* (*Saga of the Prairie*), of the same year; and *An Outdoor Overture* for high-school orchestra (also arranged for band). And then there is the highly important phase of writing music for films, including *Of Mice and Men* (1939), *Our Town* (1940), and *North Star* (1943). The *Lincoln Portrait* of 1942, for speaker and orchestra, with its declamatory style and its snatches of popular songs of the Civil War period, belongs definitely within the tendency toward an imposed simplicity. The main theme of this work is based on the ballad "Springfield Mountain."

El Salón México was a deliberate attempt to write "tourist music." Concerning the genesis of this orchestral evocation, Copland writes:

> During my first visit to Mexico, in the Fall of 1932, I conceived the idea of writing a piece based on Mexican themes. I suppose there is nothing strange about such an idea. Any composer who goes outside his native land wants to return bearing musical souvenirs. In this case my musical souvenirs must have been very memorable, since it wasn't until 1933 that I began to assemble them into the form of an orchestral work.
>
> From the very beginning, the idea of writing a work based on popular Mexican melodies was connected in my mind with a popular dance hall in Mexico City called Salón México. No doubt I realized even then, that it would be foolish for me to attempt to translate into musical sounds the more profound side of Mexico, the Mexico of the ancient civilizations or the revolutionary Mexico of today. In order to do that one must really know the country. All that I could hope to do was to reflect the Mexico of the tourists, and that is why I thought of the Salón México. Because in that "hot spot" one felt, in a very natural and unaffected way, a close contact with the Mexi-

[6] Copland, *Our New Music*, pp. 228–229.

can people. It wasn't the music I heard, but the spirit that I felt there, which attracted me. Something of that spirit is what I hope to have put into my music.[7]

So Copland joined the company of Rimsky-Korsakoff and Chabrier as a composer of "tourist music," a genre to which *El Salón México* is a vividly picturesque contribution. As for the tunes he uses, he got most of them from two books: Frances Toor's *Cancionero Mexicano*, and *El Folklore y la Música Mexicana* by Rubén M. Campos. Among the melodies he borrowed are "El Palo Verde," "La Jesucita," and especially "El Mosco," which occurs twice, immediately after the introductory measures. *El Salón México* was first performed in Mexico City on August 27, 1937.

Apart from this Mexican excursion, and a *Danzón Cubano* for two pianos (also orchestrated) which he wrote in 1942, Copland's main concern during this period was the folk music of the United States. During the 1940s American folk music was attracting widespread attention, as jazz had done two decades earlier, but with this difference: it was less controversial, it provoked no outbursts of moral indignation, it drew no imprecations from the righteous. When Copland experimented with jazz, he placed himself in the *avant-garde;* when he took up American folk music, he was moving with the prevailing trend, and this was in line with his strategy of coming closer to the public. In the light of historical perspective, it may also be found that Copland himself contributed something to the vogue of folk music, for doubtless there were some Americans, and many foreigners, who heard these tunes for the first time in the engaging musical scores that he wrote for the ballets *Billy the Kid* (1938), *Rodeo* (1942) and *Appalachian Spring* (1944).

Billy the Kid, written for the Ballet Caravan, was produced in New York on May 24, 1939. Three years later the composer made a symphonic suite from the ballet score. The ballet deals with the legendary desperado of the trans-Pecos country, of whom many a ballad tells:

> I'll sing you a song of Billy the Kid,
> I'll sing you a song of the desperate deeds that he did,
> Way out in New Mexico long, long ago,
> When a man's only chance was his own fo'ty fo'.

[7] Quoted in Program Notes of the Boston Symphony Orchestra.

Prominent in the score is the cowboy song "Bury Me Not on the Lone Prairie," which Copland uses in an idealized version to create a mood of pathos just before the scene of the final shooting.

Rodeo, written for Agnes de Mille, was produced by the Ballet Russe de Monte Carlo in New York on October 16, 1942. The heroine of the story is a "cow girl" who outdoes the men in broncobusting and thereby becomes socially unpopular. But all ends well when she meets her match. Along with more familiar cowboy songs, the score includes freely treated versions of "Sis Joe" and "If He'd Be a Buckaroo." From this ballet the composer extracted *Four Dance Episodes* for orchestra, consisting of "Corrale Nocturne," "Buckaroo Holiday," "Saturday Night Waltz," and "Hoedown."

Appalachian Spring (the title is from a poem by Hart Crane) was written on a commission from the Elizabeth Sprague Coolidge Foundation and was first performed by Martha Graham and her Company at the Library of Congress on October 30, 1944. The original score was for chamber orchestra (thirteen instruments). The composer later arranged the music as a concert suite for symphony orchestra, first performed by the New York Philharmonic-Symphony on October 4, 1945. For this suite, Copland provided the following synopsis:

(1) Very slowly–Introduction of the characters, one by one, in a suffused light.
(2) Fast–Sudden burst of unison strings in A major arpeggios starts the action. A sentiment both elated and religious gives the keynote to this scene.
(3) Moderate–Duo for the Bride and her Intended–scene of tenderness and passion.
(4) Quite fast–The Revivalist and his flock. Folksy feelings–suggestions of square dances and country fiddlers.
(5) Still faster–Solo dance of the Bride–Presentiment of motherhood. Extremes of joy and fear and wonder.
(6) Very slowly (as at first)–Transition scene to music reminiscent of the introduction.
(7) Calm and flowing–Scenes of daily activity for the Bride and her Farmer-husband.
(8) Moderate–Coda–The Bride takes her place among her neighbors. At the end the couple are left "quiet and strong in their new house." Muted strings intone a hushed, prayer-like passage.

In section 7, Copland introduces "five variations on a Shaker theme." This theme—sung by a solo clarinet—is taken from the song called "Simple Gifts," published in the collection of Shaker melodies compiled by Edward D. Andrews under the title *The Gift to be Simple* (see chapter 11 for the music of this song).

The music of *Appalachian Spring* is essentially diatonic, a tendency that is continued in Copland's Third Symphony (1946). The latter is a work in four movements, in which, according to the composer, "any reference to jazz or folk material is purely unconscious." The last movement opens with a fanfare (*Molto deliberato*) which is derived from a *Fanfare for the Common Man* that Copland wrote in 1942. Stylistically the work is closely related to *Appalachian Spring.*

The Third Symphony appears to mark the return to a phase of abstract or nonprogrammatic composition in Copland's career. To this phase belong the Clarinet Concerto (1948), first performed by Benny Goodman with the NBC Symphony on November 6, 1950, and the Piano Quartet, commissioned by the Elizabeth Sprague Coolidge Foundation and first performed at the Library of Congress on October 29, 1950. The Piano Quartet, consisting of a vivacious middle section flanked by two slow movements, breaks away from the clichés of Copland's folkish period and combines maturity of style with freshness of invention. These qualities are also evident in two vocal works, *In the Beginning* for mixed chorus (1947), and *Twelve Poems of Emily Dickinson* (1950), for voice and piano.

Copland's second opera, *The Tender Land,* based on a story of the rural Middle West and dealing with "plain, salt-of-the-earth folk," was produced by the New York City Opera in April, 1954, and was coolly received by the public and the critics. According to *Time*, the music "held as little punch as the libretto."

Whatever may be the ultimate verdict regarding the intrinsic value of Copland's music, or the degree of attention that posterity may bestow upon his compositions, he remains historically important as a musician who by the diversity and effectiveness of his output, by his impressive impact on America's musical activity at many different points, by his versatility, his adventurousness, and his industry, has participated with extraordinary completeness in the musical events of the contemporary world, not only in the concert hall, the theater, and the classroom, but also in such typical twentieth-century media of mass communication as the radio and the motion picture. Whatever posterity may say, we can only reply: "He was a musician of our times." We may turn to his compositions as to a compendium of twentieth-century trends in American music.

"Protagonist of the time-spirit"

"Gentlemen, a genius—but keep your hats on!" With this paraphrase of Robert Schumann's excited tribute to Chopin's Opus 1, Arthur Farwell began an article on Roy Harris written in 1931. It was in that year that Harris's Opus 1, a Sonata for piano, appeared in print. The composer could hardly be called precocious, for he was then thirty-three years old. True, he had written a few earlier works, which had already brought him a small measure of recognition; nevertheless at a comparatively mature age he still stood on the threshold of his career as a composer. Farwell, therefore, could approach his music in a spirit of discovery and with the thrill that comes from recognizing genius before it has been generally acclaimed.

Moved by the excitement of discovery, and by a certain "pride of authorship," for Harris had been a pupil of his, Farwell was by no means cautious in his tributes to this rising luminary of America's music. "It may be that he will prove to be the protagonist of the time-spirit," wrote Farwell. And this: "Harris is a straight-out classicist, challenging the entire subsequent epoch, neo-classicists and all, from the primal standpoint of Bach and Beethoven. . . ." Of the orchestral Toccata: "I regard it as one of the greatest emotional and intellectual achievements of modern times." No wonder that Walter Piston, after the publication of this article, found it appropriate to congratulate his colleague for "surviving the trying experience of having been hailed as a genius."

In the light of Harris's unbounded enthusiasm, unabashedly expressed, for his own music, one may be permitted to doubt that he found the experience of being hailed as a genius in the least trying. In the words of Henry Cowell, "Harris often convinces his friends and listeners of the extreme value of his works by his own indefatigable enthusiasm for them." In 1942 he wrote to Nicolas Slonimsky: "I have finished two movements of my Fifth Symphony, and it is wonderful beyond my wildest hopes." Such self-adulation is refreshing, but we need to pick our way carefully among the superlatives.

Roy Harris was born in Lincoln County, Oklahoma, on the anniversary of Lincoln's birth: February 12, 1898. This chronological coincidence, and the fact that the event occurred in a log cabin, are important ingredients of "the Harris legend," which makes him appear as a rugged product of the pioneer Middle West. The family moved to California while he was still a child, and it was there that Harris grew up, on his father's farm. His musical experience consisted chiefly of some sporadic piano lessons and playing the clarinet in a school band. He spent four years working as a truck driver for a California dairy company, exploring music in his spare time and finally, at the age of twenty-four, deciding that he wanted to be a composer. He then went to Los Angeles, where he studied harmony with Farwell and orchestration with Altschuler. His first recognition as a composer came when Howard Hanson conducted his Andante for Orchestra at Rochester in 1926. This was a signal to move on to Paris, where Harris joined the distinguished company of Nadia Boulanger's pupils.

In Paris he wrote a Concerto for piano, clarinet and string quartet, which was performed there in 1927. An accident that resulted in a broken spine caused him to return to the United States, necessitating a serious operation followed by a long convalescence, during which he composed his First String Quartet. After another sojourn in Paris, Harris returned to New York, where his music had been performed by the League of Composers; by 1934, when his First Symphony was performed in Boston, he was on the highroad to fame. Koussevitzky's interest in his music gave him an effective start in that direction.

From the beginning, Harris took himself very seriously as a composer. He felt imbued with a sense of destiny and with a feeling of moral responsibility toward his country and his times. In an article entitled "The Growth of a Composer," published in *The Musical Quarterly* for April, 1934, he stated his artistic credo: "The creative impulse is a desire to capture and communicate feeling." This statement is crucial for the appreciation of Harris's music. His compositions have grown out of a yearning for self-expression. But at the same time he feels a cosmic urge to express something beyond himself, and then he speaks of the "search for an understandable race-expression."

Harris has been extremely articulate about his aims as a composer, both in general and in connection with specific works. He has on several occasions tried to establish verbal equations between the American character and American music, and several of his compositions purport to be musical expressions of such equations. In an essay on *Problems of American Composers*, published in 1933, he develops at some length the theory that Americans have rhythmic impulses that are fundamentally different from the rhythmic impulses of Europeans, "and from this unique rhythmic sense are generated different melodic and form values." Attempting to define this American sense of rhythm, he writes: [8]

> Our sense of rhythm is less symmetrical than the European rhythmic sense. European musicians are trained to think of rhythm in its largest common denominator, while we are born with a feeling for its smallest units. That is why the jazz boys, chained to an unimaginative commercial routine which serves only crystallized symmetrical dance rhythms, are continually breaking out into superimposed rhythmic variations which were not written into the music. This asymmetrical balancing of rhythmic phrases is in our blood; it is not in the European blood. . . . We do not employ unconventional rhythms as a sophistical gesture; we cannot avoid them. To cut them out of our music would be to gainsay the source of our spontaneous musical impulses. . . . Our struggle is not to invent new rhythms and melodies and forms; our problem is to put down into translatable symbols and rhythms and consequent melodies and form those that assert themselves within us.

As regards harmonic idiom in American music, Harris has this to say:

> American composers have not as yet developed any predominant type of harmonic idiom, but I have noticed two tendencies that are becoming increasingly prevalent both with our commercial jazz writers and with our more serious composers: (1) the avoidance of definite cadence, which can be traced to our unsymmetrically balanced melodies (difficult to harmonize with prepared cadences) and our national aversion to anything final, our hope and search for more satisfying conclusions; (2) the use of modal harmony, which probably comes from ennui of the worn-out conventions of the major and minor scales and our adventurous love of the exotic.

It is typical of Harris's musical metaphysics that he ascribes an alleged avoidance of definite cadence to an alleged national aversion of

[8] The three quotations that follow are from *American Composers on American Music*, edited by Henry Cowell. Reprinted with permission of the publishers, Stanford University Press. Copyright 1933 by the Board of Trustees of Leland Stanford Junior University. Originally published in *Scribner's*.

anything final, which in turn is equated with our hope and search for something more satisfying.

Harris has been much concerned with the "social value" of music. In the same essay he writes:

> Musical literature never has been and never will be valuable to society as a whole until it is created as an authentic and characteristic culture of and from the people it expresses. History reveals that the great music has been produced only by staunch individuals who sank their roots deeply into the social soil which they accepted as their own.

There is ample evidence to indicate that Harris considers himself to be one of those "staunch individuals" who are creating an authentic and characteristic musical expression of American culture. He has made this clear in the commentaries he has appended to several of his scores. Let us now briefly review his major works, beginning with the symphonies.

The symphonies of Roy Harris

The *Symphony, 1933,* his first, was performed by the Boston Symphony Orchestra on January 26, 1934, under the direction of Koussevitzky, who called it "the first truly tragic symphony by an American." The composer gave the following summary of its three movements: "In the first movement I have tried to capture the mood of adventure and physical exuberance; in the second, of the pathos which seems to underlie all human existence; in the third, the will to power and action."

The Second Symphony, performed by the same orchestra on February 28, 1936, also consists of three movements, of which the first is a sort of bravura introduction, the second (Molto cantabile) a "study in canons," and the third a "study in rhythmic developments," which is again intended to convey "a feeling of power." The emphasis on canonic writing is characteristic of Harris, with whom canon and fugue are favorite devices.

With the performance of his Third Symphony by Koussevitzky and the Boston Symphony Orchestra on February 24, 1939, Harris achieved a resounding triumph. Its success was sensational. Within a year it received ten performances by the Boston Symphony alone, in various cities. According to Leichtentritt, thirty-three performances were given by American orchestras during the season of 1941–1942, in addition to several performances abroad. The work was soon issued in recorded form.

The Third Symphony is a relatively brief work, in one continuous movement, with a duration of approximately seventeen minutes. The composer has provided the following outline of its musical structure, divided into five sections:

I. Tragic—low string sonorities
II. Lyric—strings, horns, woodwinds
III. Pastoral—woodwinds with a polytonal string background
IV. Fugue—dramatic
  A. Brass and percussion predominating
  B. Canonic development of materials from Section II constituting background for further development of Fugue
V. Dramatic—tragic
  A. Restatement of violin theme of Section I: tutti strings in canon with tutti woodwinds against brass and percussion developing rhythmic motif from climax of Section IV
  B. Coda—development of materials from Sections I and II over pedal tympani

It will be noticed that the emphasis is upon strictly musical structure, combined with generalized emotional situations devoid of programmatic or descriptive connotations.

Musically, the Third Symphony is a powerful and fully integrated work. Historically, it marks the beginning of a new era in American symphonic music. It made a profound impression, achieved a wide acclaim and had an unprecedented acceptance. It was a serious, an individual, and a compelling musical utterance, that communicated effectively with large sections of the American public. The manager of a baseball team is said to have written to Harris after hearing a performance of the Third Symphony: "If I had pitchers who could pitch as strongly as you do in your Symphony, my worries would be over." This is a new pitch in musical criticism.

On February 21, 1941, the Boston Symphony Orchestra gave the first performance of Harris's fourth symphony, the *Folk Song Symphony* for chorus and orchestra, in which his musical Americanism finds literal expression through the use of American folk songs. It was written, moreover, with the intent "to bring about a cultural cooperation and understanding between the high school, college and community choruses of our cities with their symphonic orchestras." The folk tunes are taken from the collections of John and Alan Lomax and Carl Sandburg. The symphony consists of five choral sections and two instrumental interludes. The first choral section, "Welcome Party," is based on the Civil War song "When Johnny Comes Marching Home" (upon which Harris had composed an Overture in 1934). The second, "Western Cowboy," makes use of "The Dying Cowboy" ("Bury Me Not on the Lone Prairie") and "As I Walked Out in the Streets of Laredo." Then comes the first interlude, "Dance Tunes" for strings and percussion, in which the tunes are of the composer's invention, but strongly reminiscent of traditional fiddle tunes. The next choral section, "Mountaineer Love Song," is based on an Anglo-American folk song with Negro influence, "I'm goin' away for to stay a little while." The second interlude, for full orchestra, is a lively combination of dance tunes, including "The Birds' Courting Song" and "Hop Up, My Lady." Another choral number, titled "Negro Fantasy," features the camp-meeting hymn "De Trumpet Sounds It in My Soul." The choral finale, returns to cowboy material with "The Gal I Left Behind Me," to which Harris adds "Goodnight, Ladies," as a coda.

After a performance of the *Folk Song Symphony* in Cleveland, Herbert Elwell wrote, "This music is nothing if not 100% U.S.A." Henry Simon aptly described it as "not so much a symphony as a little concert of Americana."

In his Fifth Symphony, performed on February 26, 1943 (inevitably by the Boston Symphony), Harris clung to his obsession of expressing the American character in music. He wanted to portray qualities "which our popular dance music, because of its very nature, cannot reveal." And the composer's comments continue:

> Our people are more than pleasure-loving. We also have qualities of heroic strength—determination—will to struggle—faith in our destiny. We are possessed of a fierce driving power—optimistic, young, rough and ready—and I am convinced that our mechanistic age has not destroyed an appreciation of more tender moods. . . .

The Fifth Symphony opens with a somewhat martial introduction, followed by a chorale movement "in singing choral style, yet rhapsodic." The last movement consists of a triple fugue, that is, it is in three sections and on three subjects, with interpolated material, the whole of considerable structural complexity. This work represents an advance in technical mastery over the Third Symphony.

The Sixth Symphony (performed April 14, 1944, Boston Symphony) is another essay in musical Americana, this time based on Lincoln's Gettysburg Address, and dedicated to "the Armed Forces of Our Nation." The four movements of the symphony are titled, respectively, "Awakening," "Conflict," "Dedication," "Affirmation"—episodes that the composer conceives as making up "that great cycle which always attends any progress in the intellectual or spiritual growth of a people," and which he considers as finding "a classic expression" in the Gettysburg Address. "Awakening" refers to the beginning of Lincoln's speech, to the Revolution and the achievement of independence. "Conflict" evokes the struggle of the Civil War. "Dedication" draws its inspiration from Lincoln's tribute to the fallen: "We have come to dedicate a portion of that field as a final resting place for those who here gave their lives that that nation might live." Finally, "Affirmation" voices the spirit of Lincoln's statement of faith, that "This nation, under God, shall have a new birth of freedom, that government of the people, by the people, for the people, shall not perish from the earth."

The last movement of the Sixth Symphony, again, is cast in the structure of a fugue, by which the composer has endeavored to "reflect in architectural terms the mood of strong faith in mankind." This is an example of Harris's attempt to make musical structure serve the programmatic purpose of his symphony.

On November 20, 1952, the Chicago Symphony Orchestra, under the direction of Rafael Kubelik, gave the first performance of Harris's Seventh Symphony. This work, in one movement, received praise for its brilliant orchestration, but did not appear to mark any important step forward in the composer's creative development.

The compositions of Harris are too numerous to mention. He has written works for band, for chorus, for piano, for voice and piano, for piano and orchestra, and for various chamber-music combinations. Notable in this last category are his three String Quartets and a Piano Quintet (1936). The latter, indeed, is among his finest works. The Second String Quartet consists of Three Variations on a Theme, and is known by that title. An early Piano Sonata, dating from 1928, should also be mentioned as Harris's only work in this form and medium, up to the time of this writing.

It is interesting to remark that the Overture, *When Johnny Comes Marching Home* (1934), was written especially for recording, and had to fulfill certain conditions, not the least of which was the requirement that it should be eight minutes in length and be divided into two equal parts, each to occupy one side of a twelve-inch record (that was before the invention of the long-playing record). Another requirement, more difficult to fulfill, was that "the work should express a gamut of emotions particularly American and in an American manner."

In coping with this second problem, Harris decided that the familiar Civil War tune would serve his purpose, particularly because of its combination of ribaldry and sadness, contrasting moods that he feels are particularly American. He tells us that it was his father who planted in him "the unconscious realization of its dual nature. He used to whistle it with jaunty bravado as we went to work on the farm in the morning and with sad pensiveness as we returned at dusk behind the slow, weary plodding of the horses." This antithesis of mood provides the basis for musical contrast in the Overture. About its general organization, Harris writes: "In the treatment of the texture and the orchestration I have tried to keep the work rough-hewn, sinewy, and directly outspoken, as are our people and our civilization."

Harris, in formulating his creed as a composer, stressed the importance of the large contrapuntal forms, and stated:

> I have become increasingly convinced that music is a fluid architecture of sound and that all the elements of music—melody, harmony, counterpoint, dynamics, orchestration—must be coordinated into a swift-moving form which fulfils itself from the root idea to its complete flowering in organic ornamentation.[9]

Because the music of Roy Harris at its best embodies these principles of dynamic form and organic ornamentation, he must be counted among the truly creative figures in American music.

Assorted Americanists

Many pages could be filled simply with mentioning the names and works of composers who might be described as "musical Americanists" in the sense that they have demonstrated a consistent concern with

[9] Quoted in *The Book of Modern Composers,* edited by David Ewen, p. 453. Published by Alfred A. Knopf, Inc., New York.

the American scene and with the vernacular elements of our music. Some composers, such as Henry Cowell and Virgil Thomson, have made numerous and valuable contributions to musical Americana, but are dealt with elsewhere because of the emphasis placed on other phases of their production. Cowell is included among "The Experimentalists," while Thomson figures among "The Eclectics" as well as in the chapter on the emergence of American opera. Another composer who figures in the last-mentioned chapter, Douglas Moore, should also be mentioned here because of his repeated excursions into musical Americana, such as *The Pageant of P. T. Barnum* (5 episodes), *Overture on an American Tune, Moby Dick* (symphonic poem after Melville's famous novel), *Village Music, Farm Journal, Power and the Land* (suite from music for a documentary film), *Down East Suite* (for violin and piano), and *Ballad of William Sycamore* (poem by Stephen Vincent Benét) for baritone solo, flute, trombone, and piano. Moore's feeling for the vernacular in America's music, and for many aspects of our tradition and folklore, is wide in range, embracing the tragic grandeur of Melville and the jaunty vulgarity of Barnum's "Greatest Show on Earth," with its culmination in the garish pageantry of the circus parade. In his *Overture on an American Tune*, Moore painted a musical portrait of Babbitt, the American businessman immortalized in Sinclair Lewis's novel. Even in a work of classical form, such as his *Symphony of Autumn*, one feels that the music of Douglas Moore is permeated by the moods and tones of an American landscape. In works without programmatic connotation—the Second Symphony in A, string quartets, Quintet for winds, and Quintet for clarinet and strings—Moore cultivates a traditional style with distinction and individuality.

The late John Alden Carpenter (1876–1951), a pupil of Paine at Harvard, and, like Charles Ives, a businessman by profession, was one of the first American composers to experiment with the use of jazz inflections. He employed ragtime rhythms in his Concertino for piano and orchestra, composed in 1915, several years before the vogue for "symphonic jazz." Another experiment in the popular idiom was the ballet or "jazz pantomime" titled *Krazy Kat* (1921), inspired by the newspaper comic strip of that name. The success of this work brought a commission from Diaghilev, the impresario of ballet, to write a score employing the American musical vernacular and depicting some typical aspect of American life. Carpenter responded with

Skyscrapers, "a ballet of modern American life," which was produced at the Metropolitan Opera House in New York on February 19, 1926. These works were symptomatic of the "Jazz Age." They now appear to us as period pieces. Carpenter's musical Americanism was largely of the surface; his style was wholly dominated by European—chiefly French—influences. Although he wrote symphonies, choral works, songs, and chamber music, he will perhaps be best remembered for his amusing descriptive suite for orchestra, *Adventures in a Perambulator* (1914).

Ferde Grofé, born in New York in 1892, has composed a number of orchestral suites descriptive of the American scene. The best-known of these is the *Grand Canyon Suite* (1932), undoubtedly one of the American compositions that is most frequently performed throughout the world. Grofé has also written a *Mississippi Suite*, a *Tabloid Suite*, a *Hollywood Suite*, and a *Transatlantic Suite*. He is an extremely skillful orchestrator, as he proved when he orchestrated Gershwin's *Rhapsody in Blue*. In the realm of popular orchestration, Grofé has been credited with creating "an orchestra based on saxophones rather than strings," which is the typical radio orchestra as we know it today. Whether this places him among the great innovators in the history of orchestration, along with Berlioz and Rimsky-Korsakoff—as claimed by one of his admirers [10]—is a moot question. But there is no question as to the widespread influence of Grofé's innovations in this mass-media phase of contemporary American music.

Two other composers closely associated with radio who have successfully cultivated the American vein are Morton Gould (born in New York, 1913) and Don Gillis (born in Missouri, 1912). Gould has rather systematically exploited the various phases of the American musical vernacular, from spirituals to swing, not forgetting minstrel tunes, jazz, and Latin American rhythms, dressing up his borrowed materials in a smoothly effective and somewhat synthetically brilliant orchestration. Among his compositions in this style are *Swing Symphonietta*, *Spirituals*, *Minstrel Show*, and *Concerto for Orchestra* (1945), this last described as "boisterously Americanistic." His most recent excursion into musical Americana is the *Concerto for Tap Dancer and Orchestra* (1952). His more ambitious works include three symphonies and *A Lincoln Legend* for orchestra (1942). Gillis's con-

[10] Tom Bennett, in *Music and Radio Broadcasting*, edited by Gilbert Chase. New York, 1946, p. 77.

tributions to musical Americana include *An American Symphony*, *Prairie Poem* for orchestra, *Cowtown* (suite), *The Alamo* (symphonic poem), and Symphony No. 7 ("Saga of a Prairie School"). Inclined to be humoristic, often bright and brash, reflecting the prevailing popular tempo, Gillis's music finds a ready response among American listeners today.

Among composers who have particularly cultivated American folk music are David Guion (*b.* 1895), George Frederick McKay (*b.* 1899), Elie Siegmeister (*b.* 1909), Lamar Stringfield (*b.* 1897), and Charles G. Vardell (*b.* 1893). The last two are from North Carolina and may be said to represent a regional trend in American music. Ernst Bacon (*b.* 1898) has written two orchestral suites, *Ford's Theatre* and *From These States*, dealing with the American scene, as well as the folk operas *A Tree on the Plains* and *A Drumlin Legend*. He has also published a collection of eight American folk songs entitled *Along Unpaved Roads*, which rank among the most skillful and faithful settings of this kind.

William Grant Still has been concerned mainly with depicting the backgrounds of the American Negro in music. Born in Woodville, Mississippi, in 1893, he was raised in Little Rock, Arkansas, where his mother taught school. His racial heritage includes Indian, Negro, and European strains. Becoming a composer of "serious" music was not an easy task for Still. After considerable knocking about at odd jobs, he obtained a scholarship to study composition at Oberlin College. Later he became an arranger for W. C. Handy in New York, where he also studied composition with the modernist Edgar Varèse. Playing in theater and night-club orchestras, and arranging popular music, gave him another variety of musical experience. Out of this varied background, Still began to compose symphonic works influenced by Afro-American traditions: *Darker America* (1924); *From the Black Belt*, for chamber orchestra (1926); *Africa* (1930); *Afro-American Symphony* (1931); and the Second Symphony in G minor (1937), subtitled "Song of a New Race" and described as an expression of "the American colored man of today."

Still has written two operas, *Blue Steel* (1935) and *Troubled Island* (1949), the latter produced at the New York City Center in the spring of 1949. Haiti is the setting of *Troubled Island*, which deals with the life of the Emperor Dessalines, whose brief moment of power and glory had a tragic ending. The libretto is by the Negro poet

Langston Hughes. The West Indies, Africa, and Harlem, provide the setting for three ballets by Still. *Sahdji* (1931) has its scene in ancestral Africa and calls for a chorus that comments on the action, also a bass chanter who recites African proverbs, *La Guiablesse* (1933), based on West Indian and Louisiana Creole material, has its scene laid on the island of Martinique. *Lenox Avenue* was originally composed for radio and consisted of ten episodes for chorus, narrator, and orchestra, depicting scenes in the life of Harlem, the Negro quarter of New York. Later it was converted into a ballet and produced successfully in that form. Finally, we must mention one of Still's most impressive works, *And They Lynched Him on a Tree* (1940), for contralto, mixed chorus, orchestra, and narrator.

Ernest Bloch's *America*

One of the most fervid manifestations of musical Americanism is the work of the Swiss-born composer Ernest Bloch (*b.* 1880) titled *America* and described as "an epic rhapsody in three parts for orchestra." The score has the following dedication:

> This Symphony has been written in love for this country/In reverence to its Past—In faith in its Future/It is dedicated to the memory of Abraham Lincoln and Walt Whitman, whose vision upheld its inspiration.

Bloch's *America* was completed in 1927, eleven years after the composer first came to the United States. It received a mixed critical reception and has not entrenched itself very firmly in the symphonic repertoire. Nevertheless, the intent and scope of the work entitle it to more than casual attention.

It is not within the plan of this book to deal in detail with Bloch's career and output as a whole. Suffice it to say that he is one of the most outstanding of contemporary composers, internationally admired and respected for such works as *Trois Poèmes Juifs* for orchestra (1913), the rhapsody *Schelomo* for cello and orchestra (1916), the symphony *Israel* (1916), Suite for viola and orchestra, Concerto Grosso (1924), Violin Concerto, and chamber and choral music, as well as the opera *Macbeth* (1910). Bloch has lived in the United States from 1916 to 1930, in Switzerland from 1930 to 1939 (with frequent visits to America), and in the United States again since 1939.

The epic rhapsody *America* is an attempt to summarize and express in music the essential historical role and destiny of the United States of America. It applies the epic style to musical composition, relying on broad and massive effects, and on the impact of the work as a whole rather than on the refinements or distinction of any of its component parts. In a prefatory note to the score, the composer wrote:

> The Ideals of America are imperishable. They embody the future credo of all mankind: a Union, in common purpose and under willingly accepted guidance, of widely diversified races, ultimately to become one race, strong and great. But, as Walt Whitman has said: "To hold men together by paper and seal or by compulsion, is of no account. That only holds men together which aggregates all in a living principle, as the hold of the limbs of the body or the fibres of plants."
>
> Though this symphony is not dependent on a program, the composer wants to emphasize that he has been inspired by this very Ideal.

The score has running explanatory references at the bottom of the pages, which are intended to clarify the composer's intentions rather than to provide a descriptive "program." Part I begins with the year 1620. It evokes the soil, the Indians, the *Mayflower*, the landing of the Pilgrims, primeval nature, and Indian life (with quotation of Indian tribal melodies collected by Frances Densmore among the Pueblo, Mandan, Hidatsa, and Chippewa Indians). Part II covers the period of the Civil War, 1861–1865, and bears the subheading "Hours of Joy—Hours of Sorrow." In this section there are musical quotations from "Old Folks at Home," Virginia reels, "Hail Columbia," Creole folk songs, "Dixie," "Battle Cry of Freedom," "John Brown's Body," and "Tramp, Tramp, Tramp." Part III, bearing the date 1926, evokes the spirit of the present and the future. Its motto is, "As he sees the farthest he has the most faith." Two Negro folk songs are quoted: "I Went to the Hop Joint" and "The Coon-can Game." There is a section reflecting the "turmoil of the present time," the speed and noise of the Machine Age. Then is heard "The Call of America," symbolized in these lines from Walt Whitman:

> Then turn, and be not alarm'd O Libertad—
> turn your undying face
> to where the future, greater than all the past,
> is swiftly, surely preparing for you.

The next episode depicts the mastery of Man over the machines, his environment, and himself. The call of America to the nations of the world leads to the climax of "The Fulfillment Through Love," and at this moment the people (i.e., the audience) rise to sing the anthem that the composer has incorporated in the score: [11]

As the composer explains, the symphony is based entirely upon the anthem, which "from the first bars appears, in root, dimly, slowly taking shape, rising, falling, developing, and finally asserting itself victoriously in its complete and decisive form. . . . The Anthem . . . symbolizes the Destiny, the Mission of America."

[11] From the symphony *America* by Ernest Bloch, C. C. Birchard & Company, Publishers. Used by permission.

chapter twenty-five

The eclectics

All music is a tone experience. . . . All human music should be close to us . . . irrespective of race or epoch.

DANE RUDHYAR IN AMERICAN COMPOSERS ON AMERICAN MUSIC.

Eclecticism, in philosophy, is a system composed of doctrines selected from different sources. By analogy, an eclectic composer is one who selects his material from various sources. To a certain extent all creative artists are eclectic, because an artist does not derive his material or develop his style solely from one source or tradition. This is particularly true of modern artists, who, to begin with, have all the sources and traditions of the past to draw on; and in addition, thanks to the greatly developed facilities for cultural interchange, have at their disposal the materials and resources pertaining to all the cultural systems of the world.

Eclecticism in music, therefore, scarcely serves to define a specific school or group of composers, especially in the United States, where eclecticism is the norm rather than the exception. We are a nation made from many sources and many cultures. An American composer can be thoroughly eclectic even without seeking material beyond the borders of his own country. He can draw on the music of the Indian and of the Negro, on the heritage of Anglo-American folk song, on the Hispanic tradition of the Southwest, on the tradition of rural hymnody and on the various types of popular music, from ragtime to boogie-woogie. Many of the composers dealt with in other chapters of this book, among them Arthur Farwell, Henry Gilbert, George Gershwin, Henry Cowell, and Aaron Copland, are markedly eclectic, and what we have done is simply to emphasize certain prominent trends within their eclectic tendency, such as the folklorism of Farwell and the Americanism of Gershwin. In this chapter we shall deal with composers whose music represents divergent trends, and who have little in common with one another except a marked tendency toward eclecticism.

The first of these composers is Charles Tomlinson Griffes (1884–1920), whose predominant tendency might be described as exotic eclecticism. Griffes began by assimilating the technique of German song writers, veered to the impressionism of Debussy and the primitivism of Stravinsky, underwent the influence of the arch-eclectic Busoni, made more than a passing bow to the Russian "Five," turned briefly to American Indian themes, and found a congenial source of material in the music of the Far East. Throughout these avatars he maintained a personal style and developed a power of expression that entitle him to a distinctive place among the creative musicians of America. That he died before achieving his full creative development seems probable; that he suffered from material handicaps in his career as a composer is certain; and that his music reveals technical weaknesses may be conceded. Yet alone for such works as *The Pleasure Dome of Kubla Khan,* the *Poem* for flute and orchestra, and the Sonata for piano, his place is secure.

Charles T. Griffes was born in Elmira, New York, on September 17, 1884. At an early age he displayed a remarkable sensitivity for color, a trait that remained with him as a composer, for he came to associate certain keys with certain colors. His musical aptitude was at first channeled in the direction of becoming a concert pianist, and upon the advice of his teacher he went to Europe in 1903 to complete his training at the Stern Conservatory in Berlin. He remained in Germany four years, except for two brief visits to his home. He became increasingly interested in composing, in spite of the fact that his teacher tore up the first song that he submitted—perhaps because it was in French. He rebelled against the "terribly ordinary and common" modulations recommended by the pedantic professor at the Conservatory, and was happier when he managed to have some lessons in composition with the gifted Humperdinck, composer of the opera *Hansel and Gretel.*

When Griffes returned to the United States in 1907 the only immediate solution he could find for the problem of earning a living was to accept a position as music teacher at the Hackley School for boys in Tarrytown, New York. It was not a congenial situation. Of his pupils he wrote, "Oh! how they bore and weary me!" Nevertheless he was destined to remain at this school for the rest of his life.

As a composer, Griffes was befriended and encouraged by that generous and broad-visioned champion of American music, Arthur Farwell. After his early settings of German songs, he began to set poems by American and English authors, including Sidney Lanier ("Evening Song"), Sara Teasdale, and Oscar Wilde. He wrote a series of impressionistic piano pieces: *The Lake at Evening* (1910), *The Night Winds* (1911), *The Vale of Dreams* (1912), *Barcarolle* (1912), and *Scherzo* (1913).

Early in 1912 Griffes began to compose a work for piano based on Coleridge's poem "Kubla Khan." After frequent revisions over several years he finally decided that it would be more effective as an orchestral composition. In this form it was completed in April, 1916. But not until November 28, 1919, just a few months before the composer's death, did this symphonic poem receive its first performance.

Regarding this symphonic poem, Griffes wrote:

> I have taken as a basis for my work those lines of Coleridge's poem describing the "stately pleasure-dome," the "sunny pleasure-dome with caves of ice," the "miracle of rare device." Therefore I call the work *The Pleasure-Dome of Kubla Khan* rather than *Kubla Khan*. . . . As to argument, I have given my imagination free rein in the description of this strange palace as well as of purely imaginary revelry which might take place there. The vague, foggy beginning suggests the sacred river, running "through caverns measureless to man down to a sunless sea." The gardens with fountains and "sunny spots of greenery" are next suggested. From inside come sounds of dancing and revelry which increase to a wild climax and then suddenly break off. There is a return to the original mood suggesting the sacred river and the "caves of ice."

The passages in Coleridge's poem to which Griffes specifically refers consist of lines 1 to 11 and lines 32 to 38.

In 1915 Griffes composed his piano piece *The White Peacock*, based on a poem of that title by "Fiona Macleod," the pseudonym of a Scottish writer named William Sharp who, in the early years of the century, did much to stimulate what Gilman called "the Celtic impulse" among American composers, including MacDowell. Actually, there was nothing Celtic about a white peacock, and Griffes eventually included his tone poem in a set of four piano pieces entitled *Roman Sketches* (the other three pieces are "Nightfall," "The Fountain of Acqua Paola," and "Clouds"). *The White Peacock* was orchestrated by the composer for a choreographic number staged by Adolph Bolm at the Rivoli Theatre in New York, which ran for a week beginning on June 22, 1919. Both as a piano piece and as an orchestral tone poem, *The White Peacock* obtained wide acceptance.

Griffes felt a strong attraction for the music of the Near and Far East. While working on *Kubla Khan* he consulted all the works on Arabian music in the New York Public Library, and copied out some melodies that appealed to him. His tendency toward Orientalism was further developed in his settings for voice and piano of *Five Poems of Ancient China and Japan,* and in the writing of a Japaneses dance drama, *Sho-Jo,* for the dancer Michio Ito, based on Japanese melodies given to him by the singer Eva Gauthier (1917).

The *Poem for Flute and Orchestra,* finished in 1918, is one of Griffes's best works and marks the culmination of his Orientalism. It is, to be sure, an impressionistic and highly attenuated Orientalism, which strives for atmospheric coloring rather than for ethnographic authenticity (such as we find later, for example, in the music of Colin McPhee).

Griffes also turned briefly to American Indian music, in his *Two Sketches Based on Indian Themes* for string quartet. The first of these, Scherzo, was composed in 1916; the second, Lento, in 1918, utilizing for its main theme a farewell song of the Chippewa:

In February, 1917, a dance drama with music by Griffes, titled *The Kairn of Koridwen,* was produced in New York. The music was scored for piano, celesta, flute, clarinets, horns, and harp. This small combination acted as a challenge to the composer's resourcefulness, and he made the most of it. In the words of Paul Rosenfeld: "The unusual conjunction of timbres, split horn and piano, chromatic harp, chromatic flute and celesta, the happy superposition of conflicting tonalities, the knitting of strongly contrary rhythms that abound throughout the work, should make a musicians' holiday." [1] Actually there was so much trouble over the rehearsals and the production that it gave the musicians, including the composer, a headache rather than a holiday.

Griffes's Sonata for piano, completed in January, 1918 (revised in May, 1919), gives evidence of his impressionistic Orientalism in its use of the following scale:

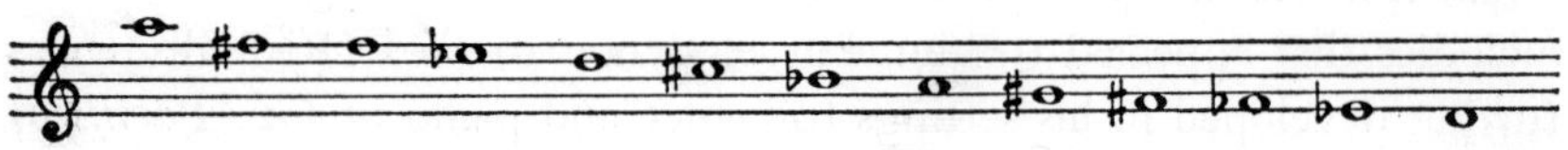

Although influenced by Scriabin, the Sonata is, on the whole, the most original as well as the most complex and ambitious of Griffes's compositions. It is in three movements: Feroce-Allegretto con moto, Molto tranquillo, Allegro vivace. Experimental in its harmonic idiom, richly expressive and strongly emotional, the Piano Sonata may be regarded as a peak of neo-romantic expression in American music.

Composers of the immediate past

In contrast to Griffes, whose music is very much alive over thirty years after his death, there is a group of composers, all born in the 1870s, who long outlived him and who were more successful than he, but whose music seems already to belong to another period. These composers were markedly eclectic, influenced by many current trends and fashions. They figured prominently in the American musical scene for many decades and therefore merit at least passing mention in these pages.

Henry Kimball Hadley (1871–1937), a native of Somerville, Massachusetts, and a graduate of the New England Conservatory of Music, was active as a conductor besides being an extremely prolific composer. Among his six operas were *Azora, Daughter of Montezuma,* produced by the Chicago Opera Company in 1917 and 1918, and *Cleopatra's Night,* produced at the Metropolitan Opera House in New York in 1920. His orchestral works include five symphonies, of

[1] From a review originally published in *Seven Arts.* Quoted by Maisel in *Charles T. Griffes,* p. 340.

which four were programmatic—(1) *Youth and Life,* (2) *The Four Seasons,* (4) *North, East, South, West,* (5) *Connecticut-Tercentenary.* The Fifth Symphony—whose three movements bore the respective dates 1635, 1735, 1935—was one of those well-meant historical-commemorative-descriptive-nationalistic lucubrations that are fortunately becoming less frequent in American music. Hadley should in any case be remembered as the founder of the National Association for American Composers and Conductors, which in turn sponsored the Henry Hadley Memorial Library of music by contemporary American composers.

Frederick Shepherd Converse (1871–1940), born in Newton, Massachusetts, was a pupil of Paine at Harvard but also studied with Chadwick in Boston and with Rheinberger in Germany. He was for many years on the staff of the New England Conservatory of Music, at first as professor of composition and later as Dean of the Faculty. For a time, Converse was much concerned with the American scene. He wrote the tone poem *California* (1918), the orchestral suite *American Sketches* (1929), and—his brightest contribution to musical Americana—the symphonic poem *Flivver Ten Million* (1927). This work depicts, in successive episodes, *Dawn in Detroit, The Birth of the Hero, May Night by the Roadside* ("America's Romance"), *The Joy Riders* ("America's Frolic"), *The Collision* ("America's Tragedy"), and *Phoenix Americanus,* an apotheosis of "the indomitable American spirit." Besides this humorous period piece, Converse wrote many symphonic works, including three symphonies, and a one-act opera, *The Pipe of Desire,* the first opera by an American to be produced at the Metropolitan Opera House (in 1910).

Ernest Schelling (1876–1939), a brilliant pianist who began his career as a child prodigy, was the composer of two symphonic works that are still occasionally played by American orchestras: *Impressions from an Artist's Life,* variations for piano and orchestra (1916), and *A Victory Ball,* symphonic poem after Alfred Noyes (1923). The latter is one of those vividly descriptive and emotionally evocative compositions, in the tradition of the Lisztian tone poem, which contrasts peacetime gaiety with the horrors of war. Other works by Schelling include *Légende Symphonique, Suite Fantastique,* the tone poem *Morocco,* and a Violin Concerto first played by Fritz Kreisler in 1917. For many years Schelling conducted the children's concerts of the New York Philharmonic-Symphony Orchestra.

David Stanley Smith (1877–1949), a native of Toledo, Ohio, studied with Horatio Parker at Yale and in 1920 succeeded him as Dean of the School of Music at that university. His approach to music was intellectual and traditionalistic within the academic convention. In addition to four symphonies and other orchestral works, such as *Fête Galante* for flute and orchestra, Smith wrote a large quantity of chamber music, including eight string quartets, and several choral works, among which are *The Vision of Isaiah* (1927) and *Daybreak* (1945). In two orchestral pieces, *1929–A Satire* and the overture *Tomorrow*, dating respectively from 1932 and 1933, he recorded his impressions of the world around him.

Some eclectics of today

Today, as yesterday, there are many eclectic composers writing music in the United States. Only a few representative figures can be cited here.

Arthur Shepherd was born in Paris, Idaho, on February 19, 1880, the son of English converts to Mormonism who had emigrated to the West in the 1870s. At the age of twelve he was sent to Boston to study at the New England Conservatory of Music. In the words of William Newman: "During the five years that followed in Boston the formal part of the training was as German as it might have been at Leipzig"—where his parents had originally considered sending him. Strong eclectic inclinations saved Shepherd from accepting late German music as the sole pathway to salvation. After periods of teaching in Salt Lake City and Boston, he became assistant conductor of the Cleveland Symphony Orchestra. He then joined the music staff of Western Reserve University in Cleveland, serving as chairman of the Music Department from 1933 to 1948.

Shepherd became interested in modern French music, particularly that of Fauré and d'Indy, and in the national folklore movement led by Farwell and Gilbert. He himself confessed that he seemed to have a strong atavistic tendency toward writing tunes "with a pronounced Celtic flavor." His First Symphony, completed in 1927 and titled *Horizons: Four Western Pieces for Symphony Orchestra* (later the composer stated that he wished this work to be known as *Nature Symphony*), is an impressive embodiment of the spirit of the West in music. It consists of four movements: "Westward," "The Lone

Prairie," "The Old Chisholm Trail," and "Canyons." The second movement makes use of the cowboy song known as "The Dying Cowboy" ("O bury me not on the lone prairee"). The last movement includes a chorale derived from a hymn of the Western pioneers.

In 1946 Shepherd composed a *Fantasia on Down East Spirituals*, described as "an excursion into the realm of American folk tunes." But his main preoccupation has not been with musical Americana. His eclectic tendencies are revealed in an extensive catalogue of works in many forms, outstanding among which are his Symphony No. 2 (1940), Violin Concerto (1946–1947), String Quartet in E minor, Quintet for piano and strings, *Triptych* for soprano and string quartet, Second Piano Sonata, Psalm 42 for chorus and orchestra, and some two dozen songs.

Among women composers, Mary Howe (*b.* 1882) and Marion Bauer (*b.* 1887) have distinguished themselves. The former has written a series of impressionistic orchestral poems, such as *Sand, Dirge, American Piece, Potomac;* some choral works (*Chain Gang Song, Fiddler's Reel*), and chamber music (including *Three Pieces after Emily Dickinson* for string quartet). Marion Bauer, who was born in the State of Washington, has worked largely within the orbit of impressionism and has absorbed various exotic elements, ranging from American Indian to African material (*A Lament on African Themes* for chamber orchestra, 1928). Typical of her rather extensive chamber-music production are the *Fantasia Quasi una Sonata* for violin and piano (1928) and the Concertino for oboe, clarinet, and string quartet (1939–1943).

Philip James (*b.* 1891) has ranged in his descriptive orchestral music from metropolitan scenes of the present in *Station WGZBX* (1932) to evocations of America's past in the overture *Bret Harte* (1936), which attempts to evoke "the romance, the boisterousness, the animation" of the Far West as depicted in the stories of Bret Harte. James has also written an *Overture on French Noëls*, a *Sea Symphony*, a setting of Vachel Lindsay's "General William Booth Enters Heaven," and considerable chamber and choral music. Another scene of metropolitan daily life is his *Skyscraper Romance* (*The Typist and the Mailman*), for women's chorus, soprano and baritone solos, and piano accompaniment, with text by Amy Bonner, published in 1949.

Harl McDonald, born in Boulder, Colorado, in 1899, joined the faculty of the University of Pennsylvania in 1927 and in 1939 became manager of the Philadelphia Orchestra. He has written orchestral and choral works, usually descriptive as in the Symphony No. 1 (*The Santa Fe Trail*), the orchestral nocturnes titled *San Juan Capistrano*, the symphonic suite *My Country at War* (1943), and the symphonic poem *Bataan* (1942). His *Lament for the Stolen*, for women's chorus and orchestra (1938) was written as an elegy for the kidnaped child of Charles Lindbergh. One of his best-known choral works is *The Breadth and Extent of Man's Empire* for mixed chorus. In his Symphony No. 2, subtitled *Rhumba*, McDonald employs Latin American rhythms.

Harrison Kerr, born in Cleveland, Ohio, in 1899, is among the many American composers who studied with Nadia Boulanger in Paris. But he is an eclectic composer who has assimilated various elements of modern music in the process of evolving his personal style. His evolution has been from a rather conventional idiom (in his student days) to a prevailingly *un*tonal (rather than *a*tonal) texture utilizing twelve-tone elements, though not according to the strict Schoenbergian canon. His use of twelve-tone techniques has been nearer to the practice of Alban Berg than of Schoenberg (cf. Chapter 28). Much of his music is characterized by chromaticism, frequent use of chords or sonorities based on superimposed fourths, dissonant counterpoint, and free use of changing meters. In his later works the harmony is not readily identifiable with any key, but there is nearly always a discernible tonal center. In general, tonal-center relationships replace the conventional key relationships of orthodox harmony.

Among the orchestral works of Harrison Kerr are *Dance Suite* (1938), which includes two African drums and seven Chinese gongs as optional percussion; Symphony No. 1, in one movement (1927–1929; revised 1938); Symphony No. 2 in E minor (1943–1945); and Symphony No. 3 in D minor (1953–1954). His chamber music includes a String Quartet (1937), Suite for flute and piano (1940–1941), Suite for cello and piano (1944–1946); Trio for clarinet, cello, and piano (1936); and Trio for violin, cello, and piano (1938). For piano he has written two Sonatas (1929 and 1943), and a set of Preludes (1938). Among his vocal compositions are *Wink of Eternity* for mixed chorus and orchestra (1937); *Notations on a Sensitized Plate* for voice, clarinet, piano, and string quartet (1935); Three Songs for contralto and orchestra, Three Songs with chamber orchestra, and Three Songs with string quartet (all 1924–1928). Since 1949 Harrison Kerr has been Dean of the College of Fine Arts of the University of Oklahoma.

Among American composers born in the last decade of the nineteenth century, two may stand as thoroughly representative of eclecticism, though each in a completely different manner. They are Roger Sessions and Virgil Thomson. Both are difficult to classify, but the former may be called an academic eclectic with neoclassical tendencies. As for Thomson, we can say only that he is unscholastic, unacademic, unorthodox, and unregenerate. Both composers are important.

"An intensely serious composer"

Roger Sessions was born in Brooklyn, New York, on December 28, 1896. But Brooklyn was not his natural habitat. He came of old New England stock, and soon after his birth the family returned to its ancestral domain in Massachusetts. Sessions, intellectually precocious, entered Harvard at the age of fourteen. Later he attended the Yale Music School, where he was a pupil of Horatio Parker in composition. Still later he studied composition with the Swiss-American composer Ernest Bloch, who influenced him deeply and whom he accompanied to Cleveland in 1921. In 1925 Sessions went to Europe and remained there eight years (except for trips to the United States in 1927 and 1928), living chiefly in Florence, Italy, but traveling through various countries, including France, Austria, and England. After returning to the United States he occupied various teaching posts and in 1945 became professor of music at the University of California in Berkeley.

One critic assures us that Sessions derives from Stravinsky, while another hailed him as an "American Brahms." If both are right, the result is an amazing conciliation of opposites, and this argues a strong character. And that is exactly what distinguishes the music of Sessions: strength of character. He has deeply absorbed certain influences, notably those of Bloch, Stravinsky, Schoenberg, and Richard Strauss. His creative personality, the interior dynamism that prompts him to emotional expression in music, is strong enough to absorb these influences and to emerge with a mode of utterance that is as personal as it is eclectic.

We may unhesitatingly agree with Mark Schubart that Sessions is "an intensely serious composer." He takes with the utmost seriousness every aspect of musical art: the theoretical, the creative, the didactic, and the interpretative. The fruits of his cogitations are found not only in his compositions and his teaching, but also in two books that he has published: *The Musical Experience of Composer, Performer, Listener* (1950) and *Harmonic Practice* (1951). The latter, of course, is a textbook intended for classroom use. In it the author acknowledges his indebtedness to Iwan Knorr, Heinrich Schenker, Paul Hindemith, and Arnold Schoenberg. Regarding the last-mentioned he writes: "It becomes always clearer that the influence of this truly extraordinary man is not limited to his most immediate or obvious followers, but has had a far-reaching effect on friend and foe alike. His *Harmonielehre*, many later writings, and above all his music, have set in motion trains of thought, as they have opened new avenues of musical sensibility, of human awareness—in a word, of musical experience—which are at the very least a challenge to all musicians of today." [2]

The last chapter of Sessions's text on harmony, "Introduction to Contemporary Harmonic Practice," is a valuable analysis of recent trends in composition, including the problem of tonality, and should be read by anyone seriously interested in the subject. In discussing various technical problems of today, he reminds us that, now as always, "It is never a question of applying a formula, but of solving a problem, in each case, in accordance with the composer's ideas and the technical necessities which these ideas create."

To illustrate what he means by a musical "idea," Sessions takes an example from his First Piano Sonata, which was begun in 1927 while he was in Italy. In his book *The Musical Experience* he writes:

> The first idea that came to me for my First Piano Sonata . . . was in the form of a complex chord preceded by a sharp but heavy up beat.

[2] Quoted by permission of the publisher, Harcourt, Brace and Company, New York.

This chord rang through my ear almost obsessively one day as I was walking in Pisa. The next day, or, in other words, when I sat down to work on the piece, I wrote the first phrase of the Allegro

as you see, the chord had become simpler—a C minor triad, in fact, and its complex sonority had given way to a motif of very syncopated rhythmic character. Later it became clear to me that the motif must be preceded by an introduction, and the melody in B minor [example 124c] with which the Sonata begins, immediately suggested itself, quite without any conscious thought on my part.

A few days later the original complex chord came back into my ear, again almost obsessively; I found myself continuing it in my mind, and only then made the discovery that the two lower notes of the chord, F# and E, formed the minor seventh of the dominant of the key of B minor, and that the continuation I had been hearing led me back to B; that the germ of the key relationship on which the first two movements of the sonata were based were already implicit in the chordal idea with which the musical train of thought—which eventually took shape in the completed sonata—had started.[3]

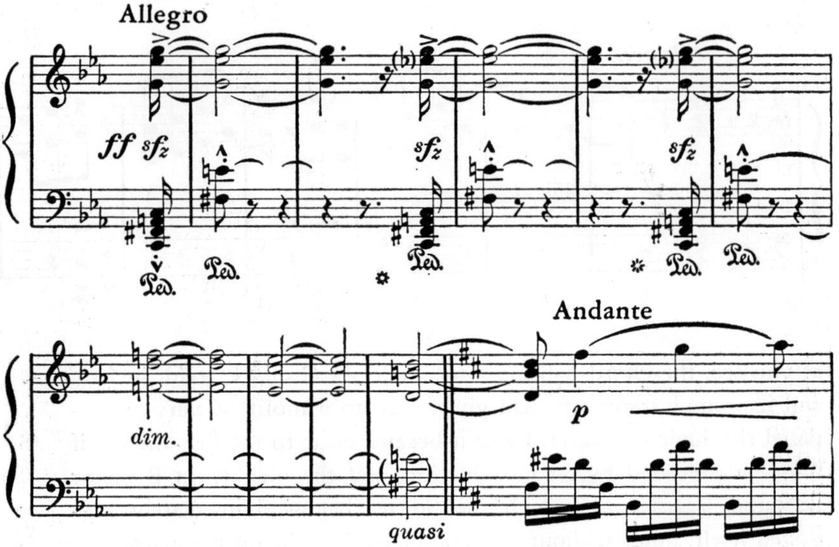

Sessions goes on to say that he has pointed out these things not only to illustrate the nature of the musical idea, but also "in order to throw some light on some of the ways in which a composer's mind, his creative musical mind, that is, works." Since Sessions is generally considered to be a "difficult" composer, these insights into his creative processes are valuable in helping us understand the basis of his musical thought.

Sessions' first important work was the orchestral score he composed for a performance of Andreyev's play *The Black Maskers* given at Smith College, Northampton, Massachusetts, in June, 1923 (he taught there from 1917 to 1921). From this music he made in 1928 a symphonic suite in four movements, which remains his best-known and most frequently performed composition. The four movements are: (1) "Dance": stridente, sarcastico, (2) "Scene": agitato molto, (3) "Dirge": larghissimo, (4) "Finale": andante moderato un poco agitato. Sessions points out that Andreyev's play, written in 1908, deals symbolically with the theme of tragic conflict within the human soul.

[3] Quoted by permission of the publisher, Princeton University Press. Musical examples from the First Piano Sonata, copyright 1931 by B. Schott's Söhne, Mainz, Germany; by permission of Associated Music Publishers, Inc.

He quotes a passage from Andreyev's diary: "The castle is the soul; the lord of the castle is man, the master of the soul; the strange black maskers are the powers whose field of action is the soul of man, and whose mysterious nature he can never fathom."

Concerning the score of *The Black Maskers*, the composer states: "The music was conceived throughout as an expression of certain moods felt behind the incidents of the play, rather than as their descriptive counterpart." There are, to be sure, definite evocations of moods and situations depicted in the play: the suggestion of malicious laughter, cries of agony and despair, the victorious trumpetings of the black maskers as they swarm over the castle, the trumpet calls that announce the death of Lorenzo (the master of the castle), and the conflagration of the final scene, when Lorenzo finds redemption in the symbolic purity of the flames. But the music stands on its own merits: it is extremely brilliant in orchestration, emotionally powerful in its dramatic expression, rich in texture. It is exciting and compelling music. Hearing it today, thirty years after it was written, one finds its impact undiminished; and one is, moreover, somewhat surprised to find that it does not sound in the least like most of the music that was being written during the 1920s—another proof of Sessions's independence and strength of character as a composer.

Among other works of Sessions are three Chorale Preludes for organ (1926), a Concerto for violin and orchestra (1932), three *Dirges* for orchestra (1938), two String Quartets, a second Piano Sonata, three symphonies, and a one-act opera, *The Trial of Lucullus*, based on a radio play by Bertolt Brecht and first performed at the University of California at Berkeley on April 18, 1947. This opera has a moral for our times, as it deals with the humiliation of a dictatorial aggressor.

The Symphony No. 2 of Sessions, composed from 1944 to 1946, is dedicated "To the Memory of Franklin Delano Roosevelt." It is in four movements: (1) Molto agitato, tranquillo e misterioso, (2) Allegretto capriccioso, (3) Adagio, tranquillo ed espressivo, (4) Allegramente. It has the dissonant contrapuntal texture, the harmonic complexity, and the rhythmic drive that are characteristic qualities of his music. Some hostile reaction was provoked by the first performance of the work at San Francisco in 1947. That is a healthy sign.

The pianist Andor Foldes, for whom the Second Piano Sonata was written, has made the following comments on this work: "The forbidding harmonies of the work and its uncompromising tonal structure will keep it from becoming very popular for the time being. . . . But regardless of its immediate acceptance, this is a work of grandeur, a composition of wide breadth and sincere, deep feeling."[4] Its three movements are Allegro con fuoco, Lento, Misurato a pesante.

In *The Black Maskers* Sessions demonstrated that he possessed all the requisites for writing overwhelmingly effective music of strong emotional and imaginative appeal. Had he turned out a series of symphonies in this vein, his popular success would have been assured. Instead, he chose to follow his true destiny as a composer, developing "the ability to conceive his musical ideas in almost abstract terms" and becoming "consciously aware of so much that previously remained below the surface." Paraphrasing what he wrote about the composer in general, we may say that Sessions, having reached the point of creative maturity, refused to lapse into self-imitation and chose rather "to strike out boldly into new territory." There the hardy listener may follow him or the timid turn away. Sessions would subscribe to the ancient Greek dictum: "The beautiful is difficult." In the music of Sessions, technique and integrity link arms, blocking the primrose path toward facile pleasures.

The unpredictable Mr. Thomson

It would be invidious to suggest that we may tread the primrose path as we approach the music of Virgil Thomson, because this might imply that he rules over a realm of facile pleasures. This would be unfair to Mr. Thomson, who really takes music seriously, however much he may try to conceal the fact. Perhaps it would be more exact to say that Mr. Thomson takes composition seriously as a métier, that he has a meticulous sense of craftsmanship and a fastidious feeling for the *mot juste* in his music as in his prose writing (he is a remarkably productive and adept writer on musical subjects), but that he refuses to write music that takes itself too seriously and that he absolutely balks at being solemn about anything whatsoever. It may seem either too obvious or too cryptic to call him the Erik Satie of American music, yet the title is helpful as an orientation. Thomson's special achievement, as Charles Seeger remarked, is the apotheosis of the commonplace, and that brings him rather close to Satie. Thomson, more-

[4] In *Notes* of the Music Library Association, March 1950, p. 313.

over, has been dubbed "our most musical Francophile," and he certainly imbibed through every pore the musical atmosphere of Paris in the 1920s, over which the spirit of Satie presided like an avuncular oracle.

Virgil Thomson was born in Kansas City, Missouri, on November 25, 1896. His musical training was orthodox. He matriculated at Harvard, where he studied music with a number of impeccable professors. He even played the organ in King's Chapel, Boston. He also displayed aptitude for winning academic awards, obtaining the Naumburg and Paine Fellowships, which permitted him to go to Paris, where he studied with Nadia Boulanger and acquired a permanent taste for French culture. After graduating from Harvard in 1922 he continued there for three years as an assistant instructor and then went to Paris again, where he remained most of the time until the outbreak of World War II. In Paris he formed a friendship with Gertrude Stein, whose *Capital, Capitals* and *Four Saints in Three Acts* he set to music (see the chapter "Toward an American Opera"). He inevitably gravitated toward the circle of Jean Cocteau and "Les Six," the group of young antibourgeois composers, followers of Satie, whose irreverent attitudes and unconventional creations embodied the spirit of '26. These young composers, among them Milhaud and Honnegger, were intrigued by jazz and the idioms of American popular music. For them, nothing was vulgar or commonplace. Or if it was, they transmuted everything they touched. Thomson found in them a stimulus for his own musical curiosity and eclecticism.

In February, 1926, at St. Cloud, Thomson completed his *Sonata da Chiesa* (literally, "church sonata," a term borrowed from seventeenth-century Italian instrumental music) for clarinet in E flat, trumpet in C, viola, horn in F, and trombone. Who but a disciple of Satie would have thought of inserting a tango as the second movement in this supposedly austere type of chamber music? That is the Thomson touch, and he carries it off most effectively, and discreetly, with just a suggestion of the tango rhythm in the clarinet and trumpet parts, played *con sordino*. The flanking movements are a Chorale and a Fugue, the former plentifully supplied with parallel fifths. This little work demonstrates Thomson's skillful and expressive use of dissonant counterpoint.

The lure of Paris did not cause Thomson to forget his American heritage. In his *Symphony on a Hymn Tune* (1928) he drew on the heritage of American hymnody, actually using two familiar hymn tunes: "How Firm a Foundation Ye Saints of the Lord" (main theme) and "Yes, Jesus Loves Me" (secondary theme). This symphony is nostalgic in its evocation of the well-worn hymns, but it is also extremely witty and subtle. The musical idiom itself is deliberately commonplace and transparent, but here and there an unexpected touch or an amusing vagary reveal the anticonventional aesthetic that prevails in most of Thomson's music. His adherence to traditional symphonic form also has in it a touch of satire and quiet maliciousness, like the subdued ridicule of someone who salutes another person too ceremoniously.

Thomson likewise drew on familiar hymn tunes in four sets of *Variations and Fugues* for organ, written at different times. In these he used the hymns "Come Ye Disconsolate," "There's Not a Friend Like the Lowly Jesus," "Will There Be Any Stars in My Crown?" and "Shall We Gather at the River?" With the exception of Charles Ives, Thomson is the only contemporary composer who has taken full advantage of the possibilities inherent in this type of musical Americana.

Hymn-tune reminiscences or resemblances run through much of Thomson's music. They can be noticed in his Second Symphony (1931; reorchestrated 1941), a beautifully integrated and balanced work, prevailingly diatonic.

In his ballet *Filling Station* (1938), Thomson turned out a period piece that captures the flavor of the popular tunes of the 1930s and that is still amusing and pungent.

Thomson is fond of composing musical portraits—he has written over a hundred of these for piano, and a set of five *Portraits* for a quartet of clarinets (1929). He has composed four Sonatas for piano, a quantity of songs, two String Quartets, a Violin Sonata, a Sonata for flute alone, a set of *Mayor La Guardia Waltzes* for orchestra, a *Stabat Mater* for soprano and string quartet, *Three Antiphonal Psalms* for women's voices *a cappella*, a *Missa Brevis* for men's voices *a cappella* and one for women's voices with percussion, and a Mass for mixed chorus *a cappella*. Scores written for the films *The River*, *The Plough That Broke the Plains*, and *Louisiana Story*, have been made into orchestral suites. His two operas are discussed in another chapter.

From 1940 to 1954 Thomson was music critic of the *New York Herald Tribune*, proving himself a lucid writer and a discerning, if often caustic, critic. He is the author of several books, including *The State of Music* (1939), *The Musical Scene* (1945), *The Art of Judging Music* (1948), and *Music Right and Left* (1951).

A dynamic New Yorker

We have now in the United States a generation of mature composers who were taught by other American composers rather than by European teachers. To this generation belongs William Schuman (born in New York City on August 4, 1910), who studied composition with Roy Harris and who at the outset of his career was definitely a disciple of that master. One also thinks of Schuman as being, in a way, spiritually akin to Sessions, whom he resembles as a composer in seriousness of purpose, intensity of expression, uncompromising utterance, dynamic energy, and rhythmic drive. He is somewhat more eclectic and flexible, for besides some of the grimmest music of our times he has also written a *Circus Overture* (for the show *Seven Lively Arts*) and the lighthearted baseball opera *The Mighty Casey*, which includes some songs in Broadway musical-comedy style.

Schuman graduated from Columbia University in 1935 and obtained his master's degree there in 1937. In 1935 he studied at the Mozarteum in Salzburg. From 1935 to 1945 he was on the faculty of Sarah Lawrence College in Bronxville, New York. Since 1945 he has been President of the Juilliard School of Music in New York City. He was twice awarded a Guggenheim Fellowship, and in 1943 he won the first Pulitzer Prize to be given for musical composition, with *A Free Song* (after Walt Whitman) for mixed chorus and orchestra. He has won many other awards and honors and is a member of the National Institute of Arts and Letters. He is the author of an essay, "On Freedom in Music," published in the volume *The Arts in Renewal* (Philadelphia, 1951).

Schuman has written some piano pieces and considerable choral music, including "*Pioneers!*" (Walt Whitman) for mixed chorus *a cappella; This is Our Time* (Genevieve Taggard) for mixed chorus and orchestra (1940); and *Te Deum* for mixed voices *a cappella* (1944). But his most important production is in the realm of symphonic and chamber music. His output in these fields comprises six symphonies, three overtures, a Piano Concerto, a Violin Concerto, four String Quartets, and the scores for several ballets: *Undertow*

(1945), *Night Journey* (1947), and *Judith* (1949)—the last two written for Martha Graham.

The Symphony No. 1 for 18 instruments (1935) and Symphony No. 2 (1937) have been withdrawn by the composer pending revision. The Symphony No. 3 (completed in January, 1941) is in neoclassical style and consists of four movements: Passacaglia, Fugue, Chorale, Toccata. In it Schuman's tendency toward the use of bitonality and polyharmony are affirmed. This tendency is further developed in the Symphony No. 4 (completed in August, 1941), which is in three movements and closely akin in style to the Third Symphony, complex in structure and markedly contrapuntal in texture. Robert Sabin aptly said of this symphony that it is "as functional, and as beautiful, in its way, as a skyscraper or an ocean liner. Yet it is neither inhuman nor unfeeling. On the contrary, it is a direct expression of the spirit of its time in art." [5] The same remarks apply to Schuman's work as a whole. One should mention a jazzy injection in the last movement of the Fourth Symphony that contributes to its vivid contemporaneity.

Schuman's Fifth Symphony, finished in July, 1943, is for strings. Its three movements are: Molto agitato ed energico, Larghissimo, and Presto leggiero. The jazzlike element, merely adumbrated in the Fourth Symphony, acquires full stylistic status in the last movement of the *Symphony for Strings*, which applies syncopation in the manner of ragtime music. The Symphony No. 6, completed on the last day of 1948, represents the peak of Schuman's achievements to date. The work is in one movement with six sections, all derived from thematic material stated at the beginning. The sections are marked Largo; Moderato con moto; Leggieramente; Adagio; Allegro risoluto, presto; Larghissimo. Though the structure of this work reveals the composer's customary formal logic and intellectual control, its emotional impact is almost terrifying in its depth and intensity. It has grandeur and passion.

William Schuman, like Virgil Thomson, merits a place among the Americanists as well as the eclectics, because of his continual preoccupation with the American scene. In his *American Festival Overture* (1939) he gave expression to a typically American mood. In his own words:

[5] In *Notes* of the Music Library Association, Dec. 1950.

> The first three notes of this piece will be recognized by some listeners as the "call to play" of boyhood days. In New York City it is yelled on the syllables "Wee-Awk-EE" to get the gang together for a game or a festive occasion of some sort. This call very naturally suggested itself for a piece of music being composed for a very festive occasion. . . . The development of this bit of "folk material" . . . is along purely musical lines.

In the *William Billings Overture* (1943), Schuman incorporates and develops themes from three choral works by the pioneer New England composer. The first is the stirring anthem "Be Glad, Then, America"; this leads to the middle section, based on "When Jesus Wept"; and the final section is on "Chester," the hymn that became the marching song of the Continental Army.

Other examples of musical Americana composed by Schuman are *Newsreel: In Five Shots* (1941) and *George Washington Bridge* (1950), both for band; music for the documentary film *Steeltown;* the ballet *Undertow* (also arranged as Choreographic Episodes for Orchestra); and the one-act opera *The Mighty Casey*.

The ballet *Judith* is presented also as a "choreographic poem for orchestra," and, together with the score for *Undertow*, stands among the most striking works of Schuman, particularly with respect to orchestration. *Judith* is like a richly colored biblical painting, and *Undertow* is exciting in its realism and satire.

Self-taught composer

Standing chronologically between Sessions and Schuman—he was born in 1906—Paul Creston has something in common with both of these composers: the importance that he assigns to rhythm, and his stress on musical content rather than programmatic intent. "I regard music as a language that begins where vocal language ends," he has stated. Even when he gives descriptive titles to his works, he is concerned with the projection of mood and emotion rather than with narration or description.

Paul Creston (*recte* Joseph Guttoveggio) was born in New York City and studied music with Randegger, Déthier, and Pietro Yon. In composition he is self-taught. He first attracted attention with his *Seven Theses* for piano (1933), which demonstrated the absolute or constructivist style that he was to pursue in *Five Two-part Inven-*

tions (1937) and *Six Preludes* (1945) for piano, the Suite for violin and piano (1939), the *Partita* for flute, violin, and strings (1937), and the orchestral *Pastorale and Tarantella* (1941) and *Prelude and Dance* (1941).

In his orchestral tone poem *Threnody*, composed in 1938, Creston combines a subjective approach (personal emotion) with the abstract development of musical ideas. This work is marked by the free use of modal materials derived from Gregorian chant, a tendency that reached its culmination in Creston's Third Symphony (1951), subtitled *Three Mysteries* (the Nativity, the Crucifixion, and the Resurrection). According to the composer's statement:

> Although the work derives its inspiration from these events, historic and mystic, it is a musical parallel of the inherent emotional reactions rather than a narrative or painting. The programmatic content, such as there may be, is for the justification of drawing from the immense wealth in Gregorian chant.

Of Creston's two earlier symphonies, the First (Opus 20) was completed in 1940, the Second (Opus 35) in 1944. Both reveal his facility in handling traditional materials and forms. The First Symphony is in the usual four movements, with a vigorous opening Sonata-allegro, a strongly rhythmic Scherzo, a lyrical Andante, and a four-alarm Finale. The Second Symphony breaks with convention by having only two movements, each of which is in two sections: (1) "Introduction and Song," (2) "Interlude and Dance." The whole is conceived as an "apotheosis" of song and dance, the foundations of music. A further tribute to the dance as abstract form is contained in *Two Choric Dances* (1938), which exist in two versions, one for chamber orchestra and one for full orchestra.

Creston has written three works for E flat alto saxophone: a Suite, a Sonata, and a Concerto (with orchestra). He has also composed a Concertino for marimba and orchestra, a *Fantasy* for piano and orchestra, *Three Chorales from Tagore* for chorus, and much chamber music. His idiom is conservative, with moderate use of dissonance.

Neoclassical eclecticism

Norman Dello Joio, born in New York City in 1913, resembles Creston in his penchant for Gregorian themes and Schuman in his use of dissonant harmony and neoclassical tendencies. An interesting contrast in the use of Gregorian material from the same source (*Mass of the Angels*) is presented in two works by Dello Joio: the Piano Sonata No. 3, and the Variations, Chaconne, and Finale for orchestra, the former composed in 1947, the latter in 1948. The treatment of the themes in the orchestral work is brilliant and colorful; in the piano sonata it is more introspective but equally imaginative. The *Fantasia on a Gregorian Theme* for violin and piano is another work in similar vein.

Dello Joio studied composition with Bernard Wagenaar and Paul Hindemith. Following in the footsteps of his father, he has been organist and choirmaster in several New York churches. For a time he taught composition at Sarah Lawrence College.

Dello Joio's neoclassical tendencies are fully manifested in his *Ricercari* for piano and orchestra (1946), which purports to be a kind of Scarlatti *redivivus*. Its three movements develop a single germinal idea harmonically, melodically, and rhythmically. Likewise in the neoclassical tradition are the *Sinfonietta* for piano and orchestra (1941) and the *Serenade for Orchestra* (1948). Following a similar tendency, but in a lighter vein, is the *Variations and Capriccio* for violin and piano, written to be, as the composer says, "earfully charming." More serious in mood are the orchestral *Magnificat* (1942) and *Epigraph* (1951), the latter described as "a piece written in memory of a man"—in other words, an elegy.

One of his most important works is *The Mystic Trumpeter*, with a text adapted from Walt Whitman, for full chorus of mixed voices, soprano, tenor, and baritone solos, and French horn or piano—a thoroughly American composition that owes much to Harris and Schuman. Dello Joio has made particularly impressive contributions to American choral music. In addition to the work just mentioned, his choral compositions include *A Jubilant Song*, *Madrigals*, and *A Psalm of David* for mixed chorus and piano (or brass, strings, and percussion). This is a setting of Penitential Psalm 51 (50 in the Vulgate), in three sections with introduction and coda, in prevailingly homophonic style.

Impressive among Dello Joio's orchestral works is the symphony entitled *The Triumph of St. Joan*, first performed by the Louisville Orchestra in December, 1951. It is in three movements: I, *The Maid;* II, *The Warrior;* III, *The Saint*. When performed in Louisville the work was mimed by Martha Graham.

In 1953 Dello Joio was commissioned to compose a large choral work for the centennial celebration of Cornell College, in Mount Vernon, Iowa. The result was a symphonic cantata called *Song of Affirmation,* with a text adapted from Stephen Vincent Benét's narrative-historical poem, *Western Star.* The cantata consists of three sections: "Virginia," "New England," and "The Star in the West." The score calls for a narrator, soprano solo, mixed chorus, and full orchestra.

An academic eclectic

Randall Thompson, born in New York City on April 21, 1899, is a composer who has assimilated various styles of the past and has combined them in a personal speech that shows a remarkable feeling for the idioms of American folk and popular music within the framework of academic traditionalism. He might have been placed with the traditionalists or the Americanists, but his output is perhaps most fully contained in the concept of eclecticism. He studied at Harvard with Hill and Spalding, and privately with Ernest Bloch. He was a Fellow of the American Academy in Rome from 1922 to 1925, and received Guggenheim Fellowships in 1929 and 1930. He has held various teaching posts, at Harvard, at the University of Virginia, at Princeton, and elsewhere. His most significant work has been done in the choral and symphonic fields, though he has also written some admirable chamber music and an attractive one-act opera, *Solomon and Balkis,* based on Rudyard Kipling's tale "The Butterfly that Stamped" (it was composed for radio production in 1942).

Two works stand out conspicuously in the production of Randall Thompson: the Second Symphony (1931) and *The Peaceable Kingdom* (1936) for mixed voices *a cappella.* The Second Symphony, in E minor, consists of four movements: 1, Allegro (in sonata form); 2, Largo; 3, Vivace (scherzo-trio); 4, Andante moderato–Allegro con spirito–Largamente (E major). The Allegro in the last movement is a modified rondo, having as its theme a diminution of the theme of the first and last sections. The composer has been sparing in his instrumentation, limiting the percussion to cymbals and kettledrums, and the brass in the scherzo to horns and one trumpet. Not until the Largamente at the end are the full sonorities of the orchestra employed. This restraint is characteristic of Thompson. He has wished to entice and delight his hearers rather than to overwhelm them. The composer insists that his symphony is simply music, with no literary or spiritual "program." One would like to say that it is delightfully civilized music, if one were certain that this would not belittle it in the eyes (or ears) of any reader (or listener). The suggestions of American popular idioms in the Vivace are as clever and engaging as they are discreet and skillful.

The Peaceable Kingdom consists of eight choruses from Isaiah for mixed voices *a cappella,* suggested by the painting of that title by the early nineteenth-century American artist Edward Hicks, who was also a Quaker preacher. Thompson selected the texts from Isaiah with a view to illustrating the spirit of the painting. The first chorus contrasts the reward of the righteous, who "shall sing for joy of heart," and the fate of the wicked, who "shall howl for vexation of spirit." The second chorus, "Woe Unto Them," is a dramatic admonition to those who "regard not the Lord." The third chorus continues to foretell the doom of the wicked: "Their children also shall be dashed to pieces before their eyes." The dramatic tension reaches its culmination in the next number, "Howl Ye," for double chorus with antiphony. The final section is also antiphonal, men's voices being opposed to women's voices in proclaiming the words of the prophet:

> Say ye to the righteous, it shall be well with him:
> for they shall eat the fruit of their doings.

Thompson's choral music includes further *Five Odes of Horace* (1924), *Americana* (1932) for mixed voices and piano or orchestra, *Alleluia* for mixed voices *a cappella* (1940), and *The Testament of Freedom* (1943) for men's voices with piano or orchestra. Each of these compositions is completely different from any of the others. The *Odes* show his mastery of part writing and his skill in the solution of the rhythmic problems presented by the text. *Americana* is a set of five choruses with texts from the *American Mercury*, dealing with five aspects of American life—fundamentalism, spiritualism, temperance, capital punishment, optimism. The satiric humor of these pieces reaches its climax in the final chorus, which proclaims the virtues of a book by Miss Edna Nethery, *Loveliness*, "all abrim with Joy, Love, Faith, Abundance, Victory, Beauty, and Mastery." Thompson's setting of *Alleluia,* written on that word alone, is a well-conceived and brilliantly executed *a cappella* choral number that has firmly established itself in the repertoire of American choirs. *The Testament of Freedom* is a setting of selected writings by Thomas Jefferson: *A Summary View of the Rights of British America* (1774); *A Declaration of the Causes and Necessity of Taking up Arms* (July 6, 1775); Letter to John Adams, Monticello, dated September 12, 1821. In this work the composer deliberately set himself to write a type of "public music" that would be as impersonal as possible and that would possess a dignified grandeur arising from simplicity of means. Hence the writing is predominantly in unison, stressing directness of expression and clarity in projection of the text.

Among Thompson's instrumental works should be mentioned his two String Quartets, the Suite for oboe, clarinet, and viola (1940), the *Jazz Poem* for piano and orchestra (1928), *The Piper at the Gates of Dawn* (1924), symphonic prelude for orchestra, and the Third Symphony (1949), which incorporates folklike material. These compositions reveal his eclectic tendencies, ranging from French impressionism to the stylization of jazz. Finally, no account of Randall Thompson would be complete that failed to mention his incidental music for the *Grand Street Follies* (1926), one of the many musical chores that he did to make a living during the two years that he was a struggling young artist in Greenwich Village.

Two composers from Cleveland

Herbert Elwell, music critic of the *Cleveland Plain Dealer* since 1932, is a Clevelander by adoption. He was born in Minneapolis, Minnesota, in 1898, and after attending the University of Minnesota he studied composition with Ernest Bloch in New York and with Nadia Boulanger in Paris. He was the recipient of a fellowship from the American Academy in Rome in 1926, and thereafter spent several years in Europe. He has taught at the Cleveland Institute of Music and at the Oberlin Conservatory of Music.

Elwell's best-known work is the orchestral suite from a ballet titled *The Happy Hypocrite* (1925), which has been frequently performed in the United States and in Europe. He has also written *Introduction and Allegro* for orchestra (1941); the cantata *Lincoln* for baritone solo, mixed chorus, and orchestra (1945); a quantity of chamber music, including *Blue Symphony* for medium voice and string quartet; and many songs and piano pieces.

Among Elwell's students in composition at the Cleveland Institute of Music was a young Negro employee of the post office in that city. His name was Howard Swanson. He was born in Atlanta, Georgia, but his parents, who were poor, moved to Cleveland when he was eight years old. After graduating from high school he got a job as greaser in a locomotive roundhouse, then as a letter carrier, and afterward as a postal clerk. After completing his studies at the Cleveland Institute of Music, he received a Rosenwald Fellowship that enabled him to study composition with Nadia Boulanger in Paris for two years. Thus, like Kerr, Elwell, and so many other American composers of our time, he became a member of what one pun-happy critic has dubbed "the Boulangerie." Abandoning Paris in the face of the German occupation, Swanson returned to the United States, where, to make his living, he worked for a time in the Internal Revenue Service of the Treasury Department. Finally, resolved to devote himself entirely to music, he resigned and began to compose intensively.

The next episode of Swanson's career reads like a classical American "success story." His dramatically expressive songs, in which the text, the melody, and the accompaniment are so skillfully interwoven, were introduced at a recital in New York in October, 1946, and immediately won critical acclaim. The songs were taken up by Marian Anderson and other celebrated singers, so that the composer's international reputation was quickly established. His Short Symphony, composed in 1948, was given its first performance by Dimitri Mitropoulos with the New York Philharmonic-Symphony Orchestra in November, 1950, and was later included in the repertoire of that orchestra when it played at the Edinburgh Festival in Scotland in the summer of 1951. Then the influential Music Critics' Circle of New York chose Swanson's Short Symphony as the best new orchestral work performed in that metropolis during the 1950–1951 season. Today the name of Howard Swanson is widely known both at home and abroad.

Swanson's Short Symphony is in three movements: Allegro moderato; Andante; Allegro giocoso—Andante con moto. It is predominantly neoclassical in texture, and one critic has described it as an attempt "to apply fugue principle to the sonata-allegro scheme." It is markedly eclectic in its alternating use of freely chromatic, diatonic, neoclassical, and slightly jazzlike elements (in the last movement). These disparate elements do not always coalesce, but the Short Symphony, in spite of its shortcomings, is a sincere and attractive work.

Another work by Swanson that has been well received is *Night Music* for woodwinds, horn, and strings. Other instrumental works are a Piano Sonata, *Nocturne* for violin and piano, Suite for cello and piano, *Soundpiece* for brass quintet, and *Music for Strings*. His songs include "The Valley" (Edwin Markham), "The Junk Man" (Carl Sandburg), "Ghosts in Love" (Vachel Lindsay), and "The Negro Speaks of Rivers" (Langston Hughes).

Some younger eclectics

Ray Green is a composer from the Middle West who gravitated toward the "New Music" group in New York and eventually became executive secretary of the American Music Center in that city. Born in Cavendish, Missouri, in 1909, he studied composition with Bloch, Elkus, and Milhaud. His early works, published by New Music Editions in the 1930s, reveal an innovating spirit impatient of conventional restrictions. To this period belong the Sonatina for Piano, Two Madrigals (one for mixed voices, the other for men's voices), and *Three Inventories of Casey Jones*, for percussion. The Madrigal for men's voices (*Sea Calm*) experiments with the use of quarter tones. In later works Green has combined his distinctly modern idioms with baroque formal structures, achieving a vigorous contemporary expression in such works as the Short Sonata for Piano, *Holiday for Four* (for viola, clarinet, bassoon, and piano; in three movements: "Fugal Introduction," "Prairie Blues," "Festival Finale"); and *Festival Fugues*, (subtitled *American Toccata for Piano*), consisting of "Prelude Promenade," "Holiday Fugue," "Fugal Song," "Prelude-Pastorale," "Jubilant Fugue."

Green is one of the composers who have effectively utilized the American heritage of folk hymnody stemming from the shape-note "fasola" tradition, as well as the background of the early American fuguing tune. He has done this notably in his *Sunday Sing Symphony*, in five movements, which evokes the whole range of communal religious feeling as manifested in rural traditions.

Leon Kirchner might be described as a Californian from Brooklyn. He was born in Brooklyn in 1919 but went West early in life. His teachers in composition were Bloch, Schoenberg, and Sessions. During his younger years he wrote a quantity of music that he afterward, with admirable self-discipline, repudiated. His list of acknowledged compositions begins with a Duo for Violin and Piano dating from 1947, and continues with a Piano Sonata (1948), a String Quartet (1949), and several pieces for piano. Aaron Copland, reviewing the Duo, characterized it as belonging "to the Bartók-Berg axis of contemporary music," and declared that Kirchner's principal claim to originality lay in "the daringly free structural organization of his compositions." [6] His music is highly dissonant in texture and rhapsodically emotional in expression, influenced by Central European folk music (probably via Bartók).

Paul Bowles, pupil and disciple of Virgil Thomson, is a composer who has made eclecticism the very essence of his music. Born in New York City in 1911, and no stranger, musically, to the commercial Broadway circuit, he is an inveterate traveler, with a preference for Africa and Latin America, and an indefatigable collector of exotic musical materials. His list of compositions is impressively long and reflects virtually every trend of contemporary music, from Futurism and Dada to jazz and folklorism, not omitting a neoclassicism stemming from Satie. Among his works are *Scènes d'Anabase* (1932) for tenor, oboe, and piano (text by St.-John Perse); *Par le Detroit* (1933), cantata for soprano, male quartet, harmonium, and percussion; *Music for a Farce* (1938); Sonata for Two Pianos (1946); *Yankee Clipper*, ballet (1946); and an opera, *The Wind Remains* (1943); after García Lorca). Typical of his neo-primitive writing is the concluding Allegro of the two-piano Sonata, based on a West African dance and employing tone clusters to evoke the percussive quality of native tribal drums. For several years Bowles has been living in North Africa, composing little but writing fiction (*The Sheltering Sky* and numerous short stories) that has won him a considerable literary reputation. His future as a composer is an interesting question of the moment in American music. He is extremely talented and his music has a powerfully evocative quality.

Roger Goeb, as one critic expressed it, "is a craftsman who can write in many styles." This may provoke the query "Why should a composer wish to write in many styles?" In the case of Goeb, Otto Luening provides what appears to be a plausible answer:

> Goeb seems to believe that in music as in other things, circumstances alter cases and that it is not only necessary but desirable to

[6] *Notes* of the Music Library Association, June 1950, p. 434.

> compose music for particular performances and particular occasions. He believes that audiences vary in their willingness to concentrate on music and that they listen to music for different reasons at different times.[7]

It follows, therefore, that the composer should adopt different styles according to the occasion.

Goeb, born in Cherokee, Iowa, in 1914, studied chemistry at the University of Wisconsin (he also learned to play most of the instruments of an orchestra), and composition with Nadia Boulanger in Paris and Otto Luening in New York. He continued with his academic musical studies, winding up with a Ph.D. from the University of Iowa in 1946. He has composed over fifty works, including *Prairie Songs* for woodwind quintet (1947), Fantasy for oboe and string orchestra (1947), Quintet for trombone and strings (1950), *Suite in Folk Style* for four clarinets (1946), *Lyric Piece* for trumpet and orchestra (1947), Symphony No. 3 (1951), *Three American Dances* for string orchestra (1952), and *Two American Dances* for orchestra (1952). His strong point is instrumentation, and his style follows the more sophisticated academic norms of today.

Ellis Kohs (born in Chicago, 1916) belongs to the growing ranks of Middle Western composers who have achieved prominence in recent years. But he became a Californian by adoption when he joined the music faculty of the University of Southern California in Los Angeles. Recognition came to Kohs when his one-movement Concerto for Orchestra was performed at the 1942 Festival of the International Society for Contemporary Music in San Francisco. His reputation was subsequently confirmed by such works as the Piano Variations (1946; based on a twelve-tone row), the Chamber Concerto for solo viola and string nonet (1949), the Capriccio for organ, and the Toccata for harpsichord or piano solo (also using the twelve-tone technique). There is also an early String Quartet (1940), structurally less convincing than the later works but still interesting for its rhythmic vitality and for the "exuberant musicalness" that Kohs brings to all his compositions.

Leonard Bernstein sprang into sudden fame as a conductor at the age of twenty-five, when he substituted for Bruno Walter at a concert of the New York Philharmonic-Symphony in 1943. As a com-

[7] In *Bulletin of the American Composers Alliance*, June 1952, p. 2.

poser he is significant above all for his dual role as a writer of both "serious" and "popular" music. Not since Gershwin has there been a composer so firmly entrenched in both fields. But Bernstein achieved his dual status by traveling in the opposite direction from Gershwin: from the serious to the popular. His whole background was academic. Born in Lawrence, Massachusetts, in 1918, he attended the Boston Latin School and Harvard University, where he studied composition with Piston and E. B. Hill. After graduating from Harvard, he spent two years at the Curtis Institute of Music in Philadelphia, where his teacher in orchestration was Randall Thompson.

Among the "serious" compositions of Bernstein are the *Jeremiah Symphony* (1944) for mezzo-soprano and orchestra; *The Age of Anxiety* (Symphony No. 2) for piano and orchestra (1949); *Hashkivenu* (1945) for tenor solo, mixed chorus, and organ; Sonata for clarinet and piano (1942), *Seven Anniversaries* for piano (1943); and the ballets *Fancy Free* (1944) and *Facsimile* (1946). These ballets are "serious" only in the loose and unsatisfactory sense in which that term is generally applied to "art music" (as distinct from folk and popular music). *Fancy Free*, produced by the Ballet Theatre in New York in 1944, proved to be enormously entertaining and drew large crowds to the Metropolitan Opera House, where it was performed. From this it was an easy transition to the Broadway popular theater, and Bernstein made it with the musical comedy *On the Town*, incorporating material from the score of *Fancy Free*.

It would be a grave mistake to regard Bernstein simply as a talented composer cultivating two disparate fields of music. Such a dichotomy would completely miss the real significance of his contribution to America's music, which lies precisely in his fusion of serious and popular elements. His symphonies undoubtedly display his innate talent but are unconvincing as major works of musical art. On the other hand, his short opera in seven scenes, *Trouble in Tahiti*, produced as a television show in 1952, is an original and truly contemporary work that could have been written only by a composer of today who has thoroughly absorbed both the academic and the popular traditions (see Chapter 30 for an account of this opera).

One wonders whether Alan Hovhaness, an American-born composer of Armenian descent, should be included among the eclectics, because he has drawn so extensively upon a single tradition, namely that of Armenian modal music. However, even within the cultural area from which he draws most of his materials and techniques, there is room for considerable eclecticism, for, as Virgil Thomson observed, "He writes in the early Christian, the medieval, and the modern Armenian techniques, possibly even a little in the pre-Christian manner of that ancient and cultivated people."

Actually, Hovhaness's mother was of Scotch origin, and Leon Kochnitzky is of the opinion that "the composer's Scottish heredity played as important a part in his artistic formation as his Armenian background." [8] This opinion is based on an analogy between the composer's evocation of the myths and rituals of a "long forgotten primitive people," and the famous "Ossianic" poems of the Scotsman Macpherson, both being taken as evidence of a cult for archaism and "make-believe." It appears, in any case, that Hovhaness did not become "Armenian-conscious" until reaching the age of thirty. He was born in Arlington, Massachusetts, in 1911, and his father was a professor of chemistry at Tufts College in Boston. He studied at the New England Conservatory of Music, and it was only in imagination that he later turned for musical inspiration to the land of his paternal ancestors, which he himself never visited.

The compositions of Hovhaness include *Prayer of St. Gregory* for trumpet and string orchestra; *Tzaizerk* ("Evening Song") for violin, flute, drums, and strings; *Avak the Healer*, for soprano, trumpet, and strings; the symphony *Anahid* (named for an ancient Armenian goddess); *Pe-El-Amarna* ("City of the Sun") for orchestra; Suite for violin, piano, and percussion; *Achtamar*, for piano; *Arevakal* ("Coming of the Sun"), concerto for orchestra; *30th Ode of Solomon*, for baritone and orchestra; and Concerto No. 5 for piano and orchestra, first performed by the National Orchestral Association in New York on February 22, 1954. In an earlier piano concerto, titled *Lousadzak* ("The Coming of Light"), Hovhaness imitates the effects of such ancient Armenian instruments as the *tar*, *kanoon*, *oud*, and *saz*. Of these, the *kanoon* is a zitherlike instrument on which sustained tones are simulated by rapid repetition of single notes. In 1953 the composer completed a cantata, *Shepherd of Israel*, for cantor, recorder (or flute), string quartet (or string orchestra), and trumpet ad libitum, written after he learned that the young composers of Israeli were interested

[8] See the very interesting discussion of Hovhaness's "Armenianism" in *The Tiger's Eye* (Westport, Conn.), No. 3 (March 1948), pp. 59–65

in musical materials and modes of expression akin to those that attracted him.

Lukas Foss, born in Berlin, Germany, in 1922, came to the United States at the age of fifteen and rapidly made a name for himself as a remarkably gifted composer of eclectic tendencies derived partly from his teacher Hindemith and partly from French neoclassical influences. He first came into prominence with a cantata, *The Prairie* (on a poem by Carl Sandburg), composed when he was nineteen. His most impressive work to date is *A Parable of Death* (1952) for tenor solo, narrator, mixed chorus, and orchestra, with texts by Rainer Maria Rilke, modeled upon the cantatas of J. S. Bach but utilizing a thoroughly modern musical idiom. Among his numerous other works are *The Song of Songs,* four settings for voice and orchestra (or piano); Symphony in G; *Song of Anguish* and *Ode to Those Who Will Not Return,* both for orchestra; Concerto No. 2 for piano and orchestra; Concerto for oboe and orchestra; String Quartet in G (1947); and *Suite for The Tempest* (Shakespeare), for chamber orchestra.

Robert Starer, born in Vienna in 1924, was taken at an early age to Israel, received his basic education there, and in 1947 came to the United States, where he studied composition with the late Frederick Jacobi and with Aaron Copland. Later he joined the faculty of the Juilliard School of Music. Hailed as "a new talent of great promise," he has been steadily producing works that have translated the promise into achievement. Among his more important compositions are a String Quartet (1947), *Five Miniatures* for brass quintet; Concertino for two voices or instruments, violin, and piano; *Kohelet* ("Ecclesiastes") for baritone, soprano, mixed chorus, and orchestra; a Sonata for piano; and the Symphony No. 2, first performed by the Israeli Philharmonic Orchestra on April 27, 1953. Like Kirchner, he moves somewhat within the orbit of Bartók, utilizing folk elements in a chromatic texture.

chapter twenty-six

The traditionalists

Will you seek afar off? You surely will come back at last,
In things best known to you finding the best, or as good as the best.
WALT WHITMAN, A SONG OF OCCUPATIONS.

Tradition is a body of usage transmitted from one generation to another. In learning, scholarship, and the fine arts, the academy or university is the recognized upholder of tradition. That is why most of the composers whom we classify as traditionalists might also be described by the term "academic." Not all traditionalists are academic, but the majority are by background, by association, or by temperament—sometimes by all three together. The academic traditionalist is usually a professor or teacher; that is to say, he has a direct professional concern with the transmitting of tradition. It has, indeed, been observed that in the United States we now have a large body of composition that might be called "professors' music." To it are generally applied such descriptive terms as "conservative," "conventional," "traditional," or "classical." All of these terms are indicative, none is definitive. "Professors' music," or, if you will, academic composition, follows many tendencies, and is often characterized by a pronounced eclecticism. To be qualified for academic sanction, an aesthetic trend or artistic style needs only the consecration of usage. This usage may pertain to the remote past, the near past, the immediate past, or even the present. If it pertains to the present, it is never the *dernier cri*, but must have gained fairly wide acceptance in order to qualify academically. Examples of academic sanction in each of these chronological categories in the realm of music, are:

1. From the remote past—the cult of medieval music
2. From the near past—the post-romantic movement
3. From the immediate past—the neoclassical revival
4. From the present—twelve-tone music

As thirty years have passed since Schoenberg developed his method of composing with twelve tones, and since the method, in one form or another, has found fairly wide acceptance, we find twelve-tone music rather well entrenched in academic circles in the second half of the twentieth century. Post-romanticism and neoclassicism, however, are the predominant academic trends. Among contemporary American composers, Howard Hanson and Samuel Barber may be taken as representing the former; Walter Piston and David Diamond the latter. It is no mere accident that both Hanson and Piston have been long and prominently identified with two important institutions of higher learning. Piston has taught music at Harvard since 1925, and Hanson has been, since 1924, director of the Eastman School of Music of the University of Rochester, founded in 1921.

The educators responsible for the policies of the Eastman School of Music were much concerned with the meaning of tradition. Charles Riker, in an official history of the school, drew a parallel between the aims of the institution and the ideas set forth by T. S. Eliot in his famous and influential essay, "Tradition and the Individual Talent." Paraphrasing a celebrated passage in Eliot's essay, Mr. Riker wrote:

> The musician and the school of music must be aware of the musical tradition, but not as something merely handed down or inherited. This tradition must be obtained by great labor, and once secured, includes a perception of the living presence of the past. In coming to grips with the old or, on the other hand, the really new work of art, one must be prepared to admit that both are measured by each other. Neither exists alone. The Eastman School, with all its commitments to the new in American music, has also its commitments to the old. One of its larger aims has been to effect a rapprochement of the two.[1]

In accordance with these policies, the Eastman School inaugurated in 1925 an annual series of American Composers' Concerts, and in 1930 an annual Festival of American Music. In 1935 the former were replaced by two annual symposia, one for the performance of works by composers from all over the country, the other for the performing of works by students, graduates, and faculty members of the school. The "commitments to the old" have resulted chiefly in the performance of music by "The Boston Classicists"—Paine, Chadwick, Foote,

[1] Riker, *The Eastman School of Music: Its First Quarter Century*, p. 58.

Parker—as well as that of various American eclectics like Henry Gilbert, Charles Griffes, Charles M. Loeffler, and Henry Hadley. Students, composers, and others who have attended these festivals have therefore been provided with an opportunity to acquaint themselves with American symphonic productions of the immediate past. Eliot himself, incidentally, does not feel that the immediate past is particularly valuable to the artist in establishing a sense of tradition. He recommends skipping several generations and picking up a more remote tradition. But in the realm of American symphonic music, the immediate past is all that we have. That is one of the difficulties encountered by the American composer in his search for "a usable past." By and large, the academic composers have not found much of a usable past in America's music.

An avowed romanticist

Howard Hanson himself uses a musical idiom that stems directly from the tradition of nineteenth-century European romanticism. This is true even when he turns to American subjects, as in the opera *Merry Mount* or the Third Symphony (1938), written in commemoration of the 300th anniversary of the first Swedish settlement on the shores of the Delaware in 1638 and "conceived as a tribute to the epic qualities of the Swedish pioneers in America." Hanson himself is of Swedish descent and he is partial to the Nordic temperament. His First Symphony (1922), titled *Nordic,* reveals the influence of Sibelius, especially in its opening movement, which "sings of the solemnity, austerity, and grandeur of the North, of its restless surging and strife, of its somberness and melancholy." In the finale of this symphony, Hanson employs themes reminiscent of Swedish folk tunes.

With his Second Symphony (1930), Hanson proclaimed himself an unabashed romanticist—in the music, in the title (*Romantic*), and in a statement that he made at the time of its première:

> The symphony represents for me my escape from the rather bitter type of modern musical realism which occupies so large a place in contemporary thought. Much contemporary music seems to me to be showing a tendency to become entirely too cerebral. I do not believe that music is primarily a matter of intellect, but rather a manifestation of the emotions. I have, therefore, aimed in this symphony

to create a work that was young in spirit, lyrical and romantic in temperament, and simple and direct in expression.[2]

There are several controversial points that might be raised in connection with Hanson's statement. But this has been cited primarily as an expression of his views, and it unquestionably makes his position clear. As a result of his musical credo, Howard Hanson has found no difficulty in "communicating" with his audience. Composers whom he calls "cerebral" also communicate emotion, but theirs is *musical emotion,* something which few listeners comprehend or are receptive to. Hanson's emotion, on the other hand, is always associated with a subjective feeling: mother love, Nordic melancholy, epic heroism, mourning for personal bereavement. Hanson's Fourth Symphony (1943), for instance, is dedicated to the memory of his father, and each of its four movements bears the name of a section of the Requiem, or Mass for the dead: "Kyrie," "Requiescat," "Dies Irae," "Lux Aeterna." Since the impulse is noble and generous and full of piety, and since the musical expression draws on a deep traditional reservoir of emotionalized musical rhetoric, communication is readily established between composer and listener.

At the time when he issued his "Romantic Manifesto," Hanson evidently felt that he was reacting against the kind of music that predominated during the 1920s. In a later statement, he declared himself a partisan of "warm-blooded music," which he contrasted with "cold-blooded music." In writing about his Third Symphony, he again returned to the attack, affirming that it, too, "stands as an avowal against a certain coldly abstract, would-be sentimental music professed by certain composers of high gifts." As eighteenth-century France had its *Guerre des Buffons* between the partisans of French and Italian opera, we in our century have had our war between the hotbloods and the coldbloods. And on the side lines are those who declare that only jazz is really hot.

Hanson was born in Wahoo, Nebraska, on October 28, 1896. He studied at the Institute of Musical Art in New York, and in 1921 obtained the American Prix de Rome for musical composition. After his three years at the American Academy in Rome he was called to be director of the Eastman School of Music, which he made a leading center of American music through the concerts and festivals men-

[2] Quoted in Bagar and Biancolli, *The Concert Companion*, p. 319.

tioned above. Besides his four symphonies, he has composed five Symphonic Poems and other symphonic works (*Prelude*, *Rhapsody*, *Legend*), a Concerto for organ and orchestra (1926), a Concerto for organ, strings, and harp (1943), a Concerto for piano and orchestra (1948), some chamber music; *The Lament for Beowulf* for mixed chorus and orchestra (1925), and *Three Poems from Walt Whitman* (from "Drum Taps") for the same.

A painter with tones

Another composer long associated with the Eastman School of Music is Bernard Rogers, who has been teaching there since 1929. He was born in 1893 in New York City, where he attended school. He studied composition briefly with Arthur Farwell, but his principal teachers were Ernest Bloch and Nadia Boulanger (in Paris). He might be described as an academic eclectic with classical tendencies. He leans strongly on tradition and on classical techniques, but has undergone numerous influences, particularly those of his teacher Bloch, the French impressionists, the modern British school (he spent some time in England), and the music of the Orient. He is an amateur painter and has been markedly influenced by visual elements in his music. For example, his tone poem *Fuji in the Sunset Glow* and *Three Japanese Dances* (1925) were inspired by Japanese prints, and *The Supper at Emmaus* (for orchestra, 1937) was inspired by Rembrandt's painting and is itself a sort of tonal painting. The same may be said of *The Dance of Salome* (1938), *The Song of the Nightingale* (1939), and *Invasion* (1943). His orchestral suite, *Characters From Hans Christian Andersen* (1944), is subtitled "Four Drawings for small orchestra" and each piece or "drawing" utilizes a different artistic medium: (1) pen and ink, (2) soft charcoal, (3) *gouache* (impressionistic), (4) brush and ink. The composer calls these pieces "acoustical illustrations."

There is a pictorial-narrative element in Rogers's oratorio *The Passion* (1944)—probably his most important work—which in six scenes depicts the Passion of Our Lord from the entry into Jerusalem to the last prayer on the Cross. The declamation in this work is dramatically expressive, particularly the use of microtonally flatted notes in the final prayer. Other biblical subjects are treated by Rogers in his cantatas *The Raising of Lazarus* (1931) and *The Exodus* (1932).

Rogers has written four symphonies: I, *Adonais* (1925); II (1928); III, *On a Thanksgiving Song* (1936); IV (1945). The date of the Fourth Symphony is significant in relation to its content and intention. It purports "to trace a line leading from darkness and despair to eventual hope and affirmation." It consists of four movements: "Battle Fantasy" (using material from *Invasion*), "Eulogy," "Fugue," "Epilogue." Rogers is but one of the many American composers whose music reflects the conflicts, the anxieties, and the aspirations of the times in which we live. His *Elegy to the Memory of Franklin D. Roosevelt* for small orchestra is an impressively moving and sincere elegiac expression and formally an admirable example of a commemorative composition.

Rogers's most often heard work is the charming *Soliloquy* for flute and strings (1922). He has also written a second *Soliloquy*, for bassoon and strings (1938). Among his orchestral works are *Five Fairy Tales*, after Andrew Lang (1935); *Two American Frescoes* (1935); *The Silver World*, suite for woodwinds and strings (1950); and *Pinocchio*, suite for small orchestra (1950). He has composed three operas: *The Marriage of Aude* (1932), *The Warrior* (1946), and *The Veil* (1950). His *Hymn to Free France* (1942) is another occasional piece revealing his interest in the issues that move the world. Rogers is the author of a valuable treatise on orchestration in which special attention is given to the orchestral color of modern music.

An eclectic traditionalist

Among the pupils of Bernard Rogers none has achieved greater prominence than David Diamond, composer of four symphonies and numerous other instrumental and vocal works that show the development of a personal idiom resulting from the assimilation and adaptation of many contemporary influences—chiefly those of Bartók, Copland, Sessions, and Stravinsky—and characterized by a transition from incipient chromaticism in the early works to a consistently diatonic style in the later compositions, with marked modal tendencies.

Diamond was born in Rochester, New York, on July 9, 1915. At the age of ten his family moved to Cleveland, where he attended the Cleveland Institute of Music. Five years later the family returned to Rochester and he then obtained a scholarship to study at the Eastman

School of Music. He also studied composition with Roger Sessions in New York and with Nadia Boulanger in Paris. He has summed up his attitude toward musical composition in these words:

> My emotional life and reactions to certain events and situations have worked hand in hand with purely abstract musical conception and manipulation of material, and it was always the material that remained foremostly important to me in my working stages.

Diamond's first important work was the Symphony No. 2, composed in 1942–1943 and consisting of four movements cast in traditional forms. Regarding it, the composer wrote: "This work was composed during the days of tense world unrest, and I am quite sure that a certain amount of exterior emotional influence has affected the quality of the symphony. . . ." And he added: "It was in no way my intention to have the musical substance represent specific emotional reactions or to conjure up programmatic fantasies. I have a horror of anything as prosaic as that, and since I have never known that method of musical composition, I can only say that the opposite is true." [3] The composer, that is, wishes to have his symphony listened to as *music;* certainly not an unreasonable or exorbitant demand, and yet one that seems to arouse a certain degree of antagonism, as though objectified emotion were somehow inferior to subjective emotion.

Diamond's Third and Fourth Symphonies followed rapidly after the Second and confirmed his adherence to traditional forms, his tendency toward cyclic procedures, his reliance on diatonic melody, and his frequent use of modality. Economy of means and clarity of texture are other features of his mature style.

In July, 1944, Diamond completed what proved to be one of his most happily conceived and successful compositions, *Rounds for String Orchestra,* in three movements: Allegro molto vivace (with syncopations reminiscent of the popular-song idiom), Adagio, and Allegro vigoroso. A round is "A species of canon in the unison, so called because the performers begin the melody at regular rhythmical periods, and return from its conclusion to its beginning, so that it continually passes round and round from one to another of them"—"Three Blind Mice" and "Row, Row Your Boat," are familiar examples. Using rondo forms and canonic devices, with lively and ex-

[3] Quoted in Bagar and Biancolli, *op. cit.,* p. 225.

pressive thematic material, Diamond has written a work as ingratiating as it is formally coherent.

To approximately the same period belong the Overture to *The Tempest* (later revised for large orchestra), the incidental music for *Romeo and Juliet,* which was made into an orchestral suite; and the Sonata for violin and piano, all prevailingly diatonic. Diamond's vocal music includes *Chorale* for mixed voices *a cappella* (poem by James Agee); *The Martyr* for men's chorus *a cappella* (poem by Melville on the death of Lincoln); *Chatterton* (poem by Keats) for voice and piano; and several songs that are less diatonic than most of his recent compositions.

Among Diamond's earlier, more complex works (as regards harmonic texture), one of the best is the *Elegy in Memory of M. Ravel* (1938) for string orchestra and percussion. It is clear that his admiration for Ravel is tinged with affection; there is Ravelian influence in much of Diamond's early music, which includes a *Suite* for chamber orchestra, a *Divertimento* for piano and small orchestra, *Heroic Piece, Variations on an Original Theme,* and Concerto (all for chamber orchestra). There are indications that Diamond may be deviating from the severe diatonicism of his output in the 1940s and resuming some of the harmonic and contrapuntal complexity of his earlier production.

Other Rochester alumni

Hunter Johnson, born in Benson, North Carolina, in 1906, graduated from the Eastman School in 1929 and four years later was awarded the American Prix de Rome, which enabled him to spend two years in Europe. His compositions include Symphony No. 1 (1929), Concerto for piano and small orchestra (1935), *Elegy* for clarinet and strings (1936), *For an Unknown Soldier,* for flute and orchestra (1944); two frequently performed ballets, *Letter to the World* (1940) and *Deaths and Entrances* (1943), both written for Martha Graham; and an important Piano Sonata, first composed in 1933–1934, rewritten in 1936, and revised in 1947–1948. The Sonata emerged as an expression of the composer's thoughts and feelings about his homeland during his stay in Rome. He said of the work: "It is an intense expression of the South . . . the nostalgia, dark brooding, frenzied gaiety, high rhetoric and brutal realism are all intermingled." As Herbert Livingston observed, the harmonic writing of the Sonata is characterized by "the frequent use of 'blue' chords containing both the major and minor third above the bass." [4]

Burrill Phillips was born in Omaha, Nebraska, in 1907, and came to the Eastman School in 1931 after a period of study with Edwin Stringham in Denver. From 1933 to 1949 he taught theory and composition at Rochester. Among his best-known works are *Selections from McGuffey's Reader* for orchestra (1934), Concert Piece for bassoon and strings (1940), Trio for Trumpets (1937), Sonata for violin and piano (1942), Concerto for piano and orchestra (first performed in 1949); Partita for piano and strings; *Tom Paine Overture;* Dance Overture; Symphony No. 1; and an opera buffa, *Don't We All?* for four singers and small orchestra (1949). In 1949 Phillips joined the faculty of the University of Illinois as associate professor of composition. His style is technically deft and conservative in manner.

Gardner Read obtained his master's degree at the Eastman School in 1937 after previous study at Northwestern University in his home town of Evanston, Illinois, where he was born in 1913. He also studied with Copland in 1941. After teaching for several years at the Cleveland Institute of Music, he became head of the music department of Boston University. He is a prolific composer of academic-eclectic tendencies. He has written some Americana, as in the orchestral works *The Painted Desert* (1933), *Sketches of the City* (1933), and First Overture (1943), which utilizes a Stephen Foster tune, "De Glendy Burk," and a Negro spiritual, "Don't Be Weary, Traveler." He has also turned to contemporary realism (*Night Flight*, 1942), and to exotic evocations (in the cantata, *The Golden Journey to Samarkand*). One of his latest works is *The Temptation of St. Anthony*, a dance-symphony after Flaubert's novel (1952). His abstract compositions include Symphony No. 1 (1936), Passacaglia and Fugue for orchestra (1938), Symphony No. 2 (1942), Concerto for cello and orchestra (1945).

Robert Palmer, born in Syracuse, New York, in 1915, was a pupil of Hanson and Rogers at the Eastman School but also studied independently with Harris and Copland. Both of these composers have influenced his style more than his teachers at Rochester. After teaching at the University of Kansas he joined the music department of Cornell University. Among his more important works are a Concerto

[4] In *Notes* of the Music Library Association, June 1950, p. 433.

for orchestra (1943), Symphonic Variations for large orchestra (1946), *Abraham Lincoln Walks at Midnight* (after Vachel Lindsay) for mixed chorus and orchestra (1945), Concerto for five instruments (1943), two String Quartets, two String Trios, and a Quartet for piano and strings (1947). His piano music includes an extremely interesting *Toccata Ostinato* (1946), which makes use of a boogie-woogie bass. Vitality, rhythmic complexity, and contrapuntal texture, are the prevailing features of his music.

Robert E. Ward, born in Cleveland, Ohio, in 1917, received his bachelor's degree from the Eastman School in 1939, then continued his studies at the Juilliard School of Music, where he has been teaching since 1946. In 1941 he studied with Copland at the Berkshire Music Center. Among his compositions are two Symphonies (1942 and 1951), *Jubilation*, an overture (1950), *Night Music* for orchestra (1949), First Sonata for violin and piano (1951), *Hush'd Be the Camps Today* for mixed chorus and orchestra (1940), and *Lamentation* for piano (1949). In 1953 he was at work on a Third Symphony, Concert Music for orchestra, and two choral pieces commissioned by the Juilliard Music Foundation. His music is rhythmically vigorous and readily communicative.

Another Eastman alumnus who joined the faculty of the Juilliard School is William Bergsma, a native of California (*b.* 1921). After two years at Stanford University he enrolled in the Eastman School, where he studied from 1940 to 1944. Two years later he transferred his activities to New York. Like many of the Rochester group, Bergsma has made his contribution to musical Americana in the folk vein, with the orchestral suites *Paul Bunyan* and *Pioneer Saga.* His abstract works include a Chamber Symphony, a Symphony completed in 1950, two String Quartets, and *Music on a Quiet Theme* for orchestra. Following a year spent in the West Indies he wrote a work called *The Fortunate Islands* (1948).

To the roster of successful Eastman School alumni must be added the name of Ulysses Simpson Kay, who studied at Rochester with Hanson and Rogers, and later with Hindemith at Yale and at the Berkshire Music Center. Winner of numerous prizes and awards, including the Ditson Fellowship at Columbia University and two fellowships at the American Academy in Rome, Kay has cultivated a mildly dissonant contemporary idiom. During World War II he served in the United States Navy. In 1954 he was invited to conduct the symphony orchestra of his home town, Tucson, Arizona (where he was born in 1917), in a performance of his work titled *Of New Horizons.* Among his other orchestral compositions are a Sinfonietta, an Oboe Concerto, and *Five Mosaics* (for chamber orchestra). He has also written a Quintet for flute and strings, a Suite for oboe and piano, a Suite for brass choir, a Sonata for piano, and *Two Meditations* for organ.

Peter Mennin, born in Erie, Pennsylvania, on May 17, 1923, attended the Eastman School of Music from 1943 to 1947, studying composition with Hanson and Rogers. From 1949 he began to have works commissioned by various orchestras and foundations. The commissioning of works by American composers has taken great strides in recent years and is one of the major factors in the creative development of American music. Moreover, the demand for his music is a vital factor in the composer's own creative attitude and productivity. Mennin has written six symphonies, of which three were commissioned, and all have been performed by major American orchestras as soon as composed. They have also been published. These facts are mentioned to show the encouragement and acceptance that await a talented young American composer today. The battle for recognition of creative talent in American music has been won.

Besides his six symphonies, Mennin has written a *Folk Overture* for orchestra (1945), a *Fantasia* for strings (1947), a *Concertato* for orchestra (1952), two String Quartets; *The Christmas Story,* cantata for mixed chorus, soprano and tenor solos, brass quartet, timpani, and strings (1949); and *Five Piano Pieces* (published in 1951). His Symphony No. 4 is entitled *The Cycle* and is written for chorus of mixed voices and orchestra. Mennin wrote the text himself, which deals with the cosmic forces of the world and eternity. If he has not completely solved the problem of writing a satisfactory choral symphony, he has in any case produced an ambitious and impressive work in a typical twentieth-century American academic style.

Mennin, like Bergsma and Ward, joined the faculty of the Juilliard School of Music (in 1947). There he found himself associated with several other rising young composers, among them Richard Franko Goldman, Robert Starer, and Vincent Persichetti.

Vincent Persichetti was born in Philadelphia in 1915 and received his musical training there. His teachers in composition were Paul Nordoff and Roy Harris. He was appointed to the Juilliard faculty in 1947. His commissioned works include a Quintet for piano and strings (1953–1954), for the Koussevitzky Foundation; an orchestral Serenade (1953), for the Louisville Symphony; a Piano Concerto for four hands, for the Pittsburgh International Festival (1952); and a score for *King Lear* (1947), for Martha Graham. In addition he has published four Symphonies, a Piano Concertino, two String Quartets, Divertimento for band, *Fables* for narrator and orchestra, Eight Serenades for various combinations of instruments, a Sonata for two pianos, a Sonata for solo violin, a Sonata for solo cello, a Sonata for harpsichord, three Piano Sonatas; *Harmonium*, a song cycle for soprano and piano; and *The Hollow Men*, for trumpet and string orchestra.

Another Philadelphian, Paul Nordoff (*b.* 1909), may be mentioned here because of his connection with the Juilliard School, where he studied composition with Goldmark. From 1938 to 1943 he taught at the Philadelphia Conservatory of Music, and later joined the music department of Michigan State College. He has written two ballets for Martha Graham: *Every Soul is a Circus* (1938) and *Salem Shore* (1944). His orchestral compositions include Prelude and Three Fugues (1932), two Piano Concertos and a Violin Concerto, a Symphony, and a Suite for chamber orchestra. One of his most ambitious works is a Secular Mass for mixed chorus and orchestra (1934). For chamber combinations he has written two string quartets, *Poem* for violin and piano, and *Poem* for clarinet and piano.

Composer from the Middle West

During the years when Howard Hanson was a Fellow of the American Academy in Rome he was accompanied by another young American composer who had also received a similar fellowship in the same year. His name was Leo Sowerby, a native of Grand Rapids, Michigan, where he was born on May 1, 1895. His father was English and his mother Canadian. He studied at the American Conservatory in Chicago, graduating in 1918. From 1921 to 1924 he was in Rome, and in 1927 he became organist and choirmaster of St. James's Episcopal Church in Chicago.

If a case were to be made for Middle Western regionalism in American art music, Sowerby would certainly be a factor in the argument. His best-known composition is the tone poem *Prairie* (1929), based on Carl Sandburg's poem of the same title. The score bears the following quotation from the poem:

> Have you seen a red sunset over one of my cornfields, the shore of night stars, the wave lines of dawn up a wheat valley?
> Have you heard my threshing crews yelling in the chaff of a straw-pile and the running wheat of the wagon boards, my corn huskers, my harvest hands hauling crops, singing dreams of women, worlds, horizons?

The composer has stated that he did not wish to write "program music" in this work, that he sought only to interpret the moods of the poetry, and that the only imaginative effort he asks of the listener is to imagine himself alone in an Illinois cornfield. In spite of the geographical tag, the music is not regional in any sense that would appear to have aesthetic relevance or stylistic cogency (as in the New England regionalism of Ives, for example).

The same observation may apply to another evocative work by Sowerby: it was composed in Italy but deals with impressions of the Canadian countryside near Lake Superior. This is the Suite in four movements, *From the Northland* (1922), consisting of "Forest Voices," "Cascades," "Burnt Rock Pool," and "The Shining Big-sea Water." The skillful impressionism of this suite, with its shimmering orchestral coloration, reminds one of an American Respighi. His Canadian forests and cascades are close to the pines and fountains of Rome.

Sowerby's overture *Comes Autumn Time* stays nearer home, but he is too eclectic, too deeply committed to the European tradition, to be an utterer of the Middle Western "barbaric yawp" in music, as Sandburg was in verse. He is more congenially employed in cultivating a conservative modernism in such works as the *Canticle of the Sun*, a cantata for mixed chorus with piano or orchestra; *The Vision of Sir Launfal*, another cantata; *Mediaeval Poem* for organ and orchestra; Concerto for violin and orchestra; and *Classic Concerto* for organ and orchestra (or piano). Sowerby has written some of the best contemporary organ music in America. Representative of his work in this field is the *Canon, Chaconne, and Fugue* for organ, dating from 1951. His chamber music comprises four String Quartets; a Trio for flute, viola, and piano; a Suite for violin and piano; and a Quintet for wind instruments. His setting of the fiddle tune "The Irish

Washerwoman," originally for piano, later orchestrated, has been frequently performed.

Another Middle Western composer, Ross Lee Finney, may be grouped with the traditionalists, though his tendencies are also markedly eclectic, and his early interest in American folk music would entitle him to a place among the "Americanists." Finney was born in Wells, Minnesota, in 1906. He studied with Roger Sessions and E. B. Hill, and in Europe (on a Pulitzer Traveling Fellowship) with Alban Berg, Nadia Boulanger, and Gian Francesco Malipiero. He became professor of music at Smith College, and after World War II (during which he served with the OSS in Europe from 1944 to 1945) he was appointed composer in residence at the University of Michigan.

Among Finney's most important contributions to musical Americana are *Pilgrim Psalms*, a cantata, and *Variations, Fugueing and Rondo* for orchestra. *Pilgrim Psalms* is for mixed chorus, soprano, alto and tenor solos, and organ or piano. Completed in 1945, this work stems from the composer's abiding admiration for the tunes of the *Ainsworth Psalter* that the Pilgrim Fathers brought with them to Plymouth. He uses fourteen tunes from the Psalter, adapting them in a style that, in his own words, "springs both from the old melodies and from my own emotional feelings." The final number calls for the participation of the audience.

The *Variations, Fugueing and Rondo*, completed in 1943, resulted from Finney's interest in the hymns and fuguing tunes of William Billings. The unifying theme is derived from Billings's hymn tune, "Berlin." As the composer writes:

> *Variations, Fugueing and Rondo* is a triptych held together by, and commenting on, this early style. The first panel is a set of variations on the hymn, developed in a free melodic manner rather than harmonically. These variations are balanced by the last panel, a Rondo which is vigorous and harmonic. Between these, and linked together by a reference to the hymn, are two contrasting panels in fugato style: the first–naively, perhaps–a picture of hell-fire and brimstone; the second, pastoral and elegiac. The whole work is framed by the Billings hymn.

In addition to various choral settings, Finney has used folk material in his Third String Quartet (1941), *Barber-shop Ballad* for radio orchestra (1937), Violin Concerto (1947), and Piano Concerto (1948).

Although still maintaining a lively personal interest in American folk songs (which he sings to his own guitar accompaniment), Finney has gradually turned away from the literal use of this material in his music. In recent years he has concentrated mainly on the writing of chamber music, and he has been increasingly concerned with the problem of chromatic integration. His Second Sonata for cello and piano, composed in 1950, was highly chromatic in texture, but free in its integration (that is to say, it did not employ strict tone-row techniques; see Chapter 28 for an explanation of these terms). In the Sixth String Quartet, completed in the same year, Finney definitely turned to strict twelve-tone writing. Since then he has continued to strive for chromatic integration on the basis of tone-rows, but remaining within the framework of tonality. A further note on his development in this direction will be found in the chapter on the twelve-tone composers.

Quincy Porter is an academic traditionalist with a marked predilection for writing string quartets: he has thus far composed eight works in this form. Born in New Haven in 1897, he graduated from Yale in 1919 and then studied composition with Horatio Parker and David Stanley Smith at the Yale School of Music. He also studied with Vincent d'Indy in Paris and with Ernest Bloch in the United States. After teaching at the Cleveland Institute of Music and at Vassar College, he joined the faculty of the New England Conservatory of Music in 1938, becoming director of that institution four years later.

In addition to his eight String Quartets, Porter has written a *Ukrainian Suite* for strings (1925), an orchestral Suite in C minor (1926), *Poem and Dance* for orchestra (1932), a Symphony (1934), *Dance in Three-Time* (1937), *Two Dances for Radio* (1938), and *Music for Strings* (1942).

A neo-romantic composer

In any writing about Samuel Barber one is likely to come across a sentence such as this: "He is one of the most frequently performed of all contemporary American composers." This has been true ever since Toscanini, in 1938, conducted the first performance of Barber's *Essay for Orchestra* (Opus 12), composed the previous year, and the *Adagio for Strings*, an arrangement of the slow movement of the String Quartet (Opus 11) composed in 1936. The *Adagio for Strings* was the only work by an American composer that Toscanini played when he toured in South America with the NBC Symphony Orchestra. The work is frankly lyrical, monothematic, with unobtrusive canonic treatment. It confirmed the composer's romantic allegiance, previously asserted in such works as *Dover Beach* for voice and string quartet (1931), Sonata for violoncello and piano (1932), Overture to *The School for Scandal* (1932), *Music for a Scene from Shelley* (1933), and the First Symphony (Opus 9), in one movement, completed in February, 1936.

Samuel Barber was born in West Chester, Pennsylvania, on March 9, 1910. He is said to have begun composing at the age of seven, and at thirteen he entered the Curtis Institute of Music in Philadelphia, where he studied composition with Rosario Scalero for six years, obtaining a thorough grounding in counterpoint. He won the Pulitzer Scholarship for music twice in succession (an unprecedented honor) and in 1935 was awarded the Prix de Rome for composition. His First Symphony received its première by the Augusteo Orchestra on December 13, 1936, while he was a Fellow of the American Academy in Rome. This symphony was also the only American work to be performed at the Salzburg Festival in 1937. After his return to the United States, Barber made his home in New York State, in a house that he called "Capricorn." This gave its name to the *Capricorn Concerto* for flute, oboe, trumpet, and strings, in the style of Bach's *Brandenburg Concertos*. Barber entered the Army in 1942. His Second Symphony is dedicated to the Army Air Forces. In 1945 he received a Guggenheim Fellowship for composition.

Barber describes his *Symphony in One Movement* as "a synthetic treatment of the four-movement classical symphony"; that is to say, the customary four movements are "telescoped" and follow one another without interruption. Barber revised this symphony in 1943. This is characteristic of his procedure, for he also revised the Second Symphony in 1947. An English critic, Arthur Jacobs, visiting the United States in 1951, had this to say about Barber's Second Symphony:

> The symphony is in that neo-Romantic style which makes Barber more readily comprehensible to conventionally-educated European musicians than are many other American composers. This is music that it seems appropriate to describe in terms of rhetoric—statement

and counterstatement, question and answer, repetition and summarization. . . . It harnesses modern discords to basically 19th-century modes of construction.[5]

Actually, the "modern discords" employed by Barber are extremely mild, especially in his compositions up to 1940. Since then he has been somewhat more venturesome in his use of dissonance and in his treatment of tonality. The *Second Essay for Orchestra* (Opus 17), composed in 1942, contains a polytonal fugue (*Molto Allegro ed energico*) that indicates a bolder concept of tonality and that points toward the tonal freedom achieved in the *Medea Suite*, which dates from 1947. His evolution has been in the opposite direction to that of such composers as Copland and Diamond, who have proceeded from complexity to simplicity. His feeling for traditional forms appears to be gradually uniting with a trend toward dissonant counterpoint and polyharmony. He is slowly catching up with the twentieth century.

Barber's trend toward a more complex texture can be observed in such works as *Knoxville: Summer of 1915*, for soprano and orchestra (Opus 24); the Piano Sonata (Opus 26), which employs twelve-tone writing; the String Quartet No. 2, and especially the cycle of five songs on poems of Rilke (in French), *Mélodies passagères*, completed in 1951.

A modern classicist

On the whole, the trend from complexity to simplicity has been more prevalent among contemporary American composers than the reverse trend. It characterizes, for example, the evolution of our leading academic traditionalist, Walter Piston. The transition becomes evident if one compares Piston's First Symphony, completed in 1937, with his Second Symphony, composed in 1943. The former employs a dissonant contrapuntal texture with twelve-tone elements and extensive use of canonic devices and fugal writing. In the Second Symphony the expression is more direct, the texture less complex, the themes boldly lyrical or dramatic, and the slow movement sings with the sustained emotional mood of a classical Adagio. Of course, with a composer as erudite and as skillful as Piston, the term "simplicity" is

[5] In *Musical America*, Apr. 15, 1951.

relative. There are details of workmanship, subtle felicities, and inner relationships in all his music that reveal themselves and attain their full effect only after repeated hearings. And the music of Piston is made for repeated hearings. That is an essential feature of its quality. It is, in a word, classical.

Walter Piston did not, at first, contemplate a musical career. His boyhood was spent in Rockland, Maine, where he was born, of Italian descent, on January 20, 1894. Wishing to become an artist, he attended the Massachusetts School of Art, from which he was graduated in 1914. After working as an artist for some time, and getting married, he decided that he wanted a college education. He then matriculated at Harvard University, where he became seriously interested in music. Although he rebelled, in the words of Elliott Carter, against "the standardized academic routine which taught harmony and counterpoint according to outmoded and unimaginative textbooks," he turned out to be a brilliant student. And when he himself became a professor of music at Harvard—where he has taught theory and composition for nearly three decades—he undertook to renovate the teaching of harmony and counterpoint in line with the evolution of modern music, summarizing his concepts in three influential textbooks: *Principles of Harmonic Analysis* (1933), *Harmony* (1941; revised edition, 1948), and *Counterpoint* (1947).

Meanwhile, after his graduation from Harvard in 1924, Piston went to Paris, where, like Copland and Thomson, he studied with Nadia Boulanger. The influence of this remarkable woman upon contemporary American music should not go unremarked. In addition to the three older men mentioned above, she has been the mentor of many of the younger composers. As far as direct teaching is concerned, the only influences that can be compared to hers, in recent years, are those of Bloch and Hindemith (the latter's courses in composition at Yale have attracted many of the younger generation). At all events, Piston found himself in Paris during that incomparably stimulating decade of the 1920s, when Satie and Stravinsky and Cocteau and the exuberant "Six" set the tone of musical derring-do. French influence on American music in the second quarter of the twentieth century is a historical fact that has to be taken into account; but it should be stressed that this was a liberalizing influence, strongly international in character. Moreover, the influence was reciprocal, for American music influenced French composers in that decade too, chiefly through ragtime, blues, and jazz. Piston, with a receptive ear for the neoclassical audacities of Stravinsky, heard nothing in Paris that would cause him to turn away from the novel and piquant idioms of American popular music.

In his Suite for orchestra (1929), his first fully characteristic work, he combined atonality with definite allusions to American popular idioms, the blues in particular. The score calls for "snare drum with wire brush" in the manner of the dance band of the 1920s. In this type of composition he was following a trend that was fairly common in that decade. But it should be observed that Piston's allusions to jazz and other popular idioms of American music became a fundamental feature of his style and were not merely the result of a passing fashion. The popular idioms have become more closely integrated into his musical texture and are used not decoratively but organically. This is splendidly illustrated in the first movement of the Second Symphony, where the syncopated rhythms actually impel one's feet to dance. The second theme of the slow movement in this symphony, played by the clarinet accompanied by muted strings, is also a striking example of the manner in which Piston has assimilated the traits of American popular song. He has never been a self-proclaimed Americanist or a cultivator of musical nationalism, but his compositions, perhaps more than those of any other composer, demonstrate the extent to which popular idioms can infuse and color even the most classical manifestations of contemporary art music in the United States.

Up to about 1939 Piston composed a number of works in neoclassical vein that gained for him an estimable reputation as a modernist but not a large following among the public. In addition to the first Suite, these works included *Three Pieces* for clarinet, flute, and bassoon (1926); *Symphonic Piece* for orchestra (1927); Sonata for flute and piano (1930); Suite for oboe and piano (1931); Concerto, and Prelude and Fugue, for orchestra (1934); Trio for violin, violoncello, and piano (1935); Concertino for piano and chamber orchestra (1937); and two String Quartets (1933 and 1935).

In 1938, Piston wrote the music for a ballet, *The Incredible Flutist*, performed at the Boston "Pops" Concerts in Symphony Hall in May of that year, and repeated with much success the following year. The scenario deals with the arrival of a circus in a village and of the strange effect that a member of the troupe, a flutist, has upon the inhabitants of the drowsy village. A Latin American locale is suggested by such musical episodes as "Siesta Hour in the Market Place," "Tango of the Four Daughters," and "Spanish Waltz." This colorful and amusing score, made into an orchestral suite in 1940, became immediately popular with audiences and has been frequently played. While this wide aceptance made Piston's name more generally familiar, it also resulted in his being best known for his least representative work. *The Incredible Flutist* is Piston's only incursion into the realm of descriptive music or music for the stage. For the rest, he has adhered strictly to absolute musical expression in the instrumental media, avoiding not only programmatic implications but also, with very few exceptions, the setting of literary texts. This consistency is rare in modern music.

During the 1940s, Piston produced the Second and Third Symphonies, the Concerto for violin and orchestra (1940), the *Sinfonietta* for orchestra (1941), the *Allegro* for organ and orchestra (1943), the *Passacaglia* for piano (1943), the *Divertimento* for nine solo instruments (1946), the Second Suite for orchestra (1948), the Third String Quartet (1947), and the Piano Quintet (1949). The Second Symphony may be regarded as the representative work of this richly productive period, not only because of its intrinsic merits—it ranks very high indeed among contemporary symphonies—but also because its immediate and far-reaching success, following its première in Washington, D.C., on March 5, 1944, immensely widened the circle of Piston's admirers and brought about his nationwide recognition (on more than a critically appreciative level) as a composer who speaks for the present as much as he relies on the past.

Piston's recent output includes a Fourth Symphony (1950), commissioned for the centennial celebration of the University of Minnesota; a Fourth String Quartet (1951); and a *Fantasy* for English horn, harp, and string orchestra.

Some Harvard alumni

Among the younger composers from Harvard, there are three who attained to considerable prominence during the last decade: Harold Shapero (*b.* 1920), Irving Fine (*b.* 1914), and Elliott Carter (*b.* 1908). Carter and Fine studied with Nadia Boulanger after graduating from Harvard. Fine first attracted attention with a set of choral settings of poems from *The New Yorker* magazine, *The Choral New Yorker.* Among his instrumental works are a Violin Sonata (1946), *Toccata Concertante* for orchestra (1947), *Music for Piano* (1947), and *Partita* for woodwind quintet (1948). Fine's idiom is dissonant but tonal. In his *Toccata Concertante* he asserts "a certain affinity with the energetic music of the Baroque concertos." This affinity with the Baroque is not uncommon among the younger American composers of today.

Harold Shapero, a native of Lynn, Massachusetts, obtained the Paine Fellowship as a pupil of Piston. He also received a Naumburg Fellowship, the American Prix de Rome, the award of the second annual Gershwin Contest, and a Guggenheim Fellowship. After graduating from Harvard he studied composition with Copland and Hindemith. He has written chiefly instrumental music, including a Symphony, a *Nine-minute Overture,* a String Quartet, a Trumpet Sonata, a Violin Sonata, a Sonatina, and Three Sonatas for piano.

Elliott Carter's principal compositions are the First Symphony (1942), *A Holiday Overture* (1944), Woodwind Quintet (1948), Sonata for cello and piano (1948), Piano Sonata (1946); Eight Etudes and a Fantasy (1950) for flute, oboe, clarinet, and bassoon; String Quartet (1951); Sonata for flute, oboe, cello and harpsichord (1952); two ballets, *Pocahontas* (1939) and *The Minotaur* (1947); and several vocal works, including *Heart Not So Heavy As Mine* (Emily Dickinson) for mixed chorus *a cappella* (1938); *The Defense of Corinth* (after Rabelais) for speaker, men's chorus and piano four-hands (1941); *The Harmony of Morning* (Mark Van Doren) for four-part women's chorus and small orchestra (1944); and *Emblems* (Allen Tate) for four-part men's chorus and piano solo (1947).

Carter has been influenced by Copland, Piston, Hindemith, and Stravinsky, which is normal for composers of his generation. Clashing tonalities, fugal writing, and sustained expressiveness characterize his music. He has been steadily developing along his own creative lines. In his Sonata for cello and piano, Carter employs a procedure that has been called "metric modulation," which consists "in the coordination of all the tempi of the work and their interrelation by notated changes of speed. . . . The large circle of speed changes is completed when the sonata concludes by returning at the very end to the speed of the first movement."

Another composer who studied with Piston at Harvard and with

Nadia Boulanger in Paris is Arthur Berger (*b.* 1912). Born in New York City, he graduated from New York University and then went to Harvard for his M.A., at the same time attending the Longy School of Music in Cambridge. The award of a Paine Fellowship from Harvard enabled him to study in France for two years, where Darius Milhaud was one of his teachers in composition. But the most powerful influence on Berger's style has been the music of Stravinsky, particularly the works of the latter's most pronounced neoclassical period.

Berger has written chiefly chamber music. This includes a Quartet in C Major for woodwinds (1941); a Serenade Concertante for violin, woodwind quartet, and orchestra of strings, two horns, and trumpets (1944; revised 1951); Duo No. 2 for violin and piano (1950); and Duo for clarinet and oboe (1952). He has also written Three Pieces for string orchestra (1945), consisting of Prelude, Aria, Waltz; and an orchestral work, *Ideas of Order* (1952), commissioned by Dimitri Mitropoulos for the New York Philharmonic-Symphony (first performed in April, 1953). This is a work of considerable structural complexity, which prompted *Time* magazine to remark that "Berger has a style of his own." If so, the style has resulted from a remarkable feat of assimilation and self-discipline.

We began this chapter by saying that tradition is a body of usage transmitted from one generation to another. But traditions are continually being renovated or created anew. The contrapuntal chromaticism of Schoenberg and the neoclassicism of Stravinsky are both deeply rooted in tradition. And they have, in turn, established two of the main traditions of twentieth-century music, which younger composers of our time have inherited and are in the process of assimilating and transforming for their own needs and idiosyncrasies. Today, in the second half of the century, dissonant counterpoint, syncopated rhythms, twelve-tone techniques, atonal excursions, and emphasis on percussion, are part of the traditional procedures of musical composition. Nowadays it is more "revolutionary" to write a simple triad than an atonal chord.

Such terms as "traditional," "conservative," "revolutionary," and "experimental," are all relative. For some, all music that is not absolutely "safe and sound" is regarded as revolutionary or experimental. Thus, after a concert of contemporary music given recently in New York, a critic wrote: "Most of the evening, one devoutly wished that the compositions had stayed in the laboratory where they belonged." Actually, the laboratory—the setting for experiments in musical invention—is quite a fascinating place (though it is, as they say of Hell, a state of mind rather than a place). In our next chapter we shall look into the musical laboratories where the "Experimentalists" have been busily at work.

chapter twenty-seven

The experimentalists

Why with the time do I not glance aside
To new-found methods and to compounds strange?
SHAKESPEARE, SONNET LXXVI.

Each decade produces at least one musical *enfant terrible*—"bad boy of music," as Antheil called himself—who breaks the traces of tradition and cavorts like a wild colt in the corral of convention. In 1912 the fifteen-year-old Henry Cowell startled an audience at the San Francisco Music Club with "tone-clusters," played by striking the keys of the piano with his forearm. A few years later, about the time of World War I, a young Philadelphian of Russian birth named Leo Ornstein drew snorts of indignation from conservative music lovers with his "revolutionary" piano pieces, assailing their ears with alarming discords and publicly proclaiming his renunciation of "form." In the 1920s, at the height of the Jazz Age, George Antheil made the headlines and reaped the ephemeral rewards of a *succès de scandale* with his *Ballet mécanique*, in which he used horns and buzz saws. In the same decade, musical circles began to be stirred by unprecedented sound waves emanating from the amazing creations of the French-born Edgar Varèse, bearing such abstract titles as *Hyperprism* and *Ionisation*. In the 1940s a young man from California, John Cage, began to attract attention with his compositions for "prepared piano" and for novel combinations of percussion instruments, including oxen bells and tin cans.

These are not, by any means, the only American composers of the present century whom we might classify as innovators or inventors, but, as they are typical specimens of their kind and have stirred up several tempests in teapots of varying importance, it will serve our purpose to present them as our first exhibit in this display of musical rarities. We may begin by disposing rather rapidly of Leo Ornstein, who was born in Russia in 1895 and was brought to the United States as a child. His earliest compositions were quite conventional, but around 1915 he began to turn out some piano pieces, such as *Wild Men's Dance* and *Impressions of Notre Dame*, which made him a center of controversy and caused at least one critic (Paul Rosenfeld) to take him seriously as a significant innovator. But Ornstein's fit of musical radicalism was of short duration and he soon passed over into the conservative camp, producing a series of works in orthodox style, such as *Lysistrata Suite* (1930) and *Nocturne and Dance of the Fates* (1936), the latter commissioned by the League of Composers, which have been performed by various orchestras without so much as rippling the surface of contemporary musical gossip. Established in Philadelphia as head of his own School of Music and teaching at Temple University, Ornstein has not produced much recently, and his youthful radicalism has acquired a sort of legendary remoteness.

George Antheil is another composer who passed from the sensationally novel to the comparatively conventional. Born in 1900, in Trenton, New Jersey, of Polish parentage, he received his early training at the Philadelphia Conservatory of Music and later studied composition with Ernest Bloch. He lived in Paris, Vienna, and Berlin, concertized as a pianist in Europe for several years, and was the recipient of a Guggenheim Fellowship in 1932 and 1933. By that time he had acquired a considerable reputation as a musical spokesman of the "Jazz Age." His *Jazz Symphony* for twenty-two instruments, composed in 1925, was one of the early attempts to treat jazz symphonically. His opera *Transatlantic* was produced at the Frankfort Opera (Germany) in 1930. This was a satire on high finance and political corruption, which the composer claims was "the first modern political opera."

It was chiefly by the performance of his *Ballet mécanique* in Carnegie Hall, New York, on April 10, 1927, that Antheil acquired his reputation as the "bad boy" of American music—a reputation that he has never completely been able either to live down or live up to. Scored for ten pianos and an assortment of mechanical noisemakers, the *Ballet mécanique* and its effect on the audience provided eye-catching copy for the alert reporters of the metropolitan dailies whose busy typewriters catapulted the composer to fame overnight. Here are the headlines into which *The New York Times* packed the gist of the news for its readers:

> Antheil Art Bursts on Startled Ears—First Performance of Ballet Mécanique in This Country Draws Varied Response—Hisses, Cheers Greet Him—Concatenation of Anvils, Bells, Horns, Buzzsaws Deafens Some, Pleases Others.

For an American composer to draw hisses and cheers from a New York audience was in itself quite an achievement. This sort of passionate reaction to new music was to be expected in Paris—where Antheil had been hobnobbing with that iconoclastic band of young composers known as "Les Six," who delighted to *épater le bourgeois*—or in Vienna, where listeners had come to blows over Schoenberg's twelve-tone music. But violent musical partisanship was not exactly in the Carnegie Hall tradition, and it was largely because of the novelty of the situation that Antheil received such instantaneous notoriety.

Neither in its aesthetic conception nor in its specific mechanistic effects was the *Ballet mécanique* a new development in modern music. At Milan, in 1913, Luigi Russolo had issued the *Futurist Manifesto* which laid the aesthetic foundations for "The Art of Noises," stating, among other things, that "We must break out of this narrow circle of pure musical sounds, and conquer the infinite variety of noise-sounds." Russolo classified the futurist orchestra into six families of noises, ranging from thunderclaps and explosions to shrieks and groans, and predicted that all these would soon be produced mechanically (as they are in radio sound effects, for that matter). The *Ballet mécanique*, as we look back on it, appears to be merely an example of Antheil's agility in identifying himself with the current fads of European music in its more extreme manifestations. Antheil himself, however, claims that his purpose in writing this work was totally misunderstood, that he never proposed to "grind out pictures of the machine age" or to project "a kind of Buck Rogers fantasy of the future." Writing to Nicolas Slonimsky in 1936, Antheil tried to explain the significance of his mechanical ballet:

> I personally consider that the Ballet Mécanique was important in one particular and that it was conceived in a new form, that form specifically being the filling out of a certain time canvas with musical abstractions and sound material composed and contrasted against

one another with the thought of time values rather than tonal values. . . . In the Ballet Mécanique I used time as Picasso might have used the blank spaces of his canvas. . . . My ideas were the most abstract of the abstract.[1]

If this interpretation is correct, then Antheil must be regarded as a precursor of the "Abstract Composers" of the post-World War II period, such as John Cage and Morton Feldman, who have been experimenting with time-space concepts in music. Antheil wrote several discussions of this subject in *avant-garde* periodicals of the 1920s: *De Stijl* (Rotterdam, 1924-1925), *transition* (Paris, 1925), and *The Little Review* (1925).

Much to everybody's surprise, Antheil's *Ballet mécanique*, in a shortened version (lasting 18 minutes instead of half an hour), was revived at a concert of the Composers Forum in New York on February 20, 1954, and was received with prolonged applause that constituted an ovation for the composer, who was present, and for the conductor of the performance, Carlos Surinach. For this performance, the number of pianos was reduced from ten to four, and the original airplane propeller, which, according to an ear-witness, "at the American première in 1927 produced more wind than noise," was replaced by a recording of the roar of a jet engine. A reviewer in *The New York Times* wrote that "the work . . . now sounds like an ebullient and lively piece that is actually pretty in places and suggests nothing so much as an amplified version of Balinese gamelan music." Thus have our ears become accustomed to the mechanistic terrors of the twenties.

Antheil's opera *Helen Retires*, to a libretto by John Erskine, produced at the Juilliard School of Music, New York, in February, 1934, with its blend of disparate styles ranging from musical comedy to modern dissonance, its pseudo jazz effects, its deliberate banality, its tunefulness and topicality, deserves, I believe, a place within the developing tradition of realistic opera in America, of which more will be said in another chapter.

Antheil also belongs to that small band of American composers who have tussled with the exigencies of Hollywood and mastered the difficult task of writing music for films, among them *The Plainsman*

[1] Quoted in Slonimsky, *Music Since 1900*, 3d ed. (New York: Coleman-Ross Company, Inc., 1949), p. 288.

and *Make Way for Tomorrow.* His Fourth and Fifth Symphonies, dating respectively from 1942 and 1946, are cast in a mold of ample rhetoric and a somewhat synthetic dynamism which make him appear as an emulator of Shostakovitch. He continues to produce works in the larger forms, including a Violin Concerto and a Piano Concerto, while working as a film composer in Hollywood and pursuing on the side a variety of esoteric hobbies, such as the study of astronomy and of glands.

Henry Dixon Cowell, born in Menlo Park, California, in 1897, has not been consistently an innovator or an experimentalist in his numerous compositions, many of which, to borrow Slonimsky's paradoxical epithet, sound "audaciously conservative." Nevertheless, he belongs in this chapter as the exploiter of "tone-clusters" on the piano (he has employed the same principle in his orchestration too), as a theorist concerned with new musical resources, as a leader of the new music movement (chiefly as founder and editor of the *New Music Quarterly*), and as a restless investigator of the unusual in music, whether it be the most primitive or the most sophisticated.

Cowell grew up without orthodox musical training and developed his novel pianistic effects as the result of self-guided experimentation on an old upright piano. From the age of sixteen he studied theory at the University of California with Charles Seeger. Later he studied composition in New York for three years, chiefly with R. Huntington Woodman and Percy Goetschius. Cowell delved into the problems of musical notation, embodying his findings and theories in a book titled *New Musical Resources* (1930), and then endeavored to put his theory into practice by inducing Professor Leon Theremin, inventor and constructor of acoustical instruments, to collaborate with him in making an instrument, called the "Rhythmicon," designed to reproduce with complete accuracy all kinds of rhythms and metrical combinations, however complex. This instrument was first demonstrated in January, 1932, at the New School for Social Research in New York. Cowell had previously composed a suite in four movements, titled *Rhythmicana*, for orchestra and "Rhythmicon."

One of Cowell's deliberately experimental works is *Synchrony* (1930), in which tone-clusters are treated orchestrally as elements in an abstract musical "construction." Slonimsky calls this work a "constructivist symphonic poem," but surely the term "symphonic poem" can legitimately be applied only to an orchestral work that has a programmatic or extra-musical factor imposed on it, whether this be descriptive or allusive, whereas a "constructivist" composition is by definition "abstract" and therefore devoid of poematic content. Cowell has on occasion written "program music," such as his *Tales of Our Countryside*, just as he has written many other kinds of music, for he is essentially an eclectic composer drawing his material from many sources, including Celtic folklore, traditional American hymn tunes and country-dances, and the folk music of many lands. Were it not for his persistent interest in new musical resources and his various acoustical experiments, we would certainly have placed him among the Eclectics, for that is where he belongs by the bulk of his production, such as his eight Symphonies, his *Irish Suite*, his *Celtic Set*, his *United Music*, his *Amerind Suite*, and his *Ancient Desert Drone*.

"A rugged individualist"

That too-abused term, "a rugged individualist," inevitably needs to be applied to Carl Ruggles, who for many years has lived in a converted schoolhouse in Arlington, Vermont, writing his own kind of music at his own deliberate pace, sublimely indifferent to current trends and changing fashions, painting pictures or working at manual crafts when not composing or arguing, and always plainly speaking his mind about everything and everyone under the sun. Henry Cowell, a close friend, describes him as "irascible, lovable, honest, sturdy, original, slow-thinking, deeply emotional, self-assured and intelligent." An anecdote told by Cowell illuminates the composer's character:

> One morning when I arrived at the abandoned school house in Arlington where he now lives, he was sitting at the old piano, singing a single tone at the top of his raucous composer's voice, and banging a single chord at intervals over and over. He refused to be interrupted in this pursuit, and after an hour or so, I insisted on knowing what the idea was. "I'm trying over this damned chord," said he, "to see whether it still sounds superb after so many hearings." "Oh," I said tritely, "time will tell whether the chord has lasting value." "The hell with time!" Carl replied. "I'll give this chord the test of time right now. If I find I still like it after trying it over several thousand times, it'll stand the test of time, all right!" [2]

[2] Prefatory Note to Harrison's *About Carl Ruggles*, p. 3.

Had Ruggles lived several generations earlier, he probably would have gone a-whaling like his New Bedford ancestors. But by the time he was born, on March 11, 1876, at Marion, Massachusetts, his family was steeped in gentility; and the boy Carl was taught to play the violin, appearing as a local prodigy at the age of nine in a concert given for President Cleveland. At Harvard he studied music with Claus, Spalding, and Timner, then went to Winona, Minnesota, where he founded and directed a symphony orchestra. As a composer, his first work of any importance was an opera, *The Sunken Bell,* after the drama by Gerhart Hauptmann. His characteristic style, based on the use of free dissonant counterpoint, is first fully displayed in the work titled *Angels,* dating from 1921 and originally scored for six trumpets (it was later revised for four violins and three cellos, or for four trumpets and three trombones, and published in this version in 1938). The list of his published works is so brief that it may be given here in full: *Toys,* for soprano and piano (1919); the two versions of *Angels,* mentioned above; *Men and Mountains,* for chamber orchestra (1924); *Portals,* for string ensemble or for string orchestra (1926); *Sun-Treader,* for large orchestra (1933); *Evocations,* for piano solo (1937–1945). Besides various early works, there are in manuscript *Vox Clamans in Deserto,* for solo voice and chamber orchestra; and *Organum,* for orchestra, completed in 1945. This output is small compared to that of most composers. Ruggles is fastidious, often works for several years over one composition, and writes only when and as he pleases.

Because he cultivates a contrapuntal texture in chromatic dissonant style, the music of Ruggles bears a family resemblance to that of Schoenberg and Alban Berg, but with a marked individuality of idiom. Spiritually his musical ancestors are J. S. Bach and Handel. The quality of Ruggles's counterpoint is perceptively described in an essay by Lou Harrison, who writes:

> It is characterized by an absolute lack of negative spacing in the voices, which is to say that no voice is ever given over to repetitious arpeggiation or figuration of any kind at all. Each voice is a real melody, bound into a community of singing lines, living a life of its own with regard to phrasing and breathing, careful not to get ahead or behind in its rhythmic cooperation with the others, and sustaining a responsible independence in the whole polyphonic life.[3]

[3] *About Carl Ruggles,* pp. 7–8.

Ruggles's melodic line is characterized by nonrepetition of the same tone (or any octave of it) until after the tenth progression, a principle observed particularly in the leading melody, less strictly in the other parts.

Ruggles seeks in music a quality of beauty which he calls the "Sublime." The main impression that his own music makes on most hearers (assuming that their ears have become accustomed to chromatic dissonance) is probably that of austerity. One recognizes an uncompromising integrity and a creative force that seems genuine though limited, and perhaps one deplores the lack of sensuous appeal. Yet the music stands there, as solid as Vermont granite, indifferent to our romantic inclinations, and one admires it either very much or not at all. Ruggles's music is very much admired and praised by a group of devoted friends and disciples who happen to be gifted musicians and persuasive writers and who are convinced that he has made a unique and enduring contribution to American music. The uniqueness of his contribution may be granted, but the test of its enduring quality—in spite of the composer's vehement protest—must be tritely left to time and posterity.

To seek new paths

John J. Becker, born in Henderson, Kentucky, in 1886, is another composer who has gone his own way, shunning the beaten path; but in contrast to Ruggles he has been prolific, producing seven symphonies, the same number of concertos, several orchestral suites, half-a-dozen large choral works, a quantity of chamber music, and some scores for the theater and for films. Most of this music remains in manuscript. The *Symphonia Brevis* (piano version) the *Concerto Arabesque* for piano and small orchestra, a Concerto for horn and orchestra, *Soundpiece No. 5* (sonata for piano), and *Soundpiece No. 2* for strings, have been published by New Music Editions.

Becker received his musical training at the Wisconsin Conservatory, obtaining the degree of Doctor of Music. After serving as music director at the University of Notre Dame and professor of fine arts at the College of St. Scholastica, he became music director and composer-in-residence at Barat College of the Sacred Heart, Lake Forest, Illinois. He has been active as lecturer, writer, editor, and conductor. His credo as a composer is summed up in the phrase

"Laws are made for imitators; creators make their own laws." A further statement of his attitude toward composing will make clear why he is included in this chapter:

> It is every composer's duty to add to the already existing musical resources. Regardless of the great orchestral works of the past, the undiscovered possibilities for new ways in the development of orchestral forms and sounds are beyond comprehension. The true creative artist must never be satisfied. He must seek new paths constantly, for only by seeking will he find for himself the way to musical truth and beauty.[4]

In his development as a composer Becker has been concerned with the renovation of a Palestrinian polyphonic style in a modern dissonant idiom. In addition to the *Symphonia* mentioned above, his religious music includes a *Mass in Honor of the Sacred Heart* for men's or women's voices *a cappella*, and *Moments from the Passion* for solos and men's or women's voices *a cappella* (this score, completed in 1945, has been published). He has also been engaged in the search for a personal orchestral idiom leading to the creation of new orchestral sounds.

Describing his methods of orchestration in an article for *Musical America*, Becker mentions certain specific devices. One of these is "the juxtaposition of contrasting instruments, that is, instruments which have no relationship to each other as far as their orchestral color is concerned." He gives as an example a passage for trumpet, horn, and bassoon in his *Concerto Arabesque*. This method he considers particularly effective for the projection of dissonant contrapuntal and harmonic passages. Another device for obtaining new and interesting effects is that of "long sustained sections of seconds, scored for instruments of the same color." Becker finds fascinating possibilities in scoring for percussion instruments and has exploited some of these possibilities in his dance work *Obongo* (1933), scored for twenty-nine percussion instruments. He has also exploited the resources of the piano as a percussion instrument. For example: "If the top line of a dissonant counterpoint or chordal movement in the orchestra is doubled in octaves by the piano played with a percussive stroke, an effect like the cutting of steel will be produced." Becker has used this effect frequently in his Third Symphony (1929).

[4] *Musical America*, Feb. 1950, p. 214.

The reader may ask why a composer should be interested in producing an effect like the cutting of steel. The answer is that an experimentally minded composer is primarily concerned with discovering or inventing new sounds, or at least sounds that are new to the traditional materials of musical composition. This is more or less true of all composers, and it is largely a matter of emphasis and degree as to whether a particular composer should be classed among the experimenters. At all events, the desire of certain contemporary composers to incorporate in their music a wider range of sounds, especially "realistic" sounds suggested by conditions in the modern world, may be compared to the incorporation in modern poetry of realistic images and words from everyday speech, supplementing the traditional poetic diction.

Experimental composers of the twentieth century have also endeavored to expand and enrich their basic materials by drawing on the resources of non-European and nondiatonic musical systems. The importance of this expanded concept of musical composition is stressed by Becker in a challenging essay titled "Imitative Versus Creative Music in America," from which we quote the following excerpt:

> If it is true that all composers must learn their craft by imitation, we can find no objection to teaching the technic of composition provided it is based upon all of the musical systems, new and old. This is not the usual method of procedure. Almost all teachers, theorists, and composers ignore the importance of the Greek, Chinese, East Indian, modal, and all of the newly evolved scales, and have insisted for generations that the diatonic is the (and not a) system upon which the entire musical art must be based.[5]

The charge of narrowness in pedagogical theory is perhaps less valid now than it was when Becker wrote his essay some twenty years ago. For one thing, there has been an increasing interest in the study of comparative musicology, which has done much to spread the knowledge of primitive and non-European musical cultures. And secondly, the systematic compilation and divulgation of new musical resources has made great forward strides, the most notable effort in this direc-

[5] Cowell (ed.), *American Composers on American Music*, p. 188. Reprinted with the permission of the publishers, Stanford University Press. Copyright 1933 by the Board of Trustees of Leland Stanford Junior University.

tion being Nicolas Slonimsky's monumental *Thesaurus of Scales and Melodic Patterns*, a work that Virgil Thomson has aptly called "a tonal vocabulary of modernism."

Charles Louis Seeger is better known as a musicologist than as a composer. Nevertheless, he was one of the first genuinely experimental composers in America, and the influence of his inventive, inquiring, and systematic mind has made itself felt in the modern musical movement of the United States. Seeger was born in Mexico City, of American parentage, in 1886. He was educated at Harvard University, where he won honors in music. From 1912 to 1919 he was professor of music at the University of California. He then taught at the Institute of Musical Art and the New School for Social Research in New York. For several years he was associated with the Federal Music Project in Washington, D.C. From 1941 to 1953 he was chief of the Division of Music and Visual Arts of the Pan American Union. His compositions include *Twenty-five Songs with Pianoforte Accompaniment* (1906–1911); *The Shadowy Waters*, overture for orchestra after W. B. Yeats (1908); *Three Choruses with Pianoforte Accompaniment* (1912); Seven Songs for voice and piano; String Quartet in two movements (1913); Sonata for violin and piano (1913); Studies in single, unaccompanied melody and in two-line dissonant counterpoint (1915–1932); two pageants for orchestra and chorus, *Derdra* (1914) and *The Queen's Masque* (1915); *Parthenia* and *Second Parthenia* for orchestra (1915–1917); Solo for clarinet (1924); and a setting of the folk ballad "John Henry" for solo voice with orchestra.

Ruth Crawford Seeger has produced a number of highly original compositions full of intellectual subtleties and formal complexities. Born in East Liverpool, Ohio, in 1901, she studied music first in Chicago and later, on a Guggenheim Fellowship (the first given to a woman for musical composition), went to Berlin and Paris. Her *Three Songs* (words by Carl Sandburg) for contralto, oboe, piano and percussion with orchestral ostinato, composed in 1930–1932, are characterized by a heterophonic and polymetrical organization of the musical materials. This means that the various parts or simultaneous sound units (such as the solo instruments and the orchestral ostinato) are treated with a high degree of independence, and that different metrical patterns are superimposed upon each other. The three songs are "Rat Riddles," "In Tall Grass," and "Prayers of Steel."

Important among Ruth Crawford Seeger's works is a String Quartet composed in 1931, consisting of four movements, of which the third employs what has been termed "contrapuntal dynamics," as illustrated in the following example:[6]

Other compositions include *Two Movements* for chamber orchestra (1926), *Nine Preludes* for piano (1926), Sonata for violin and piano (1927), and *Four Diaphonic Suites* (1930) for two cellos, two clarinets, oboe, and flute (in various combinations). She has also written *Two Chants* for women's chorus *a cappella* (1930). Her originality and independence, her technical resourcefulness and creative integrity, give to Ruth Crawford Seeger a prominent place among the experimentalist composers of America. She died in Washington, D.C., on November 18, 1953.

Trio from Canada

Three Canadian-born American composers, each an experimentalist in his own fashion, should be mentioned here. They are Colin McPhee (*b.* 1901), Gerald Strang (*b.* 1908), and Henry Dreyfuss Brant (*b.* 1913). McPhee lived for a number of years in Bali (in the 1930s) and has made a special study of the music of Bali and of Java. This interest is reflected in an orchestral work titled *Bali* (1936) and in *Balinese Ceremonial Music* for two pianos (1942). Among his

[6] *New Music, A Quarterly of Modern Compositions,* Jan. 1941, p. 12.

other works are a Concerto for piano and wind octet (1929) and a *Sea Shanty Suite* for baritone solo, men's chorus, two pianos, and two sets of timpani (1929). A gifted writer as well as musician, his book *A House in Bali* (1946) paints a fascinating picture of life on that island and contains a good deal of information on the musical traditions and ceremonial dances of the Balinese.

McPhee's most important work in Balinese style is the symphony *Tabuh Tabuhan*, in three movements, which represents what is probably the most authentic, most exciting, and most significant meeting of East and West in modern symphonic music. According to Henry Cowell, parts of this score were mistaken for boogiewoogie by members of the CBS Orchestra who performed it for a radio broadcast in 1948.

Gerald Strang, a native of Alberta, was graduated from Stanford University, then did graduate work in music at the Universities of California and Southern California. From 1935 to 1940 he was managing editor of New Music Editions and during part of that period was also assistant to Schoenberg in the music department of the University of California at Los Angeles. His compositions include two Symphonies, a *Canzonet* for string orchestra and string quintet (or quartet), a String Quartet, a Quintet for clarinet and strings, three pieces for flute and piano, percussion music for three players (interest in percussion is typical of the experimentalists), and a choral work titled *Vanzetti in the Death House*, for baritone, mixed chorus, and small orchestra. This dates from 1937 and is still in manuscript. In his *Mirrorrorrim* for piano, Strang organizes his musical material around "tonal centers" instead of the traditional tonalities.

Henry Brant studied composition with Goldmark, Brockway, Copland, Antheil, and Riegger. He settled in New York, and has been busy writing or arranging scores for radio, for films, and for ballet, as well as teaching, while collecting exotic wind instruments and performing on them as a hobby. At the age of sixteen he composed a highly intellectual and deliberately modernistic set of *Variations for Four Instruments*, of which the original feature was that they created harmonic relations obliquely instead of vertically. Brant subsequently repudiated this and other early works of his published by New Music Edition. Prior to 1950, the compositions of Brant made considerable use of jazz and of satirical materials. Representative of this period are the Symphony in B flat (1945) and the *Saxophone Concerto* (1941), both of which have been recorded recently. Brant's present tendencies, based on antiphonal and polyphonic organization, are represented by the following works: *Millennium 1* (1950) for eight trumpets, bells, cymbals; *Origins* (1952), for forty percussion instruments with sixteen players; *Stresses* (1953), for strings, harp, celesta, piano; *Signs and Alarms* (1953), for three woodwinds, five brass, and two percussion instruments; *Antiphony 1* (1953), for symphony orchestra in five separated groups; *Millennium 2* (1954), for ten trumpets, ten trombones, eight horns, four tubas, four percussion, and one soprano; *Encephalograms* (1954), for high voice, harp, piano, percussion, woodwinds, and trumpet; *Ceremony* (1954), for solo violin, oboe, cello, four solo voices (soprano, alto, tenor, baritone), with six woodwinds, pianos, and four percussion; *Galaxy 1* (1954), for vibraphone, chimes, clarinet, horn; *Galaxy 2* (1954), for two woodwinds, four brass, two percussion; *Galaxy 3* (1954), for clarinet, piano, xylophone, glockenspiel. The piece titled *Ceremony* was commissioned for the Columbia University bicentennial celebration and was first performed in New York on April 3, 1954.

Brant's compositions since 1950 have made use of two basic concepts. One of these is the concept of "antiphonal placing," or "stereophonic distribution," of the instrumental and vocal forces into various separated positions in the concert hall, so that the hearer receives the sound from more than one direction. The second concept is that of a "polyphony of tempos," conceived as a possible intensification of "antiphonal placing," but also used when the instruments are normally placed. In this kind of polyphony, each separated group or instrument has not only its own particular time signature, but also its own independent tempo. For example, in *Millennium 2*, in one place, there are as many as twenty-one different tempi heard simultaneously; but only one conductor is needed! In *Antiphony 1*, on the other hand, five conductors are required.

Brant's personal collection of odd musical instruments includes Spanish ox bells, a Persian oboe, a Chinese oboe, double ocarina, double flageolet, an American and a French dulcimer, and twenty tin whistles in different keys.

Trio from France

To match our trio of Canadian-born experimentalists, we have three composers of French origin who have been prominently identified with the *avant-garde* of music in this country. They are Carlos Salzedo (*b.* 1885), Dane Rudhyar (originally Chennevière-Rudyard, *b.* 1895), and Edgar Varèse (born in Paris, December 22, 1885). Salzedo, trained at the Paris Conservatory, is a celebrated harpist, and all his compositions feature the harp either alone or in combination with other instruments. He belongs literally among the "inventors" in this chapter, for he invented a modern harp reflecting the ingenious complexity of the machine age. He has also "invented" new sonorities for the harp, systematically exploring all its possibilities and discovering by experimentation more than a hundred different effects that had previously been unknown or unexploited. He is thus, within his special field, both an inventor and an innovator.

The compositions of Salzedo include *The Enchanted Isle* for harp and orchestra (1918), Concerto for harp and seven wind instruments (1926), *Four Preludes to the Afternoon of a Telephone* for two harps (1921), Sonata for harp and piano (1922), and a number of pieces for harp solo, among them *Short Stories in Music* and *Fantasies on Popular Folk Tunes.*

Dane Rudhyar, composer of atonal music, is also a painter, a writer, a mystic, and a student of Oriental philosophy who has attempted to achieve "a new cosmological outlook" on life. He was first heard from in America with the performance in 1917 of two orchestral pieces whose titles are reminiscent of Erik Satie: *Poèmes Ironiques* and *Vision Vegétale.* These were included in the program of a modernistic dance recital given at the Metropolitan Opera House in New York by Valentine de Saint-Point. Among other orchestral works of Rudhyar are *The Surge of Fire* (1921), *To the Real* (1923), *Ouranos* (1924), a Symphony (1928), *Hero Chants* (1930), and a Sinfonietta (1931). In 1934, while living at Chamita, New Mexico, he completed the piano score of a symphonic poem with recitation, *Paean to the Great Thunder*, the first part of a projected trilogy titled *Cosmophony*, which, according to the composer, is "designed to express stages of development of mystic consciousness." Rudhyar has recently taken up musical therapy.

Edgar Varèse, the most consistently uncompromising among American musical modernists, was born in Paris on December 22, 1885, of French and Italian parentage. An early interest in science and mathematics indicated that he might take to engineering as a career, but at the age of seventeen he had already decided that music was to be his field (which by no means meant that he had abandoned his scientific interests: his approach to music remained abstract and objective, and he experimented with sonorities as though he were a scientist in a laboratory). He studied with Roussel and d'Indy at the Schola Cantorum and with Widor at the Paris Conservatory; but it was through another teacher, of bolder vision than these, the enigmatic Ferruccio Busoni, that Varèse was influenced in the direction of an experimental modernism. He also heeded the message of the Futurist Manifesto issued in 1913, with its program for developing "The Art of Noises" through all kinds of percussive and conventionally nonmusical sonorous effects.

From the first Varèse was also an active organizer and leader of musical organizations. In Paris, in 1906, he organized the chorus of the Université Populaire and the concerts of the "Château du Peuple," both intended to bring music to the people. After the outbreak of World War I he joined the French army, was discharged, and came to the United States in 1916, where he has since remained. His first musical enterprise in America was the founding of the New Symphony Orchestra in New York in 1919. His intention was to concentrate on the performance of music by modern composers, but meeting with opposition from the board of directors, he resigned and founded, in 1921, the International Composers' Guild, which under his leadership became a consistent vehicle for the performance of new and unconventional works by composers of America and Europe. Carlos Salzedo was associated with him in this enterprise, which was discontinued in 1927. A year later Varèse and Salzedo took the initiative in founding the Pan American Association of Composers, an early and significant effort to achieve cooperation among composers of all the Americas.

The list of Varèse's orchestral compositions begins with a work titled *Amériques* and ends (as of this writing) with one titled *Equatorial*, for bass-baritone voice, organ, percussion, trumpets, trombones, and theremin. But the majority of his compositions move in a world of abstract sonorities devoid of such geographical connotations. Merely to read the titles is to stand on the threshold of that unique sonorous microcosm created by Varèse: *Arcana, Metal, Espace, Integrales, Offrandes, Hyperprism, Ionisation, Density 21.5, Octandre.* Let us attempt to explore that strange world of sounds, in which primitive forces blend with the dynamic energy of the modern industrial city.

Four representative compositions of Varèse will be examined, not in their chronological order but according to the relative degree of difficulty that they offer to the listener (though this is admittedly a subjective criterion, since reaction and receptivity will vary with different hearers). One should perhaps begin by casting off certain traditional listening habits and preconceived notions of form and harmony before exposing oneself to the music of Varèse. Listening to some African tribal music or to some of the authentic music of the Orient is recommended as a preparatory exercise, not so much because of any direct similarity that may exist but rather as a reminder that there are other musical systems that do not rely on the major and minor modes, the chords and the tonal relationships to which we have become accustomed in Western Europe and America. Though the music of Varèse is by no means "primitive," it has certain qualities that are associated with primitive music, such as the reliance upon percussion (treated with great rhythmic complexity) as a fundamental and expressive element of the sonorous texture and the complete independence of the polyphonic lines or voices from the demands of chordal harmony. Another similarity with non-Occidental music is the supreme importance given to timbre in Varèse's musical texture. As Sidney Finkelstein points out in his perceptive notes for the complete recorded works of Varèse,[7] it is out of the composer's concept of timbre that arise both his individual harmony and his individual polyphony. Since timbre depends on the creation of a series of overtones which arise naturally from each instrument, it becomes "a means of exploring the sounds in between the whole and half tones of customary pitch." The exploitation of these fractional intervals resulting from the blending of overtones is another factor for which we must be prepared in listening to the compositions of Varèse. As regards polyphony, Finkelstein expresses the idea very well when he remarks that "one layer of sound is added to another." Each instrument has its own melodic line and rhythmic pattern, and its independence is emphasized by contrasting timbres.

Dissonance is a fundamental architectonic element in the compositions of Varèse. This is probably the most disconcerting factor to the listener who hears this music for the first time. Only when one has become so accustomed to these strong dissonances that they cease to distract one's attention from other elements of style and texture, can

[7] Copyright by EMS Recordngs, New York.

one really begin to appreciate the finely balanced sonorities and the multitude of rhythmic refinements and subtle contrasts of timbre that make each of Varèse's compositions a highly organized work of art possessing an inviolable integrity of form and structure. As to why he finds it necessary to use such dissonances consistently as part of his harmonic fabric, Henry Cowell offers an explanation that is interesting because it stresses the element of tension that is always present in Varèse's music: "To introduce a consonant harmony would remove the sense of implacable, resilient hardness, and create a weak link in the chain; the let-down would be so great that the whole composition might fall to pieces." [8] The music of Varèse has the beauty and precision of an intricate machine, and creates its emotion objectively, not as a subjective projection of the composer's ego or a public display of his private feelings.

The piece titled *Density 21.5* for solo flute was composed in 1936 for Georges Barrère's new platinum flute (21.5 is the density of platinum). Since there are limits to the unconventional effects one can create with a single instrument, this may well serve as an introduction to the music of Varèse, from which the listener may pass on to larger and more complex works, in which the same type of melodic line is employed polyphonically. Here, indeed, the wide range of the instrument, from the lowest to the highest register, conveys the suggestion of widely spaced polyphony and harmonic richness, even though only a single instrument is actually used.

With *Octandre* (1924) we enter a realm of instrumental polyphony in which contrasting timbres are interwoven in complex and clashing linear designs. The composition is for flute, clarinet, oboe, bassoon, French horn, trumpet, trombone, and contrabass. It is in three short movements, the first introduced by the oboe, the second by the flute, and the third by the bassoon. Each instrument is treated independently as regards melodic line, and with the intent of emphasizing its individual tone color.

Ionisation (1924) is one of the works that has gained for Varèse the reputation of being a manipulator of percussive effects at the expense of harmony and melody. Slonimsky, who accurately labels this work as "for instruments of percussion, friction, and sibilation, of inderminate pitch," points out that it is in sonata form,

[8] Cowell (ed.), *American Composers on American Music*, p. 47.

> . . . with the first subject given out by the *tambour militaire* (the while two sirens slide over the whole range in opposite directions like two harps glissando), the second by the *tutti* of percussion instruments, the development section being built on contrasting metal and wood percussion tone-color, and the coda (after an abridged recapitulation) introducing tubular chimes and low-register pianoforte tone-clusters (like pedal points).[9]

Among the instruments used in this composition (thirteen performers play thirty-five different instruments) are low and high sirens, "lion's roar," slapstick, *bongos* (Afro-Cuban drums), *güiro* (scraper made of a serrated gourd), Chinese blocks, sleigh bells, and two anvils.

Stylistic elements of the two preceding works are combined in the composition titled *Integrales* (1926), written for two flutes, two clarinets, two trumpets, three trombones, oboe, French horn, and a battery of percussion instruments (four players). Thematic developments and other elements of formal structure may be discerned, but they scarcely obtrude on the hearer's attention, which is beset by the impact of sensational sonorities. Slonimsky speaks of "static" emotion in this work; but of subjective emotion there appears to be none. This is abstract musical design, or as abstract as music can be; for it is a paradox of music that the more "abstract" it tries to be, the more "concrete" it becomes: it winds up as pure sound, a concrete physical fact.[10]

Trio from the Far West

Among the younger experimental composers, Lou Harrison, born in Portland, Oregon, in 1917, stands about midway between Varèse and Cage, sharing the former's interest in exploring the resources of pure percussion, and the latter's penchant for subtle and distinctive

[9] Slonimsky, *Music Since 1900*, 3d ed. (New York: Coleman-Ross Company, Inc., 1949), p. 340.

[10] Cf. the recent movement in Paris known as *Musique concrète*, a refinement of the "art of noises" utilizing modern recording techniques. Consult on this subject the article "Musique Concrète" by Henry Barraud in *Musical America*, Jan. 15, 1953, which in turn is a résumé of Pierre Schaeffer's authoritative work, *A la Recherche d'une musique concrète* (Paris, Edition du Seuil, 1952). Pierre Boulez, the leader of this movement in France, has influenced John Cage. Morton Feldman is another young American composer who has been experimenting along these lines, as has Vladimir Ussachevsky (experiments with magnetic tape recorder).

quasi-Oriental sonorities. He studied composition with Henry Cowell and Arnold Schoenberg. In 1952 and 1954 he was the recipient of a Guggenheim Foundation Fellowship. On the percussive side, Harrison has written, among other things, *Canticles I–VI*, *Simfonïes I–XIV*, and First Concerto for solo flute with percussion. His *Canticle III*, first performed under the direction of Leopold Stokowski, includes such unconventional percussion media as brake-drums, iron pipes, and packing boxes, in addition to wood blocks, assorted drums, a guitar, and an ocarina for the melodic element. The result has been described by Richard Franko Goldman as "a succession of charming and obviously well-organized sounds."

There is a deeply serious, semimystical vein in much of Harrison's music. He has written a number of religious works, including several Masses, a *Motet for the Day of Ascension* (for seven stringed instruments), *Praises for Michael the Archangel* (for organ and strings), and an *Alleluia* for small orchestra. He has also composed a "Symphony on G" (1948–1954), which employs a tonally centered twelve-tone technique (see next chapter for an explanation of these terms), a Piano Sonata, Suite No. 2 for string quartet (1948), Suite for cello and harp (1949); Suite for violin, piano, and orchestra; and an opera, *The Only Jealousy of Emer* (after Yeats). He is strongly influenced by the Baroque style, especially in his Suites, and he endeavors to develop the resources of secundal counterpoint, particularly as a medium of meditative expression. He says that his Suite No. 2 for string quartet is an attempt to make secundal counterpoint "sit down quietly and think and feel."

In 1954, Harrison was invited to attend the International Composers Conference in Rome and to submit a composition for a prize offered by the Congress for Cultural Freedom. He won a divided prize for the third section of a short opera, *Rapunzel* (text by William Morris), for mezzo-soprano, contralto, baritone, and seventeen instruments. Like many of Harrison's recent compositions, this score employs the twelve-tone technique.

Harry Partch is a composer who during the past thirty years has been consistently experimenting with new musical resources and devices. He was born in Oakland, California, in 1901, raised in Arizona, and self-taught in music. His theoretical musical explorations led him to develop a new musical scale, based on microtonal intervals and giving forty-three tones to the octave (instead of the twelve tones of the conventional tempered scale). In order to have instruments that could play the music written according to his system, Partch became an inventor, creating or adapting a whole array of microtonal instruments, including electric guitars and three types of adapted reed organ with special keyboard, which he calls "chromelodeon."

Among the compositions of Partch are *Seventeen Lyrics by Li Po, San Francisco Newsboy Cries, Letter from Hobo Pablo, U.S. Highball—Account of Hobo Trip, Account of the Normandy Invasion by an American Glider Pilot* (setting of a recorded transcription), and a score for *King Œdipus* (the William Butler Yeats version of Sophocles's *Œdipus Rex*), produced at Mills College, Oakland, California, in March, 1952. The score of this last work—his most important to date—calls for various modified string instruments, a newly designed *kithara*, three specially constructed marimbas, and glass bowls struck with hammers, in addition to the instruments mentioned above.

In his score for *King Œdipus*, Partch has written neither incidental music for a play nor an opera. It is an integrated score for instruments and actors, in which the instruments often follow the lines of inflected speech, and in which the actors are required to intone on pitch according to the system of the composer's microtonal scale. In both the speech and the instrumental music there is frequent use of "gliding" up or down from one tone to another—a practice hitherto condemned in art music but often encountered in folk and primitive music (another of the many links between the modern and the primitive in art).

Concerning his score for *King Œdipus*, Partch has said: "The music is conceived as an emotional saturation that it is the particular province of dramatic music to achieve. My idea has been to present the drama expressed by language, not to obscure it, either by operatic aria or symphonic instrumentation. Hence in critical dialogue music enters almost insidiously as tensions enter."

There is an interesting similarity between Partch's conception of the role of music in drama and T. S. Eliot's conception of the use of poetry in drama. Good dramatic poetry, according to Eliot (in his book, *Poetry and Drama*), is poetry that "does not interrupt but intensifies the dramatic situation." He objects to "passages which called too much attention to themselves as poetry" and charges that "they are too much like operatic arias." His ideal, therefore, is essentially the same as that of Partch.

Partch has developed a type of composition that he calls "Satyr-play Music for Dance Theater." In this form he appears to return to the ancient Roman *satura* (from which we get our term "satire"), which originally meant "a medley full of different things" (*satur* means "full"). The original *satura* combined words, music, and miming, but without a fixed plot.

One of Partch's satyr-plays, titled *Ring Around the Moon*, is described by the composer as

> A satire on the world of singers and singing, music and dance; on concerts and concert audiences, where the occasional perception of an understandable American word is an odd kind of shock. Also a satire on the world in general, on whimsy and caprice, on music in 43 tones to the octave, on people who conceive such things, on grand flourishes that lead to nothing, on satyrs, or on nothing.

In the course of this satire, further identified as "A Dance for Here and Now," a voice utters a series of clichés, banalities, and hackneyed expressions, such as, "Well, bless my soul!" and "Shake hands now, boys, and at the sound of the bell come out fighting!"

The trilogy of satyr-plays is completed by *Castor & Pollux—A Dance for the Twin Rhythms of Gemini*, and *Even Wild Horses—Dance Music for an Absent Drama* (in three acts and eight scenes). In the latter work a voice declaims fragments from Rimbaud's *A Season in Hell.* The dances bear such unlikely labels as "Afro-Chinese Minuet" and "Cuban Fandango."

The following instruments are used by Partch in these "Plectra and Percussion Dances":

Kithara: seventy-two strings in chords of six each in a lyre-type body. Open chords and sliding tones. Completed in 1943.

Surrogate kithara: six strings each on two long resonating boxes. Sliding tones mostly. Completed in 1953.

Harmonic canons (three): forty-four strings on each, with a movable bridge for each string. Developed from 1945 to 1953.

Chromelodeon: a reed organ with a forty-three-tones-to-the-octave scale spreading over three and one-half keyboard octaves. Completed in 1941.

Diamond marimba: thirty-six blocks with bamboo resonators arranged for chordal strokes and running passages. Made in 1946.

Bass marimba: eleven Sitka spruce blocks over redwood resonators, descending to the low cello C. Completed in 1950.

Cloud-chamber bowls: tops and bottoms of pyrex carboys. Bell-like tones. Collected 1950–1952. (A carboy is a large glass bottle used for corrosive acids, etc.).

Eroica and wood-block: a Pernambuco block giving the A below cello C, and a high multiple-toned redwood block.

Adapted viola: with an attenuated neck for microtonal scales. Played like a cello. Completed in 1930.

Adapted guitars: Hawaiian type, six and ten strings. Made in 1935 and 1945.

Once the novelty of Partch's microtonal instrumentation has worn off, the listener is apt to be left with a feeling of monotony. The expressive range of his music is limited. But since he seems to be aiming at a fusion of speech and dance with music, one should perhaps more fairly judge his works in their complete lyrical-mimetic projection rather than simply as formal patterns of organized sounds.

The fact that Partch, Cowell, and Cage come from California might tend to support the claim that the climate of that state is inducive to experimentation and inventiveness in the arts. Be this as it may, John Cage was born in Los Angeles in 1912 and by the time he was twenty was already composing piano pieces in which his sole interest seemed to be the search for unusual sonorities based on subtle gradations of timbre and dynamics. He studied dissonant counterpoint and composition with Cowell for one season and then went to New York to study with Adolph Weiss, an exponent of the twelve-tone technique who had been a pupil of Schoenberg in Vienna. Since Schoenberg had meanwhile settled in Los Angeles, Cage returned to his native city and studied with the master at the University of California there; he did not, however, exert himself to acquire the tone-row technique of composition, preferring rather to develop his own system. While in New York he attended Cowell's course in comparative musicology at the New School for Social Research and this stimulated his interest in non-European musical systems, particularly those of the Far East.

Nearly all of John Cage's music has been written either for percussion or for the "prepared piano." His works for percussion orchestra include *Construction in Metal* for seven players (1939); *Second Construction* (1940) and *Third Construction* (1941), both for four players; *March* for five players (1942); *Amores* for three players

(1943); and *The City Wears a Slouch Hat* (1942), composed for radio performance. He has written several *Imaginary Landscapes,* including one for electrical orchestra with percussion and another for twelve radios.

Cage's "prepared piano" is an ordinary grand piano whose strings have been muted at various specified points with a wide assortment of miscellaneous small objects, such as bits of wood, rubber, metal, glass, screws, bolts, hairpins, rubber bands, weather stripping, and so forth. The exact type of "preparation" differs for each piece or set of pieces. Occasionally an "unprepared" tone is allowed to sound in its natural state. Virgil Thomson described the typical sound of the prepared piano as "a ping, qualified by a thud." Cage's sonorous effects are delicate, carefully calculated, controlled by an extraordinary aural sensibility, and based on an extremely subtle exploitation of overtone combinations. His prepared piano suggests the Javanese gamelan or orchestra, with its wooden chimes, its bronze slabs, its bamboo pipes and metal disks, all blended into rather limited but enchanting sonorities.

Cage's most ambitious work for the prepared piano is a set of sixteen sonatas and four interludes, composed between February, 1946, and March, 1948, which takes eighty minutes to perform. Each of the twenty pieces that make up this complex work is a self-contained unit with its own structural pattern. The basic principle of organization is that of unchanging phrase-lengths within a given piece. If Mr. Cage decides that a sonata will consist of a succession of nine-measure phrases, he adheres strictly to that pattern throughout that particular composition. Another sonata may consist of six-measure phrases, another of ten-measure phrases, and so forth. The composer explains that this system of division "corresponds to the Oriental organization of poetry in terms of breath-phrases." This principle of rhythmic organization supplants the system of harmonic organization upon which traditional Western European music is based. The end of a rhythmic phrase takes the place of a harmonic cadence. The whole scheme is rigidly controlled by the application of a preconceived plan.

Sometimes, however, the plan itself may be the result of chance. In the endeavor to create purely objective form, Cage wishes to eliminate the factors of personal choice and volition. He therefore often lets chance decide such questions as how many measures shall constitute a phrase, or what scheme of dynamics shall be followed in a given work. His favorite method for utilizing the aid of chance is "I-Chang," an old Chinese game of throwing coins or marked sticks for chance numbers (the equivalent of our dice).

Cage used "I-Chang" to determine the structure of his composition for twelve radios titled *Imaginary Landscape*, first performed in New York in 1951 and marking what was up to that date probably the most extreme manifestation of mechanistic experimentalism in music, if music it can be called. This composition requires twenty-four performers—two at each radio—plus the conductor (who at the New York performance was the composer himself). One member of the team at each radio set manipulates the tuning dial and the other handles the dial for regulating the dynamics. The wave lengths to be tuned in at any particular moment are indicated in the score; but the actual stations that will be received vary, of course, according to the location of the performance. A given pattern of wave lengths will bring in one set of stations in New York and another in Chicago or San Francisco. The results, obviously, will also vary according to the time of day or night when the composition is performed. Therefore, while such factors as wave lengths to be tuned in, dynamic gradations (ranging from pianissimo to fortissimo), and the ratio of silence to sound, are determined beforehand and rigidly controlled the actual "content" of the composition (musical or otherwise) is determined by the nature of the radio programs that are on the air at a particular time and place. That is to say, the "content" in one performance will never be identical with that of any other performance.

Virgil Thomson classifies the music of John Cage and his followers—for he already has a following among the younger musicians—as "abstract," in the sense in which this term is employed with relation to modern art. Cage himself, in March, 1952, delivered a speech at the Juilliard School in New York called "Words for Prepared Discourse," in which, with transparent confusion, he explained his own ideas on music, on composition, and on expression. Among his leading ideas seemed to be the following: (1) the most that any musical idea can accomplish is to show how intelligent the composer was who had it; (2) in the case of a musical feeling the sounds are unimportant: what counts is expression; (3) one has to stop all the thinking that separates music from living.

Some actual excerpts from Cage's discourse—which was punctuated with music (here indicated by blank spaces)—will be quoted herewith, in order that the reader may appreciate the full flavor of this possibly historic document of contemporary music:

> I have nothing to say and I am saying it and that is poetry as I need it contemporary music is changing.
>
> But since everything's changing we could simply decide to drink a glass of water. To have something to be a masterpiece you have to have enough time to talk when you have nothing to say.
>
> In other words there is no split between spirit and matter. And to realize this: we have only suddenly to awake to the fact.[11]

The influence of Gertrude Stein on John Cage's prose style is evident. Since there should always be experimentation in the arts, Cage's movement is a healthy sign, whatever its ultimate significance may be in terms of permanent artistic achievement.

[11] Quoted in *Bulletin of the American Composers Alliance*, June 1952, p. 11.

chapter twenty-eight

Twelve-tone composers

Composing with twelve tones is not nearly as forbidding and exclusive a method as is popularly believed.
ARNOLD SCHOENBERG, MY EVOLUTION (MUSICAL QUARTERLY, 1952).

Twenty years ago the small handful of courageous composers who cultivated Arnold Schoenberg's "method of composing with twelve tones" would certainly have found their proper place among the very advanced guard of the Experimentalists. Today, thirty years after Schoenberg completed his first compositions systematically employing the twelve-tone technique, the latter may be said to have definitely outgrown the stage of laboratory experimentation and to have become one of the main trends of musical composition in the twentieth century. All three of its great pioneer exponents—Arnold Schoenberg, Anton Webern, Alban Berg—have passed into history, leaving to the world a fecund musical legacy in the form of some indisputable masterpieces, a profoundly elaborated theory, and the makings of a genuinely new tradition in the art music of Western civilization.

On April 11, 1941, Arnold Schoenberg, Viennese-born composer and creator of the method of composing with twelve tones, became an American citizen. He was then sixty-six years old and had been living in the United States with his family since 1933. Until 1925 he had lived and composed and taught in Vienna, becoming known as the composer of several impressive works of post-romantic tendency, stemming from Wagner, Brahms, and Bruckner, such as *Verklärte Nacht* ("Transfigured Night") and the symphonic poem *Pelleas and Melisande*. But he also became a controversial figure, often arousing violent opposition, through his bold experiments with dissonance and his alleged undermining of the "eternal" laws of musical aesthetics. Withal, his reputation and prestige were such that in 1925 he was appointed to succeed Busoni as professor of advanced composition at the Prussian Academy of Fine Arts in Berlin. As a Jewish musician, his position in Berlin became precarious after Hitler seized power. Hence Schoenberg, anticipating the inevitable, left Germany in May, 1933, going at first to Paris. In October of the same year he sailed for America.

During his first winter in the United States, Schoenberg taught at the Malkin Conservatory in Boston. Finding the climate of the Eastern seaboard uncongenial (he suffered from asthma), he moved to Los Angeles, California, in the fall of 1934. The following summer he became professor of composition at the University of Southern California. In 1936 he was appointed professor of music at the University of California at Los Angeles, retaining this position until 1944, when he retired and was named professor emeritus. He died at his home in Brentwood on the night of July 13, 1951, at the age of seventy-six.

In the United States, Schoenberg, like many other exiled artists and scholars, had an opportunity to exercise his profession in full freedom and to contribute his valuable store of knowledge and inspiration to the enrichment of our cultural life. True, he did not feel that his music was performed often enough, either in the United States or elsewhere. He was never able to hear, for instance, a "live" performance of his Violin Concerto, composed in 1936 and first played in 1940. Shortly before his death, a tape recording of another performance was sent to him, and that is how he finally heard a performance of the concerto. Although Schoenberg may have felt somewhat isolated or neglected in his eminence as a tremendously "advanced" composer, he was certainly not a prophet without honor in his adopted land. Besides the regular academic posts that he held, he was invited to lecture at the University of Chicago and other centers of higher learning. Harvard University commissioned him to write a String Trio for the "Symposium on Music Criticism" held in 1947. In April of that year, a special citation and a cash award for distinguished achievement in music were bestowed upon him by the American Academy and the National Institute of Arts and Letters. His important treatise on harmony was published in an English translation in New York in 1948, and his volume of collected essays and addresses, *Style and Idea*, appeared in 1950.

It is not the purpose of this chapter to trace in detail the life and work of Schoenberg, most of whose career belongs to the history of music in Europe. But his residence of eighteen years in the United States gives him a definite place in the American musical scene, and we propose to review briefly the works that he composed in this country. First, however, it will be necessary to summarize, as concisely as possible, the development of Schoenberg's method of composing with twelve tones.

Schoenberg himself described his system as follows:

> The method of composing with twelve tones substitutes for the order produced by permanent reference to tonal centers an order according to which, every unit of a piece being a derivative of the tonal relations in a basic set of twelve tones, the *Grundgestalt* [fundamental form] is coherent because of this permanent reference to the basic set.[1]

The music of Schoenberg and his followers has often been called "atonal" because of this search for a fundamental principle of formal organization not based on that of "tonality" or "permanent reference to tonal centers" which has dominated Western art music for roughly two and a half centuries. The term "atonality," however, is misleading and has been repudiated by Schoenberg. Actually, as we shall see later, the method of composing with twelve tones may be adapted for use within the traditional tonal system.

Evolution of the twelve-tone method

For a long time, then, Schoenberg was seeking a method of composition, a coherent system of organizing musical materials, that would be independent of traditional tonal relationships (tonic-dominant, and so forth). In the course of this search he found it necessary to arrive at what he calls "the suspension of the tonal system." But this was a gradual process. Passages of indeterminate tonality in certain of his early works, among them *Pelleas and Melisande*, were signposts marking an "advance in the direction of extended tonality." The com-

[1] From an essay entitled "My Evolution," originally written in 1949 for the Mexican periodical *Nuestra Música*, later delivered as a public lecture at the University of California at Los Angeles, and published in the *Musical Quarterly* for Oct. 1952 (copyright by G. Schirmer, Inc.). Other quotations from Schoenberg used in this chapter are from the same source.

poser was preparing himself for a definite renunciation of a tonal center as the unifying principle of a composition. A considerable advance in this direction was made in the *Chamber Symphony* (Opus 9), particularly through "the emancipation of dissonance." This tendency was continued in the *Two Ballads* (Opus 12) and in the Second String Quartet. In the latter work, according to the composer, "there are many sections in which the individual parts proceed regardless of whether or not their meeting results in codified harmonies." Hence, "the overwhelming multitude of dissonances cannot be counterbalanced any longer by occasional returns to such tonal triads as represent a key." Here we are face to face with the suspension of the tonal system. It becomes necessary to find a new principle of organization, one that will provide unity and coherence along with variety and flexibility.

In 1915 Schoenberg sketched the *scherzo* of a symphony in which the main theme happened to consist of twelve tones. Soon afterward, in his unfinished oratorio, *Jacob's Ladder,* he planned to build all the main themes out of a row or series of six tones. Then, in the *Five Piano Pieces* (Opus 23), he began tentatively but deliberately the procedure of "working with tones," though not yet exploiting the device of a fixed series of tones or "tone-row." Only the last piece in this set actually uses a twelve-tone row. Finally, in the Suite for piano (Opus 25) and the Wind Quintet (Opus 26), both dating from the year 1924, the material is organized entirely on the basis of tone-rows, and the method of composing with twelve tones takes definite shape.

The "twelve tones" are those of the chromatic scale (obtained by playing all the white and black keys on an octave of the piano keyboard). The composer begins by arranging these twelve tones in a series or row. Once arranged in a special order, with no tones repeated, this tone-row provides the material, both melodically and harmonically, out of which the entire composition is made. It may be said, therefore, in the words of René Leibowitz, that "every twelve-tone piece is nothing but a series of variations on the original row." The tone-row may be used in its entirety or in fragments, and in any of the following basic forms, derived from traditional contrapuntal devices: [2]

[2] The tone-row given in this illustration is that used by Schoenberg in his Suite for piano (Opus 25).

I. Its original form (symbol: O).

II. Its retrograde or "backwards" form (symbol: R).

III. Its inverted or "upside-down" form (symbol: I).

IV. Its retrograde inversion or "upside-down backwards" form (symbol: RI).

Since each of these forms of the tone-row may be transposed to each of the twelve tones of the chromatic scale, a total of forty-eight possible patterns is available to the composer who employs this method of composition.

As Virgil Thomson sensibly observes:

> The device of arranging these twelve tones in a special order particular to each piece and consistent throughout, is not an added complication of twelve-tone writing but a simplification, a rule of thumb, that speeds up composition. The uses of such a "row" . . . are not necessarily intended for listeners to be aware of any more than the devices of fugal imitation are. They show up under analysis, of course, but they are mainly a composer's way of achieving thematic coherence with a minimum of effort.[3]

Among important works of Schoenberg written before his coming to America and embodying further development of the twelve-tone technique are the Suite (Opus 29) for piano, piccolo clarinet, clarinet, bass clarinet, violin, viola, and cello (1926); the Third String Quartet (Opus 30, 1926); the Variations for Orchestra (Opus 31, 1927–1928); and the opera buffa *From Today Till Tomorrow* (Opus 32, 1929).

[3] *Music Right and Left*, p. 182. Used by permission of the publisher, Henry Holt & Company, Inc.

Schoenberg's American period

In America a curious thing occurred with Schoenberg's composing: he returned in certain instances to tonal writing. His first work composed in the United States was a tonal Suite for Strings, in the key of G Major, written for student orchestra. In 1938 he composed a tonal setting of the *Kol Nidre* for solo voice, chorus, and orchestra. Another tonal work, the *Variations on a Recitative for Organ*, was written in 1941. Regarding this return to tonality, Schoenberg wrote: "A longing to return to the older style was always vigorous in me; and from time to time I had to yield to that urge." He was like an explorer who has discovered a new continent that thrills and fascinates him, but who feels now and then a longing to revisit the homeland with its familiar habits and comforts.

But Schoenberg did not by any means abandon twelve-tone writing in America. He continued to develop the twelve-tone method in such works as the Violin Concerto (Opus 36, 1936), the Fourth String Quartet (Opus 37, 1936), the Piano Concerto (Opus 42, 1942), and the String Trio (Opus 45, 1947). Another extremely interesting twelve-tone work of this period is the *Ode to Napoleon Buonaparte*, (Opus 41, 1942), for string quartet, piano, and reciter. This is a setting of Lord Byron's poem denouncing tyranny and praising the democratic spirit of George Washington. It employs a kind of "speech song" (*Sprechstimme*), a technique that Schoenberg had previously used in the poetic settings of *Pierrot Lunaire* (1912) for reciter and five instruments. The *Ode to Napoleon Buonaparte*, with string orchestra substituted for quartet, was first performed at a concert of the New York Philharmonic-Symphony on November 23, 1944.

The *Ode* gave proof that Schoenberg was not indifferent to the catastrophic struggle of the world in which he lived, and which had touched his own life so closely. Further evidence of this preoccupation is found in a work composed in 1947, entitled *A Survivor From Warsaw* (Opus 46), for narrator, men's chorus, and orchestra. The narrator takes the role of the Survivor and recounts his experience of Nazi brutality toward the Jews of Warsaw, as they are rounded up for the gas chamber, while the old and infirm are knocked down and beaten over the head with clubs. The singing of the Hebrew prayer, "Hear, O Israel," rises like an affirmation of faith and hope in the midst of this horror.

Schoenberg's last completed work was the *De Profundis* (Opus 50b), a setting of the 130th Psalm in Hebrew, for six-part mixed chorus, using the twelve-tone technique, with spoken and sung passages alternating. He left many works unfinished.

Schoenberg was less dogmatic than is generally supposed. In his lecture "My Evolution," from which we have already quoted, he said:

> In the last few years I have been questioned as to whether certain of my compositions are "pure" twelve-tone, or twelve-tone at all. The fact is I do not know. I am still more a composer than a theorist. When I compose I try to forget all theories and I continue composing only after having freed my mind of them. It seems to me urgent to warn my friends against orthodoxy. Composing with twelve tones is not nearly as forbidding and exclusive a method as is popularly believed. It is primarily a method demanding logical order and organization, of which comprehensibility should be the main result.

It is very characteristic of Schoenberg that he should warn his followers against "orthodoxy." He did not want the twelve-tone method to become a dogma but rathe. a source of creative energy. Some of his followers took his warning to heart and went their separate ways, seeking new and unorthodox procedures for twelve-tone writing. Others have endeavored to uphold strict orthodoxy and to develop a systematic body of dogma, in spite of the Master's warning. Others, again, have taken some elements of the twelve-tone technique and have combined them with traditional tonal procedures.

Schoenberg himself combined the twelve-tone technique with tonal organization in his Concerto for Piano and Orchestra, and, more remarkably, in the *Ode to Napoleon*. An earlier and striking example of a twelve-tone work that employs the functions of tonality may be found in Alban Berg's Violin Concerto (1935), which utilizes a tone-row so constructed that it includes major and minor triads as well as the whole-tone scale, as follows:

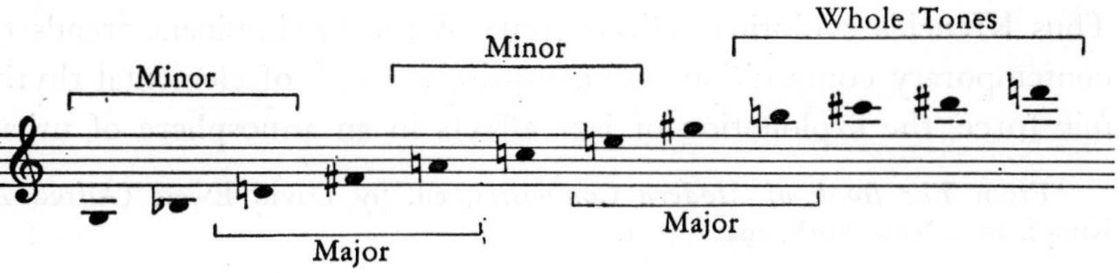

The "tonal application" of the twelve-tone technique is rapidly becoming one of the most widespread, most productive, and most significant trends in the music of our time.

Another composer from Vienna

Prominent among twelve-tone composers in America is Ernst Křenek (*b.* 1900), who, like Schoenberg, was born in Vienna, and who approached the twelve-tone technique via the unlikely route of Schubert's music. Křenek first visited the United States in 1937 and returned the following year to take up permanent residence in this country. From 1939 to 1942 he was on the music faculty of Vassar College; later he was appointed Dean of the School of Fine Arts at Hamline University, St. Paul, Minnesota.

In an autobiographical statement published in 1942, Křenek reviewed his musical evolution and attempted to explain his "apparently aimless meandering through styles." This is his self-explanation:

> After a few initial attempts in the exalted late romantic manner of my teacher, Franz Schreker, I turned soon to the more aggressive idiom of atonality, whose main organizing agency was elemental rhythmic force. I became interested in jazz, in the early twenties, and I had my greatest success when I used some jazz elements in my opera *Jonny spielt auf!* . . . I was not satisfied with either rhythmically stiffened atonality or semi-primitive jazz, and in about 1928 I went back to the early romantic vocabulary of Schubert. I was called both surrealist and reactionary, while I personally had the feeling that I was making up for things which I had missed when I had been in school. Another about-face, this time slow and deliberate, took place: through concentration, condensation, sophistication of the Schubert style, I came directly to Schoenberg's twelve-tone technique. This move seemed particularly logical to me. During the last years, I have devoted much work to the practical development and the critical interpretation of that technique, as well as to creative writing and theoretical studies.[4]

Thus Křenek's evolution reflects some of the predominant trends of contemporary composition: the neo-primitive cult of elemental rhythmic force, the exploitation of jazz effects in an atmosphere of urban

[4] From *The Book of Modern Composers,* ed. by David Ewen (Alfred A. Knopf, Inc., New York, 1942), p. 354.

sophistication, and the search for absolute values in abstract musical expression. When a third factor is added—his vein of political satire—he becomes a yet more representative musician of these times. From 1926 to 1928, Křenek composed a trilogy of one-act operas in the spirit of political satire, titled respectively *The Dictator*, *The Mysterious Kingdom*, and *Heavyweight, or Pride of the Nation.* It is interesting to observe that after his arrival in the United States he returned to the subject of tyranny and violence, this time in a more serious vein, in his chamber opera *Tarquin* (1940), described as "a new opera for the modern stage."

Anyone wishing to become acquainted with the twelve-tone technique in all its "classical" purity and strictness, but in a comparatively simple form not too difficult to grasp, might well begin by acquiring a knowledge of Křenek's *Twelve Short Piano Pieces*, written in 1938, which are a sort of *Gradus ad Parnassum* of twelve-tone writing. Considerably more formidable is the Second Concerto for piano and orchestra, composed in 1937 with strict employment of a twelve-tone row in its four basic forms. When this work received its first American performance by the Boston Symphony Orchestra on November 4, 1938, an old lady in the audience was overheard remarking to her husband, "Conditions in Europe must be dreadful." [5]

Apart from the historical opera *Charles V* (1933), Křenek's most ambitious effort to employ the twelve-tone technique in a large-scale work is his Fourth Symphony (1947), a carefully constructed composition designed to depict the conflict between the Ideal and the Real. It was the composer's intention to present in this work "a very high amount of logical coherence and intelligible significance." But these qualities are more appreciated in mathematics and in philosophy than in music, which for most people remains a language of the emotions. Hence Křenek's symphony was not received with enthusiasm.

Křenek's Third Concerto for piano and orchestra, composed in 1946, is not a twelve-tone composition but is based on traditional tonality. It is in five movements, played without interruption, and in each movement a different section of the orchestra enters into dialogue with the solo instrument. The score makes occasional excursions into jazzlike effects.

One of the most unusual bits of musical Americana was composed

[5] This anecdote is told by H. W. Heinsheimer in his entertaining book, *Menagerie in F Sharp.*

by Křenek in 1945, when he set to music *The Santa Fe Time Table* for mixed chorus *a cappella*—a monodic intonation of the names of railroad stations on the Santa Fe line from Albuquerque to Los Angeles. A more traditional contribution to musical Americana is Křenek's set of orchestral variations on the American folk hymn "I Wonder as I Wander" (1942).

Among other works written by Křenek in the United States are the *Cantata for Wartime* (1943), *The Ballad of the Railroads* (song cycle, 1944), *Five Prayers by John Donne* for women's voices *a cappella* (1944), Sonata for violin and piano (1944–1945), String Quartet No. 7 (1944), and a considerable quantity of other chamber music. He is the author of a stimulating book, *Music Here and Now* (English translation, New York, 1939), and of *Studies in Counterpoint* (1940).

Two independent twelve-toners

Stefan Wolpe is another European-born exponent of twelve-tone music, who settled in the United States about the same time as Křenek and eventually became an American citizen. Born in Berlin in 1902, Wolpe received his musical training in that city. His musical development was strongly influenced by Busoni and later by Anton Webern, whom he met after going to Vienna in 1933. He was active in Palestine for several years before going to the United States. From 1939 to 1944 he taught at the Settlement Music School in New York City.

Wolpe, like Křenek, assimilated many styles and experimented with many techniques before turning to the twelve-tone method. And then he transformed the latter for his own purposes instead of adopting it literally. According to Abraham Skulsky:

> Stefan Wolpe was the first composer to develop a newly organized harmonic system from the twelve-tone principles of Schoenberg. He employs harmonic zones or regions that result from each of the individual contrapuntal lines; the inner relationship between the harmonic zones is established by what he calls spatial organization.[6]

Wolpe first began to experiment with these "spatial" relationships in his *Studies on Basic Rows* (1934), originally written for piano and later orchestrated, in which he systematically exploited the intervalic

[6] In *Musical America*, Nov. 1, 1951, p. 6.

relationships derived from the twelve-tone technique. The Passacaglia, for example, "is built progressively on all the intervals from the minor second to the major seventh" (Skulsky).

Wolpe has been deeply influenced by his contact with the folk music of the Near East. Unlike Schoenberg, who scorned the use of folk music, Wolpe has found inspiration in Hebrew folklore and its ancient roots. A manifestation of this interest are his *Twelve Palestinian Songs* on biblical texts (1936) and the oratorio *Israel and His Land* (1939).

Among Wolpe's compositions written in America, there is the *Lament for Ignacio Sánchez Mejía*, a setting of García Lorca's splendid poem on the death of a bullfighter, for soprano, baritone, speaker, and chamber orchestra (1945). A *Toccata for Piano in Three Movements*, composed in 1941, uses basic tone-rows somewhat in the manner of his earlier Studies. Other works that reveal the development of his contrapuntal style are *Encouragements, or Battle Piece*, for piano (1946–1947); Sonata for violin and piano (1949); and Quartet for trumpet, saxophone, piano, and drums (1950).

One of the earliest followers of the twelve-tone method in the United States is Adolph Weiss, who studied with Schoenberg in Vienna from 1927 to 1929. Weiss was born in Baltimore, Maryland, in 1891, and received his musical training in Chicago and New York. A bassoonist by profession, he played with symphony orchestras in New York, Chicago, and Rochester. For his own instrument he wrote a prize-winning Concerto for Bassoon and String Quartet, which has been frequently performed. He was one of the musicians who, in the 1930s, organized the "Conductorless Orchestra" in New York City.

The early compositions of Weiss were markedly derivative, with strong impressionistic influences. After his studies with Schoenberg, he began to compose with twelve tones in such works as *Chamber Symphony* for ten instruments (1928), *Sonata da Camara* for flute and viola (1930), and Preludes for piano. In his scherzo for orchestra titled *American Life* (1929) he does not use a twelve-tone row, but builds the composition on the basis of the interval of the augmented fourth. Among other works by Weiss are a Quintet for wind instruments (1932), four String Quartets, a Concerto for trumpet; and *The Libation Bearers* (after Aeschylus) for solo quartet, mixed chorus, orchestra, and dance pantomime (1930).

The music of Wallingford Riegger

The leading native-born American composer who composes with twelve tones is Wallingford Riegger. He was born in Albany, Georgia, in 1885, but while he was still a child his family moved to Indianapolis, where his musical education began. When he was fifteen the family moved to New York. After attending Cornell University for a year, Riegger entered the Institute of Musical Art, from which he was graduated in 1907. There followed two years of advanced study at the Berlin Hochschule, an engagement as conductor of the opera in Würzburg (1914–1915), and as conductor of the Blüthner Orchestra in Berlin. When the United States entered World War I, Riegger of course returned to America. For three years he taught at Drake University in Des Moines, Iowa, then at a conservatory in Ithaca, New York. Since the early 1930s he has made his home in New York City.

Although he received several awards and commissions during the 1920s, it was not until some twenty years later, with the performance of his Third Symphony at the Columbia University Festival of American Music in 1948, that Riegger began to win the wide recognition that his music merits. Riegger's early works, such as the Piano Trio in B minor (1921), were lushly romantic. He was at that time writing the kind of conservative music that was most generally acceptable. He might have gone from one facile success to another, but instead he chose to alter his course completely. In 1927 he completed a work entitled *Study in Sonority*, for ten violins or any multiple thereof, written in a strongly dissonant idiom, and in which, instead of following the traditional tonic-dominant relationship, he invented, as Cowell observes, "a chord to play the part of tonic and another to play that of dominant." This initiated the vein of innovation that he has since pursued.

Riegger's adherence to the method of composing with tone-rows was foreshadowed in his orchestral work *Dichotomy*, composed in 1931–1932, in which he uses two different tone-rows, one consisting of eleven tones, the second of thirteen (ten different tones and three recurring tones). This impressive work, which closes with a passacaglia, is one of the most interesting and original modern American compositions for orchestra. Concerning it Riegger has written:

> Among the special things I should like to point out is what I call "cumulative sequence," a device by no means original with me, but used perhaps more consciously and to a greater degree in my work than elsewhere. . . . This is the old Three Blind Mice idea, keeping the original motive and *adding* a sequence, above or below, instead of moving the motive itself. I also use something I call "organic stretto," e.g., the telescoping of different sections, instead of the subject with itself, as in the fugue. It is like beginning a subordinate theme before the principal theme is established.[7]

In his First String Quartet (Opus 30) Riegger uses the twelve-tone technique in its strict or "classical" form, according to the purest Schoenbergian canon. Each of the four movements of this quartet employs the basic tone-row of twelve tones in one of the four fundamental forms prescribed by Schoenberg: in its original form (first movement); in its retrograde form, or "backwards" (second movement); in its inverted form, or "upside down" (third movement); and in its retrograde inversion form, or "upside-down backwards" (fourth movement). Clear and prominent statement of the tone-series at the outset, combined with ingenious variety of texture and a lively expressiveness, make this an attractive and satisfying work.

In general Riegger uses the twelve-tone method rather freely. He is by no means a dogmatic Schoenbergian. Expressiveness and strength of texture are what he seeks above all. There is in his music a fundamental honesty, both of concept and workmanship, that is best described by the word "integrity." He avoids the sensational, the cliché, and the cheap effect. His qualities of originality, invention, clarity, discipline, and expressiveness, are amply revealed in his Third Symphony, the work that brought him a wider fame when performed in 1948. In this symphony, traditional and tone-row procedures are combined, and the sense of tonality is not abandoned. This is a strong and sincere work, splendidly orchestrated, which serves to place its composer in the very front rank of contemporary American musicians.

Among other compositions by Riegger are *Canons for Woodwinds* (1931), *Fantasy and Fugue* for orchestra and organ (1930–1931); *Music for Brass Choir* for ten trumpets, four horns, ten trombones, two tubas, and timpani (Opus 45, 1948–1949); *Passacaglia and Fugue* for orchestra (1942); Duo for Three Woodwinds (1943); *New and*

[7] Quoted by Henry Cowell in *Musical America*, Dec. 1, 1948.

Old, a suite of twelve pieces for piano (1945); *New Dance* for piano and chamber orchestra (1944); several String Quartets; and a Fourth Symphony.

Riegger has written a number of vocal works, including a setting of "La Belle Dame Sans Merci" for four solo voices and eight instruments (an early work of impressionist tendency, 1924); and especially *In Certainty of Song* (1949), a cantata for mixed chorus with orchestra in praise of "the brotherhood of man," dedicated to the Interracial Fellowship Chorus of Greater New York. His stage works were written mostly for the modern dance, and are scored for various chamber combinations. They include *Frenetic Rhythms* (1932), *Theatre Piece* (1935), *With My Red Fires* (1936), *Chronicle* (1936), *Trend* (1937), and *Trojan Incident* (1937).

Wallingford Riegger has been aptly described by Cowell as "a romantic who admires strict forms." His predilection for strict classical forms and his striving for intellectual order through twelve-tone techniques have not obscured the essentially expressive quality of music. Out of the fundamental dichotomy of his temperament "he has welded together"—in the words of Irving Lowens—"an astonishingly eloquent and highly individualistic personal style from a number of widely disparate elements." [8]

Some younger twelve-tone writers

Kurt List, born in Vienna in 1913, came to the United States with the advantage—for a twelve-tone composer—of having absorbed the Schoenbergian principles at their fountainhead, as a pupil, in his native city, of Alban Berg and Anton Webern. A strict follower of the twelve-tone canon, he reveals his allegiance to both Schoenberg and Bach in his contrapuntally elaborated compositions. These include Wind Quintet for flute, oboe, clarinet, English horn, and bassoon; First Symphony for contralto, tenor, and twenty-six instruments (setting of texts by Shakespeare, Goethe, Byron, Heine, Wordsworth, Verlaine, Valéry, George, Rilke, Wayne Clark, Louise Labbé, Guillaume Apollinaire); String Quartet; *Variations on a Theme of Alban Berg* for piano; *Contrapuntal Pieces* for piano (Chorale, Passacaglia, Fugue, and Toccata); *Songs to Words by E. E. Cummings,* for voice

[8] In *Notes* of the Music Library Association, Mar. 1952, p. 325.

and piano; Second Symphony, and an opera, *The Wise and the Foolish.*

Also of Central European origin but now identified with the twelve-tone movement in the United States, is Erich Itor Kahn, whose *Ciaccona dei tempi di guerra* for piano (1943) has received frequent performances in this country. Among other works of this composer are *Two Psalms* for mezzo-soprano, *Three Madrigals* for mixed choir, and *Music for Ten Instruments and Soprano,* first performed at a concert of the International Society for Contemporary Music in New York in January, 1954.

Among the younger American twelve-tone composers, George Perle (*b.* 1915) has distinguished himself both as a theorist with original ideas and as the author of musical works possessing marked individuality of style. He studied composition with Ernst Křenek. Within the area of twelve-tone writing, which he uses freely, Perle has experimented with modal structure. He is, therefore, one of those who followed Schoenberg's advice to avoid orthodoxy. Perle, who is on the music faculty of the University of Louisville (Kentucky), has written several theoretical studies, including "Evolution of the Tone-Row" (*The Music Review,* Nov. 1941).

Perle began composing in a "free" atonal system, but soon abandoned this in order to investigate the possibilities of twelve-tone writing. From the outset he had a fundamental objection to the orthodox twelve-tone method because, in his opinion, "it failed to rationalize harmonic events." He decided that he wanted to use twelve-tone writing, but without being atonal. What he wanted was "dodecaphonic functionality" rather than "atonality" to take the place of diatonic functionality. From this premise he evolved his "Twelve-tone Modal System," which has been the basis of his composing since 1940. He has been consistently concerned with the harmonic problem in twelve-tone writing. Apart from the Third String Quartet (Opus 21, 1947), Perle has composed few works in the orthodox twelve-tone technique. Among his tonal twelve-tone works are the Second String Quartet (Opus 14, 1942) and the *Variations on a Welsh Melody* for band (Opus 30, 1952). He has written several homophonic atonal works, not based on a tone-series, including the Sonata for Solo Viola (Opus 12, 1942), Three Sonatas for Solo Clarinet (Opus 16, 1943), and Sonata for Solo Cello (Opus 22, 1947). In addition to the foregoing, his principal compositions include an important Piano Sonata (Opus 27, 1950),

Preludes for piano (Opus 2, 1947), Fourth String Quartet (Opus 24, 1948), Sonata for Viola and Piano (Opus 25, 1949), three symphonies (Opus 23, 1948; Opus 26, 1950; Opus 31, 1952), and Rhapsody for Orchestra (Opus 33, 1953).

Two American composers who happen to have been born in the same year—1916—have achieved prominence as cultivators of the twelve-tone technique, each in his own manner. They are Milton Babbitt and Ben Weber. Babbitt is from Mississippi and studied composition with Roger Sessions, Marion Bauer, and Philip James. He acknowledges that his greatest debt is to Sessions, who managed to reveal to him the path that he should take. Babbitt teaches music at Princeton University, where he formerly studied with Sessions. It is perhaps not without significance that for a time he taught mathematics at Princeton. This is in line with his statement that as a composer he likes "the overtone of complete abstraction" implicit in such titles as *Composition for Four Instruments* and *Three Compositions for Piano*, which he has given to recent works of his.

Babbitt is a strict and uncompromising twelve-tone writer. Anthony Bruno quotes him as saying,[9] "I believe in cerebral music, and I never choose a note unless I know why I want it there." And again: "The twelve-tone set [his term for the tone-row or series] must absolutely determine *every* aspect of the piece. The structural idea is the idea from which I begin. . . . I have the end in mind as well as the beginning and a middle, and the piece ends when the possibilities or resources of the particular set are exhausted." Babbitt feels that he has made a sacrifice in renouncing tonality, but he also believes that in twelve-tone music "we can structuralize rhythm as we cannot in tonality" and that, consequently, "The great achievement and the compensation for sacrificing tonality is rhythmic independence." Finally, he is convinced that "dynamics are an absolutely organic part of the piece"—that is, of any musical composition (compare Ruth Crawford Seeger's "contrapuntal dynamics" in the preceding chapter).

Ben Weber was born in St. Louis, Missouri, on July 23, 1916. He attended the University of Illinois, where, like many another future musician, he received premedical training. But at De Paul University

[9] Bruno, "Two American Twelve-tone Composers," *Musical America*, Feb. 1951, pp. 22, 170. In my discussion of Babbitt and Weber I have drawn extensively on Bruno's article, which in turn is based on personal interviews with these two composers.

in Chicago, having discovered his true vocation, he took up the study of musical theory. In composition, however, he is largely self-taught. From 1939 to 1941 he was active as a leader of the "New Music Group" in Chicago. He earns a living as an autographer for photo-offset reproduction, but in 1950 he was awarded a Guggenheim Foundation Fellowship, which enabled him for a time to devote himself entirely to composing.

Weber is much less dogmatic than Babbitt in his attitude toward twelve-tone composition. He relies more on intuition than on logic and confesses that he has a "romantic" temperament. "I tend to use the twelve-tone row melodically," he says, "and my rhythms are determined by my melody." In relation to the Great Three of the twelve-tone tradition, he is closer to Schoenberg than to Webern, and closer to Berg than to Schoenberg. He is inclined to an impassioned lyricism, which is always, however, under firm technical control, as in the *Fantasia* for violin and piano, the *Lyric Piece* for string quartet, the Suite for piano (Opus 8), and the Trio for strings. He has produced works in free atonal style, such as Five Pieces for cello and piano (1941), Variations for piano, violin, clarinet, and cello (1941), Ballade for cello and piano (1943), Second Sonata for violin and piano (1943), Symphony for cello and orchestra (1945). And he has also written numerous works in the twelve-tone technique, though seldom within the strictest canon. Among these are the First Sonata for violin and piano (1939), Suite for piano (1941), Concertino for violin, clarinet, and cello (1941), Sonata for cello and piano (1942), *Capriccio* for piano (1946), *Fantasia Variations* (Opus 25) for piano, Piano Suite (Opus 27), Concerto (Opus 32), for piano, cello, and five wind instruments; and a ballet, *The Pool of Darkness* (Opus 26), scored for flute, violin, bassoon, trumpet, cello, and piano. It will be noted that most of Weber's output consists of chamber music. He has, however, composed an *a cappella* choral setting of Rilke's Ninth Sonnet, and a *Concert Aria after Solomon*, Opus 29 (1949), for soprano and orchestra. Among his recent works are a Concerto for piano solo, cello, and wind instruments, Opus 32 (1950), and Symphony on Poems of William Blake, Opus 33 (1952). In 1953 he was at work on a Concerto for violin and orchestra.

Among American composers discussed elsewhere in this book, Walter Piston has made rather frequent use of twelve-tone writing, notably in his First Symphony and in the Partita for violin, viola, and organ. His procedure is to treat the material tonally. Ellis Kohs, Ross Lee Finney, Gerald Strang, Harrison Kerr, Lou Harrison, Virgil Thomson, Leon Kirchner, Roger Sessions, Samuel Barber (in his Piano Sonata), and Aaron Copland (in his Piano Quartet) are others who have in various ways employed twelve-tone techniques.

Finney and Kerr

The case of Ross Lee Finney is exceptionally interesting because it demonstrates how a composer may turn to twelve-tone techniques, not by adopting a doctrinaire attitude, but simply as the consequence of a natural evolution. As stated in an earlier chapter, among the teachers with whom Finney studied in Europe was Alban Berg (in 1931). But at that time Finney reacted violently against the twelve-tone technique because of what seemed to him "its opposition to tonal organization and the functionalism that occurs in music from such tonal design." Nearly twenty years passed before Finney realized that "the twelve-tone technique is not actually in opposition to tonal functionalism but is a technique concerned with chromatic integration." Finney had used a highly chromatic dissonant texture in his Second Sonata for cello and piano, but he was still seeking a method of integration, of structural organization, that would enable him to achieve emotional expression in a contemporary idiom. This he found, almost without being aware of it himself, in the Sixth String Quartet (1950), which turned out to be a work strictly conceived on the basis of the twelve-tone row. Far from being a coldly calculated plan, Finney says that this event came almost as much a surprise to him as to anyone else. As he writes:

> No work that I have ever written has sprung from logic; music springs, I feel sure, from musical ideas and gestures. The real problem, therefore, and the one that concerns me more and more, is to find a *lyric* expression within the bounds of organization that seem to me important.[10]

This would appear to offer at least one explanation for the fact that so many composers are using twelve-tone techniques as a means of integrating and organizing their musical ideas.

[10] From a letter to the author, dated Feb. 22, 1954. Other statements from Finney are from the same source.

Although he was included among "The Eclectics," Harrison Kerr must also be mentioned here because, without being a strict twelve-tone writer, his compositions since 1935 have all been more or less influenced by the twelve-tone technique. The compositions of Kerr in which this influence is most prominent are the String Quartet (1937), the Suite for flute and piano (1940–1941), the Second Symphony in E minor (1943–1945; slow movement), the Second Piano Sonata (1943), and the Violin Concerto (1950–1951). The application of the twelve-tone method is very free in these works, except in the slow movement of the String Quartet. Only rarely and briefly has Kerr used the strict Schoenbergian technique, with the tone-row appearing in all voices, and with inversion and retrograde motion. Kerr, like Finney, feels that the twelve-tone technique is compatible with tonal functionalism.

It is slightly amusing, as well as somewhat disconcerting, to learn that in some circles Kerr is regarded as a rather strict twelve-tone composer, while others have denied that he is a twelve-tone composer at all! It all depends on whether or not one judges by the canon of the strictest orthodoxy. The fact that most twelve-tone practitioners are going in the direction of greater freedom seems to indicate the desirability of revising and liberalizing our conception of twelve-tone writing. In the light of present practice it is difficult to tell, as Kerr confesses, "where ultra-chromaticism leaves off and twelve-tone technique begins." As a first step toward clarification, one should perhaps seek a new terminology.

The term "ultra-chromaticism," employed by some writers, is not entirely satisfactory. It implies a texture but not a structure; it expresses freedom but not form. Ross Lee Finney's term, "chromatic integration," is felicitous and useful. It implies both texture and form. Inherent in the term "integration" are the principles of form, structure, and organization which are indispensable to the work of art. At the same time, the composer is left free to select, within a chromatic texture, the elements and techniques and devices by which he achieves integration.

What has actually happened is that the whole scope of twelve-tone writing has widened immensely in the last ten or fifteen years. On the one hand, the older twelve-tone composers are in many cases becoming more free in the use of that technique, and on the other hand, many composers hitherto not particularly interested in twelve-tone writing have become attracted by it and are using it with increasing frequency and also, in most cases, with considerable freedom. They seem to have accepted Schoenberg's declaration that "composing with twelve tones is not nearly as forbidding and exclusive a method as is popularly believed." And, of course, the more and the more freely it is used by composers of many different tendencies and temperaments, the less forbidding and exclusive it becomes. We can safely say that free twelve-tone writing, call it "chromatic integration" or what you will, is here to stay for a while, and that it should be accepted as "standard practice" by listeners who live in the second half of the twentieth century.

chapter twenty-nine

In the orbit of Broadway

The lyrics, choreography, and music of Broadway musical entertainment have made steady progress—particularly in the last thirty-five years—toward an unmistakably American character. . . .
CECIL SMITH, MUSICAL COMEDY IN AMERICA.

This chapter is concerned with two types of musical entertainment—comic opera and musical comedy—that have Broadway as their symbol if not always as their geographical locus. Musical comedy, indeed, is indigenous to Broadway, but comic opera is not. The latter has a history that long precedes the rise of Broadway as the "Great White Way" of popular entertainment. Comic opera is an imported European product. The greatest names in the annals of comic opera are European: Offenbach, Lecocq, Von Suppé, Johann Strauss, Lehar, Sir Arthur Sullivan. The most celebrated names in musical comedy are unquestionably American: George Gershwin, Jerome Kern, Cole Porter, Richard Rodgers—to mention only the top few. Conversely, many of our most successful composers of comic opera have been European-born, like Herbert, Friml, and Romberg, or European-trained, like De Koven.

The line of demarcation between comic opera and musical comedy has not been rigidly drawn. Comic opera—or light opera, or operetta—is nearer in form and style to traditional opera, except that it employs spoken dialogue and more frivolous plots. Musical comedy is nearer to the "play with music," although it by no means follows that "the play's the thing" in musical comedy. A good libretto can help, of course, but more important are good tunes, sparkling lyrics, lavish costumes, and, naturally, beautiful girls. In the beginning, girls and comedians were the chief attractions. They are still important, but it is a sign of maturity in American popular entertainment that the libretto, the lyrics, the choreography, and the music of our musical comedies have been steadily improving in artistic quality.

Comic opera preceded musical comedy in America. The success of European works in this genre aroused emulation among American composers. A pioneer in this field was Willard Spenser (1852–1933) of Philadelphia, whose two-act comic opera *The Little Tycoon* was produced in that city on January 4, 1886. In subsequent years it was performed many thousands of times all over the country, by both professional and amateur groups. The plot concerns the efforts of a young New Yorker to marry the daughter of wealthy General Knickerbocker against the latter's opposition and preference for an English lord as a son-in-law. When the American suitor presents himself as "The Great Tycoon of Japan," the General falls for the title and grants him his daughter's hand; whereupon the bride and chorus sing, "Yes, I'll Be the Little Tycoon." It was all good clean fun. Spenser wrote several other comic operas, of which the most successful was *The Princess Bonnie* (1894).

A composer from Boston named Woolson Morse (1858–1897) was the next American to make a big impression on the popular musical stage. He had studied painting in Paris but found music more to his liking, though he continued to paint the scenery for his comic operas after becoming a composer (he is said to have composed all his music on a harmonium). Morse turned out *The Merry Monarch* (1890), *Panjandrum* (1893), and *Dr. Syntax* (1894), but his great success was attained with *Wang*, produced in New York in 1891 with De Wolf Hopper in the title role of Wang, the Regent of Siam. In spite of the Oriental setting, which established a pattern for many musical comedies, and which Morse evoked by "loud cymbals plus cacophony," the music was rather colorless and uninspired. Morse continued his exotic musical excursions with *Panjandrum*, with the Philippine Islands for its setting and De Wolf Hopper again as the leading man.

Edgar Stillman Kelley (1857–1944), known as the composer of a *New England Symphony*, a *Gulliver Symphony* and various other symphonic works, was the conductor of a comic-opera company in the 1890s and perhaps for this reason was tempted to try his hand in the popular theater. There is considerable doubt as to whether his operetta *Puritania*, produced in Boston in 1892, comes under the heading of entertainment. It dealt with the Salem witch trials, a subject that seems to appeal to American composers. It ran for upwards of a hundred performances and was not heard again. Another "serious" composer, George Chadwick of "The Boston Group," made an incursion into the popular field with a comic opera titled *Tabasco*, produced in 1894, which has been described as a "hodgepodge" and must inelegantly be termed a flop. These experiments proved that comic opera, though it might be light entertainment, could not be taken lightly by a composer. It was not something to be tossed off between symphonies. It required a solid métier and a special knack, acquired by training and experience.

De Koven and Victor Herbert

Reginald De Koven (1859–1920) made it a point to acquire the special training needed for composing comic operas. He was born in Middletown, Connecticut, and at the age of ten was taken to England, where he graduated from Oxford University in 1879. He then studied composition in Stuttgart, in Frankfort, in Vienna with Genée, and in Paris with Delibes. From these two masters he learned the technique of comic opera, and began to apply his knowledge in *The Begum* (1887) and *Don Quixote* (1889). Meanwhile he had married an American and settled in Chicago. There, on June 9, 1890, he produced the greatest success of his entire career, the romantic comic opera in three acts, *Robin Hood*. It was performed by a company called The Bostonians, who kept it as their chief support for many years. The score contains De Koven's two most enduring songs, "Brown October Ale" and "Oh, Promise Me." The work achieved more than three thousand successive performances and established De Koven's reputation so firmly that he could live on it ever after. Not that he didn't try hard enough to repeat the success of *Robin Hood*. He kept on writing comic operas, turning out a total of twenty, but none even remotely approached the success of that early effort. The work that came nearest to it was *The Highwayman*, produced in New York in 1897 and revived there, with better success, twenty years later. *Rob Roy* was produced in 1894 and *Maid Marion* in 1901, the latter a sequel to *Robin Hood*. De Koven tried his hand at grand opera with *The Canterbury Pilgrims*, libretto by Percy Mackaye, produced in New York on March 7, 1917. He also wrote what he called an American "folk opera," *Rip Van Winkle*, produced in Chicago shortly before he died (January 2, 1920).

De Koven's contemporary, Victor Herbert (1859–1924), far surpassed him in the number and permanence of his successes. Herbert was born in Dublin, Ireland, and received his musical training, primarily as a cellist, in Germany, where he was sent to study from the age of seven. In 1882 he played with the Johann Strauss Orchestra in Vienna, and from 1883 to 1886 was a member of the court orchestra in Stuttgart, where he studied composition with Max Seifritz. In 1886 he married the Viennese singer Thérèse Förster and came to the United States as a cellist at the Metropolitan Opera House. Later he held the same position with the Theodore Thomas Orchestra and the New York Philharmonic Society. From 1898 to 1904 he was conductor of the Pittsburgh Symphony Orchestra and thereafter conducted his own orchestra in New York.

In 1893 Herbert was persuaded to write a comic opera, *Prince Ananias,* for The Bostonians, who produced it in New York the following year. Its reception was sufficiently encouraging for Herbert to feel that he should continue in this path. There followed in rapid succession *The Wizard of the Nile* (1895), *The Serenade* (1897), *The Fortune Teller* (1898), *Babes in Toyland* (1903), *Mlle. Modiste* (1905), *The Red Mill* (1906), *Little Nemo* (1908), *Naughty Marietta* (1910), *Sweethearts* (1913), *The Princess Pat* (1915), *The Century Girl* (1916), *Eileen* (1917), *The Velvet Lady* (1919), and *The Dream Girl* (1924)—the list does not pretend to be complete. This is the most distinguished and most enduringly successful corpus of light opera produced by an American composer—and Victor Herbert may be considered such by virtue of his early identification with the American milieu.

Victor Herbert's mellifluous melodies and skillful orchestrations, united to better-than-average librettos, have kept the best of his light operas alive for many decades. And many of his songs have enjoyed an independent life apart from their theatrical context. *Mlle. Modiste,* produced in New York on December 25, 1905, with Fritzi Scheff in the title role, contains the largest number of hit tunes, with "The Time and the Place and the Girl," "Love Me, Love My Dog," "I Want What I Want When I Want It," and, above all, "Kiss Me Again." *Naughty Marietta,* produced on November 7, 1910, includes "I'm Falling in Love with Someone" and "Ah, Sweet Mystery of Life." *The Red Mill* has proved to be one of Herbert's most enduring works, combining an effective plot, fast action, a picturesque setting, and attractive tunes, such as "The Isle of Our Dreams" and "Because You're You."

Herbert was ambitious to achieve success in the realm of grand opera. His first attempt in this direction, *Natoma*, dealing with an Indian subject, was produced in Philadelphia in 1911 and was given two performances at the Metropolitan Opera House, in New York in February and March of that year, by the Chicago-Philadelphia Opera Company. It was also performed in Chicago and on tour. His second attempt, *Madeleine*, was produced at the Metropolitan Opera House on January 24, 1914. Although Otto Kahn, after the première, declared, "We have at last a real English opera," it received a total of only six performances. The composer died without having obtained more than a *succès d'estime* in the field of serious opera.

John Philip Sousa, the "March King," merits mention in this chapter as the composer of ten comic operas, of which the best-known is *El Capitan*, produced in 1896 with De Wolf Hopper in the title role, a Peruvian viceroy of the sixteenth century who disguises himself as a notorious bandit in order to thicken the plot. The familiar march *El Capitan* appears as a male chorus in the second act, and the last act contains what was once a topical hit, "A Typical Tune of Zanzibar."

Sousa was born in Washington, D.C., in 1854, and died in 1932. After conducting with various theater companies he became conductor of the U.S. Marine Band in 1880. Twelve years later he formed his own famous band, with which he achieved an unprecedented success at home and abroad. He composed over one hundred marches, among them *Semper Fidelis* (1888), *Washington Post March* (1889), *High School Cadets* (1890), and *Stars and Stripes Forever* (1897). His comic operas include, besides *El Capitan, The Bride-Elect, The Charlatan*, and *The Free Land*.

Backgrounds of musical comedy

Before dealing with later composers of comic opera in America, let us trace the antecedents of modern musical comedy in the closing decades of the nineteenth century. It is customary to begin the story of American musical comedy with the production of *The Black Crook* at Niblo's Garden in New York on September 12, 1866. This fabulous production was certainly a huge success and held the stage for more than a quarter of a century; but it was actually a musical extravaganza, which relied for its effect largely upon girls in tights and the flashing of many lovely legs. While girls and legs have continued to be important ingredients of musical comedy, they are not, in the best circles, regarded as the whole show. The fact is that many types of musico-theatrical entertainment went into the making of musical comedy, including old-time minstrelsy, burlesque (in its original meaning of travesty or parody, in the pre-Minsky era), farce, pantomime, extravaganza, and operetta. When *A Gaiety Girl* was produced in New York in 1894, the critic of the *Dramatic Mirror* called it "an indefinable musical and dramatic mélange," containing "sentimental ballads, comic songs, skirt-dancing, Gaiety Girls, society girls, life guards, burlesque, and a quota of melodrama." It was from this sort of indefinable mixture that musical comedy was to emerge.

Since *A Gaiety Girl* was imported from London's Gaiety Theatre, we must credit the British stage with an assist toward the creation of musical comedy. There was much give-and-take between the English and American popular theater in that early period. The American producer Edward E. Rice, who in 1876 had made American theatrical history with his production of the burlesque musical extravaganza *Evangeline* (for which he also wrote the music), followed the lead of *A Gaiety Girl* by producing, in 1897, *The Girl from Paris*, with an imported British company. The music was by Ivan Caryll, a composer of Belgian birth who settled in England and later came to the United States, where he lived as an American citizen from 1911 until his death in 1921. His biggest triumph was with *The Pink Lady*, produced in New York in 1911 and taken on tour throughout the country with immense acclaim. As Earl Derr Biggers wrote: "Everyone should see *The Pink Lady* to discover what a musical comedy should be." Caryll also achieved notable successes with *Oh! Oh! Delphine* (1912) and *Chin Chin* (1914).

Meanwhile, the American vernacular was coming along. In 1898 Edward Rice sponsored the production of an all-Negro musical comedy called *Clorindy, the Origin of the Cakewalk*, with a libretto by Paul Laurence Dunbar and a score by Will Marion Cook (1869–1944). It broke no records, but it was full of fine singing and exploited the ragtime rhythms that were then sweeping the country. People found it novel and exciting and enjoyed such numbers as "Darktown Is Out Tonight" and "That's How the Cakewalk Is Done." Although all-Negro shows have been rare on Broadway, the combination of white and Negro talent has been one of the characteristic features of the American musical stage. As for Will Marion Cook, he deserves to be remembered as one of our best popular composers. Actually, he had a thorough training in music, for he studied at the Oberlin Conservatory, in Berlin with Joachim, and in New York with Dvořák. He wrote the music for several shows that featured the celebrated team of Williams and Walker: *Dahomey* (1902), *Abyssinia* (1906), *Bandanna Land* (1907); and a number of highly successful songs, among them: "I May Be Crazy but I Ain't No Fool," "Mandy Lou," "I'm Comin' Virginia," "Swing Along," and "Rain Song." His stage works, in addition to *Clorindy*, include *Darkeydom* (1912), and an opera, *St. Louis 'ooman.*

The year 1903 saw the production of a musical comedy that, in one form or another, was to keep its hold on the American public for several decades: *The Wizard of Oz,* based on the novel by L. Frank Baum, with music by Paul Tietjens and A. Baldwin Sloane. The original production took place in Chicago, but it soon hit New York, where it owed much of its success to the performances of Fred Stone as the Scarecrow and Dave Montgomery as the Tin Woodman.

At about this time the vernacular took a large stride forward on Broadway through the activities of George M. Cohan (born July 3, 1878), member of a theatrical family that at first appeared as "The Four Cohans." Cohan was a producer, a manager, an actor, a dancer, a singer, a playwright, and a composer of songs. When he starred in *Little Johnny Jones,* in 1904, he featured one of his typical songs, "Yankee Doodle Boy." Following *Forty-five Minutes from Broadway*, produced in 1906 and epitomizing the Broadway spirit, Cohan struck his characteristic flag-waving vein with *George Washington, Jr.* (1906), which featured the patriotic song "The Grand Old Flag." Although conservative critics accused him of being vulgar, cheap, and blatant, Cohan went merrily on his way from one success to another, both with his shows and his songs. Lasting fame came to him when he composed the favorite song of World War I: "Over There." Among his other songs are "I'm a Yankee Doodle Dandy" and "Give My Regards to Broadway." He died in 1942.

Comic opera composers

Going back to the year 1903, mention must be made of the comic opera *The Prince of Pilsen,* if only for the sake of the reputation it acquired rather than for any intrinsic merit. Its composer was Gustave

Luders (1866–1913), who had been born in Germany and who came to the United States in 1885, settling in Chicago, where he met his principal librettist, Frank Pixley. The story of *The Prince of Pilsen,* such as it is, concerns a party of American girls on a tour of Europe who mistake Hans the brewer for the Prince. The ensuing antics are said to have been side-splitting in their day. Luders wrote the music for a whole string of comic operas, among them: *King Dodo, The Grand Mogul,* and *The Sho-Gun* (1904), this last with a libretto by George Ade.

Two other European-born composers may be briefly mentioned here because of the success that they achieved in the Broadway theater. They are Gustave Kerker (1857–1923) and Ludwig Englander (1859–1914); the former came to America at the age of ten, the latter at twenty-three. Kerker's outstanding success was the musical comedy *The Belle of New York,* produced in 1908. Englander made the transition from comic opera to musical comedy in such shows as *The Strollers* and *A Madcap Princess* (1904), the latter based on the best-selling novel, *When Knighthood Was in Flower.*

Much more important in the history of the American musical stage is Rudolf Friml, born in Prague in 1881, trained as a concert pianist, and a pupil of Dvořák in composition. He began in the vein of comic opera or operetta with *The Firefly* (1912), *High Jinks* (1913), and *Katinka* (1915); tried his hand at musical farce with *Tumble In* (1919) and *The Blue Kitten* (1924); and returned triumphantly to his true field of operetta with *Rose Marie* (1924) and *The Vagabond King* (1925). The former contains his best-known tunes, "Indian Love Call" and "Rose Marie I Love You." In 1928 Friml scored another hit with *The Three Musketeers.* Since then he has devoted his time mainly to writing music for films.

Another foreign-born composer who made his mark upon the American musical stage is Sigmund Romberg, born in Hungary in 1887 and originally trained as a construction engineer. Coming to America in 1909, he secured a job as staff composer at the Winter Garden in New York, writing music for *The Passing Show,* a typical (and topical) Broadway revue. He wrote the scores of several musical comedies, including *Follow Me* (1916) and *Over the Top* (1917), but his most congenial field was that of operetta, in which he produced three enduring works: *Maytime* (1917), *Blossom Time* (1921), and *The Student Prince* (1924). This last is his masterpiece, a model comic opera both for its plot and its music. *Blossom Time*, based on a highly fictionized life of Schubert and utilizing some of that composer's melodies, including a theme from *The Unfinished Symphony* and the *Ave Maria*, indulges in a sentimentality that verges on bathos; but this has not diminished its perennial appeal. Romberg obtained another notable success with *The Desert Song* in 1926, followed by *The New Moon* in 1928 and, after a long interruption, *Up in Central Park*, produced in 1945.

Irving Berlin and Jerome Kern

This brings the story of American comic opera more or less up to date, and we must now pick up the thread of musical comedy. The date of December 8, 1914, will serve that purpose as well as any, for on that date Charles Dillingham produced a "syncopated musical show" called *Watch Your Step*, with music and lyrics by Irving Berlin, featuring the dancing of the Castles (Irene and Vernon). Irving Berlin (*recte* Izzy Baline), born in Russia in 1888, was brought to America as an infant and grew up in New York's lower East Side. He got a job as a singing waiter at a place known as "Nigger Mike's" in Chinatown. Thereafter he began an extraordinarily successful career as a song writer, turning out such hits as "Alexander's Ragtime Band," "Everybody's Doin' It," "When that Midnight Choo-Choo Leaves for Alabam," "When My Baby Smiles at Me," "A Pretty Girl Is Like a Melody," "What'll I Do?" "All Alone," "Blue Skies," "Remember," and many others.

In August, 1918, on leave from the Army, Irving Berlin produced a soldier show called *Yip, Yip, Yaphank*, for which he wrote the tunes and the lyrics and which included the hit song, "Oh, How I Hate to Get Up in the Morning." Twenty-four years later this song was heard again in another soldier show put together by Berlin, *This Is the Army*, produced on July 4, 1942, with immense success. This had been originally conceived as an up-to-date version of *Yip, Yip, Yaphank*, but turned out to be something quite different. Its theme song, "This Is the Army, Mr. Jones," quickly captured the nation.

Apart from these two soldier shows, Berlin's most important contributions to American musical comedy were made with *Face the Music* (1932) and *As Thousands Cheer* (1933), both with librettos by Moss Hart and both highly topical in their allusions to the current depression, political affairs, and contemporary celebrities. *Face the Music* had police corruption in New York as the target of its satire, while *As Thousands Cheer* directed its shafts at everything from the White House to the Metropolitan Opera. One sketch was entitled "Franklin D. Roosevelt Inaugurates Tomorrow," and another, labeled "Heat Wave Strikes New York," featured Ethel Waters in a song that included the unsubtle couplet, "She started a heat wave, By making her seat wave."

After the success of these two musical shows, Berlin yielded to the lure of Hollywood and did not do another Broadway musical until *Louisiana Purchase*, produced in 1940. This too exploited the vein of political satire, with Huey Long as its target, but the satire was less pointed and pungent. In 1946 Berlin climaxed his Broadway career with a tremendous success, *Annie Get Your Gun*, featuring Ethel Merman in the role of Annie Oakley, the sharpshooting star of Buffalo Bill's Wild West Show. For this show Berlin wrote some of his most effective songs: "Doin' What Comes Naturally," "Show Business," "You Can't Get a Man with a Gun," and "They Say It's Wonderful."

As a matter of record, it should be added that one of Berlin's patriotic songs, "God Bless America," popularized by Kate Smith on the radio, swept the country in the early 1940s and became ubiquitous for a time. In 1954, Irving Berlin received a special citation of merit from President Eisenhower as the composer of many patriotic songs, especially "God Bless America."

The elaborately lavish type of musical comedy, incorporating features of the revue, is represented by *The Century Girl*, produced in 1916, with music by Victor Herbert and Irving Berlin. The producers of this show, Dillingham and Ziegfeld, tried to duplicate its success with another lavish musical comedy, *Miss 1917*, for which Herbert and Jerome Kern wrote the music. Kern, born in New York in 1885, already had a number of musical comedies to his credit, among them *The Red Petticoat* (1912), which marked the discovery of the West in American musical comedy. This was followed by *90 in the Shade* (1915), with the Philippine Islands as its alleged locale, and *Very Good Eddie* (1915), which established the vogue of the intimate type of musical show written especially for a small theater. Then, in 1917, came *Have a Heart* and *Oh, Boy*, which attempted to introduce "realism" rather than "escapism" into musical comedy. *Leave It to*

Jane (1917) dealt with what purported to be life on an American college campus, a field that was to prove fruitful for the musical stage. During the 1920s Kern wrote the scores for *Sally* (1920) in collaboration with Herbert; in which Marilyn Miller, the darling of the decade, sang "Look For the Silver Lining"; its sequel, *Sunny* (1925); *Stepping Stones* (1923), written for Fred Stone and his dancing family; *Show Boat* (1927); and *Sweet Adeline* (1929). In the 1930s he did the music for *The Cat and the Fiddle* (1931), *Music in the Air* (1932), *Roberta* (1933), and *Very Warm for May* (1939). *Roberta* revealed again the fine melodic gift of Kern in such songs as "Smoke Gets in Your Eyes" and "The Touch of Your Hand." During the last years of his life, Kern wrote mostly for the films.

Show Boat has a special place in the affections of the American public. It was composed on a commission from that vastly enterprising showman, Flo Ziegfeld, at whose theater it was produced on December 27, 1927. Oscar Hammerstein 2d prepared the libretto from Edna Ferber's novel of the same title, and Jerome Kern wrote some of his best songs for the score: "Old Man River," "Only Make Believe," "Can't Help Lovin' that Man," "Why Do I Love You?" "You Are Love," and "My Bill" (for which P. G. Wodehouse wrote the words).

Show Boat tells the story of Cap'n Andy and his theatrical troupe aboard the Mississippi steamer *Cotton Blossom,* with the love interest revolving around the romance of Magnolia, the leading lady, and Gaylord Ravenal, the dashing gambler. The second act brings the couple to the Chicago World's Fair of 1893 and the Trocadero Music Hall. Their daughter Kim turns out to be a successful singer, and as the action ends on board the *Cotton Blossom* in the year 1927, we hear her singing some of the old songs of another day.

There is general agreement that *Show Boat* is a masterpiece of its kind. In the words of Cecil Smith: "No other American piece of its vintage left so large a permanent musical legacy, and certainly no other surpassed it in quality." [1] There is less agreement as to what kind of piece it is. Smith calls it a musical comedy; McSpadden, a musical play; the *Harvard Dictionary of Music,* an operetta; J. T. Howard, hedging somewhat, calls it "almost a folk opera." My own preference is for calling it an operetta in the tradition of American musical comedy; which leaves the matter of nomenclature in the air

[1] Smith, *Musical Comedy in America,* p. 275.

but is fairly satisfactory as description. *Show Boat* received notable revivals in 1932, 1945, and 1952. It was while he was in New York, working on the production of the 1945 revival, that Kern died, on November 11.

In addition to his stage works and film scores, Kern composed an orchestral suite, *Portrait of Mark Twain*, commissioned by André Kostelanetz in 1942, consisting of *Hannibal Days*, *Gorgeous Pilot House*, *Wandering Westward*, and *Twain in His Career*. He also prepared a *Scenario for Orchestra on Themes from Show Boat*, written for the Cleveland Symphony Orchestra in 1941 at the request of Artur Rodzinski.

Youmans, Gershwin, and Porter

Vincent Youmans (1898–1946) was a composer who might have left an even stronger impression than he did on the musical-comedy stage had not illness cut short his career. His masterpiece was *No! No! Nanette*, produced in 1923, which contains those memorable songs, "Tea for Two" and "I Want to Be Happy." The score of *Hit the Deck* (1927) included one of his biggest hits, "Hallelujah." Another lasting success, the balladlike "Without a Song," made its appearance in *Great Day* (1929). In the 1930s he wrote the music for *Smiles*, *Through the Years*, and *Take a Chance*. This last featured two of his most effective songs, "Eadie Was a Lady" (sung by Ethel Merman), and "Rise and Shine" (which brought the frenzy of revivalism to the musical-comedy stage).

George Gershwin (1898–1937), whose background and achievements in the realm of "serious" music are described in Chapter 24, got off to a rather slow start with his first two musical comedies, *La! La! Lucille* (1919) and *Sweet Little Devil* (1924), in which his lack of technical preparation were apparent. He hit his stride with *Lady, Be Good* (1924), *Tip-Toes* (1925), *Oh, Kay* (1926), *Funny Face* (1927), and *Girl Crazy* (1930). With *Strike Up the Band* (1930) he and his brother Ira (who wrote the lyrics for most of his shows) turned to political and social satire that pulled none of its punches. It was hard-hitting, often bitter, very effective, and quite amusing. Gershwin was to continue this vein of satire, though with less propaganda and more humor, in *Of Thee I Sing* (1931), which spoofed the folklore of an American presidential election and its aftermath in the

White House. In 1932 *Of Thee I Sing* was awarded the first Pulitzer Prize ever bestowed for a musical play, as "the original American play performed in New York which shall best represent the educational value and power of the stage." George and Ira Gershwin went on to display once more the satirical power of the musical comedy stage with *Let 'em Eat Cake* (1933). The libretto was by Kaufman and Ryskind, and, as Brooks Atkinson wrote, "Their hatreds have triumphed over their sense of humor." This could scarcely be called musical *comedy*. Gershwin, in any case, was ready to leave the field of musical comedy, for by this time he had established his reputation as a "serious" composer. In the same year (1933) he turned out one more piece in the genre that he had cultivated with such success, *Pardon My English*, an inconsequential affair, and when he returned to the lyric theater it was with a far more ambitious effort, *Porgy and Bess* (1935). The story of that work is told in the chapter "Toward an American Opera."

Cole Porter, whom Cecil Smith calls "the genteel pornographer" of musical comedy, was born in Peru, Indiana, in 1892. He was graduated from Yale in 1913; then, after study at the Harvard Law School, he enrolled at the music school there and finally polished off his musical training at the Schola Cantorum in Paris, where Vincent d'Indy presided over a musico-mystical-aesthetic regime that was almost monkish in its austerity. It was not there that Porter acquired his encyclopedic knowledge of sex, which he displayed to a delighted public in his first complete musical-comedy score, *Fifty Million Frenchmen* (1929), for which he also wrote the sophisticated lyrics (a practice he was to continue in other works). Porter's next show, *The New Yorkers* (1930), was allegedly a "sociological musical satire" (that was a fashion of the 1930s), but it proved to be chiefly a vehicle for Jimmy Durante. Porter, at all events, continued to turn out one show after another. The list includes *The Gay Divorcée* (1932), *Anything Goes* (1934), *Jubilee* (1935), *Red Hot and Blue* (1936), *Leave It to Me* (1938), *Du Barry Was a Lady* (1939), *Panama Hattie* (1940), *Let's Face It* (1941), *Something for the Boys* (1943), *Around the World* (1946; a failure), and *Kiss Me Kate* (1948; a huge success, based on Shakespeare's *The Taming of the Shrew*). This last show included such characteristic Porter songs as "I Hate Men," "Wunderbar," and "So in Love Am I." The songs of Cole Porter are thoroughly idiosyncratic. They have a wide range of expression, from deft parody ("Wunderbar") to erotic feeling ("Night and Day"), and they are less formula-ridden than most Broadway tunes. The highly effective "Begin the Beguine" is a good example of his individual style and dramatic flair.

Rodgers, Hart, and Hammerstein

American musical comedy may be said to have reached maturity in the series of works for which Richard Rodgers wrote the music, at first in literary partnership with Lorenz Hart and later with Oscar Hammerstein 2d.

Richard Rodgers was born in New York City in 1902, the son of a physician. The usual legend of musical precocity is attached to his infancy. In the words of his press agent, "Rodgers showed his unique musical aptitude at an early age . . . he began picking out tunes on the parlor piano at the age of four." Not unique: merely standard procedure for musical geniuses. He attended Columbia University, where he met his librettist, Lorenz Hart, with whom he collaborated in the varsity show of 1918, *Fly With Me.* Rodgers left college at the end of his sophomore year, determined upon winning success in the professional theater. Meanwhile he studied composition at the Institute of Musical Art (now the Juilliard School of Music) and continued to write, in collaboration with Hart, a long series of amateur shows. Professional success seemed very distant, and he was about to accept a job as a salesman for a garment firm in New York. Then, in 1925, the Theatre Guild invited him to write the music for the *Garrick Gaieties,* and he was launched on Broadway.

The first outstanding Rodgers and Hart production was *A Connecticut Yankee* (1927), based on Mark Twain's novel of a Yankee at the court of King Arthur, in which the lyrics combined the archaic and the slangy in a blend that caught the public's fancy. There followed *Present Arms* (1928), glorifying the Marines; *Jumbo* (1935), described by Percy Hammond as "a sane and exciting compound of opera, animal show, folk drama, harlequinade, carnival, circus, extravaganza and spectacle"; *On Your Toes* (1936), remarkable for its realistic ballet, *Slaughter on Tenth Avenue; Babes in Arms* (1937), an apotheosis of youth; and *I'd Rather Be Right* (1937), in which they collaborated with George Kaufman and Moss Hart as librettists in another political satire of the 1930s. More characteristic of the

Rodgers and Hart inspiration were *I Married an Angel* (1938), *Too Many Girls* (1939; comment on college life), and especially *Pal Joey* (1940), based on a series of hard-boiled stories by John O'Hara originally published in *The New Yorker*. Woven into a libretto by O'Hara himself, the story concerns a plausible young heel who climbs to success on the crest of a love affair with a society woman, only to be let down when she grows tired of him. In the course of the show all the clichés and bromides of the entertainment business are cleverly satirized. After collaboration on one more show, *By Jupiter* (1942), which reached no high level of accomplishment, the remarkably productive partnership of Rodgers and Hart was dissolved (Hart died in 1943). They had collaborated on twenty-nine musical shows (nine of which were made into motion pictures) and had written a total of nearly four hundred songs.

A new musical-comedy team was formed when Rodgers began to collaborate with Oscar Hammerstein 2d, initiating a partnership that was to be no less memorable than its predecessor, since it resulted in *Oklahoma!* (1943), *Carousel* (1945), *Allegro* (1947), *South Pacific* (1949), *The King and I* (1951), and *Me and Juliet* (1953).

Oklahoma! was an adaptation of the regional folk play by Lynn Riggs, *Green Grow the Lilacs*, which had been produced by the Theatre Guild in 1931. The musical version started out as *Away We Go* in New Haven, but in Boston it became *Oklahoma!*, and with that title reached the St. James Theatre in New York on March 31, 1943, to remain there for nearly six years. It achieved a total of 2,202 performances, the longest run of any musical show in the history of Broadway. On the road it endeared itself to the whole nation, for it was a fine and friendly show, good-humored, colorful, clean, and clever. It contained such attractive songs as "O What a Beautiful Mornin'," "People Will Say We're in Love," and "The Surrey with the Fringe on Top." But good songs alone did not give *Oklahoma!* its lasting appeal and its historical importance in America's musical theater. Here was a genuinely American musical comedy, different in character and idiom from anything known to Europe, different even from the standard Broadway show. It was original, it was refreshing, and it was gratifying on all counts.

Rodgers and Hammerstein became more conventionally ambitious, perhaps one should say pretentious, in their next two shows. *Carousel* was based on Ferenc Molnar's play *Liliom*, much more adult and complex in its treatment of human character than the average Broadway show. The scene of the play was shifted to New England (instead of Europe), complete with clambake and other local color. The score had some good songs, such as "If I Loved You" and "What's the Use of Wond'rin'?" but Rodgers did not show himself fully equipped to deal with the dramatic exigencies of the play; so that it did not build up to an effective climax. Nevertheless, *Carousel* is a fine example of the mature American musical play, and it has continued to hold the stage with both critical and popular acclaim.

More definitely pretentious was *Allegro*, with a would-be dramatic theme involving the spiritual struggles of a young doctor torn between worldly ambition and noble humanitarianism. Needless to say, he adopts the choice of dedication and self-sacrifice. Staged with many gadgets and elaborate scenic effects, *Allegro* failed to please the public, which found it neither entertaining nor exciting.

Their next production, *South Pacific*, brought Rodgers and Hammerstein into wide favor once more. The libretto, adapted from James Michener's *Tales of the South Pacific*, provided them with a plausible story and an exotic setting for the romance of the American nurse who falls in love with an island planter. The show was a tremendous success. Its array of hit songs included the duet "Some Enchanted Evening," and the hilarious chorus, "There's Nothing Like a Dame."

With *The King and I*, based on the biography *Anna and the King of Siam*, which recounts the experiences of an English girl who was engaged as a teacher for the children of the King of Siam, Rodgers and Hammerstein continued the vein of intelligent, tasteful, clever, and skillful musico-theatrical entertainment by which they had raised American musical comedy to its highest level of achievement.

The German-born composer Kurt Weill, who died in 1950, was responsible for some of the best musical shows produced on Broadway in recent years. His two most notable successes were *Knickerbocker Holiday* (1938), with a libretto by Maxwell Anderson based on Washington Irving's *Father Knickerbocker's History of New York;* and *Lady in the Dark* (1941), for which Moss Hart wrote the book and Ira Gershwin the lyrics. The latter featured Gertrude Lawrence in the role of a successful but unsatisfied magazine editor, Liza Elliott, who seeks the advice of a psychoanalyst to solve her personal problems. Much of the action was concerned with depicting the vivid dream sequences of Liza's subconscious, as she indulges freely in wish-fulfillment. It moved far from the conventional musical-comedy pattern, but by this time it should be clear that anything goes in the American musical theater, provided that the results are effective, as they certainly were in this case.

A few words must be said here about one of the most extraordinary musical productions that ever struck Broadway, Oscar Hammerstein's adaptation of *Carmen,* with the locale changed to North Carolina and an all-Negro cast. Robert Russell Bennett edited and arranged Bizet's score for the production, which opened in 1943 under the sponsorship of Billy Rose and enjoyed a run of 231 performances. Stunningly staged, it proved that opera is welcome on Broadway when it possesses all the attributes of a good show.

American musical comedy, in its more ambitious manifestations, has made a slight approach in the direction of opera. And American opera, in its more popular manifestations, has adopted some of the traits of musical comedy. Some observers believe that at the point where these two tendencies converge, the American opera of the future will emerge. Others believe that opera and the popular theater should go their separate ways, lest the result should be an unsatisfactory hybrid. Whatever may be the final outcome, it is certain that there will be much interchange of influences among the various types of musical theater in America; in whatever happens, the American musical theater will be varied, many-sided, enterprising, and changeful.

chapter thirty

Toward an American opera

The "vernacular" is on the march.
MARK VAN DOREN, INTRODUCTION TO MADE IN AMERICA BY JOHN A. KOUWENHOVEN.

The editor of *Harper's Magazine*, writing in 1859 about the arts in America, concluded that "what is fine in the buildings of the old countries we can borrow; their statues and their pictures we will be able in good time to buy." That was the theory of the fine arts that prevailed in America for many generations: a theory that art imitated or imported from Europe was better than anything we could produce ourselves, and that the best hope for us was to imitate faithfully and borrow extensively. Few people were ready to listen to Emerson when he said: "It is in vain that we look for genius to reiterate its miracles in the old arts; it is its instinct to find beauty and holiness in new and necessary facts, in the field and roadside, in the shop and mill."

During the nineteenth century, composers such as Fry and Bristow tried to create American grand opera by a slavish imitation of the Italian models then in vogue. The choice of an American subject like the legend of Rip Van Winkle did little to mitigate the imitativeness of their music. Toward the end of the century, when the prevailing mode was Wagnerian music drama, Walter Damrosch's setting of *The Scarlet Letter* (1896) was aptly characterized as "the *Nibelungen* of New England." After an excursion into French poetic drama with *Cyrano de Bergerac* (1913), Damrosch many years later turned again to an American subject in *The Man Without a Country*, with a libretto by Arthur Guiterman after the story by Edward Everett Hale, produced at the Metropolitan Opera House on May 2, 1937; but he succeeded only in producing another conventional grand opera made from a European stereotype.

It may be objected that Damrosch, Breslau-born and European-trained, was musically too close to his native Germany to have a feeling for American elements in opera. But the native-born American composers of opera were just as conventional and just as imitative, as proved by the earliest American operas produced at the Metropolitan Opera House: *The Pipe of Desire* (1910) by Frederick S. Converse; *Mona* (1912) by Horatio Parker; *Cleopatra's Night* (1920) by Henry Hadley. Resounding public successes were achieved by the two operas of Deems Taylor, *The King's Henchman* (February 17, 1927), with a libretto by Edna St. Vincent Millay, and *Peter Ibbetson* (February 7, 1931), after the novel by Du Maurier (previously dramatized by Constance Collier). The former received fourteen performances in three seasons, the latter sixteen performances in four seasons. These records have never been surpassed by any other American composer whose works have been given at the Metropolitan Opera House.

Howard Hanson's opera *Merry Mount*, produced on February 10, 1934, achieved a total of nine performances. Based on a fictional account of happenings at Thomas Morton's colony at Merry Mount, the plot of the opera deals with the downfall of a Puritan pastor who, in attempting to save the soul of a beautiful sinner, loses his own and brings death to both himself and her. Olin Downes described the music as "at times conventional and noisily effective," and added: "It displays neither originality nor any special aptitude for the theater." This remark would apply to most American operas produced at the Metropolitan. Deems Taylor's operas displayed some aptitude for the theater—which accounts for their relative success—but they completely lacked originality—which may account for their subsequent neglect.

With dogged persistance, but with even more dismal results, the Metropolitan, on January 11, 1947, produced another American opera, *The Warrior*, music by Bernard Rogers, libretto (dealing with the story of Samson and Delilah) by Norman Corwin, a prominent radio dramatist. In spite of the reputation of both composer and librettist, the work was a flat failure: dull, stilted, and lifeless. Rogers, a composer with an excellent technical background, revealed, like so many of his predecessors, a lack of feeling for dramatic values in the musical theater. Corwin, who could certainly write effectively when he chose, became self-conscious and pretentious, as so many people do when they approach opera from the outside.

There is general agreement that opera should be good theater. It should also be good music; and theater and music should be thoroughly integrated, so that neither overbalances the other and each contributes structurally to the effectiveness of the whole. Many American operas have been condemned for not being good theater. On the other hand, when a particularly effective dramatic work has been set to music, the complaint is sometimes made that the music is more or less superfluous. Something of the sort occurred with Louis Gruenberg's operatic version of Eugene O'Neill's drama, *Emperor Jones*, produced at the Metropolitan Opera House on January 7, 1933. The play deals with a Negro Pullman porter who goes to an island in the West Indies and makes himself "Emperor" there. The mysterious and primitive forces of the island prey on his mind, and he becomes demented, while the terrors of the jungle close in around him. As Olin Downes remarked after the première, Gruenberg showed dramatic instinct and intuition for the theater, and it is this which makes his work a landmark among American operas produced at the Metropolitan. He utilized a modern orchestral idiom and drew on the dramatic resources of Afro-American rhythms and songs, as in the spiritual "Standin' in the Need of Prayer," and in the writing for chorus. Moreover, he had the wisdom to choose a subject dealing with recognizable human beings in the world of today, involved in a comprehensible dramatic situation charged with inherent psychological tensions. Critics may question the extent to which the music enhances the intrinsic dramatic power of the play, and the degree of merit that the score possesses as music. But the significance of *Emperor Jones* is that here at last an American opera appeared that was both musical and dramatic.

Gruenberg has written two other operas. The first was *Jack and the Beanstalk*, to a libretto by John Erskine, subtitled "A Fairy Opera for the Childlike," which was produced by the Juilliard School of Music in New York on November 19, 1931. The other is an opera written especially for radio performance: *Green Mansions*, after the novel by W. H. Hudson, produced by the Columbia Broadcasting System on September 17, 1937. Radio and television have played a role of considerable importance in the development of American opera. In fact, these media, together with the university workshops and the Broadway theater, have made possible the emergence of an American tradition in the lyric theater.

It may not be irrelevant to note that Gruenberg had worked for some time with the stylization of Afro-American material, as in *The Daniel Jazz* and *The Creation* (both for high voice and eight solo instruments), and *Jazz Suite* for orchestra. *Emperor Jones* was a continuation of this vein. The point is of interest because, when we reach the first indisputable masterpiece of the American lyric theater, Gershwin's *Porgy and Bess,* we find that it resulted from a similar interest in Afro-American material, combined with the cultivation of so-called "symphonic jazz" and the background of the Broadway musical show.

Gershwin's *Porgy and Bess*

Somewhere around 1929 Gershwin read the novel called *Porgy,* by Du Bose Heyward, dealing with Negro life in Charleston, South Carolina. He was attracted by the subject, saw at once its dramatic, human, and musical possibilities, and wished to make an opera of it. When the novel was made into a play, Gershwin was closer to getting the libretto that he wanted. The libretto was finally fashioned by Heyward, with the composer's brother Ira collaborating on the lyrics (as he had done for many of George's Broadway shows). The summer of 1934 was spent by Gershwin on Folly Island, about ten miles from Charleston, absorbing the music and the folkways of the Negroes. He attended services of the Gullah Negroes on nearby islands, and took part in their "shouting." He noted the cries of the street vendors in Charleston, with their fascinating melodic inflections.

Gershwin spent nine months orchestrating *Porgy and Bess.* To Rouben Mamoulian he wrote: "It is really a tremendous task scoring three hours of music." Gershwin was not doing another musical "show," he was writing a full-sized opera, and he took the job very seriously. Partly because the work was cut (by about one-fourth) for its original production, and partly because of Gershwin's use of some tunes in the Broadway manner, the notion prevailed that *Porgy and Bess* was just a super musical play rather than a "real opera." But as Alexander Steinert remarked: "It belongs in an opera house, played by a large orchestra, for which it was written." *Porgy and Bess* may not be orthodox grand opera, but it *is* opera, and some day it may be given in the large opera houses of America, as it has been given, with tremendous acclaim, in those of Europe.

It is customary to speak of *Porgy and Bess* as a folk opera. But neither this description nor any other appears on the title page of the published score. Since Gershwin does not use folk tunes to any appreciable extent (there are some traditional street cries in the score), there is no need to call his work a folk opera. *Porgy and Bess* is simply an American opera in three acts and nine scenes. If anyone doubts its operatic proportions, let it be observed that the manuscript score contains 700 pages of closely written music.

The action takes place in Catfish Row, a Negro tenement section on the Charleston water front, and on the nearby island of Kittiwah. The time is the recent past. The central figures are Porgy, a crippled Negro beggar who rides in a small cart drawn by a goat, and Bess, who comes to live with him after her man Crown, a powerful stevedore, commits murder and flees to Kittiwah Island. A character named Sportin' Life, who peddles dope, tries to induce Bess to accompany him to New York. She refuses and remains with Porgy. In the second act the people of Catfish Row are mourning for Robbins, the man killed by Crown in a crap game. But this is also a day of gaiety, for there is to be a picnic on Kittiwah Island. Bess is persuaded to go along, though her heart tells her she should stay with Porgy. As she is about to leave the island after the picnic, she hears the voice of Crown, who has been hiding and waiting to find her alone. She tries to resist him, but in the end yields, for he still attracts her strongly; and he keeps her on the island when the others leave.

After a few days Bess returns to Catfish Row, ill and delirious. Recovering, she confesses to Porgy that she has agreed to meet Crown and go away with him. His domination over her is strong, but at heart she fears him. Her real love, as she now admits, is for Porgy, and as the latter sings "You got Porgy, you got a man," he promises to protect her from Crown. Following a terrific storm, Crown suddenly returns. In the third act he reappears, attempts to enter the room where Bess is, and is intercepted and strangled to death by Porgy. When the police come to investigate, they receive no help in identifying the killer. But Porgy is taken to jail as a witness. Meanwhile, Sportin' Life again tempts Bess with "happy dust" and the lure of New York. This time, feeling alone and defeated, she succumbs and goes off with Sportin' Life. When Porgy comes back and learns that Bess has gone to New York, he calls for his goat and cart, and sets off to find her.

There are many goods tunes and memorable songs in *Porgy and Bess*. The fact that some of these songs are couched in the Broadway idiom does not invalidate their status as operatic material. We have only to think how close to the spirit of Italian popular song are many of the tunes in the operas of Verdi. Gershwin was writing an American opera, dealing with a certain segment of the American folk, and his use of the popular-song idiom, integrated into the action and the score, was entirely appropriate. The songs in *Porgy and Bess* are so excellent, and so much a part of America's music, that it is fitting to review them briefly.

"Summertime" is the lovely lullaby sung in the opening scene by Clara, wife of the fisherman Jake (who is later lost in the storm). "Gone, Gone, Gone" is a mourning-spiritual for the death of Robbins, with the call-and-response pattern faithfully reflected in solo and chorus, and with the typical melodic inflections of Negro singing. "My Man's Gone Now" is Serena's lament for her murdered husband, remarkable for its expressive use of syncopation and for the wailing glissando chorus, accompanied by a chromatic crescendo in the orchestra. "It Takes a Long Pull to Get There," sung by Jake and the fishermen, is a stylization of the Negro work song in call-and-response form, with the characteristic grunt at the end of the chorus as the men pull at the net: *to get there, huh!* It shows also the blend of work song and spiritual, as the singer first says, "I'm going out to de Blackfish banks," and at the end, "But I'll anchor in de Promise' Land."

A tune in Gershwin's best popular style is "I Got Plenty o' Nuthin'!" Porgy's song of insouciance, when he is feeling carefree and happy with love. A complete contrast is the "Buzzard Song," sung by Porgy when a great bird flies low over Catfish Row, bringing an ill omen. This is a truly dramatic aria (including high notes) both in itself and in the function it performs in the opera, marking a transition to tragedy. "Bess, You Is My Woman Now" is the love duet sung by Porgy and Bess just before she goes to the picnic, and it is in the operatic tradition. Then comes the irresistible syncopation of "Oh, I Can't Sit Down" sung by the people as they leave for the picnic, while The Charleston Orphans' Band plays on stage.

At the picnic the Negroes are dancing and making music on mouth organs, combs, bones, washboard, and washtub. Sportin' Life sings his big humorous song, "It Ain't Necessarily So" ("De t'ings dat yo' li'ble to read in de Bible"), with effective help from the chorus. When Crown appears, he and Bess sing the duet, "What You Want wid Bess," in which she expresses her loyalty to Porgy while Crown asserts his domination over her.

The cries of the street vendors—the Strawberry Woman, the Honey Man, and the Crab Man—are the folklore gems of the opera. Another spiritual, "Oh, Doctor Jesus," sung while the people are praying during the storm, over the continuous humming of men and women, reveals again the degree of skill achieved by Gershwin in the stylization of Afro-American material. Sportin' Life's "temptation song," "There's a Boat Dat's Leavin' Soon for New York," marked *Tempo di Blues*, is the product of a top-notch Broadway song writer. Finally there are the last two songs of Porgy, the first when he is seeking for Bess after his return from jail, "Bess, Oh Where's My Bess?" and the second when he starts for New York in his goat cart, in a mood of exaltation that approaches the religious fervor of the spirituals: "Oh Lawd, I'm On My Way."

Porgy and Bess was first performed at the Colonial Theatre in Boston on September 30, 1935, under the auspices of the Theatre Guild, directed by Rouben Mamoulian and conducted by Alexander Smallens. On October 10 it was brought to the Alvin Theatre in New York, where it ran for sixteen weeks, followed by a road tour of three months. It was revived in 1938 and in 1942, and was taken on a tour of Europe in 1952 with an all-Negro cast that performed it with immense success in the leading capitals. A revival at the New York City Center in 1953 was tremendously successful. *Porgy and Bess* has proved its vitality as a work for the theater, its validity as a work of art, and its stature as an American opera.

In the American folk vein

American composers, since the nineteenth century, had tried to present American subjects in operatic form, but perhaps they had tried too hard to emulate the style of "grand opera," with results that were imitative, stilted, artificial, and pretentious. Gershwin, adapting the operatic tradition to familiar material and to his own background as a composer, avoided these pitfalls. An American subject was not the open sesame to operatic success; but, other factors being equal, it could facilitate the path to that integrity of form and style, that integration of content and expression, which make for successful works of art. Douglas Moore, a composer who had frequently occupied himself with the American scene, found in a story by Stephen Vincent Benét a bit of American folklore and American humor, as well as some deeper reflection of the American spirit, which appealed to him strongly as operatic material. This story was *The Devil and Daniel Webster.*

Made into a one-act opera, with the libretto by Benét himself, and the music (scored for large orchestra) by Douglas Moore, *The Devil and Daniel Webster* was produced by the American Lyric Theatre in New York on May 18, 1939, with Fritz Reiner conducting. The author's synopsis of the plot is as follows:

> "The Devil and Daniel Webster" is laid in New Hampshire, in the forties. It begins with a country festival—the neighbors of Cross Corners celebrating the marriage of Jabez and Mary Stone. The Stones were always poor, but Jabez has prospered amazingly and they're talking of running him for governor. Everything goes well at first—Daniel Webster, the great New England hero, appears as a guest, and is given a real New Hampshire welcome. But there is another guest, too, and an unexpected one—a Boston lawyer named Scratch, who carries a black collecting box under his arm. His appearance terrifies Jabez, the song he sings horrifies the neighbors and when a lost soul, in the form of a moth, flies out of the collecting box, panic ensues. The neighbors realize that Jabez has sold his soul to the devil, denounce him, and flee. Left alone with Mary, Jabez tells how he came to make his hideous bargain. They appeal to Daniel Webster who promises to help them. But the devil—Mr. Scratch—is an excellent lawyer too. When Webster demands a trial for his client, Scratch summons from the Pit a jury of famous American traitors and renegades and a hanging judge who presided at the Salem witch-trials. It is a jury of damned souls, and Webster seems about to lose, not only the case but his own soul's salvation, when, by his powers of oratory, he finally turns the tables on Scratch and rescues Jabez. The neighbors rush in to drive the Devil out of New Hampshire, and the case ends with pie breakfast, as it should.[1]

In *The Devil and Daniel Webster*, the composer follows the tradition of *opéra comique* in having spoken dialogue alternating with the

[1] From the score of *The Devil and Daniel Webster*, for the opera by Douglas Moore, copyright 1938, 1939, by Stephen Vincent Benét; published by Boosey and Hawkes, New York.

singing. He also employs the device known technically as "melodrama," in which the spoken dialogue has an orchestral accompaniment. There are "set numbers," such as the duet between Mary and Jabez, the latter's narrative in which he tells of his deal with the devil, and Scratch's ballad, "Young William Was a Thriving Boy," with its refrain, "Listen to my doleful tale." This is a sort of parody of the doleful popular ballad, but done in traditional style, so that it is half mocking and half serious. Then there is Daniel Webster's song, "I've Got a Ram, Goliath," in the manner of the tall-tale, bragging, frontier ballad. Webster's stirring oration in the trial scene is in the form of melodrama, spoken rhythmically over a musical accompaniment. The whole trial scene is extremely effective, and the opera sweeps quickly to the boisterous climax in which the devil is driven out of New Hampshire, while Daniel Webster, joining the general chorus, sings again of his ram Goliath.

Musically, Moore has made the most of the local atmosphere, with evocation of fiddle tunes for New England country-dances, and has been faithful to the setting as well as to the folklike spirit of Benét's story. His score, straightforward and vivacious, is also lyrical when it should be and dramatic when it needs to be. These qualities have earned it frequent performances throughout the United States, by universities and music schools, at Chautauqua, at the Worcester Festival (1941), and by opera companies in San Francisco, Mobile, Cincinnati, St. Louis, and New York. In the summer of 1953 *The Devil and Daniel Webster* was selected for a long-run performance (July 18 to August 30) at Old Sturbridge Village in Massachusetts, a restored replica of a New England village as it appeared in the early nineteenth century. It was planned to make this performance a permanent feature of the Sturbridge Festival each summer. This is an encouraging sign that American opera is not only being written and produced, but that it is also finding its place in the cultural life of the nation.

Douglas Moore has composed three other stage works. One is the operetta *The Headless Horseman*, written especially for performance by schools and amateur groups (produced in 1937). Another is his musical setting of Philip Barry's play *White Wings*, produced by the Hartt Opera Guild in Hartford, Connecticut, on February 9, 1949. This is a whimsically humorous fantasy in which Moore provides a lot of singable tunes and has some fun caricaturing both nineteenth-century grand opera and American popular idioms. The third is a tragic opera in three acts and four scenes, titled *Giants in the Earth*, libretto by Arnold Sundgaard after the novel by O. E. Rolvaag, first performed by the Columbia University Opera Workshop in New York, from March 28 to April 7, 1951. The action of this opera takes place in Dakota Territory in 1873 and revolves around the spiritual conflicts of a pioneer wife who rebels against the harsh and godless world into which she has been thrust and into which her baby is born. The somber story matches the starkness of the setting. The action is possibly too circumscribed, the plot somewhat spare, for maximum theatrical effectiveness. Moore has written a masterly score, perhaps more notable for the instrumental than the vocal writing.

One often finds that the term "opera" is avoided in connection with American musical works for the stage. Thus, the two chamber operas of Ernst Bacon, *A Tree on the Plains* (1943) and *A Drumlin Legend* (1949), are described as "music-plays." Nevertheless, they are operas: there is no need to avoid the term. Both of these operas have an American setting and incorporate American musical idioms. In recent years a number of other American composers have turned to American themes and settings for their operas. Among them are Otto Luening with his four-act opera *Evangeline* (1948), Vittorio Giannini with his radio opera *Blennerhassett* (1939), Max Wald with *A Provincial Episode* (which has for its setting a small Middle Western town in the early 1890s), Lukas Foss with *The Jumping Frog of Calaveras County*, after the story by Mark Twain, and Virgil Thomson with *The Mother of Us All.*

The team of Thomson and Stein

Virgil Thomson deserves a special niche in the halls of American opera. His contributions to the American lyric theater are unique and memorable. On February 8, 1934, an enterprising organization called "The Friends and Enemies of Modern Music," produced in Hartford, Connecticut, Thomson's opera, *Four Saints in Three Acts,* with libretto by Gertrude Stein. It was sung by an all-Negro cast and created a sensation. In the same month it was brought to New York for a run of several weeks at the Forty-fourth Street Theatre. Broadcast performances in 1942 and 1947, and a highly successful revival at the Broadway Theatre in New York in April, 1952, demonstrated that the appeal of this work was the result not merely of novelty but also of its intrinsic musical merit and stagecraft. Taken on its own terms—as it must be taken—*Four Saints in Three Acts* is a lovely work. No one familiar with the writings of Gertrude Stein and the compositions of Virgil Thomson need be told that this is not a conventional opera. The composer has summarized the intent of the work in these words:

> Please do not try to construe the words of this opera literally or to seek in it any abstruse symbolism. If, by means of the poet's liberties with logic and the composer's constant use of the simplest elements in our musical vernacular, something is here evoked of the child-like gaiety and mystical strength of lives devoted in common to a non-materialistic end, the authors will consider their message to have been communicated.[2]

Thomson's delightful music greatly facilitates our participation in the unlogical landscape of words and images created by Stein's untrammeled text. The score incorporates elements from a variety of religious traditions, ranging from Gregorian chant to American folk hymnody (Thomson is thoroughly familiar with the shape-note tradition of the fasola folk). Thomson sets English words to music with marvelous clarity, precision, and fidelity to the spoken language. In spite of the deceptive simplicity of his musical idiom, his score is full of subtleties and of imaginative touches that reveal a high order of creative inspiration. *Four Saints in Three Acts* is an opera completely *sui generis*, and a masterpiece in originality and invention.

Another product of the Stein-Thomson collaboration was the opera *The Mother of Us All*, commissioned by the Alice M. Ditson Fund of Columbia University and produced at the Brander Matthews Theatre on May 7, 1947. The central figure of this opera is Susan B. Anthony, pioneer leader in the struggle for woman suffrage in the nineteenth century. The cast includes many other historical figures, several of them anachronistic: Daniel Webster, Anthony Comstock, Ulysses S. Grant, John Adams, Lillian Russell, Andrew Johnson, Thaddeus Stevens—also Virgil T(homson) and "G. S." (none other than Gertrude Stein, of course). To explain everything that happens in this opera would take too long. Daniel Webster pursues (discreetly) Angel More; John Adams courts Constance Fletcher, but

[2] Introducing a broadcast performance in 1942. Quoted in *The New York Times*.

cannot kneel to propose because he is an Adams; General Grant is stubborn; Jo the Loiterer marries Indiana Elliot and then changes names with her; and in the midst of it all, Susan B. Anthony carries on her Cause, and in the last scene but one the chorus sings:

> Susan B. Anthony was very successful we are very grateful to Susan B. Anthony because she was so successful, she worked for the votes for women and she worked for the votes for colored men and she was so successful they wrote the word male into the constitution of the United States of America, dear Susan B. Anthony.[3]

In the last scene the cast gathers around the statue of Susan B. and her comrades in the suffrage fight. At the end, Susan B.'s voice is suddenly heard from the statue and attempts to expound what it is all about (previously she had said, "I am not puzzled but it is very puzzling"). Her final message is summed up in these words: "Life is strife, I was a martyr all my life not to what I won but to what was done." If this is still puzzling, try listening to the music.

The same qualities of clarity and felicity in the setting of English are evident in this score, equally manifested in the treatment of recitative and in the arias and choruses. The musical materials utilized by Thomson are heterogeneous: revival hymnody, gospel tunes *à la* Salvation Army band style, modal melodies, popular-song idiom, and so forth. He employs the calculated cliché and the deliberate commonplace with an amazing effect of freshness. The whole score has style, and it is unmistakably the Thomson style. It is also unmistakably American.

Bearing in mind Paul Bekker's dictum that "opera is a musical work based on the genius of the language," we must concede real importance to the musical stage works of Virgil Thomson, not only for their originality and ingenuity, but above all for their fidelity to the American vernacular, both in music and in speech.

In 1947 Thomson told an interviewer that he might sometime set to music Gertrude Stein's "opera" *Doctor Faustus Lights the Lights* (1938). As he remarked to the reporter: "She's changed the story a good deal. In her version, Faust is always playing with dynamos and the lights are always going out." It is to be hoped that this opera will eventually be composed, for we should have an American

[3] Stein, *Last Operas and Plays*, p. 83. Used by permission of Carl Van Vechten, Gertrude Stein's literary executor, and of Rinehart & Company, Inc., publishers.

Faust on the operatic stage, after doing with importations for so many years.

Blitzstein and Kurt Weill

The proletarian novel of the 1930s had its counterpart in the opera of "social significance" with its themes of the class struggle and social justice. Two such operas were written by Marc Blitzstein (born in Philadelphia, 1905), a pupil of Scalero, Boulanger, and Schoenberg. The first of these was *The Cradle Will Rock*, first performed in a concert version in New York in 1937 (with piano) and ten years later brought to the stage at the City Center in New York with the original orchestration. The second was *No for an Answer*, produced at the Mecca Auditorium in New York on January 5, 1941. Regardless of the ideological content, these operas had the merit of coming to grips with problems of our times and in the musical language of our times. Moreover, they revealed a flair for the theater that was further manifested in a later, nonpolitical work: Blitzstein's operatic version of Lillian Hellman's play *The Little Foxes*, produced in 1949 at the New York City Center under the title of *Regina*. Again, the setting is familiar and unremote: a small town in Alabama in the year 1900. But the play is essentially a study of character, and this has imposed a difficult task on the composer. In coping with it, Blitzstein demonstrates a genuine musico-dramatic talent. The extent of his absolute success has been questioned, but *Regina* at this writing still holds the stage: a situation not yet so common with American opera that it may go unrecorded.

Notable contributions to the American musical theater were made by the German-born composer Kurt Weill (1900–1950), who began to be interested in American themes long before he settled in the United States and became a citizen of this country. From the outset he was attracted by American jazz idioms, which he used in his opera *Rise and Fall of the City of Mahagonny* (1930). The scene of this satiric opera is laid in Alabama; it has been called a modern morality play because of its exposé of corruption and hypocrisy.

In 1933 Weill left Germany and two years later settled in the United States, where his fame as the composer of *The Threepenny Opera* had preceded him. In this work, based on John Gay's *The Beggar's Opera,* Weill had also used elements of American popular music, including the blues. After his arrival in the United States, Weill devoted himself to writing chiefly for the popular musical stage, though he wrote the scores for at least two works that transcended the level of popular entertainment: *Street Scene* (Elmer Rice), and *Lost in the Stars.* The former is a play of humble people in New York City, the latter a musical tragedy with a libretto by Maxwell Anderson, based on the novel by Alan Paton, *Cry, the Beloved Country*, dealing with racial tensions in South Africa. In this work, Weill was exploring one of the possible paths toward the creation of American tragic opera: the elevation of the musical show, with its songs and choruses, to what Brooks Atkinson calls a "high plane of spiritual existence." *Lost in the Stars* proved that it could be done even on Broadway.

Kurt Weill also composed an American "folk opera," *Down in the Valley* (based on the familar folk song of that name), written especially for performance by schools and amateur groups.

In the summer of 1952, Weill's *The Threepenny Opera,* in an English version and adaptation by Marc Blitzstein, received a concert performance at Brandeis University. In the Blitzstein version, the locale of the work is New York in the 1870s, and the lyrics are translated into American slang.[4] As hard-hitting satire in the vernacular, this eighteenth-century comic opera with a modern twist retains its lusty vitality, its rough vigor, and its mordant wit.

The operas of Menotti

In 1937 the opera department of the Curtis Institute of Music in Philadelphia produced a one-act *opera buffa* by a young composer named Gian-Carlo Menotti. The work was entitled *Amelia Goes to the Ball* and revealed an exceptional flair for the musical theater. The little work was later performed in New York, and on March 3, 1938, it reached the stage of the Metropolitan Opera House, where its reception confirmed the appearance of a new talent in the American lyric theater.

Menotti came to the United States in 1928 from his native city of Milan, Italy, where he was born on July 7, 1911. From his boyhood in Milan he had thoroughly absorbed the tradition of Italian opera,

[4] In the revival presented at the Theater de Lys in New York in March, 1954, Blitzstein changed the locale again—back to England.

and after completing his musical training at the Curtis Institute he was ready to adapt his skills and his intuition to the field of opera in his American environment. He conceived his own operatic plots and wrote the librettos himself. He started off rather conventionally with *Amelia al Ballo* (it was originally written in Italian), but became somewhat more venturesome with the comic opera *The Old Maid and the Thief*, commissioned by the National Broadcasting Company for radio performance in 1939 (it later proved equally successful on television). He switched to tragedy, rather less successfully, with *The Island God* (one act), produced at the Metropolitan in 1942. A few years later he was commissioned to write an opera by the Alice M. Ditson Fund of Columbia University. The result was a work that made him famous: the musical tragedy in two acts titled *The Medium*, produced at the Brander Matthews Theatre on May 8, 1946.

Revised and restaged, *The Medium* was presented by the Ballet Society at the Heckscher Theatre in New York from February 18 to 20, 1947. Within a few months it broke into Broadway, with a run that began on May 1 at the Ethel Barrymore Theatre. Thereafter it enjoyed continuous success, with many performances in America and Europe, and a film version made under the composer's direction.

There are five characters, one of whom is a mute, in *The Medium*. The action takes place in the parlor of Madame Flora, an unscrupulous medium with a violent temper, a daughter named Monica, and a mute servant named Toby, an orphan whom she has taken into her household. He manipulates the machinery that sets the spiritualistic apparatus in motion, while Monica does the sound effects (voices of the dear departed). Monica is a lonely and imaginative girl who indulges in fairy-tale fantasies with Toby, who dresses himself in fantastic attire with pieces of colored silk and gaudy ornaments belonging to Madame Flora (who is called "Baba"). During a séance Baba suddenly feels a hand at her throat. She is terrified and abruptly dismisses her clients. Becoming panic-stricken and hysterical, she tries to get Toby to confess that he is the culprit. Since she can get nothing out of him, she beats him in a fit of fury. Finally Toby, in terror, hides behind the curtain of the puppet theater in the parlor. Baba takes out a revolver, and as the curtain moves, she shoots, killing Toby, who falls headlong into the room. As Baba kneels by his body, she hoarsely whispers, "Was it you? Was it you?" And the curtain falls very slowly.

The acting and singing of Marie Powers as Madame Flora contributed much to the success of this two-act musical thriller. But it can stand on its own as a taut and suspenseful psychological drama. The gay tenderness of Monica's songs in her make-believe scenes contrasts with the painful sentimentality of the séance and the brutal realism of Baba's disintegration under the influence of fear, remorse, and alcohol. Her long monologue, in which she alternately cajoles and threatens Toby, is an example of Menotti's dramatic writing at its most powerful.

Menotti adhered to tragedy in his next work, *The Consul*, a musical drama in three acts which received its première at the Schubert Theatre in Philadelphia on March 1, 1950 and began its Broadway run at the Ethel Barrymore Theatre on March 15, 1950. Nothing is more eloquent of Menotti's success than the fact that with his operas one takes a Broadway run for granted. The action of *The Consul* takes place in a large European city and the time is the present. The principal characters are John Sorel and his wife Magda. The scene alternates between the shabby apartment of the Sorels and the office of an unspecified Consulate. John Sorel is a patriot, a friend of freedom and therefore an enemy of those who have the power in his country. He and his wife are trying to obtain visas so that they can escape to a free nation. Sorel, pursued by the secret police, is forced to go into hiding. Meanwhile Magda joins the crowd of persistent, frustrated people who haunt the Consulate seeking visas. The Consul himself never appears and is too busy to see anyone. Magda's urgency and anguish are of no avail against the solid wall of indifference and routine.

In the second act, a month later, Magda is at home, her baby dying, and receives word that John is hiding in the mountains near the border. The secret police come to the apartment and attempt to force Magda into revealing the names of her husband's fellow patriots. In act three, Magda is at the Consulate again, though she is now almost hopeless. Her mother and her baby have died. John, appearing at the Consulate just after Magda has left, is taken off by the secret police. Alone in the apartment, Magda turns on the gas in the stove. As she dies, she has a vision of her husband, her mother, and the people in the Consulate, swirling wildly around her.

There can be no question about the theatrical effectiveness of *The Consul*. That can now be taken for granted in the works of Menotti.

He knows all the tricks of the trade and can apply them with unfailing craftsmanship. The opening of the first act, with a phonograph playing a sentimental French song backstage while John Sorel, injured, stumbles into the room and is greeted by a frantic Magda, is but one of many clever devices in the score. The work is musically resourceful, skillfully orchestrated, employing dissonant harmony that gives it a modern texture, while the melodies often preserve the facile contours of conventional operatic style. The treatment of the recitative, always a difficult matter in English opera, is one of the most satisfactory features of *The Consul.* Performances of *The Consul* in London and Vienna in 1951 confirmed its European success.

Another distinction came to Menotti when he was commissioned by the National Broadcasting Company to write the first opera designed especially for television production. This was *Amahl and the Night Visitors,* a short work, which was produced on Christmas Eve, 1951, by NBC-TV. This opera was suggested by Hieronymus Bosch's painting "The Adoration of the Magi." A crippled shepherd boy sees a star shining brightly in the night sky and excitedly tells his mother about it. She reproves him for "imagining things." He goes to bed, and soon the Three Kings arrive, bearing gifts for a newborn child. While the Kings sleep, the mother, wishing to help her crippled son, attempts to steal some of the gold but is discovered by a servant. When the Kings offer to let her keep the gold, since the newborn child does not really need it, she becomes remorseful. So that he also may give a gift, the boy offers his crutch. He then finds himself miraculously healed and accompanies the Three Kings on their journey.

Amahl and the Night Visitors is a chamber opera, melodious and deftly orchestrated. As in his other stage works, Menotti wrote the libretto himself. And, as in his other works for the theater, he uses the conventional devices of opera. Menotti has transplanted the conventions of European opera to America, but he has used them with a freedom and flexibility, and with a sense of contemporary values and needs that has given them a new impact and a new significance. His music is derivative, showing the influence of Puccini, Verdi, Moussorgsky, Debussy, Stravinsky, Wolf-Ferrari, Richard Strauss, Prokofieff, and others. His effects are often superficial and contrived rather than genuinely imaginative or inventive. That he is the most successful living American composer of opera is an objective fact. He has proved to many Americans, to whom the heritage of opera is not a birthright, as it was to Menotti in Milan, that opera can be good theater and that it can deal effectively both with imaginative subjects and with the burning issues of our time. The future must reveal the ultimate scope and value of his contribution toward the emergence of an indigenous American opera.

Bernstein and Schuman

Leonard Bernstein, who was mentioned in an earlier chapter as cultivating both popular and "serious" types of music, has combined elements of both in his short satirical opera, *Trouble in Tahiti,* first performed at Brandeis University and later on television (1952). As the composer points out, in this work there is no "plot" in the ordinary sense and very little "action." It presents a psychological situation, and it is essential that every single word sung or spoken by the actors be clearly heard. The principal characters are Dinah, an American suburban wife in her early thirties (mezzo-soprano), and Sam, her husband, a successful businessman (bass baritone). There is nothing unusual about this couple. They are supposed to be typical members of any American suburban community. Their marital relationship provides neither of them with the emotional satisfaction that they are seeking. Their attempt to talk things over ends only in frustration. Finally they decide to go to the movies together, although it is only to see a picture, called *Trouble in Tahiti,* which Dinah has already seen and disliked. The movie, with its "Super Silver Screen," at least offers them ready-made magic with which to escape from their own troubles.

Throughout the action, which takes place in a single day, there is a running comment by The Trio, "a Greek Chorus born of the radio commercial" (soprano, tenor, baritone), which "sings generally in a whispering, breathy pianissimo which comes over the amplifying system as crooning. . . . The Trio is refined and sophisticated in the high-priced dance-band tradition. They . . . *must never stop smiling*" (from the composer's directions in the score, published by G. Schirmer). The score employs a wide variety of popular idioms, from "scat" to the blues. It is original, extremely clever, and effective.

When William Schuman reached the age of forty, he had many important compositions to his credit, but not a single opera. He decided to write one. His subject was quickly chosen: baseball. Schuman had always loved baseball, and what could be more American? He decided to build his opera around that immortal classic of baseball,

"Casey at the Bat," by Ernest L. Thayer, which tells how the mighty Casey, in his hour of expected triumph, suddenly strikes out. He got Jeremy Gury to write a libretto (Gury also added two stanzas to Thayer's poem), and set to work. The result was the one-act opera *The Mighty Casey*, produced in Hartford, Connecticut, by the Julius Hartt Opera Guild, on May 4, 1953.

The action of *The Mighty Casey* takes place in Mudville, U.S.A., in the not too distant past. The opera is divided into three scenes. In the first, various characters are introduced, including the heroes of baseball, who are acclaimed in an "Abner Doubleday Song" (named for the inventor of the game). In the second scene the fateful game is going on, while the Watchman recites the lines of "Casey at the Bat" as he sits on the apron of the stage. In the third scene, following the catastrophe (which is lamented in a requiemlike chorus), Casey's ignominious strike-out is turned into a motive of rejoicing by his girl friend Merry, who can now have him all to herself instead of sharing him with a big-league ball club. And a little boy named Charlie still thinks that Casey is a hero.

In addition to those mentioned, the cast includes the usual quota of baseball players, three umpires, and the manager of the Mudville team, who at one point tells the umpire (in song), "I'm Fed to the Teeth." Other numbers include a teen-agers' chorus, "Case on Casey"; "Peanuts, Popcorn, Soda, Crackerjack"; "You're Doing Fine, Kid" (the catcher addressing the pitcher in a pep talk); "Oh, Somewhere in this Favored Land" (chorus following the strike-out); and "A Man" (what Merry wants), the aria sung by Casey's girl friend, who thinks that a husband is more important than baseball.

In Schuman's score, baseball is very close to Broadway. It inevitably brings up the perennial question: where does musical comedy end and opera begin? But there are many kinds of opera, and as long as we are shaping the tradition of American opera with new materials and new concepts, the field may as well be left wide open. In *The Mighty Casey*, Schuman takes a zestful swing at the American vernacular. Time will tell whether or not he has made a hit.

William Schuman has already decided on the subject of his next opera. It will be based on Theodore Dreiser's novel *An American Tragedy*. Comic or tragic, the vernacular in American opera marches on!

chapter thirty-one

Composer from Connecticut

The future of music may not lie with music itself, but rather . . . in the way it makes itself a part with the finer things that humanity does and dreams of.

CHARLES E. IVES, MUSIC AND ITS FUTURE.

In the year 1894 Antonin Dvořák, distinguished composer from Bohemia, was teaching in New York and urging the creation of an American "national" movement in music based on the use of Negro and Indian melodies. Edward MacDowell, "a glorious young figure" (so Hamlin Garland saw him), wearing a derby hat and a curled mustache, walked in Boston Common musing upon Arthurian legends and Celtic lore. Horatio Parker, erudite, fastidious, Munich-trained, fresh from the triumph of his cantata *Hora Novissima*, had just assumed his duties as professor of music at Yale University. A twenty-year-old student from Danbury went up to New Haven and matriculated in the class of '98 at Yale. His name was Charles Edward Ives.*

Young Ives was a musician, the son of a band master and music teacher in Danbury, Connecticut, where he was born on October 20, 1874. The senior Ives had an inquiring mind and an open ear. He brought up his children mainly on Bach and Stephen Foster. Conventional listening habits were not encouraged in the Ives household. When Charles was ten, his father had him sing "Swanee River" in the key of E flat major and play the accompaniment in the key of C major, in order, he said, "to stretch our ears." George Ives, the father, was a true spiritual descendant of Billings and of Benjamin Franklin: self-reliant, independent, inventive, and ingenious. He engaged in various acoustical experiments, including the investigation of

* While this book was in press, word was received of the death of Charles Ives, on May 19, 1954.

quarter tones, for which purpose he constructed a device consisting of twenty-four violin strings stretched over a wooden frame.

Receiving music lessons from his father beginning at the age of five, Charles Ives learned to play several instruments, including the organ, and from the age of twelve was employed as organist in a local church. From his father he also learned harmony, counterpoint, and fugue. He began to compose at an early age, and when he was fifteen the town band performed a piece of his "suggesting a Steve Foster tune, while over it the old farmers fiddled a barn dance with all its jigs, gallops and reels." At twenty he composed a *Song for Harvest Season*, for voice, cornet, trombone, and organ pedal—*each in a different key!*

This was the musical "baggage" that Charles Ives brought to Yale in 1894. At that time not even the most advanced European composers had begun to experiment with polytonality (the simultaneous use of different tonalities, as in Stravinsky's famous bitonal chord—C major and F sharp major—in *Petrouchka*, dating from 1911). No wonder that Parker, with whom Ives studied composition at Yale, was disconcerted and annoyed. "Ives," he testily asked, "must you hog all the keys?" Thenceforth the daring young man from Danbury kept his musical heresies to himself and satisfied his teacher by turning out an impressive batch of "correct" compositions. Perhaps the discipline was good for him. At any rate, no one could claim, later, that he did not know how to write music, that is, music "according to the rules."

After graduating from Yale, Ives had to decide whether to make music a career or an avocation. It was clear to him that he had no interest in writing the conventional music that found ready acceptance with publishers and performers and public. If he depended on music as a profession he would undoubtedly face a rough road, beset by frustration. In order to be creatively independent he decided to make himself financially independent. He entered the world of business, specializing in the field of insurance. After working in this field for several years, he organized in 1909 the firm of Ives & Myrick, which became very successful. He remained with this firm until 1930, when ill-health forced his retirement. He did his composing in the evenings, on week ends, on holidays and vacations. Often, absorbed in his creative work, he stayed up until two or three in the morning. His wife—Harmony Twitchell, whom he married in 1908—gladly renounced an active social life so that her husband could devote all his leisure to his chosen avocation.

Toward a "substantial" art

Ives himself never felt that his business career was a handicap to him as an artist. On the contrary, he felt that it was of positive value to him in every way, and not merely a matter of "expediency" (a word that he detests). It is extremely revealing, both of the man and his music, to hear what he had to say on this subject, as told to his friend Henry Bellamann:

> My business experience revealed life to me in many aspects that I might otherwise have missed. In it one sees tragedy, nobility, meanness, high aims, low aims, brave hopes, faint hopes, great ideals, no ideals, and one is able to watch these work inevitable destiny. And it has seemed to me that the finer sides of these traits were not only in the majority but in the ascendancy. I have seen men fight honorably and to a finish, solely for a matter of conviction or of principle—and where expediency, probable loss of business, prestige, or position had no part and threats no effect. It is my impression that there is more open-mindedness and willingness to examine carefully the premises underlying a new or unfamiliar thing, before condemning it, in the world of business than in the world of music. It is not even uncommon in business intercourse to sense a reflection of a philosophy—a depth of something fine—akin to a strong beauty in art. To assume that business is a material process, and only that, is to undervalue the average mind and heart. To an insurance man there *is* an "average man" and he is humanity. I have experienced a great fullness of life in business. The fabric of existence weaves itself whole. You cannot set an art off in the corner and hope for it to have vitality, reality and substance. There can be nothing "*exclusive*" about a substantial art. It comes directly out of the heart of experience of life and thinking about life and living life. My work in music helped my business and my work in business helped my music.[1]

This declaration of faith reveals, among other things, that Ives has pursued the ideal of a *nonexclusive* and *substantial* art, possessing vitality, reality, and substance. In his artistic philosophy, Ives opposes

[1] *Musical Quarterly*, XIX, 1 (Jan. 1933), 47.

"substance" to "manner," and gives a higher value to the former. He equates substance with reality, quality, spirit, as against "the lower value of form, quantity, or manner." And he continues:

> Of these terms, "substance" seems to us the most cogent and comprehensive for the higher, and "manner" for the under-value. Substance in a human-art-quality suggests the body of a conviction which has its birth in the spiritual consciousness, whose youth is nourished in the moral consciousness, and whose maturity as a result of all this growth is then represented in a mental image.[2]

As an illustration of his thesis, Ives uses a comparison between Emerson and Poe. The former, he says, seems to be almost wholly "substance" and the latter "manner."

> The measure in artistic satisfaction of Poe's "manner" is equal to the measure of spiritual satisfaction in Emerson's "substance." The total value of each man is high, but Emerson's is higher than Poe's because "substance" is higher than "manner"—because "substance" leans toward optimism, and "manner" pessimism.

Ives takes his stand with Emerson: that is an important fact to remember about him.

Ives has written a great deal about the philosophy of art, the nature of beauty, the problems of musical expression. He evidently enjoys being a homespun philosopher. By a sort of spiritual anachronism, he has preserved much of the soaring speculativeness of the Concord Transcendentalists. But as a shrewd Connecticut Yankee he keeps at least one foot on the earth. He admits that "if one tries to reduce art to philosophy" one inevitably ends by going around in a circle. And then he adds—this is a typical Ivesian touch—"But personally, we prefer to go around in a circle than around in a parallelepipedon, for it seems cleaner and perhaps freer from mathematics. . . ." It is important also to remember that Ives has a sense of humor.

It is not our purpose to expound in detail the artistic philosophy of Ives. A few pointers toward the spiritual "climate" of his music are all that we propose to extract. We have learned something of what he means by "substance," and that he considers "substance" more important than "manner." That is because he believes substance is related to character while manner is not. On the subject of expression,

[2] From *Essays before a Sonata.*

he has this to say: "The humblest composer will not find true humility in aiming low—he must never be timid or afraid of trying to express that which he feels is far above his power to express. . . ." Ives himself has often stretched the limits of musical expression to the utmost; and it is the listener who needs to be bold and adventurous in attempting to follow him. For, as Ives writes: "Beauty in music is too often confused with something that lets the ears lie back in an easy chair. Many sounds that we are used to, do not bother us, and for that reason, we are inclined to call them beautiful." Ives remarks that familiar sounds, like drugs, can be habit-forming.

The historical perspective

Today, in the second half of the twentieth century, many sounds that might have bothered us or our parents thirty or forty years ago, no longer annoy us, or annoy us less, because the ear gradually becomes accustomed to unusual combinations of sound. We have become fully accustomed to polytonal music, and more or less accustomed to atonal music. It takes a tremendous dissonance to startle us now. This chronological factor is central to our discussion of Ives's music, especially when we attempt to place it in its historical sequence. Ives, as we have seen, was far ahead of his time in that he employed tonal, harmonic, and rhythmic combinations that did not come into general use until much later. Had his music been performed immediately or soon after it was composed, it would have appeared, in most cases, as something startlingly "new" and would presumably have created as much of a furore as did the music of Schoenberg and Stravinsky in Europe. But the music of Ives did not synchronize with the musical development of the United States. When we were finally ready for his music, he was an old man, and many of his innovations were "old hat." It is a tribute to his vitality and originality, to the "substantial" quality of his music, that so much of it appeared as new as it did, after such a disconcerting time lag in its performance. Let us glance at the record.

Ives's Second Symphony, completed in 1902, did not receive its first performance until 1951, when it was played by the New York Philharmonic-Symphony under the direction of Leonard Bernstein. His Third Symphony, completed in 1911, was performed for the first time by the New York Little Symphony, Lou Harrison conducting, on April 5, 1945. The Fourth Symphony, composed between 1910 and 1916, has never been performed in its entirety. The second movement of this symphony was played at a concert of the Pro Musica Society in New York on January 29, 1927, under the direction of Eugene Goossens. The second Piano Sonata, begun in 1904 and finished in 1915, received its first complete public performance when John Kirkpatrick played it in Town Hall, New York City, on January 20, 1939. Not until 1947, when he was awarded a Pulitzer Prize for his Third Symphony, did Charles Ives approach the status of a well-known figure in American music. With the advent, some two years later, of the long-playing phonograph record, much of his music began to be recorded, and through this medium to reach a receptive audience. In 1945 Ives was elected a member of the National Institute of Arts and Letters. He was then seventy-one years old and had never heard any of his compositions performed by a full orchestra.

It might be claimed that Ives made this long neglect inevitable when he cut himself off from active participation in the musical life of the country, as well as when he wrote music that was mostly too "difficult" for the musicians and the hearers of his time. It could be argued that he chose isolation instead of having it thrust upon him. The matter might be settled by saying that he was following his destiny. However we look at it, the most significant fact is that the music of Charles Ives has entered, albeit belatedly, the main stream of America's music. Charged with vitality and substance, it flows along in the stream of enduring things that move toward the future.

However modern it may be in "manner," the "substance" of Ives's music has its sources in the past—not so much the past as history but the past as a continuing tradition, the past surviving in the present, as it does, for instance, in folklore. We can take almost the whole body of American folk and popular music, as we have traced it from the early psalmody and hymnody of New England, through the camp-meeting songs and revival spirituals, the blackface minstrel tunes, the melodies of Stephen Foster, the fiddle tunes and barn dances, the village church choirs, the patriotic songs and ragtime—and we can feel that all this has been made into the substance of Ives's music, not imitated but assimilated, used as a musical heritage belonging to him by birthright. Thanks to his early background, to the decisive influences of his formative years, and to his utter independence of conventional musical standards, Charles Ives, first and alone among American composers, was able to discern and to utilize the truly idiosyncratic and germinal elements of our folk and popular music.

This music, as we know, possesses intrinsic traits—melodic, harmonic, and rhythmic—that do not conform to the norms of European art music. These include such features as "incorrect" harmonic progressions, irregular rhythms, asymmetrical melodies, improvised embellishments, and deviations from standard pitch. Most composers and arrangers altered or discarded these traits in order to make the music conform to the academic tradition in which they had been trained; thus they destroyed or distorted all that was most vital and characteristic in the folk and popular traditions. Ives, on the contrary, by seizing precisely on the most unconventional features of folk and popular music—unconventional, that is, by academic standards—was able to create an entirely new and powerful medium of musical expression, which is at once personal and more than personal. It is personal because only he could have created it; and it is more than personal because it incorporates a vital tradition that is the cultural expression of a human collectivity through numerous generations.

Formative experiences

While his contemporaries in Boston were absorbing Brahms and Wagner, Ives was absorbing the musical experiences provided by the New England village in which he grew to manhood: the concerts of the village band, the singing of the village choir, the barn dances, the camp meetings, the circus parades. The musical impressions he received were lasting and fecund. In after years he recalled the unusual effects obtained when the village band was divided into several groups placed in and around the main square:

> The main group in the bandstand at the center usually played the main themes, while the others, from the neighboring roofs and verandahs, played the variations, refrains, and so forth. The piece remembered was a kind of paraphrase of *Jerusalem the Golden,* a rather elaborate tone-poem for those days. The bandmaster told of a man who, living near the variations, insisted that they were the real music and [that] it was more beautiful to hear the hymn come sifting through them than the other way around. Others, walking around the square, were surprised at the different and interesting effects they got as they changed position. It was said also that many

thought the music lost in effect when the piece was played by the band all together, though, I think, the town vote was about even. The writer remembers, as a deep impression, the echo parts from the roofs played by a chorus of violins and voices.[3]

Ives has always been keenly sensitive to the qualities of sound, and to the conditions that affect this quality, such as the factor of *distance*. As he points out: "A brass band playing *pianissimo* across the street is a different-sounding thing from the same band, playing the same piece *forte*, a block or so away." The *volume* of sound that the listener hears will be approximately the same, but the quality will be different. The sound of distant church bells has fascinated Ives, as it did Thoreau, who loved to listen to the Concord church bell over Walden Pond. "A horn over a lake," writes Ives, "gives a quality of sound and feeling that it is hard to produce in any other way." For the understanding of Ives's music, it is valuable to retain this reference to "sound *and* feeling," for Ives is equally interested in both. Few composers have ever attached more significance to the sheer quality of sound in music, but this does not imply a doctrine of "sound for sound's sake." Sound as a medium of expression is what Ives seeks.

It would be misleading to think of Ives as belonging to the "folklore" school of composers. He stands as far from Dvořák as he does from MacDowell. There is nothing to indicate, either in his music or in his writings, that he has any particular interest in folklore as such; in the sense, let us say, that John Powell and Vaughan Williams are interested in folklore. Folk music is for him simply one source, among many others, of material that can be utilized to create an expressive musical language. It is also a means, when creatively utilized, of renovating the idiom of art music and injecting into it new vigor. In his search for vigor and vitality, Ives does not shun vulgarity. A circus band is as valid for him as a church organ. A gospel hymn may be as inspiring as a symphony. He does not limit himself. He does not exclude. What is of value to him in the tradition of European art music he takes—and fuses it with American folk and popular traditions. He assimilates and transforms disparate elements; his art is heterogeneous, and only his creative genius gives it unity.

Ives employs polytonality, multiple cross-rhythms of great complexity, extreme dissonance, tone-clusters (chords made up of minor

[3] "Music and Its Future," *New Music Quarterly.*

and major seconds), quarter tones and other fractional intervals, wide melodic skips, asymmetrical rhythmic patterns, off-beat rhythms emphasized by dissonance, jazz effects, and other devices and procedures that were new when he used them though later incorporated into much of modern music. He arrived at these procedures independently, because he was not familiar with the "advanced" European music of his time. Besides, as already stated, some of his innovations preceded those of Schoenberg and Stravinsky in Europe. If it is true, as Stravinsky claims, that the composer's task is to "invent" music, then Ives will go down in musical history as one of the most inventive composers of modern times. But it is also necessary to observe that Ives, when it suits his expressive needs, can write with the utmost simplicity. Coming to his music so late, as we do, we sometimes have to make more allowance for his simplicity than for his complexity.

The symphonies of Ives

The Second Symphony, for example, evokes, as Burrill Phillips remarks, "in gentle and mostly lyrical language, a world long vanished. It is a world in which leisure and individuality and strength of mind had not become boisterous and shrill and psychotic. . . . The harmonic language throughout is of course dominated by the 19th century, but it is in the style of the parlor organ and the 19th-century park bandstand, not the European concert hall or opera house." This "aesthetic of the commonplace" kept Ives from uttering pretentious banalities, as did so many of his American contemporaries.

Ives composed the Second Symphony between 1897 and 1901, except for part of the last movement, which dates from 1889. The composer describes this part as "suggesting a Steve Foster tune, while over it the old farmers fiddled a barn dance with all its jigs, gallops, and reels." This symphony is in five movements: Andante moderato, Allegro, Adagio cantabile, Lento maestoso, Allegro molto vivace. It is scored for large orchestra and takes about thirty-five minutes to perform. The juxtaposition of two slow movements is characteristic of Ives; actually, because of the proportion and balance between these two movements, there is no trace of formal incongruity. It is also characteristic that Ives makes no marked attempt to exploit orchestral color in this work: he is more interested in texture than in color. In the first movement the scoring is almost entirely for strings, with only brief passages for horns and bassoons; and near the end an embellished restatement of the main theme is given to the oboe: [4]

In the last movement Ives introduces snatches of familiar American songs—"Camptown Races," "Turkey in the Straw," "Columbia, the Gem of the Ocean"—a procedure that he has followed in other scores also. Often he sets such interpolated songs in different keys, but here he does not employ polytonality.

In the same year (1901) that he completed his Second Symphony, Ives began to compose his Third Symphony, which he finished in 1904 except for some revision in 1911. The Third Symphony is considerably shorter than the Second (it requires about seventeen minutes to perform) and is scored for a small orchestra: flute, oboe, clarinet in B flat, bassoon, two horns in F, trombone, strings, and bells (ad libitum). It is in three movements: Andante maestoso, Allegro, Largo. Concluding with a slow movement is typical of Ives. The bells (or chimes) are heard in the last two measures of the work, "as distant church bells," marked with a *decrescendo* sign from *ppp* to *ppppp*—an example of Ives's insistence on dynamic nuances that verge on the impossible. The bells are heard as triads of B minor and G sharp minor, floating above the chords of B flat major and F major in the strings. This is the only touch of polytonality in the symphony.

The first and third movements are devotional in character, utilizing material originally written for the Presbyterian church service, as well as themes from familiar hymns. In the first movement there is a section, marked Adagio cantabile, based on the hymn tune "O, What a Friend We Have in Jesus." There is also a reminiscence of that old-time revival hymn, "There is a Fountain Filled With Blood." Another well-known hymn, "Just As I Am Without One Plea," figures prominently as a main theme in the third movement, treated contrapuntally with a subject derived from material in the first movement.

The contrasting middle movement, in binary form (A-B-A), has

[4] Charles E. Ives, Second Symphony, used by permission of the copyright owners. Copyright 1951 by Southern Music Publishing Company, Inc., New York.

for its principal theme an attractive and rhythmically flexible melody of folklike flavor: [5]

The middle section of this movement consists of one of those marching rhythms that are perhaps associated with memories of the band led by the composer's father.

Though its texture is fairly complex, and there are some rapidly shifting rhythms in the last movement, the Third Symphony presents no untoward difficulty for the listener. It is a work of quiet charm, mostly meditative in mood, devoid of sensational effects, appealing by its integrity and restrained eloquence, by its "substance" rather than its "manner." It sums up in symphonic form the deep-rooted tradition of American hymnody, from which our major musical impulse sprang for upwards of three centuries; and it stands, to borrow a phrase of William Carlos Williams, as a classic "in the American grain."

Ives's Fourth Symphony, composed between 1910 and 1916, has not, at this writing, been performed in its entirety. The second movement, as previously mentioned, was performed in New York in 1927. Slonimsky describes it as "employing polymetrical notation, ad libitum instrumental passages, counterpoint of two orchestral units, and the freest use of dissonance within essentially simple tonality." This work is therefore one of Ives's most "advanced" compositions and for that reason may have to wait decades before receiving adequate recognition.

From 1911 to 1916 Ives worked on a projected *Universe Symphony*, intended as "a presentation and contemplation in tones, rather than in music (as such), of the mysterious creation of the earth and firmament, the evolution of all life in nature, in humanity to the divine." He completed only the Prelude to this symphony, and left part of one movement unfinished. The attempted distinction between

[5] Copyright 1947 by Arrow Music Press, Inc., New York. Used by permission of the copyright owners.

"tones" and "music" *as such*—perhaps akin to the distinction between substance and manner?—indicates a tendency toward mysticism in Ives, a tendency that has always been present, though counterbalanced by his sense of humor and his feeling for reality. In the Second Piano Sonata, as we shall observe later, we find this tendency to transcend the limitations of music and to attain through tones to the realm of pure contemplation.

New England Impressionist

A good case could be made for considering Charles Ives as a regional composer of New England. He represents both a grass-roots regionalism, drawn from his rural environment, and an intellectual or cultivated regionalism, identifying itself with the spiritual achievements of the finest New England minds at their best moment. This latter aspect finds its fullest expression in the Second or *Concord Sonata* for piano, evoking the choice spirits of Concord in its golden decades: Emerson, the Alcotts, Hawthorne, Thoreau. Other works deal with various aspects of the New England scene, in both its historical and its natural settings.

The First Piano Sonata (composed mostly in 1902) was described by the composer as "in a way a kind of impression, remembrance, and reflection of the country life in some of the Connecticut villages in the 1880s and 1890s." It evokes such home-town scenes as the school baseball game, the farmers' barn dance on a winter's night, the "quicksteps" of the town band, a touch of ragtime, and echoes of old hymn tunes. It is in five movements, of which two are *scherzi*.

The First Orchestral Set (1903–1914), subtitled *Three Places in New England* and sometimes referred to as *New England Symphony*, consists of three tone-pictures: "The Boston Common," "Putnam's Camp," and "The Housatonic at Stockbridge." This last piece takes its name from a poem by Robert Underwood Johnson, parts of which are printed with the score. The last lines quoted are "Let me thy companion be/By fall and shallow to the adventurous sea." In a letter to Alfred Frankenstein, the composer's wife wrote as follows regarding his intentions in this piece:

> This grand old river is one of nature's masterpieces and has been an inspiring friend to Mr. Ives from his boyhood days. The music would reflect—at least he hopes it does—the moving river, its land-

> scapes and elm trees, on its way to the adventurous sea. From the beginning of the score until the sea is near, it was, in a way, intended that the upper strings, muted, be heard rather subconsciously as a kind of distant background of an autumn sky and mists seen through the trees and over a river valley.[6]

Here we have sheer musical impressionism: a term that will define Ives's prevailing mode as well as any and better than most. If one *must* tag him, let it be with the label of "New England Impressionist."

The Second Orchestral Set (1912–1915) contains three more New England sketches or impressions: "Elegy," "The Rockstrewn Hills Join in the People's Outdoor Meeting," and "From Hanover Square North–at the End of a Tragic Day, the Voice of the People Again Arose."

Another set of orchestral pieces, titled *Holidays* (1909–1913), evokes scenes of national rather than regional scope; yet their vividness owes much perhaps to the observation of local color, which makes the impressions concrete rather than generalized. The four holidays are "Washington's Birthday," "Decoration Day," "Fourth of July," and "Thanksgiving."

In his setting of Psalm 67 for mixed chorus *a cappella*, Ives created a modern expression of early New England psalmody, combining elements of the old fuguing tune with a bitonal texture (women's voices in D major, men's voices in G minor).

Ives's chamber music includes several works that are evocative of New England rural scenes. Among these is the Second Sonata for violin and piano (1903–1910), of which the three movements are titled, respectively, "Autumn," "In the Barn," and "The Revival." The Fourth Sonata for violin and piano (1914) bears the subtitle *Children's Day at the Camp Meeting;* it uses the revival hymn "Shall We Gather at the River," and conveys a lively impression of what happens when the children get out of hand.

Miscellaneous works and songs

While regionalism is unquestionably a fundamental trait of Ives's creative character, it does not encompass the entire extent of his output. Many of his compositions have no local connotations. Among

[6] Quoted by permission of Alfred Frankenstein.

these are the *Tone Roads* for orchestra (1911–1919); *Lincoln—the Great Commoner*, a setting of Edwin Markham's poem, for chorus and orchestra (1912); *General William Booth Enters into Heaven*, after the poem by Vachel Lindsay, for chorus, or solo voice, with brass band (1914); *On the Antipodes*, chorus with two pianos, organ, and string orchestra (1915–1923); *Aeschylus and Socrates*, chorus with string orchestra or quartet (1922); *The Unanswered Question* ("A Cosmic Landscape") for trumpet, four flutes, treble woodwind, and strings (1908); *Hallowe'en* for string quartet and piano (1911); *Over the Pavements* for clarinet, piccolo, bassoon, trumpet, piano, drum, and trombones (1906–1913); Second String Quartet (1911–1913); and numerous songs for voice and piano. A work that has local connotations, but not connected with New England, is the impressionistic tone poem for orchestra, *Central Park in the Dark* (1906).

The Second String Quartet has been aptly called a modern *quodlibet* (from the Latin, "what you please"). A *quodlibet* is a piece of music characterized by the quotation of well-known tunes (and texts, in a vocal composition), combined in an incongruous manner, usually with humorous intent. Ives describes this work as "String Quartet for four men—who converse, discuss, argue (politics), fight, shake hands, shut-up, then walk up the mountainside to view the firmament." Its three movements are titled, respectively, "Discussions," "Arguments," and "The Call of the Mountains." It is in the first and second movements that most of the quotations occur. One hears snatches of "Columbia, the Gem of the Ocean," and of such Civil War tunes as "Dixie" and "Marching Through Georgia." Later there are bits of familiar hymn tunes, like "Nearer, My God, to Thee," and excerpts from famous symphonies: Beethoven's Ninth, Brahms's Second, and Tchaikovsky's *Pathétique*.

Throughout these two movements Ives has a lot of verbal as well as musical fun. He gives the second violin the name of "Rollo" and makes him the scapegoat for characteristic gibes at the genteel tradition (it is significant that Ives's most damning adjective is said to be "nice"). He writes sweetly sentimental passages for Rollo, marking them Andante emasculata and, in parentheses, "Pretty tune, Ladies." When the music gets difficult, Ives writes in the margin, "Too hard to play—so *it just can't* be good music, Rollo." Finally, he throws a sop to Rollo with the words "Join in again, Professor, all in the key of C. You can do that nice and pretty." At the end of the second movement, the argument winds up violently, and the performers are directed to play *con fistiswatto.*

In the final movement the mood becomes serious. The men have had enough of discussion and argument. In a spirit of cosmic contemplation they heed "The Call of the Mountain" and commune serenely with Nature.

In 1922 Ives published *A Book of 114 Songs* in a privately printed edition, with a preface saying, among other things, "I have not written a book at all—I have merely cleaned house." Most of the songs were composed in the period between 1895 and 1901, but the earliest dates from 1888, and the latest from 1921. As indicated by the composer's quip about cleaning house, there is no attempt at selectivity or orderly arrangement in this volume. Anything goes. The songs range in mood from sentimentality to satire, from bathos to burlesque, from nostalgia to caricature. The best of them are art songs of marked originality and expressivity, each of which creates and projects a definite mood or emotion in a musical idiom that is unmistakably individual. In them we find many anticipations of modern musical devices, such as polytonality ("The Children's Hour," 1901), atonality produced by chords of fourths and fifths ("The Cage," 1906), extreme dissonance ("A Song to German Words," 1899), off-rhythms ("Walking Song," 1902), and ragtime effects ("The Circus Band," 1894).

It is necessary to stress the immense variety of mood and style in the songs of Ives. Tenderness prevails in such lyrics as "Two Little Flowers" and "Cradle Song." In "Charlie Rutledge" we have a roughhewn Western ballad of rousing dramatic effect. "The Greatest Man," in which a boy gets to thinking about his "pa," is good, homespun human stuff. And for a sustained poetic expression we may turn to a song like "The White Gulls," with its typical Ivesian harmonic texture.

Later collections of Ives's songs made selected items from the 1922 volume more readily available; and smaller collections of new songs, the latest composed in 1927, were also brought out by various publishers. An album of recorded songs issued by the Concert Hall Society contains a representative selection from 1894 to 1921. The songs of

Charles Ives are a vital and enduring contribution to art song in America.

The "Concord" Sonata

In the years 1909 and 1910 Ives composed the greater portion of one of his most important works, the Second Pianoforte Sonata, subtitled *Concord, Mass., 1840–1860.* The last movement was completed in 1915. The sonata consists of four movements: "Emerson," "Hawthorne," "The Alcotts," "Thoreau." John Kirkpatrick, the American pianist who first overcame the tremendous difficulties of this work, has called it "an immense four-movement impressionist symphony for piano." It is indeed of symphonic proportions, and we are not surprised to learn that the first movement is based on an uncompleted score of a concerto for piano and orchestra, while the third movement uses material taken from an orchestral overture titled *Orchard House.* The first edition of the *Concord Sonata* was privately printed in the fall of 1919 and appeared together with six *Essays before a Sonata* written by the composer. The volume bore the following dedication: "These prefatory essays were written by the composer for those who can't stand his music—and the music for those who can't stand his essays; to those who can't stand either, the whole is respectfully dedicated." Summarizing the intent of the sonata, Ives wrote:

> The whole is an attempt to present one person's impression of the spirit of transcendentalism that is associated in the minds of many with Concord, Mass., of over half a century ago. This is undertaken in impressionistic pictures of Emerson and Thoreau, a sketch of the Alcotts, and a Scherzo supposed to reflect the lighter quality which is often found in the fantastic side of Hawthorne. The first and last movements do not aim to give any programs of the life or of any particular work of either Emerson or Thoreau but rather composite pictures or impressions.[7]

In the foregoing passage, Ives appears as a self-proclaimed impressionist.

[7] This and other quotations from Ives in the remainder of this chapter are from *Essays before a Sonata* and from the composer's notes for the Second Pianoforte Sonata (2d ed.). Copyright 1947 by Arrow Music Press, Inc., New York. Used by permission of the copyright owner.

Ives sees Emerson as "America's deepest explorer of the spiritual immensities." From the prefatory essay on Emerson, the following excerpt may serve to establish the spiritual climate of the sonata's first movement:

> We see him standing on a summit, at the door of the infinite where many men do not dare to climb, peering into the mysteries of life, contemplating the eternities, hurling back whatever he discovers there—now thunderbolts, for us to grasp, if we can, and translate, now placing quietly, even tenderly, in our hands, things that we may see without effort. . . .

In addition to the prefatory essays, Ives includes numerous notes on the interpretation of the sonata, which reveal much about the composer as well as the music. In his first note on the Emerson movement, Ives applies his theory of "musical relativism," based on variable subjective factors:

> Throughout this movement, and to some extent in the others, there are many passages not to be too evenly played and in which the tempo is not precise or static; it varies usually with the mood of the day, as well as that of Emerson, the other Concord bards, and the player. A metronome cannot measure Emerson's mind and over-soul, any more than the old Concord Steeple Bell could. . . . The same essay or poem of Emerson may bring a slightly different feeling when read at sunrise than when read at sunset.

While refusing to identify the music with any specific passages in Emerson's writings, the composer does indicate that certain sections of the music are associated with the poetry and others with the prose. At one point the entrance of an abrupt dissonance, marked fortissimo, is described as depicting "one of Emerson's sudden calls for a Transcendental Journey." Three pages later the performer is instructed to hit a certain formidable chord "in as strong and hard a way as possible, almost as though the Mountains of the Universe were shouting, as all of humanity rises to behold the 'Massive Eternities' and the 'Spiritual Immensities.'" Here is this passage: [8]

[8] Quotations from the Second Pianoforte Sonata are used by permission of the copyright owners, Arrow Music Press, Inc.

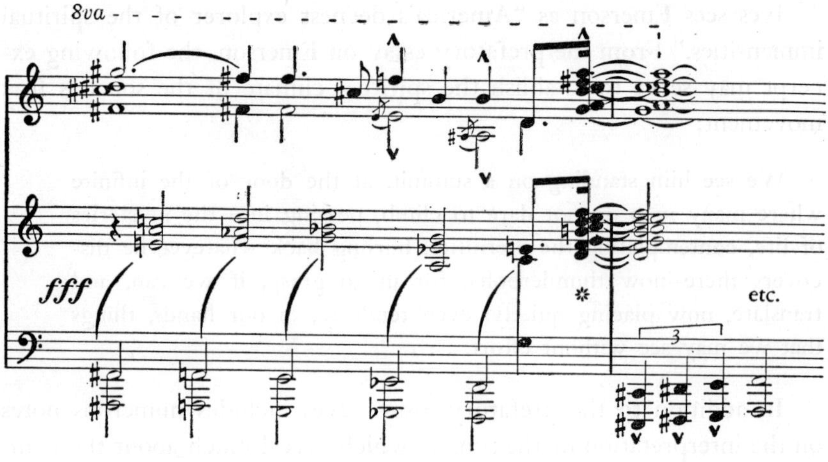

After the dramatic climax of this call to a "Transcendental Journey," there follows a meditative section leading to a mystical ending in which the upper notes in the treble clef (played by the left hand, pianissimo) are supposed "to reflect the overtones of the soul of humanity and as they rise away almost inaudibly to the Ultimate Destiny."

Concerning the second movement, a Scherzo, the composer tells us that the music makes no attempt to reflect the darker side of Hawthorne's genius, obsessed by the relentlessness of guilt:

> This fundamental part of Hawthorne is not attempted in our music . . . which is but an "extended fragment" trying to suggest some of his wilder, fantastical adventures into the half-childlike, half-fairylike phantasmal realms. It may have something to do with the children's excitement on that "frosty Berkshire morning, and the frost on the enchanted hall window" or something to do with "Feathertop," the "Scarecrow," and his "Looking Glass" and the little demons dancing around his pipe bowl; or something to do with the old hymn tune that haunts the old church and sings only to those in the churchyard, to protect them from secular noises, as when the circus parade comes down Main Street; or something to do with the concert at the Stamford camp meeting, or the "Slave's Shuffle"; or something to do with the Concord he-nymph, or the "Seven Vagabonds" or "Circe's Palace," or something else in the wonderbook—not something that happens, but the way something happens; or something personal, which tries to be "national" suddenly at twilight, and universal suddenly at midnight; or something

about the ghost of a man who never lived, or about something that never will happen, or something else that is not.

Here we meet several of the favorite Ivesian themes: the old hymn tune, the camp meeting, the circus parade. In treating the "phantasmal" aspects of Hawthorne's world, Ives avoids the merely quaint or fanciful. When he evokes a circus parade it is a real one, with all its gaudy vulgarity. His brass band blares in competition with the local Drum Corps marching along Main Street, and at one point in the score (the composer tells us), the Drum Corps "gets the best of the Band—for a moment." Another realistic touch is when certain notes "are hit hard by the left hand, as a trombone would sometimes call the Old Cornet Band to march."

There are other pure Ivesian touches in this Scherzo. When the old hymn tune is first heard it follows a furious arpeggio passage culminating in a chord marked *ffff*. The composer directs that "The first chord in the Hymn (*ppp*) is to be played before the *ffff* chord held with the right foot pedal is stopped—as a Hymn is sometimes heard over a distant hill just after a heavy storm." A little later he remarks: "Here the Hymn for a moment is slightly held up by a Friendly Ghost in the Church Yard."

The Scherzo is marked to be played "Very fast." Toward the end there is the direction, "From here on, as fast as possible," then "Rush it," and finally, "Faster if possible"! The final section Ives refers to as the "call of the cloud breakers." The hymn tune appears, very softly and slowly, as an echo, just before the final, up-rushing chord that brings the Scherzo to a close.

In connection with the third movement of the *Concord Sonata*, "The Alcotts," the composer has written about the spirit and aspect of Concord village, and about Orchard House, the family home where Louisa May Alcott wrote *Little Women* and where her father philosophized:

Concord village, itself, reminds one of that common virtue lying at the height and root of the Concord divinities. As one walks down the broad-arched street, passing the white house of Emerson—ascetic guard of a former prophetic beauty—he comes presently beneath the old elms overspreading the Alcott house. It seems to stand as a kind of homely but beautiful witness of Concord's common virtue—it seems to bear a consciousness that its past *is living*, that the "mosses of the Old Manse" and the hickories of Walden are not far away. Here is the home of the "Marches"—all pervaded with the trials and happiness of the family and telling, in a simple way, the story of "the richness of not having." . . . And there is the little old spinet-piano Sophia Thoreau gave to the Alcott children, on which Beth played old Scotch airs and played at the *Fifth Symphony*. . . .

We dare not attempt to follow the philosophic raptures of Bronson Alcott. . . . And so we won't try to reconcile the music sketch of the Alcotts with much besides the memory of that home under the elms—the Scotch songs and the family hymns that were sung at the end of each day—though there may be an attempt to catch something of that common sentiment . . . a strength of hope that never gives way to despair—a conviction in the power of the common soul which, when all is said and done, may be as typical as any theme of Concord and its transcendentalists.

"The Alcotts" is the shortest and the least difficult of the four movements of the *Concord Sonata*. The composer has provided all the clues that are needed for its understanding: the simplicity of the old home, the family hymns, the Scotch songs, and the reminiscences of Beethoven's Fifth Symphony. Remember, however, that the latter transcend the amateurish attempts of Beth Alcott at the spinet-piano, and are transmuted into the image of the Concord bards "pounding away at the immensities with a Beethoven-like sublimity."

For the final movement of his sonata, "Thoreau," the composer has given us a more detailed "program" than for the other movements. This section might have been subtitled "A Day at Walden." In his synopsis Ives does not specifically correlate the verbal description with the corresponding passages in the score. In giving the composer's synopsis below, I have taken the liberty of inserting musical illustrations that correspond to the scenes or moods described in the commentary.

And if there shall be a program let it follow his [Thoreau's] thought on an autumn day of Indian summer at Walden—a shadow of a thought at first, colored by the mist and haze over the pond:

> Low anchored cloud,
> Fountain head and
> Source of rivers . . .
> Dew cloth, dream drapery—
> Drifting meadow of the air . . .

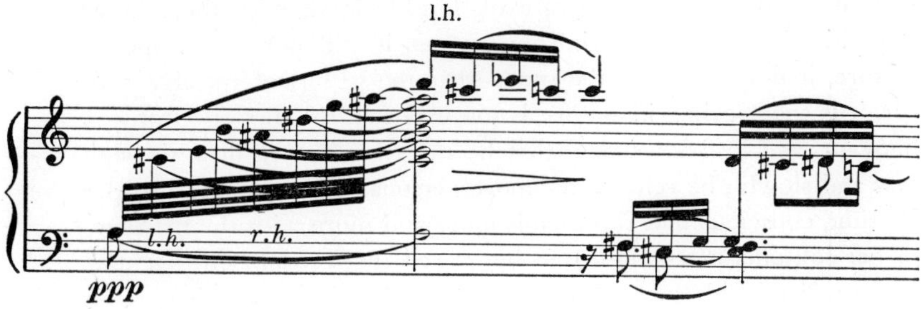

but this is momentary; the beauty of the day moves him to a certain restlessness—to aspirations more specific—an eagerness for outward action, but through it all he is conscious that it is not in keeping with the mood for this "Day." As the mists rise, there comes a clearer thought more traditional than the first, a meditation more calm.[9]

As he stands on the side of the pleasant hill of pines and hickories in front of his cabin, he is still disturbed by a restlessness and goes down the white-pebbled and sandy eastern shore, but it seems not to lead him where the thought suggests—he climbs along the "bolder northern" and "western shore, with deep bays indented," and now along the railroad track, "where the Aeolian harp plays." But his eagerness throws him into the lithe, springy step of the specie hunter

[9] Copyright 1947 by Arrow Music Press, Inc. Used by permission of the copyright owner.

—the naturalist—he is still aware of a restlessness; with these faster steps his rhythm is of a shorter span—it is still not the tempo of Nature, it does not bear the mood that the genius of the day calls for, it is too specific, its nature is too external, the introspection too buoyant, and he knows now that he must let Nature flow through *him* and slowly; he releases his more personal desires to her broader rhythm, conscious that this blends more and more with the harmony of her solitude; it tells him that his search for freedom on that day, at least, lies in his submission to her, for Nature is as relentless as she is benignant. He remains in this mood and while outwardly still, he seems to move with the slow, almost monotonous swaying beat of this autumnal day.[10]

He is more contented with a "homely burden," and is more assured of "the broad margin of his life; he sits in his sunny doorway . . . rapt in revery . . . amidst goldenrod, sandcherry, and sumach . . . in undisturbed solitude." At times the more definite personal strivings for the ideal freedom, the former more active speculations come over him, as if he would trace a certain intensity even in his submission. "He grew in those seasons like corn in the night and they were better than any works of the hands. They were not time subtracted from his life but so much over and above the usual allow-

[10] Copyright 1947 by Arrow Music Press, Inc. Used by permission.

ance." He realized "what the Orientals meant by contemplation and forsaking of works." . . . "The evening train has gone by," and "all the restless world with it. The fishes in the pond no longer feel its rumbling and he is more alone than ever. . . ." His meditations are interrupted only by the faint sound of the Concord bell—'tis prayer-meeting night in the village—"a melody, as it were, imported into the wilderness. . . . At a distance over the woods the sound acquires a certain vibratory hum as if the pine needles in the horizon were the strings of a harp which it swept. . . . A vibration of the universal lyre." . . . Part of the echo may be "The voice of the wood; the same trivial words and notes sung by the wood nymph." It is darker, the poet's flute is heard out over the pond and Walden hears the swan song of that "Day" and faintly echoes.[11]

[11] Copyright 1947 by Arrow Music Press, Inc. Used by permission.

[In these final pages, Ives has written out a part for the flute; but if no flute is used, he directs that the piano shall play the melody given in the small notes. He adds, however, that "Thoreau much prefers to hear the flute over Walden."]

Is it a transcendental tune of Concord? 'Tis an evening when the "whole body is one sense." . . . and before ending his day he looks out over the clear, crystalline water of the pond and catches a glimpse of the shadow-thought he saw in the morning's mist and haze—he knows that by his final submission, he possesses the "Freedom of the Night." He goes up the "pleasant hillside of pines, hickories," and moonlight, to his cabin, "with a strange liberty in Nature, a part of herself." [12]

Throughout this movement there are no key signatures, no time signatures, and no bar lines. But this does not mean that Ives subscribes to a principle of musical "anarchy," or that his musical discourse is merely "rhapsodic," lacking in formal cohesion. Obviously, he does not adhere to *conventional* form, but that is only one kind of form. In this connection it is well to remember that Ives called this work a "sonata" only because he could not think of a better name for it. He did not propose to write a composition in conventional sonata form. The *Concord Sonata* has *organic* form, based on thematic unity, structural parallelism, motival development, repetition, and variation. It also has *psychological* form: it follows the curves of emotion and feeling, rising to climaxes and falling to quieter moods, according to a controlled design.

In the "Emerson" and "Hawthorne" movements, Ives occasionally

[12] Copyright 1947 by Arrow Music Press, Inc. Used by permission.

uses time signatures, and therefore bar lines. In "The Alcotts" he uses a key signature in some sections, as well as time signatures. Ives is not a doctrinaire iconoclast. His object is musical expression. He will use conventional devices and commonplace materials when they suit his expressive purpose, and he will discard them when they hamper that purpose. Whatever material he employs, and whatever devices he uses, whether conventional or unconventional, we may be certain that a genuinely creative mind is at work. In the "Hawthorne" movement of the *Concord Sonata,* certain clusters of notes have to be played by using a strip of board about fifteen inches long, "heavy enough to press the keys down without striking." This is the effect that Ives felt he needed to suggest Hawthorne's "Celestial Railroad," and he adopted the only practical means to obtain that effect. Such a device is the result not of modernistic eccentricity but of Yankee ingenuity.

Past and present in the music of Ives

When Henry Bellamann wrote that "Ives is wholly of the bone and flesh of Colonial America" he overstated his case. Ives, one of the most independent artists who ever lived, cannot be circumscribed by colonialism. It is true—and this is the important thing—that Ives does have his spiritual roots deep in America's past, including all that was most "uncolonial," all that was most self-sufficient and new-seeking, in the period preceding our nationhood. But he is equally akin to the pioneer, self-made composers and singing-school masters of the late eighteenth and early nineteenth centuries; and one pictures him, in his self-reliance, his enthusiasm, his belief in the strength of Nature, and his philosophizing on the powers and properties of music, as a modern Billings. He belongs also to the great age of New England culture, blood brother to the Concord bards, achieving in music, more than half a century later, what they achieved in literature and thought. He belongs, finally, to the whole tradition of New England folkways, which he absorbed and transmuted in his music.

There is much truth in Burrill Phillips's statement that Ives "might be fairly called a historian-composer," in the sense that he evokes a past that has presumably vanished. But let us recall what Ives said of Orchard House in Concord, that "it seems to bear a consciousness that its past *is living.*" The same may be said of Ives's music: that in it the past is living. And it lives in his music because it lived for him and in him. Ives did not deliberately seek to recreate the past or to be a musical historian. He embraced the past, as well as the present, simply by identifying himself completely with the traditional culture of his environment. And the deeper he immersed himself in this tradition, the more boldly he was able to reach out toward the future. The paradox is similar to that expressed by Van Wyck Brooks in *The Flowering of New England:* "Ironically enough, it was Boston and Cambridge that grew to be provincial, while the local and even parochial Concord mind, which had always been universal, proved to be also national." Ives's outlook was local but never provincial. Like the ever-widening circles that appear when a stone is thrown into a pool of water, his music proceeds from the local to the regional, thence to the national, and finally to the universal.

Bibliography

The bibliographies for the individual chapters serve largely as a list of sources, supplementing with complete bibliographical data the brief references given in the footnotes.

The general bibliography that follows those for specific chapters is not meant to be exhaustive but is intended as a representative list of titles on American music and as a guide for the reader who may wish to pursue further special phases of the subject.

Since there is overlapping in the subject matter of certain chapters, several titles are necessarily repeated. In the case of such repetitions, only the author and title are mentioned, and the reader is referred to the chapter in which the complete listing of the imprint occurs. Thus, the following entry:

Slonimsky, Nicolas. *Music Since 1900.* (24) means that the complete listing of this work, with publisher, place, and date, will be found in the bibliography for Chapter 24.

For one, Puritan psalm singers

Bradstreet, Anne. *The Works of Anne Bradstreet in Prose and Verse,* ed. by John H. Ellis. Charlestown, Mass.: A. E. Cutter, 1867.

Cotton, John. *Singing of Psalms a Gospel Ordinance: Or a Treatise wherein are handled these four particulars. I. Touching the duty itself. II. Touching the matter to be sung. III. Touching the singers. IIII. Touching the manner of singing.* Boston, 1647.

Fisher, Williams Arms. *Ye Olde New England Psalm Tunes (1620–1820), with historical sketch.* Boston: Oliver Ditson Company, 1930.

MacDougall, Hamilton C. *Early New England Psalmody, 1620–1820.* Brattleboro, N.H.: Stephen Daye Press, 1940.

Playford, John. *An Introduction to the Skill of Musick* (11th ed.). London, 1687.

———. *The Whole Book of Psalms: With the Usual Hymns and Spiritual Songs, Together with all the Ancient and Proper Tunes sung in Churches, with some of Later Use . . .* (4th ed.). London, 1698.

Pratt, Waldo Selden. *The Music of the Pilgrims*. Boston: Oliver Ditson Company, 1921.

——. *The Music of the French Psalter of 1562*. New York: Columbia University Press, 1939.

The Psalms, Hymns, and Spiritual Songs, of the Old and New Testament: Faithfully Translated into English Meetre. For the use, Edification and Comfort of the Saints in publick and private, especially in New-England (9th ed.). Boston: Printed by B. Green and J. Allen, for Michael Perry, 1698.

Ravenscroft, Thomas. *The Whole Booke of Psalmes: With the Hymnes Evangellical and Songs Spirituall. Composed into four parts by Sundry Authors. . . .* Printed at London, 1621. 2d ed., 1633.

Scholes, Percy A. *The Puritans and Music in England and New England.* New York: Oxford University Press, 1934. Contains a wealth of valuable material and copious bibliographical references.

Sewall, Samuel. *Diary*, ed. by Mark Van Doren. New York: Macy-Masius, 1927. Also edition of the Massachusetts Historical Society in three volumes, 1876–1882.

Smith, Carleton Sprague (ed.). *Early Psalmody in America.* Series I. *The Ainsworth Psalter.* Psalm 65, with settings by Claude Goudimel. New York: The New York Public Library, 1938.

Thorndike, S. Lothrop. *The Psalmodies of Plymouth and Massachusetts Bay.* Publications of the Colonial Society of Massachusetts, vol. 1, pp. 228–238.

Warrington, James. *Short Titles of Books Relating or Illustrating the History and Practice of Psalmody in the United States.* Privately printed, Philadelphia, 1898.

For two, New England reformers

Chauncey, Nathaniel. *Regular Singing Defended, and proved to be the only true way of singing the songs of the Lord. . . .* New London: Printed and sold by T. Green, 1728.

Curwen, J. Spencer. *Studies in Music Worship.* First Series (2d ed.). London: J. Curwen & Sons, 1888.

Gould, Nathaniel D. *History of Church Music in America.* Boston: A. N. Johnson, 1853.

Hood, George. *History of Music in New England.* Boston: Wilkins, Carter and Company, 1846.

Jones, Matt B. *Bibliographical Notes on Thomas Walter's "Grounds and Rules of Musick Explained."* Reprinted from *Proceedings of the American Antiquarian Society*, Oct. 1932. Worcester, Mass.: The Society, 1933.

Kouwenhoven, John A. "Some Unfamiliar Aspects of Singing in New England." *The New England Quarterly*, VI, 3 (Sept. 1933), 567–588.

Mainzer, Joseph. *The Gaelic Psalm Tunes of Ross-shire, etc.* Edinburgh, 1844.

Metcalf, Frank J. *American Psalmody (1721–1820).* New York: C. F. Hartmann, 1917.

Millar, Patrick. *Four Centuries of Scottish Psalmody.* New York: Oxford University Press, 1949.

Staples, Samuel E. *The Ancient Psalmody and Hymnology of New England.* Worcester, Mass.: C. Jillson, 1880.

Symmes, Thomas. *Utiles Dulci. Or, A Joco-Serious Dialogue, concerning regular singing: calculated for a particular town (where it was publickly had, on Friday Oct. 12. 1772.) but may serve some other places in the same climate.* Boston: Printed by B. Green, for S. Gerrish, in Cornhill, 1723.

Tufts, John. *A Very Plain and Easy Introduction to the Singing of Psalm Tunes.* Boston, 1721. Modern facsimile edition published by Harry Dichter, Philadelphia: Musical Americana, 1954.

Walter, Thomas. *The Grounds and Rules of Musick Explained, or An Introduction to the Art of Singing by Note.* Boston: Printed by J. Franklin, for S. Gerrish, near the Brick Church in Cornhill, 1721.

For three, Singing dissenters

Andrews, Edward D. *The Gift to Be Simple.* Locust Valley, N. Y.: J. J. Augustin, Inc., 1940.

Benson, Louis F. *The English Hymn: Its Development and Use in Worship.* New York: George H. Doran Co., 1915.

Bost, George H. *Samuel Davies: Colonial Revivalist and Champion of Religious Toleration.* A part of a dissertation submitted to the Faculty of the Divinity School in candidacy for the degree of Doctor of Philosophy. The University of Chicago, 1944.

Chauncey, Charles. *Seasonable Thoughts Upon the State of Religion in New England. . . .* Boston: Printed by Rogers and Fowle for Samuel Eliot in Cornhill, 1743.

Church Music and Musical Life in Pennsylvania in the 18th Century. Publications of the Pennsylvania Society of the Colonial Dames of America, IV. (3 vols.) Philadelphia: Printed for the Society, 1926–1947.

Da Silva, Owen. *Mission Music of California.* Published under the auspices of the Franciscan Fathers of California. Los Angeles: Warren F. Lewis, 1941.

David, Hans T. "Ephrata and Bethlehem in Pennsylvania: a Comparison." *Papers of the American Musicological Society,* Annual Meeting, 1941, pp. 97–104. Printed by the Society, 1946.

———. "Musical Life in the Pennsylvania Settlements of the *Unitas Fratrem.*" *Transactions of the Moravian Historical Society,* vol. 13, parts 1 and 2, pp. 19–58. Bethlehem, Pa., 1942.

———, (ed.). *Music of the Moravians in America.* 12 vols. in blackline print. New York Public Library Music Series, 1938–1939.

Drummond, Robert Rutherford. *Early German Music in Philadelphia.* New York: D. Appleton & Company, Inc., 1910.

Foote, Henry W. *Three Centuries of American Hymnody.* Cambridge, Mass.: Harvard University Press, 1940.

Funston, John W. *The Wesleys in Picture and Story. An illustrated history of the life and times of John and Charles Wesley.* Oak Park, Ill.. 1939.

Gerson, Robert A. *Music in Philadelphia.* (University of Pennsylvania Dissertation.) Philadelphia: Theodore Presser, 1940.

Gewehr, Wesley M. *The Great Awakening in Virginia.* Durham, N.C.: Duke University Press, 1930.

Grider, Rufus A. *Historical Notes on Music in Bethlehem, Pa. (1741–1871).* Philadelphia: J. A. Martin, 1873.

Hall, Thomas Cuming. *The Religious Background of American Culture.* Boston: Little, Brown & Company, 1930.

Hess, Albert G. "Observations on the Lamenting Voice of the Hidden Love." *Journal of the American Musicological Society*, V, 3 (1952), 211–223.

Hymns on the Great Festivals and other occasions. London: Printed for M. Cooper at the Globe in Pater-noster-Row and sold by T. Trye near Grays-Inn Gate, Holborn, etc., 1746. Contains musical settings of Wesleyan hymns by John Frederick Lampe.

Jackson, George Pullen. *White and Negro Spirituals.* Locust Valley, N.Y.: J. J. Augustin, Inc., 1943.

Learned, Marion D. *Life of Francis Daniel Pastorius, the Founder of Germantown.* Philadelphia: W. J. Campbell, 1908.

Lightwood, J. T. *Hymn Tunes and Their Story.* London: C. H. Kelly, 1906.

Price, Carl F. *The Music and Hymnody of the Methodist Hymnal.* New York: Eaton and Mains; Cincinnati: Jennings and Graham, 1911.

Rau, Albert G., and Hans T. David. *A Catalogue of Music by American Moravians, 1742–1842.* Bethlehem, Pa.: The Moravian Seminary and College for Women, 1938. Includes twenty-four plates of selected compositions and pages from original manuscripts.

Sachse, Julius F. *The German Pietists of Provincial Pennsylvania, 1694–1708.* Philadelphia, 1895.

———. *The Journal of Johannes Kelpius, Magister of the Hermits of the Ridge in Pennsylvania 1694–1708.* Philadelphia, 1893. Photographically reproduced from the original in the Historical Society of Pennsylvania.

———. *Music of the Ephrata Cloister.* Lancaster, Pa.: Published by the author, 1903.

Stevens, Abel. *The History of the Religious Movement of the 18th Century, Called Methodism.* 3 vols. New York: Carlton and Porter, 1858–1861.

Stevenson, Robert M. *Patterns of Protestant Church Music.* Durham, N.C.: Duke University Press, 1953.

Sweet, William Warren. *Religion in Colonial America.* New York: Charles Scribner's Sons, 1942.

———. *Religion in the Development of American Culture, 1765–1840.* New York: Charles Scribner's Sons, 1952.

———. *The Story of Religion in America* (2d rev. ed.). New York: Harper & Brothers, 1950.

Wearmouth, Robert F. *Methodism and the Common People of the 18th Century.* London: The Epworth Press, 1945.

Wesley, John. *A Collection of Psalms and Hymns.* Charles-town, S.C.: Printed by L. Timothy, 1737.

Wesley, John. *The Journal of the Rev. John Wesley*, ed. by Nehemiah Curnock, assisted by experts. 8 vols. London: R. Culley, 1909–1916. Also an edition in Everyman's Library, 4 vols., London: J. M. Dent & Sons, Ltd.; New York: E. P. Dutton & Co., Inc., 1922–1930.

The Works of John and Charles Wesley, ed. by Richard Green. London, 1896.

For four, African exiles

Alberts, Arthur S. *Tribal, Folk and Cafe Music of West Africa.* Recorded and edited. Text and Commentaries by Melville J. Herskovits, Duncan Emrich, Richard A. Waterman, and Marshall W. Stearns. New York: Field Recordings, 1950.

Ballanta (-Taylor), Nicholas G. J. *St. Helena Island Spirituals.* New York: G. Schirmer, Inc., 1925.

Captain Canot; or, Twenty Years of an African Slaver. Written out and edited from the Captain's Journals, Memoranda, and Conversations by Brantz Mayer. New York: D. Appleton & Company, Inc., 1854.

Curtis, Natalie. *Songs and Tales from the Dark Continent.* New York: G. Schirmer, Inc., 1920.

Du Bois, William E. B. *Black Folk: Then and Now; An Essay in the History and Sociology of the Negro Race.* New York: Henry Holt and Company, Inc., 1939.

Gaines, Francis P. *The Southern Plantation: A Study in the Development and the Accuracy of a Tradition.* New York: Columbia University Press, 1924.

Gorer, Geoffrey. *Africa Dances; a Book About West African Negroes.* London: Faber & Faber, Ltd., 1935.

Hare, Maud (Cuney). *Negro Musicians and Their Music.* Washington, D.C.: The Associated Publishers, Inc., 1936.

Harrison, William P. *The Gospel Among the Slaves.* Nashville, Tenn.: Publishing House of the M. E. Church, 1893.

Herskovits, Melville J. *The Myth of the Negro Past.* New York: Harper & Brothers, 1941.

Jones, Charles C. *The Religious Instruction of the Negroes in the United States.* Savannah, Ga.: Purse, 1842.

Kolinski, Mieczyslaw. "La Música del Oeste Africano." *Revista de Estudios Musicales*, I, 2 (Dec. 1949), 191–215.

Krehbiel, Henry E. *Afro-American Folksongs.* New York: G. Schirmer, Inc., 1914.

Mordecai, Samuel. *Virginia, Especially Richmond, in By-Gone Days* (2d ed.). Richmond, Va.: West and Johnston, 1860.

Phillips, Ulrich B. *American Negro Slavery. . . .* New York: D. Appleton & Company, Inc., 1918.

———. *Life and Labor in the Old South.* Boston: Little, Brown & Company, 1929.

———. *Plantation and Frontier Documents: 1649–1863.* Cleveland: The A. H. Clark Company, 1909.

Ward, W. E. "Music of the Gold Coast." *The Musical Times* (London), LXXIII (Aug., Sept., Oct. 1932) 707–710, 797–799, 901–902.

Waterman, Richard A. "African Influence on the Music of the Americas." Reprinted from TAX: *Acculturation in the Americas.* Vol. II, *Proceedings of the 29th International Congress of Americanists.* Chicago: The University of Chicago Press, 1952.

———. *African Patterns in Trinidad Negro Music.* (Doctoral Dissertation). Department of Anthropology, Northwestern University, Evanston, Ill., May 1943. (Typewritten). Includes material from a valuable unpublished work by M. Kolinski, *Die Musik Westafrikas* (see above).

Wesley, John. *The Journal of the Rev. John Wesley, A. M.* (3)

For five, Gentlemen amateurs

Fithian, Philip Vickers. *Journal and Letters, 1767–1774,* ed. by John R. Williams. Princeton, N. J.: Princeton University Press, 1900.

Franklin, Benjamin. *Complete Works,* ed. by Bigelow. New York, 1887.

———. *Quatour pour 3 violons et violoncelle, transcription de Guillaume de Van.* Paris: Odette Lieutier, 1946.

Hopkinson, Francis. *Seven Songs for the Harpsichord or Forte Piano.* Philadelphia, 1788. Modern facsimile edition by Harry Dichter, Philadelphia: Musical Americana, 1954.

Hastings, George E. *The Life and Works of Francis Hopkinson.* Chicago: The University of Chicago Press, 1926.

King, A. Hyatt. "The Musical Glasses and Glass Harmonica." *Proceedings of the Royal Musical Association* (London). Session LXXII, 1945–1946, pp. 97–122.

Lichtenwanger, William. "Benjamin Franklin on Music." In *Church Music and Musical Life in Pennsylvania . . . ,* vol. 3, part 2, pp. 449–472 (3).

Maurer, Maurer. "A Musical Family in Colonial Virginia." *Musical Quarterly,* XXXIV, 3 (July 1948), 358–364.

Milligan, Harold V. (ed.). *Colonial Love Lyrics: Six Songs by Francis Hopkinson.* Boston: The Arthur P. Schmidt Company, 1919.

———. *The First American Composer: Six Songs by Francis Hopkinson.* Boston: The Arthur P. Schmidt Company, 1918.

Redway, Virginia Larkin. "James Parker and the 'Dutch Church.'" *Musical Quarterly,* XXIV, 4 (Oct. 1938), 481–500. Refers to Francis Hopkinson.

Smith, Carleton Sprague. "The 1774 Psalm Book of the Reformed Protestant Dutch Church in New York City." *Musical Quarterly,* XXXIV, 1 (Jan. 1948), 84–96. Refers to Francis Hopkinson.

Sonneck, Oscar G. *Early Concert Life in America.* Leipzig: Breitkopf & Härtel, 1907.

———. *Early Opera in America.* New York: G. Schirmer, Inc., 1915.

———. *Francis Hopkinson, the First American Composer.* Washington, D.C.: H. L. McQueen, 1905.

———. *Miscellaneous Studies in the History of Music.* New York: The Macmillan Company, 1921.

———. *Suum Cuique.* New York: G. Schirmer, Inc., 1916.

For six, Professional emigrants

Drummond, Robert R. "Alexander Reinagle and His Connection with the Musical Life of Philadelphia." *German-American Annals,* n. s., V, 5 (1907), 294–306.

Engel, Carl. "Introducing Mr. Braun." *Musical Quarterly,* XXX, 1 (Jan. 1944), 63–83. Deals with the musician known as William Brown.

Howard, John Tasker (ed.). *A Program of Early American Piano Pieces.* New York: J. Fisher and Brother, 1931. Compositions by Carr, Pelissier, Reinagle, Taylor, and others.

———. *The Music of George Washington's Time.* Washington, D.C.: United States George Washington Bicentennial Commission, 1931.

Johnson, H. Earle. *Musical Interludes in Boston, 1795–1830.* New York: Columbia University Press, 1943.

Konkle, Burton A. *Joseph Hopkinson, 1770–1842, Juror, Scholar; Inspirer of the Arts; Author of Hail Columbia.* Philadelphia: University of Pennsylvania Press, 1931.

Krohn, Ernst C. "Alexander Reinagle as Sonatist." *Musical Quarterly,* XVIII, 1 (Jan. 1932), 140–149.

Maurer, Maurer. "The 'Professor of Musick' in Colonial America." *Musical Quarterly,* XXXVI, 4 (Oct. 1950), 511–524.

Milligan, Harold V. (ed.). *Pioneer American Composers. A Collection of Early American Songs.* Boston: The Arthur P. Schmidt Company, 1921, 2 vols.

Parker, John R. (ed.). *Euterpeiad: or Musical Intelligencer. Devoted to the Diffusion of Musical Information and Belles Lettres.* Boston, 1820–1823.

———. *Musical Biography; or, Sketches of the Lives and Writings of Eminent Musical Characters.* Boston, 1824.

Redway, Virginia Larkin. "The Carrs, American Music Publishers." *Musical Quarterly,* XVIII, 1 (Jan. 1932), 150–177.

———. *Music Directory of Early New York City; A File of Musicians, Music Publishers and Musical Instrument-makers listed in New York directories From 1786 through 1835.* New York: The New York Public Library, 1941.

Sonneck, Oscar G. *Bibliography of Early American Secular Music.* Washington, D.C.: H. L. McQueen, 1905. Revised and enlarged by William Treat Upton, Washington, D.C.: The Library of Congress, 1945.

———. *Early Concert Life in America.* (5)

———. *Early Opera in America.* (5)

For seven, Native pioneers

Belcher, Supply. *The Harmony of Maine: being an original composition of psalm and hymn tunes, of various metres . . . with a number of fuging pieces and anthems. Together with a concise introduction to the grounds of musick, and rules for learners. For the use of singing schools and music societies.* Boston: Thomas and Andrews, 1794.

Billings, William. *The New-England Psalm-Singer: or American Chorister. Containing a Number of Psalm-Tunes, Anthems and Canons. In Four and Five Parts.* Boston: Printed by Edes and Gill, n.d. [1770].

——. *The Singing Master's Assistant, or Key to Practical Music, being An Abridgement from the New-England Psalm-Singer; together with several other Tunes, never before published.* Boston: Printed by Draper and Folsom, 1778.

Britton, Allen P. "Bibliography of Early Religious American Music" (eighteenth century). Part of a Doctoral dissertation titled *Theoretical Introductions in American Tune-Books to 1800.* Typewritten copy in Music Division, Library of Congress, Washington, D.C.

Brooks, Henry M. *Olden-Time Music.* A compilation from newspapers and books. Boston: Ticknor & Co., 1888.

Cheney, Simeon Pease. *The American Singing Book . . . the biographical department containing biographies of 40 of the leading composers, book-makers, etc., of sacred music in America. . . .* Boston: White, Smith & Co., 1879.

——. *Brother Cheney's Collection of Old Folks Concert Music, a very careful selection of the old fugue tunes and anthems together with a few new pieces. . . .* Boston: White, Smith & Co., 1879.

[Gilman, Samuel]. *Memories of a New England Village Choir . . . By a Member.* Boston: Crosby, Nichols & Co., n.d.

Goldman, Richard Franko. *Landmarks of Early American Music, 1760–1800.* New York: G. Schirmer, Inc., 1943. A collection of thirty-two compositions.

Law, Andrew. *The Musical Primer, or the First Part of the Art of Singing: Containing the Rules of Psalmody . . . together with a number of Practical Lessons and Plain Tunes.* New Haven, Conn., 1780.

Lindstrom, Carl E. "William Billings and His Times." *Musical Quarterly,* XXV, 4 (Oct. 1939), 479–497.

Lowens, Irving. "The Origins of the American Fuging Tune." *Journal of the American Musicological Society,* VI, 1 (Spring 1953), 43–52.

Lyon, James. *Urania, or a choice Collection of Psalm-Tunes, Anthems and Hymns from the most approved Authors, with some entirely new; in two, three and four Parts. . . .* Philadelphia, 1760.

Madan, Martin. *A Collection of Psalm and Hymn Tunes . . . To be had at the Lock Hospital near Hyde Park Corner.* London, 1769.

Metcalf, Frank J. *American Writers and Compilers of Sacred Music.* New York and Cincinnati: Abingdon Press, 1925.

Moore, John W. *A Dictionary of Musical Information . . . and a list of modern musical works published in the United States from 1640 to 1875.* Boston: Oliver Ditson & Co., 1876.

Pierce, Edwin Hall. "The Rise and Fall of the 'Fugue-Tune' in America." *Musical Quarterly,* XVI, 2 (Apr. 1930).

Skeel, Emily E. F. *Mason Locke Weems, His Works and Ways.* 3 vols. New York, 1929.

Sonneck, Oscar G. *Bibliography of Early American Secular Music.* (6)

——. *Francis Hopkinson and James Lyon.* (5)

——. *Early Concert Life in America.* (5)

Standish, L. W. *The Old Stoughton Musical Society*. Stoughton, Mass.: The Society, 1929.

Wright, Edith A. "James Lyons's 'Friendship.'" *Music Library Association Notes*, ser. 2, IV, 3 (June 1947), 293–295.

For eight, Progress and profit

Birge, Edward B. *History of Public School Music in the United States.* Boston: Oliver Ditson Company, 1928.

Hastings, Thomas. *Dissertation on Musical Taste; or General Principles of Taste Applied to the Art of Music.* New York: Mason Brothers, 1853. (First edition published in Albany, 1822).

Lucas, G. W. *Remarks on the Musical Conventions in Boston.* Northampton, Mass.: The author, 1844.

Mason, Henry L. *Hymn-Tunes of Lowell Mason; A Bibliography*. Cambridge, Mass.: Harvard University Press, 1944.

——. *Lowell Mason, An Appreciation of his life and work.* New York: The Hymn Society of America, 1941.

Mason, Lowell (ed.). *The Boston Handel and Haydn Society Collection of Church Music* . . . (10th ed.). Boston: Published by Richardson, Lord and Holbrook, 1831.

——. *The New Carmina Sacra: or Boston Collection of Church Music.* . . . Boston: Published by Rice and Kendall, Late Willkins, Carter and Company, 1853.

Mason, William. *Memories of a Musical Life.* New York: Century Company, 1901.

Perkins, Charles C., and John S. Dwight. *History of the Handel & Haydn Society of Boston.* Boston: A. Mudge and Sons, 1883.

Proceedings of the Musical Convention Assembled in Boston, August 16, 1838. Boston: Kidder and Wright, 1838.

Rich, Arthur L. *Lowell Mason, "The Father of Singing Among the Children."* Chapel Hill, N.C.: The University of North Carolina Press, 1946.

Scanlon, Mary B. "Thomas Hastings." *Musical Quarterly*, XXXII, 2 (Apr. 1946), 265–277.

Seward, T. F. *The Educational Work of Lowell Mason.* 1879.

For nine, The genteel tradition

Brink, Carol. *Harps in the Wind, The Story of the Singing Hutchinsons.* New York: The Macmillan Company, 1947.

Damon, S. Foster (ed.). *Series of Old American Songs.* Providence, R.I.: Brown University Library, 1936.

Fatout, Paul. "Threnodies of the Ladies' Books." *Musical Quarterly*, XXXI, 4 (Oct. 1945), 464–478. Includes numerous musical illustrations.

Hewitt, John H. *Shadows on the Wall.* Baltimore: Turnbull Brothers, 1877.

Hill, Richard S. "The Mysterious Chord of Henry Clay Work." *Music Library Association Notes*, 2d ser., X, 2 (Mar. 1953), 211–225; and X,

3 (June 1953), 367–390. Contains valuable source material and dated list of songs.

Hutchinson, John W. *Story of the Hutchinsons.* 2 vols. Boston: Lee and Shepard, 1896.

Jordan, Philip D. *Singin' Yankees.* Minneapolis: The University of Minnesota Press, 1946.

———, and Lillian Kessler. *Songs of Yesterday.* New York: Doubleday, Doran & Company, Inc., 1941.

Russell, Henry. *Cheer! Boys, Cheer! Memories of Men and Music.* London: John Macqueen, Hastings House, 1895.

For ten, The fasola folk

Aiken, Jesse B. *The Christian Minstrel. A new system of musical notation; with a collection of psalm tunes, anthems, and chants, selected from the most popular works in Europe and America. . . .* Philadelphia, 1850. In 1873, in Philadelphia, appeared what was advertised as the "one hundred and seventy-first edition" of this compilation.

———. *Harmonia Ecclesiae; or, Companion to the Christian Minstrel. . . .* Philadelphia: Published by the Proprietor, 1853.

———. *The Imperial Harmony.* Compiled with Hubert P. Main and Chester G. Allen. New York and Chicago: Bigelow & Main, 1876.

———. *The True Principles of the Science of Music, with a rare collection of a few of the best tunes that are published.* Philadelphia: J. B. Aiken, 1893.

Buchanan, Annabel Morris. "American Folk Hymnody." *The International Cyclopedia of Music and Musicians,* ed. by Oscar Thompson (6th ed.). New York: Dodd, Mead & Company, Inc., 1952.

———. *Folk Hymns of America.* New York: J. Fischer & Brother, 1938. Fifty folk-hymn settings from 17 states; with introduction, notes, bibliography, and analyses of modes and tunes.

Davisson, Ananias. *Kentucky Harmony. Or A Choice Collection of Psalm Tunes, Hymns and Anthems . . .* (4th ed.). Harrisonburg, Va.: Printed and sold by the Author, 1821.

Everett, Lemuel C., and A. B. Everett. *The New Thesaurus Musicus; or United States Collection of Church Music; constituting the most complete variety of new psalm and hymn tunes, sentences, anthems, chants, etc., for the use of the choir, the congregation, and the singing school . . . comprising also all the popular old choir and congregational tunes in general use.* Richmond, Va.: Published by the authors, 1859. (*The Thesaurus Musicus* was originally published at Richmond in 1856.)

———. *The Progressive Church Vocalist . . .* (2d ed.). New York: Published for the authors by Mason Brothers, 1855.

Hauser, William. *The Olive Leaf . . . A Collection of Beautiful Tunes.* Wadley, Jefferson Co., Georgia, 1878.

Jackson, George Pullen. *Another Sheaf of White Spirituals.* Gainesville, Fla.: University of Florida Press, 1952.

Jackson, George Pullen. *Down East Spirituals and Others.* Locust Valley, N.Y.: J. J. Augustin, Inc., 1939.

———. *Spiritual Folk-Songs of Early America.* Locust Valley, N.Y.: J. J. Augustin, Inc., 1937.

———. *White Spirituals in the Southern Uplands.* Chapel Hill, N.C.: The University of North Carolina Press, 1933.

———.*White and Negro Spirituals.* (3)

Lowens, Irving. "John Wyeth's *Repository of Sacred Music, Part Second:* A Northern Precursor of Southern Folk Hymnody." *Journal of the American Musicological Society,* V, 2 (1952), 114–131. With an Appendix containing eighteen tunes.

McIntosh, Rigdon M. *Light and Life: A Collection of New Hymns and Tunes for Sunday-schools, prayer meetings, praise meetings, and revival meetings.* Boston: Oliver Ditson Co., 1881.

———. *Tabor: or, The Richmond Collection of Sacred Music.* New York: F. J. Huntington & Co., 1866.

Metcalf, Frank J. "The Easy Instructor." *Musical Quarterly,* XXIII, 1 (Jan. 1937), 89–97.

Niles, John Jacob. *The Shape-Note Study Book.* New York, 1950.

Original Sacred Harp. Denson Revision. Haleyville, Ala.: Sacred Harp Publishing Company, Inc., 1936.

Seeger, Charles. "Contrapuntal Style in the Three-Voice Shape-Note Hymns." *Musical Quarterly,* XXVI, 4 (Oct. 1940), 483–493.

Swan, M. L. *New Harp of Columbia,* Nashville, Tenn.: L. D. Schultz, 1921. Facsimile reprint of the 1867 edition of *Harp of Columbia.*

Walker, William. *The Christian Harmony.* Spartanburg, S.C., 1866. Rev. ed. Philadelphia: E. W. Miller, 1901.

———. *The Southern Harmony, and Musical Companion.* New ed. Philadelphia: E. W. Miller, 1854. Facsimile reprint by the Federal Writers Project, Works Progress Administration, New York, 1939.

White, B. F., and E. J. King. *The Sacred Harp,* 1844. Republished as *The Original Sacred Harp.* Atlanta, Ga.: United Harp Musical Association, 1911.

Wyeth, John. *Wyeth's Repository of Sacred Music, Part Second.* (2d ed.). *Together with a plain and concise Introduction to the Grounds of Music* . . . Harrisburg, Pa.: by John Wyeth, Printer and Bookseller, 1820.

For eleven, Revivals and camp meetings

Andrews, Edward D. *The Gift to Be Simple.* (3)

Asbury, Samuel E., and Henry E. Meyer. *Old Time White Camp Meeting Spirituals.* Austin, Tex.: The Texas Folklore Society, 1932.

Bellinger, Lucius C. *Stray Leaves from the Portfolio of a Local Methodist Preacher.* Macon, Georgia: Printed for the Author by J. W. Burke & Co., 1870.

Davidson, Robert. *History of the Presbyterian Church in the State of Kentucky.* New York, 1847.

Dow, Lorenzo. *History of Cosmopolite; or, The Four Volumes of Lorenzo's Journal* . . . New York: J. C. Totten, 1814.

McDowell, Lucien L. *Songs of the Old Camp Ground*. Ann Arbor, Mich.: Edwards Brothers, 1937.

See also the bibliographies for Chapters 3 and 10, especially Benson's *The English Hymn* and the works of George Pullen Jackson.

For twelve, The Negro spiritual

Allen, William Francis, Charles P. Ware, and Lucy McKim Garrison (eds.). *Slave Songs of the United States*. New York: A. Simpson and Company, 1867. Reprinted by Peter Smith, New York, 1929.

Aptheker, Herbert (ed.). *A Documentary History of the Negro People in the United States*. New York: The Citadel Press, 1951.

Ballanta (-Taylor), Nicholas G. J. *St. Helena Island Spirituals*. (4)

Bolton, Dorothy G., and H. T. Burleigh. *Old Songs Hymnal*. New York: Century Company, 1929.

Botkin, B. A. *Lay My Burden Down: A Folk History of Slavery*. Chicago: University of Chicago Press, 1945.

Burlin, Natalie Curtis. *Hampton Series of Negro Folk-Songs*. 4 books. New York: G. Schirmer, Inc., 1918–1919.

———. "Negro Music at Birth." *Musical Quarterly*, V, 1 (Jan. 1919), 86–89.

Fenner, Thomas P., and F. G. Rathbon. *Cabin and Plantation Songs as Sung by the Hampton Students*. New York: G. P. Putnam's Sons, 1874.

Fisher, Miles M. *Negro Slave Songs in the United States* (American Historical Society Publications). Ithaca, N.Y.: Cornell University Press, 1953.

Gordon, Robert W. "The Negro Spiritual." In *The Carolina Low-country*. New York: The Macmillan Company, 1931, pp. 191–222. Also contains "Some Songs the Negro Sang," arranged by Katherine C. Hutson, pp. 225–327.

Grissom, Mary Allen. *The Negro Sings a New Heaven*. Chapel Hill, N.C.: The University of North Carolina Press, 1930.

Hallowell, Emily. *Calhoun Plantation Songs*. Boston: C. W. Thompson & Co., 1901.

Hatfield, Edwin F., compiler. *Freedom's Lyre; or, Psalms, Hymns and Sacred Songs, for the slave and his friends*. New York: S. W. Benedict, 1840.

Jackson, George P. *White and Negro Spirituals*. (3)

Jackson, L. P. "Religious Development of the Negro in Virginia from 1760 to 1860." *Journal of Negro History*, XVI (1931), 168–239.

Johnson, Guy B. *Folk Culture on St. Helena Island, South Carolina*. Chapel Hill, N.C.: The University of North Carolina Press, 1930.

Krehbiel, Henry E. *Afro-American Folksongs*. (4)

Marsh, J. B. T. *The Story of the Jubilee Singers, with Their Songs*. Boston: Houghton, Osgood & Co., 1880.

McIlhenny, Edward A. *Befo' de War Spirituals*. Boston: Christopher Publishing House, 1933.

Murphy, Jeannette Robinson. "The Survival of African Music in America." *Popular Science Monthly*, LV (Sept. 1899), 660–672.

Odum, Howard W., and Guy B. Johnson. *The Negro and His Songs.* Chapel Hill, N.C.: The University of North Carolina Press, 1925.
———. *Negro Workaday Songs.* Chapel Hill, N.C.: The University of North Carolina Press, 1926.
Parrish, Lydia. *Slave Songs of the Georgia Sea Islands.* Music transcribed by Creighton Churchill and Robert MacGimsey. Introduction by Olin Downes. New York: Creative Age Press, Inc., 1942.
Parsons, Elsie Clews. *Folk Tales of the Sea Islands, South Carolina.* Memoirs of the American Folklore Society, No. 16. Cambridge, Mass.: American Folklore Society, 1923. Includes eighteen songs.
Scarborough, Dorothy. *On the Trail of Negro Folk-Songs.* Cambridge, Mass.: Harvard University Press, 1925.
Seward, Theodore F. *Jubilee Songs, as Sung by the Jubilee Singers of Fisk University.* New York: Bigelow & Main, 1872.
Work, John W. *American Negro Songs.* New York: Howell, Soskin Publishers, Inc., 1940.
Waterman, Richard A. " 'Hot' Rhythm in Negro Music." *Journal of the American Musicological Society*, I, 1 (1948), 24–37.
Consult also the bibliography for Chapter 4.

For thirteen, The Ethiopian business

Burleigh, Henry T. *Negro Minstrel Melodies.* New York: G. Schirmer, Inc., 1910.
Damon, S. Foster (ed.). *Series of Old American Songs.* (9)
Galbreath, C. B. *Daniel Decatur Emmett, Author of Dixie.* Columbus, Ohio: F. J. Heer, 1904.
Loesser, Arthur. *Humor in American Song.* New York: Howell, Soskin, Publishers, Inc., 1942.
Nathan, Hans. "Dixie." *Musical Quarterly*, XXXV, 1 (Jan. 1949), 60–84.
———. "The First Negro Minstrel Band and Its Origins." *Southern Folklore Quarterly* (June 1952), pp. 132–144. With copious bibliographical sources.
———. *Dan Emmett and Early American Negro Minstrelsy.* (In preparation.)
Parkman, Daily, and Sigmund Spaeth. *"Gentlemen, Be Seated!" A Parade of the Old-Time Minstrels.* New York: Doubleday, Doran & Co., 1928.
Rice, Edward LeRoy. *Monarchs of Minstrelsy, From "Daddy" Rice to Date.* New York: Kenney Publishing Co., 1911.
Rourke, Constance. *American Humor; A Study of the National Character.* New York: Harcourt, Brace & Co., 1931. Reprinted by Doubleday & Co., 1953.
White, Newman. *American Negro Folk-songs.* Cambridge, Mass.: Harvard University Press, 1909.
Wittke, Carl. *Tambo and Bones, a History of the American Minstrel Stage.* Durham, N.C.: Duke University Press, 1930.
Also contemporary "Songsters" (collections) of the period.

For fourteen, America's minstrel

Foster, Morrison. *My Brother Stephen.* Indianapolis, Ind.: Privately printed for the Foster Hall Collection, 1932.

———. *Songs and Musical Compositions of Stephen Collins Foster.* Pittsburgh, 1896.

Foster, Stephen Collins. *Songs, Compositions and Arrangements.* Foster Hall Reproductions. Indianapolis, Ind.: Privately printed for the Foster Hall Collection by J. Kirby Lilly, 1933.

Gombosi, Otto. "Stephen Foster and 'Gregory Walker.'" *Musical Quarterly,* XXX, 2 (Apr. 1944), 133–146.

Howard, John T. "Newly Discovered Fosteriana." *Musical Quarterly,* XXI, 1 (Jan. 1935), 17–24.

———. *Stephen Foster, America's Troubadour.* New York: Thomas Y. Crowell Company, 1934. (New ed., 1953.)

Jackson, George P. "Stephen Foster's Debt to American Folk-Song." *Musical Quarterly,* XXII, 2 (Apr. 1936), 154–169.

Milligan, Harold V. *Stephen Collins Foster, A Biography.* New York: G. Schirmer, Inc., 1920.

Morneweck, Evelyn Foster. *Chronicles of Stephen Foster's Family.* 2 vols. Pittsburgh: Published for the Foster Hall Collection by the University of Pittsburgh Press, 1944.

Sonneck, Oscar G., and Walter Whittlesey. *Catalogue of the First Editions of Stephen C. Foster.* Washington, D.C.: The Library of Congress (Government Printing Office), 1915.

Walters, Raymond W. *Stephen Foster: Youth's Golden Gleam; a Sketch of His Life and Background in Cincinnati, 1846–1850.* Princeton, N.J.: Princeton University Press, 1936.

For fifteen, The exotic periphery

Allen, William Francis, *et al. Slave Songs of the United States.* (12)

Arpin, Paul. *Life of Louis Moreau Gottschalk.* Translated from the French by H. C. Watson. New York, 1852.

Asbury, Herbert. *The French Quarter.* New York: Alfred A. Knopf, Inc., 1938.

Cable, George W. "Creole Slave Songs." *The Century Magazine,* XXXI, 6 (Apr. 1886), 807–828.

———. "The Dance in Place Congo." *The Century Magazine,* XXXI, 4 (Feb. 1886), 517–532.

Carpentier, Alejo. *La Música en Cuba.* México, D.F.: Fondo de Cultura Económica, 1946.

Courlander, Harold. *Haiti Singing.* Chapel Hill, N.C.: The University of North Carolina Press, 1939.

Fors, Luis Ricardo. *Gottschalk.* Havana, 1880.

Goffin, Robert. *Jazz, From the Congo to the Metropolitan.* (23)

Gottschalk, Louis Moreau. *Notes of a Pianist,* ed. by his sister, Clara Gottschalk. Philadelphia: J. B. Lippincott Company, 1881.

Grenet, Emilio. *Popular Cuban Music.* Havana, 1939.
Hare, Maud (Cuney). *Six Creole Folk Songs.* New York: Carl Fischer, 1921.
Hearn, Lafcadio. *Two Years in the French West Indies.* New York: Harper & Brothers, 1890.
Hensel, Octavia. *Life and Letters of Louis Moreau Gottschalk.* Boston: Oliver Ditson Co., 1870.
Howard, John Tasker. "Louis Moreau Gottschalk, as Portrayed by Himself." *Musical Quarterly,* XVIII, 1 (Jan. 1932), 120–133.
Krehbiel, H. E. *Afro-American Folksongs.* (4)
Lange, Francisco Curt. "Vida y Muerte de Louis Moreau Gottschalk en Rio de Janeiro (1869)." *Revista de Estudios Musicales* (Mendoza, Argentina), Año II, 4, 5–6, 1950–1951.
Lindstrom, Carl E. "The American Quality in the Music of Louis Moreau Gottschalk." *Musical Quarterly,* XXXI, 3 (July 1945), 356–366.
Monroe, Mina, and Kurt Schindler. *Bayou Ballads.* New York: G. Schirmer, Inc., 1921.
Peterson, Clara Gottschalk. *Creole Songs from New Orleans.* New Orleans: L. Gruenwald Company, 1902.
Tiersot, Julien. *Chansons Nègres d'Amérique.* Paris: Heugel & Cie., 1933.
Whitfield, Irène Thérèse. *Louisiana French Folk Songs.* Baton Rouge, La.: Louisiana State University Press, 1937.

For sixteen, Europe versus America

Armstrong, W. G. *Record of the Opera at Philadelphia.* Philadelphia: Porter and Coates, 1884.
Dictionary of American Biography. Articles on Bristow, Buck, Fry, Gilchrist, Gleason, Paine, Pratt.
Goodrich, A. J. *Complete Musical Analysis.* Cincinnati: The John Church Company, 1889. Contains analyses of works by Paine, Pratt, Buck, Gilchrist, and Gleason.
Howe, M. A. De Wolfe. "John Knowles Paine." *Musical Quarterly,* XXV, 3 (July 1939), 257–267.
Huneker, James G. *The Philharmonic Society of New York and its 75th Anniversary.* New York: The Society, 1917.
Krehbiel, H. E. *Notes on the Cultivation of Choral Music and the Oratorio Society in New York.* New York: E. Schuberth and Company, 1884.
———. *The Philharmonic Society of New York.* New York and London: Novello, Ewer and Company, 1892.
Lanier, Sidney. *Music and Poetry: Essays upon Some Aspects and Interrelations between the Two Arts.* New York: Charles Scribner's Sons, 1898.
———. *The Science of English Verse.* New York: Charles Scribner's Sons, 1880.
Mason, William. *Memories of a Musical Life.* New York: Century Company, 1902.
Mattfeld, Julius. *A Hundred Years of Grand Opera in New York (1825–1925).* New York: The New York Public Library, 1927.

Mims, Edwin. *Sidney Lanier*. Boston: Houghton Mifflin Company, 1905.
New York Philharmonic Journal, ed. by Edward Jerome Hopkins. New York: The Society, 1868–1885.
Starke, Aubrey H. *Sidney Lanier: A Biographical and Critical Study*. Chapel Hill, N.C.: The University of North Carolina Press, 1933.
———. "Sidney Lanier as a Musician." *Musical Quarterly*, XX, 4 (Oct. 1934), 384–400.
Thorpe, Harry C. "Sidney Lanier: A Poet for Musicians." *Musical Quarterly*, XI, 3 (July 1925), 373–382.
Upton, William Treat. *The Musical Works of William Henry Fry in the Collections of The Library Company of Philadelphia*. A Research Bulletin of The Free Library of Philadelphia. Philadelphia, 1946.
———. *William Henry Fry, American Journalist and Composer-Critic*. New York: Thomas J. Crowell Company, 1954.

For seventeen, A romantic bard

Brown, Rollo W. *Lonely Americans*. New York: Coward-McCann, Inc., 1929.
Butler, Nicholas Murray. "Columbia and the Department of Music." *The New York Times*, Feb. 8, 1904. Reprinted by Columbia University, 1904.
Currier, T. P. "MacDowell as I Knew Him." *Musical Quarterly*, I, 1 (Jan. 1915).
Erskine, John. "Edward MacDowell." *Dictionary of American Biography*, vol. 12, pp. 24–27.
———. "MacDowell at Columbia: Some Recollections." *Musical Quarterly*, XXVIII, 4 (Oct. 1942).
Gilbert, Henry F. "Personal Recollections of Edward MacDowell." *New Music Review*, II, 132 (1912).
Gilman, Lawrence. *Edward MacDowell, A Study*. New York: John Lane Company, 1908.
———. *Phases of Modern Music*. New York: Harper & Brothers, 1904.
MacDowell, Edward. *Critical and Historical Essays*. Boston: The Arthur P. Schmidt Company, 1912.
MacDowell, Marian. "MacDowell's 'Peterboro Idea.'" *Musical Quarterly*, XVIII, 1 (Jan. 1932), 33–38.
Matthews, J. Brander. *Commemorative Tributes to Edward MacDowell*. New York: American Academy of Arts and Letters, 1922.
Page, Elizabeth F. *Edward MacDowell, His Work and Ideals*. New York: Dodge Publishing Company, 1910.
Porte, John F. *Edward MacDowell, A Great American Tone Poet*. London: Kegan Paul, Trench, Trubner & Co., 1922.
Rosenfeld, Paul. *An Hour with American Music*. (See General Bibliography.)
Sonneck, Oscar G. *Catalogue of the First Editions of Edward MacDowell*. Washington, D.C.: The Library of Congress (Government Printing Office), 1917.
———. *Suum Cuique*. (5). Includes "MacDowell vs. MacDowell."

For eighteen, The Boston classicists

Chadwick, George W. *Commemorative Tribute to Horatio Parker.* New Haven, Conn.: Yale University Press, 1921. Also in American Academy of Arts and Letters Publication No. 23, New York, 1922.

Engel, Carl. "Charles Martin Loeffler." *The International Cyclopedia of Music and Musicians,* ed. by Oscar Thompson. (6th ed.) New York: Dodd, Mead & Co., 1952.

———. "George W. Chadwick." *Musical Quarterly,* X, 3 (July 1924). (Reprinted in pamphlet form by the New England Conservatory of Music, Boston.)

Hughes, Rupert. *Contemporary American Composers; being a study of the music of this country, its present conditions and its future, with critical estimates and biographies of the principal living composers. . . .* Boston: L. C. Page & Company, 1900.

Langley, Allen L. "George Chadwick and the New England Conservatory of Music." *Musical Quarterly,* XXI, I (Jan. 1935), 39–52.

Leichtentritt, Hugo. *Serge Koussevitzky, the Boston Symphony Orchestra, and the New American Music.* Cambridge, Mass.: Harvard University Press, 1946.

Mason, Daniel G. "Arthur Whiting." *Musical Quarterly,* XXIII, 1 (Jan. 1937), 26–36.

———. *Music in My Time, and Other Reminiscences.* New York: The Macmillan Company, 1938.

Semler, Isabel Parker. *Horatio Parker; a Memoir for his grandchildren, compiled from letters and papers . . . in collaboration with Pierson Underwood.* New York: G. P. Putnam's Sons, 1942. Includes "Works of H. W. Parker, compiled by W. Oliver Strunk," pp. 318–330.

Smith, David Stanley. "A Study of Horatio Parker." *Musical Quarterly,* XVI, 2 (Apr. 1930).

Tuthill, Burnet C. "Mrs. H. H. A. Beach." *Musical Quarterly,* XXVI, 3 (July 1940), 297–310.

For nineteen, Nationalism and folklore

Carter, Elliott. "American Figure, with Landscape." *Modern Music,* May-June 1943. Deals with Henry F. Gilbert.

Downes, Olin. "An American Composer." *Musical Quarterly,* (Jan. 1918). Deals with Henry F. Gilbert.

Farwell, Arthur. *Music in America.* (See General Bibliography.)

Howard, John Tasker. *Charles Sanford Skilton.* New York: Carl Fischer, Inc., 1929.

Salter, Sumner. "Early Encouragements to American Composers." *Musical Quarterly,* XVIII, 1 (Jan. 1932), 76–105.

Upton, William Treat. *Anthony Philip Heinrich.* New York: Columbia University Press, 1939.

Waters, Edward N. "The Wa-Wan Press: An Adventure in Musical Idealism." In *A Birthday Offering to Carl Engel,* ed. by Gustave Reese. New York: G. Schirmer, Inc., 1943.

For twenty, Indian tribal music

Baker, Theodore. *Über die Musik der Nordamerikanischen Wilden.* Leipzig: Breitkopf & Härtel, 1882.

Burton, Frederick R. *American Primitive Music, with special attention to the songs of the Ojibways.* New York: Moffat, Yard and Co., 1909.

Catlin, George. *Letters and Notes on the Manners, Customs, and Condition of the North American Indians,* 2 vols. New York, 1841. (New ed. as *North American Indians,* Edinburgh: J. Grant, 1926.)

Curtis, Natalie. *The Indians' Book. An offering by the American Indians of Indian lore, musical and narrative, to form a record of the songs and legends of their race.* New York and London: Harper & Brothers, n.d. [1907].

Densmore, Frances. *The American Indians and Their Music.* New York: The Women's Press, 1926.

———. *Chippewa Music, I and II.* Smithsonian Institution, Bureau of American Ethnology, Bulletins 45 and 53. Washington, D.C.: Government Printing Office, 1910 and 1913.

———. *Mandan and Hidatsa Music.* Bureau of American Ethnology, Bulletin 80, Washington, D.C.: Government Printing Office, 1923.

———. *Menominee Music.* Bureau of American Ethnology, Bulletin 102, Washington, D.C.: Government Printing Office, 1932.

———. *Northern Ute Music.* Bureau of American Ethnology, Bulletin 75, Washington, D.C.: Government Printing Office, 1922.

———. *Papago Music.* Bureau of American Ethnology, Bulletin 90, Washington, D.C.: Government Printing Office, 1929.

———. *Pawnee Music.* Bureau of American Ethnology, Bulletin 93, Washington, D.C.: Government Printing Office, 1929.

———. *Teton Sioux Music.* Bureau of American Ethnology, Bulletin 61, Washington, D.C.: Government Printing Office, 1918.

———. *Yuman and Yaqui Music.* Bureau of American Ethnology, Bulletin 110, Washington, D.C.: Government Printing Office, 1932.

———. "The Study of Indian Music." From the *Smithsonian Report for 1941,* pp. 527–550. Washington, D.C.: Smithsonian Institution, 1942. (Publication 3671.)

Fenton, William N. *Songs from the Iroquois Longhouse: Program Notes for an Album of American Indian Music from the Eastern Woodlands.* Washington, D.C.: Published by the Smithsonian Institution, 1942.

Fewkes, J. Walter. "Additional Studies of Zuñi Songs and Rituals with the Phonograph." *American Naturalist,* Nov. 1890, pp. 1094–1098.

———. "A Few Summer Ceremonials at Zuñi Pueblo." *A Journal of American Ethnology and Archaeology,* I (1891), 1–62. Boston and New York: Houghton Mifflin Company.

Fillmore, John C. *The Harmonic Structure of Indian Music.* New York: G. P. Putnam's Sons, 1899.

Fletcher, Alice C. *Indian Story and Song from North America.* Boston: Small, Maynard & Co., 1900.

Fletcher, Alice C. "A Study of Omaha Indian Music, with a Report on the Structural Peculiarities of the Music by John Comfort Fillmore." Harvard University, *Archaeological and Ethnological Papers of the Peabody Museum*, I, 5. Cambridge, Mass.: Peabody Museum of American Archaeology and Ethnology, 1893.

Gilman, Benjamin Ives. "Zuñi Melodies." *A Journal of American Ethnology and Archaeology*, I (1891), 63–91. Boston and New York: Houghton Mifflin Company.

———. "Hopi Songs." Hemenway Southwestern Expedition. *A Journal of American Ethnology and Archaeology*, V (1908), Boston and New York: Houghton Mifflin Company.

Rhodes, Willard. "Acculturation in North American Indian Music." Reprinted from TAX: *Acculturation in the Americas*. Vol. II, *Proceedings of the 29th International Congress of Americanists*. Chicago: The University of Chicago Press, 1952.

———. "North American Indian Music: A Bibliographical Survey of Anthropological Theory." *Music Library Association Notes*, Ser. 2, X, 1 (Dec. 1952), 33–45.

———. "On the War Path, 1942." *Modern Music*, XX, 3 (Mar.–Apr. 1945), 157–160.

Roberts, Helen H. *Form in Primitive Music; An Analytical and Comparative Study of the Melodic Form of Some Ancient Southern California Songs*. New York: W. W. Norton & Company, 1933.

Schoolcraft, Henry R. *Historical and Statistical Information Respecting the History, Condition, and Prospects of the Indian Tribes of the United States*. 6 parts. Philadelphia: Lippincott, Grambo and Co., 1851–1857.

———. *The Indian in His Wigwam, or Characteristics of the Red Race of America*. New York: W. H. Graham, 1848.

Skilton, Charles S. "American Indian Music." *The International Cyclopedia of Music and Musicians*, ed. by Oscar Thompson. (6th ed.) New York: Dodd, Mead & Company, Inc., 1952.

Speck, F. G., *Ceremonial Songs of the Creek and Yuchi Indians*. With music transcribed by J. D. Sapir. University of Pennsylvania Anthropological Publications, I, 2. Philadelphia: University Museum, 1911.

———, and Leonard Broom, in collaboration with Will West Long. *Cherokee Dance and Drama*. Berkeley, Calif.: University of California Press, 1951.

Troyer, Carlos. *Indian Music Lecture: The Zuñi Indians and Their Music*. Philadelphia: Theodore Presser Company, 1913.

Wallaschek, Richard. *Primitive Music*. Chap. 1, "America." London: Longmans, Green & Co., Ltd., 1893.

For twenty-one, The rise of ragtime

Blesh, Rudi, and Harriet Janis. *They All Played Ragtime: The True Story of an American Music*. New York: Alfred A. Knopf, Inc., 1950. The definitive work on the subject to date.

Borneman, Ernest, and Bartlett D. Simms. "History and Analysis of Ragtime." *Record Changer*, Oct. 1945.

Campbell, S. Brunson. "Early Great White Ragtime Composers and Pianists." *Jazz Journal*, II (May 1949).
———. "Ragtime Begins." *Record Changer*, VII (Mar. 1948), 8, 18.
Confrey, Zez. *Modern Course in Novelty Piano Playing*. New York: Mills Music Co., Inc., 1923.
Gardner, Carl E. "Ragging and Jazzing." *Metronome* (New York), XXXV, 10 (1919), 35.
Hearn, Lafcadio. *American Miscellany;* articles and stories now first collected by Albert Mordell. 2 vols. New York: Dodd, Mead & Company, Inc., 1924. A collection of miscellaneous articles by Hearn.
Hughes, Rupert. "A Eulogy of Ragtime." *Musical Record* (Boston), No. 447 (Apr. 1899), 157–159.
Witmark, Isidore. *The Story of the House of Witmark: From Ragtime to Swingtime*. New York: Lee Furman, Inc., 1939.
See also the bibliography for Chapter 23.

For twenty-two, Singin' the blues

Ferguson, Otis. "The Man with the Blues in his Heart." *New Republic*, XCI (July 14, 1937), 277–279. About Jack Teagarden.
Gombosi, Otto. "The Pedigree of the Blues." *Volume of Proceedings of the Music Teachers National Association*, 40th ser., 70th year, pp. 382–389. Pittsburgh: Published by the Association, 1946.
Greene, Maude. "The Background of the Beale Street Blues." *Bulletin of the Tennessee Folklore Society*, VII (1941), 1–10.
Handy, W. C. (ed.). *A Treasury of the Blues*. With an historical and critical text by Abbe Niles. New York: Published by Charles Boni, distributed by Simon and Schuster, 1949. (Originally published in 1926.) A valuable historical anthology.
———. *Father of the Blues, An Autobiography*. New York: The Macmillan Company, 1941.
Lee, George W. *Beale Street, Where the Blues Began*. New York: Robert O. Ballou, 1934.
Lomax, John A., and Alan Lomax. *Negro Folk Songs as Sung by Lead Belly*. New York: The Macmillan Company, 1936.
Mezzrow, Milton, and Bernard Wolfe. *Really the Blues*. New York: Random House, 1946.
Odum, Howard W., and Guy B. Johnson. *The Negro and His Songs*. (12)
See also the bibliography for Chapter 23.

For twenty-three, The growth of jazz

Armstrong, Louis. *Swing That Music*. New York: Longmans, Green & Co., Inc., 1936.
Blesh, Rudi. *Shining Trumpets: A History of Jazz*. New York: Alfred A. Knopf, Inc., 1946.
Borneman, Ernest. *A Critic Looks at Jazz*. London: Jazz Music Books, 1946.
Condon, Eddie, and Thomas A. Sugrue. *We Called It Music*. New York: Henry Holt and Company, Inc., 1947.

Copland, Aaron. "Jazz Structure and Influence." *Modern Music*, IV (Jan.–Feb. 1927), 9–14.
———. *Our New Music.* (24)
Delaunay, Charles. *New Hot Discography* (2d ed.), ed. by W. E. Schaap and George Avakian. New York: Criterion Music Corp., 1948.
Dexter, Dave, Jr. *Jazz Cavalcade. The Inside Story of Jazz.* New York: Criterion Music Corp., 1946.
Feather, Leonard. *Inside Be-bop.* New York: J. J. Robbins & Sons, 1949.
Finkelstein, Sidney. *Jazz: A People's Music.* New York: The Citadel Press, 1948.
Goffin, Robert. *Jazz, From the Congo to the Metropolitan.* New York: Doubleday, Doran & Company, 1944.
———. *Horn of Plenty; The Story of Louis Armstrong.* New York: Allen, Towne & Heath, 1947.
Goodman, Benny, and Irving Kolodin. *The Kingdom of Swing.* Harrisburg, Pa.: Stackpole Sons, 1939.
Harap, Louis. "The Case for Hot Jazz." *Musical Quarterly*, XXVII, 1 (Jan. 1941).
Harris, Rex. *Jazz.* Baltimore: Penguin Books, Inc., 1952.
Hobson, Wilder. *American Jazz Music.* New York: W. W. Norton & Company, 1939.
Jones, Max. "Ferdinand Joseph Morton–A Biography." *Jazz Music*, II (Feb.–Mar. 1944), 86–101.
Knowlton, Don. "The Anatomy of Jazz." *Harper's Magazine*, CLII (Apr. 1926), 578–585. Reprinted in *Contemporary Thought*, ed. by Taft, McDermott, and Jensen (New York, 1929), pp. 478–490.
Lomax, Alan. *Mister Jelly Roll.* New York: Duell, Sloane & Pearce, Inc., 1950.
Miller, Paul Eduard (ed.). *Esquire's 1945 Jazz Book.* New York: A. S. Barnes and Company, 1945.
Osgood, Henry Osborne. *So This Is Jazz.* Boston: Little, Brown & Company, 1926.
Panassie, Hugues. *Hot Jazz: The Guide to Swing Music.* New York: M. Witmark & Sons, 1936.
———. *The Real Jazz.* New York: Smith & Durrell, 1942.
Ramsey, Frederic, and C. E. Smith. *Jazzmen.* New York: Harcourt, Brace and Company, Inc., 1939.
Rosenthal, George S. (ed.). *Jazzways.* New York: Greenberg, 1947.
Sargeant, Winthrop. *Jazz: Hot and Hybrid.* New and enlarged ed. New York: E. P. Dutton & Co., Inc., 1946.
Smith, Charles Edward. *The Jazz Record Book.* New York: Smith & Durrell, 1942.
Toledano, Ralph de (ed.). *Frontiers of Jazz.* New York: Oliver Durrell, Inc., 1947.
Ulanov, Barry. *Duke Ellington.* New York: Creative Age Press, Inc., 1946.
———. *A History of Jazz in America.* New York: The Viking Press, Inc., 1952.
Whiteman, Paul, and Mary Margaret McBride. *Jazz.* New York: J. H. Sears & Co., Inc., 1926.

For twenty-four, The Americanists

Armitage, Merle (ed.). *George Gershwin.* New York: Longmans, Green & Co., Inc., 1938.

Arvey, Verna. *William Grant Still.* New York: J. Fischer & Bros., 1939.

Berger, Arthur V. "The Music of Aaron Copland." *Musical Quarterly,* XXXI, 4 (Oct. 1945), 420–447.

———. *Aaron Copland.* New York: Oxford University Press, 1953.

Copland, Aaron. *Our New Music.* New York: Whittlesey House, McGraw-Hill Book Company, Inc., 1941.

Cowell, Henry (ed.). *American Composers on American Music.* [Stanford University, Calif.] Stanford University Press, 1933.

Duke, Vernon. "Gershwin, Schillinger, and Dukelsky: Some Reminiscences." *Musical Quarterly,* XXXIII, 1 (Jan. 1947), 102–115.

Farwell, Arthur. "Roy Harris." *Musical Quarterly,* XVIII, 1 (Jan. 1932), 18–32.

Gershwin, George. *George Gershwin's Song Book.* New York: Simon and Schuster, 1930.

Goldberg, Isaac. *George Gershwin, A Study in American Music.* New York: Simon and Schuster, 1931.

Levant, Oscar. *A Smattering of Ignorance.* New York: Doubleday, Doran and Company, 1940.

Luening, Otto. "Douglas Moore." *Modern Music,* May–June 1943.

Piston, Walter. "Roy Harris." *Modern Music,* Jan.–Feb. 1934.

Slonimsky, Nicolas. "Roy Harris." *Musical Quarterly,* XXXIII, 1 (Jan. 1947), 17–37.

Smith, Julia F. *Aaron Copland: His Work and Contribution to American Music.* New York: E. P. Dutton & Co., Inc., 1955.

Thomson, Virgil. "George Gershwin." *Modern Music,* Nov.–Dec. 1935.

For twenty-five, The eclectics

Broder, Nathan. "The Music of William Schuman." *Musical Quarterly,* XXXI, 1 (Jan. 1945), 17–28.

Cowell, Henry. "Paul Creston." *Musical Quarterly,* XXXIV, 4 (Oct. 1948), 533–543.

Eyer, Ronald F. "William Schuman." *Musical America,* Jan. 25, 1944, pp. 8, 25.

Frankenstein, Alfred. "William Schuman." *Modern Music,* Nov.–Dec. 1944, pp. 23–29.

Maisel, Edward M. *Charles T. Griffes; The Life of an American Composer.* New York: Alfred A. Knopf, Inc., 1943.

Newman, William S. "Arthur Shepherd." *Musical Quarterly,* XXXVI, 2 (Apr. 1950), 159–179.

Sabin, Robert. "Norman Dello Joio." *Musical America,* Dec. 1, 1950, pp. 9, 30.

Schubart, Mark A. "Roger Sessions." *Musical Quarterly*, XXXII, 2 (Apr. 1946), 196–214.
Sessions, Roger. *Harmonic Practice*. New York: Harcourt, Brace and Company, Inc., 1951.
———. *The Musical Experience of Composer, Performer, Listener*. Princeton, N. J.: Princeton University Press, 1950.

For twenty-six, The traditionalists

Alter, Martha. "Howard Hanson." *Modern Music*, Jan.–Feb. 1941.
Broder, Nathan. "The Music of Samuel Barber." *Musical Quarterly*, XXXIV, 3 (July 1948), 325–335.
Carter, Elliott. "Walter Piston." *Musical Quarterly*, XXXII, 3 (July 1946), 354–375.
Citkowitz, Israel. "Walter Piston, Classicist." *Modern Music*, Jan.–Feb. 1936.
Diamond, David. "Bernard Rogers." *Musical Quarterly*, XXXIII, 2 (Apr. 1947), 207–227.
Hanson, Howard. "Bernard Rogers." *Modern Music*, Mar.–Apr. 1945.
Riker, Charles. *The Eastman School of Music: Its First Quarter Century, 1921–1946*. Rochester, N.Y.: The University of Rochester, 1948.
Skulsky, Abraham. "Elliott Carter." *Bulletin of American Composers Alliance*, III, 2 (1953), 2–16.
Tuthill, Burnet C. "Howard Hanson." *Musical Quarterly*, XXII, 2 (Apr. 1936), 140–153.
———. "Leo Sowerby." *Musical Quarterly*, XXIV, 3 (July 1938).
Wykes, Robert. "Howard Hanson: 25 Years of Progress." *Musical America*, Apr. 1950, pp. 37, 50.

For twenty-seven, The experimentalists

Antheil, George. *Bad Boy of Music*. New York: Doubleday, Doran and Company, Inc., 1945.
Becker, John J. "Finding a Personal Orchestral Idiom." *Musical America*, Feb. 1950, pp. 126, 256.
Buchanan, C. L. "Ornstein and Modern Music." *Musical Quarterly*, Apr. 1918.
Cage, John. "Words for Prepared Discourse." *Bulletin of American Composers Alliance*, II, 2 (June 1952), 11.
Copland, Aaron. "George Antheil." *Modern Music*, Jan. 1925.
Cowell, Henry (ed.). *American Composers on American Music*. (24)
———. "The Music of Edgar Varèse." *Modern Music*, Jan. 1928.
Glanville-Hicks, P. "John Cage." *Musical America*, Sept. 1948.
Harrison, Lou. *About Carl Ruggles*. New York: Published by Oscar Baradinsky at the Alicat Bookshop in Yonkers, 1946.
New Music, A Quarterly of Modern Compositions. New York: The New Music Society Publishers.
Partch, Harry. *Genesis of a Music*. Madison, Wis.: The University of Wisconsin Press, 1949.

Pound, Ezra. *George Antheil and the Theory of Harmony*. Paris, 1925.
Seeger, Charles L. "Carl Ruggles." *Musical Quarterly*, XVIII, 4 (Oct. 1932), 578–592.
Slonimsky, Nicolas. *Music Since 1900*. 3d ed. New York: Coleman-Ross Co., Inc., 1949.
Thomson, Virgil. "The Abstract Composers." *Bulletin of American Composers Alliance*, II, 2 (June 1952), 9–10.
——. *Music Right and Left*. New York: Henry Holt and Company, Inc., 1951.

For twenty-eight, Twelve-tone composers

Bruno, Anthony. "Two American Twelve-tone Composers." *Musical America*, Feb. 1951, pp. 22, 170. Deals with Milton Babbitt and Ben Weber.
Cowell, Henry. "Wallingford Riegger." *Musical America*, Dec. 1, 1948, pp. 9, 29.
—— (ed.). *American Composers on American Music*. (24)
Hill, Richard S. "Schoenberg's Tone-Rows and the Music of the Future." *Musical Quarterly*, XXII, 1 (Jan. 1936), 14–37.
Jalowetz, Heinrich. "On the Spontaneity of Schoenberg's Music." *Musical Quarterly*, XXX, 4 (Oct. 1944), 385–409.
Leibowitz, René, *Schoenberg and His School: The Contemporary Stage of the Language of Music*. Translated from the French by Dika Newlin. New York: Philosophical Library, 1949.
Rubsamen, Walter H. "Schoenberg in America." *Musical Quarterly*, XXXVII, 4 (Oct. 1951), 469–489.
Rufer, Josef. *Composition with Twelve Notes*. Translated by Humphrey Searle. New York: The Macmillan Company, 1954.
Schoenberg, Arnold. "My Evolution." *Musical Quarterly*, XXXVIII, 4 (Oct. 1952), 517–527.
——. "Problems of Harmony." *Modern Music*, XI, 4 (1934), 167–187.
——. *Style and Idea*. New York: Philosophical Library, 1950.
Skulsky, Abraham. "Arnold Schoenberg." *Musical America*, Sept. 1951, pp. 5, 34.
——. "Stefan Wolpe." *Musical America*, Nov. 1, 1951, pp. 6, 29.
Stein, Erwin. "Schoenberg's New Structural Form." *Modern Music*, VII, 4 (1930), 3–10.

For twenty-nine, The orbit of Broadway

Adams, F. P. "Words and Music." *The New Yorker*, Feb. 8, 1930. Deals with Jerome Kern.
Armitage, Merle (ed.). *George Gershwin*. (24)
Burton, Jack. *The Blue Book of Broadway Musicals*. Watkins Glen, N.Y.: Century House, 1952.
DeKoven, Mrs. Reginald. *A Musician and His Wife*. New York: Harper & Brothers, 1926.
Gershwin, George. *George Gershwin's Song Book*. (24)
Goldberg, Isaac. *George Gershwin, A Study in American Music*. (24)

Kaye, Joseph. *Victor Herbert.* New York: G. H. Watt, 1931.
Lewiton, Mina. *John Philip Sousa, the March King.* New York: Didier, 1944.
Marks, E. B. *They All Had Glamour. From the Swedish Nightingale to the Naked Lady.* New York: Julian Messner, Inc., Publishers, 1944.
McSpadden, Joseph W. *Operas and Musical Comedies.* Enlarged ed. New York: Thomas Y. Crowell Company, 1951.
Morehouse, Ward. *George M. Cohan, Prince of the American Theatre.* Philadelphia: J. B. Lippincott, 1943.
Purdy, Claire L. *Victor Herbert, American Music Master.* New York: Julian Messner, Inc., Publishers, 1945.
Rodgers, Richard (ed.). *The Rodgers and Hart Song Book.* New York: Simon and Schuster, Inc., 1951.
Smith, Cecil. *Musical Comedy in America.* New York: Theatre Arts Books, 1950. A comprehensive history of the subject.
Sousa, John Philip. *Marching Along, An Autobiography.* Boston: Hale, Cushman and Flint, 1928.
Taylor, Deems. *Some Enchanted Evenings.* New York: Harper & Brothers, 1953. Deals with Rodgers, Hart, and Oscar Hammerstein, 2d.
Waters, Edward N. *Victor Herbert, A Life in Music.* New York: The Macmillan Company, 1955.
Woollcott, Alexander. *The Story of Irving Berlin.* New York: G. P. Putnam's Sons, 1925.

For thirty, Toward an American opera

Gershwin, George. *Porgy and Bess.* Libretto by Du Bose Heyward. New York: Gershwin Publishing Corp., 1935.
Graf, Herbert. *Opera and Its Future in America.* New York: W. W. Norton & Company, 1941.
———. *Opera for the People.* Minneapolis: University of Minnesota Press, 1951.
Hipsher, Edward E. *American Opera and Its Composers.* Philadelphia: Theodore Presser Company, 1927.
Howard, John Tasker. *Deems Taylor.* New York: J. Fischer & Brother, 1927.
Kolodin, Irving. *The Story of the Metropolitan Opera, 1883–1950. A Candid History.* New York: Alfred A. Knopf, Inc., 1953.
Kramer, A. Walter. "Louis Gruenberg." *Modern Music,* Nov.–Dec. 1930.
Lahee, H. C. *Grand Opera in America.* Boston: L. C. Page & Company, 1902.
Rosenfeld, Paul. *A Musical Chronicle.* New York: Harcourt, Brace and Company, Inc., 1923. Includes "The Fate of Mona."
Stein, Gertrude. *Last Operas and Plays.* New York: Rinehart & Company, Inc., 1948.

For thirty-one, Composer from Connecticut

Bellamann, Henry. "Charles Ives: The Man and His Music." *Musical Quarterly,* XIX, 1 (Jan. 1933), 45–58.

Carter, Elliott. "Ives Today: His Vision and Challenge." *Modern Music,* May–June 1944.
Cowell, Henry and Sidney. *Charles Ives and His Music.* New York: Oxford University Press, 1954.
Cowell, Henry. "Charles Ives." *Modern Music,* Nov.–Dec. 1932.
Ives, Charles. *Essays before a Sonata* (Second Pianoforte Sonata). Privately printed, 1919. 2d ed., New York: Arrow Music Press, 1947.
Rosenfeld, Paul. *Discoveries of a Music Critic.* New York: Harcourt, Brace and Company, Inc., 1936.
Taubman, Howard. "Posterity Catches Up with Charles Ives." *The New York Times Magazine,* Oct. 23, 1949.

General bibliography

Barnes, Edwin N. C. *American Music: From Plymouth Rock to Tin Pan Alley.* Washington, D.C.: Music Education Publications, 1936.
Bauer, Marion. *Twentieth Century Music.* New York: G. P. Putnam's Sons, 1933.
Bio-bibliographical Index of Musicians in the United States of America from Colonial Times. Washington, D.C.: Music Division, Pan-American Union, 1941.
Bliven, Bruce (ed.). *Twentieth Century Unlimited; From the Vantage Point of the First Fifty Years.* Philadelphia: J. B. Lippincott Company, 1950. Includes a chapter, "American Music," by Cecil Smith, pp. 234–253.
Chase, Gilbert. "American Music." In *Collier's Encyclopedia,* vol. 14, pp. 315–320. New York: P. F. Collier & Son Corporation, 1952. [Entered as "Music, American."]
———. "Music of the New World." *Handbook for the Broadcast Series of the Inter-American University of the Air.* 5 vols. New York: Published for the National Broadcasting Company by the Southern Music Publishing Comany, Inc., 1942–1945. Includes "Folkways in Music" (Vols. III and IV) and "Music in American Cities" (Vol. V).
———. *A Guide to Latin American Music.* Washington, D.C.: Music Division, The Library of Congress, 1945. Latin American Series, No. 5. Includes a section on Hispanic music in the United States, pp. 220–228.
Clarke, Eric. *Music in Everyday Life.* New York: W. W. Norton & Company, 1935.
Copland, Aaron. *Our New Music; Leading Composers in Europe and America.* New York: McGraw-Hill Book Company, Inc., 1941.
Cowell, Henry (ed.). *American Composers on American Music: A Symposium.* [Stanford University, Calif.] Stanford University Press, 1933.
Despard, Mabel H. *The Music of the United States, Its Sources and Its History. A Short Outline.* New York: J. H. H. Muirhead, 1936.
Eaton, Quaintance. *Musical U.S.A.* New York: Allen, Towne & Heath, 1949.
Elson, Louis C. *The History of American Music.* New York: The Macmillan Company, 1904. Rev. ed., 1915. (Also new edition, revised to 1925 by Arthur Elson.)
———. *The National Music of America and Its Sources.* Boston: L. C. Page & Company, 1899. (Also new edition, revised to 1924 by Arthur Elson.)

Ellinwood, Leonard. *The History of American Church Music.* New York: Morehouse-Gorham Co., Inc., 1953.

Encyclopédie de la Musique et Dictionnaire du Conservatoire, ed. by Albert Lavignac and Lionel de la Laurencie. Paris: Delagrave, 1913–1931. Part I, vol. 5 (1922) includes a chapter on American music by Esther Singleton.

Ewen, David. *American Composers Today*. New York: The H. W. Wilson Company, 1949.

Farwell, Arthur, and W. Dermot Darby. *Music in America.* Vol. 4 of *The Art of Music*. New York: The National Society of Music, 1915.

Fisher, William Arms. *One Hundred and Fifty Years of Music Publishing in the United States; An Historical Sketch with Special Reference to the Pioneer Publisher, Oliver Ditson Company, Inc., 1783–1933.* Boston: Oliver Ditson Company, 1933. A revision and extension of the author's *Notes on Music in Old Boston*, 1918.

Goss, Madeleine. *Modern Music-makers: Contemporary American Composers.* New York: E. P. Dutton & Co., Inc., 1952.

Hanson, Howard. *Music in Contemporary American Life.* (Montgomery Lectures on Contemporary Civilization, 1951.) Lincoln, Neb.: The University of Nebraska, 1951.

Howard, John Tasker. *Our American Music: Three Hundred Years Of It* (3d ed., rev.). New York: Thomas Y. Crowell Company, 1946. (First published in 1931.)

———. *Our Contemporary Composers: American Music in the Twentieth Century*. New York: Thomas Y. Crowell Company, 1941.

———. *A Program Outline of American Music.* New York: Thomas Y. Crowell Company, 1931.

Howe, Granville L. (ed.). *A Hundred Years of Music in America.* Chicago: G. L. Howe, 1889.

Hubbard, W. L. (ed.). *History of American Music*. Volume 8 of *The American History and Encyclopedia of Music*. Toledo, Ohio: Irving Squire, 1908–1910.

Hughes, Rupert. *Contemporary American Composers*. Boston: L. C. Page & Company, 1900. (Also new edition, revised to 1914 by Arthur Elson, under the title *American Composers.*)

Kaplan, Max. *The Musician in America: A Study of His Social Roles.* (University Microfilms Publication No. 3142.) Ann Arbor, Mich.: University Microfilms, 1951.

Kaufmann, Helen L. *From Jehovah to Jazz: Music in America from Psalmody to the Present Day*. New York: Dodd, Mead & Company, Inc., 1937.

Keppel, Frederick P., and R. L. Duffus. *The Arts in American Life*. New York: McGraw-Hill Book Company, Inc., 1933.

Lahee, H. C. *Annals of Music in America; a chronological record of significant musical events, from 1640 to the present day . . .* Boston: Marshall Jones Company, 1922.

Lavignac, Albert. *Music and Musicians*. New York: Henry Holt and Company, 1899. Includes chapters on music in America by H. E. Krehbiel, who edited the 4th rev. ed. in 1903.

Madeira, L. C. (comp.). *Annals of Music in Philadelphia and History of the Musical Fund Society from Its Organization in 1820 to the Year*

1858. Edited by Philip H. Goepp. Philadelphia: J. B. Lippincott Company, 1896.

Mason, Daniel Gregory. *The Dilemma of American Music*. New York: The Macmillan Company, 1928.

———. *Music in My Time*. New York: The Macmillan Company, 1938.

———. *Tune In, America! A Study of Our Coming Musical Independence*. New York: Alfred A. Knopf, Inc., 1931.

Mathews, W. S. B. *A Hundred Years of Music in America*. Chicago: G. L. Howe, 1889.

Morris, Harold. *Contemporary American Music*. Rice Institute Pamphlets, Vol. XXI. Houston, Tex.: Rice Institute of Liberal and Technical Learning, 1934.

Paine, J. K., Theodore Thomas, and Karl Klauser. *Music in America*. Vol. 2 of *Famous Composers and Their Works*. Boston: J. B. Millet & Co., 1901.

Reis, Claire. *Composers in America; Biographical Sketches of Contemporary Composers with a Record of Their Works*. Rev. and enlarged edition. New York: The Macmillan Company, 1947. (Originally published in 1938.)

Ritter, Frédéric Louis. *Music in America*. New York: Charles Scribner's Sons, 1883.

Rosenfeld, Paul. *An Hour with American Music*. Philadelphia: J. B. Lippincott Company, 1929.

Sonneck, Oscar G. *Miscellaneous Studies in the History of Music*. New York: The Macmillan Company, 1921. Includes "The History of Music in America."

———. *Suum Cuique; Essays in Music*. New York: G. Schirmer, Inc., 1916. Includes "A Survey of Music in America."

Slonimsky, Nicolas. *Music Since 1900* (3d ed., revised and enlarged). New York: Coleman-Ross Co., Inc., 1949. (First published in 1937.)

Spaeth, Sigmund. *A History of Popular Music in America*. New York: Random House, 1948.

Stearns, Harold E. (ed.). *Civilization in the United States*. New York, Harcourt, Brace and Company, Inc., 1922. Includes a chapter on music by Deems Taylor.

Sward, Keith. "Jewish Musicality in America." *Journal of Applied Psychology*, XVII, 6 (Dec. 1933), 675–712.

The ASCAP Biographical Dictionary of Composers, Authors and Publishers, ed. by Daniel I. McNamara (2d ed.). New York: Thomas Y. Crowell Company, 1952.

The International Cyclopedia of Music and Musicians, ed. by Oscar Thompson (6th ed.). Revised by Nicolas Slonimsky. New York: Dodd, Mead & Company, 1952.

The Year in American Music, 1946–1947, ed. by Julius Bloom. New York: Allen, Towne & Heath, Inc., 1947. Also published in 1948, edited by David Ewen.

Upton, William Treat. *Art-song in America; A Study in the Development of American Music*. Boston and New York: Oliver Ditson Company, 1930.

———. *A Supplement to Art-song in America, 1930–1938*. Boston: Oliver Ditson Company; Philadelphia, Theodore Presser Company, distributors, 1938.

A note on recordings

Recordings of works by American composers have increased in number to a surprising extent during the last few years. This has been due in part to the stimulus given to all types of recording by the advent of the microgroove or long-playing disk, but also in large part to an awakened interest in the production of our contemporary composers, as well as to a growing curiosity about our musical past. As a result there is available a large body of recorded American music, from the psalmody of the Puritans and the compositions of the first musical emigrants to the most recent works of the older and younger composers of today.

In addition to the goodly percentage of American music being issued by both the larger and the smaller commercial recording companies, there are various special recording enterprises, such as those of the Louisville (Kentucky) Symphony Orchestra and the "University Recordings" of the University of Oklahoma, which, while not dedicated exclusively to American music, yet give a very large share of their attention to it. An organization that does devote itself exclusively to the recording and distribution of American music is the American Recording Society, which was established through a grant from the Alice M. Ditson Fund of Columbia University. The ARS recordings are distributed solely on a subscription basis.

In the field of folk music, the most comprehensive single source is the Archive of American Folk Song in the Library of Congress, which, drawing on its vast and always increasing collection, periodically issues record albums copiously annotated by experts, presenting folk music of the United States in all its diversity. Catalogues of these recordings may be obtained by writing to the Recording Laboratory, Music Division, Library of Congress, Washington 25, D.C. Another valuable source of recordings of American folk music, available through commercial outlets, is the "Ethnic Folkways Library" issued by Folkways Records of New York City, which has also issued "Folkways Americana," "Anthology of American Folk Music," and "Anthology of Jazz" (historical survey of jazz in eleven volumes with three additional "Footnotes").

Since many of the older recordings of American music are not readily obtainable, and since new recordings are appearing continually, no attempt will be made here to compile a comprehensive record list, which would soon become obsolete. *The Long Player,* a periodical catalogue published by Long Player Publications of New York and distributed through record dealers, may be consulted for current recordings of American music. We will list here the releases of the American Recording Society, because it is the only label devoted exclusively to American music, and because its recordings are not available through dealers and record stores. Further information may be obtained by writing to the American Recording Society, 100 Avenue of the Americas, New York 13, N.Y.

ARS–1	Walter Piston, Symphony No. 2
ARS–2	Henry Cowell, Symphony No. 5
ARS–3	Edward MacDowell, *Indian Suite*
ARS–4	Randall Thompson, Symphony No. 2
ARS–5	Douglas Moore, Symphony in A major
ARS–6	Howard Hanson, Symphony No. 4
ARS–7	Howard Swanson, *Short Symphony* David Diamond, *Rounds* for String Orchestra
ARS–8	Virgil Thomson, *The River* Otto Luening, Two Symphonic Interludes and Prelude on a Hymn Tune (by William Billings)
ARS–9	Alexei Haieff, Concerto for Piano and Orchestra Robert Ward, Symphony No. 1
ARS–10	Howard Swanson, Seven Songs Roger Goeb, *Prairie Songs* for Woodwind Quintet Ben Weber, Concert Aria after Solomon
ARS–11	Roger Sessions, *The Black Maskers*
ARS–12	Jerome Moross, *Frankie & Johnny* Aaron Copland, *Music for the Theatre*
ARS–14	Leo Sowerby, *Prairie* (A Poem for Orchestra) and *From the Northland*
ARS–15	Stephen C. Foster, *Village Festival* and *Old Folks Quadrille* Minstrel Songs of the Nineteenth Century
ARS–18	William Bergsma, String Quartet No. 2 Arthur Shepherd, *Triptych* for Soprano and String Quartet

ARS–20	John Powell, *Rhapsodie Nègre* Daniel Gregory Mason, *Chanticleer Overture*
ARS–21	Bernard Wagenaar, Symphony No. 4
ARS–22	Charles T. Griffes, *Poem* for Flute and Orchestra Arthur Foote, Suite for String Orchestra
ARS–23	Deems Taylor, *The Portrait of a Lady* (Rhapsody for strings, winds, and piano) Paul Creston, Partita for Solo Flute and Violin with String Orchestra
ARS–24	Ernest Bloch, *Trois Poèmes Juifs* Victor Herbert, Concerto for Violoncello and Orchestra
ARS–25	Elliott Carter, Sonata for Violoncello and Piano (1948) and Sonata for Piano (1945–1946).
ARS–26	Aaron Copland, *Appalachian Spring* Samuel Barber, *Overture to The School for Scandal* and *Music for a Scene from Shelley*
ARS–27	Charles Ives, *Three Places in New England* Robert McBride, Concerto for Violin and Orchestra
ARS–28	Roy Harris, Symphony No. 3 William Schuman, *American Festival Overture*
ARS–29	Frederick S. Converse, *The Mystic Trumpeter* George W. Chadwick, *Tam O'Shanter* (Symphonic Ballad)
ARS–30	Bernard Rogers, *Leaves From Pinocchio* Robert Sanders, *Saturday Night* Burnet Tuthill, *Come Seven* (Rhapsody for Orchestra)
ARS–31	Ray Green, *Sunday Sing Symphony* Peter Mennin, Concertato for Orchestra Norman Dello Joio, *Epigraph*
ARS–32	Early American Psalmody: *The Bay Psalm Book* (Sung by Margaret Dodd Singers) Mission Music in California: Music of the Southwest (Sung by Coro Hispanico de Mallorca)
ARS–33	American Colonial Instrumental Music: John Christopher Moller, Quartet in E Flat; Joseph Gehot, Quartet in D major; John Frederick Peter, Quintet No. 1 in D major and Quintet No. 6 in E Flat major.
ARS–36	Quincy Porter, Concerto for Viola and Orchestra Norman Dello Joio, *Serenade*
ARS–37	John Alden Carpenter, *Skyscrapers* (Suite from the Ballet) Herbert Elwell, *The Happy Hypocrite*
ARS–38	Henry Brant, Symphony No. 1 Burrill Phillips, *Selections From McGuffey's Readers*
ARS–335	Horatio W. Parker, *Hora Novissima* Ernst Bacon, *Ford's Theatre*

Index

Abel, Carl Friedrich, 60
Abel, F. L., 151
Abel, Ludwig, 375
Abstract composition, 573–575, 595, 612
Adams, George Whitefield, 151
Adams, John, 61, 99, 540, 644, 645
Ade, George, 624
Adgate, Andrew, 128, 191
Adonais (Chadwick), 370
Adventures in a Perambulator (Carpenter), 511
Aeolian Hall, New York, 491
African music, 66, 68, 69, 71–76, 254–256, 469, 523, 543
  music of West Africa, 71–76, 255–256
  rhythm in, 73–75, 255–257
  singing, characteristics of, 71–72, 255
    call-and-response pattern in, 33, 71, 233, 249, 255
    harmony in, 72, 75, 255
    intervals, 72
  syncretism in, 75, 256
  (*See also* Afro-American music)
Afro-American Folksongs (Krehbiel), 248, 313, 315
Afro-American music, 65–69, 76–83, 452–458
  hymns, 64, 80–81
  influence of, 75–78, 257–258, 437–438, 457–458
  instruments, 67, 76, 469–470
  origins of, 254–256
  themes from, 388–391, 398, 401, 512
  work songs, 245–246, 435–436
  (*See also* Blues; Creole songs and dances; Jazz; Negro spirituals; Ragtime; Voodoo ceremonies in New Orleans)
Agee, James, 555
"Ah, Lovely Appearance of Death," 48–49
Aiken, Jesse B., 200, 201
Ainsworth, Henry, 16–18
Ainsworth Psalter, 17–18, 21, 39, 561
Aitken, John, 62
Alabados, 62
Alabanzas, 62
Alcott, Bronson, 672
Alcott, Louisa May, 671
Alcott family, 664, 668, 671, 672, 677
"Alexander's Ragtime Band" (Berlin), 451, 625
Allegro (Rodgers), 631–632
Alleluia (Thompson), 539
Allen, William Francis, 238–239, 243, 247
Allison, Richard, 12, 13, 20
Alsted, Johann Heinrich, 13–14
Altschuler, Modest, 503
Amahl and the Night Visitors (Menotti), 650
"Amazing Grace," 202, 224
Amelia Goes to the Ball (Menotti), 647, 648
America (Bloch), 513–515
"America" (Law), 129
American Academy in Rome, 540, 551, 557, 559, 563
American Composers' Concerts, 549
American Festival Overture (Schuman), 534–535
American Harmony (Holden), 135
American Indian music, 403–432
  characteristics of, 406–409
  in MacDowell's *Indian Suite,* 363
  modern, 430–432
  religious significance of, 227, 421, 424
  studies of, 404–406, 409–411, 414, 416
American Indians, folklore of, 121, 404, 417–430
  and German missionaries, 55, 60
  Jefferson on, 66

American Indians, music inspired by, 363, 385–386, 388–390, 399–400, 432, 514, 517, 519, 523
in New England, 5, 6, 9, 12
and Spanish missionaries, 62
American minstrelsy (*see* Minstrelsy)
American Music Center, New York, 542
American in Paris, An (Gershwin), 489, 492
American Prix de Rome (*see* Rome Prize)
American Tragedy, An (Dreiser), 652
Americana (Thompson), 539
Americanesque (Gilbert), 398
Ammons, Albert, 467
Amores (Cage), 593
Anderson, Arthur Olaf, 395
Anderson, Marian, 541
Anderson, Maxwell, 647
Andrews, Edward D., 500
Andreyev, Leonid, 528, 529
Angels (Ruggles), 577
Annie Get Your Gun (Berlin), 626
Antes, John, 60
Antheil, George, 488, 571–575, 583
Anthony, Susan B., 644, 645
Aphrodite (Chadwick), 370
Apollinaire, Guillaume, 610
Appalachian Spring (Copland), 229, 498–501
Apthorp, W. F., 350
Arcadian Symphony (Bristow), 329
Archers, The (Carr), 119
Armenian music, 545–546
Armonica (*see* Harmonica)
Armstrong, Louis, 465, 475, 477, 480–481, 483, 485, 487
Arne, Thomas A., 85, 100, 155
Arnold, Samuel, 114
Art of Noises (*see Futurist Manifesto*)
As Thousands Cheer (Berlin), 625–626
Asbury, Francis, 207
Asbury, Henry, 222
Asbury, Herbert, 306
Asbury, Samuel, 223–224
At a Georgia Camp Meeting (Mills), 450
Atkinson, Brooks, 629, 647
Atonality, 599, 611, 667
(*See also* Twelve-tone technique)
Auber, Daniel François, 331
Austin, Lovie, 465
Autos sacramentales, 62
Ayres, Frederic, 395
Babbitt, Milton, 612, 613
"Babylon is Falling" (Work), 180
Bach, C. P. E., 59, 112, 116, 117
Bach, Johann Christian, 59, 111, 116
Bach, Johann Christian Friedrich, 60
Bach, Johann Sebastian, 109, 113, 287, 359, 365–366, 377, 502, 547, 577, 653
Bacon, Ernst, 512, 643
Baker, Benjamin Franklin, 179
Baker, John C., 176
Baker, Theodore, 363, 404, 409–410, 413
Baker family, 176
Balakirev, Mily A., 387
Balinese music, 582, 583
Ballad operas, 114, 118, 204
Ballads, traditional, 14–15, 95, 248, 261, 298, 469
Ballanta-Taylor, Nicholas, 74
Ballet Caravan, 499
Ballet mécanique (Antheil), 571, 572–574
Ballet music, 337, 494, 499, 510–511, 532–533, 535, 540, 543, 545, 559, 566, 568, 630
Ballet Russe, 500, 513
Baline, Izzy (*see* Berlin, Irving)
Baltimore, 52, 116–118, 343
Balzac, Honoré de, 123
Bamboula, La (Gottschalk), 306, 310–311, 314–315
Bamboula (dance), 307–309, 398
Bananier, Le (Gottschalk), 315
Bands in New Orleans, 469–471
Banjar (*see* Banjo)
Banjo, The (Gottschalk), 315
Banjo, 66–68, 259–260, 262–263, 307, 313, 433, 439–440, 457
Baptists, 47, 53, 57, 79, 194, 211, 236, 238, 251
Barber, Samuel, 549, 562–564
Barlow, Joel, 42
Barnum, Phineas Taylor, 150, 316, 325, 327, 510
Barry, Philip, 642
Bartlett, M. L., 308
Bartók, Bela, 389, 543, 547, 553
Basie, William ("Count"), 486
"Basin Street Blues," 483
"Battle Cry of Freedom, The" (Root), 180, 249, 514
"Battle Hymn of the Republic," (Howe), 231
Battle of Trenton (Hewitt), 120
Baudelaire, Charles, 373
Bauer, Marion, 523, 612
Baum, Frank, 623

Bay Psalm Book, 14, 19–21
Bayley, Daniel, 127
"Be Glad, Then, America" (Billings), 144, 535
Beach, Mrs. H. H. A., 378
Beach, John P., 395
"Beale Street Blues," 483
"Beautiful Dreamer, Wake unto Me" (Foster), 296
Bechet, Sidney, 472, 476
Becker, John J., 578–580
Beecher, Lyman, 152, 156, 174
Beethoven, Ludwig van, 92, 152, 155, 287, 327, 332, 333, 347, 366, 502, 672
"Before Jehovah's Awful Throne," 131, 155
Beggar's Opera, The, 114, 646
"Begin the Beguine" (Porter), 630
Begum, The (De Koven), 619
Beiderbecke, Leon ("Bix"), 482
Beissel, Conrad, 57–58
Bekker, Paul, 645
Belcher, Supply, 124, 125, 132–134, 324
Bellamann, Henry, 655, 677
Belle of New York (Kerker), 624
Bellinger, Lucius C., 217, 222, 237
Bellini, Charles, 86
Bellini, Vincenzo, 167, 331–332, 338
Benavides, Fray Alonso de, 62
Benét, Stephen Vincent, 510, 538
Benham, Asahel, 124
Bennett, Robert Russell, 633
Benson, Louis, 52, 208
Bentley, John, 113
Bentley, William, 124, 140, 144–145
Berg, Alban, 524, 543, 561, 577, 597, 610, 613
  Violin Concerto, 603
Berger, Arthur V., 497, 568
Bergsma, William, 557–558
Berkenhead, John, 120
Berkshire Music Center, 557
Berlin, Irving, 451, 462, 625–626
Berlioz, Hector, 315, 322, 511
Bernstein, Leonard, 544, 651, 657
Bethlehem, Pa., 58–60
  (*See also* Moravians)
Bigard, Barney, 480
Biggers, Earl Derr, 622
Billings, William, 124, 130, 135, 139–145, 150, 155, 183, 188, 191, 324, 561, 653, 677
  on composing, 140
  fuguing tunes, 141–142
  New England Psalm Singer, 140–143
  Thoughts on Music, 141
Billy the Kid (Copland), 499
Bimboni, Alberto, 400
Birch, Raymond (*see* Johnson, Charles L.)
Bizet, Georges, 385, 633
Black, Brown and Beige (Ellington), 484
Black Maskers (Sessions), 528–530
Blackface minstrelsy (*see* Minstrelsy)
Blake, Eubie, 446
Blake, William, 394, 613
Blennerhassett (Giannini), 643
Blesh, Rudi, 444, 464, 466, 487
Blitzstein, Marc, 646–647
Bloch, Ernest, 513, 525, 538, 540, 542, 552, 562, 565, 572
Blossom Time (Romberg), 624, 625
Blue laws, 9
Blues, 72, 78, 82, 433, 435, 438, 449, 452–467, 469, 471, 478, 480, 483, 492, 495, 566
  antiphonal pattern in, 458, 465, 478
  "blue" notes, 434, 456–458
  "break" in, 455, 478
  folk, 455–456, 458, 461, 467
  scale, 72, 456–457
  singers of, 462–467
  structure of, 454–458
  "tangana" rhythm in, 461
Boccherini, Luigi, 85
Boehler, Peter, 44–45
Bohm, Carl, 450
Bolden, Charles ("Buddy"), 471–472
Bolm, Adolph, 519
Bones in minstrel shows, 259–260, 267
Bonja (*see* Banjo)
"Bonja Song," 262
Bonner, Amy, 523
Boogiewoogie, 466–467, 486, 583
  (*See also* Blues)
Borneman, Ernest, 444
Borodin, Alexander, 387
Boston, 19, 20, 39, 86
  "Classicist" composers of, 364–382
  early musical life in, 9, 13, 19–20, 27, 34, 39, 121–122, 138–142
Boston Academy of Music, 153, 155, 159, 160, 162, 179
"Boston Common" (Ives), 664
Boston "Pops" Concerts, 566
Boston Symphony Orchestra, 351, 374, 398, 493, 495, 505–508, 605
Boston University, 556
Bostonians, The, 619–620
Botsford, George, 445

Boulanger, Nadia, influence of, 565
pupils of, 494, 503, 524, 531, 540–541, 544, 552, 554, 561, 567, 569, 646
Boulez, Pierre, 589*n.*
Bourgeois, Louis, 17
Bower, Frank, 259
"Bowery Gals," 281
Bowles, Paul, 543
Bradbury, William B., 162, 179
Bradford, William, 11
Bradstreet, Anne, 8
Braham, Dave, 439
Brahms, Johannes, 334, 347, 365–367, 375, 525, 597, 659
Brandeis University, 647
Branscombe, Gena, 395
Brant, Henry D., 582–584
Brattle, Thomas, 4, 34
Brecht, Bertold, 529
Brewster, William, 12, 13
Briggs, Pete, 480–481
Bristow, George Frederick, 326–330, 634
Broady, Thomas E., 446
Brockway, Howard A., 583
Brooks, Van Wyck, 678
Brown, Bartholomew, 124
Brown, William, 113
Brown University, 129
Browne, Robert, 8
Bruckner, Anton, 597
Brunies, George, 481
Bruno, Anthony, 612
Bryan, Samuel J., 237
Bryant, Dan, 260, 268
Bryant, William Cullen, 171, 236
Bryant's Minstrels, 268, 272–273, 275
Buck, Dudley, 334–335, 338, 351
"Buffalo Gals," 171, 247
Buitrago, Juan, 348
Bull, Amos, 124
Bull, Ole, 181–182
Bulwer-Lytton, Edward, 331
Bunyan, John, 7
Bremner, James, 100, 101
Burke, Edmund, 107
Burleigh, Henry Thacker, 315, 387–390
Burlin, Natalie Curtis, 253, 395, 403, 405, 424
Burns, Barney, 263
Burton, Frederick R., 405, 410–412, 414
Busch, Carl, 400
Busoni, Ferruccio, 517, 586, 598, 606
Butler, Nicholas Murray, 352
Butler, Pierce, 232
Butts, Thomas, 49
Byles, Mather, 42, 141
Byron, George Gordon, 349, 602, 610
Cable, George W., 304, 306–310, 312–314, 398
Cadman, Charles Wakefield, 399–400
Cady, C. M., 179
Cage, John, 571, 574, 589*n.*, 593–596
prepared piano, compositions for, 571, 593, 594
Cakewalk, 78, 83, 310, 311, 433, 438
origin of, 439
Caldwell, William, 194, 197
Calhoun Industrial School, 253
California missions, 62
Calinda (dance), 312–314
Camidge, Matthew, 36, 38
Camp-meeting hymns, 40, 138, 196, 199, 208, 213–214, 219, 222, 507, 658
(*See also* Negro spirituals)
Camp meetings, 207, 209–211, 237, 251, 255, 659, 665
Campos, Ruben M., 499
"Camptown Races" (Foster), 248, 292, 295, 298, 662
Canterbury Pilgrims (De Koven), 619
Capron, Henry, 113
"Careless Love," 464, 465
Caribbean music, 302–309
Carmen (Bizet-Bennett), 633
Carmina Sacra (Mason), 150, 160
Carnegie Hall, 488, 492, 572, 573
Carousel (Rodgers), 631–632
Carpenter, John Alden, 105, 338, 488, 510–511
Carr, Benjamin, 118–120
Carr, Joseph, 118
Carr, Thomas, 118
Carrell, James P., 192–193, 196
Carreño, Teresa, 350
Carter, Benny, 484
Carter, Elliott, 565, 567–568
Carter, Robert, 85, 92, 127
Caryll, Ivan, 622
"Casey at the Bat," 652
Castle, Irene and Vernon, 625
Catholic Church music, 61–63
Catlin, George, 390, 404
Cavaliers, 5, 11
Cavendish, Michael, 20
Cennick, John, 50, 51, 208, 214
Central Park in the Dark (Ives), 666
Chabrier, Emmanuel, 499
Chadwick, George W., 351, 366, 368–372, 375–376, 379, 380, 521, 549, 619

Charleston, S.C., 45, 84, 86, 106–109, 149, 637
St. Cecilia Society, 84, 107–109
Charleston (dance), 83, 460
Charlestown, S.C. (*see* Charleston)
Charpentier, Gustave, 397
Chauncey, Nathaniel, 22, 24, 25, 35, 38
Chauvin, Louis, 442, 444
Cheney, Amy Marcy (*see* Beach, Mrs. H. H. A.)
Chennevière-Rudyard (*see* Rudhyar, Dane)
Cherubini, Luigi, 155, 159
"Chester" (Billings), 144, 535
Chestnut Street Theatre (*see* New Theatre)
"Chevy Chase," 15, 95
Chicago Musical College, 445
Chicago Opera Company, 520
Chicago-Philadelphia Opera Company, 621
Chicago Rhythm Kings, 482, 485
Chicago Symphony Orchestra, 508
Chicago World's Fair, 627
Children's Day at the Camp Meeting (Ives), 665
Chippewa Indians, tribal music of, 406–407, 409, 411–412, 414–415, 519
Chopin, Frédéric, 316, 333, 347, 387, 502
Christensen, Axel, 446
Christian Harmony (Ingalls), 137–139, 202
Christian Harmony (Walker), 201
Christian Minstrel (Aiken), 200, 201
Christy, E. P., 180, 260, 267–268, 284, 285, 292–294
Christy, George, 268
Christy Minstrels, 268, 281, 292
Chromatic integration, 562, 614–616 (*See also* Twelve-tone technique)
Church, Arthur L., 57
Circuit riding, 197, 207, 209, 223
Civil War, 257, 274, 276, 318–319, 342, 469, 508, 509, 514
songs, 178, 180, 298, 451, 498, 507
"Clare de Kitchen," 261, 279
Clark, John J. ("Juba"), 269
Clarke, H. A., 339
Clay, Henry, 167, 177
Cleopatra's Night (Hadley), 520, 635
Cleveland Institute of Music, 540, 541, 553, 556, 562
Cleveland Symphony Orchestra, 522, 628
Clifton, William, 205, 279
Clorindy, the Origin of the Cakewalk (Cook), 622
"Coal Black Rose," 171, 261, 289
Coates, Albert, 492
Cocteau, Jean, 531, 565
Cohan, George M., 623
Cole, F. L. Gwinner, 340
Cole, John, 280
Coleridge, Samuel Taylor, 518
Collier, Constance, 625
Collins, Lee, 465
Colman, Benjamin, 42
Columbia Broadcasting System, 636
"Columbia, the Gem of the Ocean," 662, 666
Columbia University, 346–347, 351–353, 355, 380, 557, 630, 644, 648
bicentennial celebration, 584
Opera Workshop, 643
"Come, Thou Fount of Every Blessing," 188, 214
"Come Where My Love Lies Dreaming" (Foster), 296, 298
Comedy Overture on Negro Themes (Gilbert), 398
Comes Autumn Time (Sowerby), 560
Composers Forum (New York), 574
Concerto in F (Gershwin), 492
Concord, Mass., 656, 660, 664, 668–672, 675, 678
Concord Sonata (Ives), 658, 664, 668–677
Concrete music, 589
Condon, Eddie, 482, 483, 485
Congo (dance), 76, 77, 312
Congo Square (New Orleans), 305–306, 313, 314
Congress for Cultural Freedom, 590
Connecticut Yankee (Rodgers), 630
Continental Harmony (Billings), 140
Contradanza, 309–311
Contrapuntal dynamics, 582, 612
Contredanse, 309, 312
Converse, Frederick S., 338, 377, 520, 635
Cook, Will Marion, 622
Coolidge Foundation (*see* Elizabeth Sprague Coolidge Foundation)
Coon songs, 78, 433, 438–440
Cooper, George, 296
Copland, Aaron, 488, 493–501, 516, 543, 553, 564, 565, 568
Appalachian Spring, 229, 500–501
and jazz, 494–496, 501
other compositions, 494–500, 501
pupils of, 547, 556, 557, 583

Corelli, Arcangelo, 85
Corelli, Marie, 338
Cornell University, 393, 556, 608
Corwin, Norman, 635
Cotton, John, 9, 14, 16, 31, 32
Cotton, Seaborn, 14
Counjaille (dance), 312
Cowboy songs, 393, 396, 523
Cowell, Henry, 190, 510, 516, 571, 575–576, 583, 608, 610
  compositions of, 575–576
  pupils of, 590, 593
  quoted, 488, 502, 576, 588, 608, 610
  use of tone-clusters, 571, 575
Cowper, William, 51
Cradle Will Rock, The (Blitzstein), 646
Crane, Hart, 500
Crawford, Ruth (*see* Seeger, Ruth Crawford)
"Creation" (Billings), 143
Creole Jazz Band, 473
Creole songs and dances, 309–314
Creston, Paul, 535–536
Crèvecoeur, St. Jean de, 324
Cromwell, Oliver, 7
Crosby, Fanny, 179
Cuban Overture (Gershwin), 493
Cui, César, 387
Culprit Fay (Gleason), 338
Cummings, E. E., 610
Curwen, John Spencer, 30, 32–36
Curtis, Natalie (*see* Burlin, Natalie Curtis)
Curtis Institute of Music, 545, 563, 647, 648
Cushing, Frank C., 404
Custis, Nellie, 110

Dada, 543
Dakota Indian music, 416
Dallas, R. C., 262
Dallas Rag, 477
Damon, Foster, 261, 262, 264, 278
Damrosch, Walter, 492, 494
  operas, 634–635
Dance in Place Congo (Gilbert), 397
Dance Symphony (Copland), 496
Dancing, 76–78, 83, 171
  in Africa, 66, 69, 71, 74
  Maypole, 10, 11
  Negro, 77, 236, 256, 304–312, 436–437 (*See also* Cakewalk; Shouts)
  among Puritans, 10, 13
  among Shakers, 210, 229–230
Danzón Cubano (Copland), 499
Dare, Elkanah Kelsay, 189
Dark Dancers of the Mardi Gras (Cadman), 400
"Dark Was the Night," 463
David, Hans T., 61
Davies, Cecilia, 91
Davies, John, 79–82
Davies, Marianne, 90–91
Davies, Samuel, 47, 48, 67, 78, 236–237
Davis, Jefferson, 276
Davisson, Ananias, 189–193, 197, 204
Day, H. W., 213
Debussy, Claude, 347, 379, 494, 496, 517
"Deep River," 380, 388
De Koven, Reginald, 617, 619
Delaval, E. H., 90
Delibes, Leo, 619
Dello Joio, Norman, 536–538
de Mille, Agnes, 500
"Denmark" (Madan), 131, 185
Density 21.5 (Varèse), 586, 588
Densmore, Frances, 405–408, 414, 416, 422, 427, 430, 514
Desvernine, Paul, 348
Déthier, Eduard, 535
Detroit Symphony Orchestra, 401
Devil and Daniel Webster (Moore), 641–642
Diaghilev, Sergei, 510
Diamond, David, 549, 553–555, 564
Dichotomy (Riegger), 608, 609
Dickinson, Emily, 501, 523, 568
Dillingham, Charles, 625, 626
d'Indy, Vincent (*see* Indy, Vincent d')
Dippermouth Blues, 480
Dissonant counterpoint, 569, 577, 579, 590, 593
Ditson, Alice M., Fund of Columbia University, 644, 648
Ditson, Oliver, 173
"Dixie" (Emmett), 259, 272, 274–277, 514, 666
Dixieland Jass Band, 468, 474, 481
Dixieland jazz, 473–476, 481, 485
Dixon, George Washington, 259, 261, 263, 266, 271, 278
Doctor Faustus Lights the Lights (Stein), 645
"Doctor Jazz," 466, 475
Dodds, Edward ("Baby"), 465, 466, 475, 480
Dodds, Johnny, 466, 474, 480
Dodecaphonic composition (*see* Twelve-tone technique)
Dodge, Ossian E., 180
Donizetti, Gaetano, 167, 331, 332
Doolittle, Amos, 124, 134

Dorn, Heinrich, 340
Dorsey, Tommy, 487
Dow, Lorenzo, 209–211
Dow, Peggy, 209, 237
Dowland, John, 20
Down in the Valley (Weill), 647
Downes, Olin, 635, 636
Drake, Sir Francis, 5, 6
Drake, Joseph Rodman, 338
Dreamland Syncopaters, 481
Dreyschock, Alexander, 333
Drumlin Legend (Bacon), 643
Du Bois, William E. B., 68
Dulcimer, The (Woodbury), 150, 163
Dunbar, Paul Lawrence, 622
Dunkers, 55
Duport, Pierre Landrin, 117
Durán, Padre Narciso, 63
Durang, John, 39
Durante, Jimmy, 629
Dutrey, Honore, 474, 480
Dvořák, Antonin, 319, 322, 355, 356, 386–392, 394, 623, 624, 653, 660
  and folk music, 389
  influence in America, 387–392
  on musical nationalism, 355, 356
  and Negro spirituals, 388–391
  New World Symphony, 388, 389, 391
  pupils in America, 387–388
Dwight, John Sullivan, 150, 168, 284, 333, 336, 391
Dwight, Timothy, 43
"Dying Cowboy," 507, 523
Dying Poet (Gottschalk), 321

Eastman School of Music, 549, 551–558
Easy Instructor, The, 187
Edmonds, Shepard N., 439
Edwards, Charles L., 398
Edwards, Eddie, 474
Edwards, Jonathan, 46
Edwin and Angelina (Pelissier), 121
Ehlert, Louis, 348
Einstein, Alfred, 349
Eisenhower, Dwight D., 626
El Capitan (Sousa), 621
Eliot, T. S., 549, 591
Eliott, John, 78
Elizabeth I, Queen of England, 5, 227
Elizabeth Sprague Coolidge Foundation, 374, 500, 501
Elkus, Albert, 542
Ellington, Edward ("Duke"), 484–486
Elson, Louis C., 368, 384, 389, 390
Elwell, Herbert, 507, 540–541
Emerson, Ralph Waldo, 145, 234, 634, 656, 664, 668–671
Emmett, Daniel Decatur, 259, 260, 263, 267–277, 284, 325
  "Dixie," 272, 274–277
  "Old Dan Tucker," 270
  walk-arounds, 270, 272–273
Emperor Jones (Gruenberg), 636, 637
Engel, Carl, 373
Englander, Ludwig, 624
English Dancing Master (Playford), 7, 10
Ephrata Cloister, 57, 58, 63
Episcopalians, 34, 79
Erskine, John, 354–356, 574, 636
Essay for Orchestra (Barber), 562
Essays before a Sonata (Ives), 668
Ethiopian melodies, 247, 248, 283–285 (*See also* Minstrelsy)
Ethiopian Serenaders, 271, 281
Evangeline (Luening), 643
Evangeline (Rice), 622
Evens, Williams, 286
Everett, A. B., 201
Everett, L. C., 201

Face the Music (Berlin), 625, 626
Falckner, Justus, 55, 56
Falla, Manuel de, 389
Fancy Free (Bernstein), 545
Farmer, John, 20
Farnaby, Giles, 20
Farrell, Bob, 261, 278
Farwell, Arthur, 392–397, 399, 405, 502, 503, 516, 518, 522, 552
  compositions, 396, 399
  and Wa-Wan Press, 394–397
Fasola folk, 137, 183–206, 214, 542, 644 (*See also* Shape-note system)
Fauquier, Francis, 85, 86
Fauré, Gabriel, 522
Federal Harmony (Swan), 135
Federal Overture (Carr), 119
Feldman, Morton, 574, 589*n.*
Fenton, William, 410
Ferber, Edna, 627
Fétis, François Joseph, 153
Fewkes, J. Walter, 404, 426
Field, A. G., 277
Fifty Million Frenchmen (Porter), 629
Fig Leaf Rag (Joplin), 442
Filling Station (Thomson), 352
Fillmore, John Comfort, 405
Films, music for, 498, 532, 535, 574
Fine, Irving, 567, 568
Finkelstein, Sidney, 587

Finney, Ross Lee, 561, 614, 615
  and twelve-tone technique, 614
Fireside Tales (MacDowell), 353
First Orchestral Set (Ives) (*Three Places in New England*), 664–665
First Piano Sonata (Ives), 664
First Piano Sonata (Sessions), 526–528
Firth & Hall, 262
Firth, Pond & Co., 275–276, 291, 295, 296, 299
Fish Wharf Rhapsody (Gilbert), 399
Fisher, William Arms, 387
Fisk University, 254
Fithian, Philip Vickers, 85, 92, 127
Flagg, Josiah, 124
Flaubert, Gustave, 556
Fletcher, Alice C., 344, 403, 405, 408, 413, 421
Fletcher, Francis, 6
Flivver Ten Million (Converse), 521
Foldes, Andor, 529
Folk hymnody, 45, 138, 189, 190, 192, 193, 196, 202, 214, 542, 644
  (*See also* Fasola folk; Negro spirituals)
Folk music, 192, 198–199, 202, 222, 224, 325, 366, 512, 562
  Arthur Farwell on, 393, 394, 396
  compositions based on, 380–381, 401–402, 498–499, 501, 506–507, 512, 514, 535, 538, 543, 561, 576
  Dvořák's interest in, 387–391
  and hymns, 33, 202–203
  and jazz, 469, 488, 490
  MacDowell on, 355, 356, 363
  minstrel songs in, 278
  and ragtime, 435
  and Stephen Foster, 248–249, 300
Folk opera, 443, 493, 512, 627, 637, 638, 641, 647
Folk Song Symphony (Harris), 506–507
Folklore, of American Indians, 121, 404, 417–430
  in music, 322, 355–356, 363, 397, 433, 510, 516, 543
  of Negroes, 69, 78, 205, 248
Fontainebleau School of Music, 494
Foote, Arthur, 338, 351, 366–368, 549
Foote, Henry W., 38
Foss, Lukas, 547, 643
Foster, Dunning, 290, 294
Foster, Henry, 296
Foster, Jane McDowell, 292, 294–296
Foster, John, 9
Foster, Morrison, 287–289, 294, 296
Foster, Stephen Collins, 132, 168, 171, 214, 219, 273, 282–300, 325, 336
  and Afro-American music, 248–249, 280, 434
  early life, 285–288
  influence of, 388, 390, 556, 653, 654, 658, 661
  marriage, 292, 295
  "My Old Kentucky Home," 294, 300
  and Negro minstrelsy, 268, 289, 291–293
  "Oh Susanna," 290–291, 298–299
  "Old Folks at Home," 292, 298–300
  summary of his music, 297–300
Foster, William Barclay, 286, 288
Four Saints in Three Acts (Thomson), 531, 643, 644
Fourth Symphony (Ives), 658, 663
Fox, George, 57
Fox, Gilbert, 119
Frankenstein, Alfred, 664
Franklin, Benjamin, 15, 25, 34, 42, 57, 85, 87–97, 105, 653
  compositions attributed to, 89
  inventor of Glass Harmonica, 88–92
  as music critic, 92–96
Franklin, James, 25, 27, 33
Franklin, Peter, 15, 92, 94
Friedenthal, Albert, 77
Friml, Rudolf, 617, 624
"From Greenland's Icy Mountains" (Mason), 155
Fry, William Henry, 105, 328–333, 634
Fuguing tunes, 10, 49, 134–136, 139, 141–143, 145, 196, 202, 542, 665
Futurism, 543
Futurist Manifesto, 573, 586

Gaiety Girl, A, 622
Gaines, Francis P., 271
Galbreath, C. B., 273
Galuppi, Baldassare, 92
García Lorca, Federico (*see* Lorca, Federico García)
Garland, Ed, 475
Garland, Hamlin, 363, 653
Garrick Gaieties, 630
Garrison, Lucy McKim (*see* McKim, Lucy)
Gauthier, Eva, 519
Gay, John, 646
Gehot, Jean, 120
Genée, Franz, 619
Geneva Psalter, 19
Genteel tradition, 130, 164–183, 184, 285, 295, 323, 354, 356, 364, 461, 666

Georgia Sea Islands, 82, 232, 236, 240
Gershwin, George, 462, 488–493, 511, 516, 545, 617, 628–691
  An American in Paris, 489, 492–493
  Concerto in F, 489, 492
  on jazz, 488–490
  Porgy and Bess, 637–640
  Rhapsody in Blue, 488, 491–492
Gershwin, Ira, 628, 629, 632, 637
Gettysburg March, 469, 477
Giannini, Vittorio, 643
Giants in the Earth (Moore), 643
Gilbert, Henry F., 362, 394–399, 516, 522, 550
Gilchrist, William Wallace, 338, 339
Gilliat, Sy, 76
Gillis, Don, 511, 512
Gilman, Benjamin Ives, 405, 425–427
Gilman, Lawrence, 347, 349, 350, 357, 361, 363, 518
Glass Harmonica (*see* Harmonica)
Glassychord (*see* Harmonica)
Gleason, Frederick Grant, 338–339
"Glendy Burk" (Foster), 285, 295, 434, 556
Gleny, Albert, 477
Glinka, Mikhail, 322, 330, 385, 387, 389
Gloria Dei Church, 55, 56
Gluck, Christoph Willibald von, 90
"God Bless America" (Berlin), 626
Godowsky, Leopold, 450
Goeb, Roger, 543–545
Goethe, Johann Wolfgang von, 92, 349, 610
Goetschius, Percy, 380, 575
Goffin, Robert, 469, 489–490
Gogol, Nikolai, 374
Goldman, Richard Franko, 558, 590
Goldmark, Rubin, 387, 388, 395, 490–491, 493, 494, 559, 583
Goldsmith, Oliver, 121
Goodale, Ezekiel, 124
Goodman, Benny, 483, 486–487, 501
Goossens, Eugene, 658
Gordon, R. W., 242, 257
Gottschalk, Edward, 301–302
Gottschalk, Louis Moreau, 302–323, 396, 439
  La Bamboula, 306, 310–311, 314
  Caribbean vagabondage, 317–318
  in Europe, 306, 315, 316
  in South America, 319–322
Gould, Morton, 511
Graham, Martha, 228, 500, 534, 537, 555, 559
Gram, Hans, 136
Grand Canyon Suite (Grofé), 511
Green, Ray, 542
Green Grow the Lilacs, 631
Greene, David, 159
"Green-sleeves," 10
Gregorian chant, 365–366, 536–537, 644
Grieg, Edvard, 347, 362, 387, 389
Griffes, Charles T., 517–520, 550
Grissom, Mary Allen, 249
Grofé, Ferde, 489, 491, 511
Gruenberg, Louis, 636, 637
Guggenheim Memorial Foundation Fellowship, 563, 568, 572, 581, 590
Guilmant, Alexandre-Félix, 393
Guion, David, 513
Guitar, 67, 457, 463–465, 467
Guiterman, Arthur, 634
Gury, Jeremy, 652
Guttoveggio, Joseph (*see* Creston, Paul)

Habanera rhythm, 310–311
Hadley, Henry Kimball, 520, 550, 635
Hagen, Peter Albrecht van, 121
"Hail Columbia," 119, 288, 514
Haiti, 277, 303, 309, 512
Hale, Edward Everett, 634
Hale, Philip, 354, 371, 372, 375, 377
Hall, Minor ("Ram"), 475
Hall, Thomas C., 46
Hallé, Charles, 315
Halleck, Fitz-Greene, 171
Hallowell, Emily, 238
Hambitzer, Charles, 490
Hamerik, Asger, 343
Hamline University, 604
Hammerstein, Oscar, 2d, 627, 630–633
Hampton, Lionel, 487
Hampton, Robert, 446
Hampton Institute, 254
Handel, George Frederic, 34, 59, 85, 96, 100, 112, 128, 131, 152, 155, 287, 332, 577
  The Messiah, 97
Handy, W. C., 455, 459–462, 512
Hanson, Howard, 337, 503, 549–552, 556–559
  Merry Mount (opera), 550, 635
Happy Hypocrite (Elwell), 540
Hardin, Lillian, 475, 480, 481
Harlem Rag (Turpin), 443, 444
Harmonic Society of New York, 327, 329
Harmonica, 85, 88–91, 121
  description of, 91
  invented by Benjamin Franklin, 88
Harmony of Maine (Belcher), 132

Harney, Ben R., 444–446
Harp of Columbia, 190
Harper, Edward, 278
Harrigan and Hart, 439
Harris, Roy, 501–509, 533, 537, 557–558
  on American music, 503–504
  compositions, 503, 505–508
Harrison, Lou, 577, 588, 589, 614, 657
Hart, Lorenz, 630, 631
Hart, Moss, 625, 632
Harte, Bret, 523
Hartt Opera Guild, 642, 652
Harvard College (*see* Harvard University)
Harvard University, 9, 13–15, 22, 25, 33, 124, 336, 378–380, 531, 538, 545, 549, 565, 567, 569, 598
  early musical studies at, 13–14
Hasse, Johann Adolph, 85, 91, 92
Hastings, Thomas, 161–162, 185, 391
  and "Ethiopian melodies," 283–284
Haupt, Karl August, 335, 369
Hauptmann, Gerhart, 577
Hauptmann, Moritz, 333, 334
Hauser, William, 197–198, 215
Hawkins, Coleman, 483
Hawthorne, Nathaniel, 11, 664, 668, 670–671, 676, 677
Hayden, Scott, 442
Haydn, Josef, 59–61, 112, 116, 120, 155, 159, 287, 365
Haydn, Michael, 155
Hearn, Lafcadio, 77, 305, 313, 435–438, 468
Heath, Lyman, 174
Heine, Heinrich, 349, 610
Heinrich, Anton Philip, 385–386, 400
Helen Retires (Antheil), 574
Hellman, Lillian, 646
Helmholtz, Hermann, 407
Hemenway, Mary, 404
Hemenway Southwestern Expedition, 404, 405
Henderson, Fletcher, 481, 483–484, 486, 487
Henderson, William J., 351, 377
Henry, Patrick, 65, 86
Henry Hadley Memorial Library of Music, 521
Herbert, Victor, 377, 617, 620, 626, 627
Heredia, José María de, 385
Herman, Woody, 487
Hermits of the Wissahickon, 55
Herrnhut, 45, 46
Herskovits, Melville, 69
Herzog, George, 354
Hesperian Harp (Hauser), 197, 198, 215
Hess, Albert, 56
Hess, Cliff, 462
Hewitt, James, 120, 121, 177, 364
Hewitt, John Hill, 176–179
Heyman, Karl, 348
Heyman, Katherine Ruth, 395
Heyward, Du Bose, 637
Hicks, Edward, 539
Higginson, Henry Lee, 373
Higginson, Thomas Wentworth, 240–241, 244
High Society, 469, 475, 480
Highwayman, The (De Koven), 619
Hilaire, Andrew, 475
Hill, Bertha ("Chippie"), 465
Hill, Edward Burlingame, 378–379, 395, 538, 545, 561
  compositions, 379
Hill, Sumner, 162
Hill, Ureli Corelli, 172
Himes, Joshua V., 220
Himmel, Friedrich H., 159
Hindemith, Paul, 526, 536, 547, 557, 565, 568
"Ho, Westward, Ho!" (Dodge), 181
Holden, Oliver, 124, 125, 135, 136, 156
Hollers, 82, 435
Holyoke, Samuel, 135–136, 188, 191
Homer, Sidney, 369
Honnegger, Arthur, 531
Hooker, Brian, 377
Hopi Indians, tribal music of, 404, 423, 426–427
Hopkinson, Francis, 97–103, 105, 119, 125, 126, 132, 364
  Seven Songs for the Harpsichord, 99–102
Hopkinson, Joseph, 119
Hopper, De Wolf, 618, 621
Hora Novissima (Parker), 376, 377, 653
Horizons (Shepherd), 522
Horn, Charles Edward, 164, 172, 176, 205, 298
Hornpipes, 16, 19, 50
"Hot" rhythm, 310, 434, 450, 474
  in Negro dancing, 435–437
  in Negro spirituals, 255, 257
  in New Orleans bands, 470–472
  (*See also* African music; Afro-American music; Jazz; Negro spirituals)
"Housatonic at Stockbridge" (Ives), 664–665
Hovey, Richard, 372
Hovhaness, Alan, 545–546

"How Firm a Foundation," 224, 532
Howard, John Tasker, 295, 354, 492, 627
Howe, Julia Ward, 231
Howe, Mary, 523
Hubbard, John, 130
Hudson, W. H., 636
Hughes, Langston, 513, 542
Hughes, Rupert, 337, 346–347, 367–368, 371, 440
Humperdinck, Engelbert, 393, 517
Hunt, Leigh, 88
Hunter, Charles H., 445
Hus, John, 46
Huss, Henry Holden, 351
Hutcheson, Ernest, 490
Hutchinson, Abby, 175
Hutchinson, John, 173
Hutchinson family, 170, 173–176, 222
Hymnody, 21, 22, 38, 43, 49, 50, 52, 67, 82, 130, 334, 532, 658
  evangelical, 40, 43, 48, 50, 51, 63, 64, 78, 208
  Methodist, 45, 52, 58
  revivalist, 45, 52, 208–209, 248, 645
  popular, 40, 48, 157, 207, 231
  (*See also* Folk hymnody; Mason, Lowell)
Hymns, 80, 81, 124, 126, 160, 162, 214
  gospel, 133, 645, 660
  (*See also* Camp-meeting hymns; Hymnody)
Hymns and Spiritual Songs (Watts), 41, 42, 208
Hyperprism (Varèse), 471, 586

"I Wonder as I Wander," 606
Ibsen, Henrik, 97
Imaginary Landscapes (Cage), 594, 595
Impressionism, 540
  in music of Griffes, 517, 519
  in music of Ives, 664, 668
  in music of Loeffler, 373–374
Incredible Flutist (Piston), 566–567
Indian Suite (MacDowell), 351, 362–363, 404
Indians, American (*see* American Indians)
Indy, Vincent d', 378, 381, 522, 562, 586, 629
Ingalls, Jeremiah, 124, 137–139, 202
Institute of Musical Art, 551, 608, 630
  (*See also* Juilliard School of Music)
Integrales (Varèse), 586, 589
International Composers Conference (Rome), 590
International Composers' Guild, 586
International Society for Contemporary Music (ISCM), 544, 611
Ionisation (Varèse), 571, 586, 588, 589
Iroquois tribes, music of, 409–410
Irving, Washington, 329, 335, 632
Island God, The (Menotti), 648
Ives, Charles E., 510, 532, 560, 653–678
  artistic philosophy, 655–657
  business experience, evaluation of, 654–655
  Concord Sonata, 658, 664, 668–677
  other compositions, 657–658, 664–667
  symphonies, 661–664
Ives, George, 653, 654

Jack and the Beanstalk (Gruenberg), 636
Jackson, George K., 152
Jackson, George Pullen, 38, 50, 81, 199, 203, 254
Jackson, John B., 194
Jackson, Tony, 446, 449
Jacobi, Frederick, 547
Jacobs, Arthur, 563
Jadassohn, Salomon, 369
James, Harry, 487
James, Joe, 196
James, Philip, 523, 612
James, William, 145
James, Willis Laurence, 434
Janis, Harriet, 444
Jasmine Concerto (Johnson), 450
Jazz, 468–487, 494–496, 504–506
  archaic, 470
  backgrounds of, 31, 72, 78, 82, 257, 304, 435, 438, 457–459, 465, 475–477
    (*See also* African music; Afro-American music; Blues; Ragtime)
  "break" in, 455
  in Chicago, 473–475, 481
  Chicago style, 482
  Dixieland, 473–476, 481, 485
  effects in musical composition, 501, 534, 540, 541, 565, 574, 604, 605, 661
  Kansas City style, 486
  in New Orleans, 433, 436–437, 449, 470–476, 479–481, 484–487
  origin of word, 468, 474
  pioneers of, 471–475
  and ragtime, 435, 477–478
  (*See also* Symphonic jazz)

"Jeanie with the Light Brown Hair" (Foster), 300
Jefferson, "Blind Lemon," 464, 465
Jefferson, Thomas, 83, 85–87, 97, 101–103, 105, 227, 262, 277, 540
 on Negro music, 66–68
Jenks, Stephen, 124
Jeremiah Symphony (Bernstein), 545
Jig, 7, 16, 19, 50, 76, 101, 144
"Jim Crow," 264–265, 284, 289
Joachim, Joseph, 373, 623
Jocelyn, Simeon, 127
"Joe Turner," 454–456
John Brown's Body, 514
Johnson, Charles L., 445
Johnson, Guy B., 218, 254
Johnson, Hunter, 555–556
Johnson, James P., 446, 450, 467
Johnson, Margaret, 479
Johnson, Pete, 486
Johnson, Robert Underwood, 664
Jommelli, Nicola, 92
Jones, Charles C., 237
Jones, Richard M., 465
Jonny spielt auf! (Křenek), 604
Jonson, Ben, 4
Joplin, Scott, 440–442, 445–448, 450, 477
Journal of Music (Dwight), 150, 168, 333
Jubilee (Chadwick), 371
"Judea" (Billings), 50
Judith (Schuman), 535
Juilliard Music Foundation, 557
Juilliard School of Music, 388, 533, 547, 557–559, 630, 636
Jullien (Julien), Louis Antoine, 327, 332
Jumping Frog of Calaveras County (Foss), 643

Kahn, Erich Itor, 611
Kairn of Koridwen (Griffes), 519
Kames, Lord, 92
Kansas City jazz, 486
Kaufman, George, 629
Kay, Ulysses Simpson, 557
Keats, John, 555
Kelley, Edgar Stillman, 394, 395, 618
Kelpius, Johannes, 55, 56
Keltic Sonata (MacDowell), 353, 359, 362
Kemble, Frances Anne, 232–234, 247, 266, 280
Kendall, Edward, 269
Kentucky Harmony (Davisson), 189–190
 supplement to, 191, 204
Keppard, Freddie, 472
Kerker, Gustave, 624
Kern, Jerome, 462, 617, 626–628
Kerr, Harrison, 524–525, 541, 614
 and twelve-tone technique, 615
Kilenyi, Edward, 490
Kimball, Jacob, 124, 150
King, A. Hyatt, 91
King, E. J., 196
King and I, The (Rodgers), 631–632
King Œdipus (Partch), 591
King Porter Stomp (Morton), 450, 487
King's Chapel, Boston, 34, 531
King's Henchman, The (Taylor), 635
Kipling, Rudyard, 538
Kirchgässner, Marianne, 92
Kirchner, Leon, 542–543, 614
Kirkpatrick, John, 319, 658, 668
Kiss Me Kate (Porter), 629
Kithara, microtonal, 590, 592
Kleber, Henry, 288
Kneass, Nelson, 290
Knickerbocker Holiday (Weill), 632
Knight, Joseph, 164
Knorr, Ivan, 526
Kochnitzky, Leon, 546
Kohs, Ellis, 544, 614
Kolinski, Mieczyslaw, 75, 254–256
Kostelanetz, André, 628
Kotzschmer, Herman, 335
Koussevitzky, Serge, 493, 494, 503, 505
Koussevitzky Foundation, 559
Krazy Kat (Carpenter), 510
Krehbiel, H. E., 244, 248–249, 254, 305, 309, 313, 315
Kreisler, Fritz, 521
Krell, William, 444
Křenek, Ernst, 604–606, 611
Krupa, Gene, 487
Kubelik, Rafael, 508

La, La, Lucille (Gershwin), 491, 628
Labbé, Louise, 610
Lady in the Dark (Weill), 632–633
La Flesche, Francis, 405
Laine, Jack ("Papa"), 474
Lalo, Edouard, 385, 389
Lamb, Joseph, 445
Lambert, Constant, 484
Lampe, John Frederick, 48, 49
"Land of the Sky Blue Water" (Cadman), 399
Lang, J. B., 367
Lang, Margaret Ruthven, 351
Lanier, Sidney, 334, 341–345, 371, 518
La Rocca, Dominique ("Nick"), 474

Law, Andrew, 127–131, 136, 186–188
  shape-note system, 129–130
Lawes, Henry, 36
Lawrence, Gertrude, 632
Leadbetter, Huddie ("Leadbelly"), 465
League of Composers, 503, 571
Lecocq, Charles, 617
Lee, "Mother" Ann, 53, 54, 227
Lee, Philip Ludwell, 106
Lehar, Franz, 617
Leibowitz, René, 600
Leichtentritt, Hugo, 506
Leipzig, 162, 333, 334, 522
Leland, John, 223
Leonora (Fry), 329, 331
Leschetizky, Theodor, 401
Let 'em Eat Cake (Gershwin), 629
Lewis, Meade Lux, 466
Lewis, Sinclair, 510
Library of Congress, 58, 114, 116, 139, 224, 252, 374, 410, 449, 500, 501
  (*See also* Elizabeth Sprague Coolidge Foundation)
Lincoln, Abraham, 276, 388, 508, 512, 555
Lind, Jenny, 327
Lindbergh, Charles, 524, 543
Lindsay, John, 465, 475
Lindsay, Vachel, 523, 666
Lining-out, 31, 32, 38, 39, 81, 349–351
  (*See also* Psalmody)
List, Kurt, 610, 611
Liszt, Franz, 186, 333, 334, 340, 349, 366, 367, 379, 490
Little, William, 186–188, 191
Little Tycoon (Spenser), 618
Livingstone, Herbert, 555
Lodge, Henry, 446
Loeffler, Charles Martin, 372–374, 550
Lomax, Alan and John, 507
London, 45, 98, 113, 162, 340, 350
Long, Huey, 626
"Long Tail Blue," 263, 264, 289
"Long Time Ago," 172, 205, 279–280, 298
Longfellow, Henry W., 17, 175, 334
Loomis, Harvey Worthington, 387, 388, 395–396
Lorca, Federico García, 543, 607
Lost in the Stars (Weill), 647
Loud, Thomas, 124
Louisiana Purchase (Berlin), 626
Louisville Orchestra, 537, 559
Love, Charles, 106, 107
Low, Seth, 352
Lowens, Irving, 610
Luders, Gustave, 623–624
Luening, Otto, 543–544, 643
Lunceford, Jimmie, 484
Luther, Martin, 45
Lyell, Sir Charles, 234
Lyon, James, 125–128, 150, 162
Lyric theater (*see* Musical comedy; Opera)

McCurry, John Gordon, 198, 199, 214–215, 219
Macdonald, A. J., 230
McDonald, Harl, 524
MacDowell, Edward A., 345–364, 373, 390, 392, 396, 404, 518, 653, 660
  in Boston, 350–351
  at Columbia University, 351–353
  compositions, 350–351, 353, 359–364
  in Europe, 348–350
  ideas on music, 356–359
  on musical nationalism, 355–356
MacFarren, G. A., 326
McGready, James, 207
McIntosh, Rigdon McCoy, 201
Mackay, Charles, 167, 168, 176
McKay, George Frederick, 512
McKim, J. Miller, 242
McKim, Lucy, 240, 243
McPartland, Jimmy, 482
McPhee, Colin, 519, 582, 583
McSpadden, J. Walker, 627
Madan, Martin, 131, 155
Maeterlinck, Maurice, 374
Mahon, John, 296
"Majesty" (Billings), 142–143
Malet, William W., 238
Malipiero, Gian Francesco, 561
Mamoulian, Rouben, 637, 640
Man without a Country (Damrosch), 634
Mainzer, Joseph, 32
"Maniac, The" (Russell), 167, 170, 173
Mann, Elias, 128
Maple Leaf Rag (Joplin), 441–442, 449–450
Marcello, Benedetto, 159
"Marching through Georgia" (Work), 180, 666
Mares, Paul, 481
Margil de Jesus, Fray Antonio, 62
Markham, Edwin, 542, 666
Marmontel, Antoine-François, 348
Marshall, Arthur, 442, 446
Mason, Barachias, 151, 334

Mason, Daniel Gregory, 153, 338, 365, 366, 375, 379–381, 402
  compositions of, 380
Mason, Johnson, 334
Mason, Lowell, 150–162, 173, 179, 187, 192, 333–334
  early life, 151
  influence of, 130, 150–151, 195–196, 200, 201, 325
  sacred music collections of, 150–152, 159
  and school music, 156–159
Mason, Timothy, 159, 187
Mason, William, 153, 333, 365
Masque of Alfred the Great (Hopkinson), 100
"Massa's in de Cold Ground" (Foster), 285, 294, 297
Massenet, Jules, 385
Mather, Cotton, 23, 25, 28, 31, 35, 42
Mather, Increase, 8
Mathews, W. S. B., 338
Matthews, Brander, 271
Maytime (Romberg), 624
Me and Juliet (Rodgers), 631
Meachum, Joseph, 53
Meignen, Leopold, 330
Melville, Herman, 325, 510
"Memphis Blues" (Handy), 460
Men and Mountains (Ruggles), 577
Mendelssohn, Felix, 327, 333, 334, 365
Mennin, Peter, 558
Mennonites, 54, 55, 63
Menotti, Gian-Carlo, 646–651
  The Consul, 649–650
  The Medium, 648–649
Merman, Ethel, 626, 628
Merry Mount (Hanson), 550, 635
Merry Mount, 10–12, 635
Mesmer, Franz Anton, 91
Metcalf, Frank J., 136, 137, 161
Methodists, 40, 44, 46, 49, 52, 79, 188, 194, 207–211, 234, 236, 251
Metric modulation, 568
Metropolitan Opera House, 377, 398, 399, 510, 520, 545, 585, 620–621, 625, 634–636, 647, 648
  American operas produced at, 634–636
Meyerbeer, Giacomo, 167, 320
Mezzrow, Mezz, 482
Michael, David Moritz, 60
Michener, James, 632
Microtonal music, 587, 590–593
Milhaud, Darius, 491, 531, 542, 569
Millay, Edna St. Vincent, 635
Millennial Harp, 217, 220–222
Miller, Glenn, 487
Miller, Paul Eduard, 472
Miller, Peter, 57
Miller, William, 220–221
Milligan, Harold Vincent, 299
Mills, Kerry, 450
Mills College, 691
Milneburg Joys (Morton), 481
Milton, John, 7, 116
Mims, Edwin, 341
Minstrel shows (*see* Minstrelsy)
Minstrelsy, 78, 170, 180, 205, 236, 246–247, 249, 257–300, 460, 622
  antecedents of, 259–264
  compositions based on, 511, 658
  first minstrel troupes, 259, 267–268
  and jazz, 469
  minstrel melodies, 277–282
  and ragtime, 433–434, 438–439
  (*See also* Emmett, Daniel Decatur; Foster, Stephen Collins; Rice, Thomas Dartmouth)
Mintz, David, 208
Mississippi Rag (Krell), 444
Missouri Harmony, 190
Mitchell, George, 475
Mitropoulos, Dimitri, 541, 569
Moffet, John, 219
Moller, John Christopher, 121
Molnar, Ferenc, 631
Mona (Parker), 377, 635
Moore, Douglas, 510, 641–643
  The Devil and Daniel Webster, 641–642
  other operas, 642, 643
Moore, William, 193
Moravians, 44–47, 50, 58–60, 63, 197
  music of, 58–59
Mordecai, Samuel, 76
Moreau de St. Méry, Mederic L. E., 110
Morgan, Justin, 124, 136, 191
Morley, Thomas, 20
Morneweck, Evelyn Foster, 287
Morris, George Pope, 171, 172, 174–176, 205, 288, 298
Morris, William, 394, 590
Morse, Woolson, 618
Morton, Ferdinand ("Jelly Roll"), 446, 449–450, 465–466, 475–478, 481, 485
Morton, Thomas, 10–12, 635
Moscheles, Ignaz, 333
Moten, Bennie, 486
Mother of Us All (Thomson), 643, 644–645

Motion pictures, music for, 498, 532, 535, 574
Mount Wollaston (*see* Merry Mount)
Moussorgsky, Modest P., 387
Mozart, Leopold, 91
Mozart, Wolfgang Amadeus, 59, 91–92, 112, 152, 155, 159, 327, 332, 365, 366
  and the Harmonica, 91–92
Murphy, Jeannette R., 252
Music Critics' Circle (New York), 541
Music for the Theatre (Copland), 495
Musica Sacra (Hastings), 161, 185
Musical comedy, 617–633
  backgrounds of, 621–623
  by George Gershwin, 628–629
  by Richard Rodgers, 630–632
  since 1914, 625–633
Musical Fund Society of Philadelphia, 118
Musical glasses (*see* Harmonica)
Musical Primer (Law), 129, 130, 186
Musique concrète, 589
"My Days Have Been So Wondrous Free" (Hopkinson), 100
"My Old Kentucky Home" (Foster), 285, 294, 297, 300
Mystic Trumpeter (Dello Joio), 537

Nathan, Hans, 263, 264, 274–275, 279
National Broadcasting Company, 630, 648
NBC Symphony Orchestra, 501, 563
National Conservatory of Music, 376, 377, 387
National Federation of Music Clubs, 377, 401
National Institute of Arts and Letters, 598, 658
National Orchestral Association, 546
Nationalism in American music, beginnings of, 332, 340, 371, 381, 385–386
  in Bloch's *America,* 513–515
  Dvořák on, 386–391
  Farwell's contribution to, 392–396
  Gilbert's contribution to, 396–398
  and jazz, 488, 489
  MacDowell on, 355–356
  in music of Charles Ives, 658–660, 677–678
  in twentieth century, 401–402, 494–495, 503–509, 534–535, 561
Natoma (Herbert), 621
Naughty Marietta (Herbert), 620
Naumann, Johann G., 92, 159
Naumberg Fellowship, 531, 568
"Nearer, My God, to Thee" (Mason), 160, 666
Negro music (*see* African music; Afro-American music; Blues; "Hot" rhythm; Jazz; Negro spirituals; Ragtime)
Negro spirituals, 232–258
  antebellum accounts of, 232–239
  and blues, 455–456, 463, 465
  compositions based on, 380, 390, 511, 556
  during and after Civil War, 238–248
  Dvořák's interest in, 388, 390, 391
  first publications of, 239–240, 243–246
  folk tradition of, 249–255
  "hot" rhythm in, 255, 257, 435, 470
  manner of singing, 232–233, 236, 238–239, 246, 250–254, 455–456
  origins of, 45, 67, 75, 78, 80–82, 209, 216
  relation to African music, 254–257
  (*See also* African music)
Nelson, Louis ("Big Eye"), 472, 477
Neoclassicism, 435, 543, 549, 566, 569
Nevin, Arthur, 400
Nevin, Ethelbert, 346, 400
Nevin, Robert, 291
Nevins, Marian (Mrs. MacDowell), 349
New England (*see* Boston; Ives, Charles E.; Mason, Lowell; Psalmody; Puritans)
New England Conservatory of Music, 369, 375, 520–522, 546, 562
New England Harmony (Swan), 135
New England Idyls (MacDowell), 353, 360
New England Psalm Singer (Billings), 140–143
New England Symphony (Ives) (*see Three Places in New England*)
New Music Editions, 542, 578, 583
New Music Quarterly, 375
New Orleans, 77, 78, 180, 301–306, 314–315, 398, 449–450, 468–469
  voodoo ceremonies in, 304–305
  (*See also* Creole songs and dances; Gottschalk, Louis Moreau)
New Orleans jazz (*see* Jazz)
New Orleans Rhythm Kings, 481
New School for Social Research, 575, 593
New Theatre, Philadelphia, 111, 114, 117, 119, 331
New World Symphony (Dvořák), 388–389, 391, 393

New York City, 316, 354, 376, 393, 533, 541–543, 545
Academy of Music, 331
early musical life in, 109, 113, 118–121, 164–165, 168, 172–174
jazz in, 483
musical comedy in, 617–633
New York City Center, 640, 646
New York City Opera, 501, 512
New York Little Symphony, 657
New York Philharmonic Society, 172, 326–330, 332, 620
New York Philharmonic-Symphony, 500, 521, 541, 544, 569, 657
New York Symphony, 492, 494
Newburgh, Brockhill, 90
Newman, William, 522
Newton, John, 50, 51, 202, 208
Niblo's Garden, 621
Nichols, George, 261, 266
Nichols, Red, 483, 487
"Night and Day" (Porter), 630
Niles, Edward Abbe, 453, 455–457
No for an Answer (Blitzstein), 646
No! No! Nanette (Youmans), 628
Noise-sounds (*see Futurist Manifesto*)
Noone, Jimmy, 474
Nordoff, Paul, 558–559
Norma (Bellini), 331, 332
Norris, Homer A., 393
Norse Sonata (MacDowell), 353
"Northfield" (Ingalls), 138–139
Notes on Virginia (Jefferson), 65–67, 262
Noyes, Alfred, 521
Nuñez, Alcide ("Yellow"), 474

Oberlin Conservatory of Music, 540, 622
O'Brien, Daniel Webster (*see* Bryant, Dan)
Octandre (Varèse), 586, 588
Ode to Napoleon Buonaparte (Schoenberg), 602, 603
Oedipus Tyrannus (Paine), 337
Oerter, Christian Frederick, 60
Of Thee I Sing (Gershwin), 626–629
Offenbach, Jacques, 617
O'Hara, John, 630
Ojibway Indians (*see* Chippewa Indians)
Ojos Criollos (Gottschalk), 311, 319
Oklahoma! (Rodgers), 631
"Old Black Joe" (Foster), 285, 292, 294, 295, 297, 298, 300
"Old Chisholm Trail," 523
"Old Churchyard," 174, 222
"Old Dan Tucker," 171, 270, 434
"Old Folks at Home" (Foster), 283–285, 292–294, 297–299, 319, 514
"Old Granite State," 222
"Old Hundredth," 18, 170, 333
Old Maid and the Thief (Menotti), 648
Old Ship of Zion, 237, 398
Oldberg, Arne, 395
"Ole Tare River," 280, 281
Oliver, Joseph ("King"), 472–477, 479–480
Oliver, Sy, 484
Olney Hymns, 51
Omaha Indians, tribal music of, 400, 413
On the Town (Bernstein), 545
On Your Toes (Rodgers), 630
O'Neill, Eugene, 636
O'Neill, Francis, 279
"Open Thy Lattice, Love" (Foster), 171, 288
Opera by American composers, in early twentieth century, 377, 399, 621, 634–635
modern, 512, 574, 636–652
in nineteenth century, 329–332, 634
one-act, 533, 535, 538, 543, 641, 647–648, 652
(*See also* Folk opera; Musical comedy)
Original Sacred Harp, 134, 139, 219
Denson Revision of, 218
(*See also Sacred Harp*)
Ornstein, Leo, 571, 572
Ory, Kid, 475, 480, 481
Over the Pavements (Ives), 666

Pachelbel, Charles Theodore, 109
Pachelbel, Johann, 109
Pagan Poem (Loeffler), 374
Paine, John Knowles, 334–338, 346, 351, 367, 379, 380, 510, 521, 549
compositions of, 337–338
Paine Fellowship, 531, 568, 569
Palestrina, Giovanni Pierluigi da, 155, 357
Palmer, Robert, 556
Pan American Association of Composers, 586
Papago Indians, tribal music of, 427–429
Paris, 86–87, 89, 306, 315–316, 331, 348, 373, 381, 393
American music performed in, 350–351

Paris, American musicians who studied in, 494, 503, 524, 531, 540, 541, 544, 552, 554, 562, 565, 569
  Conservatory, 89, 330, 348, 586
  Opéra, 87, 331
Parker, Horatio W., 366, 375–377, 386, 522, 525, 550, 562, 635, 653, 654
  compositions of, 376–377
Parker, John R., 117, 118
Parkman, Francis, 336
Parnell, Thomas, 100
Partch, Harry, 590–593
  microtonal instruments invented by, 592
Pastorius, Francis Daniel, 57
Patent notes (*see* Shape-note system)
Paton, Alan, 647
Pawnee Indians, tribal music of, 421–423
Peabody, George Foster, 394
Peabody Symphony Orchestra, 343
Peaceable Kingdom (Thompson), 538, 539
Peale, Charles Willson, 99
Pelham, Dick, 259
Pelissier, Victor, 121
Penn, John, 86
Penn, William, 57, 227
Pennington, William, 263
Perez, Manuel, 472
Pergolesi, Giovanni, 100
Perkins, Gertrude, 464
Perle, George, 611, 612
  twelve-tone modal system, 611
Perronet, Edward, 135
Perse, St. John, 543
Persichetti, Vincent, 558
Pestalozzi, J. H., 158, 159
Peter, John Frederick, 60, 61
Peter Ibbetson (Taylor), 635
Peterboro Artists' Colony, 353, 495
Peters, Samuel, 9
Peters, W. C., 264–265, 290, 291
Peyser, Herbert, 331
Pfitzner, Hans E., 393
Philadelphia, early musical activity in, 54–57, 86, 100–101, 107, 109–111, 113–117, 119–120, 125, 128
Philadelphia Conservatory of Music, 559, 572
Philadelphia Orchestra, 524
Phile, Philip, 118
Phillips, Burrill, 556, 661, 677
Phillips, Ulrich B., 83
Picasso, Pablo, 574
Picou, Alphonse, 472, 476–477
Pierce, Charles, 482
Pietists, 46, 50, 55, 57
Pilgrims, 6, 9, 16, 38, 39, 41
Pink Lady, The (Caryll), 622
Pipe of Desire (Converse), 377, 521, 635
Piston, Walter, 379, 502, 545, 549, 564–568
  compositions, 566–567
  use of twelve-tone technique, 613
Pittsburgh International Festival, 559
Pixley, Frank, 624
Plaidy, Louis, 334
Plantation melodies, 78
  Dvořák's interest in, 388, 390, 391
  in minstrelsy, 260, 265, 267, 280
  and ragtime, 433, 440
  Stephen Foster's use of, 248, 288, 289, 291–292, 294, 295
Play-party songs, 278, 315
Playford, John, 3, 7, 10, 14, 20, 29, 156
Pleasure Dome of Kubla Khan (Griffes), 517–519
Pleyel, Ignaz, 120, 155
Pockrich, Richard, 90
Poe, Edgar Allan, 176, 177, 399, 656
Poem for Flute and Orchestra (Griffes), 519
Pollack, Ben, 486
Polytonality, 564, 654, 660, 662, 667
  in blues, 548
Pond, William, 296
Pond, William A., & Co., 165
Popular music, 381, 440
  blues as, 457, 459, 461, 462
  by Gershwin, 488–493
  idioms of, in compositions, 494, 531–532, 538–539, 545, 566
  (*See also* Blues; Jazz; Minstrelsy; Musical comedy; Ragtime)
Porgy and Bess (Gershwin), 493, 629, 637–640
Port Royal Islands, 234, 238, 240, 243, 246–247, 252, 257
Portals (Ruggles), 577
Porter, Cole, 617, 629–630
Porter, Quincy, 562
Powell, John, 380, 401–402, 660
Powers, Marie, 649
Prairie (Sowerby), 559–560
Pratt, Paul, 446
Pratt, Silas Gamaliel, 340–341
Pratt, Waldo Selden, 17
Prepared piano, 571, 593, 594
Presbyterians, 47, 79, 126, 194, 207, 208, 210
President's March (Phile), 119

Prince of Pilsen (Luders), 623–624
Princeton University, 125, 126, 538, 612
Pro Musica Society, 331, 658
Prynne, William, 8
Pryor, Arthur, 438
Psalm 87 (Ives), 665
Psalm Singer's Amusement (Billings), 140
Psalmody, 3–45, 50, 66, 80–82, 101, 125, 126, 131, 239
  early New England, 3–6, 8, 16–21, 22–39
    Ainsworth Psalter, 16–19
  Bay Psalm Book, 14, 19–21
  folk style of singing in, 22–26, 28–35, 38–39, 81, 455
  Gaelic, 30, 32–33
  Negroes and, 79–82, 236–237
Pueblo Indians, music of, 423
Pugnani, Gaetano, 85
Pulitzer Fellowship, 561, 563
Pulitzer Prize, 533, 629, 658
Purcell, Henry, 14, 100
Puritans, 3–21, 30, 31, 34, 38, 41
  attitude, toward dancing, 10–12
    toward music, 6–9
    toward use of musical instruments, 7, 9–10
  (*See also* Psalmody)
Putnam, J. S., 440
Pyrlaeus, John Christopher, 60

Quakers, 47, 50, 53, 57, 210
  Shaking, 47, 53
    (*See also* Shakers)
Quarter tones, 542, 654, 661
Quincy, Josiah, 107, 108
Quiñones, Cristobal de, 62

Raff, Joseph Joachim, 337, 349
Ragas, Henry, 474
Ragtime, 433–451, 455
  antecedents of, 260, 310
  and jazz, 469, 474, 477–479
  use of, by composers, 510, 534, 566, 658, 664, 667
Ragtime Instructor (Harney), 445–446
Ragtime Nightmare (Turpin), 443
Rainey, Gertrude ("Ma"), 464, 465
Rameau, Jean-Philippe, 85
Ramsey, Frederic, 476
Rappolo, Leon, 481
Rapports, 141
Ravel, Maurice, 379, 385, 494, 496, 555
Ravenscroft, Thomas, 20, 25
Read, Daniel, 124, 125, 134, 135, 156, 188
Read, Gardner, 556
Read, Jack, 482
Red Hot Peppers, 475
Red Mill, The (Herbert), 620
Redman, Don, 484
Regina (Blitzstein), 646
Regionalism, in American music, 402, 512, 522–523
  Middle Western, 559–561
  in music of Charles Ives, 664–665
Regular singing (*see* Psalmody)
Reinagle, Alexander, 110–117, 120
  compositions of, 110, 112, 114
Reiner, Fritz, 641
Rena, Henry ("Kid"), 476
Rena, Joe, 477
Repository of Sacred Music (Wyeth), 188–189
  Second Part, 189
Revival hymns (*see* Hymnody, revivalist)
Revivalism, 46, 48, 63, 64, 79, 157, 207–231, 255, 277, 500
  (*See also* Camp meetings)
Rhapsody in Blue (Gershwin), 489, 491–492, 511
Rhapsody in Rivets (Second Rhapsody) (Gershwin), 489, 493
Rheinberger, Josef, 369, 375, 376, 521
Rhodes, Willard, 430–432
Rhythmicon, 575
Rice, Dan, 289
Rice, Edward E., 622
Rice, Edward L., 261
Rice, Elmer, 647
Rice, Thomas Dartmouth ("Daddy"), 259–261, 264–267, 271, 279, 289
  interpreter of "Jim Crow," 261, 264–265
Rich, Arthur L., 159
Richards, Frank, 478
Riegger, Wallingford, 583, 608–610
Riggs, Lynn, 631
Riker, Charles, 549
Riley, William, 34, 35
Rilke, Rainer Maria, 547, 564, 610, 613
Rimsky-Korsakoff, Nikolai, 385, 387, 389, 499, 511
Ring shouts (*see* Shouts)
Rip Van Winkle (Bristow), 329–330
Rise and Fall of the City of Mahagonny (Weill), 646
Rittenhouse, David, 54

Ritter, Frédéric Louis, 3, 188, 389
Rittinghuysen, Willem, 54
Roarke, William, 290
Rob Roy (De Koven), 619
Roberta (Kern), 627
Roberts, Luckey, 446
Robertson, Zue, 472
Robichaux, John, 472
Robin Hood (De Koven), 619
Robinson, J. Russel, 446
Robinson, Jim, 477
Robinson, Robert, 214
Rochester, N.Y. (*see* Eastman School of Music)
Rodeo (Copland), 500
Rodgers, Richard, 617, 630–632
Rodzinski, Artur, 628
Rogers, Bernard, 552–553, 557, 558
  The Warrior, 635
"Roll, Jordan, Roll," 240
Röllig, K. L., 92
Rolvaag, O. E., 643
Roman Sketches (Griffes), 519
Romanticism, 337, 349, 387, 520, 549
  in music of Barber, 563
  in music of Hanson, 550–551
  in music of MacDowell, 346–347, 349, 360, 362
Romberg, Sigmund, 617, 624
Rome Prize, American, 551, 555, 563, 568
Roosevelt, Franklin D., 529, 626
Root, George Frederick, 62, 179–180, 249
Rose, Billy, 633
Rose Marie (Friml), 624
Rosenbaum, Charles, 287
Rosenfeld, Paul, 347, 354, 359, 373, 519, 571
Rosenwald Fellowship, 541
Rossini, Gioacchino, 159, 167, 320, 332
Rounds for String Orchestra (Diamond), 554
Rousseau, Jean Jacques, 155, 158
Roussel, Albert, 586
Rudhyar, Dane, 585
Ruggles, Carl, 576–578
Russell, Henry, 164, 166–168, 170–171, 173, 175, 176, 180–182, 235, 257, 270, 295
  on Negro singing, 235–236, 246–247
Russell, Charles Ellsworth, Jr., ("Pee Wee"), 483, 486
Russell, William Howard, 238
Russolo, Luigi, 573
Sabin, Robert, 524
Sable Harmonists, 290, 291
Sacred Harp (White), 136, 190, 196, 204, 223
Sacred Harp Singers of Alabama, 139
St. Cecilia Society of Charleston, 84, 107–109
St. Cyr, Johnny, 475, 480
St. Louis, Mo., jazz in, 438
  ragtime in, 441–443
"St. Louis Blues" (Handy), 459, 461, 467
Salazar, Adolfo, 349
Salón México, El (Copland), 498–499
Salzedo, Carlos, 585, 586
Sandburg, Carl, 501, 542, 547, 560, 581
Sandys, George, 36
Santiago, Willy, 472, 477
Sarah Lawrence College, 533, 537
Sargeant, Winthrop, 457
Satie, Erik, 530, 531, 543, 565, 585
Saunders, Otis, 441
Savane, La (Gottschalk), 314, 315
Sbarbaro, Tony, 474
Scalero, Rosario, 563, 646
Scarlatti, Domenico, 537
Scarlet Letter, The (Damrosch), 634
Scharfenberg, William, 172
Schelling, Ernest, 521
Schenker, Heinrich, 526
Schmidt, Henry, 333
Schneider, Marius, 277, 300
Schoenberg, Arnold, 493, 549, 573, 583, 597–604, 661
  evolution of twelve-tone technique, 599–602
  influence of, 524–526, 569, 577, 606, 609–611, 616, 657
  life in America, 597–598
  pupils of, 542, 590, 593, 607, 646
  works composed in America, 602
Schola Cantorum, 381, 586, 629
School of Ragtime (Joplin), 446
Schoolcraft, Henry Rowe, 390, 404, 411
Schreker, Franz, 604
Schubart, Mark, 525
Schubert, Franz, 155, 366, 604, 625
Schuman, William, 533–537, 651–652
  compositions, 534–535
  The Mighty Casey, 652
Schumann, Robert, 92, 359, 365, 502
Scott, Bud, 480
Scott, James Sylvester, 443–444
Scriabin, Alexander, 494, 520
Sea Pieces (MacDowell), 353, 360

Second Piano Sonata (Ives) (*see* *Concord Sonata*)
Second Rhapsody (Gershwin), 489, 493
Second Symphony (Ives), 657, 661–662
Second Symphony (Piston), 564–567
Seeger, Charles, 190, 530, 575, 581
Seeger, Ruth Crawford, 581, 582, 612
Seguin, Anna and Arthur, 165, 168
Selby, William, 107, 122
Separatists (*see* Pilgrims)
Sessions, Roger, 525–530, 533, 542, 553–554, 561, 612
  compositions, 529
Seven Songs for the Harpsichord (Hopkinson), 99, 102
Sewall, Samuel, 3–5, 9
Seymour, Johnny, 441
Shakers, 47, 52–54, 63, 224–230
  songs of, 226–229, 501
Shakespeare, William, 16, 324, 547, 610, 629
"Shall We Gather at the River?" 532, 664
Shanewis (Cadman), 399
Shape-note system, 129, 130, 185, 187–190, 192, 194, 200–201, 542, 644
  songbooks, 134, 186–190, 197, 213
  (*See also* Fasola folk)
Shapero, Harold, 567, 568
Sharp, Cecil, 199
Sharp, William, 518
Shaw, Artie, 487
Shaw, Oliver, 151
Shelley, Percy Bysshe, 349, 563
Shepherd, Arthur, 395, 522–523
"Ship on Fire" (Russell), 168–169
Shouts, 82, 236, 256–257, 287, 435
  (*See also* Negro spirituals)
Show Boat (Kern), 627–628
Shryock, R. H., 366
Sibelius, Jan, 550
Siegmeister, Elie, 512
Simeon, Omer, 475
Simms, Bartlett D., 444
Simon, Henry, 507
Simon, Menno, 54
"Simple Gifts," 229, 500
Singing families (*see* Baker family; Hutchinson family)
Singing Master's Assistant (Billings), 140
Singing schools, 28–29, 39, 40, 57, 63, 124, 132, 145, 183–184, 186, 188, 191, 286, 334, 365
  description of, in Connecticut, 184–186
Sioux Indians, tribal music of, 407, 416–420, 430
"Six, Les" (Group of Six), 565, 573
Skilton, Charles Sanford, 400
Skulsky, Abraham, 606, 607
Skyscrapers (Carpenter), 510
Slave songs (*see* Negro music; Negro spirituals)
Slavery, 65–69, 78–79, 82–83
  (*See also* Negro spirituals)
Sloane, A. Baldwin, 623
Slonimsky, Nicolas, 502, 573, 575, 581, 588, 589, 662
Smallens, Alexander, 640
Smart and Williams, 439
Smetana, Bedřich, 387
Smith, Bessie, 464, 465, 467
Smith, Carleton Sprague, 344
Smith, Cecil, 627, 629
Smith, Charles Edward, 476, 486
Smith, Clarence ("Pine Top"), 466–467
Smith, David Stanley, 522, 562
Smith, Joshua, 208
Smith, Kate, 626
Smith, Seba, 174
Smith, William, 186–188, 191
Smith, Willy, 484
Smith and Mellor, 265
Smith College, 528, 561
Smithsonian Institution, 405, 410
Snyder, White, 261
Social Harp (McCurry), 198, 199, 214–215, 218, 219
Sonata Eroica (MacDowell), 351, 360
Sonata Tragica (MacDowell), 351, 360
Sonata Virginianesque (Powell), 401
Sonneck, Oscar G., 87
Sousa, John Philip, 438, 621
South Pacific (Rodgers), 631–632
Southern Harmony (Walker), 139, 190, 194–195, 200–205, 212, 218
Sowerby, Leo, 559–561
Spalding, H. G., 240, 247
Spalding, Walter Raymond, 538, 577
Spanier, Muggsy, 482
Spencer, Frank, 291
Spenser, Willard, 618
Spirituals (*see* Negro spirituals)
Spring Symphony (Paine), 336
Stamitz, Johann, 21, 30, 38, 59, 60, 85
Starer, Robert, 547, 558
Stark, John Stilwell, 441–444, 446
Steele, Porter, 480
Stein, Gertrude, 531, 596, 643–645
Steinert, Alexander, 637

Steinway Hall, 329
Stennett, David, 211
Sternhold, Thomas, 5
Sternhold and Hopkins, Psalter of, 17, 19, 29, 143
Sticcado pastorale, 88
Still, William Grant, 512–513
Stokowski, Leopold, 590
Stone, Fred, 637
Stowe, Harriet Beecher, 142, 143, 267, 294
Strakosch, Max, 316, 318
Strang, Gerald, 582, 583, 614
Strauss, Johann, 617, 620
Strauss, Richard, 366, 379, 525
Stravinsky, Igor, 491, 495, 496, 517, 525, 553, 565, 566, 569, 654, 657, 661
Street Scene (Weill), 647
Strike Up the Band (Gershwin), 628
Stringfield, Lamar, 512
Stringham, Edwin, 556
Stubbs, Philip, 7
Student Prince (Romberg), 624
Study in Sonority (Riegger), 608
Sullivan, Sir Arthur, 617
Sun-Treader (Ruggles), 577
Suppé, Franz von, 617
Surinach, Carlos, 576
Survivor from Warsaw (Schoenberg), 602
Swan, Timothy, 124, 125, 135, 188, 191
"Swanee River" (*see* "Old Folks at Home")
Swanson, Howard, 541–542
Sweeney, Joel Walker, 262
Swing, 477, 481, 486, 487, 511
"Swing Low, Sweet Chariot," 388–389
Symmes, Thomas, 13–15, 25, 27–30, 35, 39
Symphonic jazz, 488–491, 494, 510–511, 572, 637
Symphonic Sketches (Chadwick), 371–372
Symphony Hall (Boston), 566
Symphony on a Hymn Tune (Thomson), 531–532
Symphony in One Movement (Barber), 563
Symposium on Music Criticism, Harvard, 598
Synchrony (Cowell), 575
Syncopation, 74–75, 236, 263, 277, 279, 311, 434, 554, 566, 625
Syncretism in African music, 74, 256
Synge, John M., 399
Taggard, Genevieve, 533
Tailgate trombone, 477
Tallis, Thomas, 20, 156
Tammany (Hewitt), 121
Tans'ur, William, 140, 156
Tate, Allen, 568
Tatum, Art, 483
Taylor, Deems, 635
Taylor, Raynor, 112, 117–120
Tchaikowsky, Peter I., 366, 379, 491
Teagarden, Jack, 485
Teasdale, Sara, 518
Television, opera for, 636, 648, 650, 651
Templeton, Alec, 118
Tender Land, The (Copland), 501
Tennyson, Alfred, 344, 349
Teschemacher, Frank, 482
Testament of Freedom (Thompson), 540
Teton Sioux (*see* Sioux Indians)
Thackeray, William Makepeace, 260, 266
Thayer, Ernest L., 652
Theatre Guild, 630, 631, 640
Theodore Thomas Orchestra, 620
Theremin, Leon, 575
Third Symphony (Harris), 505–506
Third Symphony (Ives), 657, 658, 662–663
Third Symphony (Riegger), 608, 609
This Is the Army (Berlin), 625
Thomas, Theodore, 336
Thompson, H. S., 176
Thompson, Oscar, 331
Thompson, Randall, 381, 538–539, 545
Thomson, Virgil, 190, 510, 525, 530–534, 543, 565, 595
  compositions, 531–532
  operas, 643–646
  quoted, 546, 581, 594, 601
Thoreau, Henry David, 380, 660, 664, 668, 672
Three Places in New England (Ives), 664–665
Threepenny Opera (Weill), 646, 647
Tietjens, Paul, 623
Tiger Rag (Morton), 449, 474, 478, 481
Till, John C., 61
Timm, Henry Christian, 172, 328
Tipton, Louis Campbell, 395
Tomaschek, W. L., 92
Tomlinson, Eliza, 286
Tone-clusters, 543, 571, 575, 660
Tone Roads (Ives), 666
Toor, Frances, 499
Toscanini, Arturo, 562–563

Totten, John C., 208–209
Town Hall, New York, 658
"Tramp, Tramp, Tramp" (Root), 180, 514
Transatlantic (Antheil), 572
Transcendentalists, 656, 668
Tree on the Plains (Bacon), 643
Treemonisha (Joplin), 442–443
Triumph of St. Joan (Dello Joio), 537
Trouble in Tahiti (Bernstein), 545, 651
Troubled Island (Still), 512–513
Troyer, Carlos, 394–396
Tucker, Isaac, 156
Tufts, John, 25, 40
"Turkey in the Straw," 278, 662
Turpin, Thomas M., 443–444
Tuskegee Institute, 254
Twain, Mark, 630, 643
Twelve-tone technique, 524, 548–549, 562, 564, 569, 573, 590, 593, 597–616
  evolution of, 598–601
  tonal application of, 603, 604, 614, 615

Unanswered Question, The (Ives), 666
Undertow (Schuman), 535
Union Harmony (Caldwell), 194
Union Harmony (Holden), 135
Unitas Fratrem (*see* Moravians)
Universe Symphony (Ives), 663
University of California, 393, 525, 529, 598
University of Chicago, 179, 598
University of Illinois, 556, 612
University of Southern California, 544, 598
Urania (Lyon), 125–127
Ussachevsky, Vladimir, 589*n.*

Vagabond King, The (Friml), 625
"Vagrom Ballad, A," (Chadwick), 371, 372
Valéry, Paul, 610
Van Alstyne, Egbert, 449
Van der Stucken, Frank, 350–351
Van Doren, Mark, 568
Vardell, Charles G., 512
Varèse, Edgar, 512, 571, 585–589
Vassar College, 562, 604
Vaughan Williams, Ralph, 660
Verdi, Giuseppe, 320
Verlaine, Paul, 373, 610
Victory Ball, A (Schelling), 521
Vidal, Paul, 494
Viereck, J. C., 276
Virginia Harmony (Carrell), 192
Virginia Minstrels, 259–260, 267
Virginia Reel, 278, 436–437, 514
Vitebsk (Copland), 497
Vivaldi, Antonio, 85
Volunteers, The (Reinagle), 114
Voodoo ceremonies in New Orleans, 304–305
Voudou (dance), 312

Wa-Wan Press, 393–397
Wagenaar, Bernard, 537
Wagner, Richard, 186, 338, 347, 365–367, 379, 598, 659
"Wake, Nicodemus" (Work), 180
Wald, Max, 643
Walden (Thoreau), 380, 672, 675
Walk-arounds, 257, 270, 272–273, 275, 439
  by Dan Emmett, 273
Walker, William, 187, 194–197, 200–202, 204–205, 212, 218
Wallace, William Vincent, 165, 168
Waller, Thomas ("Fats"), 446, 450, 485
Walter, Bruno, 544
Walter, Thomas, 24–27, 35, 40
  The Grounds and Rules of Musick Explained, 25
Ward, Robert E., 557, 558
Ward, W. E., 72
Ware, Charles Pickard, 243, 245
Warrior, The (Rogers), 635
Washington, George, 99, 101, 102, 110, 111, 120, 127, 136, 188, 227, 602
Waterman, Richard A., 71–73, 75, 254–256
Waters, Ethel, 626
Watts, Isaac, 41–43, 52, 80–82, 127, 128, 133, 138, 143, 208, 218, 236
Webb, Chick, 486
Webb, George J., 153, 159, 160, 162, 173, 179
Weber, Ben, 612, 613
Weber, Carl Maria von, 155, 159
Webern, Anton von, 597, 606, 610, 613
Webster, Daniel, 641, 642, 644
Weems, Mason Locke, 123, 131
"Weeping Mary," 202
Weill, Kurt, 632–633, 646–647
Weiss, Adolph, 593, 606
Welsh, Nolan, 465
Wenrich, Percy, 445
Wells, Frederic P., 138
Wesley, Charles, 43–46, 48, 49, 52, 156, 191, 208, 214
Wesley, John, 43–52, 58, 79, 80, 82, 156, 208
Wesley, Samuel, 45

West African music (*see* African music)
"When Jesus Wept" (Billings), 143, 535
When Johnny Comes Marching Home (Harris), 507, 509
Whitaker, James, 53
Whitby, Henry, 260
White, Benjamin Franklin, 196, 204, 223
White, Cool, 281
White, Newman, 254
White Peacock (Griffes), 518, 519
White Wings (Moore), 642
Whitefield, George, 46, 51
Whiteman, Paul, 482–483, 491
Whiting, Arthur, 369, 375, 379
Whitlock, Billy, 259
Whitman, Walt, 325, 347, 364, 399, 513, 514, 533, 537
Whittier, John Greenleaf, 57, 336
Whole-tone scale, 603
Widor, Charles M., 379, 586
Wignell, Thomas, 114
Wilcox, Edwin, 484
Wilde, Richard Henry, 344
Wilde, Oscar, 518
William Billings Overture (Schuman), 535
Williams, Aaron, 156
Williams, William Carlos, 663
Williams and Walker, 439, 623
Williamsburg, Va., 34, 76
 Festival concerts, 85
Willig, George, Jr., 261, 265, 288
Willis, Nathaniel Parker, 171
Willis, Richard Storrs, 329–330, 332
Winslow, Edward, 8, 13
Winter, Peter von, 159
Wissahickon Hermits, 55
Witt, Christopher, 56
Wittke, Carl, 266
Wizard of Oz, The, 623
Wodehouse, P. G., 627
Wolle, Peter, 61
Wolpe, Stefan, 606, 607
Wolverines, The, 482
Wood, Abraham, 124, 125
Wood, F. C., 218
Woodbury, Isaac Baker, 150, 162–163
Woodforde, James, 88
Woodland Sketches (MacDowell), 351, 360
Woodman, R. Huntington, 575
"Woodman, Spare that Tree" (Russell), 166–167, 171, 176
Worcester Collection of Sacred Harmony (Holden), 136
Wordsworth, William, 610
Work, Henry Clay, 180
Wyeth, John, 188–189, 191

Yale College (*see* Yale University)
Yale School of Music, 525, 562
Yale University, 43, 376, 400, 522, 557, 565, 629, 653, 654
Yancey, Jimmy, 466, 467
"Yankee Doodle," 119, 120, 284, 333
Yankee Doodliad (Heinrich), 386
Yeats, William Butler, 590, 591
Yip, Yip, Yaphank (Berlin), 625
Yon, Pietro, 535
Youmans, Vincent, 628
Young, William, 107, 120
Youngs, Isaac N., 228
"You've Been a Good Old Wagon but You've Done Broke Down," 444, 464

Zedwitz, Herman, 107
Zeisberger, David, 60
Ziegfeld, Flo, 626–627
Zinzendorf, Count, 45, 46, 58
"Zip Coon," 261, 278–279, 289, 398, 434
Zuñi Indians, tribal music of, 404, 423–427

About the Author

Gilbert Chase attended Columbia University and the University of North Carolina, and also studied music privately. In Paris he was for six years music critic of the *Continental Daily Mail*, and correspondent for *Musical America* of New York and *Musical Times* of London. While abroad, he traveled extensively in Spain, and later wrote *The Music of Spain*, which was published in 1941. When he returned to the United States, Mr. Chase continued his activities in the world of music as associate editor of the *International Cyclopedia of Music and Musicians*, Latin American specialist in the Music Division of the Library of Congress, supervisor of music for the NBC University of the Air, educational director for RCA Victor, and lecturer on American music at Columbia University. In 1951, Mr. Chase joined the Foreign Service and served as Cultural Attaché in Lima, Peru. Two years later, he was appointed to the same position in Buenos Aires. He has been a member of the Advisory Committee on Music for the State Department, a member of the American Musicological Society, the French Musicological Society, the Spanish Institute of Musicology, and many other organizations. Mr. Chase is married and has three sons who are now in college.